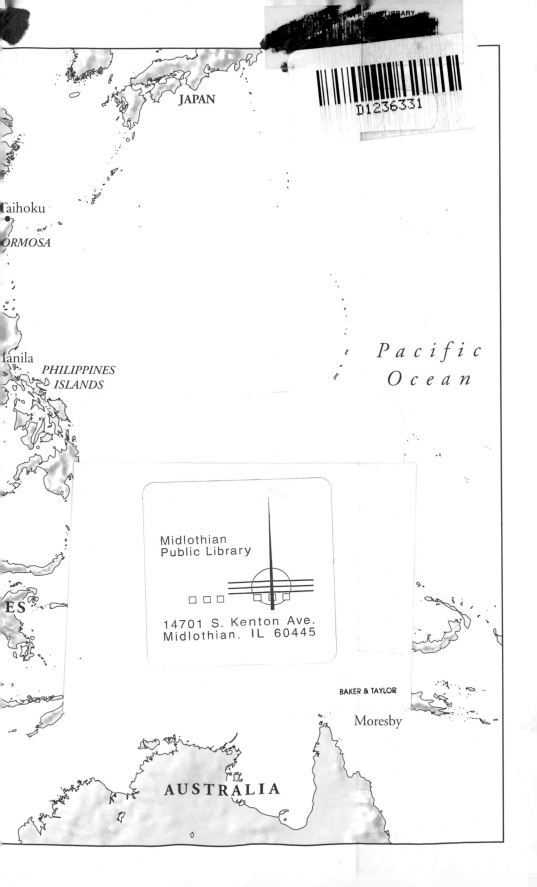

JAPAN

Taihoku

FORMOSA

Manila

PHILIPPINES
ISLANDS

*Pacific
Ocean*

ES

BAKER & TAYLOR

Moresby

AUSTRALIA

HO CHI MINH

BOOKS BY WILLIAM J. DUIKER

The Comintern and Vietnamese Communism

The Rise of Nationalism in Vietnam, 1900–1941

Ts'ai Yuan-p'ei: Educator of Modern China

Cultures in Collision: The Boxer Rebellion

China and Vietnam: The Roots of Conflict

Vietnam Since the Fall of Saigon

U.S. Containment Policy and the Conflict in Indochina

Sacred War: Nationalism and Revolution in a Divided Vietnam

Vietnam: Revolution in Transition

The Communist Road to Power in Vietnam

A Historical Dictionary of Vietnam

World History (with Jackson Spielvogel)

Twentieth-Century World History

HO CHI MINH

WILLIAM J. DUIKER

NEW YORK

Maps by Paul Pugliese / General Cartography Inc.

A list of photographic credits, constituting a continuation
of the copyright page, appears on pp. 693-695.

Library of Congress Cataloging-in-Publication Data

Duiker, William J.
Ho Chi Minh / by William Duiker.
p.   cm.
Includes bibliographical references and index.
ISBN 0-7868-6387-0
1. Há, Châ Minh, 1890–1969. 2. Presidents—
Vietnam (Democratic Republic)—
Biography. I. Title.

DS560.72.H6 D85   2000
959.704'092—dc21
[B]   00-026757

Book design by Dorothy Schmiderer Baker

First Edition
10 9 8 7 6 5 4 3 2 1

For the Vietnamese People

CONTENTS

PREFACE

I have been fascinated with Ho Chi Minh since the mid-1960s, when, as a young foreign service officer stationed at the U.S. Embassy in Saigon, I was puzzled by the fact that the Viet Cong guerrillas fighting in the jungles appeared to be better disciplined and more motivated than the armed forces of our ally, the government of South Vietnam. As I attempted to understand the problem, I became convinced that one explanation was the role played by that master motivator and strategist, the veteran Vietnamese revolutionary Ho Chi Minh. After I resigned from the U.S. government to pursue an academic career, I turned my thoughts to writing a biography of that extraordinarily complex figure, but soon realized that there were insufficient source materials available for me to produce a convincing portrayal of his life and career. I therefore put off the project until recently, when an outpouring of information from various countries around the world persuaded me that it was now possible to undertake the task.

In the course of completing this book, which has now been underway for over two decades, I have received assistance from a number of sources. The College Fund for Research in the College of Liberal Arts, as well as the Institute for the Arts and Humanistic Studies at The Pennsylvania State University, provided me with financial support on a number of occasions to undertake research on the subject in France and Vietnam. Through the assistance of Mark Sidel of the Ford Foundation, I was pleased to accompany Marilyn Young and A. Tom Grunfeld on a 1993 trip to Hanoi to explore Ho Chi Minh's relationship with the United States. I would also like to thank the Social Science Research Council and its Indochina Scholarly Exchange Program for awarding me with a grant in 1990 to conduct research on Ho Chi Minh in Hanoi. While I was there, the Institute of History, the University of Hanoi, and the Institute of Marxism-Leninism kindly made arrangements for me to discuss topics of mutual interest with scholars and researchers interested in Ho Chi Minh and the history of the

Vietnamese revolution. The Institute of International Relations sponsored an earlier visit in 1985, which included a fascinating visit to Ho Chi Minh's birthplace in Kim Lien village. Among those individuals who have assisted me in my research in Hanoi, I would like to thank Nguyen Huy Hoan of the Ho Chi Minh Museum, Nguyen Thanh of the Revolutionary Museum, and Tran Thanh of the Institute of Marxism-Leninism, all of whom agreed to lengthy interviews. At the University of Hanoi, historians Phung Huu Phu, Le Mau Han, Pham Xanh, and Pham Cong Tung graciously provided me with their time and research materials relating to Ho Chi Minh's life and thought. The late Ha Huy Giap of the Ho Chi Minh Museum and Dang Xuan Ky, then director of the Social Sciences Institute, kindly answered my questions regarding their personal recollections of President Ho. Do Quang Hung, Ngo Phuong Ba, Van Tao, and Tran Huu Dinh at the Institute of History and Luu Doan Huynh of the Institute of International Relations were generous with their time in helping to explore key issues in my research. I would particularly like to thank Vu Huy Phuc, who with patience and good humor served as both escort and fellow researcher during my visit to Vietnam in 1990. More recently, Mr. Hoang Cong Thuy of the Vietnam-American Friendship Society helped to put me in touch with other individuals and sources as I followed the trail of Ho Chi Minh. Duong Trung Quoc of *Xua Nay* magazine provided me with several useful issues of his magazine. Nguyen Quoc Uy of the Vietnam News Agency has kindly authorized me to reproduce in this book a number of photographs under VNA copyright.

I have visited a number of libraries and archives around the world in pursuit of elusive information on Ho Chi Minh's many travels. In the United States, I would like to thank the staff at the Orientalia Section in the Library of Congress, and Allan Riedy, director of the Echols Collection at the Kroch Library in Cornell University. At the U.S. National Archives in College Park, Maryland, John Taylor and Larry McDonald gave me valuable assistance in locating OSS and State Department records dealing with U.S.-Vietnam relations during and immediately following World War II. In France, I am grateful for the help I received at the Bibliothèque Nationale and the Archives Nationales in Paris, and especially at the Centre des Archives, Section Outre-Mer, in Aix-en-Provence. During my visit to Moscow in 1990, Gennadi Maslov, Yevgeny Kobelev, and Oxana Novakova were quite helpful in discussing issues relating to Ho Chi Minh's years in the USSR, while Sophie Quinn-Judge and Steve Morris provided me with important documents that they had managed to locate in the Comintern archives. Li Xianheng at the Revolutionary Museum in Guangzhou provided me with the fruits of his own research on Ho Chi Minh's years of residence in that city and took me for a fascinating visit to the training institute where Ho Chi Minh had taught over seventy years ago. Thanks are also due to Tao Bingwei and Ye Xin at the Institute of International Studies in Beijing for a lengthy interview in 1987 on Sino-Vietnamese relations. Bob O'Hara helped me to obtain relevant documents from the Public Record Office in London. While the search turned up little of interest, I feel comfortable that he explored every possible avenue on my behalf. I would also like to thank Professor Laura Tabili of the University of Arizona for providing useful guidance in seeking out other possible sources of information on Ho's elusive years of residence in Great Britain, as well as the staff at the Hong Kong branch of the PRO for enabling me to make use of its archival materials dealing with Ho Chi Minh's period of imprisonment there in the early 1930s. Ambassador T.N. Kaul was useful in discussing his recollection of the meeting between Jawaharlal Nehru and Zhou Enlai in the summer of 1954.

I have become indebted to a number of fellow scholars and researchers who share my interest in Ho Chi Minh and the history of the Vietnamese revolution. In some cases, a mere listing of their names appears to be an all too insufficient mark of gratitude, since many of them have provided me with crucial documents, or with access to their own research on related topics. Nevertheless, I would like to cite their names here. In the United States, Douglas Pike and Steve Denny of the Indochina Archives, now located at Texas Tech University, gave me useful assistance during an earlier visit to their archives when it was located in Berkeley. Others who have been of help are the late King C. Chen, Stanley Karnow, Bill Turley, Gary Tarpinian, and Mai Elliott. John McAuliff of the U.S.-Indochina Reconciliation Project was kind enough to invite me to attend the conference of Vietminh and OSS veterans held at Hampton Bays, New York, in 1998. A number of those who attended that conference, including Frank White, Henry Prunier, Carlton Swift, Mac Shinn, Frank Tan, George Wicks, Ray Grelecki, and Charles Fenn, as well as a delegation of Vietminh veterans and scholars who were also in attendance, shared their own fascinating experiences of that period with me. On an earlier occasion, I had the good fortune to discuss Ho Chi Minh with Archimedes (Al) Patti, whose own recollections, contained in his book *Why Vietnam? Prelude to America's Albatross* (Berkeley: University of California Press, 1980), are an irreplaceable source of information on the subject. Bob Bledsoe, chairman of the Department of Political Science at the University of Central Florida, graciously permitted me to examine the Patti archives, which are now held at his University. I would like to thank Al's widow, Margaret, for her permission to reproduce photos from that archive in this book.

In France, a number of people have helped me in a variety of ways, including Georges Boudarel, Daniel Hémery, Christiane Pasquel Rageau, and Philippe Devillers, as well as Chris Goscha and Agathe Larcher. Stein Tonnesson was of great assistance in sharing the fruits of his own research at the Centre des Archives, Section Outre-Mer, in Aix-en-Provence. I would like to thank Professor Bernard Dahm of the University of Passau for inviting me to attend a conference on Ho Chi Minh at his institution in 1990. Liang-wu Yin and Chen Jian kindly provided me with Chinese-language materials that were crucial in understanding Ho Chi Minh's relationship with China. Russian scholars Ilya Gaiduk and Anatoly Sokolov gave of their time or sent me useful materials relating to Soviet-Vietnamese relations. Professor Motoo Furuta of the University of Tokyo sent me a number of important documents that were not available to me in the United States. David Marr of the Australian National University has on several occasions provided me with documents, articles, and, in one case, a taped recording of Ho Chi Minh's famous speech at Ba Dinh Square in early September 1945. I would like to thank Yu Pen-li and Liu Hsiang-wang, who, in addition to their many obligations as my graduate students at Penn State, took the time to provide me with useful materials related to Ho Chi Minh's activities in south China.

At Hyperion, I am grateful to David Lott, associate managing editor, for his care in guiding this book through production; to copyeditor Trent Duffy, for his painstaking work and help with standardizing references; to Lisa Stokes and Phil Rose, for their art direction on the handsome interior and jacket designs; and to Paul Pugliese, Dorothy Baker, and Archie Ferguson, respectively, for the elegant maps, interior design, and jacket. Mark Chait was prompt and efficient in attending to my countless queries during the publication process. I would especially like to thank my editor, Will Schwalbe, who provided me with steady encouragement in bringing this project to fruition. From the beginning, he made it clear that his greatest concern was to help me create a book of the highest quality. His patience, good humor, and sound advice were much appreciated.

I would like to thank my daughters, Laura and Claire, for not complaining about the many hours (and years) that they spent listening to their father pontificate about Vietnam. Finally, I am everlastingly grateful to my wife, Yvonne, who was not only the first to read the manuscript, but who also showed her usual patience in putting up with Ho Chi Minh on those many occasions when he must have seemed almost like a member of the family.

LIST OF ORGANIZATIONS MENTIONED

IN THE TEXT

ANNAM COMMUNIST PARTY (ACP). Short-lived party established in In-
dochina in 1929 after the dissolution of the Revolutionary Youth
League. Eventually assimilated into the Vietnamese Communist
Party (VCP) established in February 1930.

ARMED PROPAGANDA BRIGADES (APBs). Armed revolutionary units created under Indochinese Communist Party (ICP) leadership in December 1944 in preparation for an uprising at the end of World War
II. Succeeded by the Vietnamese Liberation Army (VLA).

ARMY OF NATIONAL SALVATION. Armed revolutionary units created under ICP control in North Vietnam in 1944 to struggle against French
and Japanese occupation of Indochina. Eventually combined with the
APBs (see above) into the Vietnamese Liberation Army (VLA).

ARMY OF THE REPUBLIC OF VIETNAM (ARVN). Formal name for the
armed forces of the Republic of Vietnam (RVN) from 1956 until
1975.

ASSOCIATED STATE OF VIETNAM (ASV). Formal government established
by the Elysée Accords in 1949. The government, established under
Chief of State Bao Dai, was autonomous but lacked some of the
credentials for total independence from France. The ASV cooperated
with France in the conflict with the Vietminh Front during the
Franco-Vietminh War. It was replaced by an independent government in South Vietnam after the Geneva Conference of 1954.

ASSOCIATION OF LIKE MINDS (also called THE SOCIETY OF LIKE
MINDS, or TAM TAM XA). Radical organization established by Viet-
amese émigrés and nationalists living in south China in 1924. It was
eventually replaced by Ho Chi Minh's Revolutionary Youth League.

ASSOCIATION OF MARXIST STUDIES. Paper organization established by
the ICP at the time of its apparent dissolution in November 1945.

In fact, the ICP continued to exist in secret until its reappearance as the Vietnamese Workers' Party (VWP) in 1951.

CAO DAI. Syncretic religious organization founded in Cochin China after World War I. It opposed efforts by all political forces to bring it under outside control. It continues to exist in Vietnam today, although under strict government supervision.

CAMBODIAN PEOPLE'S REVOLUTIONARY PARTY (CPRP). Revolutionary organization established in Cambodia under Vietnamese tutelage in the early 1950s. It was one of three organizations that succeeded the ICP after the latter's dissolution in 1951. The CPRP's armed forces were popularly known as the Khmer Rouge (Red Khmer). The organization was replaced by a Khmer Communist Party in the mid-1960s.

CENTRAL OFFICE FOR SOUTH VIETNAM (COSVN). Headquarters unit for Communist operations in South Vietnam during the Franco-Vietminh conflict and later the Vietnam War. First created in 1951, it was disbanded after the fall of Saigon in 1975.

CHINESE COMMUNIST PARTY (CCP). Formal name for the branch of the Communist Party established in Shanghai, China, in 1921.

COMMUNIST INTERNATIONAL (COMINTERN, or CMT). Revolutionary organization established in Soviet Russia in 1919. With its headquarters in Moscow, the CMT directed revolutionary activities by its member parties throughout the world until its dissolution in 1943. The ICP was formally admitted to membership in 1935.

COMMUNIST PARTY OF INDOCHINA (DONG DUONG CONG SAN DANG, or CPI). Short-lived revolutionary organization established by breakaway members of the Revolutionary Youth League in 1929. It was eventually merged with the ACP and the Tan Viet Party into the Vietnamese Communist Party (VCP), which was founded by Ho Chi Minh in February 1930.

COMMUNIST PARTY OF THE SOVIET UNION (CPSU). Formal name for the revolutionary party established under the guidance of Vladimir I. Lenin in the 1920s.

CONSTITUTIONALIST PARTY. Politically moderate party set up by reformist elements in Cochin China in the early 1920s. Its goal was to achieve autonomy for Vietnam under a benign French tutelage. Its leader, Bui Quang Chieu, became a vocal critic of the ICP and was assassinated by Vietminh elements during the August Revolution of 1945.

DAI VIET PARTY. Nationalist organization established during World War II. At first pro-Japanese, it eventually recruited supporters among non-Communist elements in Vietnam to struggle against the French colonial regime, and continued to exist as a formal political organization in the RVN until the fall of Saigon in 1975.

DEMOCRATIC REPUBLIC OF VIETNAM (DRV). Independent government established by Ho Chi Minh and his Vietminh Front in northern Vietnam in September 1945. Driven out of Hanoi by the French in December 1946, it was granted legal authority in North Vietnam by the Geneva Conference of 1954. It was renamed the Socialist Republic of Vietnam in July of 1976.

DONG KINH NGHIA THUC (HANOI FREE SCHOOL). School established by patriotic intellectuals to promote reform during the first decade of the twentieth century. It was eventually disbanded by the French. Members of the school sponsored the establishment of the Duc Thanh school in Phan Thiet, where Ho Chi Minh taught briefly in 1910.

DONG MINH HOI (full name: VIET NAM CACH MENH DONG MINH HOI; in English, VIETNAMESE REVOLUTIONARY LEAGUE). Vietnamese nationalist organization founded under Chinese Nationalist sponsorship in August 1942. It included several Vietnamese nationalist parties and was the brainchild of Chinese general Zhang Fakui, who hoped to use it against Japanese forces in Indochina. Although Ho Chi Minh sought to use it for his own purposes, it eventually competed with the ICP for political control in Vietnam after World War II. By the time of the outbreak of war in December 1946, it had become moribund.

FATHERLAND FRONT (MAT TRAN TO QUOC). Broad-based front organization created by the DRV in 1955. It supplanted the Lien Viet Front and the latter's famous predecessor, the Vietminh Front, as a means of mobilizing support for party policies in Vietnam.

FRENCH EXPEDITIONARY FORCES (FEF). Military forces employed by France in Indochina during the Franco-Vietminh war.

HOA HAO. Syncretic religious movement founded by the Buddhist mystic Huynh Phu So in 1939. Strongly anti-French, it also opposed Communist efforts to control it after World War II. It continues to exist in the Socialist Republic of Vietnam (SRV) under the watchful eyes of authorities.

HOPES OF YOUTH PARTY (THANH NIEN CAO VONG). Short-lived nationalist party set up by Nguyen An Ninh in Saigon in the mid-1920s. Eventually dissolved.

IMPERIAL ACADEMY (QUOC TE GIAM). Training school for Confucian bureaucrats run by the imperial court in Vietnam. Originally founded in the eleventh century in Hanoi, it was transferred to Hué by the Nguyen Dynasty in the nineteenth century. Ho Chi Minh's father served at the school briefly as an instructor.

INDOCHINESE COMMUNIST PARTY (DANG CONG SAN DONG DUONG, or ICP). Communist party founded by Ho Chi Minh and colleagues in October 1930. The original name adopted in February was the Vietnamese Communist Party (VCP). The ICP was formally dissolved in November 1945 and then reemerged in 1951 as the Vietnamese Workers' Party (VWP).

INDOCHINESE FEDERATION (LIEN BANG DONG DUONG). Plan developed by the ICP in the mid-1930s to create a federation of revolutionary states of Vietnam, Laos, and Cambodia. After World War II it was replaced by the concept of a "special relationship" among the three states.

INDOCHINESE UNION (UNION INDOCHINOISE). Administrative structure established at the end of the nineteenth century to supervise French rule in Indochina. It included the colony of Cochin China and the protectorates of Annam, Tonkin, Cambodia, and Laos.

INTERNATIONAL CONTROL COMMISSION (ICC). Watchdog organization set up by the Geneva Conference to police the cease-fire reached in July 1954. Composed of representatives from Canada, India, and Poland.

KHMER COMMUNIST PARTY (KCP). Communist organization founded in the mid-1960s by radicals led by Pol Pot in Cambodia. It replaced the Cambodian People's Revolutionary Party (CPRP) that had been founded in 1951.

KHMER ROUGE. Popular name for the revolutionary armed forces in Cambodia. Sometimes identified with the Khmer Communist Party.

LAOTIAN PEOPLE'S REVOLUTIONARY PARTY (LPRP). Revolutionary organization established under Vietnamese tutelage in the early 1950s. It was popularly known as the Pathet Lao.

LIEN VIET FRONT (MAT TRAN LIEN VIET). Front organization set up by the ICP in 1946 to broaden the party's appeal, it eventually merged with the Vietminh Front in 1951 and was replaced in 1955 by the Fatherland Front.

NATIONAL ACADEMY (QUOC HOC). Prestigious secondary school established in 1896 in Hué to provide future court officials with training in French language and civilization. Ho Chi Minh attended the school from 1907 to 1908.

NATIONAL DEFENSE GUARD (VE QUOC QUAN). Brief name for the Vietnamese Liberation Army (VLA) shortly after the August Revolution of 1945. The name was selected to avoid problems with Chinese occupation forces.

NATIONAL FRONT FOR THE LIBERATION OF SOUTH VIETNAM (MAT TRAN DAN TOC GIAI PHONG MIEN NAM, or NLF). Broad alliance of resistance groups founded under DRV tutelage in South Vietnam in 1960. It was dissolved after reunification of the country in 1976.

NATIONAL LIBERATION COMMITTEE (UY BAN GIAI PHONG DAN TOC). Committee of Vietminh representatives established at the Tan Trao conference to prepare for the August uprising. Ho Chi Minh served as chairman.

NATIONAL SALVATION ASSOCIATIONS (CUU QUOC HOI). Mass organizations set up by the ICP to mobilize support against the French during and after World War II. After 1954, they were simply called mass associations.

NEW VIETNAMESE REVOLUTIONARY PARTY. Also known as the Tan Viet Revolutionary Party, the organization was founded in the late 1920s by anti-French nationalists. It eventually merged with the ICP.

PATHET LAO. Popular name for the revolutionary armed forces in Laos. During the Vietnam War, the Pathet Lao cooperated with insurgent forces in Vietnam against the United States.

PEOPLE'S ARMY OF VIETNAM (PAVN). Regular army created in the DRV after the Geneva Conference of 1954. It succeeded the Vietnamese Liberation Army (VLA) that operated in Indochina during the Franco-Vietminh War.

PEOPLE'S LIBERATION ARMED FORCES (NHAN DAN GIAI PHONG QUAN, or PLAF, or VIET CONG). Established in 1961, formal name for the armed forces of the revolutionary movement during the Vietnam War. (See also VIET CONG.)

REPUBLIC OF VIETNAM (VIET NAM CONG HOA, or RVN). Formal name for the non-Communist government founded in South Vietnam after the Geneva Conference. It replaced Free Vietnam in 1956. The RVN collapsed in 1975 and was assimilated into the Socialist Republic of Vietnam (SRV) in July 1976.

REVOLUTIONARY YOUTH LEAGUE OF VIETNAM (VIET NAM THANH NIEN CACH MENH DONG CHI). Early Vietnamese revolutionary organization founded by Ho Chi Minh in South China in 1925. Combining nationalist and Marxist themes, it was replaced by a formal Communist Party in 1930.

SOCIALIST REPUBLIC OF VIETNAM (CONG HOA XA HOI VIET NAM, or SRV). Formal name for the united Vietnamese state created in 1976 after the end of the Vietnam War.

SOUTHEAST ASIA TREATY ORGANIZATION (SEATO). Multinational alliance established under U.S. auspices in 1954 to defend the area against Communist expansion. It is now moribund.

VANGUARD YOUTH MOVEMENT (THANH NIEN TIEN PHONG). Mass youth movement established under Japanese auspices in Cochin China during World War II. It was directed by Pham Ngoc Thach, a clandestine member of the ICP, and was used in support of the August uprising in Saigon in 1945.

VIET CONG (VIET COMMUNISTS). Pejorative name used to describe insurgent forces in South Vietnam during the Vietnam War. The formal name was the People's Liberation Armed Forces, or PLAF.

VIETMINH FRONT (VIET NAM DOC LAP DONG MINH, or LEAGUE FOR THE INDEPENDENCE OF VIETNAM). Front organization created under ICP leadership in May of 1941. During World War II and in succeeding years it struggled to obtain independence from French rule.

VIETNAMESE COMMUNIST PARTY (DANG CONG SAN DONG DUONG, or VCP). Original name for the party founded by Ho Chi Minh in February 1930. Replaced by the Indochinese Communist Party (ICP) in October 1930, it was revived in December 1976.

VIETNAMESE DEMOCRATIC PARTY (DANG DAN CHU VIET NAM). Small non-Communist political party established under ICP auspices, as part of the Vietminh Front in 1944. Technically it existed to represent the interests of patriotic intellectuals.

VIETNAMESE LIBERATION ARMY (VIET NAM GIAI PHONG QUAN, or VLA). Formal name for the resistance forces organized by the ICP during the war against the French after World War II. First founded in December 1944, it was replaced by the People's Army of Vietnam (PAVN) after the Geneva Conference of 1954.

VIETNAMESE LIBERATION LEAGUE (VIET NAM GIAI PHONG DONG MINH). Front organization established by Ho Chi Minh in south China in 1941. It was designed to unite anti-French elements under ICP leadership, but was later dominated by anti-Communist elements in the area. Eventually it was replaced by the Dong Minh Hoi.

VIETNAMESE NATIONAL ARMY (VNA). Formal name for the armed forces organized by the Associated State of Vietnam under Chief of State Bao Dai. It was replaced after the Geneva Conference by the Army of the Republic of Vietnam (ARVN).

VIETNAMESE NATIONALIST PARTY (VIET NAM QUOC DAN DANG, or VNQDD). Non-Communist nationalist party established in Tonkin in 1927. For the next several decades it was one of the Communist Party's major political rivals in Indochina. Now disbanded.

VIETNAMESE RESTORATION PARTY (VIET NAM QUANG PHUC HOI). Anticolonialist party established by Phan Boi Chau in 1912. It replaced his monarchist Modernization Society when Chau decided to form a republic instead. After several unsuccessful uprisings, it eventually declined in influence and disappeared.

VIETNAMESE WORKERS' PARTY (DANG LAO DONG VIET NAM, or VWP). Formal name for the Communist Party in Vietnam after its revival in 1951. It was replaced by the Vietnamese Communist Party (VCP) in 1976.

HO CHI MINH

INTRODUCTION

On the morning of April 30, 1975, Soviet-manufactured North Vietnamese tanks rumbled through the northern suburbs of Saigon and headed toward the presidential palace in the heart of the city. Seated on the tanks, soldiers dressed in combat fatigues and the characteristic pith helmet with the single gold star waved the flag of the Provisional Revolutionary Government (PRG).

Just after noon, a row of tanks rolled slowly along Thong Nhut Avenue past the American Embassy, from the roof of which the last U.S. marines had lifted off by helicopter only two hours before. The lead tank hesitated briefly before the wrought-iron gate in front of the presidential palace and then crashed directly through the gate and stopped on the lawn before the ceremonial staircase that gave entrance into the palace. The young tank commander entered the building and met briefly with President Duong Van "Big" Minh. He then ascended to the roof of the palace where he replaced the flag of the Republic of Vietnam on the flagpole with the red and blue banner of the PRG.

The long Vietnam War had thus finally come to an end. After nearly a decade of bitter and often bloody fighting that left 50,000 of their comrades dead, the last American combat troops had finally departed after the signing of the Paris Agreement in January 1973. The agreement quickly broke down, and over the next several months the armed forces of the Saigon regime clashed repeatedly with soldiers of the Viet Cong and North Vietnamese Army (formally known as the People's Army of Vietnam, or PAVN), over 100,000 of whom had been tacitly permitted to remain in the South as the result of the agreement. In December 1974, emboldened by success on the battlefield and by growing evidence that the United States would not reenter the conflict, Party leaders (the Vietnamese Communist Party at that time was known as the Vietnamese Workers' Party, or VWP) approved a plan drawn up by the PAVN general staff for a two-year campaign to bring down the Saigon regime by the spring of 1976. But the first probes along the Cambodian border and in the Central Highlands in early 1975 elicited such a weak response from Saigon that at the end of March Hanoi instructed its commanders in the South to seek final victory before the close of the dry season at the end of April. Saigon's defenses in the northern part of the country collapsed with lightning suddenness, and by mid-April North Vietnamese troops were marching rapidly southward toward Saigon. South Vietnamese President Nguyen Van Thieu resigned on April 21. His replacement, the elderly Saigon politician Tran Van Huong, lasted only seven days and was in turn replaced by "Big" Minh in the forlorn hope that the popular southern general might be able to induce the North Vietnamese to accept a compromise peace settlement. Minh's peace feelers were contemptuously ignored in Hanoi.

The Communist triumph in Saigon was a tribute to the determination and genius of VWP leader Le Duan and his veteran colleagues in Hanoi. Equally crucial to success were the North Vietnamese troops and Viet Cong guerrillas—the simple *bo doi* (the Vietnamese equivalent of the GI), who for a generation had fought and died for the revolutionary cause in the jungles and swamps of South Vietnam. But above all it was a legacy of the vision, the will, and the leadership of one man: Ho Chi Minh, founder of the Vietnamese Communist Party, leader of the revolutionary movement, and president of the Democratic Republic of Vietnam (DRV) until his death in 1969, six years before the end of the war. In tribute to his contribution, after the fall of Saigon his colleagues would rename it Thanh pho Ho Chi Minh, or the City of Ho Chi Minh.

Agent of the Comintern in Moscow, member of the international Communist movement, architect of victory in Vietnam, Ho Chi Minh is unquestionably one of the most influential political figures of the twentieth century. Yet at the same time he remains one of the most mysterious of men, a shadowy figure whose motives and record have long aroused controversy. For three decades, debate has raged over the deceptively simple question of his underlying motives for a lifetime of revolutionary activity. Was he primarily a nationalist or a Communist? Was his public image of simplicity and selflessness genuine, or a mere artifice? To his supporters, Ho was a symbol of revolutionary humanitarianism, an avuncular figure devoted to the welfare of his compatriots and to the liberation of all the oppressed peoples of the world. To many who met him, Vietnamese and foreigners alike, he was a "sweet guy" who, despite his prominence as a major world leader, was actually a selfless patriot with a common touch and a lifelong commitment to the cause of bettering the lives of his fellow Vietnamese. Critics, however, pointed to the revolutionary excesses committed in his name and accused him of being a chameleon personality, a wolf in sheep's clothing.

The question of Ho Chi Minh's character and inner motivations lies at the heart of the debate in the United States over the morality of the conflict in Vietnam. To many critics of U.S. policies there, he was a simple patriot leading the struggle for Vietnamese independence and a vigorous opponent of global imperialism throughout the Third World. Supporters of the U.S. war effort raised doubts about his patriotic motives by alluding to his long record as an agent of Joseph Stalin and five decades of service to the world revolution. The nationalist image that he so assiduously cultivated, they allege, was simply a ruse to win support at home and abroad for the revolutionary cause.

For Americans, the debate over Ho Chi Minh arouses passions over a war that is now past. For Vietnamese, it conjures up questions of more fundamental importance, since it defines one of the central issues in the Vietnamese revolution—the relationship between human freedom and economic equality in the emerging postwar Vietnam. Since the end of the Vietnam War, Ho Chi Minh's colleagues, some of whom are still in power in Hanoi today, have tirelessly drawn on his memory to sanctify the Communist model of national development. Ho's goal throughout his long career, they allege, was to bring an end to the global system of capitalist exploitation and create a new revolutionary world characterized by the utopian vision of Karl Marx. A few dissenting voices, however, have argued that the central message of his career was the determination to soften the iron law of Marxist class struggle by melding it with Confucian ethics and the French revolutionary trinity of liberty, equality, and fraternity. In justification, they point to one of Ho's slogans, which is seen everywhere on billboards in Vietnam today: "Nothing is more precious than independence and freedom."[1]

The debate over Ho Chi Minh, then, is at the heart of some of the central issues that have marked the twentieth century, an era of nationalism, revolution, egalitarianism, and the pursuit of human freedom. The complexities of his character mirror the complexity of the age. He remains a powerful force in postwar Vietnam, revered by millions and undoubtedly detested by countless others. For good or ill, Ho Chi Minh managed to reflect in his person two of the central forces in modern society—the desire for national independence and the quest for social and economic justice. Although all of the evidence is not yet in, it is past time to expose this dominating figure of the twentieth century to historical analysis.

The problems encountered by any biographer who embarks on this quest are intimidating. Although Ho's name is instantly recognizable to millions of people throughout the world, there has long been a frustrating lack of verifiable sources of information about his life. Having passed much of his adulthood as a revolutionary in opposition to the French colonial regime in Indochina, Ho spent many years in exile and others living a clandestine existence inside his own country. During much of that period he lived and traveled incognito under a variety of pseudonyms. It has been estimated that during his lifetime Ho adopted more than fifty assumed names.[2] Many of his writings were penned under such names, while countless others have been lost or were destroyed in the course of a generation of conflict.

Ho Chi Minh contributed to the confusion by assuming a tantalizing mystery about his life. For years he denied that the unknown public figure who emerged immediately after World War II as President Ho Chi Minh was in actuality the same person as Nguyen Ai Quoc, the founder of the Indochinese Communist Party (ICP) and a prominent Comintern agent of the prewar period. Even after his true identity was revealed, Ho remained extraordinarily secretive about key events in his past life, and his few ventures into the field of autobiography, one of which was published in several languages by the DRV in the late 1950s, were written under assumed names. Only in recent years have researchers in Hanoi been able to confirm that these works were indeed written by Ho Chi Minh himself.[3]

The problem of compiling a biography of Ho Chi Minh has been compounded by the inaccessibility of existing sources. Because Ho traveled and lived in several countries in the course of his life, information on his activities is scattered on several continents. Ho himself spoke several foreign languages and his voluminous writings (including pamphlets, articles, reports, and letters) were written in a variety of languages, including English, French, Chinese, and Russian, as well as in his native Vietnamese.

Until recently, much of this information was not available to scholars. Even today, archival materials held in Hanoi are generally closed to both Vietnamese and foreign researchers. Information relating to his activities in China and the USSR was also off-limits and was rarely divulged by either the Chinese or the Soviet governments. Virtually the only interval of his life that had been subjected to careful exploration was a brief period that he spent in France after World War I. The opening of French colonial archives during the early 1970s placed those years for the first time under public scrutiny. More recently, voluminous collections of his writings have been published in Vietnam, but such compilations are by no means complete, while official editing of some passages raises doubts about their accuracy. The archives of the Comintern in Moscow have been partially opened to scholars, but detailed records of his relations with Soviet leaders remain closed to outside observers.[4]

Yet another question about Ho Chi Minh concerns the character of his leadership. Although Ho was the founder of the ICP and a leading figure in the international Communist movement, he was not as dominant a personality as many other modern revolutionary leaders, such as Lenin, Stalin, or Mao Zedong; he appeared to lead by persuasion and consensus rather than by imposing his will through force of personality. Nor did he write frequently about his ideas or inner motivations. In contrast to other prominent revolutionary figures, Ho Chi Minh expressed little interest in ideology or intellectual debate and focused his thoughts and activities on the practical issue of freeing his country and other colonial societies from Western imperialism. For that reason, Ho has often been dismissed by scholars—and sometimes by his own contemporaries—as a mere practitioner, rather than as a revolutionary theoretician. The distinction never seemed to bother him. To an interviewer who once asked why he had never written an ideological treatise, he playfully replied that ideology was something he would leave to Mao Zedong. During his later years, serious works on doctrine or strategy published in Vietnam were usually produced by his colleagues Vo Nguyen Giap, Truong Chinh, or Le Duan.

Given the controversial nature of the topic and the paucity of reliable sources, it is hardly surprising that no serious biography of Ho Chi Minh has been published in English over the last twenty years. At the height of the Vietnam War a number of biographical studies were published, but most of these were aimed at the mass market and did not attempt to make detailed use of existing source materials. In North Vietnam several official or semiofficial biographies were published, but all were marred by a blatant effort to present their subject in mythic proportions, as a saint rather than as a political figure, more caricature than reality.[5]

Today, as the passions of the Vietnam War have begun to subside and additional source materials have become available in various parts of the world, there are modest grounds for optimism that a more definitive understanding of Ho's life is becoming possible. (The nature of those sources is discussed briefly in a note on sources at the end of this book.) While by no means have all of the mysteries about his life been resolved, the assiduous biographer is now in a position to piece together a number of hypotheses to explain several of the questions that have persistently been raised about his life and character. I have tried to address these questions, either in the text or, for those issues of more academic interest, in the endnotes.

It is at once clear that for much of Ho's early life—the period prior to his arrival in Paris at the end of World War I—almost the only available source material comes from those autobiographical works mentioned above or from historical sources in Vietnam, where the attempt to present him as a legend and a gift to the ages remains a growth industry supported by the regime. Some critics raise doubts as to whether any of the information on his life that has been published by official sources in Vietnam can be trusted. After carefully examining the evidence, I have decided that significant parts of this material are reliable, although the details often remain in doubt, and some accounts are undoubtedly apocryphal. To avoid endless discussions of the reliability of various facts regarding his activities, I have therefore decided to present my own account of his life in narrative form, while relegating debates about the evidence to the endnotes. Where there are reasonable grounds to doubt a particular version of events, the issue is dealt with in the text. I hope that this will also help to convey the dramatic character of Ho Chi Minh's life and its importance in shaping the history of Vietnam and the twentieth century.

There remains the issue of political bias. Just as it has been impossible for the last generation to approach the Vietnam War in a dispassionate manner, it is equally difficult for the biographer to paint a picture of the man who brought about the Communist victory there without exposing his own political leanings. Over the decades since I have become familiar with Ho Chi Minh's life, I have developed a respect for his talent and his commitment as a revolutionary without suspending my ability to judge him as a revolutionary, as a politician, and as a man. I have gradually become convinced that, as is so often the case, the truth is much more complex than the public image would lead one to believe. Although it is always tempting to seek out some single thread (the "hidden figure in the carpet," in Leon Edel's classic phrase), I prefer to let the facts speak for themselves. I have therefore not tried to invent imaginary thoughts or conversations that might have suited my own interpretation of his inner character. Like so many great figures in history, the real Ho Chi Minh was a man of complexities and contrasts, with some unique gifts and characteristics that set him apart from other important individuals of his time.

Some readers will undoubtedly be disappointed that there is not a greater focus on the final years of his life at the height of the Vietnam War. In fact, Ho Chi Minh's role in creating the conditions for that conflict are vastly more important than his influence in Hanoi during the course of the war itself, when he was frequently ill or in China for medical treatment. Many readers will find, therefore, that substantial parts of this book refer to individuals and events with which they are not familiar. I hope that they will feel compensated by a greater awareness of the underlying causes of the war and its consequences.

There is an element of mystery in all great men. And few enjoyed that mystery more than Ho Chi Minh himself. In an interview with the Vietnam scholar Bernard Fall in 1962, Ho responded to one of Fall's questions: "An old man likes to have a little air of mystery about himself. I like to hold on to my little mysteries. I'm sure you will understand that."[6] From his seat in the pantheon of revolutionary heroes, Ho Chi Minh will be delighted to know that, at least in this biography, the air of mystery that has always surrounded him remains intact.

I | IN A LOST LAND

He entered the city quietly, with no fanfare. While his followers roamed the streets, celebrating their victory or accepting the surrender of enemy troops, he settled in a nondescript two-story commercial building in the Chinese section of town. There he spent several days in virtual seclusion, huddled over the battered typewriter that he had carried with him during a decade of travels from Moscow to south China and finally, in the first weeks of 1941, back to his homeland, which he had left thirty years before.

By the end of the month he had completed the speech that he planned to make to his people announcing the creation of a new nation. Shortly after 2:00 P.M. on September 2, he mounted the rostrum of a makeshift platform hastily erected in a spacious park soon to be known as Ba Dinh Square on the western edge of the city. He was dressed in a faded khaki suit that amply encased his spare emaciated body, and he wore a pair of rubber thongs. Thousands had gathered since the early morning hours to hear him speak. In a high-pitched voice that clearly reflected his regional origins, he announced the independence of his country and read the text of its new constitution. To the few Americans who happened to be in the audience, his first words were startling: "All men are created equal; they are endowed by their creator with certain unalienable rights; among these are life, liberty, and the pursuit of happiness."

The time was the late summer of 1945, shortly after the surrender of Japanese imperial forces throughout Asia. The place was Hanoi, onetime capital of the Vietnamese empire, now a sleepy colonial city in the heart of the Red River delta in what was then generally known as French Indochina. For two decades, Nguyen the Patriot had aroused devotion, fear, and hatred among his compatriots and the French colonial officials who ruled over them. Now, under a new name, he introduced himself to the Vietnamese people as the first president of a new country.

At the time, the name Ho Chi Minh was unknown to all but a handful of his compatriots. Few in the audience, or throughout the country, knew of his previous identity as an agent of the Comintern (the revolutionary organization, also known as the Third International, founded by the Bolshevik leader Lenin twenty-six years before) and the founder in 1930 of the Vietnamese Communist Party. Now he described himself simply as "a patriot who has long served his country." For the next quarter of a century, the Vietnamese people and the world at large would try to take the measure of the man.

The forces that initiated his long journey to Ba Dinh Square had begun to germinate in the late summer of 1858, when a small flotilla of French warships, joined by a small contingent from Spain, launched a sudden attack on the city of Da Nang, a commercial seaport of medium size on the central coast of Vietnam. The action was not totally unexpected. For decades covetous French eyes had periodically focused their gaze on Vietnam: missionaries on the lookout for souls to save, merchants scouring the globe for new consumer markets and a river route to the riches of China, politicians convinced that only the acquisition of colonies in Asia would guarantee the survival of France as a great power. Until midcentury, the French government had sought to establish a presence in Vietnam by diplomatic means and had even sent a mission to the imperial capital at Hué, about fifty miles north of Da Nang, in an effort to persuade the Vietnamese emperor to open his country to French influence. When the negotiations stalled, the government of Emperor Louis Napoleon decided to resort to force.

The country that French warships had attacked was no stranger to war or foreign invasion. Indeed, few peoples in Asia had been compelled to fight longer and harder to retain their identity as a separate and independent state than had the Vietnamese. A paramount fact in the history of the country is its long and frequently bitter struggle against the expansionist tendencies of its northern neighbor, China. In the second century B.C., at a time when the Roman republic was still in its infancy, the Chinese empire had conquered Vietnam and exposed it to an intensive program of political, cultural, and economic assimilation. Although the Vietnamese managed to restore their independence in the tenth century A.D., it took several hundred years for Chinese emperors to accept the reality of Vietnam's separate existence; in fact, this happened only after Vietnam's reluctant acceptance of a tributary relationship with the imperial dynasty in China.

Vietnam's long association with China had enduring consequences. Over a millennium, Chinese political institutions, literature, art and music, religion and philosophy, and even the Chinese language sank deep roots into Vietnamese soil. The result was a "Confucianized" Vietnam that to the untutored observer effectively transformed the country into a miniature China, a "smaller dragon" imitating its powerful and brilliant northern neighbor. The Vietnamese monarch himself set the pace, taking on the trappings of a smaller and less august Son of Heaven, as the emperor was styled in China. The Vietnamese ruling elite was gradually transformed into a meritocracy in the Chinese mold, its members (frequently known as mandarins) selected (at least in theory) on the basis of their ability to pass stiff examinations on their knowledge of the Confucian classics. Generations of young Vietnamese males were educated in the very classical texts studied—and often memorized—by their counterparts in China. Their sisters, prohibited by rigidly patriarchal Confucian mores from pursuing official careers—or indeed almost any profession—were secluded within the confines of the family homestead and admonished to direct their ambitions to becoming good wives and mothers.

Vietnam's passage into the Chinese cultural universe was probably not an especially wrenching experience, for the social and economic conditions that had helped to produce Confucian civilization in China existed to a considerable degree in Vietnam as well. Like its counterpart to the north, Vietnamese society was fundamentally agrarian. Almost nine of every ten Vietnamese were rice farmers, living in tiny villages scattered throughout the marshy delta of the Red River as it wound its way languidly to the Gulf of Tonkin. Hard work, the subordination of the desires of the individual to the needs of the group, and a stable social and political hierarchy were of utmost importance. The existence of a trained bureaucracy to maintain the irrigation system and the road network was considered essential, but there was relatively little need for commerce and manufacturing. Although indigenous elements were never eliminated in Vietnamese culture, to untutored eyes the country appeared to be a mirror image in microcosm of its giant neighbor to the north.

But if the Vietnamese people appeared willing to absorb almost whole the great tradition of powerful China, they proved adamant on the issue of self-rule. The heroic figures of traditional Vietnam—rebel leaders such as the Trung sisters (who resisted Chinese rule in the first century A.D.), the emperor Le Loi, and his brilliant strategist Nguyen Trai, who fought against the Ming dynasty 1400 years later—were all closely identified with resistance to Chinese domination. Out of the crucible of this effort emerged a people with a tenacious sense of their national identity and a willingness to defend their homeland against outside invasion.

One of the lasting consequences of the Vietnamese struggle for national survival was undoubtedly the emergence of a strong military tradition and a willingness to use force to secure and protect national interests. In the centuries after the restoration of national independence from China in A.D. 939, the new Vietnamese state, which called itself Dai Viet (Great Viet), engaged in a lengthy conflict with its neighbor to the south, the trading state of Champa. Eventually the Vietnamese gained the upper hand, and beginning in the thirteenth century they pushed southward along the coast. By the seventeenth century, Champa had been conquered and the territory of Dai Viet had been extended to the Ca Mau Peninsula on the Gulf of Siam. Vietnamese settlers, many of them ex-soldiers, migrated southward to create new rice-farming communities in the fertile lands of the Mekong River delta. Dai Viet had become one of the most powerful states in mainland Southeast Asia, and the Vietnamese monarch in his relations with neighboring rulers began to style himself not simply as a king but as an emperor.

But there was a price to pay for the nation's military success, as territorial expansion led to a growing cultural and political split between the traditional-minded population in the heartland provinces of the Red River delta and the more independent-minded settlers in the newly acquired frontier regions to the south. For two centuries, the country was rent by civil war between ruling families in the north and the south. In the early nineteenth century the empire was reunified under a descendant of the southern ruling family bearing the name of Nguyen Anh, who adopted the reign title Gia Long. At first the new Nguyen dynasty attempted to address the enduring legacy of civil strife, but by midcentury regional frictions began to multiply, supplemented by growing economic problems such as the concentration of farmlands in the hands of the wealthy, and exacerbated by incompetent leadership in the imperial capital of Hué.

The Vietnamese civil war had occurred at a momentous period in the history of Southeast Asia, as fleets from Europe, sailing in the wake of the Portuguese explorer Vasco da Gama, began to prowl along the coast of the South China Sea and the Gulf of Siam in search of spices, precious metals, and heathen souls to save. Among the Europeans most interested in the area were the French, and when in the nineteenth century their bitter rivals, the British, began to consolidate their hold on India and Burma, French leaders turned covetous eyes toward Vietnam.

In 1853 the third emperor of the Nguyen dynasty died, and the Vietnamese throne passed into the hands of a new ruler, the young and inexperienced Tu Duc. It was his misfortune, and that of his people, that on his shoulders was placed the responsibility of repulsing the first serious threat to Vietnamese independence in several centuries. Although well-meaning and intelligent, he was often indecisive and nagged by ill health. When French troops landed at Da Nang harbor in the summer of 1858, Tu Duc's first instinct was to fight. Contemptuously rejecting an offer to negotiate, he massed imperial troops just beyond French defenses on the outskirts of the city. Admiral Charles Rigault de Genouilly, the French commander, had been assured by French missionaries operating in the area that a native uprising against imperial authority would take place, but it failed to materialize. At first, the admiral hoped to wait out his adversary, but when cholera and dysentery began to thin out the European ranks, he decided to abandon the city and seek a more vulnerable spot farther to the south. Early the following year the French resumed their attack at Saigon, a small but growing commercial port on a small river a few miles north of the Mekong River delta. Imperial troops in the area attempted to counterattack, but their outdated weapons were no match for the invaders, and after two weeks Vietnamese resistance collapsed.

Although the first reaction of the emperor had been to fend off the aggressors with military force, the defeat in the south left him disheartened. Despite appeals from advisers at court for a policy of continuing defiance, Tu Duc decided to negotiate, and in 1862 he agreed to cede three provinces in the Mekong delta to the French, eventually to be known (with the addition of three more provinces a few years later) as the French colony of Cochin China. The first round had gone to Paris.

For a few years the imperial court at Hué maintained a precarious grip on independence, but when the French resumed their advance in the early 1880s, launching an attack on the citadel at Hanoi and occupying several major cities in the Red River delta, the court seemed paralyzed. The sickly Tu Duc had died just before the reopening of hostilities, and in the subsequent leadership crisis the court split into opposing factions. Over the next few months several new monarchs, most of them children, were enthroned and unseated in rapid succession. Ultimately, power was seized by the influential regent Ton That Thuyet, who put his own protégé, Ham Nghi, on the throne in hopes of continuing the resistance. In response to a Vietnamese request, the Qing dynasty in China sent imperial troops to aid its vassal, but the Vietnamese were nonetheless unable to prevail. In 1885 China withdrew its armed forces and signed a treaty with France expressly abandoning its long-standing tributary relationship with Vietnam. In Hué, a more pliant emperor was placed on the throne to replace the young Ham Nghi, who fled with his recalcitrant adviser Ton That Tuyet into the mountains in the interior to continue the struggle. In the meantime, the now dominant peace faction at court concluded a new treaty with France conceding to the latter political influence throughout the entire remaining territory of Vietnam. The French transformed their new possession into the protectorates of Tonkin (comprising the provinces in the Red River delta and the surrounding mountains) and Annam (consisting of the coastal provinces down to the colony of Cochin China far to the south). In Annam, the French allowed the puppet emperor and his bureaucracy to retain the tattered remnants of their once august authority. In Tonkin, colonial rule reigned virtually supreme. For all intents and purposes, Vietnam had become a French possession.

The French conquest of Vietnam was a manifestation of a process of European colonial expansion which had begun after the Napoleonic Wars and accelerated during the remainder of the nineteenth century as advanced Western states began to enter the industrial age. Driven by a desperate search for cheap raw materials and consumer markets for their own manufactured goods, the capitalist nations of the West turned to military force to establish their hegemony throughout the region. By the end of the century, all of the countries of South and Southeast Asia except the kingdom of Siam—later to be known as Thailand—were under some form of colonial rule.

The surrender of the imperial court did not end the Vietnamese desire for independence. Centuries of resistance to China had instilled in the Vietnamese elite class a tradition of service to king and country as the most fundamental of Confucian duties. Many civilian and military officials refused to accept the court's decision to capitulate to superior military force and attempted to organize local armed forces to restore Ham Nghi to power. In Ha Tinh province, along the central coast of Annam, the scholar-official Phan Dinh Phung launched a Can Vuong (Save the King) movement to rally support for the deposed ruler and drive the French from his native land. When his friend Hoang Cao Khai, a childhood acquaintance who had decided to accommodate himself to the new situation, remonstrated with Phung to abandon his futile effort and prevent useless bloodshed, the latter replied in the lofty tones of the principled Confucian patriot:

I have concluded that if our country has survived these past thousand years when its territory was not large, its wealth not great, it was because the relations between king and subjects, fathers and children, have always been regulated by the five moral obligations. In the past, the Han, the Song, the Yuan, the Ming [four of the most powerful of past Chinese dynasties] time and again dreamt of annexing our country and of dividing it up into prefectures and districts within the Chinese administrative system. But never were they able to realize their dream. Ah! If even China, which shares a common border with our territory and is a thousand times more powerful than Vietnam, could not rely upon her strength to swallow us, it was surely because the destiny of our country had been willed by Heaven itself.[1]

But the existence of two claimants to the throne created a serious dilemma for all those Vietnamese who were animated by loyalty to the monarchy. Should they obey the new emperor Dong Khanh, duly anointed with French approval at Hué? Or should they heed the appeal of the dethroned ruler Ham Nghi, who from his mountain hideout had issued a call for the support of all patriotic elements in a desperate struggle against the barbarians? The dilemma of choosing between resistance and accommodation was a cruel one and created a division in the traditional ruling class that would not heal for over half a century.

At the heart of the anti-French resistance movement was the central Vietnamese province of Nghe An. A land of placid beaches and purple mountains, of apple green rice fields and dark green forests, Nghe An lies in the Vietnamese panhandle between the South China Sea and the mountains of the Annamite cordillera along the Laotian border to the west. It is a land of hot dry winds and of torrential autumn rains that flatten the rice stalks and flood the paddy fields of the peasants. It is paradoxical that this land, so beautiful to the eye, has often been cruel to its inhabitants. Crowded into a narrow waist between the coast and the mountains, the Vietnamese who lived in this land, over 90 percent of whom were peasants scratching out their living from the soil, found life, at best, a struggle. The soil is thin in depth and weak in nutrients, and frequently the land is flooded by seawater. The threat of disaster is never far away, and when it occurs, it sometimes drives the farmer to desperate measures.

Perhaps that explains why the inhabitants of Nghe An have historically been known as the most obdurate and rebellious of Vietnamese, richly earning their traditional sobriquet among their compatriots as "the buffalos of Nghe An." Throughout history, the province has often taken the lead in resisting invaders, and in raising the cry of rebellion against unpopular rulers. In the final two decades of the nineteenth century, Nghe An became one of the centers of the anti-French resistance movement. Many of the province's elites fought and died under the banner of Phan Dinh Phung and his Can Vuong movement.

The village of Kim Lien is located in Nam Dan district, in the heart of Nghe An province, about ten miles west of the provincial capital of Vinh. The district lies along the northern bank of the Ca, the main river in Nghe An province. Much of the land is flat, with rice fields washed by a subtropical sun stretching to the sea a few miles to the east, but a few hillocks crowned by leafy dark-green vegetation rise above the surrounding plain. Clumps of palm trees dot the landscape and provide shade for the tiny thatch huts of the peasants huddled in their tiny hamlets. Within each individual hamlet, banana trees, citrus, and stands of bamboo provide sustenance in times of need and materials for local construction. Still, the farmers of the district were mostly poor in the nineteenth century, for it was a densely populated region, and there was inadequate land to feed the population.

It was here, in 1863, that Ha Thy Hy, the second wife of the well-to-do farmer Nguyen Sinh Vuong (sometimes called Nguyen Sinh Nham), gave birth to a son, who was given the name Nguyen Sinh Sac. Vuong's first wife had died a few years earlier, after bearing her husband's first son, Nguyen Sinh Tro. To raise his child, Vuong married Ha Thy Hy, the daughter of a peasant family in a neighboring village. By the time Sac was four, his mother and father had both died, and he was brought up by his half brother Tro, who had already taken up farming on his father's land. The farmer's life was difficult for Tro and his neighbors. When a typhoon struck, the land was flooded, destroying the entire harvest; times of drought produced stunted rice plants. As a result, many farmers in the village worked at other tasks as a sideline, such as carpentry, bricklaying, weaving, or metalworking. Yet there was a long tradition of respect for learning in the area. A number of local scholars had taken the Confucian civil service examinations, and several offered classes in the classics as a means of supplementing their meager income.

At first, the young Nguyen Sinh Sac had little opportunity to embark on his own career as a scholar. Although the family history, carefully carved in Chinese characters on wooden tablets placed, in accordance with tradition, beside the family altar, recorded that many members had successfully taken the civil service examinations in earlier times, apparently none had done so in recent generations. Sac's half brother Tro had little interest in learning. Yet it soon became clear that Sac was eager for education. After leading his brother's water buffalo back from the fields in the late morning, he often stopped off at the school of the local Confucian scholar Vuong Thuc Mau, where he tied up the animal and lingered outside the classroom, listening to the teacher conduct his lessons. In his spare time, young Sac attempted to learn Chinese characters by writing them on the bare earth or on the leaf of a persimmon tree.[2]

By the time he was an adolescent, Nguyen Sinh Sac's love of learning had become common knowledge throughout the village and came to the attention of Hoang Duong (also known as Hoang Xuan Duong), a Confucian scholar from the nearby hamlet of Hoang Tru who often walked over the mud-packed footpaths to Kim Lien to visit his friend Vuong Thuc Mau. Noticing the young lad on the back of a water buffalo absorbed in reading a book while his friends played in the fields, Hoang Duong spoke with Nguyen Sinh Tro and volunteered to raise the boy, offering him an education through the classes that he taught in his own home. Tro agreed, and in 1878, at age fifteen, Nguyen Sinh Sac moved to Hoang Tru village, where he began formal study in the Confucian classics with his new foster father and sponsor. The event was hardly an unusual one, since it was customary for the talented sons of poor farmers to be taken under the wing of more affluent relatives or neighbors and provided with a Confucian education in a local school. Should the child succeed in his studies and rise to the level of a scholar or government official, relatives and neighbors alike could all bask in the glow of the recipient's prestige and influence.

Like many other scholars in the area, Master Duong (as he was known locally) was part teacher, part farmer. The roots of the Hoang family were in Hai Hung province, just to the southeast of Hanoi in the Red River delta, where many members were renowned for their learning. After moving to Nghe An in the fifteenth century, Hoang Duong's forebears continued the tradition of scholarship. His father had taken the civil service examination three times, eventually receiving the grade of *tu tai* ("cultivated talent," the lowest level of achievement in the examination and the Confucian equivalent of a bachelor's degree in the United States today).

While Hoang Duong taught his students in two outer rooms of his small house, his wife, Nguyen Thi Kep, and their two daughters, Hoang Thi Loan and Hoang Thi An, tilled the fields and weaved to supplement the family income. Like their counterparts in villages throughout the country, none of the women in Master Duong's family had any formal education, since the arts of scholarship and governing—reflecting time-worn Confucian principles introduced from China—were restricted exclusively to males. In Vietnam, as in China, it was a woman's traditional duty to play the role of mother and housekeeper, and to serve the needs of her husband. This had not always been the case, since Vietnamese women had historically possessed more legal rights than their Chinese counterparts, but as Confucianism became increasingly dominant after the fifteenth century, their position in Vietnamese society became increasingly restricted. Within the family, they were clearly subordinate to their husbands, who possessed exclusive property rights and were permitted to take an additional wife if the first failed to produce a son.

Within these constraints, Nguyen Thi Kep and her daughters were probably better off than most of their neighbors, since they had absorbed a little literary knowledge. Kep's own family also had a tradition of scholarship. Her father had passed the first level of civil service examination just like her father-in-law had. As the wife of a local scholar, Kep was a respected and envied member of the local community. In most respects, however, her life, and that of her daughters, differed little from their less fortunate neighbors, who spent their days knee-deep in the muddy fields beyond the village hedgerow, painstakingly nursing the rice seedlings through the annual harvest cycle.

In this bucolic atmosphere, young Sac grew to adulthood. He quickly showed himself adept at Confucian learning, and when he displayed a romantic interest in Master Duong's attractive daughter Hoang Thi Loan, the family eventually consented to arrange a marriage, although Kep was apparently initially reluctant because of Sac's status as an orphan. The wedding ceremony took place in 1883. As a wedding gift, Master Duong provided his new son-in-law with a small three-room thatch hut on a small plot of land next to his own house. A one-room structure nearby served as the family altar, where the males in the family were expected to pay fealty to the family ancestors. The house built for the newlyweds was cozy and clean, with the living space in the front room, the kitchen in the rear, and an outside room for Sac's study. The family was somewhat more affluent than most in the village but did not hire laborers for their rice fields or the small vegetable garden. During the next seven years, while her husband continued his studies, Hoang Thi Loan bore three children—a daughter, Nguyen Thi Thanh, born in 1884; a son, Nguyen Sinh Khiem, in 1888; and then, on May 19, 1890, a second son, Nguyen Sinh Cung, who would later be known as Ho Chi Minh. (In Vietnam, children are given a "milk name" at birth. When they reach adolescence, a new name is assigned to reflect the parents' aspiration for their child).[3]

While Nguyen Sinh Sac studied in preparation for taking the civil service examinations, his wife, Loan, as was the custom, tended the rice fields and raised the children. According to the recollections of her contemporaries, she was diligent and family oriented, both traditional Confucian virtues, but she was also gifted and intellectually curious. She had some acquaintance with Vietnamese literature and often lulled her children to sleep with traditional folk songs or by reciting passages from Nguyen Du's famous verse classic *Truyen Kieu* (The Tale of Kieu), a poignant story of two lovers caught in the web of traditional morality.

In 1891, Nguyen Sinh Sac traveled to the provincial capital of Vinh to sit in candidacy for the *tu tai*, but he failed to pass. His performance was sufficiently encouraging, however, for him to continue his studies after his return home, and to teach classes to local children in his home to help support the family. When his father-in-law, Master Duong, died in 1893, adding to the family's financial burdens, Sac was forced to delay his preparations for retaking the examination. While his older sister helped with the household chores, little Nguyen Sinh Cung enjoyed himself, playing in the fields or roaming around his father's school. At night, before being placed in his hammock, his grandmother read him local tales of heroism. Cung was intelligent and curious, quick to absorb knowledge.

In May 1894, Sac took the examinations in Vinh a second time and received the grade of *cu nhan*, or "recommended man," a level higher than the *tu tai* and the equivalent of a master of arts degree. The achievement was unusual for a local scholar, and on his return to Hoang Tru village he was offered a small plot of land as a traditional reward given by the community to successful candidates in the civil service examinations. Since he had only three acres of rice land as part of his wife's dowry, Sac accepted, but he refused offers to arrange an expensive banquet in his honor, preferring instead to distribute water buffalo meat to poor villagers.

It was commonplace for recipients of the prestigious *cu nhan* degree to seek an official position in the imperial bureaucracy, thus "honoring the self and enriching the family" (*vinh thanh phi gia*), but Nguyen Sinh Sac preferred to continue his studies while earning a modest income as a local instructor of the classics. In the hallowed Confucian tradition of wifely sacrifice—in the expressive Vietnamese phrase, *vong anh di truoc, vong nang theo sau*, or "the carriage of the husband goes before, that of his wife after"—Hoang Thi Loan continued to work in the family's rice fields while raising the family.

In the spring of 1895, Nguyen Sinh Sac traveled to Hué to take the imperial examinations (*thi hoi*), the highest level of academic achievement in the Confucian educational system. He did not pass but decided to remain in the city in order to enter the Imperial Academy (Quoc tu Giam) in preparation for a second effort. The academy, whose origins dated back to the early years of national independence in Hanoi, served as a training place sponsored by the court for aspiring candidates for the imperial bureaucracy. Sac had no funds to pay his tuition or room and board, but fortunately the school offered a few modest scholarships to help defray living costs and with the assistance of a friend he was able to obtain one. Sac returned briefly to Nghe An to bring Loan and their two sons back to Hué, so that his wife could seek work to help the family meet expenses.

In those days, the trip from the Nghe An provincial capital of Vinh to Hué was both arduous and dangerous. The journey lasted about a month, and the road wound through dense forest and over mountains infested by bandits. It was quicker and more comfortable to travel by sea, but to poor villagers like Nguyen Sinh Sac, the cost of passage by ship was prohibitive. The family thus decided to make the trip on foot, covering at most about thirty kilometers a day and walking in groups with several other travelers for protection against bandits and wild animals. With his short legs, the five-year-old Cung found it difficult to keep up the pace, so his father sometimes carried him, entertaining him with stories of mythical creatures and the heroic figures of the Vietnamese past.

Hué, originally known as Phu Xuan, had once been the headquarters of the Nguyen lords who had ruled the southern half of the country during the two centuries of civil war. After the founding of the Nguyen dynasty in 1802, Emperor Gia Long had decided to transfer the capital there from its traditional location in the Red River valley as a means of demonstrating his determination to reunify the entire country under Nguyen rule. A small market town nestled on the banks of the Perfume River about midway between the two major river deltas, it had become an administrative center after becoming the seat of the imperial court, but was still much smaller in size than the traditional capital of Hanoi (then known as Thang Long), and probably contained a population of fewer than ten thousand inhabitants.

After arriving, undoubtedly exhausted, in Hué, Nguyen Sinh Sac was able to arrange temporary lodgings at the house of a friend. Eventually, however, the family moved into a small apartment located on Mai Thuc Loan Street, not far from the eastern wall of the imperial city, on the northern bank of the Perfume River. The Imperial Academy was located on the southern bank, about seven kilometers west of the city. But Sac seldom attended school, spending most of his time studying at home. In his spare time he taught the classics to his own boys and the children of local officials. Reflecting the intense respect for education that characterized Confucian societies, he put extra pressure on his sons, admonishing them to study hard and pay strict attention to their calligraphy. According to the accounts of neighbors, little Cung had already begun to display a lively interest in the world around him, joining his brother to watch the imperial troops perform their drills and trying to sneak into the imperial city for a closer look inside. Observing a royal procession as it left the palace on one ceremonial occasion, he returned home to ask his mother whether the emperor had injured his leg. When asked why he had posed the question, Cung replied that he had just seen the ruler being carried by bearers in a sedan chair.

In 1898, Sac failed in his second attempt to pass the metropolitan examination and decided to accept temporary employment as a teacher at a neighborhood school in the hamlet of Duong No, just east of the city. His wife, Loan, remained in the apartment in Hué to supplement the family's meager income by weaving and taking in washing. The school at Duong No had been founded by a well-to-do local farmer, who gave permission for Sac's own two sons to attend the classes. It was apparently at that time that the boys were first exposed to the Confucian classics in the Chinese language.

In August 1900, Sac was appointed by the imperial court to serve as a clerk for the provincial examinations in Thanh Hoa, a provincial capital almost five hundred kilometers north of the imperial capital. The assignment was considered an honor, since *cu nhan* were not usually allowed to serve as proctors. Sac's elder son, Khiem, went with him; Cung remained with his mother in Hué. On his return from Thanh Hoa to Hué, Sac stopped briefly in his home village of Kim Lien to build a tomb for his parents.

The decision was costly. Back in Hué, his wife had given birth to her fourth child, a boy named Nguyen Sinh Xin (from *xin*, meaning literally "to beg"). But the ordeal weakened her already fragile constitution, and despite the help of a local doctor she became ill and died on February 10, 1901. Neighbors later recalled that during the Tết (the local version of the lunar new year) holidays, the young Cung ran crying from house to house asking for milk to feed the baby, and that for weeks his normally sunny disposition turned somber.[4]

On hearing the news of his wife's death, Sac returned immediately to Hué to pick up his children and take them back to Hoang Tru village, where he resumed his teaching. For a while, young Cung continued to study with his father, but eventually Sac sent him to a distant relative on his mother's side, a scholar named Vuong Thuc Do. By then, little Cung had begun to make significant progress in his studies. He was able to recognize quite a few Chinese characters—the essential medium for a Confucian education and still used to write the colloquial Vietnamese language—and enjoyed practicing them. It was clear that the boy was quick-witted and curious, but his father was concerned that he sometimes neglected his studies and sought out other amusements. Cung's new instructor may have been some help in that regard. Vuong Thuc Do genuinely loved his students and reportedly never beat them—apparently quite unusual in his day—and he regaled his protégés with stories of the righteous heroes of the past, one of whom was his own older brother, who had fought with Phan Dinh Phung's Can Vuong movement against the French.

After a few months in Hoang Tru, Sac returned to Hué; his mother-in-law, Nguyen Thi Kep, kept the children. Sac's daughter, Nguyen Thi Thanh, who had stayed in the village with her grandmother when the rest of the family moved to Hué, was now fully grown but had not married, so she remained at home to reduce the burden on the family. Cung helped out in the house and garden, but still had time to play. In summertime he joined his friends in fishing in the local ponds, flying kites (many years later, local residents would recall that when on windless days many of his friends quickly grew discouraged, Cung would still try to keep his kite in the air), and climbing the many hills in the vicinity. The most memorable was Mount Chung, on the summit of which sat the temple of Nguyen Duc Du, a general of the thirteenth century who had fought against an invading Mongol army. It was here, too, where the patriotic scholar Vuong Thuc Mau, at whose doorstep Sac had first discovered his love of learning years before, had formed a band of rebels in 1885 to fight under the banner of the Can Vuong movement. From the heights of Mount Chung, climbers had a breathtaking view of rice fields, stands of bamboo and palm trees, and the long blue-gray line of the mountains to the west. There was only one sad interlude in this, the happiest period of young Cung's childhood. His younger brother Xin continued to be sickly, and died at the age of only one year.

Back in Hué, Nguyen Sinh Sac applied to retake the imperial examinations and this time he earned the degree of doctorate, second class (known in Vietnamese as *pho bang*). The news caused a sensation in Hoang Tru, as well as in Sac's native village of Kim Lien. Since the mid-seventeenth century, the villages in their area had reportedly produced almost two hundred bachelor's and master's degree holders, but he was the first to earn the *pho bang* degree. On his return, the residents of Hoang Tru planned a ceremonial entry into the village, but Sac, whose dislike of pomp and circumstance was now becoming pronounced, again declined the honor. Despite his protests, the village arranged a banquet to celebrate the occasion. At his request, however, some of the food was distributed to the poor.

According to tradition, the honor of claiming a successful examination candidate went to the home village of the candidate's father. In Sac's case, of course, this meant that the village that could now label itself "a civilized spot, a literary location" (*dat van vat, chon thi tu*) was his father's birthplace of Kim Lien, rather than Hoang Tru, where he now resided. To reward their native son, the local authorities of Kim Lien had used public funds to erect a small wood and thatch house on public land to entice him to live there. Sac complied, using it as a new home for himself and his three surviving children. It was slightly larger than his house in Hoang Tru, consisting of three living rooms, with one room reserved for the family water buffalo and a small room containing an altar for Hoang Thi Loan. A couple of acres of rice land were included with the house, as well as a small garden, where Sac planted sweet potatoes.

The award of a *pho bang* degree was a signal honor in traditional Vietnamese society and often brought the recipient both fame and fortune, usually in the form of an official career. Nguyen Sinh Sac, however, had no desire to pursue a career in the bureaucracy, especially in a time of national humiliation. Refusing the offer of an official appointment at court on the grounds that he was still in mourning for the death of his wife, Sac decided to stay in Kim Lien, where he opened a small school to teach the classics. The monetary rewards for such work were minimal, and Sac contributed to his financial difficulties by giving generously to the poor residents in the village. Sac did adopt one concession to his new status, however, taking on the new name Nguyen Sinh Huy, or "born to honor."[5]

For young Cung, Sac's decision came at a momentous time in his life; at the age of eleven, he was about to enter into adolescence. As was traditional in Vietnamese society, to mark the occasion his father assigned to him the new name Nguyen Tat Thanh, or "he who will succeed," on the village register. At first the boy continued to study the classics with his father, but eventually he was sent to attend a local school taught by his father's friend Vuong Thuc Qui, the son of the scholar Vuong Thuc Mau, who had committed suicide by throwing himself into a pond to avoid being arrested by the French. Although a degree holder like Sac, Qui had also refused appointment as an official and taught in his home village, where he secretly took part in subversive activities against the puppet government in Hué. In teaching his students, he rejected the traditional pedantic method of forcing his students to memorize texts, but took great care to instruct them in the humanitarian inner core of Confucian classical writings while simultaneously instilling in their minds a fierce patriotic spirit for the survival of an independent Vietnam. To burn his message into their souls, prior to beginning each day's lecture he lit a lamp at the altar of his father along the wall of his classroom.

Nguyen Tat Thanh thrived under his new tutor, penning patriotic essays at Qui's direction and helping to serve the guests who frequently came to lecture on various subjects. Unfortunately, the experience was a short one, for Qui soon closed the school and left the village to take part in rebel activities. Thanh briefly studied with another teacher in a neighboring village, but his new tutor's teaching methods were too traditional for the boy's taste, and he soon returned to study with his father, whose attitude toward learning was much more tolerant. Like his friend Vuong Thuc Qui, Sac was critical of the technique of rote memorization and once remarked that studying a text "branch and leaf" was a worthless activity far removed from the reality of life. Don't just follow the road to an official career, he advised his students, but try to understand the inner content of the Confucian classics in order to learn how to help your fellow human beings. To a friend Sac once remarked, "Why should I force my students to memorize the classics just to take the exams? I won't teach my kids that way."[6]

Young Thanh was undoubtedly delighted with his father's attitude, for he much preferred to read such popular Chinese favorites as *Romance of the Three Kingdoms*, a romantic tale of heroism during the period of turmoil following the fall of the Han dynasty, and *Journey to the West* (sometimes translated into English under the title *Monkey*), an account of the Buddhist monk Xuan Zang's trip through Central Asia to India in search of classical Buddhist texts. (While Thanh was attending school at Duong No village, an older student who had been instructed to keep an eye on him found it necessary to tie a string to his charge so that he could be located when he sneaked out to play. On most occasions, it turned out that Thanh had already learned his lesson by heart.[7])

Nguyen Tat Thanh's education was not limited to the classroom. His father's house was located near the workshop of a local blacksmith named Dien, who taught the boy how to use the forge and frequently took him bird hunting. Dien's penchant for telling stories turned his forge into one of the most popular gathering spots in the vicinity, and in the evening Thanh often joined with other village youngsters to sit at Dien's feet while Dien recounted the heroic but ultimately futile efforts of local Can Vuong bands to drive the barbarians from their homeland. With others in the audience, Thanh heard about the glorious achievements of warriors long dead like Le Loi and Mai Thuc Loan, who had fought to protect their homeland against invaders. He listened with sorrow to the story of Vuong Thuc Mau's suicide, and how the Can Vuong leader Phan Dinh Phung, his dwindling forces driven deep into the mountains along the Laotian border, had finally died of dysentery in 1896, thus bringing a tragic end to the movement. But he thrilled to hear that several members of his father's family had served and died fighting for the cause.

By now, Thanh had begun to absorb an intense feeling of patriotism. While living with his parents in Hué, he had attended memorial services at a nearby temple for martyrs who had been killed during the war of resistance against the French, and he joined the others in weeping bitterly over their sacrifice. After returning to his home village in 1901, he was irritated to discover that most of the classical texts available locally dealt with Chinese rather than Vietnamese history, and he walked to the provincial capital of Vinh to buy books about the history of his own country. When he discovered that they were too expensive to purchase, he tried to memorize key passages so that he could quote them to friends back in Kim Lien.

Until now, the boy's acquaintance with the French had been limited to observing them as a child on the streets of Hué; contemporaries later recalled his curiosity at that time as to why even the most prestigious of Vietnamese officials had to bow and scrape before all Europeans. Sometimes, he and his brother watched raptly as French construction workers erected a steel bridge over the Perfume River just east of the imperial city. On occasion, the workers would joke with the boys and offer them candy, inspiring Thanh to ask his mother why some foreigners were so much more friendly than others. On his return to his home village, however, Thanh's dislike of foreigners intensified when he heard tales of the mistreatment of laborers recruited by the French to work on a new highway under construction that wound westward through the mountains into Laos. Although Thanh and his brother, as the sons of a member of the scholarly class, were exempted from conscription for public labor projects, many other villagers were not so fortunate. The lucky ones returned home broken in body and spirit. Many others, their health ravaged by malaria, malnutrition, or overwork, did not return at all. Although corvée labor had traditionally been required of peasants in precolonial times, such projects had usually been more modest in scope and in the length of service required. The road into Laos—the "road of death," as it became known to the Vietnamese—became a major source of popular antagonism to the new colonial regime.

One of Nguyen Sinh Sac's close acquaintances was the renowned scholar and patriot Phan Boi Chau, a native of a village only a few kilometers from Kim Lien. Chau's father had been a *tu tai*, and Chau had received training in the classics as a youth. But to young Chau, the plight of his country was much more important than the promise of an official career. While still an adolescent, he had organized the youth of his village into a tiny militia to follow the example of their elders in attacking the invading French. He later acknowledged his humiliation when French troops entered the village to suppress the movement and forced him to flee to the surrounding woods in the company of a crowd of refugees.

Eventually, Chau continued with his classical studies and in 1900 he passed the regional examinations "with honors" (giai nguyen). But, like Nguyen Sinh Sac, Phan Boi Chau had no aspirations for an official career and soon began to travel throughout the central provinces of the country to organize fellow scholars into a coherent movement to oppose the feudal court and its protector, the French colonial regime. By now he had begun to read the reformist writings of Chinese progressives such as Kang Youwei and Liang Qichao, and became convinced that Vietnam must learn from the West in order to survive.

During his travels, Phan Boi Chau frequently stopped in neighboring Kim Lien to visit Nguyen Sinh Sac and Vuong Thuc Qui and discuss the matters of the day. Articulate and affable, he was a persuasive advocate of the patriotic cause, and he undoubtedly made an impression on young Thanh, who often served his father and his guest as they sat on rattan mats in the living room of Sac's house with a jug of rice wine or a pot of tea. The impressionable young man was already acquainted with some of Chau's patriotic writings and was inspired by his rebellious spirit and his contempt for feudal traditions and the decrepit monarchy in Hué.[8]

As his writings at the time vividly demonstrate, Phan Boi Chau had already concluded that the Vietnamese must eventually abandon the traditional system that had evolved over a thousand years and adopt modern institutions and technology from abroad. But he also believed that only the country's scholarly elite could lead the people to adopt such changes and that, to obtain the people's assistance, his own movement must borrow some of the hallowed trappings of past centuries. As a result, when in early 1904 he established a new organization called the Modernization Society (Duy Tan Hoi) to provide a focus for his efforts to attract support from patriotic scholars around the country, he selected a dissident member of the Nguyen royal house, Prince Cuong De, to serve as the titular head of the organization, the stated goal of which was to drive out the French and establish a constitutional monarchy.

Like many of his progressive contemporaries in China, Phan Boi Chau found a model for his program in Japan, where reformist elements from among the aristocratic class had rallied around Emperor Meiji to promote the modernization of traditional Japanese society. Like many Vietnamese, he had been impressed with the success of Japanese armed forces in the recent war against tsarist Russia, viewing it as proof that Asian peoples possessed the capacity to defeat Western invaders. Chau was firmly convinced that Vietnam would require assistance from abroad to bring his plans to fruition. At the end of 1904, he left for Japan and took steps to establish a school in Yokohama to train young Vietnamese patriots for the coming struggle for national independence. The following summer he returned to Hué and began to scour the country for prospective recruits.[9]

Sometime shortly after his return to Vietnam, Phan Boi Chau visited Kim Lien and asked Nguyen Tat Thanh and his brother to join his movement, now popularly known as Journey to the East (Dong Du). Thanh, however, rejected the offer. According to some accounts, his decision was based on the grounds that relying on the Japanese to evict the French was equivalent to "driving the tiger out of the front door while welcoming the wolf in through the back door." Other sources suggest that it was his father who made the decision. In his own autobiographical account, written under a pen name, Ho Chi Minh later explained that he preferred to go to France to see the secret of Western success at its source.[10]

Thanh's decision to reject Phan Boi Chau's offer may have been motivated by one of Chau's own remarks. When Thanh had asked how Japan had realized its own technological achievements, Chau replied that the Japanese had learned from the West. Shortly afterward, Thanh told his father that he wanted to study the French language. Sac was reluctant, since at the time only Vietnamese collaborators had bothered to learn the foreigner's tongue. But Sac himself had already begun to obtain a superficial acquaintance with Western culture when he joined a book club to read the writings of Chinese reformist intellectuals seeking to persuade the Qing court to change its ways, so he was eventually convinced by his son's arguments.

At first, opportunities for Thanh to pursue his new objective were limited. During the summer of 1905, he began to study French language and culture with the help of one of his father's scholarly friends in Kim Lien village. Then, in September, Sac enrolled both his sons in a Franco-Vietnamese preparatory school at Vinh. On the instructions of Governor-General Paul Doumer, the French administration had just decided to establish elementary-level preparatory schools to teach the French language and culture in all the provinces of central Vietnam. Doumer's objective was to attract students from the Confucian schools in the area and provide a core of potential recruits for the new colonial administration; funds were made available to provide scholarships for needy students. Although Nguyen Sinh Sac had devoted his career to traditional education, he had by now become convinced that the younger generation must adapt to the new reality and learn from the country's new masters. He frequently quoted from the fifteenth-century Confucian scholar Nguyen Trai, who had once pointed out that it was necessary to understand the enemy in order to defeat him. During the next academic year, Thanh and his brother made their first serious acquaintance with French language and culture. They also began to study *quoc ngu*, the transliteration of spoken Vietnamese into the Roman alphabet, which had first been introduced by Jesuit missionaries in the seventeenth century and was now being popularized by progressive scholars as an alternative to the cumbersome Chinese characters that had been in use for centuries.

Since receiving his *pho bang* degree in 1901, Nguyen Sinh Sac had steadily refused an official appointment by the court on the grounds of illness or family responsibility but, summoned once again in May 1906, he decided that he could no longer refuse, and accepted the offer. Leaving his daughter in charge of the house in Kim Lien, Sac returned with his two sons to the capital, arriving in June. Once again, they traveled on foot, but it must have been much easier than the previous occasion, since the boys were now teenagers. En route, Sac recounted stories about

Nguyen Trai and other famous historical figures, while Thanh quizzed his older brother on the names of all the Vietnamese dynasties.[11]

The city that they had returned to had changed considerably since they last lived there. The imperial palace, with its imposing gray walls and massive flag tower, still dominated the northern bank of the placid Perfume River, which wound its way down from the lavender hills of the Annamite cordillera to the west. From the sampans on the river, lissome prostitutes with the flowing black hair so admired by Vietnamese everywhere called out to prospective customers on the riverbank. But there were some visible changes. A massive typhoon, that periodic scourge of the entire central coast, had battered the region two summers previously, destroying vegetation and leaving a mossy residue along the riverbanks. Along the south bank, directly across the river from the imperial city, the nondescript shops in the old commercial section of town were rapidly being replaced by white stucco European-style buildings to house the offices of the French advisers.

On their arrival in Hué, Sac and his two sons lived briefly in the house of a friend, but were eventually assigned a small apartment near the Dong Ba gate on the east wall of the imperial city. The building, constructed of wood with a tile roof, had once been an infantry barracks, but was now subdivided for the living quarters of junior officials at court. Sac's apartment was small, just big enough for a bed and a table. There was no separate kitchen or running water, so the family members had to go to the local well or a nearby canal located just outside the Dong Ba gate. They ate simply, their meals consisting primarily of salted fish, vegetables, roasted sesame seeds, and cheap rice. Young Thanh did much of the cooking. While such conditions were better than those of most of their rural compatriots, they were undoubtedly much more primitive than the accommodations enjoyed by more affluent officials at court.[12]

Shortly after his arrival in Hué, Sac talked with his longtime patron Cao Xuan Duc, an official at the Institute of History who had given him assistance during his first period of residency in the imperial capital. Through Duc's intervention at court, Sac was appointed to work as an inspector in the Board of Rites (Bo Le), with responsibility for supervising students at the Imperial Academy. It was not an especially prestigious position for someone of his academic rank, since most of the *pho bang* in the class of 1901 had by now moved on to become district magistrates or to assume more senior positions in the bureaucracy. But Nguyen Sinh Sac's long refusal to accept an official appointment had undoubtedly drawn attention at court and perhaps triggered suspicion of his loyalty to the imperial house.[13]

For Sac, in any event, the experience of working at court was evidently an exceedingly unpleasant one. He had become increasingly uneasy about the morality of serving a monarchy that was only a puppet in the hands of a foreign ruler. What, he wondered, was the contemporary meaning of the traditional phrase "loyalty to the king, love of country" (*trung quan ai quoc*)? He had begun to speak to friends about the need for the reform of the old system, which in his view had become increasingly corrupt and irrelevant, and he advised his students against pursuing an official career. Mandarins, in his view, existed only to oppress the people.

Nguyen Sinh Sac's despair about the decrepitude of the traditional system was only too justified. The Confucian bureaucratic model had always depended upon the effectiveness of moral suasion as a means of maintaining the competence and the integrity of officials selected through the civil service examination system. In theory, local mandarins, indoctrinated since childhood into a system of social ethics based on service to the community, personal rectitude, and benevolence, would adopt such principles in applying their authority to those in their charge. Familiar tendencies toward bureaucratic arrogance and self-seeking conduct could be kept under control by the actions of a humane and energetic ruler at the apex of the system. By the end of the nineteenth century, however, the weakness at court had led to a general breakdown in the effectiveness of Confucian institutions in Vietnamese society, and in the prestige and authority of the emperor himself. Lacking a sense of direction from Hué, mandarins found it all too easy to use their authority to line their own pockets, or those of their friends and relatives. Communal lands traditionally made available to poor families were now seized by the wealthy, who were often able to obtain exemptions from the taxes paid annually to the government by each village.

Sac was by no means the only Confucian scholar to hold the imperial court in contempt. It was at this time that the voice of the imperial official Phan Chu Trinh first came to public attention. Trinh had received a *pho bang* degree in the same year as Nguyen Sinh Sac. Born in the province of Quang Nam in 1872, Trinh was the youngest of three children. His father was a military officer who had taken the civil service examination but had failed to earn a degree. Convinced that the old ways were useless, Trinh's father had joined the ranks of the Can Vuong, but he was eventually suspected of treason by his fellow rebels and executed. Trinh himself accepted an assignment at the Board of Rites in 1903, but he was disturbed by the corruption and incompetence of court officials and the mandarins who maintained government authority in the countryside. He publicly raised the issue to students preparing for the 1904 imperial examinations. He began to read the writings of the Chinese reformists, and in 1905 he resigned from office in order to travel around the country and consult with other scholars on the future course of action.

Eventually, Trinh crossed paths with Phan Boi Chau in Hong Kong and followed Chau to Japan, where he approved of Chau's efforts to train a new generation of Vietnamese intellectuals to save the country from extinction, but not of his friend's decision to rely on the support of a member of the imperial family. In Trinh's view, it made more sense to cooperate with the French in the hope that they would launch reforms to transform traditional Vietnamese society. In August 1906 he penned a public letter to Governor-General Paul Beau, pointing out what he considered the "extremely critical situation" in the country.

In this letter, Trinh conceded that the French presence had brought a number of advantages to the Vietnamese people, including the first stages of a modern system of transport and communications. But by tolerating the continuing existence of the imperial bureaucracy in central Vietnam, he argued, the colonial regime perpetuated a corrupt and decrepit system, and then compounded the problem by treating the Vietnamese people with condescension and contempt, thus arousing considerable public hostility. Trinh pleaded with Governor-General Beau to launch legal and educational reforms to bring an end to the old system and introduce modern political institutions and the Western concept of democracy. In doing so, he would earn the lasting gratitude of the Vietnamese people.

> It is with a heart filled with anguish and because there is no one with whom I may speak freely that I have decided to take up the pen to express my feelings to you very frankly. If the French government is really determined to treat the Annamite people more liberally, it cannot but approve my initiative and adopt my advice. It will invite me to present myself before its representatives to explain my case at ease. And on that day I will open my whole heart. I will show what we suffer and what we lack. And I dare to hope that this will mark the awakening, the resurrection of our nation.[14]

Phan Chu Trinh's public letter aroused a commotion in educated circles throughout the country, where resentment against the colonial authority was growing. Behind the mask of the "civilizing mission," French efforts to exploit the economic resources of Indochina and introduce foreign ways had aroused discontent in all strata of Vietnamese society. Traditional scholar-elites were angered at French attacks on Confucian institutions. Peasants chafed at new taxes on alcohol, salt, and opium, which the government had imposed as a means of making Indochina a self-supporting enterprise. The tax on alcohol was especially onerous, as the Vietnamese, forbidden from distilling the rice wine that had been used in family rituals for centuries, were now forced to purchase expensive wines imported from France. For those peasants who left their native village to seek employment elsewhere, a new environment often did not result in improved circumstances. Conditions in the rubber plantations in Cochin China were harsh and frequently led to disease or the death of the worker. Although recruitment was voluntary in principle, in practice it was often coercive and carried out by violence. The situation for factory workers or coal miners was little better, because salaries were low, working hours were long, and living conditions were abysmal.

Still, it was Phan Chu Trinh's hope that the French could be brought to realize their responsibility to carry out their civilizing mission in Indochina. He was not alone in seeking answers in the West to the plight of his nation. Early in 1907, a group of progressive intellectuals in Hanoi formed the Hanoi Free School (Dong Kinh Nghia Thuc). Patterned after an academy recently established by the Japanese reformer Fukuzawa Yukichi in Japan, the school was an independent institution aimed at promoting progressive Western and Chinese ideas to the next generation of Vietnamese. By midsummer, the school had opened over forty classes and enrolled one thousand students. In the meantime, Phan Boi Chau continued to be active in Japan, attracting young Vietnamese to his training program and writing inflammatory tracts that were sent back to Indochina to arouse the patriotic spirit of his people. Among them was *Viet Nam vong quoc su* (Vietnam: History of a Lost Land). Ironically, it was written in Chinese characters.

For a few months, the activities of the Hanoi Free School were tolerated by French officials in Tonkin, but eventually they began to suspect that its goals were not limited to education, and the school was ordered to close its doors in December. But the French could do nothing to silence the growing debate among concerned Vietnamese over how to guarantee the survival of their country. Nguyen Sinh Sac himself was increasingly angry, remarking in a lecture at the Imperial Academy that working in the bureaucracy was the worst kind of slavery—officials were nothing but slaves working at the behest of a slave society. But Sac found it difficult to come up with a solution. Many years later Ho Chi Minh would recall that his father frequently asked rhetorically where the Vietnamese could turn—to England, to Japan, or to the United States— for assistance.[15]

Shortly after his return to Hué, on the advice of Cao Xuan Duc, Sac enrolled his two sons in the Dong Ba upper-level elementary school. The school was part of the new Franco-Vietnamese educational system and was conveniently located just outside the citadel walls in front of Dong Ba gate. It had originally been part of a market that occupied the area, but when the market moved to a new location in 1899, the building was transformed into a school. It contained five rooms, four used as classrooms and the other for an office. Technically, young Thanh did not possess the academic credentials to enroll in the school, since he had not yet received any Western-style educational training; however, because he had learned a little French from his tutor in Kim Lien and performed well in his interview, he was admitted as an entry-level student. He apparently was not sufficiently proficient in French to read the sign, attached to the wall in front of the school, with the famous words of the French Revolution: Liberty, Equality, and Fraternity.

Classes at the school were taught in three languages: Vietnamese, French, and Chinese. At the higher levels, use of the Chinese language was reduced. Some conservatives were opposed to the relatively limited role assigned to Chinese, but Thanh and his father were probably pleased at the decision. Thanh's French tutor in Kim Lien had already advised him: "If you want to defeat the French, you must understand them. To understand the French, you must study the French language."[16]

With his wooden shoes, brown trousers and shirt, and long hair, Thanh undoubtedly cut a rustic figure among his more sophisticated schoolmates—many of whom wore the traditional tunic and trousers of the scholar or wore Western-style uniforms available for purchase at the school—so he soon decided to cut his hair in the fashionable square-cut style and dress like the others to avoid ridicule. He discarded the conical bamboo hat worn by peasants in favor of the preferred hat of woven latania leaves. A friend recollected many years later that Thanh studied hard and played little. He asked permission to write his exercises after classes at an instructor's home and reviewed his lessons with friends at night. One of those friends recalled that he often remarked to friends who became discouraged, "Only through hardship can we succeed." He worked especially hard on the French language, practicing his accent with his friends and writing the French and Chinese equivalents to Vietnamese words in his notebook. The hard work apparently paid off: He needed only one year to finish a two-year course.

In the fall of 1907, Thanh and his brother passed the entrance examinations and were enrolled in the Quoc Hoc (National Academy), the highest level Franco-Vietnamese school in Hué. The academy had been established by decree of Emperor Thanh Thai in 1896 and was placed under the authority of the French *résident supérieur* (the equivalent of regional governor) of central Vietnam. It consisted of seven levels, four of them primary, and culminated in a final level reserved for advanced students. By setting up the school, the court hoped to replace the Imperial Academy and produce Western-educated candidates for the imperial bureaucracy, so the curriculum was focused on French language and culture. Locals dubbed it "the heavenly school."

Living and learning conditions at the school, which was located on the south bank of the river across from the main gate into the imperial palace, hardly corresponded to its prestigious reputation. The main building, which had once served as an infantry barracks, was dilapidated and had a thatch roof, which leaked when it rained. It contained several classrooms, a large lecture hall, and an office. Surrounding the building were several bamboo and thatch huts. The entryway to the school opened on Avenue Jules Ferry, a major thoroughfare that ran along the riverbank into the city, and was marked by a two-story wooden portico in the Chinese style, with the name of the school inscribed in Chinese characters.

The student body at the school was highly diverse. Some, like Thanh and his brother, were scholarship students who had to walk to school. Others came from wealthy families and boarded at the school or arrived every morning in horse-drawn carriages. In the tradition of the time, students were treated harshly, sometimes even brutally. The first director was an entrepreneur by the name of Nordemann, who was married to a Vietnamese woman and spoke the Vietnamese language. His successor, a Monsieur Logiou, had once been a member of the French Foreign Legion.

Although in later years Thanh would comment in highly critical terms about the school and the brutal behavior of some of its teachers, he continued to work hard and prospered through the experience, taking classes in history, geography, literature, and science, while improving his knowledge of the French language. His classmates would recall that he always sat in the back of the room and often did not pay attention to what was going on in the classroom. But he was notorious for asking questions in class and was quite adept at foreign languages, so most of his instructors liked him. Classmates also recalled that some of his questions were quite provocative, as he sought to probe the meaning behind the classical writings of the French enlightenment philosophers. One of his favorite teachers was Le Van Mien, a recent graduate of the Ecole des Beaux Arts in Paris. Although Mien was frequently critical of the policies of the colonial regime, his familiarity with French culture had earned him a favorable reputation among French residents in the imperial capital and protected him from official censure. At the National Academy he informed his students that the French people behaved in a more courteous manner at home than did their counterparts in Indochina, and he regaled Nguyen Tat Thanh with his accounts of the great city of Paris, with its libraries, its museums, and its books on various subjects, which could be read by anyone without official restrictions. Such accounts spurred the young man on to greater achievements, leading one of his instructors to praise Thanh as "an intelligent and truly distinguished student."

Still, Thanh's outspoken demeanor and rustic manners caused problems with some of his more sophisticated fellow students, who teased him as a bumpkin because of his heavy regional accent. At first, Thanh did not react, but on one occasion he lost his temper and struck one of his tormentors in anger. A teacher scolded him for losing his patience and advised him to turn his energy to more useful purposes such as the study of world affairs. Indeed, Thanh had become increasingly interested in politics, and after class he would frequently go down to the river, where crowds gathered to discuss the latest news about Phan Boi Chau and recite together his poem "A-te-a," which described a future Asia free of white rule and appealed to the reader to mobilize for national independence.

A major source in stimulating Thanh's patriotic instincts was his Chinese-language instructor, Hoang Thong, whose anti-French views had become widely known at the school. Thong warned students in his classes that losing one's country (*mat nuoc*) was more serious than losing one's family, since in the former case the entire race would disappear. Thanh visited Thong at his home and avidly read books from his library, including collections of reformist writings by French, Chinese, and Vietnamese authors. According to some accounts, Hoang Thong was involved in clandestine political activities and put Thanh in touch with local resistance groups opposed to the imperial court and the French colonial regime.

While the degree of Thanh's involvement in such activities cannot be substantiated, it is clear that he was becoming increasingly vocal in his criticism of authority. On several occasions he spoke publicly before a crowd of students in the school courtyard, criticizing the servile behavior of the imperial court and calling for a reduction in the onerous agricultural taxes that had been imposed on local farmers. When one student reported his behavior to the authorities, Thanh was called to the office of the school superintendent and given a severe reprimand.[17]

Indeed, by the fall of 1907, the political situation had grown increasingly tense. Emperor Thanh Thai, who had originally been placed on the throne by the French in 1889, was forced to abdicate on suspicion of involvement in rebel activities. But rumors flew throughout the capital that his eight-year-old successor, the emperor Duy Tan, was even more anti-French. As if to signal his youthful determination to bring reforms to his country, his choice of a reign title was a Vietnamese word for "modernization," an act that seemed to proclaim his spiritual kinship with the Emperor Meiji in Japan.

For many progressive Vietnamese, however, it was probably too late to link the royal family to patriotic activities. Nguyen Quyen, a scholar at the Hanoi Free School, had recently written a poem calling on all Vietnamese to cut their hair in a symbolic rejection of the feudal past (at the time, many Vietnamese wore their hair in a bun, the traditional manner favored for centuries). Thanh, who had now begun to cut his classes, joined with friends to circulate among the crowds, giving haircuts, not always on request, to local passersby. Years later, Ho Chi Minh still remembered their chant:

> Comb in the left hand,
> Scissors in the right,
> Snip! Snip!
>
> Cut out the ignorance,
> Do away with stupidity,
> Snip! Snip![18]

Such behavior undoubtedly contributed to the anxiety of French officials and led to the decision by the government in Tonkin to order the Hanoi Free School to close its doors.

Up until now, most of the discontent had been centered among intellectuals. In the early months of 1908 it began to spread to rural areas, where peasants in the provinces along the central coast began to voice discontent at rising taxes, forced labor requirements, and official corruption. In his letter to Beau, Phan Chu Trinh had warned that the mass of the population, crushed by the exactions of local authorities, lived in "black misery." In some areas near the coast, forced labor requirements were especially onerous; for instance, peasants were ordered to spend substantial time clearing sand from harbors after a recent typhoon. In mid-March, large crowds congregated at the office of the district magistrate in Quang Nam province and then marched to the provincial capital of Hoi An, a once thriving seaport a few miles south of Da Nang. The protest movement was actively supported by progressive intellectuals, who had begun to open schools and commercial establishments throughout central Vietnam to educate the young in modern ideas and to raise money for their activities. Now they began to incite peasants to withhold tax payments to the authorities.

As word of the first demonstrations got out, the movement quickly spread from Quang Nam to nearby provinces. In some cases, the demonstrations became violent, as protesters occupied official buildings or the residences of local mandarins. In turn, the imperial authorities ordered soldiers to disperse rioters, which led to several deaths and hundreds of arrests. Occasionally, peasants forcibly cut the hair of passersby, thus inducing French observers to label the movement "the revolt of the short hairs."

By spring, the wave of peasant unrest began to lap at the gates of the imperial capital of Hué. In the first week of May, peasants in the suburban village of Cong Luong demonstrated against high taxes. When a local mandarin arrived with a contingent of troops, riots broke out and the official was seized. The next day a large crowd led him in a bamboo cage to the capital, where they gathered in front of the office of the French *résident supérieur* to demand a reduction of taxes and corvée labor requirements.

The incident was the occasion for Thanh's first direct involvement in political action, although he had undoubtedly followed events closely through the local rumor network. When on May 9 a group of students gathered on the riverbank in front of the National Academy to watch the large groups of peasants who were flooding into town from the suburbs, Thanh suddenly collared two friends and suggested that they join the crowd to serve as interpreters for the peasants in their protest to the French authorities. On the way into the city, he turned his latania hat upside down as a sign of the need to overthrow the status quo. By the time they arrived at the office of Levecque, the *résident supérieur*, the situation was already tense, with angry peasants confronting local officials and nervous troops. Suddenly the officer in charge ordered his militia unit to rush the crowd and drive it back with batons. Thanh, who had moved to the front in an effort to translate the peasants' demands to the authorities, was struck several times.

When the crowd continued to press forward, Levecque agreed to permit a representative from among the demonstrators to enter his office to negotiate conditions for the crowd's withdrawal. Thanh served as interpreter. But the talks failed to resolve the dispute and the people outside refused to disperse, even after Emperor Duy Tan attempted to intervene. Eventually French troops arrived and opened fire on the demonstrators occupying the new bridge over the Perfume River, causing numerous casualties.[19]

That night, Thanh went into hiding at the house of a friend. The next day his fellow students at the National Academy, many of whom had undoubtedly heard about his activities the day before, assumed that Thanh would be absent, but when the bell rang twice to announce the start of classes, Thanh suddenly arrived and took his assigned seat. At 9:00 A.M. a French police official arrived at the school with a detachment of troops and demanded the "tall dark student" who had taken part in the demonstration the day before. When he saw Thanh sitting in the back of his class, he recognized him and said, "I have orders to request that this troublemaker be dismissed from school." It was Thanh's last day at the academy.

In the weeks after the events in Hué, the political crisis intensified. In late June, followers of Phan Boi Chau attempted to stage a coup by poisoning French officials attending a banquet in Hanoi. The instigators hoped that rebel forces in the area could promote a general uprising during the ensuing disorder and seize key installations in the city. But the dosage was too weak to achieve its purpose, and none of the French guests at the banquet died, although a number were temporarily disabled. In the meantime, the plot was inadvertently divulged by one of the perpetrators, provoking the French authorities to declare martial law throughout the area. In the ensuing confusion, Chau's troops in the suburbs scattered, while others were seized by government forces. Thirteen Vietnamese involved in the plot were executed, and others received lengthy prison sentences. Panicky officials rounded up all scholar-intellectuals who were suspected of being in sympathy with the movement, and even Phan Chu Trinh was arrested in Hanoi and transferred to Hué to be put on trial. Prosecutors wanted him executed, but the *résident supérieur* intervened; he was given a life sentence and imprisoned on the island of Poulo Condore, off the coast of Cochin China. In early 1911 he was released and permitted to live in exile in France.

After the riots, Nguyen Sinh Sac was reprimanded for "the behavior of his two sons at the Quoc Hoc school." As a *pho bang* from the same class as Phan Chu Trinh, Sac was watched closely by the court, but the authorities found nothing specific to connect him with the disturbances. As a stratagem to remove him from Hué, in the summer of 1909 he was appointed district magistrate in the district of Binh Khe, in Binh Dinh province about 200 miles to the south of the capital. Although a relatively prosperous region, it had once been the site of a major rebellion against the Nguyen royal house and was now used to detain vagabonds and other undesirables. Thanh's brother, Khiem, was also placed under surveillance, and in 1914 he was convicted of treasonous activities and spent several years in jail. Even his sister, who was still living in Kim Lien, was interrogated on suspicion that she had harbored individuals suspected of complicity in the riots.

After his dismissal from school, Thanh disappeared for a few months. There were reports that a friend tried to find him a job at a limestone plant but was unable to do so because his name was on a police blacklist. Presumably he found some employment or lived with friends, but he did not return to his home village because it was now being watched by the authorities.

Eventually Thanh decided to leave Annam and travel south to the French colony of Cochin China, where he might hope to evade the watchful eyes of the imperial authorities. It may be that he had already decided to go abroad in order to find the secret of Western success at its source, in which case the safest port of departure would be the thriving commercial port of Saigon, which was under French control rather than that of the imperial government. In July 1909 Thanh stopped en route at Binh Khe, where his father had just taken up his post as district magistrate. To avoid arrest Thanh had walked the entire distance from Hué, performing odd jobs to obtain food. By some accounts, however, the meeting with his father was apparently not very successful, for Sac had become increasingly morose and had taken to drink. Sac scolded his son for his recent actions and caned him.[20]

After a brief stay at Binh Khe, Thanh went on to the nearby coastal city of Qui Nhon, where he stayed at the home of Pham Ngoc Tho, an old friend of his father. Thanh studied briefly at a local school there and then, at his host's suggestion, took an examination for a position as a teacher at a local school, using his milk name, Nguyen Sinh Cung, to avoid disclosing his identity. The chairman of the examination board had taught Thanh while he was at the Dong Ba school in Hué and was undoubtedly sympathetic to him, but the provincial governor somehow discovered the ruse and removed his name from the list of candidates for the position.[21]

Frustrated in finding employment in Qui Nhon, Thanh continued south to the port city of Phan Rang. There he sought out the scholar Truong Gia Mo, who had worked at court with Nguyen Sinh Sac in Hué and was also a friend of Phan Chu Trinh. Thanh was apparently anxious to leave the country as soon as possible, but his host persuaded him to accept a job as instructor at the Duc Thanh school in Phan Thiet, about seventy miles further down the coast and just north of the border between Annam and Cochin China. Because Thanh had run out of travel money, he agreed. Before leaving for Phan Thiet, however, he had an emotional experience. When another typhoon battered the port of Phan Rang, French officials ordered Vietnamese dockworkers to dive into the water to salvage ships. According to Ho Chi Minh's later account, many Vietnamese died in the process, to the apparent amusement of Europeans watching from the shore.

The Duc Thanh school had been founded in 1907 by patriotic local scholars who hoped to imitate the success of the Hanoi Free School. The school building was located on the south bank of the Phan Thiet River, about three miles from the South China Sea. The main building was a brick house on the property of a poet who had recently died. The school was now run by his two sons, and a bookstore was established nearby to support the school and to sell works that promoted the new reformist ideas. On the storefront was the slogan: "Get rid of the old, introduce the new and the modern." Classes at the school were taught in *quoc ngu*, but there were courses in the French and the Chinese languages, as well as in the social and natural sciences, art, and physical education.[22]

Still on the run from imperial security forces, Thanh arrived in Phan Thiet before the lunar new year (Têt) holiday early in 1910 and began employment as an instructor of Chinese and *quoc ngu*. As the youngest member of the Duc Thanh school faculty, he was also assigned other duties, including instructor of martial arts. According to recollections of students from the school, Thanh was a very popular teacher, treating his charges with respect and advising fellow instructors not to beat or frighten them. Dressed in the white pajamas and wooden sandals popular at the time, he used the Socratic method to encourage students to think and express their own ideas. He introduced his students to the ideas of Voltaire, Montesquieu, and Rousseau, the writings of whom he had absorbed during his schooling at the National Academy in Hué. Outside the classroom he was very accessible, eating with students and teachers in a temple located on the school grounds. He boarded at the school and lived like a student. He frequently took his pupils on historical and nature walks in the woods and along the shoreline in the vicinity. It was a bucolic environment, but contemporaries recalled that the noxious smell emanating from the local fish-sauce factory was sometimes quite strong, providing a distinct distraction to the learning process.

The curriculum at the school had a nationalist agenda. Every morning, each class elected a student to sing a patriotic song, which was then discussed by all in attendance. Thanh introduced topics connected with Vietnamese history in his lectures and recited verses from popular works such as "the haircut song" (*ca hot toc*) and Phan Boi Chau's poem "A-te-a." To open his classes he called on students to recite from poems from the anthology of the Hanoi Free School:

> Oh, Heaven! Can't you see our suffering?
> The nation is in chains, languishing in grief,
> Foreigners have doomed it to hunger,
> They've robbed it of everything it had.[23]

As in the country at large, however, it was not the goal of national independence, but the means to that end that was the most controversial subject for debate. The faculty at the school was divided between advocates of Phan Chu Trinh's reformist approach and Phan Boi Chau's program of violent resistance. Nguyen Tat Thanh was one of the few who did not choose sides, preferring, he later wrote, to travel abroad to understand the situation first. According to one Vietnamese source, he respected both Phan Chu Trinh and Phan Boi Chau, but had reservations about both approaches, dismissing the former's trust in French goodwill as naïve and the latter's reliance on Japan and members of the royal family as misguided.[24]

Early in 1911, before the end of the school term, Nguyen Tat Thanh disappeared. The precise reasons for his sudden departure are not clear, although it may have been connected with news of the projected arrival of his father in Cochin China. Sometime in early 1910, Sac had been recalled from his post at Binh Khe. After his posting there the previous summer he had initially been popular with the local population, releasing prisoners who had been arrested for taking part in demonstrations, protecting peasants from demands by rapacious landlords, and punishing local bullies. He was lenient in his treatment of those accused of petty crimes, remarking that it was ridiculous to spend time on such matters when the entire country had been lost. But he was stern in his judgments of the rich and the powerful. On one occasion in January 1910, he sentenced an influential local figure to 100 strokes of the cane. When the man died a few days later, his relatives complained to friends at court, and Sac was summoned to Hué for trial. On May 19, the regency council charged him with abuse of office and sentenced him to caning and a four-grade demotion in rank. In August the sentence was changed to demotion in rank and formal dismissal from office. To support himself, Sac taught school briefly in Hué. To friends he did not appear to be bitter at his dismissal; he remarked to one acquaintance, "When the country is lost, how can you have a home?" In January 1911, he submitted to French authorities a request to travel to Cochin China, probably hoping to see his son. The request, however, was rejected by the authorities, perhaps because of a lingering suspicion that he was involved in rebellious activities. According to one French police report written at the time:

> Nguyen Sinh [Sac] . . . is strongly suspected of complicity with Phan Boi Chau, Phan Chu Trinh and others. His son, who two years ago was a student at Dong Ba, has suddenly disappeared. He is believed to be in Cochin China. Nguyen Sinh [Sac] may intend to rejoin him and confer with Phan Chu Trinh.[25]

Sac ignored the refusal, and on February 26, 1911, he went to Tourane (the new French name for Da Nang) and embarked on a ship for Saigon, where he found employment giving Chinese-language lessons and selling medicinal herbs.[26]

Was Nguyen Tat Thanh aware of his father's decision to go to Cochin China, thus persuading him to leave Phan Thiet for Saigon in the hopes of finding Sac there? One of his colleagues at the school later recalled that Thanh had said that he was going to celebrate the Tết holidays with his father. Or did he fear that his real identity had been uncovered by local authorities, who had already placed the school under surveillance? Whether or not they became aware that Nguyen Tat Thanh was teaching at the school is not known for certain, but shortly after Thanh's disappearance, a French official arrived at the school to ask about his whereabouts. Thanh, however, had given no hint of his departure to his students, leaving only a short note asking that his books be given to a fellow teacher. Friends at the school later speculated that he may have left Phan Thiet on a boat carrying fermented fish sauce to Saigon. Shortly thereafter, the school was temporarily forced by the authorities to shut its doors.[27]

A few days after leaving Phan Thiet, Nguyen Tat Thanh arrived in Saigon. The city was undoubtedly an eye-opening experience for the young man from rustic Nghe An province. Once a small trading post on the Saigon River, after the French conquest it was named the capital of the new colony of Cochin China. As the colony grew steadily in population—by 1910 Cochin China contained about one quarter of the total population of 12 million settled throughout the three regions of Vietnam—the city of Saigon grew with it, and by 1900 it had become after Hanoi the largest city in French Indochina. Soon it would surpass the ancient capital in size, with a population of several hundred thousand people.

The growth of the city was based above all on its nearby economic advantages. In the years since the French conquest, Cochin China had become the source of wealth for a new entrepreneurial class composed of Europeans and Vietnamese, as well as of ethnic Chinese, whose ancestors had settled in the area in previous centuries. Much of the profit came from the opening of rubber plantations along the Cambodian border (rubber tree seedlings had been brought to Indochina from Brazil during the last quarter of the nineteenth century), and from the expansion of rice cultivation as a consequence of French efforts to drain marshlands in the Mekong River delta. Purchased by wealthy absentee landlords, these virgin lands were then leased to sharecroppers (many of them immigrants from the densely populated provinces in the north) at exorbitant rents. The rice paid by the tenants to the owners was then processed in Chinese-owned rice mills and shipped to the northern provinces or exported. By the first quarter of the twentieth century, Cochin China was the third largest exporter of rice in the entire world.

Attracted by the profits from the growing trade in rubber and rice, several thousand Europeans settled in Saigon in the hopes of carving out their own fortunes. There they competed with Chinese merchants and a newly affluent Vietnamese bourgeoisie in providing goods and services for the growing population. With its textile mills, cement factories, and food processing plants, Saigon was rapidly becoming the primary industrial and commercial base of all Vietnam. In the downtown area, imposing buildings erected in the French provincial style housed the bureaus of colonial officials. Wide avenues, laid out in grid fashion, were lined with plane trees to provide protection from the hot tropical sun.

Behind high stucco walls were the imposing homes of the Europeans and those few Vietnamese who had managed to take advantage of the presence of the foreign imperialists. The remainder of the population—factory workers, stevedores, rickshaw pullers, rootless peasants from the surrounding countryside—huddled in squalid slums along the Ben Nghe canal or along the edges of the city.

On arrival in Saigon, Thanh took up lodgings in an old granary. The owner, Le Van Dat, was a manufacturer of woven sleeping mats and had ties with members of the Duc Thanh school in Phan Thiet. There Thanh apparently located his father, who was temporarily living at the warehouse until he found more permanent accommodations. Eventually, through other contacts from the school, Thanh moved to a building on Chau Van Liem Street, near the Saigon wharf, a rat's nest of wooden shacks with tin roofs nestled between a canal and the Saigon River. With his father's encouragement, Thanh now began to make plans for going abroad. In March, he heard about a school established by the French in 1904 to provide vocational training in carpentry and metalwork. Perhaps in the hope of saving sufficient funds to finance a trip abroad, Thanh briefly attended the school. However, when he discovered that he would need to complete the entire three-year program to obtain competence, he abandoned his classes and took a job selling newspapers with a fellow villager from Kim Lien named Huang.

The workers' village where Thanh had been living was not far from Saigon's Nha Rong pier, where great ocean liners docked en route to Europe and other ports in Asia. He decided to find a job on one of those liners as his ticket to travel abroad. Ho Chi Minh described it many years later in his autobiography, allegedly written by the fictitious Tran Dan Tien:

> While I [an alleged friend of Thanh, quoted by the author] was finishing my studies at the Chasseloup-Laubat school in Saigon, . . . I met a young man from central Vietnam. I had met him at a friend's house. Being of the same age, we soon became buddies. I took him in front of the cafés frequented by the French, where we watched the electric lights. We went to the movies. I showed him the public fountains. So many things that young Quoc [Nguyen Tat Thanh] had never seen. One day, I bought him some ice cream. He was astonished because it was the first time he had ever eaten it.
>
> A few days later, he suddenly asked me a question:
> "Hey, Lê, do you love your country?"
> Astonished, I replied, "Well, of course!"

"Can you keep a secret?"

"Yes."

"I want to go abroad, to visit France and other countries. When I have seen what they have done, I will return to help my compatriots. But if I leave alone, there will be more risk if, for example, I get sick. . . . Do you want to come with me?"

"But where will we find the money for the voyage?"

"Here's our money," he said showing me his two hands. "We will work. We'll do whatever is necessary to live and travel. Will you join me?"

Carried away by enthusiasm, I accepted. But after long reflection on what our adventure would entail, I didn't have the courage to keep my promise.

I haven't seen him since. I have always thought that he went abroad, but by what means I can't tell you. Much later, I learned that that young patriot full of ardor was none other than Nguyen Ai Quoc [Ho Chi Minh], our future president.[28]

During the next few months, Thanh frequently went to the harbor to watch the ships entering and leaving. There were two steamship companies whose ships operated out of Saigon—Messageries Maritimes and Chargeurs Réunis. The latter employed Vietnamese to serve as waiters and kitchen helpers on its vessels, and its advertisements stated that the itineraries included such romantic cities as Singapore, Colombo, Djibouti, Port Said, Marseilles, and Bordeaux. Through a friend from Haiphong who worked with the company, Thanh was able to obtain an interview with the captain of the Chargeurs Réunis liner *Amiral Latouche-Tréville*, which had just arrived at Nha Rong pier from Tourane. He had already packed two sets of seaman's clothing in a small suitcase, which had been given him by a friend in Phan Thiet.

On June 2, a young man who called himself simply "Ba" showed up at the pier. Captain Louis Eduard Maisen was skeptical about the applicant, who looked intelligent but was frail in build. When Ba insisted that he could "do anything," Maisen agreed to hire him as an assistant cook. The next day Ba reported for work and was immediately assigned a full day of work, washing dishes and pans, cleaning the kitchen floor, preparing vegetables, and shoveling coal. On the fifth, the *Amiral Latouche-Tréville* passed by the marshy banks of the Saigon River out to the South China Sea en route to its next destination, the British naval port of Singapore.[29]

Why had Nguyen Tat Thanh decided to leave on his long journey abroad? In remarks to the Soviet journalist Ossip Mandelstam many years later, Thanh (by then operating under the name Nguyen Ai Quoc) remarked, "When I was about thirteen years old, for the first time I heard the French words 'liberté,' 'égalité,' and 'fraternité.' At the time, I thought all white people were French. Since a Frenchman had written those words, I wanted to become acquainted with French civilization to see what meaning lay in those words." Later he gave a similar response to a question from the U.S. journalist Anna Louise Strong:

> The people of Vietnam, including my own father, often wondered who would help them to remove the yoke of French control. Some said Japan, others Great Britain, and some said the United States. I saw that I must go abroad to see for myself. After I had found out how they lived, I would return to help my countrymen."[30]

Hagiographers in Hanoi have made much of scattered remarks contained in his reminiscences characterizing his decision to leave Vietnam as a mission to save his country. Given his notorious proclivity to dramatize events in his life for heuristic purposes, it is advisable to treat such remarks with some skepticism. Still, there seems little doubt that as he left Saigon in the summer of 1911, he was full of patriotic passion and keenly aware of the injustices committed by the colonial regime against his compatriots. To Thanh, there seemed to be no solution to such problems inside the country. Perhaps they could be found abroad.

II | THE FIERY STALLION

Although Nguyen Tat Thanh's activities following his departure from Saigon are not well recorded, evidence suggests that he spent most of the next two years at sea. Exposure to the world outside Vietnam had a major impact on his thinking and attitude toward life. Over a decade later, when he began to write articles for French publications, his descriptions of the harsh realities of life in the colonized port cities of Asia, Africa, and Latin America were often shocking, dealing with the abject misery in which many people lived and the brutality with which they were treated by their European oppressors. By the beginning of the twentieth century, much of the world had been placed under colonial rule, and the port cities of Africa and Asia teemed with dockworkers, rickshaw pullers, and manual laborers, all doing the bidding of the white man. It may have been during this period of travel abroad that the foundations of his later revolutionary career were first laid.

The trip on the *Amiral Latouche-Tréville* from Saigon to Marseilles lasted several weeks. Conditions at sea were often harsh; the ship was small for an ocean liner, measuring only about 400 feet long and weighing less than 6000 tons. In his autobiographical writings, which are virtually the only source for this period in his life, Thanh recalled storms with waves "as big as mountains," which on occasion nearly washed him overboard.

His days at sea were often long and tedious. He rose early in the morning and did not finish work until after dark. As he recounted in the third person many years later:

As a cook's help he had to work daily as follows: From 4 o'clock in the morning he cleaned the big kitchen, then lit the boilers in the hold, brought the coal in, fetched vegetables, meat, fish, ice, etc., from the hold. The work was pretty heavy because it was very hot in the kitchen and very cold in the hold. It was particularly arduous when the ship was tossing in a rough sea and he had to climb up the gangway with a heavy bag on his shoulders.[1]

Yet Thanh seemed to bear it all with good humor and enthusiasm. In a letter written to one of his acquaintances in Saigon, he joked: "The hero goes joyfully through his day doing what he pleases, polishing the brass and the washroom and emptying the buckets of human waste." After finishing his chores about 9:00 P.M., he read or wrote until midnight, or sometimes helped illiterate shipmates write letters to their families. The Vietnamese agronomist and journalist Bui Quang Chieu, later a leading figure in one of the chief rival organizations to Ho Chi Minh's communist movement, recalled meeting him on the voyage and asking why someone so intelligent should wish to seek employment that required such hard labor. Thanh smiled and remarked that he was going to France to seek a reversal of the recent dismissal of his father by the imperial government.[2]

After stops in Singapore, Colombo, and Port Said, the *Amiral Latouche-Tréville* docked in Marseilles harbor on July 6, 1911. Here Thanh received his wages—about ten francs, a sum barely adequate to feed and house him in a cheap hotel for a few days—and disembarked with a friend to get his first glimpse of France. For the first time, he saw electric trams ("running houses," as the Vietnamese then called them). For the first time, too, he was addressed as "*monsieur*" when he stopped at a café on the city's famous Rue Cannebière for a cup of coffee. The experience inspired him to remark to his friend: "The French in France are better and more polite than those in Indochina." At the same time, he discovered that there was poverty in France, just as there was in French Indochina. Then, as now, Marseilles was a rough city, its streets filled with sailors, vagabonds, merchants, and thieves of all races. Seeing prostitutes board the ship to consort with the sailors, he remarked to his friend: "Why don't the French civilize their compatriots before doing it to us?"[3]

Thanh returned to the ship before it departed for Le Havre; it arrived there on July 15. A few days later it sailed to Dunkirk, and then eventually returned to Marseilles, where it docked in mid-September. From there, he wrote a letter to the president of the French Republic. The incident is sufficiently curious to present the letter in full:

Marseilles
September 15, 1911

Dear Mr. President:

I have the honor to request your assistance in being admitted to take courses at the Colonial School as an intern.

I am now employed with the company Chargeurs Réunis (*Amiral Latouche-Tréville*) for my subsistence. I am entirely without resources and very eager to receive an education. I would like to become useful to France with regard to my compatriots, and at the same time to enable them to profit from instruction.

I am a native of the province of Nghe An in Annam. In anticipation of your response, which I hope will be favorable, please accept, Mr. President, my profound gratitude.

Nguyen Tat Thanh
Born in Vinh, 1892 [sic],
Son of M. Nguyen Sinh Huy (doctor of letters)
Student of French and Chinese characters

The Colonial School, which had been established in 1885 to train officials for government service in the French colonies, contained a *"section indigène"* for colonial subjects, with about twenty scholarships available for students from French Indochina. Some scholars have wondered why a young man like Nguyen Tat Thanh, who so clearly opposed French rule over his country, would wish to enter a colonial school to be of service to France; they have speculated that he might have been prepared to sell his patriotism for a bureaucratic career. Yet in light of his past attendance at the National Academy in Hué, there is nothing especially surprising in Thanh's behavior. Although his hostility to French colonial rule in Indochina seems already well established, he had clearly not decided what route to take for the liberation of his country and, by his own account, was still eager to obtain an education in order to improve his understanding of the situation. In a letter written sometime in 1911, he told his sister that he hoped to continue his studies in France and return to Indochina in five or six years. Moreover, as his letter to the president indicates, his ultimate objective was to be useful to his own country. It may have been that, not for the last time, he was willing to disguise his real intentions in order to seek his ultimate objective.[4]

From Marseilles, Thanh returned to Saigon on the *Amiral Latouche-Tréville*. He left the ship when it arrived in mid-October and attempted to establish contact with his father. Sac had not found steady employment since being dismissed from his position at court, and on one occasion may have been arrested for drunkenness. After working for a while on a rubber plantation in Thu Dau Mot, near the Cambodian border, he began selling traditional medicines throughout Cochin China. Although he may have been in the vicinity of Saigon when his son arrived, there is no indication that either was aware of the other's whereabouts. On

October 31, 1911, Thanh wrote a letter to the French *résident supérieur* in Annam, explaining that he and his father had been separated by poverty for more than two years and enclosing the sum of fifteen piastres to be forwarded to him. He received no reply.[5]

From Saigon, Thanh went back to sea and returned to Marseilles, where he learned that his application for admission to the Colonial School had been rejected. The application had been forwarded to the school authorities, who replied that candidates for admission had to be recommended by the governor-general of Indochina, a regulation that undoubtedly removed Thanh from consideration. He then decided to remain with the ship until it went into dry dock at Le Havre. Most of the sailors signed on with another ship and returned to Indochina; Thanh remained in Le Havre and accepted employment as a gardener at the home of a shipowner in Sainte-Adresse, a small beach resort (later to be portrayed on canvas by the French impressionist painter Claude Monet) a few miles west of the city. In his free time, he read journals in the shipowner's library and studied French with the shipowner's daughter. Sometimes he went into town to visit with other Vietnamese. At some point, he may even have traveled to Paris to meet Phan Chu Trinh. According to some reports, his father had given Thanh a letter of introduction to his fellow *pho bang* graduate before Thanh's departure from Vietnam. Trinh, after his release from prison in Indochina, had arrived in Paris sometime in the spring of 1911. If they did meet, they undoubtedly discussed the exciting news from China, where revolutionaries under the leadership of Sun Yat-sen had just overthrown the Qing dynasty and established a Western-style republic.[6]

Thanh got along well with the family of his host, and the latter was able to help him return to the employ of the shipping company Chargeurs Réunis on a ship leaving for Africa. Although a friend warned him that it was hotter in Africa than in Vietnam, Thanh still suffered from wanderlust ("I want to see the world," he replied) and decided to go. During the next several months, he visited countries throughout Africa and Asia, including Algeria, Tunisia, Morocco, India, Indochina, Saudi Arabia, Senegal, Sudan, Dahomey, and Madagascar.

He was fascinated by what he saw, and learned what he could while his ship was in port. As he reported in his reminiscences:

Ba was observant of everything. Every time the boat was in the port, he did his utmost to visit the town. When he came back, his pocket was full of photos and matchboxes, for he liked to collect these things.

He was often reminded of the horrors of the colonial system. At Dakar, he saw several Africans drown while being ordered by the French to swim out to the ship during a storm. He later wrote:

> The French in France are all good. But the French colonialists are very cruel and inhumane. It is the same everywhere. At home I have seen such things happening in Phan Rang. The French burst out laughing while our compatriots drowned for their sake. To the colonialists, the life of an Asian or an African is not worth a penny.[7]

During his years at sea, Thanh made visits to several ports of call in the Western Hemisphere. Many years later he told a Cuban acquaintance that he had visited Rio de Janeiro and Buenos Aires. At some point, his ship stopped at port cities along the East Coast of the United States, including New York City, where Thanh decided to leave the ship and seek employment. He eventually stayed several months in the United States.

Ho Chi Minh's visit to America remains one of the most mysterious and puzzling periods in his entire life. According to his own account and in recollections to acquaintances, he spent a period of time in New York City, staring in awe at the modern skyscrapers of the Manhattan skyline and strolling with friends in Chinatown, where he was impressed by the fact that Asian immigrants in the United States appeared to have equal rights in law if not in fact. He worked as a laborer (earning, he claimed, the princely salary of forty dollars a month) and as a domestic servant to a wealthy family, yet found time to attend meetings of black activists such as the Universal Negro Improvement Trust in Harlem, an organization founded under the sponsorship of the famous Jamaican-born black nationalist Marcus Garvey. Many years later, he told a delegation of peace activists who were visiting Hanoi at the height of the Vietnam War that he had been strongly moved by the plight of black peoples around the world and had contributed generously to the movement." Asked by a member of the delegation why he had gone to New York, he replied that at the time he thought that the United States was opposed to Western imperialism and would readily agree to assist the Vietnamese people in overthrowing the French colonial regime. Eventually he concluded that there was no help here.[8]

In later years, Ho Chi Minh would claim that he had also lived in Boston, where he worked briefly as a pastry chef in the Parker House

Hotel, and that he had made a short visit to the Southern states, where he observed the lynching of blacks by the Ku Klux Klan. Living in Moscow in the 1920s, he wrote an article that described these events in vivid detail. Unfortunately, none of the details of his trip to the United States can be corroborated. Virtually the only incontestable evidence that confirms his presence there is in the form of two communications that he sent. The first letter, signed Paul Tat Thanh and addressed to the French *résident supérieur* in Annam, was dated December 15, 1912 and postmarked New York City. The second was a postcard from Boston, which was mailed to Phan Chu Trinh in France; it mentioned that he was working as a cook's helper in the Parker House Hotel.[9]

Thanh probably left the United States in 1913. By his own admission, his stay apparently had little influence on his worldview, since he later told the U.S. journalist Anna Louise Strong that during his visit to the United States he knew nothing about politics. After another stopover in Le Havre, he arrived in Great Britain to study English. In a brief note to Phan Chu Trinh in France, he indicated that for the last four and a half months he had been in London studying the English language and consorting with foreigners. In four or five months, he wrote, "I hope to see you again." The letter was not dated, but it must have been written before the outbreak of war in August 1914, since he asked Trinh where he expected to spend his summer vacation.

In a second letter, Thanh commented on the start of what would turn out to be World War I. He noted that any country that tried to meddle in the issue was bound to get drawn into the war and concluded: "I think that in the next three or four months, the situation in Asia will change, and change drastically. So much the worse for those who fight and agitate. We have only to stand aside." He may have anticipated that the conflict would lead to the collapse of the French colonial system.[10]

In his first letter to Phan Chu Trinh, Thanh also remarked that he had to work hard in order to avoid going hungry. His first job was as a snow sweeper at a school. "What a hard job," he later wrote in his autobiography. "I sweated all over and yet my hands and my feet were freezing. And it was not easy to break up the icy snow, for it was slippery. After eight hours' work I was completely exhausted and hungry." He quickly abandoned that job for another as a boiler operator. But that was even worse:

From five o'clock, another friend and myself had to go to the basement to light the fire. All day long we had to feed coal into the boiler. It was terrifying. I never knew what the people were doing upstairs because I'd never been up there. My workmate was a quiet man, probably he was dumb [mute]. Throughout the working day he never spoke. He smoked while working. When he needed me he made a sign but never said a word. It was terribly hot in the basement and terribly cold outside. I did not have enough warm clothes and therefore caught cold.

Finally, he was able to find work in the kitchen at the Drayton Court Hotel in central London. Later he switched to the Carlton Hotel and worked under the famous chef Auguste Escoffier. If the following story in Ho Chi Minh's autobiography is accurate, he must have had promise as a chef:

Each of us had to take turns in the clearing up. The waiters, after attending the customers, had to clear all the plates and send them by means of an electric lift to the kitchen. Then our job was to separate china and silver for cleaning. When it came to Ba's turn he was very careful. Instead of throwing out all the bits left over, which were often a quarter of a chicken or a huge piece of steak, etc., Ba kept them clean and sent them back to the kitchen. Noticing this, the chef Escoffier asked Ba: "Why didn't you throw these remains into the rubbish as the others do?"

"These things shouldn't be thrown away. You could give them to the poor."

"My dear young friend, listen to me!" Chef Escoffier seemed to be pleased and said, smiling: "Leave your revolutionary ideas aside for a moment, and I will teach you the art of cooking, which will bring you a lot of money. Do you agree?"

And Chef Escoffier did not leave Ba at the job of washing dishes but took him to the cake section, where he got higher wages.

It was indeed a great event in the kitchen for it was the first first time the "kitchen king" had done that sort of thing.[11]

In his spare time, Thanh used his sparse savings to take English lessons with an Italian teacher, often sitting, as he remarked, "in Hyde Park with a book and a pencil in his hands." He was also becoming active in political organizations. Various reports indicate that he was involved in labor union activities and became a member of the Overseas Workers' Association, a secret organization of mostly overseas Chinese laborers committed to improving working conditions in British factories. He also claims to have taken part in street demonstrations in favor of Irish independence and a variety of leftist causes. It is probable that he first learned of the writings of the German revolutionary Karl Marx during this period.[12]

Above all other causes, Thanh continued to be concerned with the plight of his country. In a short poem that he sent to Trinh on a postcard he wrote:

> In confronting the skies and the waters
> under the impulse of will that makes a hero
> One must fight for one's compatriots.[13]

Unbeknownst to Thanh, his letters to Phan Chu Trinh had fallen into the hands of the authorities in France. In the late summer of 1914, Trinh and his close colleague, the lawyer Phan Van Truong, had been arrested by the French government on suspicion of meeting with German agents. Athough they were later released for lack of evidence, French police searched their apartment in Paris and discovered the communications from a Vietnamese named N. Tat Thanh residing at 8 Stephen Street, Tottenham Court Road, in London. In the course of their investigation, police also discovered that in one letter to Trinh (no longer extant), Tat Thanh had complained about conditions in Indochina and promised that in the future he would seek to carry on Trinh's work. At the request of the French Embassy in London, British police carried out surveillance, but could not locate anyone by that name at the address given. They did locate two brothers, named Tat Thanh and Thanh, at a different address. They proved to be engineering students who had just left to pursue their studies in Bedford, and were apparently not involved in political activities.[14]

The wartime years in Great Britain are among the least documented of Thanh's life. Accounts of his activities rely almost exclusively on his autobiographical writings of many years later. Some historians do not believe that he ever actually lived in Great Britain, but suspect he invented the experience as a means of strengthening his credentials as a revolutionary from a working-class background. This seems unlikely, since he rarely sought to disguise his family background as the son of a Confucian scholar. Although it has proven impossible to verify any of

the anecdotes contained in his account of the period, enough evidence
exists to confirm that he did live in London, although the precise nature
of his activities there remains somewhat of a mystery.[15]

The date of Thanh's return to France has long been a matter of dispute. French authorities were not aware of his presence until the
summer of 1919, when he became involved in an incident that made
him the most notorious Vietnamese in the land. In his autobiography,
Ho Chi Minh wrote that he returned to France while the war was still
under way. Several of his acquaintances in Paris maintained that he arrived in 1917 or 1918, and an agent assigned by the police to follow
him in 1919 reported that he had "long been in France." Most sources
place the date sometime in December 1917.[16]

His motives for returning to France are not entirely clear, although
in terms of his nationalist goals the change was certainly a logical one.
During the war thousands of Vietnamese had been conscripted to work
in factories in France as replacements for French workers serving in the
armed forces. From fewer than one hundred in 1911, the number of
Vietnamese living in France had grown rapidly during the war. For a
patriot determined to play a role in the liberation of his country, France
was a logical site for operations and for the recruitment of avid followers.
In Phan Chu Trinh and his colleague Phan Van Truong, Thanh already
had useful contacts who could serve as his entrée into the Byzantine
world of Vietnamese émigré politics in Paris. Because of the notoriety
brought by his open letter to Paul Beau in 1906, Trinh was the acknowledged leader of the émigré community in France. Following his
arrest on suspicion of treason at the beginning of the war, Trinh had
behaved with circumspection, although rumors persisted that he was still
active in the Vietnamese independence movement.

After his arrival in France, Thanh soon became involved in agitation
among Vietnamese workers. Social unrest was on the rise as a result of the
length and brutality of the Great War; in 1917 there was a serious mutiny
in the French army, and radical elements began to distribute antiwar propaganda and organize labor unions throughout the country. Factory and
shipyard workers from the colonial countries, because of their low pay and
the dismal conditions in which they lived, were particularly susceptible to
such agitation. A militant young Vietnamese inflamed with anticolonial
zeal would have been especially useful in such activities.[17]

How Thanh became involved is not clear. It is possible that he returned as a delegate of the Overseas Workers' Association to establish liaison with workers' groups in France. In that case, it is not unlikely that he may have traveled back and forth between the two countries on several occasions. Or he may have simply established contact independently with some of the leading figures in leftist circles in Paris, who made use of his obvious enthusiasm to assist them in their own activities.

Boris Souvarine, later to become a prominent historian but then a radical activist in Paris, recalled that he first met Thanh shortly after Thanh's arrival from London and places the year as 1917. Thanh had found lodgings in a dingy hotel on a cul-de-sac in Montmartre, and had begun to attend meetings of one of the local chapters of the French Socialist Party; it was there that he met Souvarine, who introduced him to Léo Poldès, founder of a speaking group called the Club du Faubourg. Thanh began to show up regularly at the club's weekly talks, which addressed a wide variety of subjects, from radical politics to psychology and the occult. These took place at various meeting halls in Paris. He was so painfully shy (Souvarine recalled that he was "a timid, almost humble young man, very gentle, avid for learning") that other participants dubbed him the "mute of Montmartre."

Eventually, however, Poldès encouraged him to speak publicly as a means of conquering his timidity. On his first occasion, when he was called upon to describe the suffering of his compatriots under colonialism, Thanh was so nervous that he stuttered. But although few in the audience understood what he was saying, they were sympathetic to his theme. At the close of his talk there was wide applause. He was soon invited to speak again.[18]

Souvarine's account tallies with that of Léo Poldès himself, who told the U.S. writer Stanley Karnow that he had first seen Thanh at a meeting of the Club du Faubourg. There was, he recalled, "a Chaplinesque aura about him—at once sad and comic, *vous savez* [you know]." Poldès was struck by his bright eyes and his avid interest in all things. Thanh overcame his stage fright and took an active part in discussions at the weekly meetings of the club. On one occasion he criticized the views of an advocate of hypnotism, arguing that the French colonial authorities habitually used opium and alcohol to hypnotize the peoples of Indochina. He became acquainted with many of the leading figures in the radical and intellectual movement in Paris, such as the socialist writer Paul Louis, the militant activist Jacques Doriot, and the radical novelist Henri Barbusse, who in his writings had movingly described the abysmal conditions for soldiers at the front.[19]

By now, Nguyen Tat Thanh was almost thirty years old. His worldly experience was limited to teaching, cooking, and a few menial jobs. It was probably difficult for Thanh to find employment in France, since he had no work permit. Various sources say that he sold Vietnamese food, manufactured signs, taught Chinese, and made candles. Eventually he was given a job as a photo retoucher (adding colors to black-and-white photographs, a popular innovation at the time) in a shop managed by Phan Chu Trinh. In his free time he frequented the reading room of the Bibliothèque Nationale or the library of the Sorbonne. Thanh was a voracious reader, and he especially enjoyed the works of Shakespeare, Charles Dickens, Victor Hugo, Emile Zola, Leo Tolstoy, and Lu Xun, in addition to those of Barbusse. He was living almost literally out of a suitcase, and apparently moved frequently from one shabby hotel or flat to another in working-class sections of the city.[20]

Paris at war's end was a fascinating place for a young Asian interested in politics. The French capital still had some pretensions of being the political as well as the cultural hub of the Western world. Many of the most famous radical figures of the nineteenth century had lived and operated in Paris, and the brutalities of the recent war had energized their ideological heirs into escalating their verbal attacks on the capitalist system. Along the Left Bank, intellectuals and students from France and the world over gathered in cafés and restaurants to discuss politics and plan revolutions. Some had been secretly recruited as French agents to spy on their colleagues and report any subversive activities to the police.

Among the various exile communities that had been established in Paris at the end of the war, the Vietnamese were one of the most numerous. By the end of the war there were approximately fifty thousand Vietnamese in France. While most worked in factories, a few hundred, often the children of wealthy families, had come to study; because of the highly politicized atmosphere within the intellectual community in France, such students were ripe for political agitation. Still, although national feelings were high among Vietnamese living in France, little had been done to channel this to the cause of independence. During the war France had asserted that it was the duty of every able-bodied subject of the far-flung colonial empire to come to the defense of the mother country; as a result, some of the more militant elements thought they should demand a quid pro quo—support for the French in Europe in return for increased autonomy or even independence for Vietnam following the war. Others had gone much further, flirting with German intelligence agents in the hopes that a French defeat would undermine the overseas administrative apparatus and lead to an overthrow of colonial authority.

The French appeared to have some evidence that Phan Chu Trinh and his compatriot Phan Van Truong may have tried to test both possibilities. Truong, born in 1878 near Hanoi in Ha Dong province, had been trained as a lawyer, settled in France in 1910, and became a French citizen. Just before the outbreak of war, he and Trinh formed an association of Vietnamese exiles. Trinh, predominantly a man of ideas, never displayed much capacity for organizational politics. The group, called the Fraternal Association of Compatriots (Hoi dong Than ai), did not achieve much recognition among Vietnamese living in and around Paris, recruiting only about twenty members and scheduling few activities. But there were rumors—apparently taken seriously by the French intelligence services—that the two had given some thought to organizing a movement to promote a general insurrection in Vietnam. It was for that reason that shortly after the start of the war they were briefly detained in prison on suspicion of taking part in treasonable activities. This was the arrest that resulted in Thanh's correspondence falling into the hands of the authorities. After their release, Trinh and Truong refrained from launching a major challenge to the colonial authority in Indochina—and it would be a decade before anyone else would do so. Whether because of decisive French preventive action or incompetence, the Vietnamese community in France did little during the war to further the cause of national independence. For all practical purposes, the community was politically stagnant.

Thanh was quick to change that. Up until 1919, although he had made the acquaintance of a few of the great figures of the Vietnamese anticolonial movement, his only political achievment was to serve briefly as an interpreter during the peasant demonstrations in Hué. Unimposing in appearance, shabbily dressed, Thanh was hardly an arresting figure to a casual passerby. Yet friends remember that he did possess one remarkable physical characteristic, which implied that this was no ordinary man—a pair of dark eyes that flashed with intensity when he spoke and seemed to penetrate the soul of the observer. One acquaintance even mentioned that Thanh's intensity frightened his wife.

That summer, with the benign approval of his two older colleagues, Thanh formed a new organization for Vietnamese living in France: the Association of Annamite Patriots (Association des Patriotes Annamites). Because Thanh was still relatively unknown, Trinh and Phan Van

Truong were listed as the directors of the organization, but Thanh, as secretary, was almost certainly the guiding force. The first members were probably intellectuals, but Thanh was reportedly able to employ his own contacts to recruit some working-class Vietnamese, including a number of naval hands from the seaports of Toulon, Marseilles, and Le Havre.[21]

On the surface, the association did not espouse radical objectives. Indeed, the founders hoped to avoid such an orientation in order to win broad support within the Vietnamese community and avoid suspicion by the authorities. The adoption of the word "Annam" instead of the traditional "Vietnam" into the title was probably a signal to the government that it did not represent a serious danger to the colonial enterprise. Yet from the start Thanh was determined to use the association to turn the Vietnamese community into an effective force directed against the colonial regime in Indochina. He had already contacted members of other national groups living in Paris, such as Koreans and Tunisians, who had founded similar organizations of their own to seek independence from colonial rule.

It was a propitious time to form such an organization. After the end of World War I, Paris had become the worldwide center for agitation by anticolonial groups. Debates on colonialism took place regularly within the French National Assembly. (In an address given in Hanoi in April 1918, the silver-tongued governor-general of Indochina, Albert Sarraut, then serving briefly for the second time in that position, promised the Vietnamese people that they would soon see a perceptible expansion of their political rights.) The issue was also raised in January 1919, when the leaders of the victorious Allied powers began to gather at the Palace of Versailles to negotiate a peace treaty with the defeated Central Powers and set forth the principles by which to govern international relations within the postwar world. U.S. President Woodrow Wilson had encouraged the aspirations of colonized nations throughout the globe by issuing his famous Fourteen Points declaration, which called, among other things, for self-determination for all peoples.

By early summer, a number of nationalist organizations with their headquarters in Paris had already issued manifestos to publicize their cause. Thanh and his colleagues in the Association of Annamite Patriots decided to take advantage of the situation and issue a statement of their own. With the assistance of Phan Van Truong, who offered to polish Thanh's still inadequate French, Thanh drafted an eight-point petition that appealed to the Allied leaders at Versailles to apply President Wilson's ideals to France's colonial territories in Southeast Asia. Entitled the "Revendications du peuple annamite" (Demands of the Annamite People), the document was fairly moderate in tone; it made no mention of national independence but demanded political autonomy for the Vietnamese, as well as the traditional democratic freedoms of association, religion, press, and movement, amnesty for political prisoners, equal rights for Vietnamese with the French in Vietnam, and the abolition of forced labor and the hated taxes on salt, opium, and alcohol. The declaration was dated June 18, 1919, and the author of the petition was Nguyen Ai Quoc, of 56 Rue Monsieur-le-Prince, in the name of the Association of Annamite Patriots. Although to a Vietnamese reader the name was clearly a pseudonym meaning "Nguyen the Patriot," the real identity of the author was unknown, except to a handful of his collaborators.

There has been considerable debate among Ho Chi Minh's biographers and other observers of modern Vietnamese history as to whether Nguyen Tat Thanh was the author of the document, or whether it was a group effort undertaken by several members of the Vietnamese group at Phan Chu Trinh's apartment in the Villa des Gobelins. French authorities at the time were equally puzzled; they had never encountered the name before. Some speculated that the real author was Phan Van Truong, identified as the "evil force" (*mauvais esprit*) behind the group and allegedly its most intelligent member. In his own reminiscences, however, Ho Chi Minh claimed that he had been the author, although he admitted that Phan Van Truong had helped him to draft it in intelligible French.[22]

Whether or not Thanh was the author of the petition is perhaps not so important as the fact that it was he who was primarily responsible for publicizing it and who would within months become identified with the name Nguyen Ai Quoc, a pseudonym that he would use with pride for the next three decades. He personally delivered the petition by hand to key members of the National Assembly and to the president of France, and he walked the corridors of the Palace of Versailles to submit it to the delegations of the great powers. To make sure that it would have maximum impact, he arranged to have it published in *L'Humanité*, a radical newspaper supportive of socialism. He also enlisted the aid of members of the General Confederation of Labor in order to get six thousand copies printed and distributed on the streets of Paris.[23]

The petition received no official response from the French authorities. Although the colonial question continued to be a major issue in debates within the National Assembly and aroused considerable controversy during the peace conference at Versailles, in the end the conferees took no action to address the problem. Colonel House, President Wilson's senior adviser in the U.S. delegation at Versailles, wrote a brief reply to Nguyen Ai Quoc's note, acknowledging receipt of the letter and thanking the author for sending it on the occasion of the Allied victory. A second note the following day said only that the letter would be brought to the attention of President Wilson. There was no further communication from the U.S. delegation on the matter. Woodrow Wilson, in fact, had encountered stiff resistance to his Fourteen Points at Versailles, and was forced to accept compromises to reach a peace agreement, a decision that aroused anger and disappointment throughout the colonial world.[24]

Still, the petition caused consternation in official circles in Paris. On June 23, the president of France wrote to Albert Sarraut, now back in Paris after his stint as governor-general of Indochina, noting that he had received a copy and asking Sarraut to look into the matter and ascertain the identity of the author. In August the *résident supérieur* in Tonkin cabled Paris that copies of the petition were circulating in the streets of Hanoi and had provoked comments in the local press. In September, Thanh ended speculation as to the petition's authorship by publicly identifying himself as Nguyen Ai Quoc in the course of an interview with the U.S. correspondent of a Chinese newspaper stationed in Paris. He did so, however, without revealing his real name. At about the same time, Thanh made the acquaintance of Paul Arnoux, a police official responsible for tracking the activities of Vietnamese émigrés in Paris. While attending an address by a French academic who criticized colonial policy in Indochina, Arnoux met an intense young man handing out leaflets. After several talks with Thanh in a café near the Opéra, Arnoux contacted the Ministry of Colonies and suggested that Albert Sarraut arrange to meet with him.

On September 6, Thanh was called to the Ministry of Colonies on Rue Oudinot for an interview, while police agents operating secretly within the Vietnamese exile community snapped his photograph and began to probe for information on his real identity.[25]

It is difficult to know whether Nguyen Ai Quoc, as he would henceforth call himself, had any real hopes that his plea for justice and self-determination for the Vietnamese people might receive a response, or whether he merely counted on the impact of the petition to popularize the cause of anticolonialism and radicalize the Vietnamese community in France. It is not improbable that he initially hoped that his petition might bring about positive changes in Indochina. He had an optimistic side to his character and seemed determined to believe the best about his fellow human beings, and even about his adversaries. This attitude was not limited to his compatriots, or even to fellow Asians, but extended to Europeans as well. During a brief trip to Germany, Switzerland, and Italy that he took around this time, he remarked to a friend that "all are human beings. Everywhere we meet good and bad people, honest and crooked people. If we are good people, we will meet good people everywhere." It was, he was convinced, the colonial relationship that debased and corrupted human nature. There is no doubt, however, that he was disappointed by the lack of response to his petition: Nguyen Ai Quoc complained to colleagues a decade later that many people had been deceived by Woodrow Wilson's "song of freedom."

It may be, too, that like many other Vietnamese he had been seduced by the words of Governor-General Albert Sarraut. In the interview which he had held with the U.S. reporter of the Chinese journal *Yi Che Pao* in September, Thanh had complained about the deplorable conditions in Indochina, but conceded that the first step was to obtain freedom of speech in order to seek to educate the population and then work for autonomy and national independence.[26]

Still, there is evidence that his patience and optimism were short-lived. The day after his interview with Sarraut, he sent him a copy of the petition with a cover letter:

> As a follow-up to our talk yesterday, I send you herewith a copy of the Demands. Since you were kind enough to tell me that you were disposed to talk frankly, I am taking the liberty to ask you to indicate to us what has already been accomplished regarding our eight demands. . . . Because I maintain that the eight questions continue to be unresolved, none of them having yet received a satisfactory solution.
>
> Please accept, dear M. governor-general, the assurance of my profound respect.
>
> Nguyen Ai Quoc[27]

A few days later, two police agents were assigned to track Nguyen Ai Quoc's every movement and political activities. By December he had been tentatively identified as Nguyen Tat Thanh, son of the ex-mandarin Nguyen Sinh Sac and the same elusive young man who had been expelled from the National Academy for seditious activity in 1908.

Whatever his motivations in authoring and promoting the petition, Nguyen Ai Quoc achieved publicity for the cause of Vietnamese self-determination. News of the petition spread quickly within the Vietnamese community in France and had a dramatic effect among his compatriots. Older patriots marveled at the audacity of the young photo retoucher. Younger ones showed new enthusiasm for the cause. The more prudent viewed him as a "wild man" and began to avoid him. What, they may have whispered, could you expect from a hardheaded buffalo from Nghe An?

Frustrated demands for national independence drove countless patriotic intellectuals from colonial countries in Asia and Africa into radical politics. Although it is probable that Ho Chi Minh was no exception, in his case it also is clear that his interest in socialist politics predated his involvement in the drafting of the petition. His involvement in labor union activities while living in England could well have provided the contacts through which he became active in similar circles soon after his arrival in Paris. Michel Zecchini, a member of the French Socialist Party (FSP) at that time, met Nguyen Tat Thanh at the end of World War I and noted that Thanh was already acquainted with such FSP luminaries as Marcel Cachin, Paul Vaillant-Couturier, Léon Blum, Edouard Herriot, Henri Barbusse, and Karl Marx's grandson Jean Longuet. It was through FSP contacts that he was finally able to obtain papers and a work permit. According to Zecchini, however, he was not accepted as a full-fledged member of the FSP until after he had obtained notoriety as Nguyen Ai Quoc in June 1919. As the author of the famous petition, Comrade Nguyen (or Monsieur Nguyen, as he was sometimes called) had earned a measure of respect.

Ho Chi Minh was probably attracted to the French socialists because, in his words, they "had shown their sympathy toward me, toward the struggle of the oppressed peoples." At the same time, his ideological bent toward socialism can be seen as a natural consequence of his dislike of capitalism and imperialism. Like many Asians, his first experience with the capitalist system was a product of the colonial exploitation of his country, which had produced such a brutal impact on the lives of many of his compatriots. Such views were undoubtedly strengthened by his years at sea, sailing from port to port through the colonial world, and perhaps by his period of residence in Great Britain and the United States. In later years he frequently commented on the exploitative nature of American capitalism, although he occasionally expressed admiration for the dynamism and energy of the American people. It seems likely that, as with many Asian nationalists, his initial interest in socialism came as a result of discovering its hostility toward the capitalist order.[28]

Yet the trend in Asian nationalist circles toward socialism should not be ascribed totally to expediency. For many Asian intellectuals, the group ethic of Western socialist theory corresponded better to their own inherited ideals than did the individualist and profit-motivated ethic of Western capitalism. And nowhere was this more pronounced than in Confucian societies like China and Vietnam. Chinese and Vietnamese nationalists from scholar-gentry families often found the glitter of the new commercial cities more than vaguely distasteful. In the Confucian mind, Western industrialism was too easily translated into greed and an unseemly desire for self-aggrandizement. By contrast, socialism stressed community effort, simplicity of lifestyle, equalization of wealth and opportunity, all of which had strong overtones in the Confucian tradition. Under such conditions, the philosophical transition from Confucius to Marx was easier to make than that to Adam Smith and John Stuart Mill, who stressed such unfamiliar concepts as materialism and individualism.[29]

In 1920, Monsieur Nguyen began to attend regular meetings of the FSP and the General Confederation of Labor, as well as the Ligue des Droits de l'Homme (an organization not unlike the American Civil Liberties Union), and to take an even more active role in political discussions. There are ample signs, however, that he began to find the attitude of many of his colleagues exasperating. To Nguyen Ai Quoc, the central problem of the age was the exploitation of the colonial peoples by Western imperialism. He discovered that for most of his French acquaintances, colonialism was viewed as only a peripheral aspect of a broader problem—the issue of world capitalism. Marx had been inclined toward Eurocentrism, and most of his progeny in Europe had followed his lead. The colonies, after all, represented economic wealth to France, and jobs to her workers. So Monsieur Nguyen elicited little response when he raised the colonial questions at political meetings, leading him to exclaim to one colleague in his frustration, "If you don't accuse colonialism, if you don't side with the colonial peoples, how can you make revolution?"

A serious split was developing within the ranks of the socialist movement between moderate leaders such as Jean Longuet and Léon Blum and more militant figures like Marcel Cachin and Paul Vaillant-Couturier, who appeared to hold more radical visions of the future of human society. Nguyen Ai Quoc sided with the radicals. One of the issues over which the two camps divided was the Bolshevik revolution. A militant group within the party began to coalesce around support for several key initiatives: opposition to the Versailles peace settlement; the creation of a new and more radical international socialist movement (in 1889, Marx's original First International had been replaced by a more moderate Second International, aimed at achieving socialism by parliamentary means); sympathy for the oppressed peoples of the colonial areas; and firm support for the Bolshevik revolution. At the end of 1919 a committee to advocate adherence to Lenin's new Third International— which took a firm stand in favor of the necessity of violent revolution and the formation of a dictatorship of the proletariat—was formed within the FSP. Nguyen Ai Quoc took an active part in the proceedings, and frequently attended meetings to collect money to help defend the Soviet revolution from its capitalist enemies.

Nguyen Ai Quoc was still a novice in the world of radical politics. A number of his colleagues during those formative years later remarked that at the time he knew almost nothing about theory, or the differences between the Second and Third Internationals. On one occasion he asked Jean Longuet to explain the meaning of Marxism. Longuet demurred, saying that the question was too complex and suggesting that he read Marx's *Das Kapital*. Nguyen Ai Quoc thereupon went to a library near the Place d'Italie and borrowed a copy of that magnum opus, which he read along with a number of other Marxist works. Afterward, he remarked in his autobiography, he kept a copy of *Das Kapital* under his head as a pillow.

It was, however, Lenin's famous "Theses on the National and Colonial Questions," presented to the Second Comintern Congress in the summer of 1920, that set Nguyen Ai Quoc on a course that transformed him from a simple patriot with socialist leanings into a Marxist revolutionary. In an article written for a Soviet publication in 1960, he admitted that during discussions between advocates of the Second and Third Internationals within the FSP he "could not understand thoroughly" the course of the debates. All that mattered to him was which side supported the colonial peoples. Then, in the middle of July 1920, someone gave him a copy of Lenin's "Theses," which had just been published in *L'Humanité*. The result, he recounted, was electric:

There were political terms difficult to understand in this thesis. But by dint of reading it again and again, finally I could grasp the main part of it. What emotion, enthusiasm, clear-sightedness, and confidence it instilled in me! I was overjoyed to tears. Though sitting alone in my room, I shouted aloud as if addressing large crowds: Dear martyrs, compatriots! This is what we need, this is the path to our liberation.

Shortly after, he sent a letter to the Committee for Affiliation with the Third International, requesting admittance as an individual member. The application was accepted.[30]

Cut loose from its ideological baggage, Lenin's message was simple and direct. Communist parties in the West, in their struggle to overthrow the capitalist system in advanced industrial countries, should actively cooperate with nationalist movements in colonial areas in Asia and Africa. Many of these movements, Lenin conceded, were controlled by the native middle class, who, in the long run, were not sympathetic to social revolution. So any alliances with bourgeois nationalist groups should be implemented with care, and only on condition that local Communist parties maintain their separate identities and freedom of action. But given such limitations, Lenin viewed the national liberation movements of Asia and Africa as natural, albeit temporary, allies of the Communists against the common enemy of world imperialism. It was the ability of the Western capitalist countries to locate markets and raw materials in underdeveloped countries that sustained the world capitalist system and prevented its ultimate collapse.

Imperialist control over colonial areas not only put off the inevitable day when the social revolution would destroy injustice and inequality in the West, it also prevented the emergence of progressive forces in African and Asian societies. The local bourgeoisie, prevented from playing an active role in industrial and commercial development in their own society by the Western imperialist dominance, remained weak and undeveloped; it was thus unable to play its assigned progressive role in waging the capitalist revolution against feudal forces in society, a necessary first step in the advance to global communism. The colonial middle class would need help from other progressive forces—such as the poor peasantry and the small but growing urban proletariat—to overthrow feudalism and open the door to industrial and commercial development.

In effect, Lenin was calling on his fellow Communists in the West to join hands with Asian and African nationalists in a common revolutionary endeavor. The alliance was temporary; once imperialism and its feudal allies in underdeveloped societies were overthrown, the Communist movement should detach itself from its alliance with the bourgeois political forces, who would now become increasingly reactionary, and struggle to achieve the second, socialist stage of the revolution.

Lenin was offering assistance to the Vietnamese and other peoples at a time when they sorely needed it. And he was clearly enunciating the view—so central to Nguyen Ai Quoc's own worldview—that the colonial areas were a vital defense line in the world capitalist system. Cut off the tentacles of colonialism in the far-flung colonies, and the system itself could be overthrown.

Socialists in Paris, with few exceptions, tended to dwell on words rather than deeds. Lenin was not a theorist, but a man of action. To Nguyen Ai Quoc, he was clearly an extraordinarily inspiring figure, and one worthy of his allegiance.

With the help of French acquaintances like the radical journalist Gaston Monmousseau and Jean Longuet, who helped to polish his distinctive unadorned and direct style, Nguyen Ai Quoc began to contribute articles to leftist journals in Paris in the late summer of 1919, and continued to be a prolific supporter of progressive causes until his departure from France nearly four years later. His first article, entitled "La question indigène" and printed in *L'Humanité* on August 2, 1919, was a critique of French policies in Indochina, policies that, in his words, had brought the Vietnamese people nothing but misery. Although in theory the French were performing a civilizing mission, in actuality their educational policies were simple indoctrination and kept the Vietnamese people unprepared for future competition with their neighbors. In the meantime, the Japanese government had astutely prepared its own people to develop their economic capacities. Eventually, he noted prophetically, Japanese businessmen will arrive in Indochina and make Vietnamese lives even more difficult.

Nguyen Ai Quoc had a point. At the end of World War I, the educational system that had recently been put in place by the French to provide their Indochinese subjects with exposure to Western knowledge reached only a small percentage of the population. Only 3,000 of the more than 23,000 communes in Vietnam had a village school in the Western style. Traditional education in the Chinese classics continued to be offered by Confucian scholars in rural areas, but after the civil service examinations were abolished at French order in the second decade of the century, such an education had lost its primary vocational purpose. Education at the higher level was available to Vietnamese living in the cities, but it was essentially limited to a handful of high schools that catered to the sons and daughters of the elite class.

As for Sarraut's strategy of broadening political participation, Thanh continued, it was actually no policy at all. When people attempt to stand up to protest, as they did in 1908, they are bloodily repressed. Don't the French realize, he concluded, that it is time to emancipate the natives and help prepare them for future competition from their neighbors?[31]

Nguyen Ai Quoc followed up that article with another entitled "Indochina and Korea" in *Le Populaire* and then with "Lettre à Monsieur Outrey" in the same journal in October. Like its predecessor, these two pieces, while harshly critical of some French policies, were essentially moderate in terms of proposed solutions. They made no reference to the use of violence or of a Leninist alliance between peasants and workers. In the October article, the author refers favorably to the policies and remarks of former Governor-General Albert Sarraut and declares his opposition to Maurice Outrey, a colonial official and representative of Cochin China in the French National Assembly, who was rumored to be eager to replace Sarraut as governor-general. Outrey had criticized the Association of Annamite Patriots in that chamber, while denying that the French colonial regime suppressed the Annamites. Whom, Nguyen Ai Quoc asked satirically, do you represent? The twenty million Annamites whom Outrey did not know even by name, except for a few functionaries and a fistful of wealthy electors in Cochin China? Between Outrey's views and those of Sarraut, he concluded, there is "an immense distance."[32]

Nguyen Ai Quoc's job as a photo retoucher apparently did not require long hours for, while writing these short pieces, he also began to prepare a longer manuscript titled *Les opprimés* (The Oppressed), a lengthy critique of French policy in Indochina. Seldom, it would seem, has an author's abortive efforts to write a book been so well documented, since the police were amply informed of his progress through periodic reports by agents. He began writing it in late 1919 with the help of the anticolonial publicist Paul Vigné d'Octon and pored over newspaper and periodical articles in the Bibliothèque Nationale to obtain useful statistics and quotes. When an acquaintance warned Quoc against unattributed quotations, he retorted that he hoped other publishers would demand compensation for such quotes, since that would help publicize the book. Another advised him against using such a confrontational title, but he insisted on retaining it.

According to agent reports, Nguyen Ai Quoc lacked adequate funds to obtain editorial help and intended to publish the manuscript himself. Shortly after finishing it, however, he returned home one night to find it missing. Some biographers have speculated that it was stolen by a police agent. That seems probable, although there are no such indications in police files. Although there are no clear indications of the contents, it is likely that he used much of the material from his notes in a later book called *Le procès de la colonisation française* (French Colonialism on Trial), which he published in 1925. This book was a much harsher critique of French colonial policies and reflected clearly the influence of Marxism on his worldview.[33]

Nguyen Ai Quoc had moved into Phan Chu Trinh's apartment on the Villa des Gobelins in July 1919, shortly after the publication of the petition to the Allied powers. Located in a comfortable middle-class district near the Place de l'Italie on the Left Bank, it was undoubtedly a step up from his previous seedy accommodations. He shared it not only with Phan Chu Trinh but several other colleagues as well.

But the move presented some problems. As early as December 1919, a police agent within the group's entourage reported that an angry debate had taken place between Nguyen Ai Quoc and Phan Chu Trinh at the flat over the proper course to follow. Quoc argued that Vietnamese officials were as docile as sheep and had become the accomplices of the French in attempting to restrain the masses and exploit them. Trinh retorted that this was too superficial a view. The Vietnamese people, he felt, were still too weak and lacked the capability to oppose the French. Opposition at this point, he argued, would be tantamount to suicide. "Brother Quoc," he admonished, "allow me to observe you are still very young, and all can see that you are too headstrong. You want twenty million of our compatriots to do something when they have no weapons in their hands to oppose the fearsome weapons of the Europeans. Why should we commit suicide for no purpose?"

To Phan Chu Trinh, it was still necessary to rely on the French to hasten the modernization of Vietnamese society, which remained under the influence of the dead hand of Confucian tradition. But Quoc felt that the French were the primary enemy and could not be trusted to carry out their promises of reform. "Why," he asked,

> don't our twenty million compatriots do anything to force the government to treat us as human beings? We are humans, and we must live as humans. Anyone who does not want to treat us as his fellow man is our enemy. We don't want to live together with them on this earth. If others don't want to live with us as fellow humans, then it is really useless to live humiliating lives and be insulted on this earth.

As for the view that the Vietnamese had to rely on the French to carry out needed reforms, Nguyen Ai Quoc argued that they had done very little to educate the populace or prepare it for self-rule. "You are all older and more experienced than I," he conceded, "but our compatriots have been demanding that for sixty years and have received what? Very little!"[34]

Despite the growing gap between their political views, Nguyen Ai Quoc still respected Phan Chu Trinh and tried to persuade him to change his views. On several occasions, he took his older colleague to radical meetings in Paris. The police now kept Quoc constantly under surveillance and continued their efforts to obtain precise information on his background. The authorities remained convinced that Nguyen Ai Quoc was the same Nguyen Tat Thanh who had taken part in the disturbances in Hué in the summer of 1908. They had interviewed his father, his sister, and his brother, and were looking for telltale markings on his body to verify his identity. For example, they heard he had a scar on his ear from a childhood accident. While he was in the hospital in 1920 for an abscess on his right elbow, the police attempted to photograph him.[35]

On August 17, 1920, Albert Sarraut, now minister of colonies, wrote a note to the prefect of police asking for more precise information on Nguyen Ai Quoc. "He has no right," exclaimed Sarraut in exasperation, "to meddle in our politics under an assumed name." The following month, Quoc was called into the ministry again for interrogation. According to his own later account of the incident:

One day I wrote a letter to a man of letters and four days later, I received a letter from the Ministry of Colonies, signed by a Monsieur Guesde, in which he told me he had received my letter and asked me to come to his office. What, I wondered, I don't know M. Guesde! I have never written to him nor to any one in the Ministry. Then an idea came to me. I told myself, M. Guesde does not know me, so to make my acquaintance and buy me off, he seeks an excuse to have me come to his office.

A few days later I went to the Ministry of Colonies. M. Guesde was not there, and in fact was on a trip to England. M. Pasquier [then a senior ministry official] received me and inquired whether I wanted something from the government. If so, he would try to help me.

I need nothing, I replied, except the eight articles of the petition that I presented to the peace conference. If you could intervene with the French government to grant our demands, we would be infinitely grateful. M. Pasquier did not reply to my question and changed the conversation.[36]

Pasquier's reaction to this conversation is unknown. But the growing frustration of the authorities is revealed in a report about Nguyen Ai Quoc written by Pierre Guesde to the minister of colonies on October 12. Quoc had been summoned to the prefecture of police three days after his interview at the Ministry. At the police station, he declared that he had been born on January 15, 1894, in Vinh, and that his six brothers and sisters were all dead.

"Who is this Nguyen Ai Quoc?" Guesde exploded.

He frequently changes his name and is currently hiding his identity behind an assumed name that cannot fool anyone who is even slightly familiar with the Vietnamese language. He claims that he has no documentation from the administrative authorities of Indochina that would identify him, but he interferes in our politics, takes part in political groups, speaks in revolutionary reunions, and we don't even know in whose presence we are! The information that he provides is clearly false.

In fact, Guesde said, after exhaustive efforts the authorities were in possession of clear evidence that Quoc was actually Nguyen Tat Thanh, "a dangerous agitator" who took part in the demonstrations in Annam in 1908.[37]

For over a generation, the socialist movement in France had been composed of progressive thinkers of varying hues: activist followers of the nineteenth-century revolutionary Auguste Blanqui, who advocated immediate insurrection and ignored the problem of building a future society; reformists, who followed the evolutionary road of Eduard Bernstein and the Second International; theoretical radicals, who traced their roots more to the French Revolution than to the thought of Karl Marx; and trade union leaders, who waged a class struggle aganst the captains of industry but had little use for ideology. World War I dealt a fatal blow to whatever lingering degree of common interest had previously existed within this heterogeneous group, and when Lenin issued his challenge to socialists everywhere to follow him in a holy war against capitalism, he forced party members to choose sides.

At the FSP conference held in Strasbourg in February 1920, a major discussion took place over whether to follow the relatively moderate Second International or Lenin's new Third International, the Comintern. Nguyen Ai Quoc was present, but took no part in the debate. Put to a vote, a strong majority wanted to leave the Second International, but a similar majority expressed opposition to joining the Comintern. As yet, the French left was not ready to make a choice.

During the following months, the debate over the future course of the socialist movement intensified. That summer, two prominent members of the party, Marcel Cachin and General Secretary Louis Frossard, attended the Second Comintern Congress in Moscow, which had approved Lenin's "Theses on the National and Colonial Questions." On their return to France they convened a massive rally on August 13 to discuss the results of the congress. Among the thirty thousand who jammed the grounds of the Paris circus in the western suburbs of the city was Nguyen Ai Quoc. He heard Marcel Cachin speak strongly in favor of adhesion to Lenin's new Communist International, claiming that it alone would liberate the enslaved peoples of the world and carry the struggle to the heart of global imperialism.[38]

Such words were undoubtedly welcome to Nguyen Ai Quoc, although he may have been disappointed that Lenin's eighth condition for admission to the new Comintern—calling on Communist parties in imperialist countries to carry on an active struggle against the imperialist policies of their own governments—received little attention at the meeting. He was probably heartened in September, however, to hear the news regarding the recent Conference of the Nationalities of the East held in Baku, where Platovich, a speaker representing the Comintern, had called for an active struggle to liberate the oppressed peoples of Asia.[39]

The FSP had scheduled a national congress to take place at Tours in late December to decide on possible affiliation with Lenin's Comintern. In the months leading up to the congress, Nguyen Ai Quoc attended all the district sessions and heard all the arguments on either side of the issue. There were three factions within the party, with moderates and radicals at each extreme and a group identified with Jean Longuet in the middle. Nguyen Ai Quoc contributed rarely to the debates. When he did, it was invariably to complain about the lack of attention to the colonial question. On one occasion, according to his own account, he appealed for unity of purpose in pursuit of the common cause:

Dear friends, you are all good socialists. You all wish to liberate the working class. Well, whether it is the Second International, the Second and One Half International, or the Third International, it all comes down to the same thing. Are they not all revolutionary? Don't they all struggle in favor of socialism? Whether you prefer one or the other, you must in any case unite. So why all the con-

troversy? While you spend your time debating, comrades, my compatriots are suffering and dying.

When selections for representatives to the congress were made, he managed to get invited as the representative of a small group of party members from Indochina.[40]

The congress opened on December 25, 1920, in a large riding school
next to the St. Julian Church on the south bank of the Loire River. The
cavernous hall was festooned with portraits of the old socialist warhorse
Jean Jaurès and banners proclaiming the unity of the working class
throughout the world. The speakers' platform at the front of the hall
consisted of a makeshift table composed of planks stretched across saw-
horses. The 285 delegates and other assorted guests—representing more
than 178,000 members throughout the country—were seated at long
wooden tables arranged according to their political persuasion. Nguyen
Ai Quoc was seated with the leftist faction, led by the fiery Marcel
Cachin.

Debate began that day, with the decision on whether to join the
Comintern the main topic on the agenda. As the only Asian, dressed in
a dark suit many sizes too large for his slim physique, Nguyen Ai Quoc
must have seemed out of place among the hundreds of bearded Europeans. Indeed, it did not take long for him to create a commotion at the
congress. On the first day, a photographer took his picture, and the
photograph was printed in the next day's issue of the Parisian newspaper
Le Matin. Alerted to his presence, the police appeared immediately with
orders to place him under arrest, but several of the delegates gathered
around him and prevented them from seizing him. Eventually the police
abandoned the effort.[41]

Nguyen Ai Quoc rose to speak on that same day. He spoke for twelve
minutes without the use of notes. He went straight to the point, criticizing French colonial policies for oppressing and exploiting his
compatriots. Anyone who protests, he said, is arrested, and prisons out-
number schools and are always jammed with detainees. The people have
neither freedom of speech nor the right to travel. They are forced to
smoke opium and drink alcohol for the profit of the French government,
which taxes both products. French socialists, he said, must take action
to support the oppressed colonial peoples.

At this point, Nguyen Ai Quoc was interrupted by Jean Longuet.
The socialist leader protested that he had already spoken in favor of the
natives. "I have imposed the dictatorship of silence," Quoc replied in a
humorous play on Marx's concept of the dictatorship of the proletariat,

and added that the party must actively promote socialist propaganda in all colonial countries. He said that a decision to join the Comintern would affirm that the party had correctly estimated the importance of the colonial question. He ended with an appeal: "In the name of all humanity, in the name of all socialists of the right and the left, we appeal to you, comrades, save us!"

After Nguyen Ai Quoc concluded his speech, Jean Longuet took the floor once again and reiterated that he had publicly supported the Vietnamese cause in the National Assembly and said that the issue was now being debated in that body. But Paul Vaillant-Couturier, a rising star in the radical movement and one of Nguyen Ai Quoc's most vocal supporters, retorted that what was needed now was not simply parliamentary debate, but action by the congress on behalf of the oppressed nations.[42]

On the twenty-seventh, Marcel Cachin formally proposed that the FSP accept Lenin's conditions for joining the Comintern, and Nguyen Ai Quoc spoke in support of the motion. Two days later, the motion carried by a majority of over 70 percent of the delegates. Those delegates who opposed entry into the Comintern stormed out of the hall in protest. Those who remained voted to bolt from the FSP and found a new French Communist Party (FCP). But there was no further discussion of the colonial question and the leadership rejected a proposal, undoubtedly promoted by Nguyen Ai Quoc, to issue a public declaration of support to the colonial peoples.[43]

At the Tours congress, Nguyen Ai Quoc had put his colleagues on notice that he was determined to become an outspoken advocate of greater attention to the needs of the colonial peoples as a crucial component of the struggle to overthrow capitalism. He had demonstrated in both public and private comments that he was concerned not simply about the success of the world revolution, but also about the fate of his own country. That spirit was reflected in a comment to one of his acquaintances at the time: "I have not had the good fortune to follow courses at the university. But life has given me an opportunity to study history, the social sciences, and even military science. What should one love? What should one despise? For we Vietnamese, it is necessary to love independence, work, and the motherland."[44]

But it did not take long for him to become disillusioned in his hope that all the new members of the new party would follow his lead. In February 1921, he became ill and spent some time in the hospital. After his release, he penned an article titled "Indochine" for *La Revue Commun-*

iste, which was published in April. In the article, he criticized some members of the FCP for not giving enough attention to the problems of promoting revolution in the colonies and for not studying the problem in a systematic manner. He argued that although the French were trying to destroy the spirit of the people of Indochina, the peoples of Indochina were not dead, and indeed "the peoples of Indochina still live and will live forever"—hardly an expression of Marxist proletarian internationalism. The article demonstrated clearly that he had abandoned the hope that change could be brought about without violence. While conceding that Indochina was not yet ripe for revolution—primarily because the people lacked education and had no freedom of speech or action—he contended that under the mask of passive docility "there is something that is bubbling and rumbling and that will at the appropriate moment explode in a formidable manner." It is up to the elites, he argued, to hasten that moment. "The tyranny of capitalism," he concluded, "has prepared the terrain; socialism has only to sow the seeds of emancipation."[45]

In a second article with the identical title in May, Nguyen Ai Quoc discussed the question of whether communism could be applied in Asia in general, and in Indochina in particular. This was a particularly pertinent issue, because at that time most European radicals still believed that in most "backward" countries revolution would be long delayed. Even Joseph Stalin, in an article published in *Pravda* the same month, had said that the advanced nations, *after* liberating themselves, had the duty to liberate the "backward peoples."

In his article, Nguyen Ai Quoc took issue with such views, arguing that Marxist and Leninist doctrine and strategy had current relevance in Asia as well as in the West. In Japan, he pointed out, the first Asian country to become capitalist, a socialist party had just been formed. China, still under the thrall of European and American capital, had just awakened, and a new revolutionary government led by the rebel leader Sun Yat-sen in south China promised to give birth to "a reorganized and proletarianized China." Perhaps one day soon, he predicted, Russia and China will march together. As for other suffering peoples in Asia, Korea was still at the mercy of Japanese capital, while India and Indochina were in the hands of English and French exploiters.

Nguyen Ai Quoc's prediction of future collaboration by the Russian and Chinese people was certainly prophetic. For the moment, he was commenting on recent events in China, which had led Sun Yat-sen to form an alliance with a military leader to establish a revolutionary regime in the southern port city of Canton. Sun had been living in exile for several years, after the military leader Yuan Shikai aborted the effort of Sun's followers to build a Westernized China and seized control over the reins of power himself. After Yuan's death in 1916, China fell into civil disorder, with military warlords seizing control of various parts of the country.

There were solid historical reasons, Nguyen Ai Quoc argued, why communism could acclimatize itself more easily in Asia than in Europe. In his view, Asians, although viewed by Westerners as backward, better understood the need for a total reform of contemporary society. They also harbored an historical sympathy for the idea of community and social equality. Ancient China had practiced the "equal field" (in Chinese, *jing tian*) system, dividing all farmland into equal parts and setting aside a separate plot for common ownership. More than four thousand years ago, the Xia dynasty had inaugurated the practice of obligatory labor. In the sixth century B.C. the great philosopher Confucius anticipated the Comintern and preached the doctrine of equality of property. World peace, the Master had predicted, would not come until the establishment of a universal republic. "One need not fear of having little," he preached, "but of not having equal distribution of goods." Confucius' disciple Mencius continued to follow the Master's doctrine, formulating a detailed plan for the organization of production and consumption. In response to a question by his sovereign, Mencius said that the needs of the people came first, those of the nation next, while those of the monarch came last.

Such traditions, Quoc asserted, continued to influence Asian societies. Vietnamese law, for example, placed limits on the sale and purchase of land, and a quarter of all farmlands were reserved as communal property. So, he concluded, on the day when millions of oppressed Asians wake up, they will form a colossal force capable of overthrowing imperialism, and they will aid their brothers of the West in the task of total emancipation from capitalist exploitation. Asia would play an active role in carrying out the world revolution.[46]

Nguyen Ai Quoc also used his pen to puncture the myth of the grandeur of French civilization. In an article written in September entitled "La civilisation supérieure," he ridiculed the French revolutionary trinity of liberty, equality, and fraternity, citing specific examples of French cruelty as recounted in the diary of a French soldier. In a short piece published in October in *Le Libertaire*, he recounted a personal example that he had witnessed as a student at the National Academy in Hué in 1908, where a fellow student was brutally humiliated by one of his French instructors. This took place, he remarked sarcastically, under a sign in every classroom that said, LOVE FRANCE, WHICH PROTECTS YOU (Aimez la France qui vous protège).[47]

Nguyen Ai Quoc's increasing radicalism kept him under the watchful eyes of the French authorities. Sometime in early 1921 he was summoned once again to the Ministry of Colonies for an interview with Albert Sarraut. "If France returned Indochina to you," the minister declared, "you would not be able to govern yourselves because you are not sufficiently well armed." "To the contrary," Quoc replied. "Look at Siam and Japan. These two countries do not have a civilization more ancient than our own; yet they rank among the nations of the world. If France returned our country to us, it would see without doubt that we would know how to govern it!" At these words, Sarraut changed the subject.[48]

Nguyen Ai Quoc's decision to join the French Communist Party added to existing tensions at the apartment on the Villa des Gobelins, where not all of his colleagues agreed with his opinions. During the congress at Tours, Tran Tien Nam, once one of his closest friends, remarked to a female acquaintance that Quoc's extremist views were not approved or widely shared by others at the flat. During the next several months police agents contined to report that angry discussions periodically took place there.[49]

The dispute between Nguyen Ai Quoc and his colleagues finally reached a climax in July, after growing more intense for several months. On June 6, he had taken part in a demonstration at the Père Lachaise Cemetery, in a working-class district in eastern Paris, to commemorate the deaths that had occurred there during the suppression of the Paris Commune in 1871. Quoc was badly beaten by the police, but managed to flee the scene. News of the incident made a number of his acquaintances nervous to be seen in his company. A couple of weeks later Tran Tien Nam, one of the more moderate members of the group, moved out of the apartment, claiming that Nguyen Ai Quoc's political views had become too radical for his comfort.

On July 11, 1921, police agents reported that an angry discussion had taken place betweeen Nguyen Ai Quoc and his friends; it lasted from nine in the evening until early the following morning. The next day, trailed by police agents, Quoc left the apartment to stay with his friend Vo Van Toan at 12 Rue Buot. A week later, his friend Paul Vaillant-Couturier assisted him in finding a small apartment at 9 Impasse Compoint, a cul-de-sac in the Batignolles, a working-class area in northwestern Paris.[50]

Nguyen Ai Quoc's new lodgings were spartan in the extreme, a significant step down from the relatively spacious and comfortable accommodations he had shared on the Villa des Gobelins. The one-room apartment was just large enough to hold a bed, a small table, and a wardrobe. Its single window looked out on the wall of the adjoining building, and he had to crane his neck out of the window to see the sky. There was no electricity, so he used an oil lamp; no water, so he used a basin to wash his face, and washed his clothes outside. For heat he used a brick that he warmed up in his landlady's furnace and then wrapped in a newspaper. His meals consisted of a little salted fish or meat twice a day. Sometimes he limited himself to a piece of bread and cheese.[51]

Nguyen Ai Quoc's break with the group on the Villa des Gobelins and the move to a new location apparently also necessitated a change of job. He had continued to work as a photo retoucher with Phan Chu Trinh until July 1920. Then, according to his written statement to the police on September 17, he became a decorator of Chinese frescoes for a Chinese furniture maker in the Latin Quarter. When the employees at the shop went out on strike in September, he took a new job at a photo shop on Rue Froidevaux. Then, after moving out of the Villa des Gobelins in the summer of 1921, he took a job at a photo shop a few doors from his new apartment on Impasse Compoint. As an apprentice, he earned only forty francs a week.[52]

Nguyen Ai Quoc's straitened circumstances did not appreciably affect his life. He continued to attend political meetings regularly, to attend art shows, and to frequent the Bibliothèque Nationale. In the course of his activities, he met such celebrities as the singer-actor Maurice Chevalier and the short story writer Colette. According to police reports, he often entertained visitors, cooking dinners of green vegetables mixed with soy sauce, accompanied by jasmine tea, at a small stove on a table in the corner of his apartment. Although his salary left him with little excess after paying his monthly rent, he still managed to travel to various meetings around the country, suggesting that he was receiving a subsidy from the Communist Party.

Nguyen Ai Quoc's break with the Gobelins group may have been precipitated in part by the disagreement over the decision of the FCP to form a new Colonial Study Commission (Comité des Etudes Coloniales) to promote Marxism in the French colonies. Nguyen Ai Quoc became an active member and in the middle of June 1921, he took Phan Chu Trinh to one of the meetings of the commission. A few weeks later, he attended a second meeting at Fontainebleau, thirty-five miles south-east of Paris. It was on his return two days later that he had the final fight at the apartment.[53]

One of the immediate results of the formation of the Colonial Study Commission was the creation of a new organization to represent colonial subjects living in France, the Intercolonial Union (Union Intercoloniale). For several months Nguyen Ai Quoc had been considering the estab-lishment of such a group. In a conversation with an acquaintance while he was in the hospital in February 1921, he mentioned the need to form an organization under cover of a mutual assistance association to unite the colonial peoples in their struggle for independence. For sev-eral months, his Association of Annamite Patriots had been cooperat-ing informally with a group of nationalists from the French colony of Madagascar and had created an action committee to coordinate their joint political activities. Similar groups had been established by other Africans living in Paris and London. Now, at the behest of the com-mission, this pattern of informal cooperation was formalized with the creation of the Intercolonial Union, which proclaimed itself as the pri-mary voice for the interests of all the colonial peoples residing in France. At its inception in July 1921, the union consisted of about two hundred members. Most came from Madagascar and Vietnam, although there were also a few North Africans and West Indians. The stated goals of the organization were moderate—according to its manifesto, it sought only to inform the colonial peoples of events taking place in France and to research all political and economic problems in the colonies—but its ultimate objective was to seek the destruction of the French colonial empire.[54]

From the beginning, Nguyen Ai Quoc was the driving force behind the new organization. He was elected to the executive committee along with a number of other prominent members of the FCP, such as his compatriot Nguyen The Truyen, Max Bloncourt, a member from Mad-agascar, and the Algerian Hadj Ali. Quoc was a member of the steering committee and regularly attended its meetings, which were held initially on the Avenue de Valois, near Park Monceau. Partially funded by the FCP, the union's headquarters were located at 3 Rue des Marché des Patriarches, a narrow street near the Gare d'Austerlitz on the Left Bank. With considerable effort, he was able initially to hold together the di-vergent interests represented by the group. As agent reports in French police files show, this was not easy. National jealousies and rivalries constantly disrupted the activities of the group, while leftists of European extraction sometimes complained that they were unfairly prevented from joining because of racial barriers. Some Vietnamese members charged that there was too much emphasis on cross-cultural activities and demanded the reestablishment of a purely Vietnamese organization. Africans retorted that Asian members were condescending and arrogant. Nguyen Ai Quoc was finding out that it was difficult to bring together the disparate force of the colonial peoples into a single disciplined organization.[55]

Attendance at the meetings of the general assembly gradually declined from a peak of 200 to fewer than 50 at each session. At one session in February 1923, there were only 27 members in attendance. Two were French, and two were women, both allegedly the mistresses of male activists. Nguyen Ai Quoc had his own female liaisons, although whether any of his women friends took part in radical activities is uncertain. He did have one small success: Phan Van Truong, his onetime collaborator in drafting the petition to the Allied leaders at Versailles, agreed to join.[56]

Organizational work within the Intercolonial Union was by no means Nguyen Ai Quoc's only activity during his final years in Paris. Through his association with French radicals he had learned the value of the press in publicizing the revolutionary cause; in early 1922, with encouragement from the Colonial Study Commission and other members of the Intercolonial Union, he decided to found a new journal specifically directed to appeal to colonial subjects residing in France, and to serve as a mouthpiece for the colonial peoples throughout the French empire. Called *Le Paria* (The Pariah), it was printed in French, but the title on its masthead was also presented in Chinese and Arabic. The first issue appeared on April 1, 1922, and others followed monthly; later, as financial problems accumulated, it appeared less frequently. Simple in form and in style, its aim was to inform readers of news and views on colonial affairs.

The tireless Nguyen Ai Quoc was chief editor of the journal. He was also its primary contributor and, when others were not available, he occasionally even became its major distributor, drawing pictures, wrapping the journal, and delivering it to subscribers. As he later recalled:

There was one time when I was the editor, chief treasurer, and distributor of *Le Paria* as well as the person who sold it. The comrades from Asian and African colonies wrote articles and solicited contributions and I did practically everything else.

Through the pages of *Le Paria* Nguyen Ai Quoc continued to improve his journalistic style. In editorials for the paper—sometimes two or three to each issue—he wrote about world affairs. Sometimes it was an article of a critical nature on some aspect of colonial life, such as atrocities committed by the French administration in Africa or Indochina. At other times it would be a piece on life in Soviet Russia—always painted in idyllic terms, although, of course, he had never been there.

There was nothing fancy in his writing. He had learned the importance of employing a simple and direct writing style by reading Leo Tolstoy, whose novels ranked among his favorites. His articles had no subtlety. Relying heavily on facts and figures to make his point, he appeared to his readers to be a walking statistical dictionary on life in the colonies—from the level of capitation taxes in the Ivory Coast to the colonial budget for French Indochina. When he did not attempt to bury the enemy in statistics, he employed sarcasm, but his words lacked the ironic twist of his contemporary Lu Xun, the talented Chinese writer. He tended to ignore theory and relied instead on a straightforward and invariably indignant criticism of the colonial system and its brutal effects on those who were ground under its wheels.

In later years, it became a puzzle to many students of his life that a man with so much personal magnetism and subtlety of character could adopt a writing style that was so pedestrian and heavy-handed. Yet here lies a key to his personality and to his political effectiveness over the years. Unlike many other Marxist leaders, Nguyen Ai Quoc saw his audience as composed not primarily of intellectuals, but of ordinary people—workers, farmers, soldiers, and clerks. He had no desire to impress readers with his intellectual brilliance, but rather he tried to persuade them in simple but vivid terms to share his vision of the world and his views on how to achieve change. At its worst, his writing makes turgid reading for the sophisticated reader. At best, there is sometimes a raw power, particularly when he describes the horrors of the colonial system.

Le Paria soon became well known as a major voice for the oppressed in France. As Nguyen Ai Quoc himself later wrote,

We sold the newspaper to Vietnamese workers who could not read French; however, they liked to buy the paper because they knew it was anti-West and, after they purchased it, they would have French workers read it to them. Also, there were places in Paris where we could sell the paper and earn a profit. Because we were all comrades, they sold the paper for us and took no money in return so they sold quite a few papers because practically every *Le Paria* printed was purchased by the French Ministry of Colonies.[57]

Anyone caught reading the material was immediately subject to arrest. Nonetheless, Nguyen Ai Quoc attempted to sneak copies into the colonies; at first he arranged to have sailors known to be sympathetic to the revolutionary cause carry it in their luggage. When the French authorities caught on, a new method had to be found. In the end, copies were sent by inserting them in toy clocks. It was an expensive means of spreading propaganda, but it served its purpose.

Lack of funds, however, was a persistent problem. The paper received a regular subsidy from the Intercolonial Union, but it was evidently expected to be at least partially self-supporting. In general, it did not sell well. The first issue had about 300 subscribers, but later it sank to about 200, out of about 1000 copies printed for each issue. Some were sold at meetings of the union, and several hundred were sent by various means to the colonies. The remainder had to be sold in small shops. When that proved inadequate, they were given away. Still, the police were concerned about the journal, which they viewed as Communist propaganda. All known subscribers were placed on a police blacklist.[58]

Nguyen Ai Quoc continued to write articles for other leftist newspapers and periodicals in Paris. He also briefly turned his hand to fiction. In 1922, Khai Dinh, the Vietnamese emperor, was invited to France on a ceremonial visit in conjunction with the Exposition Coloniale that was to be held in Marseilles from April through August. There were rumors of a possible attempted assassination, and some suspected Nguyen Ai Quoc or Phan Chu Trinh of being involved in the plot. In an effort to avoid unfavorable publicity, Albert Sarraut tried to persuade Phan Chu Trinh not to express his opposition to the visit, but Trinh ignored the request and wrote a public letter to the emperor that was highly critical of his role as puppet ruler of a conquered country. Nguyen Ai Quoc also used the occasion to promote his own objectives, editing articles by others on the visit and penning his own letter, which was published in the August 9, 1922, issue of *Journal du Peuple*. The letter portrayed Khai Dinh as a colonial knicknack on display at an exposition, kept in a shopwindow while his people groveled in the mud. He also produced a play titled *Le dragon de bambou*, which ridiculed the emperor and the imperial trip to France. The play, described by contemporaries as eminently forgettable, played briefly at the Club du Faubourg. When the news reached Indochina, it served to further divide Nguyen Ai Quoc from his father. On being informed of Quoc's comments, Sac reportedly remarked that any son who did not recognize his sovereign did not recognize his father.[59]

The visit of Emperor Khai Dinh did provide a final opportunity for Nguyen Ai Quoc and Phan Chu Trinh to stand on the same side of a political issue, but they could not agree on how best to liberate their homeland. In February 1922, Trinh sent an anguished letter to his young colleague while briefly visiting Marseilles. The letter did not touch on the ideological differences that had clearly emerged between the two, but focused on the question of tactics.

While defending his own approach, which concentrated on the importance of arousing the spirit and knowledge of the Vietnamese people through education, Trinh conceded that he was a conservative and a "tired horse" when compared with Quoc, a "fiery stallion." But he argued that Quoc was wasting his time by remaining abroad and writing articles in a language that few Vietnamese understood. That, he said, was Phan Boi Chau's error when he sought to recruit patriots for study in Japan. Quoc should go home, he advised, and appeal to the people inside the country. If so, he concluded, "I am convinced that the doctrine that you cherish so much can be diffused among our people. Even if you fail, others will take up the task."[60]

Nguyen Ai Quoc was too wrapped up in his own evolving career within the French revolutionary movement to heed Trinh's advice. Within a few years, he had emerged from obscurity to become a leading force within the radical movement in France and the most prominent member of the Vietnamese exile community. With the aid of Georges Pioch, a prominent radical intellectual connected with the Club du Faubourg, he had polished his speaking skills, and he began to take an active part in debates with prominent members of the FCP. At the Party's first congress, held in Marseilles in late December 1921, he gave an address on the colonial question and was elected as a representative of the district of the Seine.

Shortly after Quoc arrived in Marseilles to attend the congress, two plainclothesmen tried to seize him, but he managed to elude their grasp and enter the building where the meeting was to convene. At the end of the congress he was escorted by delegates through police patrols to a secret location until he could return to Paris.

In the capital, police continued their surveillance of Nguyen Ai Quoc's movements, and in November, probably as the result of pressure from the police, he was dismissed by his employer from his job at the photography shop adjacent to his apartment. While he was unemployed he sought other forms of work, but eventually he was able to resume his work in photography by setting up an office in his own apartment. He worked only in the morning so that he could devote himself to political activities for the remainder of the day.[61]

As a leading member of the FCP and its most prominent representative from the colonies, Nguyen Ai Quoc continued to be a source of considerable interest to the French security services. His daily routine was closely watched by the police, and two agents were assigned to follow him at all times. On June 22, 1922, Albert Sarraut invited him once again to the Ministry of Colonies for an interview. During the meeting the minister alternately threatened and bribed him. Sarraut opened the conversation by declaring that troublemakers connected with "Bolshevik" elements in France who were planning to cause problems in Indochina would inevitably be crushed. But, he added, he admired people like Nguyen Ai Quoc who had a firm purpose and the will to achieve it. But with willpower, he added, must come understanding. Let bygones be bygones, Sarraut concluded. "If you happen to want anything, I am always at your service. Now that we know each other, you can apply directly to me." Nguyen Ai Quoc stood up and thanked the minister, then remarked, "The main thing in my life and what I need most of all is freedom for my compatriots. May I go now?"[62]

A few days later Quoc wrote a public letter to the Ministry, which was published in *Le Paria*, *L'Humanité* (now the mouthpiece of the French Communist Party), and *Le Peuple*. Expressing his gratitude that the French authorities had provided him with his own private "aides-de-camp" (obviously a reference to the police surveillance), he commented that

At a time when Parliament is trying to save money, and cut down administrative personnel; when there is a large budget deficit; when agriculture and industry lack labor; when attempts are being made to levy taxes on workers' wages; and at a time when repopulation demands the use of all productive energies; it would seem to us antipatriotic at such a time to accept personal favors which necessarily cause loss of the powers of the citizens condemned—as *aides-de-camp*—to idleness and the spending of money that the proletariat has sweated for.

To alleviate this problem, he added, he was giving public notice of his daily activities:

Morning: from 8 to 12 at the workshop.
Afternoon: in newspaper offices (leftist of course) or at the library.
Evening: at home or attending educational talks.
Sundays and holidays: visiting museums or other places of interest.
There you are!

Hoping that this convenient and rational method will give satisfaction to your Excellency, we beg to remain. . . .

Nguyen Ai Quoc[63]

It is unlikely that Sarraut saw any humor in Nguyen Ai Quoc's note. There is no doubt that he continued to show an interest in his whereabouts. On one occasion Sarraut sent a cable to Governor-General Maurice Long in Indochina, declaring that the government was giving consideration to a proposal to arrest Nguyen Ai Quoc and return him to his native land. Long took issue with the idea, however, arguing that it would be easier to keep track of his activities in France. When Sarraut suggested exile in one of the French spheres of influence in south China, Long replied that he would be able to influence events in Indochina from such a nearby location.[64]

By then harassment from the authorities was probably only a minor irritant for Nguyen Ai Quoc. What was probably more frustrating was the attitude of many of his colleagues toward the common struggle. Despite his efforts, the French left still did not seem to take colonial affairs seriously. After its well-publicized beginning, the Colonial Study Commission lapsed into virtual desuetude. Party journals rarely made references to colonial problems. Even *L'Humanité*, he complained, did not accord to the cause of the oppressed colonial peoples the place that it merited. Bourgeois newspapers, he wrote, give more attention to colonies, and there were many militants "who still think that a colony is nothing but a country with plenty of sand underfoot and of sun overhead, a few green coconut palms and colored folk, and that is all."

The result of the Party's failure to address the colonial question, Quoc lamented, was a lack of mutual understanding between the working class in France and their counterparts in the colonies. French workers regarded the native as "an inferior and negligible human being, incapable of understanding and still less of taking action." Still, he conceded, prejudice ran in both directions. In the colonies, all Frenchmen, regardless of class, were regarded as "wicked exploiters."[65]

Nguyen Ai Quoc persistently prodded his colleagues on the colonial issue. At the FCP national congress held in Paris in October 1922, he and a number of other representatives from the colonial territories submitted a resolution urging that the colonial question be given more attention within the world Communist movement. But even after the Tours conference and the departure of the moderates, a Eurocentric attitude still prevailed among the radical elements who had joined the Communist Party. Occasionally the leadership would make a few halting efforts to organize the Vietnamese working community in France (most of whom consisted of manual laborers, shiphands and stevedores, and cooks). A few Vietnamese were raised to prominent positions in the party. But little else was done.

Nguyen Ai Quoc's frustration over this issue may have contributed to the increasing anti-French tone in his writings. On returning from Marseilles at the end of 1921, where he had seen the miserable conditions of Vietnamese dock workers, he began to sign articles with a new pseudonym, Nguyen o Phap, which means "Nguyen Who Detests the French." On one occasion he stormed out of an angry interview with a senior Party member responsible for dealing with colonial questions. In response, the rising young French Communist Jacques Doriot quietly advised him to tone down his rhetoric.[66]

In March 1923, Nguyen Ai Quoc moved out of his tiny apartment on Impasse Compoint and into the headquarters of *Le Paria*, now located at the Intercolonial Union's head office on the Rue du Marché des Patriarches. The move may have been motivated by convenience to his job or the need to conserve funds. The journal's office was on the ground floor; he took a room on the floor above at a cost of one hundred francs a month. It would be his last residence in Paris.[67]

He was receiving help in the publication of the journal from another rising young star in the Vietnamese nationalist movement, Nguyen The Truyen. Born in 1898 near Hanoi, Truyen arrived in Paris in 1920 to study engineering. A year later he joined the FCP and began to collaborate with Quoc at the Intercolonial Union. For a while he was almost certainly Quoc's closest colleague within the Vietnamese community.

The previous October, while attending the Party congress in Paris, Nguyen Ai Quoc had met Dmitri Manuilsky, a senior official of the Comintern in the USSR. At the congress, Manuilsky heard Quoc publicly criticize the lack of attention given to the colonial question within the Party. When, many months later, Manuilsky was ordered by the executive committee of the Comintern to prepare a report on the national and colonial questions for presentation at the Fifth Comintern Congress in the summer of 1924, he thought of the fiery young Vietnamese in Paris. Nguyen Ai Quoc was invited to Moscow at the request of Comrade Manuilsky to work for the Comintern.[68]

For Nguyen Ai Quoc, the invitation to Moscow was a reward for his efforts on behalf of the Party, and perhaps an opportunity to return to Asia to promote the revolutionary cause in Vietnam. But he approached the issue with his customary caution. To avoid giving away the news of his trip to the police, he announced to his friends that he was going to the South of France on a three-week vacation to rest. Then, having carefully set a regular pattern of behavior to lull his two "aides-de-camp" into relaxing their surveillance, on June 13 he left a movie house secretly by the rear door and hurried to the Gare du Nord, where he was handed his luggage by a friend and then caught a train for Berlin, posing as a wealthy Asian merchant with a cigar. He arrived in Berlin on the eighteenth, where his money disappeared quickly because of the murderous rate of inflation in postwar Germany. With the assistance of contacts from the local German Communist Party, he continued on to Hamburg. There he boarded the passenger liner *Karl Liebknecht* en route to Soviet Russia. He arrived in Petrograd on June 30, bearing a visa in the name of Chen Vang, a Chinese merchant.[69]

Nguyen Ai Quoc's sudden departure from Paris caught the police by surprise. The men tailing him initially reported to the Ministry of Colonies that he had left his house empty-handed but did not return. They then fell for his ruse and assumed that he was on vacation in the South. Only many weeks later did they realize that he had gone to Soviet Russia. His disappearance also confused his acquaintances in Paris. He had sent a letter to friends stating that he had left France and apologizing for the fact that he had not informed his colleagues of his impending departure. He hinted that he was going under cover and that he would not return for many years. In the meantime, he promised to send letters.[70]

In leaving Paris for Soviet Russia, Nguyen Ai Quoc had made a final symbolic break with his friend Phan Chu Trinh's path of reform and embraced the revolutionary cause of Vladimir Lenin. But his old mentor from the Villa des Gobelins wished him well. In a letter to a Vietnamese acquaintance in September, Trinh defended Quoc from his critics: "Although Nguyen Ai Quoc is young, and his acts are not subject to wise reflection," he wrote, "that has no importance, because Nguyen Ai Quoc has the heart of a patriot." Quoc had chosen the lonely and difficult path of liberating his compatriots, Trinh concluded, and all must respect his stout heart.[71]

III | APPRENTICE REVOLUTIONARY

In the late summer of 1923, Soviet Russia was still recovering from nearly seven years of war, revolution, and bitter civil conflict. Outside of Petrograd, Moscow, and a handful of other major cities in the European areas of Russia, the October Revolution had been, in Leon Trotsky's memorable words, a "revolution by telegraph." In the rural villages and market towns scattered about the vast Russian empire, Lenin's Bolsheviks—numbering only about fifty thousand at the moment of insurrection—had scant support from the millions of Russian peasants, who had little understanding of the ideas of Karl Marx and even less interest in the fate of the world revolution.

Initially, the new revolutionary leadership attempted to establish its legitimacy by announcing the inauguration of the new government in cablegrams to all administrative units. But it soon became evident that it would take more than a piece of paper to extend revolutionary power to the far reaches of the old tsarist empire. Within weeks of the storming of the Winter Palace in October 1917 (according to the Russian calendar), opposition forces began to appear: White Russian elements loyal to Tsar Nicholas II and the old monarchical system; nationalist forces among the minority ethnic groups along the fringes of the old empire, from Ukraine to Central Asia; and even foreign troops stationed in Russia to assist in the battle against Germany.

The Bolshevik government hastily mobilized manpower from among workers and poor peasants to build up the Red Army; after three years of bloody fighting it was finally able to suppress counterrevolutionary forces and establish firm control over the new Soviet state. But in the process, it had alienated key elements in Russian society, including peasants whose harvests were requisitioned by the state to feed the soldiers of the Red Army and the working population in the cities, members of non-Russian ethnic groups whose leaders were defeated and pitilessly run down by Soviet security forces, and others arrested and executed by Feliks Dzerzhinsky's secret police, familiarly known as the Cheka (Chrezvychainyi Komitet, or Extraordinary Commission).

As the country tried to recover from the Civil War, Lenin reluctantly recognized that Soviet Russia needed to go through its own capitalist stage before beginning the difficult transition to socialism. In 1921 he pushed through a moderate program of social and economic development known as the New Economic Policy, or NEP. The key elements in the program were the use of a combination of capitalist and socialist techniques to increase production, while at the same time promoting the concept of socialist ownership and maintaining firm Party control over the political system. Key industries and utilities and the banks remained in the hands of the state, but private enterprise operated at lower levels. The forced requisition of grain, which had caused serious unrest in rural areas, was replaced by a tax on production. The land remained in private hands.

Nguyen Ai Quoc's first days in the new socialist paradise that he had so glowingly described in articles written in France must have been somewhat unnerving. After disembarking from the *Karl Liebknecht* on the dock at Petrograd, he was interrogated by a suspicious young immigration officer. Lacking official papers except for the visa in the name of the fictitious Chinese merchant, which had been approved by the Soviet consulate in Berlin, and having no personal contacts in the city, he was held in detention for several weeks "in an atmosphere of tension" until his identity was finally verified by a representative of the FCP stationed in Moscow. He was then given permission to travel and proceeded to Moscow by train late in July. After being given temporary accommodations in a hotel near the Kremlin, he was assigned to work in the Far Eastern Bureau (Byuro Dalnego Vostoka, or Dalburo for short) at Comintern headquarters, located opposite the Rumyantsev Museum (now the Lenin Library).[1]

The Dalburo had been created as the result of a proposal at the Comintern's Second Congress in 1920 raised by Maring (real name Hendrik Sneevliet), a delegate of Dutch nationality who was later to achieve prominence as an adviser to the Chinese Communist Party. A strong believer in the importance of the colonial areas to the future of the world revolution, Maring had proposed the establishment of propaganda bureaus for the Middle East and the Far East, as well as the opening of a Marxist Institute in Moscow to provide training for prospective Asian revolutionary leaders. With Lenin's theses about to be approved, Maring's proposal was also adopted, and the following June, at a meeting of the Comintern Executive Committee, the Dalburo was established under the direction of the Russian orientalist scholar G. Safarov.[2]

In the ensuing months, Comintern leaders took a number of other steps to promote the establishment of revolutionary movements in Asia and Africa. All Communist parties in Western Europe were instructed to establish colonial commissions to evaluate the situation and support the struggle of the oppressed peoples in their own colonies (thus the Colonial Study Commission had been established in France). In the meantime, plans were initiated to establish training institutes in Soviet Russia to indoctrinate radicals from Asia and Africa and prepare them to return to their own countries to carry out revolutionary operations.

By then, the Comintern had already begun to engage in some preliminary operations in East Asia. In the spring of 1920, the Comintern agent Grigory Voitinsky was sent to China to get in touch with Chinese revolutionaries. Other agents based in Vladivostok traveled to Shanghai, Saigon, and Singapore to establish contact with radical elements and assist them in conducting revolutionary operations. In November, two Russians who had just arrived in Saigon were reportedly expelled on suspicion of carrying on such activities.[3]

With his now characteristic flair for the dramatic, Nguyen Ai Quoc wasted no time in making his presence felt. Shortly after his arrival in Moscow, he wrote a letter to the FCP Central Committee, criticizing his colleagues for ignoring the decisions of the Fourth Comintern Congress to expand their activities on colonial issues. While conceding that the FCP had initially responded to the order of the Comintern by creating the Colonial Study Commission as well as a regular column on the colonial question in the Party journal *L'Humanité*, he complained that in recent months the column had been canceled and that in his absence the commission was virtually moribund. "The declarations issued at national congresses in favor of the colonial peoples have helped to consolidate their sympathy with the Party," he pointed out, but "it is not reasonable to constantly repeat the same thing while doing nothing." The colonial peoples, seeing much promise with a minimum of performance, would begin to ask whether the Communists were serious or just bluffing. He concluded the letter by reminding the recipient that one key condition for joining the Comintern was to carry on systematic agitation to support the liberation of colonial peoples.[4]

Quoc also wrote a report to the presidium of the Comintern Executive Committee, detailing his ideas on how to promote the revolutionary struggle in Indochina. As he described it, the situation was hardly promising. Tonkin and Cochin China were controlled directly by the

French, while Annam, still nominally under the authority of the imperial court, was in reality under colonial domination as well. The urban proletariat represented only 2 percent of the total population and was not yet organized. There was a tiny middle class, living mainly in the large cities of Hanoi and Saigon and in provincial capitals scattered throughout the country; however, it was dominated economically by the overseas Chinese. The petty bourgeoisie, consisting of small merchants, clerks, low-level government functionaries, and artisans, were small in number and indecisive in their political views, although they did tend to support the cause of national independence. The peasants were severely oppressed and, if organized, had a high revolutionary potential. But the primary source for political activism was intellectuals and the patriotic scholar-gentry. It was they, he said, who had fomented all revolts in the past. The immediate need was therefore to establish joint action between such "national revolutionary" patriots and a Communist party.[5]

Nguyen Ai Quoc's recommendations were pure Leninism, as reflected in the latter's "Theses on the National and Colonial Questions." But given the existing state of affairs in Moscow, where attention to the colonial areas had declined substantially since the heady days of the Second Comintern Congress, it is doubtful that his ideas attracted much interest among his superiors. Still, influential Soviet officials were gradually becoming aware of the ambitious young revolutionary from Indochina and, in light of the fact that he was one of the few Asian Communists then living in Moscow, of the uses to which he could be put. During the summer of 1923 there had been a flurry of interest in Lenin's concept of a government of workers and peasants in societies that had not yet passed through the Industrial Revolution. In Prague, populist elements had established a "Green International" in 1922 to encourage the formation of peasant parties with modern political programs, and some radical elements in eastern Europe were convinced that the Comintern must come up with a similar "international" organization to compete with the Green International for the support of peasant groups in the area. Prominent in this effort was the Polish Communist Thomas Dombal (also known as Dabal), who had been arrested by the Polish government and was sent to Moscow in the spring of 1923 in an exchange of prisoners with Soviet Russia.

Given the fact that most Bolsheviks, reflecting the views of other European Marxists from Karl Marx on down, had always suspected that peasants were "bourgeois" at heart in their commitment to the concept of private property, few Comintern officials had much interest in Dombal's ideas, but they agreed for the time being to promote them. In preparation for holding an organizational conference, they took advantage of an international agricultural exhibition that had opened in Moscow in August, and decided to scour the meeting hall for foreigners with rural interests who could be recruited to serve as delegates to such a conference. Nguyen Ai Quoc, who was seemingly interested in everything that was going on in Moscow, had attended the exhibit when it first opened in August, and predictably he was selected as a delegate representing Indochina to the International Peasant Conference, which convened in Moscow on October 10, 1923. He had already signaled his views on the role of the peasantry in his report to the Comintern Executive Committee, when he remarked that because they had been so badly exploited, they were "very patriotic."[6]

The conference was held in the Andreyevskiy Palace, within the walls of the Kremlin, and Nguyen Ai Quoc was in the audience as one of the more than 150 delegates from forty different countries. Mikhail Kalinin, a party hack who had recently been appointed as the figurehead president of the Russian Federation, gave the opening speech, while the veteran Bolshevik Grigory Zinoviev, then head of the Comintern, presented the official Party position on the role of the peasants in the world revolution.

Nguyen Ai Quoc addressed the conference on the thirteenth. The speech, given in French because his knowledge of Russian was still inadequate, made no reference to the possible adoption of a "rural strategy" in colonial areas, nor to the need for a specific role for the peasantry in the revolutionary process in Asia, but simply expressed in plain and unadorned terms the difficult conditions of the rural population in many colonial Asian societies, pointing out that peasants were the worst victims of imperialist oppression in the region. The Comintern, Quoc asserted, would become a genuine Communist International only when it included representatives of the Asian peasantry as active participants.[7]

At the close of the conference, the organizers agreed to create a new Peasant International (in Russian, Krestyanskii Internatsional, or Krestintern for short). Its purpose was to "establish and maintain firm ties with cooperatives and economic and political organizations of the peasants of all countries," and to "coordinate peasant organizations and the efforts of the peasants to realize the slogan for building a workers' and peasants' government." An International Peasant Council was also created and Nguyen Ai Quoc was elected as one of the eleven members of its presidium. The post of general secretary of the larger body itself was given to a prominent Bolshevik bureaucrat, Alexander P. Smirnov. Dombal was named his assistant.[8]

In December 1923, Nguyen Ai Quoc began to take courses at the Communist University of the Toilers of the East. Founded on Lenin's order in 1921 as a result of decisions taken at the Second Comintern Congress the previous year, it was originally placed under the jurisdiction of Joseph Stalin's People's Commissariat of Nationalities, and thus became popularly labeled abroad as the dreaded "Stalin School." Under Stalin's direction, it soon became the leading institute for training Asian revolutionaries invited to Soviet Russia to study, as well as cadres of non-Russian ethnic stock from the eastern regions of the old tsarist empire. A second institute, the International Lenin School, was established to provide training for advanced cadres from Western European countries.

In 1924 Nguyen Ai Quoc published a brief article in the French journal *La Vie Ouvrière* describing the nature of the school, and this information, in addition to material gathered by the French intelligence services at the time and recent scholarship by Russian researchers in Moscow, provides a reasonably clear picture of the school and its activities. At the time he studied there, there were more than 1000 students from sixty-two different nationalities. Most of those enrolled were from Soviet-occupied areas in Central Asia, but there were some foreigners as well, including a few Chinese and Koreans. There were apparently no students from Indochina prior to Quoc's arrival. Nearly 900 were members of Communist parties, and about 150 were women. About half came from peasant families, while the remainder were divided between workers and "proletarian intellectuals."

There were 150 instructors at the school, teaching a variety of courses, including the natural and social sciences, mathematics, the history of revolution and the workers' movement, and Marx's theory of historical materialism. Instruction was not provided through lectures, but through use of the Socratic technique, with students assigned individual topics to be prepared with the assistance of the instructor and discussed in class. Textbooks included Lenin's *The State and Revolution*, Stalin's *October Revolution and the Tactics of Russian Communism*, and I. M. Yaroslavskii's *Russian History: A Short Course*. The school was housed in ten buildings, with the headquarters located in an old convent on Tverskaya (now Gorkii) Street, and the dormitories and cafeterias situated nearby at an old prefecture of police.[9]

The school was run on strict military discipline, and students not only took part in classroom studies but also received military training and were taught such useful revolutionary activities as how to instigate strikes and disseminate propaganda. Classes were initially taught in French or in their own native language, but later students were expected to be conversant in Russian (a requirement that was not always met). Lodging was free, but all students were expected to take their turn performing various administrative tasks or working in the kitchen. Party cells were established among party members to monitor their behavior and guarantee ideological orthodoxy. On arrival, each student was assigned a pseudonym, and his or her real identity was to be known only by security personnel at the school.

It was not all labor. The school year ran from September to early July, and included three weeks of vacation at Christmas and one week off in the spring. A cinema was available to the students two days each week, and two rest camps were established in the Crimea for them to engage in work-study activities during their summer vacation. Some were taught cattle breeding there, while others cultivated the hundred acres assigned to provide the food served at the camp. During their vacation, students helped local peasants bring in the harvest or took part in other community services. Still, many of the students, perhaps unaccustomed to the intense cold of Russian winters, became ill, and some were dismissed for that reason from the program. One Vietnamese student contracted tuberculosis and requested a transfer to a city in the southern part of the country.

As Nguyen Ai Quoc described it in his article, the school was an idyllic place to study. There were two libraries containing over forty-seven thousand books, and each major nationality represented at the school possessed its own section with books and periodicals in its own national language. The students were "serious and full of enthusiasm," and "passionately longed to acquire knowledge and to study." The staff and the instructors treated the foreign students "like brothers" and even invited them to "participate in the political life of the country."[10]

Quoc was not happy with all aspects of the school. Shortly after taking part in the third anniversary celebration of the school in April 1924, he wrote a letter to Comrade Petrov, secretary of the Dalburo, complaining that there were virtually no Vietnamese in attendance and suggesting that a separate annex for Asian students should be established at the school. The Stalin School, he pointed out, was the mold that would shape the minds of the next generation of Asian revolutionaries and would become the basis on which a Communist "federation" of the East would eventually be founded.[11]

The Stalin School ran on two levels—a basic three-year program in Marxism-Leninism and the sciences, and a "short course" of seven months for temporary students. Nguyen Ai Quoc took the latter, presumably because he was also working at the Comintern and did not intend to remain in Moscow for an extended period of time. He also participated in a number of other organizations recently established by the Soviet state, such as the Red Labor International, the Youth International, and the Women's International. Clearly, the Comintern leadership viewed him as their token colonial who could provide an Asian dimension to the countless front organizations being formed during those heady days. In early May 1924, he was invited to take part in the annual May Day celebrations and to speak on international worker solidarity in the festivities in Red Square. Two months later, he took part in the third congress of the Red Labor International as a representative for Indochina. He also attended an international women's congress, where he briefly talked with Lenin's widow, Nadezhda Krupskaya.[12]

Through these myriad activities, Nguyen Ai Quoc gradually emerged as a well-known fixture in Moscow, and became acquainted with key luminaries of the international Communist movement, such as the veteran Bolshevik Nikolai Bukharin, the Finnish Communist Otto Kuusinen, the Bulgarian Comintern leader Georgi Dimitrov, and Ernst Thälmann, a leading member of the German Communist Party. He also met a number of Chinese comrades studying at the school (including the future prime minister Zhou Enlai, whom he had first encountered in Paris), as well as Sun Yat-sen's chief military adviser, Chiang Kai-shek, who visited Moscow for three months in the late summer and fall of 1923.

In general, Quoc's acquaintances seemed to like him. Ruth Fischer, a prominent German Communist, commented that although he was not impressive on first acquaintance, he soon won the respect and affection of all by his "goodness and simplicity." More a pragmatist than a theoretician, he appeared adept at avoiding the bitter factional disputes that were already beginning to plague the Soviet leadership and eventually led to the crippling of the Bolshevik Party (now about to be renamed the Communist Party of the Soviet Union, or CPSU) and of the Comintern itself during the next decade. The period of the NEP was a relatively brief interlude when the future must have looked bright to many

Soviet citizens and foreigners alike. With the Civil War at an end, the regime had abandoned its policy of coercion and the oppression of potential rivals and began to encourage the people to take part in economic construction ("enrich yourselves" was a popular slogan of the time). Cultural life was still rich and varied, as Soviet writers, artists, and composers sought to formulate a new revolutionary medium that could accurately express the dramatic changes taking place in the country. A few years later, at Stalin's insistence, this period suddenly came to an end.

Quoc had apparently not suffered any loss of intensity in his own revolutionary beliefs. The journalist Ossip Mandelstam, who interviewed him for the magazine *Ogonyok* in December 1923, noted that the slight young man, so imbued with the subtle qualities of the Confucian intellectual class, had large and penetrating dark eyes, and when he spoke of conditions in his country his whole body appeared to go into convulsion and his eyes seemed to reflect a strange fierce brilliance. In the interview, Quoc pronounced the word "civilization" with an attitude of supreme disgust, and harshly criticized the Catholic Church in Indochina for appropriating almost one fifth of the country's arable land. According to Boris Souvarine, the French Communist who later left the revolutionary movement, Nguyen Ai Quoc had now become "an accomplished Stalinist."[13]

Only one of his acquaintances at the time expressed a low opinion of Quoc. The prominent Indian Communist M. N. Roy, who later served as a Comintern representative in China and (in the view of many observers) whose incompetence was a major factor in the defeat of the Chinese Communists at the hands of Chiang Kai-shek in 1927, felt that the young Vietnamese was unimpressive in mind as well as in body and was a poor student to boot. Ironically, Quoc was one of the few in Moscow who shared Roy's thesis that the Asian revolution was the necessary first step in the overthrow of world capitalism.[14]

Nguyen Ai Quoc also had the time to do a considerable amount of writing, contributing regularly to French leftist journals and also to the Soviet press, publishing a number of articles in *Inprecor* (International Press Correspondence, the official mouthpiece of the Comintern). The topics of his articles were varied, but always had a revolutionary slant. He wrote about imperialist oppression in China, of the activities of the Ku Klux Klan in the United States, of the idyllic life of the population in the Soviet Union, and of course about the colonial exploitation of the native peoples of Asia and Africa. In collaboration with Chinese students at the Stalin School, he edited the short pamphlet *Kitai i kitaiskaya molodezh* (China and Chinese Youth), published in 1925 in Chinese and

French as well as in Russian. He also reportedly wrote a history of Indochina under French rule, which remained unpublished in the Comintern archives.[15]

Nguyen Ai Quoc's major writing project during his stay in Moscow, however, was *Le procès de la colonisation française* (translated into English as "French Colonialism on Trial"). Presumably based on articles that he had written while living in Paris as well as on his manuscript entitled *Les opprimés*, which had disappeared prior to publication in 1920, the book was completed in Moscow and published in Paris by the Librairie du Travail in 1926, long after he had left France for Moscow. It is a rambling indictment of colonial conditions throughout the world, ending with a spirited appeal to the youth of Indochina to rise up against their exploiters. Much of the material in the book relates to Indochina, but there are several references to the African colonies. Although it is probably the best known of all Ho Chi Minh's writings, it is so poorly organized and badly written that one biographer has speculated that it may have been written by another Vietnamese and then printed under his name. But in its tone and style, it is too similar to other writings of Ho Chi Minh for most scholars to doubt that it is essentially his work. The most that can be said about it is that it shows evidence of having been written in haste.[16]

In all of his public utterances, Nguyen Ai Quoc still seemed to be a true believer. His writings on the Soviet Union are uniformly full of praise, and his admiration for Lenin seemed boundless. He had apparently been very disappointed at being unable to meet the Bolshevik leader before his death. When he was asked the purpose of his visit on his arrival in Petrograd in July 1923, Quoc had replied that he wished to meet Lenin and was disheartened to hear that the Soviet leader was ill. The following January, he learned to his great sorrow that Lenin had died. As an Italian acquaintance, Giovanni Germanetto, recounted the story:

> Moscow, January 1924. The Russian winter is at its height. The temperature sinks at times to 40 degrees below zero. A few days ago Lenin died. That morning, a quiet knocking on our door in Lux Hotel aroused me. The door opened and a frail young man entered.
>
> He said he was Vietnamese and his name was Nguyen Ai Quoc. He also said he intended to go to Trade Union House and see off Lenin. . . .
>
> I told him he was too lightly dressed for the freezing cold outside. I said he should wait, we'd get him some warm clothing.

Ai Quoc sighed, and sat down to have tea with us, and finally went to his room. We thought he had taken our advice and had stayed indoors.

Somewhere around ten at night I heard a soft knocking on the door again. It was Comrade Ai Quoc. His face was blue, and the ears, nose, and fingers on the hands were blue, too, from the fierce cold.

Ai Quoc said he had just seen Comrade Lenin. He was trembling from the cold as he explained that he could not wait until tomorrow to pay homage to the best friend of the colonial peoples. . . . He finished by asking if we didn't happen to have some hot tea.

According to Ho's Soviet biographer, Yevgeny Kobelev, after returning from Lenin's funeral Nguyen Ai Quoc locked himself in his room and wrote an essay expressing his grief at the death of the generous Bolshevik leader who had spared his time and effort to concern himself with the liberation of the colonial peoples. "In his life," he concluded, "he was our father, teacher, comrade, and adviser. Now he is our guiding star that leads to social revolution. Lenin lives on in our deeds. He is immortal."[17]

Only in bits and pieces do we find suggestions that not everything enthralled him. On moving to the Lux Hotel in early December 1923, he had been assigned to a small room occupied by four or five fellow students that evidently displeased him. The following March he wrote a letter complaining about the conditions—by day he was kept awake by the noise, and by night by insects, which kept him from sleeping—and he declared that he was withholding his rent of five rubles a month as a form of protest. He was eventually resettled in another room.[18]

On a more important note, Nguyen Ai Quoc was not always pleased with strategy decisions. For months he had been bombarding his acquaintances on the issue of colonialism. In February 1924, he wrote to a friend at Comintern headquarters (possibly Dmitri Manuilsky) to thank him for raising the colonial issue at the FCP conference in Lyons. On the same day, he wrote Comintern General Secretary Grigory Zinoviev asking for an interview to discuss the colonial problem. Receiving no answer, he wrote a second letter complaining that he had received no answer to his request for an interview. There is no indication that Zinoviev answered his request.[19]

What he wanted to discuss with Zinoviev is not known for certain, but in an article published in the April issue of *Inprecor* titled "Indochina and the Pacific," Quoc had declared that although at first sight the Asian question was of no concern to European workers, in fact the problem of Indochina and Asia had importance for workers in all countries. Colonial exploitation of the region, he said, served not only to enrich capitalists and unscrupulous politicians, but also risked bringing about the outbreak of a new imperialist war. Such actions represented a threat to workers in Indochina and Asia, and also to the international proletariat as well.[20]

In referring to the relationship between conditions in Europe and Asia, Nguyen Ai Quoc—deliberately or not—was stepping into a minefield that had already aroused angry debates in Comintern meetings since the Second Congress in 1920. Spokesmen for the peoples of the colonial East such as M. N. Roy had argued incessantly that a resolution of the "Eastern question" was essential for the ultimate fate of the world revolution, but many European Communists retorted that the revolution in Asia could not be unleashed until Communist parties had already come to power in European countries.

At first, advocates of an Asian-based strategy had the benefit of friends in high places—including Lenin and even Joseph Stalin—who were apparently sympathetic to their views. But by 1924 Lenin was dead and Stalin had become preoccupied with the inner-party struggle for primacy in Moscow. Zinoviev, the current head of the Comintern, appeared bored by the issue. The Dutch Communist Maring had left the Comintern and even Manuilsky, Nguyen Ai Quoc's original sponsor, was a Ukrainian who had little knowledge of Asia and concentrated his activities on conditions in the Balkans.

There was also little interest in the role of the peasantry. After a strong start, the Krestintern had fallen into disrepute and was not taken seriously among the worker-oriented party bureaucrats, or apparatchiks, in Moscow. Even Nikolai Bukharin, one of the more enlightened of Bolshevik leaders, laughingly referred to Thomas Dombal as a "peasant visionary." Nguyen Ai Quoc tried to keep the issue alive, speaking on the issue of the peasantry at a meeting of the Krestintern in June 1924, but he had little response. In a remark to a friend, he laughingly referred to himself as a "voice crying in the wilderness."[21]

The Fifth Congress of the Comintern, held in the early summer of 1924, provided Nguyen Ai Quoc with a rare opportunity to air his views within the larger body of the organization. The congress, in fact, may have been the initial reason for his original summons to Moscow, since Dmitri Manuilsky had seen him as a possible source of information in connection with his own forthcoming speech on the colonial question at the conference. Since there was no Communist Party in Indochina, Quoc attended the conference as a member of the FCP delegation.[22]

The Fifth Congress opened on June 17 and held its sessions in the Bolshoi Theater in downtown Moscow.[23] Over five hundred delegates representing nearly fifty countries attended. The Comintern leadership was becoming increasingly sensitive to charges of neglect from Asian comrades and decided to devote a special session to the colonial question and issues connected with the non-Russian nationalities, in addition to appointing a committee to deal with the issue. But the congress was taking place at the height of the first power struggle between Stalin and his rival Leon Trotsky, and leading members of the CPSU were so preoccupied with the struggle inside the Kremlin that they gave little attention to the Eastern question. In his opening speech, General Secretary Zinoviev, soon to be one of Stalin's new challengers for Party leadership, mentioned the national and colonial issue only in passing, while Manuilsky's address on the national and colonial question focused primarily on the countries in eastern Europe. Perhaps at the urging of Nguyen Ai Quoc—who had probably been harassing him to raise the issue—he did criticize the FCP for its inadequate attention to the colonial question.

Right from the start, Nguyen Ai Quoc made his presence known. In the opening session, when the delegate Vasili Kolarov was reading the text of a draft resolution that would be prepared for publication after adjournment, Quoc rose to ask whether the congress would address a special appeal to the colonial peoples. Kolarov testily replied that the colonial question was already on the agenda, and thus could be raised by any delegate at the conference. But Nguyen Ai Quoc pursued the issue and asked that any address contain the words "to the colonial peoples." The proposal was accepted by the delegates.

On June 23, Nguyen Ai Quoc took the floor. "I am here," he told the delegates,

> in order to continuously remind the International of the existence of the colonies and to point out that the revolution faces a colonial danger as well as a great future in the colonies. It seems to me that the comrades do not entirely comprehend the fact that the fate of the world proletariat, and especially the fate of the proletarian class in aggressive countries that have invaded colonies, is closely tied to the fate of the oppressed peoples of the colonies. Since this is the case I will take every opportunity that presents itself or, if necessary, create opportunities to point out to you the importance of the colonial question. . . .

You must excuse my frankness, but I cannot help but observe that the speeches by comrades from the mother countries give me the impression that they wish to kill a snake by stepping on its tail. You all know that today the poison and life energy of the capitalist snake is concentrated more in the colonies than in the mother countries. The colonies supply the raw materials for industry. The colonies supply soldiers for the armies. In the future, the colonies will be bastions of the counterrevolution. Yet in your discussions of the revolution you neglect to talk about the colonies. If one wants to break an egg or a stone, one will be careful to find an instrument whose strength corresponds to the object one wishes to break. Why is it that where the revolution is concerned you do not wish to make your strength, your propaganda, equal to the enemy whom you wish to fight and defeat? Why do you neglect the colonies, while capitalism uses them to support itself, defend itself, and fight you?[24]

On July 1 Quoc took the floor once again to underscore Dmitri Manuilsky's initial criticism of European Communist parties for their failure to address the colonial issue. In a lengthy report he singled out not only the French but also the British and Dutch parties for their inadequate efforts to conduct a vigorous colonial policy and establish contacts with revolutionary elements in colonial societies. Pointing to the fact that Party journals in France had missed many opportunities to bring the issue to the attention of their readers, he called for a number of specific measures to improve their performance. As in his speech at the peasant conference, he refrained from asserting a central role for the countryside in the coming revolution, but he did make an effort to show that the peasantry would play an active role:

In all the French colonies, famine is on the increase and so is the people's hatred. The native peasants are ripe for insurrection. In many colonies, they have risen many times but their uprisings have all been drowned in blood. If at present the peasants still have a passive attitude, the reason is that they still lack organization and leaders. The Communist International must help them to revolution and liberation.[25]

With his performance at the Fifth Comintern Congress, Nguyen Ai Quoc had brought himself to the attention of the leaders of the world Communist movement. The Soviet painter N. I. Kropchenko asked him to pose for a portrait, which appeared in the journal *Rabo-*

chaya Gazeta (Workers' Gazette) at the end of July, while *Pravda* reported his comments under the provocative title, "From Words to Deeds, the Speech of Indochina Delegate Nguyen Ai Quoc." For the moment, Quoc was still following official policy, but it would not be long before his emphasis on the importance of the peasantry to the revolution in Asia would be considered heretical and would be severely punished in Moscow.[26]

As it turned out, the congress made no major changes in Comintern policy, but it did show a heightened awareness of the colonial problem. The leadership appeared conscious of the need to increase propaganda and recruitment in colonial areas and set up a commission on international propaganda. Nguyen Ai Quoc was named one of its founding members. The congress, however, did not include any special declaration on the colonial issue in its final resolution—a deficiency that would be remedied at the next congress four years later. But the Comintern did issue a broad appeal to "the slaves of the colonies," as Nguyen Ai Quoc had proposed at the opening session.[27]

Whether or not in response to Nguyen Ai Quoc's criticism, the Comintern leadership also turned its attention to bringing more Asian revolutionaries to study in the USSR. In the years following the congress, increased numbers of Asians—including more than one hundred Vietnamese—would be sent to Moscow or Leningrad (as the city of Petrograd was named after Lenin's death) for training and eventual return to their homeland for revolutionary work. The first group of three Vietnamese apparently arrived from France in mid-1925.

The central apparatus for the Soviet program to train Asian revolutionaries continued to be the Stalin School. For its part, the FCP was instructed to remedy its own shortcomings. The Colonial Study Commission was reorganized as the Colonial Commission, with Jacques Doriot at its head. In early 1925 the Party established its own clandestine colonial school near the Porte de Clignancourt in the northern suburbs of Paris to train revolutionaries from the colonies in preparation for eventual schooling in the Soviet Union. In the first class, one of the eight students was Vietnamese. Over the next several years, groups of five to ten Vietnamese arrived in Moscow each year. The majority came from France, but a few traveled directly from Indochina.

Nguyen Ai Quoc's attendance at the Fifth Comintern Congress symbolized the end of his apprenticeship as a revolutionary and the beginning of his emergence as an Asian leader of international standing in the world communist movement. He was now the recognized spokesman for the Eastern question and for increased attention to the problems of the peasantry. As gratifying as that may have been to his ego and to his desire to orient the Comintern toward assigning greater attention to the colonial question, he now felt that he had accomplished his task in Moscow and was ready to return to Asia to launch the process of building a revolutionary movement in Indochina.

Nguyen Ai Quoc had originally gone to Moscow under the impression that he would remain only briefly before returning to his homeland. In a letter to the Comintern Executive Committee written in April 1924, he had lamented that neither the Comintern nor the FCP knew very much about the situation in the French colonies. It was vital, he maintained, to establish contact with such areas, and he recommended himself to undertake the task of serving as a liaison. The letter is sufficiently revealing about his intentions to quote at length:

> It was decided on my arrival in Moscow that after three months' stay here, I would leave for China to establish contact with my country. I am now in my ninth month here, and my sixth month of waiting, and yet the question of my departure has not yet been decided.
>
> I don't feel that it is necessary to speak to you of revolutionary or nationalist movements old or new; of the existence or nonexistence of workers' organizations, or of the activities of secret societies and other groups, because I have no intention here of submitting a thesis; but I would like to point out the necessity for us to study the situation in a careful manner, and if nothing exists, to CREATE SOMETHING.
>
> My trip would thus serve as a voyage of investigation and study. I must attempt a) to establish contacts between Indochina and the Comintern, b) to study the political, economic and social situation in that colony, c) to establish contact with organizations that are already in existence there, and d) to try to organize a base for information and propaganda.
>
> How can I hope to fulfill that task? First, I must go to China. Then to undertake whatever actions that the possibilities present. What will be the necessary sum for my support? I will probably have to move often, to carry on relations with various groups, to pay for correspondence, to buy publications appearing in Indochina, to arrange for room and board, etc. etc. After consulting with Chinese colleagues here, I estimate that I will require a budget of ap-

proximately US$100 a month, not including the transportation from Russia to China. I have not included taxes.

I hope that this will provide you with a basis for discussion of the subject of my return to the Far East.[28]

Nguyen Ai Quoc's aspirations to return to Asia were probably intensified by conversations with the Soviet agent S. A. Dalin, who had just returned from propaganda activities in Guangzhou (then known to Westerners as Canton), where the Chinese patriot Sun Yat-sen had recently established the temporary headquarters of his revolutionary movement. The previous year, Sun had signed an agreement to host a Soviet advisory mission under the Comintern agent Mikhail Borodin in Canton to assist in the reorganization of Sun's Kuomintang party along Leninist lines. Dalin had been a member of the team that arrived in Canton with Borodin in October. On his return to Moscow, Dalin stayed at the Lux Hotel, where he met Nguyen Ai Quoc and talked to him about conditions in south China. Quoc was undoubtedly delighted to hear that there were a substantial number of Vietnamese émigrés in the area engaged in activities directed at destroying the French colonial regime in Indochina.[29]

For a variety of reasons, however, Quoc's departure kept being delayed. In April 1924 he had been sent to Yakutsk, in Soviet Siberia, to escort a Chinese delegation en route to Moscow. Shortly after his return, his patron Dmitri Manuilsky called him in for an interview. "So, comrade," Manuilsky greeted him, "are you anxious to fight?" Quoc took the occasion to press his point with his friend, arguing that conditions existed for "a party of the Bolshevik type" in Indochina. The workers' movement was on the rise, and there were many Vietnamese émigrés living in south China. Quoc proposed to organize them into the nucleus of a future Communist Party. Manuilsky gave his assent, but with the proviso that Quoc would also use his experience in assisting other nationalities in the area as well. Shortly after, Nguyen Ai Quoc was appointed as a member of the Far Eastern Secretariat of the Comintern Executive Committee.[30]

Still, the bureaucratic wheels moved slowly. In a letter to Grigory Voitinsky on September 11, Quoc complained that his trip to China had been delayed "for this and that reason" and "from one week to the next," and then "from one month to the next." He was also disappointed to discover that the Dalburo could not provide him with the funds for his trip or with an official position with the Comintern mission in Canton. Original plans called for him to serve in some capacity with the Kuomintang, but when that fell through, the trip was again delayed. Impatient to get under way, Quoc finally offered to seek employment on his own initiative after his arrival in Canton so long as the Dalburo could provide him with travel fare. On September 25, under the urgings of the FCP representative in Moscow, the Dalburo accepted his request: "Comrade Nguyen Ai Quoc needs to go to Guangzhou [Canton]. Expenses will be paid by the Far Eastern Bureau."[31]

Nguyen Ai Quoc had finally managed to persuade the Comintern to authorize him to return to Asia to carry on revolutionary work. Still, as he told a friend, the arrangement had its "awkward points," since he would be forced to operate illegally in Canton, under the watchful eyes of the Sûreté in the French concession in the city (during the nineteenth century, European nations had pressured the Qing government to provide them with concession areas at various points along the coast, where foreigners could carry on their activities under European jurisdiction). He would have to provide for his own expenses in a country that he had never visited, and do so in a language that he could read and write, but not speak. To provide himself with cover and a source of limited funds, he visited the offices of the Soviet news agency ROSTA and agreed to send to Moscow articles on conditions in China.[32]

Sometime in October, Nguyen Ai Quoc left Moscow by train from Yaroslavskii Station. As had happened before, he left without informing his friends, simply asking Thomas Dombal to let out the word that he was ill, since he would be living in China illegally. To further cover his tracks, he wrote a letter to a French acquaintance, explaining that he was returning to France since he was not permitted to go to Indochina. The letter was duly reported by an agent to the Sûreté.[33]

The trip to Vladivostok on the single-track Trans-Siberian Express ordinarily took about three weeks, since the train was forced to stop frequently to add coal or water, and sometimes to remain on a siding for traffic coming from the other direction. From his window, Quoc could see the vast damage caused to Siberian towns and villages by the bitter Civil War between the Bolsheviks and the White forces, which had ended only four years earlier. On several occasions, Red Army units bearing machine guns boarded the train and inspected the passengers in search of counterrevolutionary elements. After a brief stop in Vladivostok, where he stayed at the Lenin Hotel on the main avenue in the city, he boarded a Soviet ship bound for China. The ship docked in Canton on November 11, 1924.[34]

IV | SONS OF THE DRAGON

T he Asia that Nguyen Ai Quoc returned to late in 1924 was different from the Asia that he had left thirteen years earlier. Whereas the colonial system in South and Southeast Asia had survived World War I intact, the situation in China had changed dramatically. In the fall of 1911, a major convulsion had brought about the disintegration of the old imperial system in Beijing. Four months after Nguyen Ai Quoc's departure from Saigon's Nha Rong pier that June, an insurrection sparked by members of Sun Yat-sen's revolutionary party led in quick succession to the collapse of the Manchu dynasty and the rise of a new government in China. But the partisans of Sun Yat-sen had been unable to take advantage of the situation. Outmaneuvered both politically and militarily by General Yuan Shikai, the commander of the Manchu armed forces, in February 1912 Sun was forced to offer General Yuan the presidency of a new republic to be established in Beijing.

Yuan, who eventually hoped to declare a new dynasty in his own name, tried to restore law and order by relying on traditional autocratic methods of governing. This provoked clashes with Sun's party, whose members occupied almost half the seats in the newly established parliamentary body, called the National Assembly. In January 1914, Yuan abruptly dissolved the parliament and attempted to rule by fiat. Sun's party was declared illegal and Sun fled to Japan. But after Yuan died suddenly of illness in 1916, China began to disintegrate, as regional military commanders, popularly known as warlords, seized control in various provinces around the country. Although a fragile government continued to reign in Beijing, social and intellectual ferment began to build throughout the country; in 1919, major student demonstrations erupted in the capital and several other major cities. That same year, Sun Yat-sen successfully established a base for his revolutionary party—now renamed the Kuomintang, or Nationalist Party—in Canton, capital of

Guangdong province, under the protection of Chen Jiongming, the local warlord. In April 1921, Sun formally declared the establishment of a new national government, with himself as president.

In the two years immediately following the Bolshevik revolution, the new Soviet government in Moscow was in no position to take advantage of the events taking place in China, and it was more concerned with establishing control over the vast territories of the onetime Russian empire in Siberia, now temporarily occupied by a variety of anti-Communist forces. But by the spring of 1920 Soviet rule over the area had been consolidated, and a Far Eastern Secretariat was established in Irkutsk to direct Communist operations throughout the vast region of East Asia and the Pacific. That April, Grigory Voitinsky, then a Comintern agent stationed in Irkutsk, left for Beijing. After a brief stay he went on to Shanghai, where he helped to set up a provisional organization composed of revolutionaries operating in the area. The following summer, radicals from around the country gathered in Shanghai and created a formal Chinese Communist Party (CCP).

One of the first decisions facing the new party was whether to cooperate with Sun Yat-sen's new revolutionary regime in Canton. Some members, convinced that key members of Sun's entourage were essentially counterrevolutionary in their instincts, were reluctant to join forces with the Kuomintang. But the Dutch Communist Maring, who had succeeded Voitinsky as chief Comintern representative in China, was insistent; in January 1923, Sun Yat-sen and Soviet representative Adolf Joffe signed an agreement in Shanghai that created a united front between the two parties and arranged for Soviet assistance in completing the reunification of China. The arrangement, described as a "bloc within," called for members of the CCP to join the Kuomintang, which remained the dominant political force in Canton.[1]

Beginning in late 1923, the two parties, with the assistance of Mikhail Borodin's new Comintern mission, started preparations for a northern expedition to depose the rapacious warlord regimes into which China had been divided since the death of Yuan Shikai. While the CCP was the junior partner in the alliance and lacked the following and the prestige of the Kuomintang, it was clearly a new and dynamic force in Chinese politics, a party with a future if not a past.

In French Indochina, changes were also taking place, although not at the same pace as in China. The population of the three zones was increasing rapidly. From about 7 million in 1880, it rose to approximately 16 million in 1926, with 6 million in Tonkin, 5 million in Annam, and about 4 million in Cochin China. Although well over three quarters of the population still lived in the countryside, there was a steady increase in the size of the urban population, which reached the level of about 1 million people in the mid-1920s. Most of them lived in the metropolitan cities of Saigon and Hanoi.

In the thirteen years since Nguyen Ai Quoc left Saigon, the movement to restore Vietnamese independence had lost ground. With the arrest and eventual exile of Phan Chu Trinh to France, the most prominent advocate of nonviolent reform had been at least temporarily silenced. In the meantime, Phan Boi Chau's once promising organization, which had enlisted the support of many of Vietnam's most prominent patriots, had gradually faded in importance after several abortive uprisings and then the arrest and imprisonment in south China of the nationalist leader himself.

On hearing the news of the 1911 revolution in China, Chau had dropped his plan to institute a constitutional monarchy and instead established a new political party—called the Restoration Society, or Quang Phuc Hoi—aimed at creating an independent republic on the Sun Yat-sen model. Clearly Chau hoped for Chinese assistance in overthrowing the French; during a meeting with Sun Yat-sen in Canton sometime in early 1912, Sun had promised him that Vietnam would be the first to receive Chinese assistance once the revolutionaries consolidated their power in China. Shortly after, however, Phan Boi Chau was arrested by a local warlord on the charge of carrying out subversive activities. By the time Chau emerged from prison in 1917, Sun Yat-sen's party had fallen from power and Sun himself was in Japan. With his hopes for foreign assistance once again dashed, Phan Boi Chau appeared to lose his bearings. In despair, he even offered to cooperate with the French, provided that they lived up to their promises to carry out political and economic reforms in Indochina. By the early 1920s, his revolutionary apparatus in Vietnam had virtually disintegrated. He remained in exile in China, surrounded by a small coterie of loyal followers, a figure of increasing irrelevance. The era of Phan Boi Chau had clearly come to an end.[2]

The collapse of Phan Boi Chau's movement and the exile of Phan Chu Trinh were indicative of broader changes taking place in Vietnamese society; the passing of the era of the two Phans coincided with the decline of the traditional scholar-gentry class, which had dominated Vietnamese politics for centuries. Although, under the urging of such patriotic figures as Chau and Trinh, many members of the Confucian elite had cast off their old beliefs and attempted to involve themselves in mass politics, as a class they were never truly comfortable in such a role; many found it difficult to acclimate themselves to the changing conditions created under French colonial rule. Phan Boi Chau enthused in print over a movement comprising "ten thousand nameless heroes" who would drive the French into the sea, but to the end his party was composed primarily of the well-born and the well-educated, and few peasants took part. Although his movement attempted to promote commerce and industry as a means of enriching Vietnamese society, its senior members were representative of the traditional landed aristocracy. Well-meaning patriotic scholars in flowing robes opened shops to raise funds and encourage local commerce and then alienated customers with their condescending ways.[3]

By the end of World War I, the influence of the scholar-gentry class (which had about 20,000 people at the end of the previous century) within Vietnamese society was beginning to wane. The Confucian civil service examinations had been abolished in all three territories and was replaced by a new educational system imposed by the French. *Quoc ngu*, the transliteration of spoken Vietnamese into the Roman alphabet, was now being actively promoted by both Christian missionaries in Cochin China and reformist intellectuals in Tonkin and Annam and was increasingly accepted as a useful replacement for the cumbersome system of Chinese characters. While most young Vietnamese continued to receive a traditional education in their rural villages, the children of many scholar-gentry elites, now deprived of the Confucian road to upward mobility, were trained in new Franco-Vietnamese schools such as the National Academy in Hué, where instruction was given in the French language. Many went to France to complete their schooling.

At the same time, a new and more Westernized Vietnamese middle class emerged. Some had established commercial or manufacturing companies to cater to the needs and desires of wealthy families living in the major cities. Others worked for European firms, entered the professions, or obtained a position in the bureaucracy. Although many members of this new urban elite admired Phan Boi Chau and his followers for their patriotism, they privately ridiculed their elders for their conservative, old-fashioned ways. Equally committed to the cause of national independence, the members of this new generation were uprooted from their past and more sophisticated in their knowledge of the West. Many wore Western-style clothing, drank French wines, and conversed in the French language. As the French journalist Paul Monet wrote, members of this new generation were "the prototypes of our [French] culture, deprived of traditional beliefs and uprooted from ancestral soil, totally ignorant of Confucian morality, which they despise because they don't understand it."[4] French officials frequently referred to such developments as a sign that the civilizing mission was succeeding, but they would soon find out that this generation would represent a more formidable challenge than its parents'.

Senior French administrators had inadvertently contributed to the growth of Vietnamese frustration at the consequences of colonial rule. In 1919, Nguyen Ai Quoc's future adversary Albert Sarraut, then serving as governor-general of Indochina, had quickened Vietnamese hearts with his promise of a new era of reform. "I will treat you like an older to a younger brother," he had told his charges, "and slowly give you the dignity of a man."[5] Such words inspired hope in Vietnam and even earned the temporary admiration of Nguyen Ai Quoc in Paris, who still harbored a lingering admiration for the culture that had produced the revolutionary slogan of "liberty, equality, and fraternity."

After Sarraut left Hanoi for Paris to become minister of colonies, however, his promises of reform remained unfulfilled. The new educational system, for example, received little funding from the colonial administration and consequently had only a limited impact on the local population. Village schools were particularly underfunded, and the majority of young Vietnamese received less than four years of education. In the mid-1920s, only about 5,000 students throughout the entire country had received the equivalent of a high school education. Such statistics underlined the hypocrisy of the French claim that they were carrying out a civilizing mission in Indochina; whereas under the traditional system about a quarter of the population was able to decipher texts written in Chinese characters, in the decade following World War I the literacy rate in either *quoc ngu* or the traditional characters has been estimated at only about 5 percent of the population.

In the meantime, although many Vietnamese had contributed to the French cause during World War I, the colonial authorities still refused to grant their subjects the right to take an active role in the political process in their own country. The approximately 10,000 colonial officials in Indochina were still paid substantially more than their Vietnamese counterparts for equal work. Many among the 40,000 Europeans who lived and worked in Indochina—some of whom had arrived with little more than the shirts on their backs—all too often behaved with arrogance and condescension toward the local population. Foreigners, including over 200,000 overseas Chinese who had settled predominantly in the cities and market towns, continued to dominate the urban economy. In disgust, one French writer declared Sarraut's reformist policies—which were sometimes described as the "politics of collaboration"—a fraud, while French President Raymond Poincaré admitted that they had been implemented solely for form's sake.[6]

In the meantime, the mass of the population was suffering from increased taxes and the government monopolies on the manufacture and sale of opium, salt, and alcohol, which had increased the retail prices of all three products. In Cochin China, absentee landlords who had purchased virgin lands in the Mekong delta charged exorbitant rates of interest to their new tenants, sometimes over 50 percent of the annual crop, while maintaining their own residences in Saigon. Throughout the entire country, there were over half a million landless peasants, as compared with about fifty thousand landlords. In a book titled *Forceries humaines* that he wrote at mid-decade, the author Georges Garros remarked that under similar provocations the French people would have revolted. Truly, as Nguyen Ai Quoc had remarked in frustration to the journalist Ossip Mandelstam during his 1923 interview in Moscow, Vietnam was "a nation plunged into darkness."

Frustration with the situation brought about a new wave of political activism in the mid-1920s. Leading the charge was a generation of young middle-class intellectuals who had been educated under the French school system. Like their counterparts in the rest of the colonial world, many had a complex relationship with Western culture, admiring much about it but resenting it as well. Many of them read French popular novels and magazines, including periodicals written in *quoc ngu* such as *Phu nu Tan Van* (Women's News) that catered to the Westernized tastes and attitudes of educated youth. But they also resented the condescension with which the French treated their colonial subjects and questioned why the vaunted French concepts of liberty, equality, and fraternity, which they had learned in school, could not be applied in Indochina as well.

The first signs of ferment appeared in Saigon, which, of all the cities of Vietnam, had been the most directly affected by the French colonial presence. A high percentage of the European population in Indochina had settled there because Cochin China was a colony, and thus under direct French administration, and because of the opportunity for material profit offered by the rubber, tea, and coffee plantations that had been established in nearby regions. At the same time, there were more factory workers there than in any other part of the country. In Saigon the gap between rich and poor, native and foreign, was most starkly delineated. Here even the most affluent Vietnamese had reason to resent the grip that foreigners possessed over the economy. Overseas Chinese merchants controlled the rice mills and the banks and pawnshops, while Europeans owned most of the larger factories and dominated the import-export trade. The wealthy agronomist Bui Quang Chieu, whom Nguyen Ai Quoc had briefly met during his first voyage to Europe, took the lead in focusing this resentment. An absentee landlord with his residence in Saigon, Chieu was also involved in various other business transactions and founded a journal titled *La Tribune Indigène* to represent the interests of the local commercial elite. A few years later, he joined with acquaintances in founding the Constitutionalist Party, the first formal political party in French Indochina. While Bui Quang Chieu and his colleagues hoped to press the French to grant a greater role for the Vietnamese people in the political process, an additional goal was to reduce the hold of Chinese merchants over the economy of Cochin China.[7]

As in many other societies in Southeast Asia, Chinese merchants had long been a dominant force in the urban economies of Vietnam, Laos, and Cambodia. The descendants of settlers who had immigrated in past centuries to the area from coastal regions in south China, they were often encouraged to take part in manufacturing and commercial activities by local monarchs who discouraged such practices among the local populace. Usually they were settled in urban ghettos and continued to maintain key components of Chinese culture, including Confucian ethics and the Chinese language. When Bui Quang Chieu and his colleagues focused their attention on reducing the influence of the overseas Chinese rather than on that of the colonial authorities, they were adopting an attitude that was reflected in several other colonies in the region.

A potentially more dangerous adversary than Chieu, from the point of view of the French, was the Paris-trained intellectual Nguyen An Ninh. The son of a Confucian scholar from Cochin China who had connections with the Hanoi Free School and later served in Phan Boi Chau's movement, Ninh studied law in France, where he claimed to have met Nguyen Ai Quoc and developed an intense interest in politics. On returning to Saigon in the early 1920s, he founded a journal called *La Cloche Fêlée* (The Cracked Bell) with the aim of arousing the patriotic spirit of the Vietnamese people and spurring the French to grant political reforms. Like Phan Chu Trinh, Nguyen An Ninh was a fervent admirer of Western culture and convinced that it could serve as a corrective to the traditional Confucian system, which he believed had stifled the creativity of his compatriots and contributed to their conquest by the French.

During the early and mid-1920s, the charismatic young journalist was wildly popular among the educated youth of Cochin China; his occasional speeches were eagerly awaited. In an October 1923 address at the Salle d'Enseignement in Saigon, he called on his listeners to launch a new culture unencumbered by the imported ideas of Confucius, Mencius, and Lao-tzu. Like Mahatma Gandhi in India, Ninh argued that the solution to Vietnamese problems was essentially spiritual, and that the answer could only come from within the people.

The impact of Nguyen An Ninh's activities on the youth of Cochin China was increasingly worrisome to the French authorities; eventually he was summoned to talk with Lieutenant Governor Maurice Cognacq, who warned him that his efforts were closely monitored by the authorities, and that if he persisted in his activities they would use the necessary means to compel him to desist. The Vietnamese people were too simpleminded, Cognacq suggested, to understand Ninh's message. If Ninh wanted to make intellectuals, he added sarcastically, go to Moscow. Cognacq's warning, however, was ignored; Nguyen An Ninh resumed his campaign.[8]

On the day that Nguyen Ai Quoc arrived in Canton by ship from Vladivostok in mid-November 1924, the city was in turmoil, with thousands jamming the streets near the waterfront to demonstrate their support for Sun Yat-sen's government and see the president off on a trip to Beijing. Since February 1923, Sun had put into effect the "bloc within" strategy which had been negotiated with the Comintern agent Maring a few months previously. Sun moved the Kuomintang to the left by adding a number of members of the CCP to positions of responsibility. After the arrival of Comintern agent Mikhail Borodin from Moscow in October, the party was reorganized along Leninist lines and a new military academy was established on Whampoa (Huangpu) Island to provide a trained officer corps. Chiang Kai-shek, one of Sun Yat-sen's most trusted young lieutenants, was named commandant of the school, which was located a few miles downriver from the city; Zhou Enlai became the school's political commissar.

Sun Yat-sen's move to the left, however, had not come without cost; relations between his government and representatives of European interests in Canton began to deteriorate. To many Western merchants and diplomats in the city, Sun's decision to establish a formal relationship with Soviet Russia and the CCP provided conclusive evidence that he and his party were fundamentally anti-Western and had become the cat's-paw of Moscow.

During the next few months, the situation became increasingly tense. In the summer of 1924, strikes against British firms in Canton broke out in response to an incident provoked by the British authorities, who had imposed police controls to suppress street demonstrations on Shamian Island, a European concession area along the banks of West River. Sun's government declared its support for the strikers. That fall, the Canton Merchants' Association, dominated by European commercial interests, established a militia to provide the Western community with protection against Sun's military forces, and clashes broke out between militia units and government troops.

In the meantime, the situation outside Canton suddenly changed, as Wu Peifu, a warlord who had for many years controlled parts of north China, was overthrown by the "Christian general" Feng Yuxiang. Although Feng was a warlord as well, he was viewed in Canton as somewhat more sympathetic to the Chinese revolutionary cause than Wu Peifu; when Feng invited Sun Yat-sen to Beijing to negotiate a peace settlement, Sun agreed.

Although Nguyen Ai Quoc had not been sent to China in an official capacity, he was not without contacts. He immediately got in touch with Mikhail Borodin, who invited the new arrival to settle in his own lodgings at the Baogong Guan, a spacious Western-style villa surrounded by a garden across from Kuomintang headquarters in the heart of the city. On the ground floor of the building were offices for the twenty Comintern representatives sent from Moscow. On the second floor was Borodin's private apartment, where Quoc established his own lodgings. To protect himself against French surveillance or arrest by the local authorities as an illegal alien, Quoc posed as a Chinese named Ly Thuy. Only Borodin and his wife were aware of his true identity.

Borodin had become acquainted with the young Vietnamese revolutionary at the Lux Hotel when both were living in Moscow the previous year. Both spoke English (Borodin had spent some time as a labor organizer in Chicago before World War I), and they shared a common interest in their desire to promote the growth of the revolutionary movement in Asia. As head of the Comintern mission to Sun Yat-sen's government in Canton, Borodin could be very useful to his younger colleague.[9]

After getting settled in his new lodgings, Nguyen Ai Quoc was assigned to work at the office of the Soviet news agency ROSTA, which was located on the ground floor at Comintern headquarters at the Baogong Guan. Quoc penned articles for the agency, which were sent back to Moscow and published under the pseudonym Nilovskii; he also served informally as an interpreter and the local representative of the Peasant International. His primary objective, however, was to create the nucleus for a new Vietnamese revolutionary party to be built on the Leninist model. He could then embark on the more long-term goal of putting some order into the Vietnamese resistance movement and transforming it into a force responsive to his wishes.

The revolutionary strategy that had been drawn up by the Comintern at the Second Congress in Moscow provided him with general guidelines for setting the process in motion. One of the provisions was that some measure of cooperation should be realized with existing non-Communist nationalist groups operating in the vicinity, an objective that he had set forth in his reports to Comintern leaders in Moscow. But Nguyen Ai Quoc was already aware that these guidelines were not fully adequate to meet his own needs. At a meeting held to discuss the colonial question at the Fifth Comintern Congress in the summer of 1924, he had asked Dmitri Manuilsky, the Comintern's reigning colonial expert, what Asian Communist operatives should do where no mass nationalist party existed. It is doubtful that Manuilsky, who had little experience in Asian affairs, had ever thought about the question. Still, he did attempt an impromptu elaboration of Leninist "united front" strategy, suggesting that where no mass nationalist movement was already in existence, the local Communist party should take the initiative to form one under its own leadership.[10]

It would not be easy to carry out Manuilsky's suggestion in Indochina. As Nguyen Ai Quoc had reported to Comintern colleagues while he was still living in Moscow, the Vietnamese working class, presumably the leading force in a future Marxist-Leninist party, was still at an embryonic stage, numbering only about 2 percent of the population, including coal miners, who were scattered widely throughout the three territories of Tonkin, Annam, and Cochin China. In political awareness, Vietnamese workers were well behind their counterparts in neighboring China and manifestly lacked the capacity to take the lead in waging a popular uprising against French colonial rule.

Nguyen Ai Quoc had noted in Moscow that it was the patriotic intellectuals who had led the initial Vietnamese resistance to the colonial system. Unfortunately, few had any awareness of Marxist ideology. In France, the presence of socially radical views among the intelligentsia dated back at least to the revolution of 1789; in Russia, they had sprouted during the middle of the nineteenth century with the Narodniks; even in China, radical ideologies from the West like anarchism and communism had become familiar to leading members of the progressive movement by the turn of the twentieth century. But in Vietnam, shielded as it was from dangerous foreign ideas by rigid French censorship, such revolutionary ideas began to penetrate only in the years following the First World War. Even then, when Vietnamese intellectuals began to hear about the Bolshevik revolution, it was mainly in negative terms, through news reports that were heavily distorted by French censorship. Books about Karl Marx or Soviet Russia were prohibited in Indochina, while articles in local newspapers and periodicals that mentioned such subjects were routinely confiscated by French officials. Only those fortunate enough to obtain furtively circulated copies of Karl Marx's works or Nguyen Ai Quoc's journal *Le Paria* were able to read about the other side of the issue.

The lack of detailed knowledge about Marxism prevented the average Vietnamese from learning about the Bolshevik revolution. And the social composition and the world perspective of the Vietnamese elite made it difficult for Marxist ideas to win serious acceptance once these ideas became more familiar. For most Vietnamese intellectuals, urban life was a relatively new experience. Indoctrinated in Confucian ideology, which harbored a built-in bias against such urban pursuits as commerce and industry, they were not likely to see the relevance of Marxist doctrine to the problems of predominantly rural Vietnam. Still, Marxism found a receptive attitude among those who were looking for a persuasive alternative to the Confucian worldview; it did not hurt that Marxists harbored a profound antipathy to Western imperialism. As one Vietnamese nationalist said, "We will not go to communism, but to the Communists, for here, as in other countries, since the Communists promise to bring self-determination to all peoples, they will be awaited as saviors." But as a rule, their attitude was fairly naïve. Another Vietnamese patriot was quoted as saying: "If the West hates them, the Russians and Communists must be good."[11]

Nguyen Ai Quoc was aware of the problem. In 1922, he had commented in an article written in Paris that only a few intellectuals in colonies such as Vietnam understood the meaning of communism, and most of those who did were members of the native bourgeoisie and preferred to "bear the mark of the collar and to have their piece of bone." To most people in the colonies, he noted, Bolshevism "means either the destruction of everything or emancipation from the foreign yoke. The first sense given to the word drives the ignorant and timorous masses away from us; the second leads them to nationalism. Both senses are equally dangerous."[12]

The implication was that Vietnam was not yet ready for the formation of a Communist Party. The masses "are thoroughly rebellious, but completely ignorant. They want to free themselves, but do not know how to go about doing so." The educated elite was restive but not ready for Karl Marx. Time was needed so that the Vietnamese people could be brought gradually to realize that social revolution was the answer to their problems. In the meantime, a political party should be formed that could represent, in embryonic form, the ideals of Marx and Lenin but that could appeal to the public on the basis of the one major issue that could elicit a favorable response: national independence.

The most famous Vietnamese dissident then living in China was Phan Boi Chau. After his release from jail in 1917 and his brief flirtation with the idea of an accommodation with the French, Chau had returned to the anti-French views that he had held prior to his arrest. Now aging but still physically robust, with a brown beard and glasses, the fifty-five-year-old warrior settled in Hangzhou, a scenic resort southwest of Shanghai, at the home of Ho Hoc Lam, a supporter who later played a key role in the movement during World War II. Although Phan Boi Chau no longer possessed the nucleus of a patriotic anticolonial organization inside Indochina, his name still exerted a charismatic appeal; during the early 1920s a number of ambitious young Vietnamese patriots fled to south China to join the ranks of his followers. Most prominent among them were Le Hong Phong, Le Van Phan (better known within the revolutionary movement as Le Hong Son), Le Quang Dat, and Truong Van Lenh—all of them eventually to become founding members of Nguyen Ai Quoc's first revolutionary organization.[13]

Once in south China, these young firebrands quickly became impatient with the inefficiency of Phan Boi Chau's organization; in March 1924, eight months prior to the arrival of Nguyen Ai Quoc in Canton, they decided to branch out on their own, forming a new party called the Tam Tam Xa (the Association of Like Minds, but literally the Society of Beating Hearts). As in the case of most patriotic organizations established in Vietnam early in the twentieth century, the leaders of the new party were members of the traditional scholar-gentry elite. Radicalized by the student demonstrations that erupted in the mid-1920s, they had decided to drop out of school to take part in anticolonial activities. Several of them had worked as manual laborers before deciding to emigrate abroad. Virtually all of them were natives of Nguyen Ai Quoc's home province of Nghe An.

Activist in temperament and hasty in inclination, the members of the new organization scorned ideology as irrelevant to the immediate need for revolution. Their philosophy was a Vietnamese equivalent to that of Auguste Blanqui's insurrectionist movement in nineteenth-century Europe, which had sought—usually without success—to promote uprisings in France, Italy, and Spain. Their ultimate goal was to use propaganda and acts of terrorism to arouse a popular upheaval to overthrow French colonial rule in Indochina.[14]

One of the first projects envisaged by the new party was the assassination of the French governor-general of Indochina, Martial Merlin, on the occasion of his visit to Canton after an official tour of several cities in East Asia in mid-June of 1924. With advice and financial assistance from Lam Duc Thu, a thirty-six-year-old native of Tonkin who had come to Canton to meet Phan Boi Chau a few years earlier, the group launched plans to kill Merlin by exploding a bomb during ceremonies in the European concession area of Shamian Island. Although married to a rich wife and a good deal older than his colleagues, the heavyset Thu (real name Nguyen Cong Vien) was seen as a useful member of the organization because of his apparent ability to raise funds and his contacts with the French. Because he came from a family that had resisted the French conquest, his loyalty to the cause of anticolonialism was not questioned. The headquarters of the organization was located in medical shop run by Thu and his wife in a small alley off De Zheng Road and not far from Comintern headquarters.

Initially it had been decided that the darkly handsome young revolutionary Le Hong Son would be selected to carry out the operation, since he had already assassinated a double agent within the party; because of his intensity he was reportedly feared even by his own colleagues as the organization's "hit man." But Le Hong Son was already well-known to the authorities, so the job was eventually assigned to Pham Hong Thai, a young Vietnamese who had recently arrived from Indochina to join the terrorist organization. Son of an official from Nghe An province who had joined Phan Dinh Phung's Can Vuong movement, Thai studied at a Franco-Vietnamese school in Hanoi as a youth and soon became enamored of revolutionary ideals. After leaving school, he sought employment as a garage mechanic and then worked in a coal mine. In early 1924 he fled to China with his friends Ho Tung Mau and Le Hong Phong; there they all became charter members of the Tam Tam Xa.

Apparently avid for martyrdom, Pham Hong Thai agreed to take responsibility for delivering the bomb to its intended target. On the evening of June 19, French officials in the concession had arranged a banquet at the Hotel Victoria on Shamian Island to welcome Governor-

General Merlin and introduce him to prestigious members of the local business community. The banquet was to take place in a large dining hall that was located adjacent to the street. At about 8:30 P.M., just as the soup was about to be served, Thai threw the bomb through a window into the banquet hall. The scene was described by a local newspaper:

> The explosion was terrible and was heard throughout Shamian Island; its force was so strong that all the knives and forks on the banquet table were propelled on the assistants, causing a number of horrible wounds. . . . A witness who was near the hotel at the moment of the attempt and who ran to bring assistance described the scene to us in these simple words: terrifying, simply terrifying. The guests lay on their chairs or simply on the ground with horrible wounds.

Five guests were killed by the blast (three died on the spot, and the others later from injuries) and dozens were wounded. Yet Governor-General Martial Merlin was miraculously spared. In attempting to flee to the mainland, Pham Hong Thai jumped from a bridge into the Pearl River and drowned. Merlin left for Hanoi on a French cruiser the following day to avoid the possibility of a new attack during funeral ceremonies for the young assassin.[15]

Merlin may have escaped death because of his uncanny resemblance to one of the other guests, who was killed by the bomb. But suspicions were aroused among the plotters that a traitor within their ranks had passed information about the assassination attempt to the French. Their suspicions were fixed on Lam Duc Thu, whose extravagant habits and contacts with French officials made him suspect. Le Quang Dat, one of the members of the Tam Tam Xa, mentioned his fears to Le Hong Son, but Son replied that Lam Duc Thu had used his contacts with the French to obtain funds for the organization's clandestine activities. For the moment, Thu's relations with the organization continued.[16]

The bombing of the Hotel Victoria was the first attempt by Asian revolutionaries to assassinate a senior European colonial official, and it sent shock waves throughout the French community in Indochina. In Hanoi, the colonial press blamed the attack on Soviet agents. But the incident made Pham Hong Thai a martyr to anti-imperialism. Sun Yat-sen's government erected a tomb for the young Vietnamese patriot at a cemetery in Canton devoted to martyrs of the Chinese revolution; Phan Boi Chau issued a statement implying that Thai was a member of his own organization and declared that the assassination attempt was in retaliation for the brutal acts carried out by the French in Indochina. Was it worse, Chau asked rhetorically, to kill or to oppress? Later he wrote a somewhat fanciful account of Thai's life.[17]

Phan Boi Chau also used the publicity aroused by the Shamian incident to revive his own political organization in south China, which had become virtually moribund during his years in prison. In July 1924 he traveled to Canton to take part in the ceremony to erect a tomb for Pham Hong Thai. While there, he talked with some of his followers about replacing his Restoration Society with a new political organization to be known as the Vietnamese Nationalist Party (Viet Nam Quoc Dan Dang, or VNQDD), in imitation of Sun Yat-sen's Kuomintang. Chau returned to Hangzhou in September.

Nguyen Ai Quoc arrived in Canton five months after the assassination attempt on Shamian Island. A few days later, in the pose of a Chinese reporter named Wang Shan-yi, he contacted the members of the Tam Tam Xa. Their radical activism undoubtedly struck a sympathetic chord with the young revolutionary. The fact that they lacked an ideological focus was all the more convenient, of course, since it left ample room for Marx and Lenin. And it did not hurt that many of the leading members of the group were from his home province. Quoc was apparently impressed with Le Hong Son and Ho Tung Mau, but especially with Le Hong Phong, the stocky and broad-shouldered son of an educated family from Nghe An province whom Phan Boi Chau had personally recruited to study abroad.

It apparently did not take Quoc long to convert the others to his views. In a letter to the Comintern headquarters in Moscow dated December 18, 1924, he reported that he was already in touch with some Vietnamese "national revolutionaries" and had begun to cooperate with them. By February of the following year, he had formed a secret group composed of nine members and labeled the Indochinese Nationalist Party (Quoc Dan Dang Dong Duong). Some had already been sent back to Indochina to find additional recruits, while others had joined Sun Yat-sen's army or applied for membership in the CCP. Five of them he described as candidate members of a future Communist Party. He emphasized, though, that he badly needed additional funds and propaganda materials to carry out additional activities.[18]

It was probably through the members of the Tam Tam Xa that Nguyen Ai Quoc was able to get in touch with Phan Boi Chau. Although Quoc did not approve of the old rebel's methods, he probably saw him as a useful tool in building up his own organization. For his part, Chau had undoubtedly heard of the remarkable exploits of the mysterious

Nguyen Ai Quoc while he was living in Hangzhou, although he was presumably not immediately aware of Quoc's real identity as the son of his old friend Nguyen Sinh Sac. Moreover, Chau had recently become interested in socialism and the ideas of Karl Marx, although by all accounts his understanding of Marxist ideology was quite rudimentary.[19]

Nguyen Ai Quoc arrived in Canton two months after Phan Boi Chau's departure for Hangzhou in September, but undoubtedly learned of his address from members of the Tam Tam Xa. According to French intelligence sources, Nguyen Ai Quoc traveled to Shanghai in January 1925 in an effort to meet Chau. The Sûreté, however, reported that no contact between the two took place at that time.

By then, Chau had become aware of the real identity of Ly Thuy, for sometime in February or March he wrote Quoc a letter from Hangzhou, praising the latter's work and reminding him of their earlier meeting in Kim Lien village two decades previously. Chau also expressed a desire to collaborate with his younger compatriot and offered to come to Canton to meet with him. In his response, Quoc attempted to explain the need for a reorganization of Chau's party, and presented his own strategy and the Leninist doctrine that lay behind it. Chau agreed to cooperate and provided the younger man with a list of the members of his organization.[20]

But Nguyen Ai Quoc quickly recognized that Phan Boi Chau and many of his older colleagues could not serve as the basis for the new revolutionary movement that he envisioned. He soon concentrated all his efforts on transforming the Tam Tam Xa into a new Marxist-Leninist revolutionary organization. His first step was to set up a nucleus of dedicated followers into a new Communist Group (Cong san Doan), which operated under cover of the larger organization he had just created. Among the charter members were five key figures from the Indochinese Nationalist Party including Le Hong Son, Le Hong Phong, and Ho Tung Mau. Together they drew up a list of individuals from five different provinces inside Indochina who could serve as the basis for a revolutionary organization inside the country. Envoys were to be sent from Canton to escort them to China for training in organizational methods; afterward, the recruits would return to their home provinces. Other promising members of the movement would be sent to Moscow for indoctrination in revolutionary theory and practice at the Stalin School. Quoc also initiated steps to establish a revolutionary base in Siam, as well as in several cities elsewhere in south China, which would serve as a possible temporary headquarters in case of a disruption of operations in Canton. Finally, he planned to recruit members from among the Vietnamese sailors serving on vessels sailing up and down the coast of the South China Sea to provide a reliable means of communication between the headquarters and various units inside Indochina.[21]

The sudden appearance of this energetic young stranger at Comintern headquarters did not fail to come to the attention of French authorities in Canton, and in Indochina as well. By mid-February of 1925, reports that the new arrival who called himself Ly Thuy was in contact with radical elements among the Vietnamese exile community in south China led to nervous appeals from French authorities in Hanoi and Canton to the Ministry of Colonies to verify the current location of Nguyen Ai Quoc. At first, Paris reported that Quoc was still in Moscow, but within weeks French authorities began to suspect that the mysterious Ly Thuy was indeed Nguyen Ai Quoc in a new incarnation. In Canton, a newly arrived French police official with the code name "Noel" urged his agents to confirm the stranger's identity.

The most valuable of Noel's agents was Nguyen Ai Quoc's colleague Lam Duc Thu, who, despite his patriotic credentials, had agreed to serve as an informant for the French. Under the code name "Pinot," Thu would provide the French with useful information on the activities of the Viet-namese revolutionary movement for the remainder of the decade. At first, Thu was frustrated in his effort to obtain clues to the real identity of the new arrival. Ly Thuy, he reported, was very cautious and refused to have his photograph taken. But in March he was able to obtain a pho-tograph of Ly Thuy as part of a large group of people in front of Kuom-intang headquarters. Sûreté agents confirmed from it that Ly Thuy was indeed Nguyen Ai Quoc.[22]

By late spring, Nguyen Ai Quoc's attempt to create a new revolu-tionary organization based on Marxist-Leninist principles and under the guidance of the Comintern was well under way. According to the rec-ollection of one of the primary participants, a formal decision to create a new revolutionary party was reached sometime in early June. A few days later, the first meeting of the organization was held at Lam Duc Thu's house in downtown Canton. Included as founding members were the core members of Quoc's Communist Group. Although the formal name of the new organization was still under discussion, it would soon come to be known as the Vietnamese Revolutionary Youth League (Hoi Viet Nam Cach Mang Thanh Nien).

Nguyen Ai Quoc also began publication of a journal—*Thanh Nien* (Youth)—to publicize the league's ideas; a training institute was estab-lished in downtown Canton to provide a school for the indoctrination of new recruits. Quoc also imitated the tactic that he had used with some success in Paris by founding a broader alliance of radical activists from several colonial and semicolonial countries of Asia. Working with the Indian Comintern agent M. N. Roy and the Kuomintang leftist leader Liao Zhongkai, in late June he collaborated in the formation of the Society of Oppressed Peoples of Asia (Hoi Lien hiep cac Dan toc bi Ap buc). Liao Zhongkai chaired the organization, and Nguyen Ai Quoc served as general secretary and treasurer. Composed of members from Korea, India, China, and the Dutch East Indies (many of whom had been attracted to Canton, known popularly as "Moscow East" because of Sun Yat-sen's relationship with the Comintern), as well as from Indochina, the society held its first meeting in Canton in mid-July. A proclamation issued on the occasion consisted of a blistering denunciation of the evils of imperialism and an appeal to the oppressed masses to support world revolution.[23]

The league was Nguyen Ai Quoc's main enterprise during his brief stay in Canton. It was skillfully crafted to address his assessment of the prevailing situation in Indochina. The immediate need was to attract patriotic intellectuals and other national revolutionary elements to the cause in order to provide key personnel for the creation of a formal Communist Party. For practical reasons, the primary basis for that appeal would be the struggle for national independence. Yet it was also necessary to win the support of oppressed workers and peasants, for whom national independence had little relevance compared to the desperate struggle to survive in their daily lives. The league would also need to lay the foundations for the second stage of socialist revolution. Items in the *Thanh Nien*—many of them written by Nguyen Ai Quoc himself—carefully laid the groundwork for a new vision that would transcend the issue of national independence and incorporate a broader objective of world revolution.

The program of the Revolutionary Youth League was thus focused on the twin pillars of nationalism and social revolution. In linking these two issues, Nguyen Ai Quoc was adhering to the Leninist model that had been approved by the Second Comintern Congress in 1920. But where Lenin had seen the reference to nationalist sentiment primarily as a tactical maneuver to win the support of nationalist elements against the common adversary of world imperialism, the program of the league and many of the articles in its journal appeared to assign an equal if not greater importance to the issue of nationalism than to that of the future world revolution.

The strong emphasis on nationalism in the league's program, a characteristic that would henceforth become an integral part of Nguyen Ai Quoc's image as a patriot and a revolutionary, is one among several factors that over the years have led some observers to question his dedication to Marxist ideology and the struggle to build a Communist utopia. Indeed, during the late 1920s doubts about his dedication to Marxist doctrine even surfaced in Moscow and among some members of his own organization; as we shall see, a few years later such criticisms would begin to appear in print.

There are valid reasons for the argument that Nguyen Ai Quoc was above all a patriot. In 1960 he himself conceded in the short article "My Path to Leninism" that it was the desire for Vietnamese independence that had drawn him to Marxism in the first place. And where his mentor Lenin appeared to view relations between Communists and bourgeois nationalists as a tactical maneuver to strengthen Communist parties in societies with a small working class, Nguyen Ai Quoc often appeared to view the issue of national independence almost as an end in itself, with the Communist utopia a mere afterthought that could be postponed to the indefinite future. The socialist revolution in Vietnam, he often remarked, would take place in due time.

Yet there is also persuasive evidence that the young Nguyen Ai Quoc viewed Marxism-Leninism as more than just a tool to drive out the French. Although he rarely referred to Marxist doctrine in his writings, during his years in Paris and his ensuing period of training in Moscow an increasing fervency appeared in his comments about the future world revolution, which, in his mind, would bring to a definitive end the exploitative system of world capitalism. Quoc believed that the struggle against the forces of imperialism throughout Asia would culminate in a global revolution. In an interview with a Soviet journalist just before his death, Ho Chi Minh conceded that his youthful revolutionary zeal might have been excessive, remarking ruefully that on one occasion while he was living in the USSR, he had scolded a young woman for wearing a silk dress and high-heeled shoes. As he recalled, she responded spiritedly that she had made everything with her own hands. "Is it really so bad," she asked, "that young people now have the chance to eat and dress well?"[24] After decades, her comment still remained in his memory.

If it is fair to say that he was both a nationalist and a Marxist at this time, how did he reconcile patriotism with the demands of Marxist internationalism? The answer can be found in Lenin. In defining the concept of a two-stage revolution in his "Theses on the National and Colonial Questions," Lenin had set forth the concept of a "federation" to serve as a period of transition between national independence and the final stage of communism, when there would be "complete unity of the working people of different nations." Lenin viewed federations created in the early 1920s between revolutionary Russia and Finland, Hungary, and Latvia, and between Azerbaijan and Armenia, as possible models for other countries to follow. Eventually the Comintern posited the creation of a network combining independent states and "federated unions" as an example of how such alliances might be established during a transitional period to global communism in the distant future. Nguyen Ai Quoc undoubtedly became aware of such theories while he was living in the Soviet Union in 1923–1924, and he referred to the concept in a letter to the Comintern Executive Committee in May 1924, when he attempted to justify a proposal for expanding the recruitment of Asian revolutionaries to the Stalin School as laying "the basis on which a Communist Federation of the East will be founded."[25]

A second reference by Nguyen Ai Quoc to the issue of a transitional federation appeared in a document that has recently been discovered in the archives in Moscow. While the author of the document is identified only as "Nguyen," it is almost certain that it was written by Quoc sometime in 1924. In the report, "Nguyen" discussed the idea of a future Vietnamese Communist Party and declared that, given the importance of the national issue there, it was crucial to "raise the banner of indigenous nationalism in the name of the Comintern." To a bourgeois observer, he noted, this would appear to be "an audacious paradox," but it was actually "marvelously realistic." For the moment, he argued, it was impossible to come to the assistance of the Vietnamese people without deferring to the fundamental fact of their unique social experience. By the time their struggle for national independence had triumphed, he predicted, "the bulk of the world will long since have been sovietized, and thus inevitably this nationalism will be transformed into internationalism."[26]

After his arrival in Canton, Nguyen Ai Quoc referred to this concept once again in a draft program for the future Revolutionary Youth League, which was written in February 1925. The draft contained a pledge to be taken by all candidates for the new organization: first, to take part in the struggle to overthrow imperialism and reestablish national independence; then, to turn attention to the struggle to erase class distinctions and participate in the world revolution, "the final goal for which we are fighting." The pledge appeared in the program of the league as finally promulgated in June and was mentioned in an early article published in *Thanh Nien* in July: "After the political and social revolution, there will still remain oppressed peoples. There will still be differences between nations. It is then necessary to have a world revolution. After that the peoples of the four corners of the earth will befriend one another. It will be the age of world fraternity."[27]

Why did Nguyen Ai Quoc believe in the need for a world revolution? Why would a nonviolent approach to national independence not suffice? His thoughts on these issues do not often appear in print, but a letter that he wrote from Canton to Nguyen Thuong Huyen, a young disciple of Phan Boi Chau living with the old patriot in Hangzhou, provides some interesting insight into his views. Huyen was the grandnephew of Nguyen Thuong Hien, a patriotic scholar who was once head of the Hanoi Free School. In the spring of 1925, Huyen sent Quoc a copy of an article on revolution that he had recently written for possible publication and asked for his comments. In the essay Huyen found the origins of the revolutionary concept in the Chinese classic *The Book of Changes*, where it was implied that revolution was the equivalent of dynastic change. He thereupon concluded that the struggle against the colonial regime had failed because of French brutality, and that independence could best be achieved by means of nonviolent tactics similar to the boycott movement adopted by Mahatma Gandhi in British India.

In his reply, Nguyen Ai Quoc expressed his skepticism about the Chinese origins of the concept (Quoc saw the sources of revolution in Western culture) and offered his own definition, which contrasted revolution with reform. Reform, Quoc pointed out, involves changes brought about in the institutions of a particular country. Whether or not reform is accompanied by violence, some of the original order always remains. Revolution, on the other hand, entirely supplants one system with another. Dynastic change is thus not equivalent to revolution, since the victors retain the monarchical system. As for Gandhi, Quoc added, the Indian spiritual leader was clearly a reformer rather than a revolutionary, since he demanded that the British reform Indian institutions but did not arouse the Hindus to revolt as a means of recovering their independence, nor did he demand that the British carry out comprehensive changes in the Indian government. Only after the British rejected his demands, Quoc noted, did Gandhi call for a boycott.

As for Huyen's remark that revolution had failed in Vietnam because of French brutality, Quoc replied with some exasperation:

What do you expect? Do you expect them to give us the liberty to do anything, to use all means to drive them out? Do you expect them to take no action to prevent us from attacking their own interests? Instead of blaming others, I think it is more reasonable to blame ourselves. We must ask ourselves, "For what reasons have the French been able to oppress us? Why are our people so stupid? Why hasn't our revolution succeeded? What must we do now?" You compare us with success stories in Egypt and India, but they are like autos with wheels and a chauffeur, while we are just a chassis. India and Egypt have political parties with members, study groups, peasant associations, and so forth. And they all know how to love their country. So Gandhi can create a boycott. Can we do the same? Where are our parties? We still have no party, no propaganda, no organization, and you want us to boycott the French?

Nguyen Ai Quoc concluded with an aphorism from La Fontaine about the rats that dared not attach a bell to the cat to provide prior warning of an attack. How about the sons of the dragon (meaning the Vietnamese people), he asked, "are we like mice? How humiliating."[28]

In Hangzhou, Phan Boi Chau had observed the emergence of the Revolutionary Youth League with some interest. Nguyen Ai Quoc had promised to keep the older patriot abreast of his activities, and they agreed that Chau would arrange a trip to Canton sometime during the summer of 1925. In a letter that he had written to Quoc early in the year, Chau had praised the younger man's great wisdom and considerable experience and declared that he was gratified to know that someone would continue his work now that he was old and out of fashion. Yet Chau also made it clear that he wanted to be involved with the movement; in a separate letter to Ho Tung Mau, one of Nguyen Ai Quoc's colleagues, he obliquely criticized Quoc in the form of a warning to his younger compatriots not to move too quickly.

Even before Phan Boi Chau could complete his plans to come to Canton, he was complaining that Nguyen Ai Quoc was ignoring him. In mid-May Chau left Hangzhou on a train to Shanghai, but the French authorities in China had been apprised of his plans through an informer within his own entourage. On arrival at the Shanghai railway station, which was in the International Concession of the city, Chau was arrested by French security agents disguised as taxi drivers and returned to Hanoi for trial on the charge of treason.[29]

The episode has provoked one of the most long-lasting and contentious debates in the tangled history of Vietnamese nationalism. From the beginning, many members of the Revolutionary Youth League suspected that the man who had betrayed Phan Boi Chau to the French was his personal secretary, Nguyen Thuong Huyen. Chau himself made a similar claim in his memoirs. But some non-Communist nationalist sources have argued that the culprit was Nguyen Ai Quoc's close associate Lam Duc Thu, or even that Nguyen Ai Quoc himself had connived with Thu in deliberately betraying Chau in order to obtain the reward money and create a martyr for the nationalist cause. This charge has been repeated by a number of Western writers, although no concrete evidence is available to confirm it. Communist sources have consistently denied the allegation, repeating that the plot to betray Phan Boi Chau had been initiated by Nguyen Thuong Huyen, a man who eventually left the revolutionary movement to work with the French.[30]

The argument has raged largely along ideological lines. Evidence in French archives is not conclusive, but tends to exonerate Nguyen Ai Quoc of any responsibility for the affair. There is some plausibility to the charge that Lam Duc Thu was the informer, since he was already playing that role as a member of the league and reportedly assumed responsibility for the act in later years. But that assumption is probably without merit; a Sûreté report written at the time confirms that there was a French informer—presumably, but not certainly, Nguyen Thuong Huyen—living in Ho Hac Lam's household in Hangzhou. He would have had better information on Chau's movements and could have provided such information to the French. Thu was well-known as a braggart and may have taken credit for the arrest to inflate his own importance. In all likelihood, it was Huyen who betrayed Chau.[31]

In any event, it seems unlikely that Nguyen Ai Quoc would have seen an advantage to having Phan Boi Chau seized by the French. This is not to deny that he was capable of betraying the old patriot if he believed it would serve the interests of the revolutionary cause. Phan Boi Chau's value was obviously limited by his age, his lack of political sophistication, and his reluctance to countenance a violent approach. By 1925 he was clearly more valuable as a symbol of Vietnamese nationalism than as an actual participant in the resistance movement, and the anger aroused in Vietnam by his arrest and conviction could provide welcome publicity to the revolutionary cause. On the other hand, the league did not make much of the arrest of Phan Boi Chau in its propaganda, and continued to focus more attention on the heroic martyrdom of Pham Hong Thai, whose fate served as a prime motivational tool in the indoctrination of recruits in Canton.

Could financial needs have motivated Nguyen Ai Quoc to turn Chau in to the French authorities, as some allege? This charge should not be rejected out of hand, since Quoc was receiving only a limited subsidy from the CCP and sometimes was compelled to use his own private funds to carry out his activities. On the other hand, it seems unlikely that Quoc would have risked the possibility that the French might divulge the plot themselves to discredit the league and its mysterious leader. All in all, he must have felt that Chau would be more useful at liberty, where he could have served as a figurehead, an easily manipulated front man for a Communist-dominated united front, than in prison in Vietnam. It is notable that in statements made in exile to the end of his life, Chau continued to hold Nguyen Ai Quoc in high esteem and never suggested publicly that he might have held the younger man responsible for his seizure in Shanghai.[32]

Phan Boi Chau's trial opened before the Hanoi Criminal Commission on November 23, 1925. The defendant was assisted by two lawyers, but despite the presence of large crowds who demonstrated in favor of Chau—when the prosecution demanded the death sentence, one old man even offered to die in his place—he received a life sentence of hard labor. Chau was fifty-eight years old. The following day, there were demonstrations throughout the country, and students in Hanoi printed tracts to distribute on the streets. A few days later, a new governor-general arrived in Hanoi. A member of the Socialist Party and a critic of French colonial policy, Alexandre Varenne had no desire to open his term of office with a cause célèbre, and after sending a cable to France for permission, in December he commuted Chau's sentence to house arrest in Hué.

Before reducing the sentence, Varenne sought to induce the old rebel to cooperate with the colonial regime. Initially Chau refused, but he later mellowed and, although he continued to maintain contacts with leading members of the nationalist movement, he frequently issued statements that could be construed as favorable to the French. In one address that he presented to students at the National Academy in Hué, Chau praised the high quality of French education in Indochina. Such remarks aroused anger in nationalist circles and provoked Nguyen Ai Quoc in Canton to remark that they were "utter nonsense." According to information provided to the French by an informer, some nationalists even debated whether to take violent action against him. Chau finally died in 1940.[33]

While the Phan Boi Chau trial was under way, the old reformist Phan Chu Trinh returned to Indochina after more than a decade abroad. His arrival in Saigon was the occasion for mass rejoicing, and his speeches over the next few months, which continued to make the case for a policy of nonviolent reform, aroused considerable emotion. When he finally died of cancer early in 1926 at the age of fifty-three, his funeral became the occasion of a mass national outpouring of grief; thousands lined the streets to watch his bier as it was carried from Saigon to a grave site near Tan Son Nhut Airport in the northern suburbs of the city. Nguyen Ai Quoc apparently did not approve of such mass actions, arguing that they distracted public attention from more important issues. According to one Sûreté report, when he heard about the demonstrations surrounding the funeral of Phan Chu Trinh, Quoc remarked that they had probably been exaggerated by the French press to embarrass Governor-General Varenne, who was seeking to put a more human face on French colonial policies in Indochina.[34]

Through Nguyen Ai Quoc's efforts, his close colleagues in the Indochinese Communist Group were gradually exposed to Marxist-Leninist ideas. At the same time, a steady stream of patriotic young Vietnamese was recruited and brought to Canton, where they received training and indoctrination at the training institute, which had the impressive title of Special Political Institute for the Vietnamese Revolution. Its first location was in a building on Ren Xing Street. When that became too small, the school was moved to a larger three-story building owned by Communist sympathizers on Wen Ming Street, just across from Guangdong University (now the Lu Xun Museum) and close to CCP headquarters. In Chinese style, the ground floor served as a commercial establishment. Classes were held on the second floor in a large classroom with chairs, a table, and portraits of Communist luminaries on the walls. Behind the classroom was a small office and a bed for Nguyen Ai Quoc. The third floor was a dormitory for the students. A hidden trapdoor provided a secret exit to the street in case of a police raid. The kitchen was located in the garden behind the building.[35]

Most of the Vietnamese teachers at the school, such as Ho Tung Mau and Nguyen Ai Quoc himself, were themselves members of the Revolutionary Youth League, but occasionally visitors from the Soviet mission, such as Vasily Blücher (Galen), P. A. Pavlov, M. V. Kuibyshev, and V. M. Primakov, or from the local CCP mission, such as future leaders Liu Shaoqi, Zhou Enlai, and Li Fuqun, as well as the rural organizer Peng Pai, were invited to give guest lectures. One third of the school costs was borne by the CCP, while the remainder was provided for from other local organizations or through contributions by Vietnamese cadets studying at the Whampoa Academy, who donated a part of their monthly scholarship. The curriculum at the institute was closely patterned after similar training institutes in the USSR, with classes in such subjects as the rise of capitalism, the ideology of Marxism-Leninism, the organization of the Revolutionary Youth League, and the current world situation. To provide familiarity with local conditions, courses were taught on the ideology of Sun Yat-sen (which Nguyen Ai Quoc described to students as a relatively primitive form of socialism) and the Chinese language. One of Nguyen Ai Quoc's own courses was on the Leninist concept of the united front.

According to the recollections of many students, Nguyen Ai Quoc, who taught under the pseudonym of Vuong (in Chinese, Wang), was the most popular teacher in the school. They remembered him as slender, with bright eyes and a warm voice, friendly and good-humored, although he rarely laughed. Vuong was exceptionally approachable and patient with his students. He would explain difficult words and give long explanations of unfamiliar concepts. He seemed unusually well read, and a walking almanac when it came to statistics. One of his students remembered: "With dates and figures at his fingertips, he could tell us that the French colonialists had stolen so many tons of rice to send to the metropolis, that the Banque de l'Indochine netted fabulous profits, that Governor-General Varenne had shipped to France crates and crates of precious antiques from archaeological excavations."[36]

As in Paris, Nguyen Ai Quoc was not only instructor, but also moral adviser, surrogate parent, and resident cheerleader. He taught his charges how to talk and behave in a morally upright manner (so as to do credit to the revolutionary cause), how to speak in public, how to address gatherings of workers, peasants, children, and women, how to emphasize the national cause as well as the need for a social revolution, how to behave without condescension to the poor and illiterate. He anxiously checked on their living and eating conditions to make sure that they were healthy and well cared for; when they were gloomy and despondent, he cheered them up. One ex-student recalled his incurable optimism. When students appeared discouraged at the petty corruption of Vietnamese mandarins and the general ignorance and lethargy of the village population, he replied, "It's just these obstacles and social depravity that makes the revolution necessary. A revolutionary must above all be optimistic and believe in the final victory."[37]

After the conclusion of their training program, which usually lasted three to four months, the students accompanied Nguyen Ai Quoc on a ceremonial visit to the graves of seventy-two Chinese revolutionary martyrs at the Hoang Hoa knoll, outside of Canton, and in front of the tomb of the martyred patriot Pham Hong Thai, they recited their ritual vows to serve the revolutionary cause. Then most of them returned to Vietnam. A few of the more talented students, such as former Tam Tam Xa member Le Hong Phong, were sent to Moscow for further schooling. Still others found employment in the Chinese police or armed forces or were assigned to the famous Whampoa Academy, run by the Kuomintang with Comintern assistance. Nguyen Luong Bang, a member from a family of laborers, was instructed to find employment on a steamship line to set up a communications link between Hong Kong and the Vietnamese port city of Haiphong. By the spring of 1927, more than seventy students had passed through the school.[38]

Back in Vietnam, graduates from the institute sought to spread the league's revolutionary doctrine among their friends and acquaintances and to find new recruits to dispatch to Canton. As most of the alumni came from scholar-gentry backgrounds, it was inevitable that the majority of their first recruits were the same. French intelligence sources estimated that 90 percent of the students were what they described as petty bourgeois intellectuals, with the remainder workers or peasants. They came from all parts of the country, but there was a strong contingent from Nguyen Ai Quoc's native province of Nghe An and other parts of central Vietnam. By 1928 the Revolutionary Youth League had an estimated 300 members inside Indochina, with 150 in Cochin China (notably in Saigon and the large delta towns of My Tho and Can Tho), 80 in Annam (especially in Nghe An, Ha Tinh, and Quang Ngai), and 70 in Tonkin (Bac Ninh, Thai Binh, Nam Dinh, Hanoi, and Haiphong). A year later, the number had increased to over 1700.[39]

With the formation of the league, Nguyen Ai Quoc had taken the first step toward the realization of the socialist revolution in Vietnam. It was clearly a small and cautious step, but it was necessary to start somewhere. As he had written a few years earlier: "To say that that area [i.e., Indochina], with more than twenty million exploited people, is now ready for a revolution is wrong; but to say that it does not want a revolution and is satisfied with the regime . . . is even more wrong."[40]

Nguyen Ai Quoc was experienced enough to realize that propaganda would play a central role in building up his embryonic movement. The journal *Thanh Nien* helped to popularize his message. Printed in Canton, it was issued weekly and sent by sea to Vietnam. A total of 208 issues were published between June 21, 1925, and May 1930. It was written in his now familiar simple style and was enlivened by Chinese slogans and cartoons that satirized the French colonial regime and the rickety monarchy in Hué. As with *Le Paria*, Nguyen Ai Quoc wrote many of the editorials himself, although they were unsigned. The league also published two other journals, the biweekly *Linh Kach Menh* (Revolutionary Soldier) and the monthly periodical *Viet Nam Tien Phong* (Vietnamese Vanguard).[41]

In line with the stated goals of the Revolutionary Youth League, *Thanh Nien* placed primary emphasis on the issue of national independence. But some articles did refer in general terms to the global problem posed by imperialism and capitalism, suggesting obliquely that only communism could bring about liberation and social happiness. In an early issue, Nguyen Ai Quoc made the point that revolution was the only cure for his country's malaise: "Revolution is the change from bad to good; it is the entirety of all the acts by which an oppressed people becomes strong. The history of all societies has taught us that it was always by revolution that it was possible to give a better form to government, education, industry, organization of the society, etc." Only in an issue printed in the early summer of 1926 did the journal begin to speak openly of communism as a solution to the problems afflicting the peoples of Indochina.[42]

For students attending the training program, he undertook a more serious work. At that time, there was virtually nothing on Marxism-Leninism in the Vietnamese language; despite Nguyen Ai Quoc's frequent pleas for assistance, he received very little propaganda material from Moscow. To remedy that deficiency, he wrote a basic text to be used in a course at the institute dealing with the fundamental tasks of the Vietnamese revolution. This short pamphlet, titled *The Revolutionary Path* (Duong Kach Menh in Vietnamese), provided an introduction to Marxism-Leninism and explained its relevance to Vietnam. Although most copies were used by his students in Canton, a few were eventually sent to Vietnam to be distributed with *Thanh Nien*.[43]

In the pamphlet, Nguyen Ai Quoc's message was tantalizingly simple. Given the lack of sophistication of his students and their unfamiliarity with Western terminology (the Vietnamese *kach menh* was only introduced in the early twentieth century and was the Vietnamese equivalent of the Chinese word for "revolution" *ge ming*, which literally means "to change the mandate"), it is not surprising that he began with a brief definition of revolution. Revolution, he stated, is to destroy the old and build the new, or to destroy the bad and construct the good.

The author then launched into a brief explanation of the typology of revolution. There were, he noted, three types of revolution in the world:

1. Capitalist, such as the uprisings in France, Japan, and the United States

2. Nationalist, as in nineteenth-century Italy and the 1911 revolution in China

3. Class, represented by the Bolshevik revolution in Russia

All such revolutions, he continued, will eventually take place in two separate stages, with a first or "nationalist" stage and a second stage of "world revolution," when workers and peasants throughout the globe unite to overthrow the capitalist order and bring about happiness and unity to the people of all nations.[44]

The idea of a two-stage revolution, of course, is pure Lenin, but Nguyen Ai Quoc added some nuances of his own. First, although he was careful to declare that the nationalist stage of the world revolution would be followed by a socialist stage to bring about social happiness and global unity, Quoc was not specific about when that second stage would take place, and indeed implied that in Vietnam it would not take place until the entire world was ready to move from nationalism into a final stage of internationalism. This presumably reflected his belief at the time that the second stage would not take place in Vietnam until the majority of countries in the world had already passed through their own socialist revolutions. In his own formulation of the two-stage concept, Lenin had assumed that the first stage would relatively quickly "grow over" into the second one, as it had in Soviet Russia.[45]

Second, as we have already seen, Nguyen Ai Quoc ascribed somewhat more value than Lenin to the issue of national independence in the revolutionary process, presenting it in this instance as the desired consequence of the collaboration among many classes within Vietnamese society. He predicted that similar struggles for national liberation would eventually break out elsewhere in Asia. Which classes of people would *lead* the revolutionary surge in Vietnam? That, of course, was one of the key issues in the debate over strategy in the Comintern. Lenin had based his strategy on the concept of the four-class alliance, with its core the close link between workers and peasants. In *The Revolutionary Path*, Nguyen Ai Quoc singled out the latter (those who work hard and do not receive the fruits of their labor) as the prime enemy of the capitalists (who do not work yet receive all the benefits). But he appropriated Lenin's idea of a multiclass united front of progressive classes to bring about the first stage of the revolution. Included in this alliance could be

students, petty merchants, and even small landlords. Such groups, however, would not be reliable allies of the workers and peasants in carrying
out the second stage of the revolution, because they would oppose the
socialist stage. As he wrote in *The Revolutionary Path*, the workers and
peasants are the leading force of the revolution:

> This is because, first, the workers and farmers are more heavily op-
> pressed; secondly, the workers and peasants are united and therefore
> possess the greatest strength; and thirdly, they are already poor; if
> defeated, they would only lose their miserable life; if they win, they
> would have the whole world. That is why the workers and farmers
> are the roots of the revolution, while the students, small merchants,
> and landowners, though oppressed, do not suffer as much as the
> workers and farmers, and that is why these three classes are only the
> revolutionary friends of the workers and farmers.[46]

Finally, although Nguyen Ai Quoc followed Lenin's lead in stressing
the need for proletarian leadership, particularly during the second stage
of class revolution, underlying the entire pamphlet is the implied message that the rural classes were a crucial element in the revolutionary
partnership. This, of course, was a position that he had voiced with
limited success in Moscow. He argued that the lack of a close alliance
between town and country had doomed the revolutionary cause both
during the Paris Commune of 1870–1871 and the 1905 revolution in
Russia. Only when the two classes united, as had taken place during the
Bolshevik revolution in 1917, could a revolution succeed. This, he
maintained, was especially true in a country like Vietnam, where 90
percent of the population lived on the land and were grindingly poor.
Like the proletariat in Karl Marx's *Communist Manifesto*, Nguyen Ai
Quoc's peasants had nothing to lose but their chains. All they required,
as he had pointed out in articles written in France, was leadership and
organization.[47]

Nguyen Ai Quoc conceded that victory would not be easily achieved,
because it would be difficult to change a thousand-year-old society into
a new one. The most important thing was to have a revolutionary party
that could mobilize and organize the oppressed masses within the country and maintain contact with its counterparts all over the world. As a
boat cannot advance without a good oarsman, he wrote, the revolution
could not succeed without a solid party. A handful of rebels, he continued, can achieve little simply by assassinating a few government officials.
Such actions lead only to more repression, not to liberation. The

key to a solid party lay in its doctrine. A party should have an ideology that can be understood and followed by all party members. A party without ideology is like a man without intelligence, or a boat without a compass.

In the opening section of *The Revolutionary Path*, the author lists several characteristics that defined "the behavior of the revolutionary." It is interesting to compare this list with the famous "catechism of a revolutionary" written by the nineteenth-century Russian terrorist Sergey Nechayev. Nechayev emphasized the role of the revolutionary as the blind instrument of the revolutionary cause. He must be ruthless, even Machiavellian, in the promotion of his goal. He must show absolute obedience to his party, and be prepared to abandon all ties with friends and family. He must also be prepared to sacrifice generally recognized standards of morality, to lie and to cheat in the interests of the revolution. While many of Nechayev's excesses were condemned by others in the Russian radical movement, the catechism as a whole was much admired by Lenin, and became the bible of his Bolsheviks.

There were a number of similarities between Nguyen Ai Quoc's ethical rules of conduct and those of Lenin, as influenced by Nechayev. Both stressed the obligation of the party member to be courageous, bold, and persevering, and to subordinate his own needs to the requirements of the revolutionary cause. The main difference lay in the spirit behind these two sets of revolutionary standards. Where Lenin assumed that contemporary standards of morality had little relevance to the revolutionary code of conduct, and indeed that on some occasions there were irreducible contradictions between the two, the ethical core in Nguyen Ai Quoc's list of behavioral norms was strongly reminiscent of traditional Confucian morality: be thrifty, be friendly but impartial, resolutely correct errors, be prudent, respect learning, study and observe, avoid arrogance and conceit, and be generous. Indeed, except for references to the party, Quoc's revolutionary commandments could easily be accepted as behavioral norms in any devout Confucian home.[48]

It might be said, of course, that Nguyen Ai Quoc's list of revolutionary ethics was simply a means of dressing new concepts in familiar clothing; it is not unlikely that the thought crossed his mind. After all, it was obvious that the bulk of the early recruits to his cause came from scholar-gentry families. Although most had rejected traditional Confucian ideology, they were still influenced subliminally by many of its core values, and Quoc always sought to tailor his message to the proclivities of his audience. Still, the standards of personal conduct that were taught at the institute became a crucial aspect of his legacy to the Vietnamese

Communist movement and should not be dismissed as window dressing. To many of his colleagues, it was Quoc's personal demeanor, his image of goodness and simplicity, his unfailing optimism, his seriousness and devotion to the cause, that were best remembered after his death. Nguyen Ai Quoc's revolutionary ethics became the hallmark of his influence on his party and, for many, served as a distinguishing characteristic of Vietnamese communism.

Nguyen Ai Quoc's message possessed a deep inner logic for Vietnam. By itself, the country seemed powerless to achieve its own liberation. Even the intrepid nationalist Phan Boi Chau had gone abroad, at first to Japan and then to China, for assistance. It was reassuring to read in *The Revolutionary Path* that the Vietnamese people would have help from the revolutionary masses throughout the world as they struggled to achieve their own liberation. It was deeply satisfying, as well, to be told that the West, too, still had to undergo a period of social turmoil.

The pamphlet's criticisms of previous nationalist movements were particularly meaningful to young Vietnamese patriots. The weakness of nationalist organizations was only too clear; all had been notoriously deficient in ideology, with most identifying simply with the general cause of modernization and national independence. Few had attempted to go into specifics on the projected nature of a future independent Vietnam. Unlike the case in other societies in the region, the Vietnamese nationalist movement could not rally around the symbols of a common religious faith. Buddhism, which denied the essential reality of the material world and preached a philosophy of denial, had little relevance as an agent for change. Confucianism, although deeply entrenched as a set of social and political maxims among the Vietnamese elite, had been widely discredited as a result of the pusillanimous surrender of the imperial court to the French invaders. As a result, most non-Communist nationalist organizations tended to be defined by regional identity, by tactics, or by personality. The actions of their members, while sometimes courageous, often seemed meaningless gestures of hatred against an all-powerful enemy who could scatter the rebel forces with a slap of the hand.

The Revolutionary Path was Nguyen Ai Quoc's first major effort to introduce Marxist-Leninist doctrine to his countrymen. As an ideological statement, it has little to offer a serious student of modern Vietnam or an historian of the world Communist movement. As Quoc once admitted to a colleague, the description of Marxist-Leninist doctrine and practice in the pamphlet was primitive and in some cases confusing. The unsophisticated presentation and the ideological ambiguities in Quoc's treatment of the two-stage concept and the four-class alliance have led some to question his understanding of Marxist-Leninist doctrine or, alternatively, his commitment to its precepts. Because he was not precise in describing the "leading role" to be played by the working class (a key tenet of Leninism) in the Vietnamese revolution, some observers have interpreted the pamphlet as an early example of "peasant communism," an unorthodox approach to Marxist-Leninist revolutionary strategy later to be attributed to Mao Zedong.

It would be a mistake, however, to attempt to read too much into Quoc's views as expressed in this book. He was attempting to popularize Marxist ideas in a society that was predominantly rural and lacking in political sophistication. It is probable that Nguyen Ai Quoc—along the lines of his now familiar conviction that in propaganda, simpler is better—was making a deliberate effort to create a popular or "vulgar" Marxism that could be understood by the Vietnamese people in the context of their own circumstances. Although it is hardly a testament to the sophistication of his comprehension of Marxist theory, as an attempt to introduce Marxist-Leninist doctrine to the beginner it was an effective instrument.[49]

During his years in Moscow, Quoc had already demonstrated his conviction that the peasants in Vietnam, as in all of Africa and Asia, were the primary victim of Western colonialism and, as such, were destined to be closely allied with the working class. In the pamphlet he stated that support of the peasants would be a crucial prerequisite for victory. He probably justified his views as an orthodox interpretation of Leninism, even though the official line in Moscow had since departed from this view. In any case, Quoc obviously had relatively little interest in theoretical questions; his remarks in *The Revolutionary Path* may have simply been intended as an elaboration of comments he had made in Moscow a few years previously.

Still, in stressing the role of peasants, Nguyen Ai Quoc was taking a major step within the Vietnamese resistance movement. Other national leaders and groups had given only lip service to the role of the rural masses in the Vietnamese struggle for liberation. Phan Boi Chau had voiced his desire for peasant support, but Chau's appeal was generalized, and he had taken no concrete steps to put it into practice. In voicing his determination to focus attention on the rural masses, Quoc was attempting to alert his compatriots, as well as fellow revolutionaries throughout the colonial world, to the importance of the countryside in the coming revolution in Asia.

Within a few months of his arrival in Canton, Nguyen Ai Quoc had recruited a handful of young radicals who would provide the future leadership for a new and vigorous movement of national resistance. From his vantage point in south China, the situation must have looked hopeful. Beginning in 1925, the long simmering discontent of the Vietnamese people against their colonial rulers suddenly broke into open protest. Sparked by the arrest and trial of Phan Boi Chau and the funeral of Phan Chu Trinh, which followed a few months later, anti-French sentiment rapidly rose to a level that had not been seen since prior to the outbreak of World War I.

In these conditions, several embryonic political parties, such as the Youth Party in Cochin China, began to emerge. In Annam and Tonkin, a Tan Viet ("New Vietnamese") Revolutionary Party was formed by former members of Phan Boi Chau's organization, in cooperation with a handful of patriotic young students in Hanoi. The Tan Viet party included within its ranks members possessing a wide spectrum of tactical orientations and ideological convictions—from reformists to advocates of violent revolution, from advocates of the Western model to evolutionary Marxists and followers of the Leninist road. The one common denominator was resistance to French rule and dedication to the cause of national independence.

In the meantime, Nguyen An Ninh, the young journalist who had angered Lieutenant Governor Maurice Cognacq with his provocative attitude, continued to stir up the populace with his fiery speeches and articles. He lectured his audience on one occasion that they were responsible for their own sufferings, because "you have not been able to impose your ideas, you have not dictated to the government your will." Describing the collaboration that Albert Sarraut had once offered to the Vietnamese as similar to the relationship between a buffalo and its master, he warned:

> Do not place too much hope in the socialist governor-general [i.e., Alexandre Varenne] that has been sent you; he has come to cheat you, he has much to say, but he will give you nothing. There is no collaboration possible between French and Annamites. The French have nothing more to do here. Let them give us back the land of our ancestors, let them give us the floor and let us control ourselves.

Our country has given birth to innumerable heroes, of men who knew how to die for their land! Our race is not yet extinguished![50]

Ninh's speech aroused memories of Phan Boi Chau, who had lambasted the French from his exile in Japan. The French believed they had to react. On March 24, 1926, just as the funeral cortege prepared to transport Phan Chu Trinh's body to its final resting place, Nguyen An Ninh was placed under arrest.

That same afternoon, the French ocean liner *Amboise* docked in Saigon. Among its passengers was Bui Quang Chieu, the Constitutionalist Party leader whom Nguyen Ai Quoc had met on the *Amiral Latouche-Tréville* nearly fifteen years previously. Like Nguyen An Ninh, Chieu had been disappointed at the failure of Governor-General Alexandre Varenne to live up to his extravagant promises, and in early 1926 he had traveled to Paris to appeal for political and economic reforms. In talks with officials there, he warned that if the situation in Indochina did not improve, the French would be evicted in fifteen years. Chieu also held talks with radical nationalists in the Vietnamese exile community centered around Nguyen The Truyen, Nguyen Ai Quoc's successor at the Intercolonial Union, but in the end he refused to cooperate with him. The experience apparently unnerved him; when he returned to Saigon he appeared suddenly reluctant to heed the demands of street crowds to increase pressure on the colonial government, and his speech on arrival consisted of an appeal for Franco-Vietnamese harmony. With Nguyen An Ninh in jail and Bui Quang Chieu unwilling to carry the torch, the urban unrest in Cochin China quickly died down, leading one young patriot to cry in despair, "Have we all forgotten Phan Chu Trinh?"

For Nguyen Ai Quoc, who had observed with interest the rapid escalation in anticolonial agitation among his compatriots from his own vantage point in Canton, the situation offered opportunity, but also a challenge. How much should his fledgling revolutionary organization cooperate with nationalist elements inside Indochina and abroad? Despite the reservations expressed by M. N. Roy and others in Moscow, who argued that it was dangerous to cooperate with bourgeois nationalist groups, Nguyen Ai Quoc was initially determined to cast a wide net to mobilize support against the colonial regime. In the report he had written in Moscow in 1924, he had remarked that it was the spirit of nationalism that had caused the 1908 revolt in central Vietnam, taught coolies to protest against their conditions, aroused the determination of Vietnamese merchants to compete with Europeans and the overseas

Chinese, and provoked students to demonstrate and join Phan Boi Chau's organization. The torch, he wrote, was now passing from one generation to another. As young Vietnamese began to use the tactics of the West, he believed, their activities could be used for his purposes.[51]

Nguyen Ai Quoc had turned his attention to the problem of broadening the base of his movement by allying with other anticolonial organizations soon after his arrival in Canton, attempting to establish relations with nationalist elements around Nguyen Hai Than, a follower of Phan Boi Chau who had recently assisted Chau in his effort to transform his old Restoration Society into a new Vietnamese Nationalist Party modeled on Sun Yat-sen's organization in China. Quoc had also discussed with Lam Duc Thu the possibility of contacting nationalist elements inside the country. In central Vietnam, he sought contacts with what he termed "young and modern types" (presumably the Tan Viet party), but he also wanted to approach moderate elements in Cochin China such as Bui Quang Chieu and Khanh Ky (an old acquaintance from Paris) to see if they would cooperate. His colleagues warned him to be cautious in establishing relations with Chieu until it was clear that Chau was receptive, but Quoc countered that if Chieu agreed to cooperate he might be willing to provide funds.[52]

For Nguyen Ai Quoc, however, nationalist parties presented a delicate problem. How far should the Revolutionary Youth League cooperate with them? The Second Comintern Congress in 1920 had concluded that such bourgeois liberation movements should be supported "only when they are genuinely revolutionary and when their exponents do not hinder our work of education and organizing the peasantry and the broad mass of the exploited in a revolutionary spirit." But some leading members of the organization, such as the French Communist Jacques Doriot, had different advice. In a letter to one of the league's front organizations dated March 4, 1927, Doriot recommended a broader approach. "Although your party should always keep in mind that the fundamental forces of the struggle in Indochina were the working class, the peasantry, and the petty bourgeoisie of the towns," he noted,

do not forget that under the domination of imperialism, it is all the people (workers, peasants, shopkeepers, intellectuals) with the exception of a tiny minority of profiteers—who have an interest in the struggle against imperialism. Don't neglect any effort to attract them and organize them every day for the struggle. Don't refuse any cooperation. On the contrary, do everything to inspire it.[53]

Nguyen Ai Quoc followed Doriot's advice, but with caution. In keeping with the Comintern line of cooperating only with those bourgeois nationalist groups that were "truly revolutionary," under his direction the league became notably cautious about forming alliances. After his initial expression of interest in Bui Quang Chieu, Quoc scorned "national reformist" groups such as Chieu's Constitutionalist Party, which he described in one report to Moscow as opposed to communism and in favor of cooperation with France. Toward more radical parties, such as the Youth Party in Cochin China and the Tan Viet in central Vietnam, the league was somewhat more conciliatory, sending representatives to negotiate a possible alliance.

But the league's negotiating position was uniformly hard-line. It rejected the idea of a merger of equals and simply offered rival leaders a subordinate role in the league. While talks were under way, league members actively attempted to lure the delegates of rival parties into their own organization. When members of these rival groups came to Canton to study at the training institute, they were instructed not to resume contacts with their comrades on their return to Vietnam. It is hardly surprising that the leaders of such nationalist parties were put off by such tactics and spurned alliances with the Revolutionarly Youth League on the terms offered.[54]

Because Nguyen Ai Quoc was compelled to remain in China to avoid capture by the French Sûreté, his involvement in direct negotiations with the leaders of groups inside Vietnam appears to have been minimal. But it is likely that the final decisions were his. Remarks that he made to colleagues and students at the school in Canton suggest that his attitude toward rival parties combined a cautious willingness to cooperate in the cause of resistance with a fundamental suspicion of their ultimate motives. He frequently commented that alliances with such parties could be useful, but for tactical purposes only.[55]

While promoting efforts to build up the Vietnamese revolutionary movement, Nguyen Ai Quoc also sought to carry out his proletarian duty by cooperating with progressive elements in south China in the Chinese revolution. Before Quoc's departure from Moscow, Thomas Dombal had asked him to serve as the Peasant International's representative in Canton and to assist his hosts in mobilizing Chinese peasants. For a while, it appeared that this work could be accomplished with the cooperation of the Kuomintang, whose representatives in Moscow had sought assistance in drafting a peasant program from the Peasant International. Dombal also suggested that Quoc establish peasant unions in all regions of Guangdong province, most of which was by then under the control of the Canton regime.

To carry out such duties, after his arrival in Canton, Quoc began to visit the Peasant Movement Institute, a training unit that had been established by the Kuomintang government in 1924 to promote rural revolution against the warlord regimes to the north. The institute was located in an old Buddhist temple not far from the Revolutionary Youth League headquarters in Canton, and Quoc reported on its activities in articles that he sent back to Moscow. In the course of his work on peasant conditions in China, he became acquainted with Peng Pai, a prominent CCP activist and one of the leading cadres at the institute. Peng was a chief promoter of the Hai Lu Feng Soviets, peasant organizations that had been established in 1923 under his urging in two coastal districts east of Canton. Nguyen Ai Quoc was enthusiastic about the experiment, and on one occasion he visited the area and wrote an article on the subject. In return, Peng sometimes lectured at Quoc's institute.[56]

Nguyen Ai Quoc had arrived in China at a time when the revolutionary movement there was in a period of rapid flux. During the summer of 1925, massive labor strikes took place in Canton as a response to the so-called May 30 incident in Shanghai in which British police had fired on Chinese demonstrators, killing several of them. Nguyen Ai Quoc took part in the demonstrations, giving speeches of encouragement to the demonstrators and declaring—in heavily accented Cantonese—that the Indochinese people were on their side. He also took part in more formal activities, such as the Second National Congress of the Kuomintang, held in January 1926 at the instigation of left-wing elements to counter the growing influence of anti-Communist forces within the party. Quoc addressed the gathering and described current conditions in Indochina. The French, he declared, were trying desperately to prevent news of the unrest in China from coming to the attention of the Vietnamese people. Still, he promised, his compatriots and all other colonial peoples of Asia were eager to unite with the Chinese people in fighting their common oppressors. That statement, however, was more hyperbole than reality. By now, the Society of Oppressed Peoples of Asia, which he had helped found the previous year, had succumbed to bitter squabbling among various national groups—a reminder to Quoc of his problems with the Intercolonial Union in Paris—and had disintegrated.[57]

By the spring of 1927, Nguyen Ai Quoc had been in Canton for over two years. He had become a prominent and respected member of the revolutionary community, and had developed close relationships with such CCP members as Zhou Enlai, the youth organizer Zhang Tailei, and the left-wing Kuomintang leader Liao Zhongkai. His life in south China, at least for the moment, had taken on an air of stability, and (perhaps for that reason) he had given some thought to taking a Chinese wife to help him learn the Chinese language and take care of his domestic needs. To locate a suitable partner, he had apparently discussed the issue with his close colleague Lam Duc Thu, who had lived in China for many years and had a broad range of acquaintances among the local population. Quoc insisted, however, that he did not wish to follow the traditional Chinese marriage custom—he refused to pay for a wife.

Shortly after, Lam Duc Thu introduced Quoc to a young Chinese woman named Tang Tuyet Minh, the daughter of a wealthy Cantonese merchant by his third concubine. Evicted from the house after her father's death, Tuyet Minh lived in difficult circumstances until she was befriended by Lam Duc Thu's wife, who in turn introduced her to Nguyen Ai Quoc. The young woman had little education and some of his colleagues opposed the match, but Quoc ignored their advice and decided to propose marriage. After the wedding, the couple lived together in Quoc's room at Borodin's villa. Although Tuyet Minh was physically attractive (one acquaintance described her as svelte, with clear skin, shoulder-length black hair, a round face, and a small mouth), she had little interest in national affairs, and after a few unsuccessful attempts, her husband soon gave up the effort to convert her to his political beliefs. There were reports that Quoc had one daughter as a result of the marriage.[58]

In any event, Nguyen Ai Quoc's days in Canton were coming to an end. While he was struggling to fan the flames of discontent in Vietnam, the situation in China was in rapid transition. For several years, the CCP had cooperated in an uneasy alliance with Sun's Nationalist Party in the southern provinces of China. This alliance had been held together primarily by the force of Sun's own personality and his working relationship with Comintern adviser Mikhail Borodin. But Sun died of liver cancer in March 1925, while in Beijing to negotiate with the warlord Feng Yuxiang, and after a brief power struggle, Chiang Kai-shek, Sun's military adviser and commander of Whampoa Academy, succeeded him. For tactical reasons, Chiang temporarily maintained the alliance with the

CCP, despite growing anti-Communist sentiment within the conservative wing of the Kuomintang. However, Chiang was himself suspicious of the Communists; perhaps because of his visit to the Soviet Union in 1923, he was well aware of Moscow's long-term goals to use the alliance with his party and then throw it away. On April 12, 1927, in the midst of the jointly sponsored Northern Expedition against the warlord governments in central and northern China, the alliance began to come apart. When the left wing of the Kuomintang called for Chiang Kai-shek's dismissal, he ordered the massacre of thousands of Communists and sympathizers in Shanghai, China's largest city, as his troops arrived there.

Chiang's actions were immediately echoed in Canton. The following day, military units commanded by the Nationalist commander Li Jishen rounded up two thousand suspected Communists throughout Guangdong province. The Whampoa Academy was occupied and hundreds of suspected leftists, some of them Vietnamese students associated with the Revolutionary Youth League, were rounded up and shot. Nguyen Ai Quoc's friend Zhang Tailei was one of the victims. When Li's troops blockaded the houses of officials working at the Soviet consulate, Mikhail Borodin and several of his advisers left for Wuhan, where the Canton government had moved its headquarters during the previous winter.

At first, French authorities thought that Nguyen Ai Quoc had followed Borodin and his entourage to central China. In actuality, Quoc had remained in Canton, perhaps in the conviction that as a Vietnamese who had good relations with many Kuomintang officials he would be safe from arrest. To help ensure his security, he took refuge in a secret location and supported himself by selling newspapers. But sometime in late April or early May, he was alerted by Truong Van Lenh, one of his close collaborators from the Tam Tam Xa and now an official with the local municipal guard, that he might soon be arrested. Lenh advised him to flee Canton as soon as possible.[59]

Ironically, it was one of Nguyen Ai Quoc's presumed allies within the Vietnamese exile community who had identified him as a Communist to Li Jishen's police. Since his arrival in Canton, Quoc had sought to establish cooperative relations with Nguyen Hai Than and other veteran members of Phan Boi Chau's VNQDD. Than was a close friend of Lam Duc Thu, and once lived at his house. By the spring of 1926, Quoc's relations with Than had become strained, because Than had become increasingly critical of the Revolutionary Youth League's Communist orientation; Quoc was also angry about Than's alleged efforts to weaken or absorb his own organization. In late 1926, Truong Boi Cong, one of the leading members of the Kuomintang, arrived in Canton from Beijing to exhort Nguyen Hai Than to form a new political party to focus on national independence and combat the influence of the league. The split between the two Vietnamese groups widened, and it was allegedly Nguyen Hai Than who alerted Chinese authorities to Nguyen Ai Quoc's presence in early May.

Curiously, Lam Duc Thu himself, although a regular informant on league activities for the Sûreté, never betrayed Nguyen Ai Quoc to the French, perhaps because of the risks involved if his role as an agent were to be divulged. He did arrange to have photographs of key members of the league taken, however. Once he managed to deliver them to the French consulate, these photos (they are now located in the French archives) undoubtedly aided the colonial authorities in identifying Nguyen Ai Quoc's colleagues. Quoc's carelessness in allowing such photos to be taken and his apparent trust in Lam Duc Thu were later sharply criticized by some of his colleagues.[60]

On May 5, 1927, Nguyen Ai Quoc left his secret location and caught a train to Hong Kong, leaving his wife in Canton. On the same day, his residence was raided by Chinese officials. Once again he was on the move.[61]

V | THE MAGIC SWORD

As he looked out the window of his railway car at the rice fields, newly green with the first shoots of the spring rice harvest, Nguyen Ai Quoc, en route to Hong Kong, most likely had mixed feelings with regard to his current situation. The results of the last two years of work in Canton had undoubtedly been gratifying in some respects. He had created a solid foundation for a future Communist party in Indochina and had trained nearly a hundred dedicated militants, some of whom had already returned to all three regions of Vietnam to build up a revolutionary network. However, Chiang Kai-shek's preemptive attack on the CCP in Canton was a severe setback for the young organization. Continued operations by the Revolutionary Youth League in south China were now difficult, and its headquarters would have to be moved. He himself was embarked on a journey into the unknown, and his own contacts with his colleagues might be severed, perhaps for many years.

Nguyen Ai Quoc (still operating as Ly Thuy) may initially have hoped to remain in the British crown colony of Hong Kong for an extended period of time in order to maintain his links with other members of the league and find a new location for its headquarters. But the local authorities were suspicious of his papers and ordered him to leave within twenty-four hours. The next day he left by ship for Shanghai. That great commercial city was still gasping under the "white terror" that Chiang Kai-shek had launched the previous month against Communist elements in the area. To escape detection, Nguyen Ai Quoc rented a room in a luxury hotel and dressed the part of a wealthy bourgeois. With his funds rapidly running out, he was eventually able to catch a ship for Vladivostok.[1]

In Vladivostok, which still served as the headquarters for Soviet revolutionary operations in the Far East, Nguyen Ai Quoc met his old friend

Jacques Doriot, one of the rising young stars of the French Communist Party. He also encountered the Comintern agent Grigory Voitinsky, who had been promoting the formation of the Communist movement in China. Doriot proposed that Quoc return to Europe and then proceed to Siam in order to try to reconstruct the movement in Indochina with the assistance of the FCP and league activists operating there. Voitinsky suggested that he return to Shanghai to work with Vietnamese troops stationed in the French concession in the city.

Nguyen Ai Quoc listened politely to Voitinsky, but he had a strong preference for Doriot's proposal. Indeed, before his departure from Canton he had already concluded that he had only two choices—to remain in China under risk of arrest or to go to Siam to restore contact with the movement in neighboring Indochina. He left by rail for Moscow, arriving in early June. There he sent a formal travel request to the Dalburo, arguing that he would prefer to go to Siam, rather than returning to China. The most important task, he argued, was to strengthen the movement inside Indochina, where the news of the recent events in China had undoubtedly caused discouragement. Quoc felt that he could influence events in Indochina more effectively from Siam than from Shanghai.[2]

In his request to the Dalburo, Nguyen Ai Quoc had declared that he would require funds for a trip to Siam, and from there on to Indochina for "a time of residence estimated in the colony of about two years." While waiting for a decision from the Comintern, he was assigned a temporary position at Comintern headquarters, and in his spare time he wrote for publication in *Inprecor* a number of articles on conditions in Indochina. After a rest at a convalescent home at Eppatoria, near Crum on the shore of the Black Sea, where he received medical treatment for an unknown ailment, he received approval from the Stalin School to set up a separate section for the Vietnamese students whom he had earlier arranged to send from Canton. Among the five who were now in Moscow was Tran Phu, an intense and thin-faced young militant from Quang Ngai province. The son of a court official, Tran Phu had attended the National Academy in Hué and joined one of the minor nationalist parties in central Vietnam. Sent by his colleagues to Canton to negotiate with Nguyen Ai Quoc on forming an alliance, he decided to join the league and was sent to Moscow in 1927, where he soon made an impression with his intellectual brilliance and dedication.[3]

In November 1927, Nguyen Ai Quoc received a reply from the Comintern to his travel request. Instead of Siam, he was instructed to proceed to Paris to assist the FCP in drafting an effective program of action to build up the revolutionary movement in Indochina, not only among Vietnamese residents in France but also by establishing a base in Siam or elsewhere in the region. No funds were appropriated, however, for his prospective return to Asia.

En route to France, Quoc stopped briefly in Berlin, where he helped German comrades there to set up a branch of the new Anti-Imperialist League, a cover organization for Soviet operations abroad. He then proceeded under an assumed name to Paris, where he reported to FCP headquarters in Montmartre. The FCP offered him neither employment nor financial assistance, which clearly irritated him. In a letter sent to a colleague in Moscow the following May, he expressed his frustration with the French Party's continuing failure to address colonial issues. While he admitted that the FCP had devoted some attention to colonial problems, he complained that most of the progress was just on paper. To make the point, he cited his own experience:

> While I spent a month and a half in Paris, Doriot was in prison, and I had no opportunity to talk with others. I frequently asked for an address so that I could contact them after I returned to the Far East, but they refused. They claim that the Colonial Commission has a budget for colonial operations, but I hear that the box is empty. I think that the finances of the Colonial Commission should be investigated and that it should regularly submit reports to other comrades on its operations and plans. Further, it must organize a more effective means to contact our people in Indochina so that I can stay in touch with them.[4]

Nguyen Ai Quoc may have intended to remain in France until he had managed to obtain funds to return to Asia, but acquaintances warned him that the Sûreté, which had heard rumors that he had returned to France, was intensifying its efforts to locate him. In early December, he went to Brussels to attend a meeting of the executive council of the Anti-Imperialist League. There is no record that he spoke publicly at the conference, but he did take the opportunity to make the acquaintance of a number of the delegates at the conference, including the Indonesian nationalist Sukarno, the Indian nationalist Motilal Nehru (father of the future Indian prime minister Jawaharlal Nehru), and Sun Yat-sen's widow, Soong Qingling. He also renewed his friendship with the Japanese Communist Katayama Sen, whom he had known in Paris and Moscow. Madame Soong in particular would prove useful to him at a crucial moment in the not distant future.[5]

After the conference adjourned in mid-December, Nguyen Ai Quoc returned briefly to France, and then left by train for Berlin. On arrival, he wrote a letter to Thomas Dombal in Moscow, explaining that he hoped to return to Indochina in two or three weeks and asking for funds from the Peasant International to help cover his travel expenses, as well as for a plan of action to assist him in his future work. But Dombal's reply, which did not arrive until early January, was noncommittal about Quoc's request for assistance. Protesting that he did not have a clear idea about the situation in Indochina, Dombal suggested that Quoc should first direct his attention to the task of mobilizing the peasantry in the provinces on both sides of the Chinese border, organizing peasant associations and carrying out propaganda, but he made no mention of the possibility of financial aid.[6]

During the next several months, Nguyen Ai Quoc remained in Berlin while waiting for a more definitive answer to his request. To keep his expenses at a minimum, he lived with an acquaintance who was a member of the German Communist Party. He produced articles on various subjects, including an account of Peng Pai's Hai Lu Feng Soviet movement in Guangdong province, and made plans to write a recollection of his experience working with the peasant movement in China. In a letter to a comrade in Moscow, Quoc estimated that the book would be about 120 pages long and divided into five separate sections. By April, however, with his funds running out, he was becoming increasingly impatient and sent off a quick note to the Dalburo reporting on his situation. The note was cryptic, but expressive:

> Can't work in France, useless in Germany, but needed in Indochina, so I have already requested to return there. In letters to comrades I have already provided a budget for travel and work. When Doriot passed through Berlin, he promised to give attention to my situation. I told him if there were no operational funds, at least give travel money so I can leave, because for over a year I have wandered aimlessly from country to country while there is much to do in Indochina. But up to now, I have received no direction from comrades or a reply from Doriot. I am now in a difficult situation, 1) limitless waiting (await directive for four months), 2) have nothing

on which to live, so told MOPRE [the Comintern division directed to provide help to revolutionary comrades] but they say they can't give me unlimited assistance, just eighteen marks a week (that sum is not enough to live on . . .). So please send me as soon as possible a detailed directive on what I must do and when I can leave.[7]

Two weeks later, he finally received a letter from Moscow granting him permission to return to Indochina, with funds for travel and three months' room and board to be provided by the FCP. In mid-May he wrote the Dalburo that he had received permission to leave and would depart at the end of the month.[8]

In early June, Nguyen Ai Quoc left Berlin and traveled by train through Switzerland to Italy. Many years later he recalled the journey:

When [I] requested a permit to travel through Italy, the fascist government asked a lot of complicated questions. At the border, the guards looked at a book called *The Anti-Comintern Dictionary* which contained two thousand pages, which gave the names of revolutionaries of all countries from A to Z. They didn't see [my] name there, so let me through.

Passing through Milan, he continued on to Rome, where he was taken to the police station, interrogated, and (according to his own account) beaten almost senseless. Afterward, the chief interrogator shook his hand and offered him a cigarette, then resumed the questioning. Those lacking in experience, Nguyen Ai Quoc later warned readers, can easily fall into the capitalist trap. After his release, he went on to Naples, where he boarded a Japanese ship for Siam at the end of June.[9]

Nguyen Ai Quoc arrived in Bangkok sometime in July 1928. Because Siam was not a European colony and had a relatively stable society, the government permitted relatively free movement for foreigners, even for a revolutionary of Nguyen Ai Quoc's notoriety. The kingdom also possessed a considerable population of Vietnamese nationals (overseas Vietnamese were known in Vietnamese as Viet Kieu), mostly living in the flat and dry Khorat plateau in the northeastern part of the country. This helped Nguyen Ai Quoc circulate freely without attracting undue attention. In the northeast, members of the Revolutionary Youth League, under his orders, had already begun to establish a local branch of operations among the Viet Kieu community. Significantly, it took only about two weeks to travel on foot from northeast Siam over the Annamite mountains to central Vietnam.

Anticolonialist Vietnamese had been using the area as a sanctuary for many years. Most of the more than twenty thousand Vietnamese living in Siam then had originally migrated around the turn of the century. Many had supported the Can Vuong and Phan Boi Chau's anti-colonial movement. After a number of his own followers had begun to settle there, Chau had visited Bangkok in 1908 and asked the royal government to allow them to engage in farming. Many Siamese officials distrusted the French and sympathized with the Vietnamese cause, so they approved his request and a Vietnamese farm was founded at Phichit, in the Chao Phraya valley north of Bangkok. A few years later, Chau's Restoration Society set up a branch office in Siam, and a number of Vietnamese radicals—including future members of the league such as Ho Tung Mau, Le Hong Son, and Pham Hong Thai—passed through the country on their way to China. After his arrival in Canton from Moscow in 1924, Nguyen Ai Quoc had begun making plans to set up a base of the Revolutionary Youth League in the area. In 1925, Ho Tung Mau had been sent there to set up four branches, at Phichit and in Vietnamese communities located at Nakhon Phanom, Udon Thani, and Sakon Nakhon in the northeast. Where the community was well orga-nized, cooperatives were established to carry on cultivation and manu-facturing for the common good.[10]

In August 1928, a Vietnamese dressed in simple local clothes and calling himself Father Chin arrived unannounced in Bandong, in the district of Phichit, about two hundred miles north of Bangkok. The village contained about two dozen Vietnamese families, who had estab-lished a branch of the league there in 1926. The stranger remained in the village about two weeks, visiting each family and relating to them the world situation and conditions inside Indochina.[11]

In September, having decided that the community was too small to serve as a base of operations, Nguyen Ai Quoc (still posing as Father Chin) left Bandong and went to Udon Thani in the northeast. The ar-duous trip took fifteen days, including a ten-day trek along jungle paths. The travelers in the small group carried their own provisions, as well as their luggage. At first, Father Chin had difficulties and lagged behind the others, his feet raw and his breath short. But through sheer willpower he persisted; by the end of the trip he showed his mettle, managing on occasion to walk as far as seventy kilometers in a single day.[12]

Udon was a much larger town than Bandong, and had a larger Viet-namese community as well as convenient communications links with other urban centers in the Khorat plateau. As a result, the local branch of the league, which had been established in 1926, operated as the headquarters for all league operations in Siam. Keeping the name Father Chin (only a handful of members of the Vietnamese community knew his real identity), Quoc instructed his followers on the need to broaden their organization and build a mass base for the league by appealing to the entire local population and not just radical youths.

Nguyen Ai Quoc remained in Udon for several months, initiating changes in the working habits and lives of his compatriots. Most Vietnamese in northeastern Siam were urban merchants or artisans who were unaccustomed to hard physical labor. Few had contact with the local population or had bothered to learn the Thai language. Quoc made strenous efforts to change these habits, attempting to set an example by engaging in hard physical labor (when the government authorized the establishment of a local school, he helped to build it by carrying bricks). In the evenings, he talked to villagers about world events and conditions in Indochina. The local Vietnamese community gradually began to improve relations with the surrounding Thai population by digging wells, felling trees, and building schools. Quoc himself made an effort to learn the Thai language, setting a strict schedule to memorize ten words a day, and he established schools for Vietnamese residents to learn Thai and to appreciate local customs. He assured his compatriots that the Siamese people sympathized with the struggle in Indochina, since Siam survived as an independent state only under the benign tolerance of the colonial powers in the area.

Nguyen Ai Quoc also began to take steps to increase his compatriots' political awareness, writing poems and dramas that vividly described the loss of Vietnamese independence at the hands of the French. Operating through the guise of the Than Ai (friendship) association, an organization that had been established by league members in the area, he traveled constantly, setting up new cells for league operations from Mukdahan in the east to Nong Khai, just across the Mekong River from the Laotian administrative capital of Vientiane. To improve the league's propaganda, he reorganized the local Vietnamese-language journal *Dong Thanh* (One Heart), renaming it *Than Ai* and simplifying its style to make it more accessible to local readers.[13]

In early 1929, Nguyen Ai Quoc went to Sakon Nakhon, where there were more overseas Vietnamese than in Udon. According to the recollections of league members living in the area, however, the Viet Kieu at Sakon Nakhon were less politically enlightened than in Udon. Many were Christians; others were Buddhists or believers in the spirit of the traditional Vietnamese military hero Tran Hung Dao. Noticing that many still made offerings at local temples to cure their ailments, Quoc introduced them to modern medicine and invited doctors to visit the area. Yet he had no compunctions about using local beliefs for his own purposes, and writing verses for a song about Tran Hung Dao:

At the temple of Dien Hong and before the genies, the sermon
 is given,
The people, with one heart, are resolved for all,
And whoever should wish to seize Vietnam
Must first kill us to the last man.

So long as one Vietnamese remains on this soil

The mountains and the waters of Vietnam will remain his
 Fatherland.[14]

French authorities were not aware of Nguyen Ai Quoc's whereabouts during the two years after he left Canton in May 1927. Reports surfaced that he had been in Moscow, however, and eventually the Sûreté confirmed that he had spent a brief period of time in Paris in late 1927. But they lost track of him after his departure from Brussels in December. During 1928 and 1929, however, they did hear rumors about his presence in Siam and about a stranger circulating through Viet Kieu villages in eastern Siam. Quoc had to be very careful in his actions; both the French and the imperial government in Hué were looking for him. On October 10, 1929, a tribunal in Vinh condemned him in absentia to death on the charge of fomenting rebellion in Annam. In his reminiscences, Quoc claimed that the French knew he was in Siam, but since they didn't know exactly where he was, they sent police to locate him. On one occasion, he was closely pursued and had to hide in a pagoda, with his hair cut short in order to disguise himself.[15]

While Nguyen Ai Quoc was on his way to Siam, his colleagues in south China struggled to keep the Revolutionary Youth League in operation. Most of the members of the organization had been arrested, but were soon released, and managed to resume their activities in Canton under the leadership of Le Hong Son and Ho Tung Mau. They moved their headquarters, however, to a narrow alley near Ren Xing Street, near the Da Dong Gate and the original location of the training institute. In December 1927, desperate CCP activists launched a new uprising in the city. A number of members of the league took part in the operation, and several were killed by Nationalist troops as the government cracked down. Others, including Le Hong Son, were arrested and placed on trial for subversion. But the Nationalist authorities were unable to prove their case against them in court, and those detained were eventually released, although they were ordered to leave China. In the meantime, Ho Tung Mau had moved the headquarters of the league to Hong Kong, where it temporarily lost contact with the CCP and the Comintern in Moscow.[16]

Despite that setback, by early 1928 the league had become an established fixture in the Vietnamese resistance movement. The organization extended its network inside the country, and continued negotiations with non-Communist nationalist parties on forming a united front against the French colonial regime. Talks with these other nationalist groups, however, were persistently marked by mutual suspicion and difficulties arising from the league's insistence that all other parties must accept its leadership. In December 1927, a new party called the Viet Nam Quoc Dan Dang (Vietnamese Nationalist Party, commonly known as the VNQDD), was established by radical nationalists in Hanoi. Although the new party had taken the same name as Phan Boi Chau's exile organization in China, now virtually moribund, it was a separate group, composed of young teachers and journalists in Tonkin and northern Annam. In the months following its creation, the VNQDD held talks with the league. On one occasion, it even sent delegates to Siam to talk with league representatives, but the latter apparently failed to show up for the meeting. There were in any case some serious differences in ideology: VNQDD leaders had adopted the moderately socialist "three people's principles" of Sun Yat-sen as their formal program, rejecting the Marxist concept of class struggle. There were also differences on the tactical level, since VNQDD leaders insisted on keeping the leadership of their organization inside the country. As a result, competition between the two groups soon became fierce.[17]

Beyond its difficulties in establishing a common stand with other anticolonial groups inside Vietnam, the league was beginning to encounter serious internal fissures. Although it had rapidly become the most dynamic force within the Vietnamese nationalist movement, attracting new recruits from all three regions of Vietnam as well as from among the Viet Kieu abroad, under the surface discontent was brewing. The league had been constructed with two competing agendas, with the potential contradictions finessed by its agile founder, Nguyen Ai Quoc. Although inspired by the desire for national independence, the league leadership under Quoc was ultimately committed to the internationalist goals of Marxism-Leninism. To a Marxist, the fundamental conflict in the modern world was rooted in class inequalities between the oppressed peoples and their exploiters. Yet much of the league's propaganda had focused on the issue of national independence, and the nature of its following tended to reflect that fact, since many of its early followers were converts from other nationalist parties.

Nguyen Ai Quoc's desire to adapt Lenin's theses combining the dual issues of nationalism and class struggle to conditions in Indochina continued to be reflected in the leadership immediately after his departure from Canton in the spring of 1927. But while some of his successors, such as the Tam Tam Xa veterans Ho Tung Mau and Le Hong Son, had apparently become avid Marxists, others, like the veteran nationalist Lam Duc Thu, had not. This split became increasingly visible in the spring of 1928, when the league held an informal meeting at Lam Duc Thu's home in Hong Kong. At that meeting, Thu took over the leadership of the organization and was able to push through a platform that stressed nationalism over social revolution.[18]

For the first three years of the league's existence, competition between nationalism and social revolution had been contained. But after the meeting in Hong Kong the conflict broke out into the open, resulting ultimately in the destruction of the league. At first the discontent was centered within the leading group of the league's regional committee in Tonkin; its first secretary was Tran Van Cung. A native of Nghe An and a former member of the Tan Viet Revolutionary Party who had taken part in the December 1927 Canton uprising and served time in a Chinese jail, Cung had attended the meeting at Lam Duc Thu's house in Hong Kong and had been distressed by what he considered the ideological flabbiness of the line adopted by the new league leadership. He didn't believe it possible to talk of national independence and love of country and expect to earn the support of poor peasants and workers. He felt it necessary to address their practical economic interests. Cung's argument was not well received at the meeting. On his return to Hanoi, he persuaded other members of the Tonkin regional committee of the correctness of his views, and they began to plot a response.[19]

One source for their concern was the composition of the organization's membership. In Cung's view, the league had not been making a sufficient effort to recruit followers from among the small but growing industrial proletariat. The labor organizer Ton Duc Thang was a prominent exception. After working as a naval mechanic in France during World War I, he had returned to Indochina to set up a union among dockworkers in Saigon, and a few "red" unions had been established in factories in the industrial cities in central Vietnam. Elsewhere, however, relatively few workers had been introduced into the league. Recruitment continued to rely primarily on the activities of returning students from China—most of whom were from scholar-gentry families—who spread support for the movement among friends and relatives.[20]

Likewise, there was relatively little activity by league members in rural areas, although a few peasant associations were set up in 1928. Even though anti-French riots had been breaking out in various areas of the countryside since the French takeover at the end of the last century, the league had not made a major effort to build a base outside the cities. The vast majority of members of the league (the Sûreté estimate was 90 percent) came from the urban bourgeoisie.

A second source of discontent on the part of Tran Van Cung and his colleagues was the dilatory attitude taken by the league leadership in moving toward the establishment of a formal Communist Party, a decision that they felt was absolutely necessary to firm up the ideological underpinnings of the Vietnamese revolutionary movement. According to Cung, when he had raised the issue at the May 1928 meeting in Hong Kong, Lam Duc Thu had brushed him off with a simple "We'll see."

Such radical discontents had apparently begun to surface before the convening of the Sixth Comintern Congress, held in Moscow the summer of 1928. But the congress—the first to be held since the 1924 meeting, which had been attended by Nguyen Ai Quoc—undoubtedly added impetus to the complaints, for the decisions reached in Moscow signaled a major shift in direction for global Communist strategy. Disappointed by recent events in China, where the Leninist alliance between Nationalists and Communists had ended in a bloody massacre of CCP militants, and impelled by domestic political considerations to adopt a more leftist line in internal affairs, Joseph Stalin (who was now engaged in a major struggle with Leon Trotsky for dominance over the Soviet Communist Party) compelled the delegates at the congress to abandon the broad united front strategy that had been originally initiated at the Second Congress eight years earlier. Communist parties in colonial areas were now instructed to reject alliances with bourgeois nationalist parties on the grounds that the native bourgeoisie had turned away from revolution and could no longer be trusted as an ally of the proletariat. Furthermore, Communist parties themselves must be purged of their unreliable petty bourgeois elements and "bolshevized." Practically speaking, this meant that working-class representation in all communist organizations should be increased, and Party rectification movements initiated to cleanse them of impure elements. Party members with middle-class origins should be required to undergo a process of "proletarianization" (often that meant literally to put on overalls and attempt to find work in factories) to increase their awareness of the proletarian outlook.[21]

The Sixth Congress, under Stalin's prodding, claimed to see the rise of a new revolutionary wave on the horizon, as growing economic instability in Europe raised the specter of a new world depression. Communist and proto-Communist organizations throughout the world were instructed to do their utmost, not only to increase their own capacity to respond to the rising level of discontent in their own societies, but also to encourage the heightening of revolutionary awareness by initiating strikes and mass demonstrations among the workers and the poorer peasantry, and to set up Party cells in factories, schools, and villages, all in preparation for a future revolutionary upsurge.

Since it was not yet a formal Communist Party, the Vietnamese Revolutionary Youth League did not have a formal representative at the Sixth Congress, but three Vietnamese did attend the meeting as representatives of the FCP. One was Nguyen Van Tao, a native of Nghe An who had been expelled from school in Saigon for radical activities during the mid-1920s and later traveled secretly to France. Speaking under the name of An, Tao presented a major address at the congress. Tao argued that, although some felt that Vietnam was not ready for a Communist Party, there was in fact a small and growing proletariat in the country and a Communist Party was urgently needed, because the local bourgeoisie could not lead the revolution. In fact, such "national reformist" organizations as the Constitutionalist Party and the Parti Annamite de l'Indépendance (formed in Paris by Nguyen Ai Quoc's onetime colleague Nguyen The Truyen) were "absolutely dangerous" in arguing for the peaceful evacuation of Indochina by the French, since such an eventuality might reduce popular support for a genuine social revolution. After the Sixth Congress adjourned, the Comintern sent a secret directive to the league through the FCP providing instructions for future activities.[22]

The decisions of the Sixth Congress, when they became available in Vietnam at the end of the year, sharpened the debate and intensified the determination of the radical faction in Tonkin to further its bid to transform the league into a more ideologically focused Communist Party. The leader of the agitation continued to be Tran Van Cung, who had become convinced by his own experience working as a factory laborer that vague patriotic slogans would not induce urban workers to support the league. The organization must emphasize issues of primal importance to workers— higher salaries, better working conditions, reduced working hours—in order to win strong labor support. And this could not be done, he felt, without the transformation of the league into a full-fledged Communist Party.

The issue came to a head at the first formal congress of the Vietnamese Revolutionary Youth League, held in Hong Kong in May 1929. The seventeen delegates at the congress represented about 1200 members, with 800 from Tonkin, and 200 each from Annam and Cochin China. Soon after his arrival, Tran Van Cung met with Le Hong Son to suggest that the league be disbanded and replaced by a Communist Party. Le Hong Son was not adamantly opposed to the proposal. As a member of Nguyen Ai Quoc's inner Communist group from the beginning and one of the most formidable figures within the movement, Son was certainly committed to the eventual transformation of the league into a full-fledged Marxist-Leninist organization. For a variety of reasons, however, he felt that the congress was not an opportune time to make such a decision. In the first place, as he told Tran Van Cung in private, many delegates at the Hong Kong congress were either too politically unsophisticated or insufficiently radical to become sincere members of a new party. Second, the formation of a Communist Party at the Hong Kong congress would obviously come to the attention of Chinese authorities in neighboring Guangdong province and encourage them to increase their repressive measures against the league. Le Hong Son counseled caution and the launching of a gradual and covert process to transform the league into an organization that could more effectively carry out the directives of the Sixth Comintern Congress.[23]

The headstrong Cung, however, remained determined to take the issue to the floor of the congress. When he and other Tonkin delegates brought their proposal formally before the meeting, they found their primary opponent to be Chairman Lam Duc Thu, who remained unalterably opposed to the formation of a Communist Party and rejected the proposal out of hand. In a burst of anger, Tran Van Cung and all but one member of the Tonkin delegation left the congress, having announced their determination to form a party among their own followers back in Vietnam. Soon after their return to Hanoi, they established a new organization, called the Indochinese Communist Party (Dong duong Cong san Dang, or CPI), and began to compete with the league for recruits, claiming that the latter was composed of "false revolutionaries" who "have never carried their efforts to the proletarian masses or adhered to the Comintern."[24]

In the meantime, the remaining delegates at the congress tried to deal with the distressing rift. Most of them had been sympathetic in principle to Tran Van Cung's position, but were reluctant to speak out against their older colleague Lam Duc Thu. After the departure of the Tonkin delegates, the congress drafted a program of action and a resolution which stated that a Communist Party was needed in Indochina, but that the time was not ripe because of the unsophisticated nature of the Vietnamese working class and its lack of understanding of revolutionary theory. After approving the resolution, the delegates formally requested recognition by the Comintern and then adjourned.[25]

The dispute soon degenerated from crisis into absurdity. During the months following the congress, the new CPI began to lure members away from the league, forcing the leadership in Hong Kong to realize that they had made a serious tactical error in failing to recognize the degree of support for a Communist Party among the rank and file inside Vietnam. In August, when Ho Tung Mau and Le Quang Dat were released from jail in Canton, they returned to Hong Kong and, with the agreement of Le Hong Son, decided to create a secret Communist Party of their own within the body of the league—to be called the Annam Communist Party (An nam Cong san Dang, or ACP) and to consist of the most advanced members within the organization. Executive leadership was vested in a "special branch" consisting of Le Hong Son, Ho Tung Mau, Le Quang Dat, and two others. Because the group did not trust Lam Duc Thu, he was not consulted on the matter.[26]

The first cells of the new party were formed in Cochin China in August 1929, and it was here that, despite its name, the ACP recruited most effectively. But the split within the movement remained to be healed. That same month, Ho Tung Mau sent a letter to Tran Van Cung and the CPI leadership suggesting that delegates of both new parties should meet in Canton to discuss reunification. But the CPI leaders answered contemptuously that they were "too busy" to attend. In frustration, Ho Tung Mau suggested that the Comintern should be asked to find the means of creating a unified Communist Party:

> If we don't pay attention to forming a united Communist Party right away, then I fear we will evolve into two separate parties, one in the north and one in the south. Once two parties are formed in the country, it will be hard to achieve unity. At that time how will we be able to rely on the Third International to resolve the problem? Would it not be better to resolve it ourselves?[27]

Radical members of the Tan Viet Party in central Vietnam now added to the confusion by getting into the act. In a desperate effort to preserve their own following, many of whom had fled to their rivals, they renamed their own organization the Indochinese Communist League (Dong duong Cong san Lien doan). Thus, there were now three competing Communist Parties in French Indochina in addition to the league, which was now virtually moribund. It was at this point that Le Hong Son, still in Hong Kong, heard that Nguyen Ai Quoc was in Phichit. As the founder of the league and its most widely respected leader, Quoc might be able to use his formidable negotiating skills to find a way to resolve the problem. Without informing Lam Duc Thu, Son instructed his colleague Le Duy Diem to go to Siam to find Nguyen Ai Quoc and ask him to return to Hong Kong to help sort out the mess. Diem left at the end of August.[28]

The reaction from Moscow to the bewildering events taking place in Vietnam was predictable. On October 27 it dispatched a blistering directive to the ACP leadership, criticizing it for its failure to prevent the disintegration of the revolutionary forces in Vietnam into three rival factions. The lack of a united party at this time of promise, it said, was a serious danger to the development of communism and was "entirely mistaken." The Comintern directive openly supported Tran Van Cung's faction in Hanoi and asserted that the objective conditions for a socialist revolution were already present in Vietnam and that "the absence of a Communist Party in the midst of the development of the workers' and people's movement is becoming very dangerous for the immediate future of the revolution in Indochina." The league was criticized for showing "indecisiveness and indifference" and for not making greater efforts to recruit among Vietnamese workers. Finally, Moscow concluded that "the most urgent and important task of all the Communists in Indochina is the formation of a revolutionary party possessing the class characteristics of the proletariat, that is a popular Communist Party in Indochina." To resolve the immediate dilemma, it suggested that a unity conference be convened under the chairmanship of a representative of the Comintern, who would be sent as a mediator.[29]

The sense of urgency emanating from Moscow was undoubtedly strengthened by events taking place in the capitalist world, where the economic crisis that had been brewing as a result of bank failures in Austria had recently been intensifying. When news of the sudden collapse of the stock market in New York City reached the USSR, it must have appeared to Soviet leaders that the long anticipated final disintegration of the capitalist system was finally at hand.

Throughout the remainder of 1929, the three factions continued to dispute with one another, while competing for followers and exchanging insults (the most common was "Menshevik," a reference to Lenin's relatively moderate rivals within the Russian revolutionary movement prior to the Bolshevik revolution). One letter from Cung's group claimed that the ACP and the league were antirevolutionary and must be dispersed and fused with the CPI. If the Comintern insisted on the reunification of the movement, CPI leaders would agree to do so, but would point out the difficulties involved. From Hong Kong, Ho Tung Mau, representing the ACP, tried to placate his rivals, arguing that the membership of the league in the spring of 1929 had been too heterogeneous to create a formal Communist Party; since many league members lacked the revolutionary qualities required of a good Communist, it would have been folly to suggest a Communist Party at that time. To simply establish a secret Communist Party that would be labeled as "Bolshevik" in principle, he warned, would be just the same old league under a new name.

But the CPI was not ready to compromise. In early October, it repeated its demand that Ho Tung Mau must disband the league entirely. Cung argued that he and his colleagues had realized that no one at the May conference except themselves wanted to form a secret party. They had made the proposal to "mark in the history of the revolution that the Revolutionary Youth League was not Communist, and to enable the masses to see the differences between the League and the true Communists." When the conference rejected their proposal, they decided to quit the league and set up their own organization. With regard to finding a solution to the split, Cung suggested that any individual with the proper revolutionary credentials could be accepted into the CPI. Others could wait and try again. He also said that the CPI was willing to cooperate with the VNQDD on a temporary basis, but considered it to be a purely nationalist organization. Cooperation could take place only if the VNQDD agreed not to oppose CPI efforts to lure its members to its own party. As to the possibility that Nguyen Ai Quoc might return to Hong Kong to seek reunification, "If he returns," Cung declared enigmatically, "we will follow toward him the same as toward you."[30]

At the end of October, the CPI sent a representative, Do Ngoc Dzu, to Hong Kong at Ho Tung Mau's request to meet with ACP leaders in an attempt to reach a solution without outside intervention. But Dzu, presumably acting on orders, continued to insist that unity could take place only if the ACP was first dissolved, whereupon its members could apply to enter the CPI as individuals. Not surprisingly, the ACP delegates declined the offer.[31]

While the dispute was going on, the ACP leadership in Hong Kong awaited the visit of the inspector that the Comintern had referred to in its letter of October 27. They had already been informed by letter from a colleague in Moscow that their request for admission into the Comintern would not be granted until the inspection had been completed. In fact, the Dalburo, which had opened a new branch office in Shanghai (also known as the Far Eastern Bureau, here FEB) in the fall of 1928, had just decided to create a new structure to govern its relations with the various communist organizations in the region. The plan called for the creation of a new organization called the Federation of Communist Groups of Insulinde, with headquarters in Singapore. All Communist organizations in Asia that were not already organized into a national party (such as the fledgling organizations in Southeast Asia, including Indochina) were to be placed under the control of this organization, which would itself be under direct supervision of a "secretariat of the oppressed peoples of the East" attached to the FEB in Shanghai. Apparently, ACP leaders became aware of this plan sometime in the fall; a letter written by Ho Tung Mau in mid-November indicates that a Chinese delegate en route from Singapore to Shanghai to discuss the issue had stopped in Hong Kong on November 2 and told them about the project. The Vietnamese, however, were not happy about the idea. The South Seas (Nan Yang) Communist Party, which had been created in Singapore in the mid-1920s and would presumably have provided the direction for the new regional bureau there, was composed primarily of overseas Chinese from Singapore and was under the general supervision of CCP headquarters in Shanghai. Thus, in effect, the Vietnamese revolutionary movement would be placed under the ultimate direction of the CCP. In the view of many Vietnamese comrades, Chinese revolutionaries had a tendency to focus exclusively on their own objectives and were often condescending in their attitude toward the activities of other nationalities. Le Hong Son ordered Le Quang Dat to go to Shanghai to argue the ACP's case to be named a national party directly under the FEB.[32]

On December 16, 1929, Ho Tung Mau and one of his colleagues met with a representative of the Comintern who had arrived in Hong Kong on a tour to inspect all the communist organizations in the region. The representative advised his hosts that neither the Revolutionary Youth League (or its successor, the ACP) nor the CPI and the Indochinese Communist League yet merited the title "Communist" and could not be officially recognized by the Comintern. Until a united party had been created, directives for all Marxist groups in Indochina would be provided by the CCP.[33]

In Siam, Nguyen Ai Quoc had heard about the split within the league from two delegates to the May 1929 congress, and in September he had written a letter to the leaders of the new CPI, declaring bluntly that he could have no confidence in any people except true Communists. They could demonstrate their good faith, he wrote, by seeking affiliation with the Comintern, and he invited them to send representatives to a meeting to be held in 1930 in Vladivostok. But CPI leaders, who received the letter from a Vietnamese émigré arriving from Siam and read it out loud during a Party meeting in Hanoi, took no decision on the matter. Quoc tried twice to go to Vietnam, but was unable to cross the border because of police vigilance. He was about to make a third attempt when a colleague recently arrived from Hong Kong (presumably Le Duy Diem) informed him about the urgency of the situation. Quoc immediately left for Bangkok, and embarked on a ship for Canton.[34]

Nguyen Ai Quoc arrived on January 20, 1930, checked into a hotel, and wrote his colleagues in Hong Kong, asking them to come to meet him in Canton. Presumably, he was afraid of being apprehended by the ever watchful British police at the border. Eventually, however, they convinced him that it was safer to meet in Hong Kong, where British authorities were relatively tolerant of the activities of aliens residing in the territory so long as they did not offer a perceived threat to the stability of the crown colony itself. Living conditions in Hong Kong were generally more comfortable than in neighboring China, and the predominantly Chinese population was relatively quiescent, although labor strikes had broken out on several occasions during the 1920s. Ho Tung Mau sent one of his followers to Canton to escort Quoc back to Hong Kong by train, where he settled in a hotel room in Kowloon.[35]

After arriving, Nguyen Ai Quoc went immediately to Le Hong Son's apartment, where he familiarized himself with the situation and held discussions with Mau and other League members. He criticized them for their isolation from the masses and their failure to anticipate the split, which he described as "puerile." He also got in touch with the local CCP headquarters. Then he invited members of the three warring factions inside Indochina to come to Hong Kong to prepare for the fusion of the three groups into a new party.[36]

By the end of January 1930, representatives from the ACP and the CPI inside Indochina had arrived in Hong Kong. Delegates from the Indochinese Communist League had left Indochina by ship, but were arrested en route on suspicion of gambling. On February 3, the conference convened in a small house in a working-class district in Kowloon. Later it became necessary to shift to other locations, including one session that reportedly took place under a soccer stadium in Kowloon. There were two delegates each from the ACP and the CPI. Le Hong Son and

Ho Tung Mau attended the conference as representatives from the old Revolutionary Youth League headquarters in Hong Kong.[37]

According to accounts by the participants, agreement was surprisingly easy to achieve. Nguyen Ai Quoc opened the meeting by identifying himself and then gently lectured the delegates for having permitted the break to take place. He assigned responsibility for the split to both sides, and emphasized that the main problem at the moment was to restore unity to the movement. It soon became evident that the existing differences between the members of the two factions were based more on personal pique and regional sensitivities than on ideology. Members from Tonkin and Cochin China harbored suspicions of each other's true revolutionary credentials (northerners frequently disparaged southerners as lazy and easygoing, while the latter criticized their northern compatriots for being dour and stubborn), while both resented the dominant position that members from Nguyen Ai Quoc's native Nghe An province occupied within the leadership of the movement. With the ACP leadership, undoubtedly chastened by Moscow's criticism in its October letter, now convinced of the need to create a formal Communist Party, the only major issue remaining to be resolved was how to end the split and integrate the factions, including the absent Indochinese Communist League, into a single party on mutually satisfactory terms. Here Nguyen Ai Quoc's position as Comintern representative served him to advantage. He suggested that the simplest solution was neither the absorption of one party by the other nor the merger of the existing parties, but the dissolution of both and the formation of a new organization, with a new program and new statutes, and into which all who approved the aims and met the standards could be accepted as members. There was a quick and probably relieved acceptance of the proposal by all the delegates.[38]

The only remaining point of contention was the name to be given to the new united party. Nguyen Ai Quoc had already given some thought to the issue prior to convening the conference. In a note to himself dated January 6, he had listed five main points to be brought up at the founding conference; one was to agree on a new name for the party. At the meeting, he followed up on his idea, contending that neither of the names of the existing parties was adequate, since "Indochina" implied all of Southeast Asia, while "Annam," a Chinese term meaning "pacified south," was now used by the French for its protectorate in central Vietnam. He suggested that a new party should have a new name, Vietnamese Communist Party (Dang Cong san Viet Nam, or VCP). Quoc had already settled on the suitability of that term prior to convening the conference. Not only was Vietnam the formal name of the country under the independent Nguyen dynasty in the nineteenth century, it also conjured up the image of the first state of Nam Viet, which had emerged in the Red River valley prior to the Chinese conquest in the second century B.C. The name was immediately accepted.[39]

With the most thorny problems out of the way, the remaining issues were resolved without difficulty. Further sessions, allegedly held "in an atmosphere of unity and love," drafted the new party's program of action, regulations, and statutes. Nguyen Ai Quoc had seen a brief report of the results of the Sixth Comintern Congress and was at least generally aware of the changes in the general line of the movement at that time. But he had apparently not received a copy of a lengthy critique of the Revolutionary Youth League's 1929 program that recently had been written at Comintern headquarters in Moscow. "Tâches immédiates des Communistes indochinoises," which had apparently been written sometime in December, was sent to FCP headquarters in Paris, but for some reason not to league headquarters in Hong Kong. Le Hong Phong, one of the cofounders of the league, who was now in the USSR for training, had obtained a copy in Moscow and sent it to a colleague in Cochin China. Unfortunately, it did not arrive until after the close of the unity conference.[40]

The Comintern criticized the league's program for vagueness on a variety of counts. Although it conceded that the only possible revolution in Vietnam now was a bourgeois democratic revolution, it was vital that the working class play the leading role in the struggle. To establish its dominance over the movement, the future Communist Party must combat with all its vigor "national reformist" influence (e.g., the Constitutionalist Party) and seek to profit from divisions within the local bourgeoisie. The document was also critical of the program's interpretation of the Leninist two-stage revolution. With regard to the theory of accession to power in several phases, it said, this theory "is a form of reformism and not of communism, since it is impossible to predict the existence of stages in the revolutionary movement which would enable it to pass from a minimal success to a direct attack on the regime." Such an approach, it warned, "in reality only serves to place a brake on the actions of the masses and to weaken them instead of stimulating them." In any event, it declared, the theory of a revolution divided into stages would leave the direction of the struggle in the hands of a small number of Communist intellectuals, a result that would be contrary to the elementary principles of Marxism. "It is the masses who make revolution," Moscow intoned, "and the Communists are just there to instruct, organize, and direct the masses." Finally, it concluded that it was not necessary to wait until the ACP was completely organized before provoking a revolutionary uprising.[41]

The appeal that was drawn up at the February 1930 conference showed that the shift in strategy previously adopted by the Sixth Congress in July 1928 had had some effect on Quoc's own thinking. While the appeal was addressed to the majority of the population in Vietnam (workers, peasants, soldiers, youths, students, oppressed and exploited "brothers and sisters"), it deleted Quoc's old idea of a proletariat-peasant vanguard (thus implying a broader class revolution) and openly stated that the new organization was "a party of the proletariat" that would struggle to overthrow French imperialism, feudalism, as well as the counterrevolutionary bourgeoisie, and to create a "worker-peasant and soldier government." That government would gradually give way to the second, or socialist, stage of the revolution.[42]

Still, Nguyen Ai Quoc was clearly not yet ready to abandon entirely the broad Leninist united front approach that he had advocated during the life of the league. A strategy document approved at the conference called for efforts to win the support of intellectuals, middle peasants (a Party term for farmers who had enough land to live on, but not to hire laborers), the petty bourgeoisie, as well as nationalist groups such as Nguyen An Ninh's Hope of Youth party. Even rich peasants and small landlords could be rallied to the cause so long as they were not clearly counterrevolutionary. Only the Constitutionalist Party, led by the moderate reformer Bui Quang Chieu, was clearly defined as reactionary.[43]

From remarks in a February 18 letter to the FEB, written several days after the close of the conference, it seems clear that Nguyen Ai Quoc believed that the documents drawn up at the unity conference were in conformity with the new Comintern line. In fact, however, they departed from Moscow's new strategy in several respects; although Quoc was still a devoted adherent to the Leninist strategy in the colonial areas, Moscow had moved on. It was a departure that would soon emerge as a major source of difficulty for him in coming years.

At the end of the conference, the meeting had selected a provisional central committee, and then the delegates prepared to return to Indochina to set up a local apparatus for the new party. A few days later, Nguyen Ai Quoc left for Shanghai. Prior to departure, he had written to Le Quang Dat, telling him he intended to deal with the FEB about its relationship with the new party in Indochina. Then, in his letter of February 18, he reported the results of the unity conference to Hilaire Noulens, the new chief of the FEB in Shanghai. The league—which

Quoc described as "the eggshell from which come [*sic*] the young Communist bird"—had now formally been abolished and a new party had been formed. It had 204 members in Tonkin and Annam, 51 in Cochin China, 15 in China, and 40 in Siam. Mass organizations for students, peasants, and workers that had been created by the league and its successor parties during the late 1920s now contained over 3,500 followers.[44]

With the formation of the new party in February 1930, Nguyen Ai Quoc was prepared to move to the next stage of the revolution in Vietnam. As he described it in this letter to Noulens, the Party was only one of several political parties and factions in Vietnam, including the Constitutionalists, the Indochinese Communist League (soon to be dissolved, with most members joining the VCP), the Hanoi-based VNQDD, and the now defunct Revolutionary Youth League. Although the Communist Party was still young and small, he declared, it is "the best organized and the most active of them all." Now that the fighting between the two dominant Communist factions had been brought to an end, he expressed confidence that the VCP, armed with a correct policy and newfound internal unity, would begin to progress rapidly. Nguyen Ai Quoc's magic sword, the weapon that the fifteenth century patriot Le Loi had used to free his compatriots from their external enemies, was now finally within his grasp.

VI | RED NGHE TINH

To Nguyen Ai Quoc, the creation of the Vietnamese Communist Party was the fulfillment of a dream, the culmination of a process that had begun with his departure from the Saigon wharf almost twenty years previously. With the outbreak of the Great Depression in the West and the rise of a new era of activism inside Indochina, it must have indeed appeared that, as the Comintern had recently predicted, the period of temporary stability in the world capitalist order had come to an end, ushering in a new era of global revolution.

But the creation of the VCP raised questions in his mind that needed to be answered. Where was the new party to fit within the organizational structure of the Comintern? Was it going to be placed under the guidance of the new secretariat headquartered in Singapore or, as Nguyen Ai Quoc hoped, would it be accepted as an independent party directly under the authority of the Far Eastern Bureau in Shanghai? In addition, what was his own new role to be? Would Moscow expect him to continue to serve as a representative of the Comintern or to take charge of the new Vietnamese party? If the latter were to be the case, where would he be based, since he could not return to Indochina under pain of arrest and possible execution?

It was partly to seek answers to these questions, as well as to report to his superior Hilaire Noulens on the formation of the new organization, that he left for Shanghai on February 13, 1930, only a few days after the close of the unity conference. Dressed in a thin suit hardly appropriate for the chilly Shanghai winter, he rented a room in a cheap hotel and sought to establish contact with Noulens, whose FEB office was located in a European-style building along bustling Nanjing Road, the main commercial thoroughfare in the city.

With the local authorities, both Chinese and Western, on the lookout for radicals, meeting his superior was difficult. On the eighteenth, in a mood of obvious frustration, Quoc sent a detailed letter to Noulens, reporting on the creation of the new party and concluding with a post-script written in his somewhat eccentric English:

> I wish to see you as soon as possible, 1) because this report was written already two days and not reach you. There is too much delay. 2) we can resolve all these question in some hours, and I have spent already five days. 3) I am obliged to wait, doing nothing, while work is waiting for me, elsewhere.

In the letter, Nguyen Ai Quoc also registered his firm disagreement with Moscow's plan to place the VCP under the new Southeast Asian secretariat to be based in Singapore, arguing that Vietnam's geographical proximity to China and the fact that the strength of the Party was based primarily in the northern part of the country made it more appropriate to designate it as an independent organization located directly under the FEB through a suboffice located in Hong Kong. The Comintern wanted to create regional parties, regardless of ethnic or national origins, while Quoc wanted each party to have its own national character.

Presumably Quoc was eventually able to meet with Noulens, because a few days later he wrote to the Dalburo in Moscow declaring that he had already presented his report. Evidently he was also able to win Noulens's tentative agreement to place the VCP under a new Southern Bureau, to be established under his direction in Hong Kong. But not all of his questions had been answered:

> Now I don't know what exactly is my position. Am I a member of the PCF or the PCV [the French Communist Party or the Vietnamese Communist Party]? Until new orders arrive, I will continue to direct the work of the PCV. But under what title? I am not directly involved in the activities of the PCV because I can't return to Indochina. At this moment they have honored me by condemning me to death *à contumace* [in absentia]. Is my mandate with the Comintern terminated? If not, will I be connected with the regional bureau here? Please ask the Executive Committee for a decision.[1]

Before leaving, Nguyen Ai Quoc contacted Nguyen Luong Bang, a graduate of the league's training institute in Canton who was now working in Shanghai, in order to provide him with instructions on how to agitate and spread revolutionary propaganda among the more than four thousand Vietnamese troops who were then serving under the command of European officers in the French concession there. Quoc warned his colleague to be circumspect in seeking to organize them under Party leadership. Soldiers often had good intentions, but could be impetuous. He also emphasized the importance of maintaining contacts with local representatives of the Chinese Communist Party, whose help might occasionally be needed.

While awaiting word from Moscow on his own new role, Nguyen Ai Quoc returned to Hong Kong to set up the suboffice of the FEB that he had mentioned in his letter. According to his Soviet biographer, Yevgeny Kobelev, the office of the Southern Bureau was located on the second floor of a modest stone building on Hong Kong Island and operated under the disguise of a commercial firm. He took lodgings in a small flat near the airport, located across from Hong Kong Island, on Kowloon peninsula. As a cover for his own activities, he posed as a journalist and called himself L. M. Vuong. While in Hong Kong, he sought to restore contact with Communist organizations elsewhere in Southeast Asia. In his February 18 report to Noulens, he had already suggested that the VCP should maintain close links with Singapore and send a Vietnamese Party member to work there. He also asked some of his local CCP contacts for the addresses of some leading Chinese Party members in Siam, so that links with them could be established as well.

Sometime in late March, Nguyen Ai Quoc left Hong Kong on a swing through Southeast Asia to bring about the reorganization of the South Seas (Nan Yang) Communist Party, which had been decided upon by Moscow the previous year. Traveling via Bangkok, he went first to Udon Thani, in the Khorat plateau, where he reported to his compatriots on the founding of the VCP and gave them instructions on future operations in the region. According to Hoang Van Hoan, then a young VCP activist, Quoc passed on Comintern instructions that all Communists should participate in the revolutionary activities of the country where they resided in order to make contributions to the international Communist revolution. Quoc suggested that members of the now defunct league working in the area should join the soon-to-be-established Siamese Communist Party to help carry out the first, or bourgeois democratic, stage of the Siamese revolution. To assuage the fears of those Vietnamese who feared that they would no longer be identified with the struggle to liberate Vietnam, he suggested that the league's office in Udon Thani be transformed into a provincial committee of the VCP.

In mid-April, Nguyen Ai Quoc returned to Bangkok, where he presided over a meeting to establish a new Siamese Communist Party and select a provisional executive committee, which would include one Vietnamese member from the Udon Thani group. He then proceeded on to Malaya and Singapore, where he attended a conference of the South Seas Party, which had been ordered to transform itself into a new Malayan Communist Party. Both the Malayan and Siamese parties were to be placed under the FEB in Shanghai, through Nguyen Ai Quoc's Southern Bureau in Hong Kong. He returned to Hong Kong in mid-May.[2]

While Nguyen Ai Quoc was busy assisting in the birth of Communist parties throughout the region, the situation inside Indochina was becoming increasingly tense. The first clear sign of trouble came in early February, when a revolt provoked by the VNQDD broke out at military posts in various parts of Tonkin. From the start, the leaders of the VNQDD had appeared to be in a hurry. Scorning the painstaking Leninist approach of building up a mass organization with popular roots throughout the country, they created an elite corps of revolutionaries dedicated to the violent overthrow of French colonial authority by means of a military insurrection. Crucial to their plans was the subversion of native Vietnamese troops serving in the colonial army.

The colonial army, which had been created in 1879 by Ly Myre de Villers, the French Governor of Cochin China, consisted of about 30,000 troops, two thirds of whom were ethnic Vietnamese. It was divided into thirty-one battalions, all of which were commanded by French officers. There was also a militia force of about 15,000 troops serving under French noncommissioned officers. Many of the Vietnamese troops had been drafted, sometimes involuntarily, by local mandarins who were required to meet an assigned quota of conscripts from their own region, regardless of the means employed. By the late 1920s, many of the Vietnamese troops serving in the ranks harbored feelings of deep resentment against the brutality of their French officers and were susceptible to the appeal of nationalism.

By 1929, the VNQDD had begun to stockpile weapons at secret depots scattered throughout the country. Most such arsenals, however, were quickly located and destroyed by the French. Then the party's problems began to escalate. When a French recruiter for plantation labor was assassinated while leaving the home of his mistress on a public street in Hanoi, the authorities suspected the VNQDD of being implicated in the plot. Hundreds of party members or followers were arrested and charged with complicity in the assassination.

Convinced that unless they acted quickly their movement would be crushed, party leaders decided to incite a revolt. By now they possessed a core following among Vietnamese troops serving in French military camps throughout Tonkin: there were more than one thousand cells, each with three to five members. In early February 1930, planned uprisings among native troops broke out at several small military posts in the Tonkin highlands, including the camp at Yen Bay, a small town located along the Red River northwest of Hanoi. The mutiny was a disaster. The insurgents at Yen Bay had planned to poison their French officers and NCOs and then launch their uprising in the middle of the night. But one participant took fright and divulged the plot to the post commandant in advance. Although the commandant was initially skeptical, he decided to take precautionary measures. As a result, when the attack broke out shortly after midnight on the morning of February 10, the French were prepared. By midmorning the rebels had been routed and the authorities had the situation under control. Other attacks at scattered outposts nearby were put down with equal ease. Most of the leaders of the party were captured; thirteen of the ringleaders were executed on June 17, 1930.[3]

Conceptually, the uprising had been badly flawed. There had been no plans for inciting the population to rise, and no fall-back measures in case of defeat. Communications links were unexpectedly disrupted at the last minute, so there was virtually no coordination between the plotters at various posts in the region. Worst of all, there was little response to the revolt in the country at large, and those members of the party who escaped capture were forced to flee across the border into China, where they split into two factions—one dedicated to the original strategy of fomenting an armed uprising, the other inclined toward a reformist approach. For a brief moment, the French were able to breathe a sigh of relief.

But the lack of public response to the Yen Bay mutiny was deceptive, for discontent with conditions in Indochina was brewing. Preliminary signs had appeared with the rise of student activism in the major cities during the mid-1920s. Although there had been a steady increase in the number of students (in 1930, there were about 7,000 public schools enrolling a total of over 340,000 students), unrest among Vietnamese youth had been sharpened by a variety of factors, including the lack of educational opportunities at higher levels. The vast majority of students were enrolled in elementary schools in their home villages.

There were still fewer than 5,000 students attending high school, and only about 500 were enrolled at the University of Hanoi, the sole institute of higher learning in Indochina. Students were also frustrated at the lack of attractive job opportunities after graduation, and the fact that in many vocations Vietnamese were paid less than their European counterparts for similar work. Such sentiments undoubtedly added to the rising chorus of protest among Vietnamese in all three regions against foreign domination.

After the student activism of the mid-1920s subsided, it was quickly replaced by a new wave of worker discontent. Under the impact of a rise in French capital investment, the commercial and manufacturing sector had been growing rapidly in Indochina, particularly since the end of World War I. The primary beneficiaries of this rise in business activity were the thousands of Europeans residing in Indochina, as well as the large community of overseas Chinese. Inevitably, however, the effects began to be felt among the native population, most notably in the growth of a small but increasingly vocal urban middle class. At the same time, a proletariat numbering almost 200,000 by the late 1920s was forming. Some worked in factories in the big cities, producing consumer goods such as matches, textiles, furniture, and food products. Others were employed in the coal mines along the coast east of Hanoi (there were about 50,000 coal miners in 1929, five times the level at the end of World War I), on the docks in Saigon and Haiphong.

The working conditions for workers on the tea and rubber plantations in the Central Highlands and along the Cambodian border were especially bad. As one observer described them:

> On all the rubber plantations, the workers had to get up at 4 o'clock in the morning. . . . Many people did not have time to eat their breakfast, yet when the gongs sounded at about 5 o'clock or a little after urging them out for the roll call all the workers had to be out in the yard by that time—for nobody was allowed to be late. The roll call took only about 20 minutes, but what a very nerve-racking twenty minutes this was! The workers' hearts thumped with fear since during roll call the supervisors and the French owners would try to find fault with them in order to have an excuse to scold them or beat them up.

After the roll call, workers proceeded to the rubber lots to begin their day's labor. Each worker had a personal responsibility for a group of 280 to 350 trees daily. Each tree first had to be tapped, then the latex had to be collected into large pails and carried back to the collection center.

Those who were too weak to fulfill their quota were often beaten, unless they were able to bribe their supervisors to ignore the infraction. Afternoons were spent performing odd chores for the owners, such as weeding or cleaning up the residential area. Not until near sundown were the workers able to return to their compounds. "For the above reasons," remarked the observer, "on the rubber plantations the people had a habit of saying that children did not have a chance to know their fathers, nor dogs their masters."[4]

The social effects of early industrialization are rarely pleasant in any society—conditions in the industrial cities of nineteenth-century Europe amply attest to that. The situation in Vietnam was no exception, for the living and working conditions for the new laboring class were almost uniformly atrocious, whether in the sweatshops of Hanoi and Haiphong, in the mines at Hong Gai along the Gulf of Tonkin, or on the rubber plantations in Cochin China. The recruitment of laborers often involved coercion and the means employed were frequently brutal, as press gangs sometimes accosted innocent passersby and forcibly bundled them into trucks for delivery to the work site. Salaries were barely at subsistence levels and working hours were long, sometimes more than twelve hours a day, seven days a week. Many members of the new working class were peasants who had been forced to abandon their farms because of debt or foreclosure by their landlord. Their new employment, however, was rarely an improvement, and frequently involved physical brutality, undernourishment, and a total absence of safety precautions. It was a situation that Charles Dickens would have recognized and deplored.

As bad as things were when capital was flowing into Vietnam, they became worse when the shock waves of the Great Depression began to have an impact on the Indochinese economy; French capital fled the country, leading to a rapid increase in unemployment. In some enterprises over half the workers were laid off. Many were forced to flee back to the overcrowded villages whence they had come, searching for a way out of their grinding poverty. Others took to protest. By the end of the 1920s, labor strikes were becoming an increasingly common phenomenon. The strikers' goals varied according to local circumstances, but most prevalent were a reduction in working hours, improved working conditions, the prohibition of cruel treatment by plant foremen (they often flogged employees who were too sick or exhausted to perform their duties), and the abolition of piecework. In some cases, the agitation was promoted by political activists of the Revolutionary Youth League or the Tan Viet Party, but for the most part it was spontaneous.

Although such sporadic strike activity was undoubtedly disquieting to the French, in itself it was no major cause for alarm, because workers were still too poorly organized and isolated from one another to coordinate their activities. More significantly, however, unrest was beginning to appear in rural areas, particularly in the coastal plains of central Vietnam. The last major expression of peasant unhappiness in the area had occurred more than two decades earlier, during the so-called Revolt of the Short-Hairs in 1908. Since that time, rural conditions had not improved. High taxes and high rents, along with mandarin venality and corruption, were a particular characteristic in Annam, where the old imperial bureaucracy still retained considerable local authority.

Detested French monopolies on the sale of salt, opium, and alcohol all contributed to peasant resentment. One French official admitted that peasants were being forced to buy salt from the government at ten times the original price. In his book *Le procès de la colonisation française* (French Colonialism on Trial), Nguyen Ai Quoc quoted a letter from Governor-General Albert Sarraut instructing all French provincial residents to arrange for alcohol and opium "houses" to be constructed in each village in areas under their jurisdiction. Some villages, Sarraut complained, were almost completely without spirits and opium. "It is only through complete and constant understanding between your administration and ours," he intoned, "that we shall obtain the best results, in the best interests of the Treasury." No wonder, Quoc observed sarcastically, that the worthy Mr. Sarraut called himself the "little father of the natives" and was adored by them.[5]

French official reports frequently enthused over the improvements brought to rural areas of Indochina by the colonial regime; in a prime example, the steady rise in the export of rice and rubber (rubber exports increased from 200 tons in 1914 to over 10,000 tons in 1929) was cited as a testimony to the benefits of French rule for the rural population. But other statistics demonstrated that the average Vietnamese farmer benefited little from French agricultural policies. With the commercialization of agriculture, land ownership was increasingly concentrated in the hands of wealthy absentee landlords, particularly in the newly expanded cultivated areas in the Mekong delta, while small farmers were frequently forced into tenancy.

In many instances, landlords forced their tenants to perform labor over a period of several weeks a year, or to contribute gifts or money at festival time. Many landlords also served as local moneylenders, charging exorbitant rates of interest to villagers, who were forced to borrow in order to feed their family or purchase seeds for next year's harvest. Village commune lands, long used as a safety valve to provide small plots for the landless poor, were absorbed by influential landlords through legal and illegal manipulation. In one case, wrote Nguyen Ai Quoc, a French official confiscated several hectares of land from one village and turned them over to a Catholic village nearby. When the plundered peasants lodged a complaint, they were jailed. Some observers critical of the French colonial regime have claimed that despite the rise in grain production throughout the country during the first quarter of the twentieth century, the per capita consumption of rice actually declined during the same period. While such estimates might be exaggerated, even French officials at the time conceded that by the beginning of the 1930s, there was a high level of peasant misery in some areas. In a few villages in Quoc's home province of Nghe An, where overpopulation had become a serious problem, over half of the population had no land.[6]

To these chronic conditions were now added three new factors: disastrous floods in central Vietnam, drought conditions in other regions, and a severe fall in the price of rice. With rice losing value in the Great Depression, land values themselves tumbled and countless acres of land were simply abandoned by their peasant owners. French reports conceded that in some districts one third of the population was suffering from hunger.

A pervasive sense of disquiet—and in some cases desperation—affected much of Vietnamese society as the new decade dawned. In March 1930, riots broke out at the Phu Rieng rubber plantation, situated in the "terre rouge" zone in western Cochin China near the Cambodian border. A few weeks later, labor strikes erupted at a thread factory in Nam Dinh, a manufacturing center in Tonkin, and at a match factory at Ben Thuy, an industrial suburb of Vinh, the capital of Nghe An province. As a result of official efforts to suppress the unrest, several demonstrators were killed and scores wounded. The incident at Vinh was of particular significance, because many of the workers involved were recent migrants from rural areas and still had close ties with their relatives in the neighboring villages. As problems in the countryside began to intensify, peasants began to join worker riots and mount demonstrations of their own. In Thanh Chuong district, a few miles to the north of Nguyen Ai Quoc's home village of Kim Lien and one of the areas suffering most from the economic malaise in the central provinces, several thousand angry farmers marched to a local plantation whose owner had allegedly confiscated communal land and brutalized his workers. Property was destroyed and a hammer-and-sickle flag was placed on the administration building. When units of the French Foreign Legion arrived to suppress the attack, dozens of demonstrators were killed or wounded.

According to a French report written after the suppression of these riots, the aims of the demonstrators were diverse. Many of the leaders were intellectuals motivated by the desire for national independence or the creation of a "Communist paradise." Peasants tended to join the movement out of misery and desperation, or as the result of a generalized hatred of the French that had been deliberately aroused by outside agitators. Thai Van Giai, an activist who was later captured by the authorities and interrogated, said, "The masses aren't Communists, but they are discontented. The landlords exploit the peasants. The government hasn't introduced irrigation to increase land productivity. And the mandarins live off the population." Asked why the peasants resented the French, he replied, "The people know nothing about the French administration, which is too far removed from their daily lives. They know only the mandarins, whom they despise."[7]

From the start, Communist organizers had played a major part in provoking the unrest in central Vietnam. In late 1929, the CPI leadership had sent one of its leading members, a Nghe An native named Nguyen Phong Sac, to central Vietnam to help organize the workers in the Vinh area. To carry out his assignment, he took employment at the Ben Thuy match factory. In February 1930, only two weeks after the unity conference in Hong Kong, a provincial committee was founded in Nghe An and began to form cells in factories and peasant associations in the villages. Lacking firm directions from the Party leadership, local cadres acted on their own initiative. As Thai Van Giai commented to his captors a few months later:

> The Communist Party prepared the movement. It founded cells, spread tracts and organized meetings. It was able to act in total liberty in the villages where no one interfered with them. Notables did not dare to act out of fear, while the mandarins didn't pay any attention to us and the French were ignorant of what was taking place.

Asked how the demonstrations were organized, Giai said that activists beat the drum at the communal house to mobilize the local population. Those who were hesitant or resisted were intimidated with batons. In a few cases, he conceded, houses or pagodas were burned down, while some of those opposed to the demonstrations were tortured or killed, but that was not standard procedure. Assassinations of suspected Vietnamese collaborators were conducted secretly, because the Party "didn't want to frighten the masses."[8]

To many zealous young Party members at the time, Moscow's recent prediction that Asia was on the verge of revolt must have seemed clairvoyant. In its advice to leaders of the Revolutionary Youth League in late 1929, the Comintern had stated pointedly that the lack of an organized Communist Party should not prevent revolutionaries from giving their active support to a spontaneous uprising led by workers and peasants. Above all, Moscow reasoned, the league should not fall behind the masses in its revolutionary activism. As for the need to ascertain whether the situation favored the revolutionary forces, the Comintern could provide little assistance, beyond the suggestion that the final decision on such questions could be reached only by the leadership on the spot.

The Comintern had undoubtedly been impressed by continued unrest in China, where rebel groups under the ambitious CCP leader Mao Zedong had just taken refuge from the fury of Chiang Kai-shek's suppressive efforts in the mountains of Jiangxi province, southwest of Shanghai. For the newly created VCP, however, the rising crisis in Vietnam was fraught with dilemmas as well as opportunities. Despite Moscow's gratuitous comment that it was "not necessary to wait" until a Communist Party had been completely organized before inciting a revolt, the new party was certainly ill prepared for a major confrontation with the French colonial regime. It had just survived an emotionally scarifying split within the movement, and its leaders were untried and uncertain. A formal central committee had not yet been created, and the Party's local apparatus was just in the process of formation. Until such a committee could be formed, the existing leadership remained in Hong Kong, far removed from events inside the country. If the Party attempted to spark a revolt in the central provinces, there was no guarantee that the rest of the country would follow. Even if hostility and discontent among the workers and peasants could be translated into action, it was unclear whether the restless urban bourgeoisie would come to their assistance or simply watch in silence while the French restored order in rebellious areas. To a revolutionary with a sense of history, conditions in Vietnam probably resembled those in the Russia of 1905 rather than 1917.

Such at any rate was the view of prudent members of the Party leadership. Even the firebrand Tran Van Cung, head of the rump group that had broken with the league to form the CPI in 1929, was cautious. According to French intelligence reports, when VNQDD leaders contacted Cung to solicit his support for their own planned uprising in February 1930, he had rejected their proposal on the grounds that conditions for revolution were not ripe. When some local members of Cung's party wanted to take part in the Yen Bay insurrection, their leaders advised them against it.

Nguyen Ai Quoc almost certainly agreed. For one thing, the VNQDD lacked a disciplined party organization. For another, as he had warned Nguyen Luong Bang in Shanghai, it was important to be careful in attempting to mobilize soldiers because of their unreliability. In a comment to comrades in Siam a few weeks after the Yen Bay uprising, he remarked that he and other delegates attending the February unity conference in Hong Kong had attempted in vain to contact the VNQDD leadership to advise them against an insurrection.[9]

For Party operatives involved in riding the wave of anger and unrest in the central provinces, doubts and hesitancies about the immediate future were a luxury they could ill afford. Urged on by Nguyen Phong Sac, the militant activist who had now been assigned responsibility for the Party's newly organized regional committee for Annam, cadres in the area continued to stoke the fires of revolution in the countryside.

By early September, the unrest threatened to get out of hand. Demonstrators in several districts along the Ca River northwest of Vinh, acting under instructions from the Party's provincial committee, began to take power into their own hands, evicting the local authorities and forming village associations to establish peasant power at the local level. Such hastily organized peasant councils, known as "soviets" in the Bolshevik style and usually dominated by the poorer peasants in the village, abolished debts and tax collections, and ordered reductions in land rents and the confiscation of communal lands previously seized by landlords and "local bullies"; at the same time, village self-defense militia units were formed to maintain law and order. Meanwhile, labor strikes continued to spread in factories at Ben Thuy, while students in Vinh and at the National Academy in Hué organized student unions and voiced their support for the cause.[10]

In some cases, zealots took even more severe action, seizing the land of landlords and assassinating "local tyrants," abolishing traditional village customs such as expensive funeral and wedding ceremonies, and exacting stiff punishments for "backward" habits such as gambling, stealing, and prostitution. In a few cases, they even formed voluntary "collectives" (*hop tac xa*) to mobilize the population to work together and share the harvest among the village's families.

Faced with the threat of a total loss of government power throughout the central provinces, the French authorities dispatched units of the Legionnaires to bolster the imperial civil guard. On September 12, when thousands of demonstrators began to march from the village of Yen Xuyen toward the provincial capital—reportedly to seize the local office of the Bank of Indochina—imperial troops were dispatched to bar the route to

Vinh, while French fighter planes bombed the column of marchers. After an all-day battle—described by acting French Governor-General René Robin as "the most critical day"—the route between Vinh and Yen Xuyen was littered with hundreds of dead and wounded Vietnamese.[11]

While the Party's local organs were preoccupied with the task of how best to respond to the unrest in the Vietnamese countryside, leading elements were preparing to hold the first session of its provisional central committee in Hong Kong. The original plan drafted at the unity conference in February had called for the immediate establishment of three regional committees, in Tonkin, Annam, and Cochin China. Each committee would then select representatives for a nine-man provisional Central Committee to meet somewhere in Tonkin as soon as all delegates had been named. When Tran Phu, the bright young student from the Stalin School in Moscow, returned to Hong Kong in March, Nguyen Ai Quoc conferred with him and then sent him on to Vietnam to assist the activities of internal Party leaders.

An initial attempt to hold the meeting in April, however, proved abortive, and when it was postponed until July, the site was shifted to Hong Kong. But two of the delegates were arrested en route to the Hong Kong conference, so the date was postponed once again, until late October. To make final preparations, Tran Phu returned to Hong Kong in September to confer with Nguyen Ai Quoc and report on the situation in Indochina. Perhaps because of his familiarity with Marxist-Leninist doctrine, a consequence of his years in the USSR, Phu had been selected by the regional committee in Tonkin as a member of the provisional Central Committee, and he had been asked to write a draft political program based on the latest twists of the Comintern line, replacing the original drawn up by Nguyen Ai Quoc at the February unity meeting. Ideological differences between the two versions were destined to play a significant role in the debate that would take place at the forthcoming conference.[12]

Soon after Nguyen Ai Quoc and Tran Phu made a quick trip to Shanghai to report to Noulens and obtain his approval for the new Party program, delegates began to arrive in Hong Kong to attend the Party's first formal meeting since February (it would be known hereafter as the first plenary session of the Central Committee). It was probably through the reports of these delegates that Nguyen Ai Quoc received his first detailed account of the rising current of unrest inside the country. During the spring and summer, he had spent considerable time out of Hong

Kong, either in Southeast Asia or in Shanghai, and had not been able to observe the situation in detail. After assimilating this information, he wrote a report to Moscow on the events taking place in Indochina. He urged the Comintern to call on all comrades to support the suppressed masses in the beleaguered districts of central Vietnam. So far, the demonstrations there had attracted little attention in the world press, although news of the unrest had reached Paris.[13]

But there is ample reason to believe that Nguyen Ai Quoc had serious misgivings about the recent trend toward armed violence within the movement. Although the rapidly escalating crisis in the central provinces confirmed his oft stated prediction that the rural population of Indochina was on the verge of revolt against its feudal and colonial oppressors, the Party was hardly in a good position to provide the leadership necessary to turn it into a serious threat to the colonial regime. During his years in Canton, Nguyen Ai Quoc had already witnessed at first hand the heavy price of faulty preparation. In an article titled "The Party's Military Work among the Peasants," which he had written while living in Berlin in 1928, he had drawn upon his experience in south China to analyze the conditions under which a successful revolution might take place in a preindustrial society like Vietnam. In that article, he had stressed the vital importance of an effective alliance between urban workers and peasants. Although he conceded that peasants could not achieve victory without proletarian leadership and the active participation of workers, he also insisted that

the victory of the proletarian revolution is *impossible* in rural and semirural countries if the *revolutionary proletariat is not actively supported* by the mass of the peasant population. . . . In China, in India, in Latin America, in many European countries (Balkan countries, Rumania, Poland, Italy, France, Spain, etc.) the decisive ally of the proletariat in the revolution will be the peasant population. Only if the revolutionary wave sets in motion the rural masses under the leadership of the proletariat, will the revolution be able to triumph. Hence the exceptional importance of Party agitation in the countryside.[14]

This, of course, was a familiar message, one that colleagues of Nguyen Ai Quoc had heard before. And it was a message that was fully in accordance with current Comintern guidelines, as Moscow had passed them on to Asian Communist parties earlier in that year. In partial response, in the summer of 1930 the CCP, under the urging of its new general secretary Li Lisan, had launched a major effort to spark combined urban and rural uprisings against government-held regions in central and southern China, seeking a victory in one or more provinces.

But Moscow's sanction for Asian uprisings based on the formation of a worker-peasant alliance raised as many questions as it answered. Under what precise conditions would a successful rebellion of this type occur? And what policies should be adopted to maximize the chances of success? Lenin had always fended off such questions, remarking that revolution was an art, not a science. In his 1928 article cited above, Nguyen Ai Quoc agreed, quoting Lenin to the effect that armed violence in rural areas, as in urban ones, should not be unleashed "at any given moment," but only during classical revolutionary conditions, when "the yoke of the ruling classes has become intolerable, and the village masses are in a state of revolutionary ferment and ready to fight actively against the established order." Again taking his cue from Lenin, Quoc had pointed out that spontaneous actions by peasants were symptoms that the oppressed masses refused to continue in the old way, and that the country was about to enter "an immediately revolutionary situation."

But even if a Communist Party should determine that classical conditions for a successful revolution existed, it must still decide what actions to take to increase the likelihood of success. In his article, Nguyen Ai Quoc conceded that "general recipes and universal formulae for organization and tactics" were inapplicable, since conditions in one country would inescapably differ from those elsewhere. Above all, it was "the duty of the proletarian party always to take account of the concrete conditions of the moment," and to understand thoroughly the political situation and the particularities of the local population and culture, so that the proper tactics and strategy could be adopted.

One of Lenin's prerequisites for a successful revolt was that support for an overthrow of the old order should be widespread throughout the country. But Nguyen Ai Quoc had observed from his own experience in China that a revolutionary upsurge might break out initially in one province and then spread gradually to other regions. To maximize the chances of success, he recommended a particular course of action should the first stage of a revolt break out in a province where there were a number of industrial areas surrounded by a substantial rural population. At the appropriate moment, when revolutionary conditions emerged, the peasants should organize military detachments and then join with urban workers and peasants from other areas to take part in operations around the country. The armed struggle in rural areas would thus gradually take on a mass character and pass from defensive to offensive action. Quoc conceded that in some countries, where there was an infinite diversity of geographical, economic, and political conditions, the revolutionary seizure of power would not take place in the space of a few weeks or even months, but might involve a prolonged period of revolutionary agitation throughout the country.

To Nguyen Ai Quoc's experienced eye in Hong Kong, the situation in central Vietnam in the first nine months of 1930 undoubtedly displayed a number of the telltale signs that he had outlined in his article two years earlier. The unrest in the central provinces had already led to the emergence of an informal alliance between workers and peasants, while signs of similar activity were beginning to appear in other parts of the country. On the other hand, his optimism must have been tempered by a realistic skepticism over the prospects of success. As he had stated in many earlier articles, the level of political awareness and organization in Vietnam was much more rudimentary than in semicolonial countries like China. Vietnam was much smaller than China, and there was thus less likelihood that a victory could be sustained in one area. Moreover, the French were a more formidable adversary than the fragile warlord government in China. Finally, despite Moscow's confidence, he must have felt that his new revolutionary party was ill prepared to take advantage of the situation.

Thus, when reports of the unrest in central Vietnam came to Nguyen Ai Quoc's attention in the late summer of 1930, he reacted to the news with caution. In discussions with colleagues in Hong Kong just prior to the October meeting of the Central Committee, he declared that without further information on the situation he was not in a position to advise Party operatives inside Indochina on how to respond. Members of the CCP living in Hong Kong who were consulted recommended vigorous action, noting that their party had taken advantage of such opportunities in China. But Quoc was still dubious that conditions in Indochina were sufficiently ripe to move into a stage of general insurrection, even though he admitted that it might be appropriate to elect soviet organizations in rebellious villages and to redistribute farmland to local peasants. Quoc's recommendation received a mixed reception from his colleagues, some of whom were even more cautious and doubted that conditions warranted any intervention by the Party at all.[15]

Whatever his inner doubts about the consequences, however, Nguyen Ai Quoc felt that the Party was both morally and politically obligated to come to the support of the rebellious forces in the central provinces. Only by demonstrating that the VCP—and the VCP alone—stood firmly on the side of the downtrodden masses in their struggle against their oppressors could the Party solidify its relationship with the Vietnamese people and prepare the groundwork for a future revolution. If maximum publicity for the revolt could be achieved throughout the world, it would help to demonstrate the fragility of the French presence in Indochina and convince Moscow that the peoples of Indochina could make an importance contribution to the revolutionary wave in Asia.

For Nguyen Ai Quoc, then, the proper approach would be to establish a delicate balance between caution and foolhardiness, providing firm support for the rebellious elements in the central provinces, while simultaneously attempting to minimize the damage in the likelihood that the unrest would eventually be put down. Sometime in September, VCP leaders in Hong Kong sent a message to the regional committee in central Vietnam, offering this advice:

> In Thanh Chuong [and] Nam Dan at this time, the executive committee [i.e., of the Nghe An provincial committee] is already advocating violence (setting up soviets, dividing land, etc.); such policies are not appropriate, because the preparation of the Party and the masses throughout the country is inadequate, and there is no armed violence. Isolated violence in many regions at this time is premature and just blind adventurism. But with things as they are, we must thus behave in such a way as to preserve the party and soviet influence so that even if they lose, the meaning of the soviets will penetrate deeply into the minds of the masses and the influence of the party and the peasant associations will still be maintained.[16]

When the regional committee in central Vietnam received the directive for transmittal to its provincial committee is not clear. In what may have been a response to such criticism, in early October its official journal *Nguoi Lao kho* (The Oppressed) published an editorial addressed to the Party's local operatives in the region. "This," it said, "is not the time for violence," and those who maintained that it was were mistaken. Not only was support for the revolutionary cause not at a high level throughout the region, it pointed out, but the masses had little revolutionary experience, while the various village militia units that had been recently organized lacked both discipline and adequate weaponry. The Party would require a favorable general situation like a major war, the editorial concluded, to wage a successful revolt.[17]

But the Nghe An provincial committee, the primary unit in charge of directing Party operations on the spot, had a different perspective. In a circular issued in early October, it instructed its own local units to continue carrying out a policy of armed violence against reactionary elements, arguing that otherwise the masses would become discouraged and betray Party cadres to the authorities. Violence, it concluded, inspired fear in the Party's enemies and lent strength to the revolutionary cause, while struggle was the movement's only current means of subsistence. The committee circular instructed all units to continue with the confiscation of communal lands still in the hands of landlords and to carry out selective assassinations of reactionary officials. However, the provincial committee stressed too that such decisions must be cleared with higher authorities beforehand.[18]

In the shadow of the spreading insurrection in central Vietnam, Party leaders in Hong Kong continued their preparations for the first plenary session of the Central Committee. By late September, delegates from Cochin China had arrived, but there was no sign of their colleagues from Tonkin and Annam. With Nguyen Ai Quoc's approval, the former made plans to return to Indochina, but just before their departure several Tonkinese delegates arrived from Haiphong, so it was decided to go ahead with the meeting.[19]

Before convening the conference, Nguyen Ai Quoc and Tran Phu made one final trip to Shanghai to report on the situation to Noulens and to consult with him on the nature of the decisions to be adopted at the conference. Tran Phu returned to Hong Kong in early October, while Nguyen Ai Quoc remained in Shanghai for a few more days of consultations before returning on a U.S. ship in midmonth.[20]

On October 20, a few days after Nguyen Ai Quoc's return to Hong Kong, the Central Committee convened in a small flat on Khai Yee Street on Hong Kong Island. By then, delegates from all three regions of the country, and representing a total Party membership of about 900, were in attendance (although one delegate who had managed to make it to Hong Kong got lost and could not find the location of the meeting). Nguyen Ai Quoc served both as chairman and representative of the Comintern. Also in attendance, as an alternate, was an attractive, dark-skinned young Party member named Nguyen Thi Minh Khai, who had been sent to Hong Kong in April 1930 to serve as Nguyen Ai Quoc's assistant at the Southern Bureau.[21]

The primary topic for discussion was the adoption of a new political program to replace the provisional document that had been drafted under Nguyen Ai Quoc's direction at the unity conference in February. That Quoc's February program was not in full accordance with current strategical thinking in Moscow had already seemed clear from the critique sent by the Comintern to Paris in December 1929. That critique, which was not in Nguyen Ai Quoc's hands when he convened the unity conference, had pointed to a number of ideological shortcomings in the manifesto of the Revolutionary Youth League—shortcomings that were still reflected in the February program. In Moscow's view, the manifesto had not only placed insufficient emphasis on the central role of the working class in the Vietnamese revolution, it also held to the now discredited Leninist theory of a two-stage revolution.[22]

The majority of the delegates at the plenary session apparently accepted Moscow's views on the alleged shortcomings of the February program, for a circular message to all echelons issued by the new Central Committee after the close of the plenum, on December 9, was harshly critical of the united front strategy adopted at the February conference. Whereas the united front strategy had included seeking the support of bourgeois elements and petty landlords in the cause of national independence, the circular (which was probably written by Tran Phu) now emphasized that such elements were reactionary to the core and would ultimately betray the revolutionary cause. The circular was also critical of the fact that after the unity conference, all factions within the revolutionary movement had been united together in an indiscriminate manner rather than by selecting only the purest revolutionary elements from each faction.[23]

The new political program, which was passed unanimously, was designed explicitly to remedy the shortcomings of its predecessor. In formulating a new definition for the united front—to be labeled the "anti-imperialist united front" (*mat tran phan de*)—it declared that the chief allies of the Vietnamese working class were the poor and middle peasants. Cooperative activities with petty bourgeois intellectuals and parties were authorized, but these should be undertaken only with care, since the majority of such elements—based on the tragic experience of the CCP in 1927—could be expected to abandon the revolution at its moment of climax and side with the imperialists. Relationships with such parties were permitted, but only if they did not hinder efforts by the Party to propagandize among the masses. Every effort should also be made to oppose their "narrow nationalism" and to destroy their influence on the masses. Moreover, it declared, all "petty bourgeois" tendencies such as terrorism, a predilection for assassination, or a lack of confidence in the masses, should be rigorously weeded out of the Party (this criticism, which frequently appeared in directives sent from the USSR to Communist parties throughout the world, referred to Moscow's belief that radical intellectuals often tended to rely on dramatic acts of violence rather than on painstaking efforts to build up the revolutionary movement among the population; it also reflected Nguyen Ai Quoc's own criticism of the methods used by the Party's rivals, such as the VNQDD, to weaken the colonial regime).²⁴

Also resulting from the October conference was a name change for the VCP. At Moscow's insistence, it was now to be renamed the Indochinese Communist Party (Dang Cong san Dong duong, or ICP). Although it seems clear that one reason for the switch was to bring the Party's strategy into line with the Comintern's belief that revolutionary movements in smaller countries should pool their efforts by forming regional parties to seek liberation from colonial rule, it is likely that another consideration was that dropping the reference to "Vietnam" shifted attention away from the cause of national independence—now viewed in Moscow as a "petty bourgeois" concern—to class struggle. After the close of the conference, the Central Committee issued a public statement to explain the reasons for the change:

> Although Vietnam, Cambodia, and Laos are three separate countries, in reality they form only one region. In an economic sense they are tightly linked together, while politically they have all been ruled and oppressed by the French imperialists. If the workers and all the laboring masses in the three countries want to overthrow the imperialists, the monarchs, and the landlords to restore their independence and liberate themselves, they cannot struggle separately. So the Communist Party, the vanguard of the working class and the leader of all the masses in waging the revolution, must also not just separately represent Vietnam, Cambodia, or Laos. If the enemy of the revolution is composed of a united force, then the Communist Party must also concentrate the force of the workers in all Indochina.²⁵

After changing the Party's program and the name, the conference turned its attention to the situation inside Indochina. The unrest in the central provinces presented the leadership with a dilemma. It was by now increasingly apparent that the outbreak in the coastal provinces in central Vietnam was not likely to result in a nationwide rebellion against French rule. Although a few isolated outbreaks of violence against authority had taken place in scattered rural districts in the south, the peasantry remained quiet in the north, even in the impoverished villages in the Red River delta. The same was true in urban areas. In Saigon and

Hanoi, a few workers had gone on strike in response to the plight of their compatriots in the central provinces, but on the whole the population in the cities appeared apathetic. The urban middle class watched the events in Annam with fascination or in horror, but it did not rise. Since the VNQDD had fallen into disarray after the Yen Bay debacle, there was literally no organized nationalist group in Vietnam with the capacity or the inclination to rally the populace against imperialist oppression—except for the Communist Party itself. Moreover, it seemed clear that the image of dark violence and class war that emanated from the soviet movement in the central provinces had frightened off many otherwise sympathetic observers, a fact which undoubtedly confirmed in the minds of Marxist hard-liners that the bourgeoisie was vacillating and could not be counted on as a loyal ally of the revolutionary forces.

Under the circumstances, Party leaders in Hong Kong were inclined toward caution. A resolution issued at the close of the October plenum declared that revolutionary activists in local areas must make every effort to expand the movement into all regions of Indochina in order to concentrate the strength of the masses against the "white terror" waged by the colonial authorities. But at the same time it instructed them urgently to oppose all tendencies toward premature violence and blind adventurism, erroneous tendencies that were ascribed to impure and unreliable elements introduced into the Party after the unity conference. Such elements, the resolution charged, placed too much emphasis on the struggle against imperialism and not enough on the issue of class struggle. The most important thing now, the Central Committee reasoned, was to strengthen the Party's roots with the oppressed masses so that a future uprising would have a better chance to succeed. To do that, propaganda should focus on issues central to rural concerns, such as opposing oppressive taxes, reducing land rents, and eliminating monopolies.[26]

Then, in a separate communiqué specifically directed to Party activists in the rebellious provinces of Nghe An and Ha Tinh, the conference expressed its view of the newly formed soviets:

> If the masses are at the point when they take action spontaneously, then the Party has no option but to lead them immediately. But in this case, the executive committee [probably of the Nghe An provincial committee] is actually advocating such actions, and that is very mistaken, because: a) although the situation in a few areas is revolutionary, the overall level of consciousness and the struggle of workers and peasants in the region is not uniformly high, b) al-

though there is a high level of consciousness and enthusiasm in some villages, there are not enough weapons.

Given the overall situation in Vietnam and the comparative strength and preparedness of the revolutionary forces and the enemy, the communiqué concluded that to advocate violence in just one region was not correct policy. In the central provinces, Party operatives should use the favorable situation caused by widespread hunger and imperialist brutality to broaden the mass struggle, but without recourse to acts of premature and isolated violence, while preparing for a military uprising to achieve total victory in the future.[27]

At the close of the first plenary session, the delegates elected a permanent Central Committee, as well as a Standing Committee composed of Tran Phu, Nguyen Trong Nghia, and the central Vietnamese activist Nguyen Phong Sac, even though the latter had not attended the meeting in Hong Kong. At first, the Standing Committee, which was expected to provide leadership for the Party in the interval between sessions of the Central Committee, was to be located at Haiphong, but when a delegate from Tonkin pointed out that security was inadequate there, it was decided to establish the Party headquarters in Saigon, where communications links with France and China would be relatively convenient to maintain. Tran Phu, now emerging as a dominant figure in the party, was named to the pivotal post of general secretary, while Nguyen Ai Quoc was to remain in Hong Kong as the representative of the Comintern's Southern Bureau.[28]

Nguyen Ai Quoc could not have been unaware that the decisions reached at the plenary session represented a clear and even flagrant rejection of some of his own ideas and the character of his leadership. It must have galled him that, in some instances, the criticism was clearly unwarranted. During his years as a leading member of the league, he had attempted to raise the ideological level of its members and had persistently urged all cadres operating in Vietnam to seek out qualified workers for membership and training. To be accused implicitly of ideological softness by younger and less experienced colleagues must have rankled.

In fact, the new Comintern line was not simply a repudiation of Nguyen Ai Quoc himself, but a clear departure from Lenin's own 1920 strategy of focusing on the issue of national independence and seeking the active cooperation of progressive elements within the middle and the rural scholar-gentry classes. In the new era, at a time when efforts to establish an effective alliance with nationalist parties in China and the Dutch East Indies had proven abortive, the ideas of Nguyen Ai Quoc, the most experienced revolutionary in all of Indochina, no longer seemed relevant.

Despite the affront, he took the setback with good grace. According to the recollection of one participant at the conference, Quoc "was modest and listened to and respected the opinions of the collective," opinions that in many instances contrasted sharply with his own. In private conversations with his colleagues before the plenary session, he admitted that the decisions at the unity conference had been superficial and hastily adopted, but he assigned some responsibility for such "gaps" to regional committees of the league in Vietnam, who had not communicated conditions inside the country to him. Afterward, in his capacity as Comintern representative in Hong Kong, he reported the results of the plenum to Hilaire Noulens in Shanghai.[29]

Still, Nguyen Ai Quoc may have succeeded in introducing his own ideas into the minds of his colleagues. In mid-November, the new Standing Committee issued a decree instructing the Party's lower echelons on how to form the new anti-imperialist front. The document contained tantalizing hints that Quoc's views on the composition of the united front still survived within the Party. The decree stressed the importance of building a broader united front with the various classes in Vietnamese society—and especially in the frontline areas in the central provinces. In the recent past, the directive pointed out, cadres had not had a clear understanding of the purpose of the united front; they were forming "red unions" and "red peasant associations" without grasping the importance of creating mass organizations for intellectuals, the middle class, and patriotic landlords. Moreover, it added, some Party members had failed to see the progressive character of national revolutionary parties such as the VNQDD, which had been so cruelly oppressed earlier in the year. Such groups were often timid and in some areas of the country had shown opposition to the revolution, but in other areas, such as in the central provinces of Annam, they were often progressive in their inclinations. It was important to recognize, the decree concluded, that national revolution was an integral part of class revolution.[30]

Whatever effect this decree had on the views of Party members with regard to the composition of the united front, however, was probably negated by the Central Committee December circular, which explained the decisions reached at the plenary session and the mistakes committed by the February unity conference. The circular was highly critical of the role of the bourgeoisie in the Vietnamese revolution. Although some members of the local bourgeoisie opposed the imperialists, they lacked the strength to resist firmly; when the revolution developed, they would shift to the imperialist cause. The influence of the bourgeoisie on the masses was thus very dangerous and must be unmasked. Landlords were similarly reactionary in their views, and their land must be confiscated and given to poor and middle peasants.[31]

During the late fall and winter of 1930–1931, French efforts to repress the unrest escalated. Popular demonstrations were brutally suppressed, villages that had supported the revolt were attacked and occupied by government troops, and the imperial court ordered mass arrests of individuals suspected of supporting the uprising. Party committees in the central provinces reported a decline in morale and in support for the movement among the mass of the population. In desperation, Party activists ignored Quoc's advice and increasingly turned to acts of terrorism, including attacks on government installations or the assassination of individuals suspected of being sympathetic to the imperialists.

Shortly after the new year, the Standing Committee, now established in Saigon, sent out new instructions to the three regional committees, warning them against panic or succumbing to the rising strain of pessimism within the revolutionary movement. The purpose of the struggle, it emphasized, was to wage revolution. Only if Party members waged revolution and set up soviet power would it obtain long-term benefits. Charges that the masses were discouraged were misguided, for history proved that if the masses are revolutionary, then the struggle can never be suppressed. The Standing Committee fended off appeals from the local echelons for their superiors to do something—anything—to protect the masses from their oppressors, explaining that the Party had no method, no magic wand, to bring about a successful revolution. It had no army, no fighter planes; all it possessed was a means of arousing the masses to seek their own liberation, to use their own strength to carry on the struggle, to organize themselves to oppose oppression.

The directive concluded with a list of instructions to local Party branches on how to avoid panic and to promote mass struggles, such as labor strikes and peasant demonstrations, that would oppose the enemy's white terror. It pointed out that the masses were in a revolutionary frame of mind and ready to be led; otherwise, they would act on their own and ignore the Party, which would have to follow at their tail. At the same time, the Standing Committee continued to discourage the use of armed violence, and took issue with those who said that the movement must obtain weapons to defend itself from the enemy. Although the masses were revolutionary, the country was not in a direct revolutionary situation, and the village militia was not a red army. The militia could help by distributing propaganda, by promoting unity within the movement, and by demonstrating a willingness to sacrifice. And for those purposes, weapons were not necessary.[32]

Back in Hong Kong, Nguyen Ai Quoc was exerting his efforts to focus world attention on the trials of his compatriots inside Vietnam. In reports to Moscow, he described himself as constantly badgering acquaintances at the FEB in Shanghai to publicize the uprising and instruct workers' organizations around the world to demonstrate their support for their comrades in Indochina. In an article titled "Red Nghe Tinh" (Nghe Tinh Do, a reference to the two neighboring provinces of Nghe An and Ha Tinh where the rebellion was strongest), written in early 1931, he alluded to the explosive power of combined worker-peasant discontent in central Vietnam and concluded that the revolt there indeed merited the word "red."[33]

But Nguyen Ai Quoc was frustrated at his inability to play a more active role in directing the movement. Problems were escalating rapidly in his relations with Tran Phu, who had been quick to criticize Nguyen Ai Quoc in Hong Kong for the latter's "nationalist" tendencies and his failure to keep abreast of the latest Comintern line. Quoc had managed to swallow his irritation at his younger colleague's condescension, but Phu's obvious desire to elbow him aside and seize control over the future direction of the Party must have offended him deeply.

The tension between the two men broke into the open as the new year began. In a letter to Quoc in January 1931, Tran Phu complained about the absence of reliable communications between Saigon and the FEB in Shanghai. Who, Phu asked testily, is responsible for the rupture of this link? If Quoc can't put the Standing Committee in touch with Shanghai and Comintern headquarters in Moscow, what was his function in Hong Kong? Is there not some other way that Shanghai and Moscow could contact the committee? At the very least, Phu declared, the Standing Committee in Saigon needed to receive the letters the FEB and Comintern had promised to send them. In closing, Phu complained at the tone his older colleague had employed at the beginning of Quoc's previous letter.[34]

Although Nguyen Ai Quoc may have been irritated at the patronizing tone of Tran Phu's messages, he sought to respond faithfully to

Phu's complaints, declaring in an undated letter to Noulens in Shanghai that "our firm" in Saigon "needs letters from you." Quoc noted that "the firm" had been put into operation only recently and had not received any follow-up orders. Without directives and official support from its parent firm, it would be very difficult for representatives in Saigon to carry out their task in all branches of their operation. So it was vital for them to receive letters as soon as possible.[35]

Nguyen Ai Quoc shared many of his younger colleague's frustrations. In another letter to Noulens a few days later, he complained about a lack of directives from the Comintern, pointing out that for several months no messages had arrived at the Hong Kong office from any organization under the direction of Moscow, or even from the FCP, which still played the informal role of a patron for the ICP. The people of Indochina, he lamented, were becoming convinced that their suffering, their struggles, their millions of arrests and their hundreds of deaths were being completely ignored by their comrades around the world. They felt abandoned and forgotten and had come to believe that they could expect nothing from international solidarity. Pleading for further directives, Quoc concluded with a request to be transferred to Shanghai.[36]

In early March 1931, a visitor to Hong Kong brought some temporary relief. Joseph Ducroux, a Comintern agent operating under the code name Serge Lefranc and working with the Comintern's Pan Pacific Trade Union Secretariat in Shanghai, arrived in the crown colony to confer with Nguyen Ai Quoc as the first stop on a swing through Southeast Asia to consult with leading members of Communist parties throughout the region. Lefranc and Nguyen Ai Quoc had become acquainted in the early 1920s, when both were connected with the Federation of Young Communists in Paris, and Nguyen Ai Quoc took the occasion of their meeting to unburden himself to his guest. Lefranc immediately passed on his host's complaints to Noulens. Offering his support to Nguyen Ai Quoc's request for additional operating funds, Lefranc concluded: "We must also consider how best to use him. He can do more than liaison and translations and here he can only do that. He can carry out no genuine [political work] because as a liaison agent he is isolated from Indochina." Noting that Nguyen Ai Quoc was one of the most experienced and effective agents in the area, Lefranc proposed that he be transferred to Shanghai to handle Indochinese affairs under the direct guidance of the FEB, with someone else appointed to do the liaison work in Hong Kong. As for the situation in Indochina, Lefranc remarked that since October the ICP had received no directives from Moscow and the leadership of the Party was virtually isolated. If Nguyen Ai Quoc were in Shanghai, he concluded, perhaps the operations of the Party could be improved.[37]

Two weeks later, Lefranc traveled to Saigon. Tran Phu, who had been alerted to his expected arrival by Nguyen Ai Quoc, ordered Ngo Duc Tri, a colleague who had attended the October conference, to meet Lefranc in front of the Saigon Palace Hotel. Tri, who had replaced Nguyen Phong Sac on the Standing Committee because Sac was preoccupied with the revolt in central Vietnam, could be expected to recognize Lefranc because the two had met while studying at the Stalin School in Moscow. Tri met with Lefranc in Lefranc's hotel room on March 23 and then made arrangements for him to confer with the other two members of the Standing Committee at Tran Phu's house the following day. After receiving their report on the situation in Indochina, Lefranc passed on funds to assist the Party in its operations and informed them that Noulens would arrange a meeting with ICP leaders as soon as possible. He also told them that Nguyen Ai Quoc would soon be transferred to Shanghai to facilitate communications between the Party leadership and the Comintern. After sending a postcard to Nguyen Ai Quoc to let him know of his whereabouts, Lefranc left Saigon on the twenty-seventh.[38]

By now, French efforts to restore law and order in the central provinces were beginning to bear some results, and although colonial officials freely admitted that the Communists were still popular among the local population there, the combination of government attacks on rebel-held villages and violent acts committed by supporters of the movement in response was beginning to have an effect. Local Party committees were running out of cadres, weapons, and operating funds, and a sense of desperation was becoming pervasive within the movement. Such conditions began to influence many fence-sitters, who started to cooperate with the authorities. The police were also having some success in capturing leading members of the Party and obtaining information through their interrogation (often supplemented by physical torture). Prisoners were often beaten with clubs, suspended by chains from prison walls, or even given electrical shocks on sensitive parts of the body. French successes in suppressing the unrest sowed panic and division inside the movement, and the fear of spies within the ranks became endemic. When Nguyen Duc Canh, a veteran of the revolutionary movement who had attended the May 1929 conference of the league, was seized by imperial authorities in Ha Tinh province, the ICP provincial committee reported that it had decided to assassinate him in prison so that he could not betray others in the movement. In another message, the same committee reported that any Vietnamese suspected of holding favorable views of the imperialists—

whether a merchant, a landlord, or even a household servant—should be condemned to death.[39]

At the end of March 1931, Tran Phu convened the Second Plenum of the Party Central Committee in Saigon. Although the precise nature of the discussion was not recorded, the resolution issued at the close of the meeting declared bravely that the movement was progressing because of the world situation as well as through the urgent efforts of the Party. But it conceded that serious problems existed. The movement in the northern provinces was almost totally moribund because of an absence of Party leadership in Tonkin, a problem that the Central Committee ascribed to the vestiges of "petty bourgeois" influence (a legacy from the Revolutionary Youth League) within the regional leadership. As a result, local operatives had failed to recruit effectively among factory workers and the rural poor. The resolution concluded by calling for efforts to broaden the class struggle among the peasants, to create more Party cells in factories, and to eradicate the influence of nationalist parties among the masses.[40]

A few days following the end of the plenum, the Sûreté located the headquarters of the Standing Committee in Saigon and launched a raid while the Standing Committee was consulting with members of the regional committee of Cochin China. Everyone at the meeting was arrested except for General Secretary Tran Phu, who had fortuitously gone to the toilet in the garden just as the police arrived and managed to elude his pursuers by escaping through the back gate. Among those seized was Ngo Duc Tri, who betrayed a number of his comrades under interrogation. By April 17, Tran Phu was the only remaining member of the Party leadership still at large.[41]

That day, Tran Phu addressed a rambling report to the FEB in which he recounted these disastrous events. Characteristically, he placed the primary blame for the Party's misfortunes on unnamed internal elements who, he charged, continued to act on the basis of the erroneous policies promulgated by the previous leadership. The ICP, Phu complained, was not yet a proletarian party, but a party of all the oppressed classes. The lack of workers in the organization had led to "petty bourgeois thinking" and opposition to the policy line by leading elements within the regional committees in north and central Vietnam. Still, Tran Phu expressed optimism for the future of the movement, estimating that there were about 2,400 full-fledged Party members at the time of writing, compared with only 1,600 the previous October. More than 63,000 peasants had joined the movement as compared with 2,800 in the autumn. To handle such responsibilities, he asked for more operating funds.[42]

While Tran Phu was maneuvering desperately to keep out of the clutches of the Sûreté, Hilaire Noulens in Shanghai and Nguyen Ai Quoc in Hong Kong were trying to stay abreast of the situation. Sometime in April, Noulens wrote to Quoc, confirming that he had received Quoc's reports about the serious problems in Indochina and remarking that he was in the midst of preparing a detailed report on the situation that he would shortly send to Hong Kong. In the meantime, he expressed his dissatisfaction with the lack of information that he was receiving from Quoc about the situation in Indochina. We lack information in your letters, he complained, about inner Party life and the activities of various associations. There was also too little information on why and how people were arrested, so that lessons could not be drawn on how to avoid such arrests in the future. Noulens concluded that it was "not practical" for Nguyen Ai Quoc to transfer to Shanghai at this time. All the preparatory measures that had been agreed upon must be carried out before it would it be appropriate to speak of holding another meeting.[43]

On April 20, 1931, as yet unaware of the new wave of arrests in Indochina, Nguyen Ai Quoc wrote to the ICP leadership in Saigon with a list of criticisms forwarded from Noulens. Responding to a suggestion from the regional committee in central Vietnam that the name of the Party not be formally changed until separate organizations had appeared in Cambodia and Laos, Quoc justified the move, explaining that the Comintern's directive called on the new Party to help form cells among working-class elements in both protectorates.

Nguyen Ai Quoc was still unhappy about his own role. In a second letter to Saigon, mailed on the twenty-fourth, he complained that he was "just a letter box" and commented that he had asked the FEB to replace him and assign him to a new task. In the meantime, he responded testily to Tran Phu's complaints with a list of his own, pointing out that if reports from the Standing Committee arrived in Hong Kong regularly, he would not need to rely on information provided by local Party committees. Unfortunately, he said, the Standing Committee was not communicating with Quoc's Southern Bureau on a regular basis, and no information on the situation in central and north Vietnam had arrived in Hong Kong since December. Although Quoc conceded that circumstances in Indochina were difficult, he stressed the importance of providing information to administrative units outside the country on the situation inside Indochina. Otherwise, there would be no means for such units to provide advice and instructions.[44]

Tran Phu never received the message. On April 18, the day following his own rambling letter to Shanghai, he was arrested by the French authorities. A few months later, he died in prison. There were varying interpretations of his death: The colonial administration reported to Paris that he had died of tuberculosis, but sources in the Party charged that torture may have been the cause. Ngo Duc Tri and Nguyen Trong Nghia, the other members of the Standing Committee, were both in prison. With Nguyen Phong Sac having been executed in April, the Party was almost totally bereft of leadership inside the country.[45]

The French crackdown on unrest in the central provinces continued relentlessly. According to Sûreté reports, by the late spring of 1931 at least 2,000 activists were dead, and an astounding 51,000 followers of the movement were reported to be in detention. Party documents seized by the French displayed a growing sense of desperation, discouragement, and mutual infighting, as local authorities were increasingly emboldened to strike back at the rioters. As a Party historian later recorded:

> In Quang Ngai regular demonstrations of 300 to 500 people took place during the early months of 1931. . . . After the month of May, violent demonstrations were generally accompanied by the execution of traitors. But the most important demonstration took place at Bong Son, in Binh Dinh province, on July 23. Three columns of demonstrators, armed with machetes, sticks and guns, marched along the main road, felling trees to make barricades, cutting telegraph wires and setting fire to cars encountered along the road. Several notables were executed.[46]

Offering a dismal counterpoint to the suppression of the movement by the colonial regime, a widespread drought swept over the central provinces. A French report written in July 1931 stated that, with the destruction of the rice crop, 90 percent of the population in Nghe An's Nam Dan district were dying of hunger. Even moderates like Bui Quang Chieu were revolted by the brutality of the French suppression. Although the central provinces were now quiet, declared his newspaper *La Tribune Indochinoise*, it was "the silence of death."[47]

On May 12, 1931, Hilaire Noulens sent Nguyen Ai Quoc his long awaited critique of the evolving situation in Indochina. Noulens accused Party leaders of departing from Comintern guidelines in a number of respects. "Putschism"—what the party labeled the advocacy of premature rebellions against colonial regimes—had nothing to do with communism and such putschist actions as shooting at police and acts of individual terrorism would only do damage to the movement in spite of their superficially heroic character. Meetings were too long and concerns for secrecy were often lax, while organizational work among the masses was frequently neglected. Still, Noulens promised to do his utmost to bring the situation in Indochina to the attention of the world revolutionary movement. In the meantime, he concluded, "by all means write us about your work, your achievements and mistakes, etc."[48]

While waiting for news of his request for a transfer, Nguyen Ai Quoc remained in Hong Kong. He had been living for months in the apartment on Kowloon peninsula, and had become romantically involved with Nguyen Thi Minh Khai, the alternate at the October 1930 plenary conference. Like Nguyen Ai Quoc himself, "Duy" (as she was then known within the movement) bridged the gap between past and present. Born in 1910 into an illustrious family in Ha Dong province, near Hanoi, she was the granddaughter of an official in Bac Giang who had received a *pho bang* degree. Her father, Nguyen Van Binh, had learned to speak French but, after failing the civil service examinations, decided eventually to accept employment as a railroad official at Vinh sometime after 1907. After enrolling in a girl's elementary school at Vinh, Minh Khai transferred to a coeducational high school at age fourteen. She was introduced there to revolutionary ideas by Tran Phu, who persuaded her to join the Tan Viet party. High-spirited and physically attractive, after her arrival in Hong Kong, she soon caught Quoc's attention.[49]

Not much is known about Minh Khai's romantic relationship with Nguyen Ai Quoc, or whether they ever participated in a formal wedding ceremony. Quoc's previous relationship with Tuyet Minh, his Chinese wife in Canton, had apparently come to an end after his departure from China in April 1927, although there are some indications that she encountered him by chance after he settled in Hong Kong in early 1930. If so, the relationship was not resumed. Lam Duc Thu, Nguyen Ai Quoc's onetime colleague in the league, told his Sûreté contact that Tuyet Minh considered Quoc too old for her taste and had agreed to marry him only out of financial need. Quoc's feelings on the matter are unclear, but about a year after his departure from Canton, he wrote her a short note, which Thu passed on to the French: "Although we have been separated for almost a year, our mutual feelings remain, although unspoken. I want to take this occasion to send you these few words of reassurance, and to ask you to give my best wishes to your mother."[50]

With Nguyen Ai Quoc's relationship with Tuyet Minh at an end, in the spring of 1931 he struck up a liaison with his young Vietnamese colleague and requested permission from the FEB to get married. In a letter to Quoc in April, Noulens replied that he needed to know the date of the marriage two months in advance. Not long after that, however, Minh Khai was arrested by the British police in Hong Kong on suspicion of involvement in subversive activities. Because she claimed to be a Chinese citizen by the name of Tran Thai Lan, she was transferred to Chinese authorities in Canton and incarcerated for several months before being released for lack of evidence.

Nguyen Ai Quoc's reaction to Minh Khai's arrest and extradition remains a mystery. He referred briefly to the incident in a letter to Noulens in late April or early May, remarking laconically that one of the comrades in charge of communications in his office had been detained by the authorities. He then turned to his own situation and reiterated his request for a transfer. "Just do what you can for me," he asked, "even though it is a bother."[51]

While Nguyen Ai Quoc was awaiting news about his request, the Comintern agent operating under the code name Serge Lefranc was continuing his journey throughout Southeast Asia. After his stop in Saigon, he visited several other countries in the region and then sailed on to the British colony of Singapore on the U.S.S. *President Adams*. Although posing as a commercial traveler, his real purpose was to confer with members of the newly established Malayan Communist Party (MCP) and convey information on its activities to Nguyen Ai Quoc in Hong Kong and Hilaire Noulens in Shanghai, both of whom had been eager for months for such news. Alerted to his arrival by a letter from Nguyen Ai Quoc, the MCP leader Fu Dajing, an overseas Chinese who had earlier cooperated with Nguyen Ai Quoc in establishing the Siamese Communist Party, arranged to meet Lefranc secretly on the sidewalk at Collier Quay, along the Singapore waterfront.[52]

British authorities in London had long been aware of Lefranc's tour and had attempted to locate him during short stops that he made in India and Ceylon, but they had lost track of him. Now, however, they had a stroke of luck. Fu Dajing was under police surveillance in Singapore because of his relationship with the Indonesian Communist Tan Malaka. When informed that Fu and a colleague had met with a European named Lefranc on Collier Quay, the local police concluded that Lefranc might be the Joseph Ducroux whom London had been warning them about. After placing Lefranc and his local contacts under arrest, they searched his hotel room and seized all of his papers. Lefranc had been careless about his wastepaper, and had in his possession letters from Nguyen Ai Quoc in Hong Kong (under the pseudonym of T. V. Wong), and from Noulens in Shanghai. Based on that evidence, Lefranc and his accomplices were tried in Singapore and sentenced to terms in prison, while the local police telegraphed the information to British police in Hong Kong and Shanghai.[53]

At 2:00 A.M. on June 6, British police arrived at Quoc's apartment in the crowded residential quarter of Kowloon. There they found a man in a second-floor flat in company with a young Vietnamese woman. The man claimed to be a Chinese by the name of T. V. Wong while the woman identified herself as his niece, Ly Sam. Numerous political tracts and manifestos seized in the apartment, however, suggested strongly that the man was indeed Nguyen Ai Quoc, the veteran Comintern revolutionary. The woman was later identified as Ly Ung Thuan, the wife of Party member Ho Tung Mau. Nguyen Ai Quoc's arrest was a major setback, which not only ruptured his fragile contacts with Party members inside Indochina but also threatened to throw him into the arms of the French, or of the imperial government in Annam. If that should occur, his future role as a Comintern agent and the leader of the Vietnamese revolutionary movement would be in serious jeopardy.[54]

VII | INTO THE WILDERNESS

T he 1931 arrest of Nguyen Ai Quoc in Hong Kong was part of a widespread series of operations by colonial authorities to round up Communist activists throughout eastern Asia. It had begun in early June, with the arrest in Singapore of Serge Lefranc, the Comintern agent who had been undertaking a tour of Southeast Asia on behalf of its Pan Pacific Trade Union Secretariat in Shanghai. On June 5, Le Quang Dat, the ICP member who had been assigned by Quoc to serve as liaison with the FEB, was arrested in the French concession in Shanghai. Early the following morning, Nguyen Ai Quoc and his colleague Ly Sam were seized in Hong Kong. A few days later, Hilaire Noulens and his wife were detained by municipal police in the International Settlement in Shanghai. Noulens, whose real identity was somewhat of a mystery to colonial authorities, declared himself to be a Belgian citizen, but it soon became clear that he possessed several passports under various names and nationalities, and his claim was denied by the Belgian consulate in Shanghai.

Although there was no evidence that Noulens was guilty of any offense in the International Settlement, European security officials were convinced of his secret role as Comintern representative in the Far East, and after a few days in detention in Shanghai, Noulens and his wife were turned over to Chinese authorities in neighboring Jiangsu province, where he was sentenced to life imprisonment at a trial in Nanjing. As a result of efforts by the Soviet-sponsored International Red Aid, Noulens and his wife were eventually released from prison and returned to Moscow.[1]

Meanwhile, Nguyen Ai Quoc (claiming to be the Chinese journalist Song Man Cho) was detained without warrant, as the local police sought to obtain evidence that might link him with subversive activities promoted by the Comintern. Although he had not committed any known offense in Hong Kong, British policy did not permit the use of British territory to foment unrest in neighboring countries. Local officials were convinced that the detainee was actually Nguyen Ai Quoc; some hoped to find a means to turn him over to French authorities in Indochina. Since an existing Franco-British agreement did not permit extradition for political offenses, the only recourse was to obtain a warrant to banish him from Hong Kong territory. After determining to their own satisfaction that Song Man Cho was really Nguyen Ai Quoc, the Hong Kong government decided six days after his apprehension to make a formal request for a warrant of deportation. In those days, banishment under deportation warrant was usually carried out on a specific ship to a specified port and often took place under armed guard.[2]

Although Nguyen Ai Quoc did not produce a passport, he claimed to possess one under the name of Song Man Cho and insisted that he was not Vietnamese but Chinese. The normal procedure in such cases was to conduct a banishment inquiry to establish true identity and place of birth before reaching a determination on how to dispose of a case. Such an inquiry convened on July 10, 1931. Speaking in English, the prisoner denied that he was Nguyen Ai Quoc and claimed that he had been born at Tung Hing, a small town in Guangdong province near the Indochinese border. He declared that he had indeed been to France, but had not visited Soviet Russia, nor had he ever been connected with the Comintern. He insisted that he was a nationalist, not a Communist. He denied knowing Serge Lefranc, but admitted having signed a postcard that had been found in the latter's pocket in Singapore. Arguing strenuously against being deported to Indochina, he demanded extradition to Great Britain.

Before the end of the banishment hearing, Nguyen Ai Quoc began to receive legal assistance from an unexpected source. There are several versions of how the young Hong Kong solicitor Frank Loseby became involved in the case. One version maintains that a clerk in his office was Vietnamese and casually mentioned it to his employer. In his own memoirs, Ho Chi Minh explained that he and Loseby had an unnamed mutual friend in Hong Kong. Sources in Hanoi today, however, maintain that Loseby was retained formally on Nguyen Ai Quoc's behalf by the International Red Aid and the League Against Imperialism, another Moscow-based organization that provided support for prominent radicals arrested in capitalist countries.[3]

Loseby immediately became involved in the proceedings. Denied the possibility of an extradition order, the government of French Indochina (which had been following the inquiry closely) requested through the French consulate general in Hong Kong that it be informed when and how Nguyen Ai Quoc would eventually be deported from the crown colony. Loseby, however, warned Hong Kong authorities that if normal deportation procedures were followed, Nguyen Ai Quoc and Ly Sam, the young woman who had been arrested with him, would undoubtedly be placed in serious jeopardy, since the French would seize him at his point of disembarkation and return him to Indochina for trial. Loseby therefore requested that Quoc and Ly Sam be allowed to leave under their own arrangements, and to a destination of their choice. The governor of the colony reluctantly agreed. On July 24, he telegraphed the Colonial Office in London with the proposal that Nguyen Ai Quoc be set free, on condition that he leave Hong Kong within seven days. To deport Quoc to Indochina, the governor declared, would simply be a disguised form of extradition and "repugnant to British principles."[4]

By now, however, press reports sponsored by the Comintern and its affiliates had brought Nguyen Ai Quoc's arrest to broad public attention throughout the world. Jules Cambon, the French ambassador in London, had expressed his government's concern over the issue, stating that Quoc was "an international danger" and should not be permitted to remain at large. Although Paris had no legal grounds on which to make a formal request for his extradition to Indochina, Cambon wanted the British to know French views on the matter. He also reiterated the request of the French consul general in Hong Kong that Nguyen Ai Quoc be deported in a manner "to facilitate the task of the governor-general of Indochina." The British Foreign Office, which was eager to please the French on a matter relating to joint anti-subversive activities, agreed with the consul general's proposal and suggested that Quoc be deported to Annam, as Paris had requested.[5]

The Foreign Office request provoked a flurry of memos within the Colonial Office in London over the merits of turning Nguyen Ai Quoc over to the French. Some officials felt that since he had committed no offense against British law, the only ground for deporting him was that he was a Communist. That, in the words of one official, was the equivalent of "putting his neck in the French noose." But others argued that he should be turned over. As one colonial official noted in August:

> Personally I am in favor of sending this man to his native country as the F.O. suggests. He is one of the worst agitators who was put into the bag in the round-up following the Le Franc seizure in

Shanghai and it is probably only bad luck that we have not got enough evidence to imprison him for revolutionary activities in Hong Kong.

All one's sporting instincts of course are in favor of letting the man go to Russia instead of in effect handing him over to his enemies, but I think that this is a case for suppressing those instincts. Revolutionary crime in Annam is a really low-down dirty business, including every kind of murder, even burning public officers alive and torturing them to death. For much of this crime Nguyen is personally responsible, and it is not in his favour that he has directed the affairs from afar instead of having the guts to go and take a hand in things himself.

Apart from the fact that if he is allowed to go free, he will continue to foment this kind of crime, I do entirely agree with the F.O. and the French government that it is in the general interest of civilization in the East that the Colonial Powers should stand together and help one another to suppress this kind of crime, which is highly infectious.[6]

As a result of the request by the Foreign Office, the crown colony's governor issued a new order to deport Quoc directly to Indochina. To forestall that possibility, Loseby had already instituted a suit in the Superior Court of Hong Kong for a writ of habeas corpus as a means of forcing a public trial. On August 14, the Superior Court convened to hear the case. During the proceedings, which lasted several weeks, Loseby challenged the government's new deportation order, claiming that the banishment inquiry had followed improper procedures by asking the defendant questions of a political nature that went beyond the purview of the original purpose of the inquiry. When Chief Justice Sir Joseph Kemp warned Hong Kong officials that he might rule against the existing deportation order, a new one was immediately drawn up under a different section of the Deportation Ordinance of 1917. The Court approved the change, noting that although a deportation order whose consequence was tantamount to extradition might be objectionable on the grounds of policy, it was not contrary to British law. Nguyen Ai Quoc's request for a writ of habeas corpus was thereupon denied, and he was once again subject to deportation to Indochina. Ly Sam was ordered released and permitted to leave Hong Kong by her own arrangements.[7]

Frank Loseby had already anticipated this judgment by the Supreme Court, however, and he now gave instant notice of appeal to the Privy

Council in London on the ground that the decision represented an abuse of executive power. In accepting the case, the Privy Council provided Nguyen Ai Quoc with a change of scenery. Since the appeal would not be considered for several months, he was now transferred from Victoria Prison to the Bowen Road Hospital. Loseby informed the authorities that if the deportation order to Indochina under section 6 of the Deportation Ordinance were to be canceled, Quoc would agree to leave on his own initiative. He requested permission to go temporarily to Great Britain.

Although Nguyen Ai Quoc was not visibly ill, he was worn out and emaciated. In his memoirs, he complained that in Hong Kong he was housed in a virtual dungeon, where he was regularly maltreated and was fed meals of bad rice, rotten fish, and a little beef. Sometimes he fell momentarily into despair when it appeared that he would not be released. Hunting for bugs, he related, was his only amusement. To pass the time he also sang songs or wrote poetry and letters to friends on scraps of paper that he managed to find in prison.

According to some sources, however, in the Bowen Road Hospital he was lodged in relative comfort and was regularly visited by the colonial secretary and his wife (who was a friend of Mrs. Loseby), as well as by a number of other Europeans. Because hospital fare was inadequate, Frank Loseby arranged to have meals brought in from a local restaurant. Nguyen Ai Quoc spent his idle hours reading and reportedly writing a book in English on his personal philosophy. Unfortunately, the book was lost by the Losebys during World War II.

As usual, Nguyen Ai Quoc missed no opportunity to propagandize on behalf of the future revolution. British visitors frequently visited the prison or the hospital to stare at the "strange" Bolshevik. Chinese employees and their friends occasionally stopped by as well, but they were more respectful. As Quoc related it in an autobiographical account:

> One day, a Chinese nurse who was assigned to care for Uncle [as the author referred to himself in the book] asked him secretly: "Uncle, what is communism? What did you do as a Communist to get yourself arrested?" The nurse knew that Communists were not smugglers, thieves, or murderers, so she couldn't understand why Communists were arrested.
>
> "To put it simply," Uncle replied, "Communists hope to make it so that Chinese nurses will not have to take orders from their British superiors." The nurse looked at Uncle with wide eyes and replied, "Really?"[8]

While in detention, Nguyen Ai Quoc was permitted to send and receive correspondence. A few weeks after his arrest he sent a letter to Lam Duc Thu, the former Revolutionary Youth League member who had lost the trust of his revolutionary colleagues out of growing suspicion that he was a French intelligence agent. Quoc explained that he had been in prison for three weeks and was deeply ashamed. "I have no parents," he lamented. "Who will be a witness to my innocence?" Quoc appealed to his onetime colleague to do all in his power to restore his freedom and pledged his eternal gratitude.

Apparently Nguyen Ai Quoc's request was in vain. Several months later, Thu reported to his French contact officer that Quoc had asked him for HK $1,000 to enable him to travel to Europe after his release. When Thu replied that he had no money to provide assistance, Quoc asked Thu to persuade his wife to sell some of her possessions. He also asked Thu to help reorganize the Party, but Thu replied that he could do little, since Party members remained suspicious of him. Despite this rebuff and the fact that Nguyen Ai Quoc must have known that Lam Duc Thu was a renegade, he maintained the correspondence. In late November, he wrote his former comrade that he was in poor health and vomited blood regularly. If the condition persists, he lamented, "I fear to die in prison. But I keep my thoughts fixed on Heaven." He advised Lam Duc Thu not to visit him in order to avoid getting in trouble with the authorities.[9]

It may indeed have been a lonely time. His most recent love interest, the young Nguyen Thi Minh Khai, was now in prison in China. His father had died two years before, virtually penniless, in Cochin China. Quoc did manage to keep in touch with his brother and sister through an occasional exchange of letters. His brother, Khiem, had been imprisoned by the French for subversive activities in 1914. After being released in 1920, Khiem was kept under police surveillance in Hué, where he practiced medicine and taught geomancy, a vocation that allowed him secretly to engage in clandestine activities. He must have been in financial need, for in 1926 Quoc secretly sent him a small amount of money with the assistance of Phan Boi Chau.

Quoc's sister, Nguyen Thi Thanh, had also encountered continuing problems with the authorities. Arrested on the charge of possession of firearms in 1918, she was released in 1922 but placed under surveillance; she also settled in Hué where, like her brother Khiem, she practiced medicine while secretly taking part in the anti-French resistance. When her father died in 1929, she visited Kim Lien briefly to console remaining members of the family.[10]

With the decision on Nguyen Ai Quoc's fate now in the hands of the Privy Council in London, British officials continued to discuss the issue. Opinion at the Colonial Office favored the governor's advice that he be released and permitted to leave Hong Kong on his own accord. But the Foreign Office was still concerned about how to square such an action with the French and asked that the Hong Kong authorities detain Quoc until the French could be queried about the charges levied against him. In the meantime, the Colonial Office agreed to delay further action on his release until the Privy Council had decided on the matter.[11]

On December 22, the new French ambassador in London, Jacques Truelle, responded to the British request for information on the current charges against Nguyen Ai Quoc in Indochina. Truelle told the Colonial Office that the minister of colonies in Paris was in possession of recent information that had confirmed French suspicions that Nguyen Ai Quoc was indeed the Comintern's liaison agent with all Communist parties in Southeast Asia. Among such parties, he noted pointedly, was the Communist Party of Malaya, which was a British colony. As for Quoc's alleged crimes in Indochina, Truelle noted that the imperial government in Annam had accused him of being the primary instigator of the rebellion that had recently taken place in the central provinces. At first, the provincial tribunal in Vinh had condemned him to death, but in October 1929, after review by the Supreme Tribunal in Hué, the sentence was reduced to forced labor in perpetuity. In February 1930, the tribunal had decided that Nguyen Ai Quoc would be judged anew after his arrest by French authorities. At a new trial, noted Truelle, the charges that would be levied against Quoc would include plotting and instigating rebellion against the royal Annamite government, provoking murder and pillage, and the propagation of subversive doctrines. These accusations, he declared, were based on the evidence contained in several documents, some containing Quoc's signature, that were in the possession of the French authorities. Truelle assured London that these charges would not be definitive until approved by the French *résident supérieur* in Annam. If Nguyen Ai Quoc were to be convicted of criminal activities, Truelle assured his British colleagues, the *résident supérieur* would make sure that no sentence of capital punishment would be carried out.[12]

At the end of 1931, Nguyen Ai Quoc's appeal finally came before the Privy Council in London. His case was advocated by D. N. Pritt of the law firm Light and Fulton, while the government of Hong Kong was represented by the prominent Labour Party politician Stafford Cripps. According to Quoc's attorney, Cripps soon realized what a bad

showing the case would make for the Hong Kong government and approached Pritt with the proposal that the matter be resolved by allowing
Nguyen Ai Quoc to leave the colony "under his own steam." But the
legal adviser at the Colonial Office privately accused Cripps of refusing
to argue the case because he sympathized with the politics of the defendant. Some writers have even speculated that Nguyen Ai Quoc was released after giving his assent to becoming a British agent.

Nguyen Ai Quoc's attorney agreed to accept the offer of a compromise. The British government agreed to pay for the costs of his appeal
to the Privy Council and to assist him in going where he wished. Nguyen
Ai Quoc had already expressed his willingness to accept this solution, so
an arrangement was reached between the two sides on the morning of
the hearing, June 27, 1932; the matter was thus never argued in open
court.[13]

Although he was now eligible for release from police custody,
Nguyen Ai Quoc continued to be nervous about the possibility that the
French authorities would try to seize him en route to London. Since
Soviet ships did not call at Hong Kong, Loseby asked the government
to arrange temporary asylum for him in Great Britain, and British officials in Hong Kong initially informed him that there would be no objection to such an arrangement. Problems immediately arose, however,
when his travel plans were broached with British authorities. Nguyen
Ai Quoc was worried that if he took passage on a ship that passed
through the Suez Canal, French agents might seize him at Port Said in
Egypt; he requested permission to travel to Europe via Australia and
South Africa. Neither country, however, was willing to accept him. Nor,
as it turned out, was Great Britain. Officials in Hong Kong had initially
informed Loseby that there would be no objection to making temporary
asylum in Great Britain en route to the USSR. That later turned out to
be an error. The British government had originally indicated that he
would *not* be welcome in England, but the word "not" had been inadvertently deleted from the message.[14]

Forced to abandon his plans to go to England, Nguyen Ai Quoc
turned his attention to finding other means of reaching Moscow. He
decided to go to Singapore and board a Soviet ship sailing from there to
Vladivostok. By now, however, the authorities had become exasperated
at the delay in getting rid of their troublesome guest—the negotiations
on his passage and future whereabouts had lasted several weeks, with
one British official remarking to a Sûreté official, "Nobody wants him"—

and on the evening of December 28, 1932, he was removed from the hospital and set free on the street with instructions to be out of the colony within twenty-one days.

After staying briefly with the Losebys, Nguyen Ai Quoc (posing as a traditional Confucian scholar with a newly grown wispy beard) took up lodging at the Chinese YMCA in Kowloon. In an effort to minimize the danger of French surveillance, the Losebys put out the word that Nguyen Ai Quoc had died of tuberculosis in the hospital. The Comintern had already done its part; *The Daily Worker*, published in London, announced his death in prison in its August 11, 1932, issue. With the assistance of Mrs. Loseby, Quoc found passage on a ship to Singapore.

But problems continued to dog him. On his arrival in Singapore on January 6, 1933, he was immediately seized by immigration officials and sent back to Hong Kong on the S.S. *Ho Sang*. Disembarking at Hong Kong, he was recognized and detained on the grounds that he had arrived without proper papers. The authorities decided to ignore his technical breach of the departure order, however, and—despite the protests of local police officials—set him free again on January 22, with orders to be out of the colony within three days. The Losebys arranged a clandestine residence for him, this time in the New Territories, while seeking an alternative route out of the colony. They found passage for him, accompanied by an interpreter, on a Chinese ship scheduled to leave for Xiamen on the twenty-fifth. To avoid the prying eyes of the French security services, Quoc was escorted after dark to the docks by plainclothesmen. From there a motor launch hired by the government took him out to Lei Yue Mun Strait, just outside the harbor, where the ship was waiting for him.[15]

On arrival in Xiamen (a foreign concession port in Fujian province then widely known to foreigners as Amoy) the next morning, Nguyen Ai Quoc and his interpreter disembarked and checked into a YMCA in the Chinese section of town. After passing the Tết holidays with friends, he spent several weeks of restless inactivity. After obtaining funds from a wealthy local Chinese who was an acquaintance of Loseby, he was finally able to travel by ship to Shanghai. That great commercial and industrial metropolis, once the scene of a powerful left-wing labor movement, had been cleansed of radicals in Chiang Kai-shek's "Shanghai massacre" in April 1927; the few remaining members of the CCP who resided in the city were in hiding from Chiang's security forces. To avoid security officials in the French concession, Quoc stayed at a sumptuous hotel while posing as a wealthy businessman. To preserve his meager funds, he ate alone and washed his clothing in his hotel room. Quoc was well advised to be careful, for Sûreté officials had dismissed reports of his demise and were now hearing rumors that he was in south China, Indochina, or Siam. On the chance that he was in Shanghai, French concession police there had intensified their efforts to locate him and offered a substantial reward for his arrest.[16]

With the local CCP headquarters driven under cover, Nguyen Ai Quoc found it difficult to make contacts with Chinese comrades who might fund his future travel, but by good fortune he discovered that Paul Vaillant-Couturier, his close colleague and patron from the early days of the French Communist Party, was in Shanghai as a member of a visiting delegation of antiwar representatives of the French National Assembly. Quoc had learned previously from friends in the CCP that, in extremis, he could get in touch with them by contacting Sun Yat-sen's widow, Soong Qingling. Since her husband's death, Madame Soong, who now lived in a large villa on Rue Molière in the French concession of the city, had covertly developed a close relationship with the CCP.

Lacking an alternative, Nguyen Ai Quoc decided to make use of this connection. Renting a taxi, he ordered the driver to drive to Rue Molière, where he surreptitiously placed an unsigned letter in her mailbox. As he recounted it later, the stratagem almost resulted in disaster:

> On his way back to the taxi, [Quoc] saw that the French police had blocked the streets in the neighborhood and were interrogating all the pedestrians. The taxi driver appeared hesitant. Uncle cried, "Let's go!" Fortunately, because the taxicab was a luxurious model, it was not stopped by the police for inspection. Once more, a narrow escape!

The ruse worked, and he was able to establish contact with Vaillant-Couturier, who arranged to meet him in a city park. After recovering from his surprise in learning that, contrary to news reports, his old friend was still alive, Vaillant-Couturier put Quoc in touch with underground representatives of the CCP, who were in turn able to arrange passage on a Soviet steamship bound for Vladivostok. Since the French police were watching the docks closely, Quoc boarded the ship dressed as a prosperous Chinese businessman.[17]

After traveling by train across the frozen tundra of Siberia from Vladivostok, Nguyen Ai Quoc arrived in Moscow sometime in the spring of 1934. A five-year plan to develop the Soviet economy had been approved at a Party congress in 1928, as well as a program of collectivization and socialist industrialization to be carried out throughout the country. To short-time visitors and citizens who did not venture outside of Moscow, Leningrad, or other large cities, the situation probably appeared much improved over what it had been during the previous decade. Visiting journalists filed glowing reports; the dramatist George Bernard Shaw, for example, described it as a "great social experiment" after a trip to the USSR in the mid-1930s. Nguyen Ai Quoc appeared to agree, declaring in his reminiscences that under the socialist system, the USSR was making the transition from a backward agricultural society into an advanced industrial powerhouse.[18]

For millions of Soviet citizens, however, the reality was far different. In his determination to collectivize agriculture, in the early 1930s Stalin had ordered the destruction of the private farm economy. Rich peasants, known in Russian as *kulaks* (or "fists," for their grasping ways), were to be "liquidated as a class." Those who resisted collectivization were killed or shipped to Siberia. Thousands more were forced to work in slave labor gangs to carry out massive civil engineering projects such as the Karelian Canal, which connected the Gulf of Finland to the White Sea and finally opened for shipping in 1933. Although there were more goods on the shelves of state stores in urban areas, the authorities had requisitioned grain from the peasants to feed the cities or to export abroad to pay for machinery; as a result, a crisis developed in the countryside. Famine began in the Ukraine in 1932; over the next two years, 5 to 7 million people died of hunger.

By the mid-1930s, resistance to Stalin's draconian efforts to transform Mother Russia into a socialist economic powerhouse had become widespread within the Communist Party of the Soviet Union itself. At the Seventeenth Congress of the CPSU in 1934, a movement to replace Stalin with the popular Leningrad Party chief Sergey Kirov rapidly gained momentum. But Stalin had already consolidated his power over the Party apparatus and moved with force against his rivals, whom he suspected of plotting against his leadership. Leon Trotsky had already been forced into exile; other key leaders, such as Lev Kamenev and the onetime Comintern head Grigory Zinoviev, were being isolated. In December, Kirov was assassinated at Stalin's order, and massive purge trials began to deplete the corps of old Bolsheviks who had joined with Vladimir Lenin to wage the 1917 Revolution. In 1935, more than 100,000 suspected "enemies of the state" were arrested in Leningrad alone.

On the surface, the tension within the Party did not seem to affect Nguyen Ai Quoc personally. On arrival in Moscow, he had received a hero's welcome at the secretariat of the Dalburo, now under the directorship of the Finnish Communist Otto Kuusinen. Vietnamese students at the Stalin School (now renamed the Institute for the Study of the National and Colonial Questions) had received reports of Quoc's death "from advanced tuberculosis" and had already organized a funeral ceremony for both him and for Tran Phu, the ICP general secretary who had died in a French prison in the fall of 1931.

Nguyen Ai Quoc was immediately placed in charge of the 144 Vietnamese students now studying at the institute, with an office on the fourth floor of a house on Moskovskii Boulevard. There he attended lectures, wrote articles, and oversaw the students. As one of the students, Nguyen Khanh Toan, recalled:

> He maintained an extremely close contact with the Vietnamese group. Normally, he came during the evening to recount his experiences in putting an emphasis on revolutionary morality and, in particular, on solidarity. Some of the youngest members, out of pique or arrogance, used to squabble over minor issues. It was Uncle Ho who arbitrated such conflicts. He sought to inculcate in everyone a few essential principles: to combat pride, egoism and egocentrism, indiscipline, anarchism, and to reinforce unity and the need to place the interests of the revolution above all else. He often advised us: "If you are incapable of maintaining solidarity in this little group, how will you able to talk of unifying the masses to combat the colonialists and save the nation after you return to your country?"[19]

Living within the cocoon represented by the school, Quoc may have been unaware of the tragic conditions faced by millions of Soviet citizens living in the countryside. Students at the institute were still being treated much better than the remainder of the population. They received free clothing and shoes, lived in relatively spacious quarters in their dormitories, and were well fed at the school cafeteria. They received free medical care, free vacations in the Crimea, and 140 rubles per month to handle other expenses.

Still, Nguyen Ai Quoc badly needed a rest. Acquaintances at the institute later recalled that on his arrival in Moscow, he appeared to be haggard and sick, perhaps a continuing legacy of his months in prison in Hong Kong. In September 1934, he traveled to the Crimea, where he enrolled for medical treatment in a sanatorium. After remaining there for several weeks, he returned to Moscow and entered Lenin University, a school for advanced party cadres of fraternal Communist parties. There were two different programs at the school, one for three years and the other for six months. He enrolled in the latter course under the name of Lin (in Russian, Linov). For the next several months he attended lectures, taught courses on morality, and wrote articles, while continuing to arbitrate the problems of his fellow Vietnamese at the various institutes or at the Dalburo.

Little is known about his personal life during these first months in Moscow. He was initially placed in a residence hall with a group of Chinese cadres, but after he complained that he was having difficulty in understanding them, he was eventually shifted to a dormitory for French speakers. Although still frail and sickly in appearance, he led an active social life, attending art exhibits and literary programs and taking part in periodic visits to local sites of interest, including a collective farm in Ryazan. According to his Soviet biographer, he performed exercises every day to strengthen his frail physique and had a dumbbell and a chest expander in his room.[20]

It used to be thought that Nguyen Ai Quoc managed successfully to avoid the turbulent impact of the Stalinist purge trials that rocked the country during the mid-1930s. According to the French writer Jean Lacouture, Nguyen Ai Quoc was "remote from the quarrels and purges rending the Soviet Communist Party and the International." Other early biographers concur.[21]

Recently, however, reports have surfaced that Nguyen Ai Quoc did come under suspicion during this period and may even have been brought to trial. Sources in Moscow state privately that sometime during his stay in the USSR in the mid-1930s, he was investigated by a tribunal composed of his old acquaintance and sponsor Dmitri Manuilsky, the Machiavellian CCP militant Kang Sheng, and the Comintern administrator Vera Vasilieva. What he might have been charged with is unclear, although it was undoubtedly well-known that he held ideas counter to the general line espoused at the Sixth Comintern Congress of 1928. That in itself was probably sufficient to place him under suspicion by Stalin. The fact that he was a close colleague of Mikhail Borodin, himself a victim of the purge trials, may also have been held against him. Finally, it may also have been that his unexpected release from prison in Hong Kong in December 1932 had aroused suspicions in Moscow that he might have made a deal with the police to obtain his freedom.[22]

In any event, perhaps as the result of support from Manuilsky and Vasilieva, he was apparently cleared of any charges. Vasilieva, who had long served as a liaison between Vietnamese students in Moscow and the Comintern apparatus, came staunchly to his defense, arguing that he was guilty only of inexperience. Perhaps that explains her enigmatic comment, in an undated letter to ICP leaders in south China while he was in Moscow, that "as far as Quoc is concerned, we feel that in the coming two years he must apply himself seriously to his studies and will not be able to handle anything else. After he finishes his studies, we have special plans to use him."[23]

While Nguyen Ai Quoc was in Moscow, those of his colleagues who were still at large were striving to restore the Party apparatus inside Indochina. The Comintern Executive Committee had recognized the new ICP as a member in good standing in April 1931, the same month that the Party's senior leadership had been seized by the French in Cochin China. For the next several months, the Party apparatus was in a state of total disarray. To relieve the problem, Comintern officials in Moscow instructed fraternal Communist parties to do what they could to publicize what had come to be known as the Nghe-Tinh revolt. Workers in all countries were called upon to demonstrate in favor of their oppressed comrades in Indochina. More concretely, over thirty Vietnamese students currently enrolled in various training programs in Moscow were instructed to return by various routes to Indochina in order to provide the foundation for a new Party central committee. Most (twenty-two out of thirty-five, states one source) were arrested en route or deserted to the French. Among those who arrived safely was Le Hong Phong, Nguyen Ai Quoc's protégé from the Tam Tam Xa, who had studied at an aviation school in Leningrad and then transferred to the Stalin School in 1929. Phong left the USSR in the summer of 1931; after stopovers in Berlin and Paris, he finally arrived in Longzhou, a border town in Guangxi province in south China, in April 1932. With two other colleagues from the Stalin School in Moscow, Ha Huy Tap and Phung Chi Kien, he eventually moved to nearby Nanning and in the summer of 1933 the three set up a new Overseas Executive Committee (Ban chi huy hai ngoai). According to Comintern directives, the new organization was to serve as a temporary liaison bureau between the Dalburo in Moscow and the Party apparatus inside the country.[24]

In the meantime, Party bases were established in other areas to help restore its internal apparatus. By the mid-1930s, the population of the three regions of Vietnam had grown to over 18 million, with over 4 million in Cochin China, 5 million in Annam, and the remainder in Tonkin. In Cochin China, the task of reconstruction fell on the shoulders of Tran Van Giau, an ambitious young Stalin School graduate who had returned to Saigon from Moscow in early 1933. He immediately set out to revive the Party organization throughout the southern provinces. Following the current line in the Soviet Union, cadres were instructed to concentrate their efforts among workers in urban areas. The Great Depression had led to a high level of unemployment in the factories, however, and few workers dared to enroll in the cause.[25]

The Party had relatively more success in rural regions, most notably in parts of the Mekong delta, where popular resentment against the demands of rapacious landlords and corrupt officials was strong. Nevertheless, a handful of Communist intellectuals in Saigon took advantage of a gradual relaxation of official restrictions on indigenous political activities. A Party newspaper called *La Lutte* was established, with assistance from Vietnamese followers of Leon Trotsky who had studied in Paris. Party leaders in Saigon were even successful in running candidates for positions on the municipal council. In mid-1933, a new regional committee for Cochin China was established, with subcommittees for the eastern and western provinces, and a small school was created to train cadres. The intense Tran Van Giau, who was the driving force behind such activities, was arrested by the French in October, but was released shortly after for lack of evidence.

Official reports to the ministry of colonies in Paris displayed the frustration of the local security services at their inability to counter ICP activities. As one report declared: "The Sûreté stands powerless at the birth and expansion of the danger. It can only give the alarm. Its services cannot take suppressive action unless they receive orders from government authorities." But the Sûreté did have one success. Since the suppression of the Nghe-Tinh revolt, the notorious Party assassin Le Hong Son, one of the original members of the Tam Tam Xa, had been moving from one country to another to avoid capture by the French. Expelled from Burma in July 1931, he had gone to Siam and then on to Shanghai to establish contact with the CCP headquarters. But he was arrested by police in the French concession. After intensive interrogation, he was handed over to imperial Vietnamese authorities in Hué, and in February 1933 he was executed at the provincial capital of Vinh.[26]

Tran Van Giau's modest achievements in Cochin China were in stark contrast with conditions elsewhere in Indochina. In both Annam and Tonkin, police surveillance and popular apathy made it difficult for Party cadres to carry on operations. In central Vietnam, a small number of Communist operatives who had infiltrated from Siam attempted to revive the Party's moribund organization. Some of the new recruits were former members of the ICP who had recently been released from prison (according to French reports, at one time there were more than two thousand radicals in prison in Vinh alone), but in general Party leaders were suspicious of the loyalty of ex-prisoners. According to a contemporary report by the provincial committee of Nghe An, "of one hundred old Communists, only one is capable of staying true to the doctrine of the Party." By mid-1934, three regional committees, each with responsibility for from four to seven provinces, had been set up in Annam. In Tonkin, ICP activities were virtually nonexistent until 1934, when Party cells began to appear in the mountains of the Viet Bac, as the area north of the Red River delta was known. Shortly after, from his base in China, Le Hong Phong was able to reestablish a regional committee for Tonkin.

Meanwhile, in Siam a group of Party members operating in the Vietnamese communities in the Khorat plateau—a legacy of Nguyen Ai Quoc's activities in the region in the late 1920s—established a temporary central committee to provide direction for the movement and set up a training institute to prepare new recruits for operations in Vietnam. They then set out to establish themselves as the direct liaison between Party operatives in Cochin China and Annam and the outside world. Similar committees were established in Laos and Cambodia.[27]

One of the most important tasks for Party leaders as they sought to recover from the disastrous effects of the Nghe-Tinh revolt was to formulate a new strategy. In mid-1932, Le Hong Phong and other senior cadres living in south China drafted a new Party program of action, which was eventually printed by lithograph to be circulated among the Party faithful in Indochina. In keeping with the mood in Moscow at the time, the tone of the document was decidedly sectarian and leftist, emphasizing the antifeudal revolution over the anti-imperialist struggle and expressing heavy suspicion about the role of nationalist parties in the Vietnamese revolution.

Opinions published in the Party press at that time reflected a similar line. An article in the journal *Bolshevik*, the official mouthpiece of the Overseas Executive Committee, was strongly critical of petty bourgeois attitudes, such as the idea that the national revolution must take place before the socialist revolution. The author of the article—probably the recent Stalin School graduate Ha Huy Tap—also criticized Party cadres inside Indochina for placing too much attention on mobilizing peasants in rural areas and called for more emphasis on recruiting workers into the movement. Peasants, the author charged, were "greedy for personal property; very amorphous and slow from an ideological and practical point of view, very disunited, i.e., very badly qualified to assume the direction of the revolutionary movement."

Although these criticisms were ostensibly directed at unnamed Party cadres inside Indochina, the chief concern of the editors of *Bolshevik* was the views and past policies of Nguyen Ai Quoc himself. One article noted that "certain comrades" inside Indochina had argued that rich peasants and capitalists were essentially anti-imperialistic and thus could become part of the revolutionary movement; it then flatly stated that such views had been promoted by Nguyen Ai Quoc at the unity conference in February 1930, but were justifiably repudiated by the new Party leadership later that year. The ICP, the journal emphasized, was a party of the proletariat, and not of all the working masses; although the "most advanced elements of other classes can be incorporated into its organization, it must attempt to preserve a proletarian majority." As for the issue of national independence:

> The Communist Party directs the class struggle and not that of race. . . . As the Communist Party is the party of the proletariat, and as it struggles to maintain the political line of internationalism, it must combat theories and national propaganda and prohibit the usage of clichés of this genre: to advocate the restoration of the country and the renaissance of the race of dragons and fairies" [a phrase often used to designate the Vietnamese people] and so forth. We struggle against French imperialism, but that does not imply support for nationalism.[28]

Another article, undoubtedly written by Ha Huy Tap, was even more explicit. We owe much to Nguyen Ai Quoc, it noted,

> but our comrades should not forget the nationalist legacy of Nguyen Ai Quoc and his erroneous instructions on the fundamental questions of the bourgeois democratic revolutionary movement in Indochina, as well as his opportunist theories which are still rooted in the spirit of the adherents of the league and the Tan Viet. . . . Nguyen Ai Quoc did not understand the directives of the Communist International; he did not fuse the three Communist organizations of Indochina from top to bottom, and did not put into prior discussion the tactics that the Communist International had to apply to extirpate the opportunist dreams of these sections. The brochure

entitled "Political Principles" [i.e., the political program adopted in February 1930] and the statutes of the unified Party did not exactly follow the instructions of the Communist International.

Nguyen Ai Quoc also advocated such erroneous and collaborationist tactics as "neutrality with regard to the bourgeoisie and the rich peasants," "alliance with the middle and small landowners," and so forth. It is because of such errors from January to October 1930 that the ICP followed a policy that in many respects was in opposition to the instructions of the Communist International, even though it had energetically led the masses in revolutionary struggle, and it is equally because of this that the policy followed by the soviets of Nghe An was not consistent with the Party line.[29]

In June 1934, Le Hong Phong and Ha Huy Tap convened a meeting in the Portuguese colony of Macao to consult with leading cadres from inside the country over future policies and to prepare for the Party's first national congress. In the resolution issued at the end of the conference, so-called national reformists—including such diverse figures as Bui Quang Chieu, the patriotic journalist Huynh Thuc Khang (later to be a member of Ho Chi Minh's government in Hanoi), and the radical intellectual Nguyen An Ninh—were all accused of being the accomplices of imperialism. Such elements, the resolution charged, were particularly dangerous because they "posed as defenders of the working masses, adversaries of the government, propagandists for constitutional reforms and partisans of Franco-Annamite collaboration and the union of classes, with the sole aim of turning the masses from the revolutionary road." It was the task of all Party members, the document concluded, to undermine the influence of such groups, including Trotskyite elements, members of the old Revolutionary Youth League, and remnants of the Tan Viet party.[30]

In attacking "nationalist" tendencies within the Party and the efforts of some cadres to recruit actively in rural areas, the Overseas Executive Committee was undoubtedly trying to reflect the ideological line currently in fashion in Moscow. Yet just as the committee in its zeal tried to bring Party members serving inside the country into line with strategic guidelines issued in the Soviet Union, attitudes were beginning to shift in Moscow. In October 1934, for example, an article written under the pseudonym "Orgwald" was published in *Communist International*, the Comintern's official journal. In the article, "Entretien avec les camarades indochinois," which had originally appeared in another journal in July 1933, the author criticized the ICP leadership for its sectarian attitudes toward the united front. It is one thing to express opposition to the national reformists, Orgwald noted, since their leaders are clearly counterrevolutionary and should be unmasked; but it is a mistake to call for the overthrow of the bourgeoisie, because the petty bourgeoisie and perhaps even some members of the national bourgeoisie might be willing to cooperate with the Party if it used anti-imperialist slogans.[31]

Whether ICP leaders obtained a copy of this article is unclear. In any case, they had every reason to be confused about the current line, for another piece, labeled "Letter to Indochinese Comrades" and allegedly written by a leading member of the Chinese Communist Party, had appeared in the August 5, 1934, issue of the same publication. After devoting the bulk of the letter to a criticism of the inadequacy of the Party organization and the need for increased discipline and work with the masses, the author turned to the question of the united front and its importance in carrying on the revolutionary struggle. But in defining the nature of the front, the letter was ambiguous. Like the 1932 program of action (to which it specifically referred in a favorable manner), it was highly critical of "national reformists," even those who hid their real character under "leftist" and "nationalist" slogans. These reformists, it affirmed, must be pitilessly opposed.[32]

Such views, which presumably had official approval from high-level sources in Moscow, must have sown confusion in the minds of the recipients. In a letter to ICP comrades written on March 17, 1935, the Comintern's Vietnam specialist, Vera Vasilieva, confirmed that the Orgwald note and the CCP letter represented basic policy guidance, along with the ICP's own 1932 program of action. Vasilieva's letter was probably intended to serve as a set of guidelines for Party leaders in preparation for their upcoming national congress.

At its June 1934 Macao meeting, the Overseas Executive Committee had approved plans to hold the first national congress of the party in Hong Kong in January 1935. However, according to French sources, the Comintern asked that the meeting be postponed until the following March. In the late summer of 1934, Party leaders began to draw up draft documents to be discussed at their congress, now scheduled to take place in Macao; instructions were sent out to all echelons to select delegates, who were ordered to arrive there by March 15. Party leaders hoped that Moscow would send a delegate to attend the meeting as a formal representative from the Comintern. In the early autumn of 1934, an ICP delegation composed of Le Hong Phong, Nguyen Thi Minh Khai (who had been released from jail in Canton and was now operating under the name of Van), and Hoang Van Non (a Party member from Cao Bang province) left for Moscow to attend the Seventh Comintern Congress, which was scheduled to be held the following summer.[33]

With Le Hong Phong en route to Moscow, Ha Huy Tap now became the senior Party official in charge of preparing for the national congress. A native of Nghe An province, Tap had joined the Tan Viet party and then defected to the Revolutionary Youth League. While at the Stalin School, he developed a flair for theory and became a vocal critic of the ideological shortcomings of the league. Described by French security officials as proud, shifty, and "suspicious to an extreme," Tap immediately began to encounter problems in his relations with his colleagues, who derisively labeled him "Mr. Short" because of his small stature. Relations were especially strained with Tran Van Giau. In September 1934, Giau arrived in Macao, partly to report on conditions in Cochin China and partly to play a formative role in preparations for the national congress. Tran Van Giau probably considered the feisty Tap an upstart, while Tap was suspicious of Giau's arrogance and independent ways. Eventually, Tap began to fear that Tran Van Giau was a French spy, reporting his suspicions in a letter to Moscow. Only later, when Giau's residence was searched by the French authorities, did Ha Huy Tap concede that his suspicions had been unfounded.[34]

As it turned out, the danger from *provocateurs* came from elsewhere. One of the Party cadres in Macao, a cook by the name of Nguyen Van Tram, stole a substantial amount of money from ICP coffers and fled to Hong Kong. Because Tram had been given the responsibility for selecting the site of the congress in Macao, Party leaders were forced to change the venue on the suspicion that he might have divulged the location to the French, whose agents were active within the Portuguese colony. Ha Huy Tap also suspected a second member, Nguyen Huu Can, of reporting on ICP activities to the French consulate there. To minimize the damage, Tap instructed all Party units in Indochina and Siam to take extra security precautions and sent Tran Van Giau back to Cochin China to reorganize the ICP apparatus there. He also attempted to confuse the Sûreté by passing false information to Can, complaining that the Party was in trouble and could not hold its national congress as scheduled.[35]

The national congress had been scheduled to convene on March 18, but because of the growing fear of disclosure (and perhaps because some delegates were delayed en route), at the last minute it was postponed until March 27. Attending the meeting, in addition to Ha Huy Tap, were Hoang Dinh Giong, Phung Chi Kien, and ten other delegates.

There was no representative from the Comintern or from the other Communist parties.

The delegates to the Macao congress represented a total of about eight hundred Party members operating in Indochina and Siam. The majority were ethnic Vietnamese, although a few, like Hoang Dinh Giong and Hoang Van Non, were members of the mountain minorities, or were overseas Chinese. Most were relatively young, in their twenties or thirties, and only a few were women. The presence of Nguyen Thi Minh Khai, Quoc's love interest and one-time assistant at the Southern Bureau in Hong Kong, within the Party leadership suggests that barriers to advancement on the basis of sex were not yet a factor.

Although accurate statistics are lacking, it appears that the percentage of members from worker or peasant backgrounds was increasing, although the ruling clique within the Party was dominated by members from scholar-gentry backgrounds, many of whom had studied within the Franco-Vietnamese school system and now operated as full-time revolutionaries. As we shall see below, Nguyen Ai Quoc had already complained that Party members who lacked any formal education often found it difficult to grasp the ideological complexities of Marxist-Leninist doctrine and were sometimes unreliable under pressure. Prejudice against those Party members from rural backgrounds was especially strong within the leadership, a legacy of accepted wisdom in Moscow as well as of traditional attitudes within the Vietnamese scholar-gentry class. Workers and peasants could be highly useful, however, as a means of facilitating the effort to penetrate factories and farm villages to spread propaganda for the cause.

Despite the winds of change emanating from Moscow, the decisions reached at the Macao congress made no changes in existing Party strategy. The political resolution, which reaffirmed the correctness of the narrow united front approach that had first been set forth in the 1932 program of action, called on Party comrades to infiltrate national reformist parties in order to undermine their leadership and lure their followers to the ICP. New Party statutes were approved, as well as resolutions on correct work among the masses. At the close of the meeting, a new nine-member Central Committee was selected, with Ha Huy Tap to serve as general secretary. The new committee was to be relocated in Saigon, where Ha Huy Tap maintained his residence. Le Hong Phong's Overseas Executive Committee, which was to be retained as the liaison between the Central Committee and the Comintern, would be transferred to Shanghai.[36]

Ha Huy Tap took the occasion provided by his reports to Moscow on the results of the congress to deliver a few more shots at Nguyen Ai Quoc. In a March 31 letter to the Dalburo, he noted that Party members in Indochina and Siam were waging an open struggle against the legacy of the "national revolutionary" ideology of the Revolutionary Youth League and its former leader Nguyen Ai Quoc. That legacy, he warned, "is very strong and constitutes a very serious obstacle to the development of communism." A pitiless struggle against Quoc's opportunistic theories was therefore indispensable. The Communist parties in Indochina and Siam were both going to write a brochure against these tendencies. Tap proposed that Nguyen Ai Quoc draw up a self-critique to admit his past errors.

A few weeks later, Tap returned to the attack, remarking that several delegates at the Macao congress held Quoc at least partly responsible for the arrest of more than one hundred members of the ICP and the league, since Quoc had known that his colleague Lam Duc Thu was a spy, but had continued to use him. Quoc, he charged, had also carelessly asked each student at the training institute in Canton to provide him with a photograph, as well as the names and addresses of relatives. That material had later fallen into the hands of the French; Nguyen Ai Quoc, he charged, "could never disavow his responsibility" for such actions. To the degree that Quoc's ideas became clear to Party members and the masses, Tap concluded, such ideas would be criticized ever more severely.[37]

Nguyen Ai Quoc probably read such reports after their arrival in Moscow. What he thought about Tap's criticisms of his own actions is not known, but his general attitude is indicated in a letter that he wrote in January 1935 to someone in the Dalburo, complaining that the theoretical knowledge of students from Southeast Asia who had been studying in Moscow was quite low. Many did not understand the bourgeois democratic revolution, or why the land revolution and the cause of anti-imperialism were linked together. Although Quoc admitted that such shortcomings had been true within the ICP in 1930 and 1931, the problem had recently become more serious because of the youth and lack of experience of many Party members. Whether or not he was taking a passing swipe at young colleagues such as Ha Huy Tap or the now deceased Tran Phu is unclear. In any event, he suggested that a brochure be drawn up to enlighten them on ideological matters.[38]

O n July 25, 1935, the Seventh Congress of the Communist International opened in the cavernous House of Trade Unions in Moscow. On the walls were gigantic portraits of Marx, Engels, Lenin, and Stalin, as well as red banners with gold Cyrillic letters proclaiming the forthcoming victory of the proletarian revolution. The purge trial of Bolshevik leaders Lev Kamenev and Grigory Zinoviev, past head of the Comintern, was under way as the congress convened. Both would later be executed. Because of tensions surrounding the trial, delegates to the congress were all housed together in the Lux Hotel, and were not permitted to enter the Kremlin.

Three ICP delegates attended the congress: Le Hong Phong (known variously at the congress as Litvinov, Hai An, Chajan, or Chayan), Nguyen Thi Minh Khai (Van, or Phan Lan), and Hoang Van Non. Two additional delegates had been sent from Vietnam after the departure of these three, but they failed to arrive. Comintern headquarters had decided that each Vietnamese delegate would address the congress. In her speech, Nguyen Thi Minh Khai referred to the exploitation of women that was taking place in colonial areas throughout Asia and emphasized the importance of women in the future revolution in the region; Hoang Van Non spoke on mass struggle. As chairman of the delegation, Le Hong Phong presented a major address on the past shortcomings of the ICP and its current tasks. Among those errors was the fact that many Party members continued to express "putschist" and sectarian ideas inherited from earlier "national revolutionary" parties such as the VNQDD, as well as from previous Communist groups (presumably Tran Van Cung's first incarnation of the Indochinese Communist Party), and did not link the Party directly to the masses.[39]

While none of the speakers from Vietnam appeared to reflect the fact, the primary purpose of the Seventh Comintern Congress was to adopt a new strategy for Communist parties around the world, an approach that would be more in tune with the ideas that Quoc had espoused during the life of the Revolutionary Youth League than with those expressed by the Sixth Congress in 1928. The main reason for the policy shift was the growing danger represented by the rise to power of Adolf Hitler and his National Socialist (Nazi) Party in Germany. When Hitler was first named chancellor in January 1933, Stalin was convinced that he represented an extremist wing of the capitalist class in Germany and thus reflected the final virulent stage of global imperialism; his ascendancy, Stalin believed, would thus lead rapidly to the transfer of power to the German Communist Party. By 1935, however, Stalin had been disabused of such illusions, and he now viewed Nazi Germany as a mortal threat to the survival of the USSR.

Reflecting the importance of the new menace from the west, as well as the growing danger posed by the emergence of a militantly anti-Communist government in Japan, in 1935 the Kremlin decided to repudiate the ultraleftist line that had been approved at the Sixth Congress in 1928 and adopt a new strategy designed to create a united front of antifascist forces from around the world. At the Seventh Congress, the new line was carefully orchestrated by the latest general secretary of the organization, the Bulgarian Communist Georgi Dimitrov. The previous strategy, which had called for proletarian revolutions and the creation of "soviet governments" in the colonies, was discarded; the new task was to mobilize a broad alliance of progressive and democratic forces around the world to oppose the growing danger of malignant fascism. Communist parties were instructed to join with progressive government or nationalist parties in broad anti-imperialist fronts against the common danger from Nazi Germany and Japan.

Viewed from that perspective, Le Hong Phong's criticism of putschism and adventurism, characteristics that could be ascribed to the current leftist leadership of the ICP, had thus been carefully orchestrated by Moscow to send a clear message to Phong's colleagues in Macao. At the close of the final session of the congress, the ICP was admitted to full membership in the Communist International, while Phong himself was elected a member of the presidium of the organization.

Nguyen Ai Quoc had attended the congress as an observer from the secretariat of the Dalburo, under the name of Linov. He evidently did not address the congress, but was probably active behind the scenes talking to delegates, and he took part in a banquet sponsored by Maurice Thorez, a leading figure in the French Communist Party, to celebrate the formal admission of the ICP to the Comintern. The shift in global strategy announced at the congress was undoubtedly gratifying to Quoc, and a much needed confirmation of the correctness of the broad united front approach that he had earlier adopted with the Revolutionary Youth League in Canton. His role as observer at the congress was not necessarily inconsistent with his continuing responsibility as the Comintern's senior spokesman for Southeast Asian affairs. Still, it must have been galling to sit on the sidelines while one of his protégés emerged in the limelight as the leader of the ICP in the new era.[40]

To make matters worse, Nguyen Ai Quoc's intimate relationship with his young colleague Nguyen Thi Minh Khai had apparently come to an end. Letters and confidential reports from the ICP leadership in Macao to the Dalburo in the months leading up to the congress had mentioned that "Quoc's wife" (*la femme de Quoc*) would be among the delegates attending the meeting, thus implying that the two had been married prior to their arrest in Hong Kong in 1931. Perhaps, as the Soviet writer Yevgeny Kobelev has speculated, she fell in love with the handsome Le Hong Phong on the journey. Perhaps, too, Quoc and Minh Khai had drifted apart during their four years of separation after her arrest in Hong Kong in the spring of 1931. Other sources suggest that after his own arrival in Moscow, Nguyen Ai Quoc had been assigned a "temporary wife" by Comintern headquarters; it was also rumored that he had fathered a daughter by a lady friend in the USSR.

Whatever the truth of the matter, shortly after the adjournment of the Seventh Congress, Le Hong Phong and Nguyen Thi Minh Khai were formally married at a district registrar's office in Moscow. After the wedding, Phong left for China to report on the meeting to the Party leadership. Minh Khai remained in Moscow for several months, finally departing for France en route to Hong Kong with her colleague Hoang Van Non in the summer of 1936. To delude suspicious French agents, the two posed as a wealthy Chinese couple on a vacation. From Hong Kong she sailed on to Shanghai to join Le Hong Phong, and eventually returned with him to Saigon, where she became a member of the Party's regional committee for Cochin China. In so doing, she and her husband came a step closer to their future fate as two of the primary martyrs of the Vietnamese revolution.[41]

The relationship between Nguyen Ai Quoc and Nguyen Thi Minh Khai is one of the most puzzling in his life. In later years he never mentioned the issue to his colleagues, and official sources in Hanoi vigorously deny that a marriage between the two had ever taken place. Yet internal documents provide fairly strong evidence to the contrary, although it is possible that the two had never undergone a legal marriage ceremony and simply passed off their relationship to colleagues as man and wife. Whether the combination of losing his Party leadership role and his wife to Le Hong Phong was "doubly humiliating," as one observer suggests, is another matter. In his long career Quoc had already demonstrated a predilection for casual affairs so long as they did not interfere with his political objectives, and he may have seen the relationship as a temporary one from the start.

Prior to their departure for China, Minh Khai and Hoang Van Non met with Nguyen Ai Quoc to take a message back to Le Hong Phong in Shanghai. By that time, the decisions reached at the Seventh

Comintern Congress had already begun to bear fruit, as a new Popular Front government had been formed in Paris in July 1936 under the Socialist Party Prime Minister, Léon Blum. Although the FCP was not formally a part of the governing coalition, it supported the new government, which promised to oppose fascism, to support the USSR, and to end laws in France limiting free speech and association. It also called for the formation of a commission of inquiry to look into conditions in the colonies and suggest reforms. Conditions in Indochina offered a promising opportunity for the revival of the ICP. According to his Soviet biographer, Quoc gave his ICP colleagues some concrete advice:

> The Popular Front victory in France is a rare chance, and we must not fail to use it. The main thing now is to secure complete unity inside the party, especially between its homeside and overseas units. On reaching Saigon, please tell Le Hong Phong the following three things:
>
> One. The Popular Front victory in France is sure to bring about positive changes in the situation in Indochina. For this reason the overseas Central Committee should go home at once and assume the guidance of the patriotic movement. It should leave no more than a token group of comrades abroad to maintain contact with the outside world.
>
> Two. The Trotskyites have betrayed their reactionary essence everywhere, and in Vietnam as well. Our Party must dissociate itself from them most resolutely. There must be no compromises.
>
> Three. Every effort must be made to form an antifascist and antiwar democratic front. It must embrace all patriotic forces, all those who want to fight for the country's salvation. But never forget when striking up alliances that the vital interests of the Party and the working class come first.[42]

In stressing the importance of the broad united front strategy, which had been enunciated at the Seventh Comintern Congress, Nguyen Ai Quoc was unquestionably expressing his own convictions; in warning his colleagues of the need to maintain strict Party control over the revolutionary movement he was following the practices that he had adopted during the life of the league; but in singling out the Trotskyites as renegades who had betrayed the interests of Marxist-Leninist doctrine, he was probably deferring to the wishes of the Comintern, and specifically of Joseph Stalin himself, who for several years had waged a bitter battle against the influence of Trotsky and his followers within the international Communist movement. Although Quoc undoubtedly agreed with Stalin that Trotsky's emphasis on an "uninterrupted revolution" led by proletarian elements alone against hostile forces throughout the world was unrealistic, he must have felt that, on balance, Trotsky's followers in Indochina had more in common with the ICP than with their adversaries. Had it been left to him, Nguyen Ai Quoc would probably have sought to co-opt Vietnamese Trotskyites into accepting ICP leadership.

While his colleagues returned to Asia, Nguyen Ai Quoc remained in Moscow. But he was obviously restless for action. In an interview in September 1935, he told the Soviet journalist Ilya Ehrenburg that he had only one wish, and that was to return as soon as possible to his fatherland. For a while, the situation was promising. He asked for permission to return shortly after the close of the Seventh Congress, but the request was denied on the grounds that the situation in Indochina was too complicated. In the summer of 1936 he submitted a second request to be permitted to return via Berlin and France. If the plan went awry, he promised to go to Shanghai to establish contact with the Comintern office there, and then seek a route home. The Comintern's personnel office invited him to fill out a travel form, but eventually the plan was canceled because of the outbreak of the Spanish Civil War, an event that had repercussions in France.

While waiting for an answer to his request, in the fall of 1936 Nguyen Ai Quoc enrolled in a course at the Institute for the Study of the National and Colonial Questions (the former Stalin School); he thereupon moved from his lodgings at the Lenin University to a small single room on Bolshaya Bronnaya. His study program included courses in philosophy, history, and the Russian language. But he was also given a work assignment by the Indochinese office of the Dalburo to study peasant conditions and produce Vietnamese translations of Marx's *Communist Manifesto* and Lenin's *Leftism: An Infantile Disorder*. Perhaps that is why he was one of two students who did not sign up for a summer trip planned by the school. During the academic year 1937–1938, he enrolled in additional courses at the institute while also working at the Dalburo. With the help of instructors at the institute, he also prepared research materials for writing a work to be titled "The Land Revolution in Southeast Asia."[43]

After two decades of revolutionary work, Nguyen Ai Quoc chafed at his current situation. For an activist with little interest in theory, months spent on translating the works of Communist luminaries or attending classes dealing with abstract ideological matters must have been a trying experience. In June 1938, nearly three years after the close of the Seventh

Congress, he wrote a colleague at the Comintern in desperation. It had been seven years since he was arrested, and the beginning of the eighth year of his inactivity. Quoc asked for help in changing his sad situation. "Send me somewhere, or keep me here. Do of me what you consider useful. But I beg you not to leave me too long without activity and aside and outside the Party." To make his case, he asked for an interview with a responsible Comintern official. With help from a sympathetic Vera Vasilieva, his request was finally granted, and he was instructed to return to China by rail through Central Asia. On September 29, 1938, he resigned from the school. The following day, the personnel office at the institute recorded the fact that student number 19, named Lin, was now released.[44]

Why had Nguyen Ai Quoc finally been released from his purgatory in Moscow after so many years of inactivity? Without the opening of additional archives in Russia this must remain a subject for speculation, for information on his life in Moscow during the mid-1930s is pitifully sparse. Perhaps he had been under observation because of lingering rumors that he might have agreed to become a British agent as the price for release from prison in Hong Kong. It is also not unlikely that Quoc had been in disfavor with Stalin for his unorthodox approach to sacred doctrine. If so, the evolution of the world situation and the new Comintern strategy now rendered the veteran revolutionary potentially more useful in carrying out Soviet policies in East Asia. Although his specific instructions are unknown, it seems probable that he was expected to provide Moscow with information on the rapidly changing situation in China. Under intense pressure from the military forces of Chiang Kai-shek, in October 1934 the CCP had abandoned its base south of the Yangtze River, beginning its Long March to Yan'an in north China. Nguyen Ai Quoc may have viewed his new duty of reporting to Moscow on the activities of his Chinese comrades as an important assignment, but it must have appeared secondary to the task of assisting his own compatriots in carrying out the next stage of the Vietnamese revolution.

VIII | A CAVE AT PAC BO

The China to which Nguyen Ai Quoc was returning in the fall of 1938 was a far different place than the country he had left nearly five years before, for it was now a country at war. The conflict had originated with the Mukden Incident in 1931, when militant elements within the Japanese army suddenly occupied Manchuria and created the puppet state of Manchukuo. During the next few years, Japanese troops began to expand steadily southward, bringing substantial parts of China's northeastern provinces around the old imperial capital of Beijing under Japanese military administration. Initially, Chiang Kai-shek had resisted appeals from his compatriots to abandon military operations to eradicate Communist-controlled areas south of the Yangtze River—operations that had led in late 1934 to the forced exodus of Communist forces on their famous Long March to their new base area at Yan'an, in north China—and then seek to create a national consensus to resist Japanese aggression. But in early 1937, after a bizarre kidnapping of the Nationalist leader by his own military officers while he was on a visit to Xian, Chiang was prevailed upon to sign a second united front with the CCP and turn national attention to the menace from Japan. A few months later, open warfare broke out after an armed clash at the Marco Polo Bridge south of Beijing.

Although the Japanese threat placed the Chinese people in extreme peril, it represented a window of opportunity for Nguyen Ai Quoc. In the first place, the establishment of the second united front between the Nationalist government and the Communists could provide him with increased freedom of movement as he sought to restore contacts with Vietnamese revolutionaries operating in south China. Secondly, it raised the specter of a general war in Asia, which could rapidly expand into Southeast Asia and bring an end to half a century of French rule in Indochina.

Leaving Moscow by train sometime in the early fall of 1938, Nguyen Ai Quoc traveled eastward across the vast grasslands of Soviet Central Asia. After stopping in Alma-Ata, the capital of Kazakhstan, he continued on to the Chinese border, where he joined a caravan heading through Ürümqi in Chinese Turkistan to Lanzhou, once the eastern terminus of the Silk Road and now a bustling rail center and capital of Gansu province. At Lanzhou he received assistance from local representatives of the CCP, who made arrangements for him to continue on to Xian. There he was greeted by Wu Xiuquan, head of a local office of the People's Liberation Army (PLA), which served the CCP as a contact point for visitors arriving from the USSR. As Wu recalled it in his memoirs: "I was told by higher authorities that I must meet an important Asian, but I didn't know his name. Higher authorities demanded that I treat him carefully and with respect, and that I must escort him safely to Yan'an."[1]

After a two-day stay in Xian, which had just suffered its first air raid by Japanese bombers, Nguyen Ai Quoc joined a group of travelers who were being transported by bullock and horse cart on a two-hundred mile trek northward into the mountains to Yan'an. Because there were many Kuomintang troops along the route, Quoc was disguised as an "escort" for the horse carts, which were ostensibly transporting clothing and footwear to the impoverished peoples living in the hills; he thus covered much of the route on foot.

As Nguyen Ai Quoc recalled many years later, Yan'an in 1938 was flooded with nearly 200,000 PLA troops, most of whom were housed in the numerous caves that studded the loess-covered hillsides throughout the region. Many senior CCP cadres also lived in the caves, which were warmer in winter and cooler in summer than ordinary housing in the area. It was difficult for him to distinguish Chinese officers from enlisted men, however, since they all wore the same dark blue uniform and cloth shoes. Quoc was housed in the Apple Garden (Tao Yuan), a relatively spacious seven-room villa later to be occupied by CCP Chairman Mao Zedong. In Yan'an, he met a number of Chinese acquaintances whom he had known in Moscow, but he apparently did not meet Mao himself, although the latter was rapidly becoming the dominant force within the CCP.[2]

After about two weeks in Yan'an, Nguyen Ai Quoc headed south in a caravan of five automobiles carrying the retinue of the PLA military commander Ye Jianying. Danger came not from the Japanese, who had just seized Shanghai and were advancing up the Yangtze River toward Hankou, but from elsewhere. Although the united front between the CCP and Chiang Kai-shek's Nationalist Government had been in operation for over a year, the truce was a fragile one, and was not always observed with scrupulous care by the local Kuomintang authorities. To disguise his identity, Quoc adopted the Chinese name Hu Guang and posed as the orderly of a senior officer traveling with the group. According to Communist sources, during the course of their journey government troops periodically harassed the caravan until nearby PLA units forced them to withdraw.[3]

Nguyen Ai Quoc's destination was Guilin, a rustic city in the heart of Guangxi province famous for the sculptured limestone hills that surround it and have historically provided an inspiration for classical Chinese landscape painters. There he took up residence at the local headquarters of the CCP's Eighth Route Army in Lu Ma village, located just outside the municipal boundaries. He was assigned employment as a journalist and public health cadre at the local National Salvation Office (a mass organization subordinated to the CCP-Kuomintang united front). One of his Chinese acquaintances later recalled:

> I worked with Ho Chi Minh at the Eighth Route Army headquarters in Guilin from the end of 1938 to the spring and summer of 1939, and we lived together in a large house to the west of Lu Ma village. At that time he used the name of Hu Guang, and from his accent I thought he was Cantonese. Our office was like a club, but not just any club, since it also performed the function of carrying out political education and culture . . . and it had many cadres responsible for economics and finance, health, journalism, and so forth. Ho Chi Minh was responsible for hygiene but was a journalist as well, and was therefore one of the leading officials in our organization. I remember that in his inspections of sanitation conditions he took his job seriously, and had very high standards. If sanitation conditions weren't good, he could be quite blunt in his criticism. He was also responsible for editing our journal, *Shenghuo Xiaobao* [Life Journal]. . . . He designed the cover and made up the title. . . . He also wrote many articles as well as Chinese poetry in the classical style.

While Quoc was in Guilin, his friend continued,

he gave me a very sharp impression. Every day he rose early, and then swept the floor. . . . It was a dirt floor, so when he swept it raised a cloud of dust, and Hu Guang had to cover his mouth with a cloth to protect his mouth. . . . Serving as a health inspector and a journalist took a third to a half of Hu Guang's time. For the remainder of the time he either read books or typed on his typewriter. He had a foreign typewriter. I could tell that he was very proficient at it. . . . At that time I also didn't know Hu Guang's real identity. Later I came to realize that he had connections, because on one occasion I criticized him on some small matter in the office. In those days, in our office mutual criticism and self-criticism were an expected form of behavior. But the next day, [a CCP official] came to me and asked if I had criticized Hu Guang. Why [he asked] are you just haphazardly criticizing people? Thus I realized that Hu Guang was not just an ordinary person, but had connections.

Nguyen Ai Quoc was careful to cultivate the friendship of his colleagues. On his arrival, he had discovered that only English-language typewriters were available at the Eighth Route Army club in Guilin. Fortunately, one of his Chinese colleagues periodically traveled on official business to Hong Kong and Haiphong, and in the course of one visit was able to purchase a French typewriter, which he brought back for Quoc's use. In gratitude, Quoc took his friend to dinner at a local restaurant, and even splurged on two bottles of wine.[4]

Some of Nguyen Ai Quoc's articles, written in French under the name of P. C. Line, were sent to Hanoi, where they were published in the French-language Vietnamese newspaper *Notre Voix*. Most dealt with conditions in wartime China, attacking the Japanese and praising the indomitable courage of the Chinese people in resisting aggression. One early piece, written in December 1938, sarcastically described Tokyo's "civilizing" efforts in China, pointing to the massacre that had taken place at Nanjing earlier in the year as an example of Japanese brutality. Another praised the spirit of cooperation as exemplified in the CCP-Kuomintang united front, while a third pointed out that although Japanese technological superiority had resulted in early military success, the Japanese army's mechanized equipment was now becoming bogged down on primitive Chinese roads and thus getting increasingly useless. The Japanese government had promised victory in three months, he said, and then six months. But, he noted, the war continued without letup.[5]

Notre Voix was published legally under the direction of ICP leaders based in Hanoi, and its appearance was just one of the consequences of the shift in French colonial policies that had taken place after the formation of the Popular Front in 1936. With leftist parties taking part in the new government in Paris, political prisoners were released early from jail in Indochina, and political parties of all orientations were authorized to take part in limited organizational activities.

The policy shift in Paris, together with the change of strategy in Moscow at the Seventh Comintern Congress, took ICP leaders somewhat by surprise. At the Macao congress in March 1935, Ha Huy Tap and his colleagues had adopted a strongly sectarian approach that reflected the leftist line promulgated at the Sixth Congress in 1928, on the clear assumption that such a strategy would continue.

On his return from Moscow in the spring of 1936, Le Hong Phong immediately convened a meeting of the ICP Central Committee in Shanghai to discuss the results of the Seventh Congress. He explained the significance of the recent policy shift in Moscow and proposed steps to bring the Indochinese party into line with the new strategy. At his urging, the committee approved the creation of a new Indochinese Democratic Front (Mat tran Thong nhat Dan chu Dong duong) to oppose global fascism and reactionary French colonialism. The resolution was silent on the approach to be adopted toward rival political parties, but after the conference, the Central Committee sent an open letter to all Party members explaining the new policy. Letters had already been sent to the VNQDD and other nationalist parties proposing cooperation in the common goal of achieving national independence and bringing about social reforms.[6]

Although internal sources insist that the Central Committee had unanimously approved the new line as ordered by Moscow, it must have been a bitter pill to swallow for members such as Ha Huy Tap who had been weaned on a more doctrinaire approach. There was also some resistance from within the ranks, primarily from Party members who had spent time in prison and thus had bitter personal experiences with the French colonial regime.

Whatever their reluctance, Party leaders approved the new strategy, and after the conference the Central Committee moved back to Indochina, where it set up a new headquarters in Hoc Mon village, a northern suburb of Saigon. Le Hong Phong, still serving as Comintern representative to the ICP, returned with them. During the next two years, the

Party moved more and more into the open, while seeking to increase its membership among all progressive strata of Vietnamese society. "Mutual assistance associations" representing the interests of various social groups such as farmers, workers, youth, and women, were established in towns, villages, factories, and schools to serve as training grounds and recruitment centers for potential followers, as well as a cover for ICP activities. Party newspapers, run by promising young cadres such as Vo Nguyen Giap, Truong Chinh, and Tran Huy Lieu, were established in all major cities to present the new moderate line in an effort to seek the support of the patriotic middle class.

In some respects, the stratagem was a success. During the next two years Party membership increased severalfold, and the percentage of followers from among the working class and the peasantry skyrocketed. But the colonial government had only a limited tolerance level for nationalist activities, and when ICP newspapers became more strident in their criticism of official policies, the authorities struck back. A number of prominent critics, including the radical nationalist Nguyen An Ninh and Le Hong Phong himself, were arrested and held briefly, then released.

The vagaries of colonial policy, which sparked periodic tensions within the Party over the relative importance of overt and clandestine activity, became the chief topic at Central Committee meetings held at Hoc Mon in 1937 and 1938. At a meeting held in March 1938, the issue came to a head. General Secretary Ha Huy Tap was the most prominent critic of the new Popular Front strategy, while Le Hong Phong was its most vocal advocate, arguing in favor of a policy of cooperation with all progressive nationalist parties. In the middle was Nguyen Van Cu, a young Party member from the Red River delta who wanted to maintain a balance between overt and covert activity, to cooperate with other progressive organizations while continuing to oppose the Constitutionalists. In the end, Cu's views won the day. Ha Huy Tap, whose confrontational personality and suspicious nature had by now alienated most of his colleagues, was replaced by Nguyen Van Cu as general secretary.[7]

Nguyen Ai Quoc had observed the changes taking place in Indochina from his temporary base in south China. To avoid the possibility that the Sûreté might become aware of his whereabouts, he had feared to identify himself as the real author of the articles by P. C. Line, but he hoped that Party members on the editorial board at *Notre Voix* (some of whom might have been familiar with Lin, his Moscow pseudonym) would recognize the style and divine the name of the author. In July 1939, he became bolder, sending through an acquaintance a short mes-

top: A view of downtown Hanoi in the early twentieth century. In the background is the Municipal Theater, built by the French, which would eventually play a central role in the Vietnamese revolution.

bottom: Adjacent to the French sector of colonial Hanoi, with its European-style modern buildings, was the native city. Inhabited primarily by Chinese merchants and artisans, it retained its individual character under colonial rule, and continues to do so today.

A portrait taken of Ho Chi Minh's father as a young man. Although he was trained as a Confucian scholar, Nguyen Sinh Sac's modernist inclinations are apparent from his attire, as he wears the popular jacket popularized by his contemporary, the Chinese revolutionary Sun Yat-Sen.

After Nguyen Sinh Sac married Hoang Thi Loan in 1883, his father-in-law built a small two-room house adjacent to his own family home in Hoang Tru hamlet and gave it to the new couple as a wedding present. Here Ho Chi Minh was born on May 2, 1890. Although neither of the original houses has survived, they were reconstructed in 1959, when Ho had become president of the Democratic Republic of Vietnam.

top: In this room in the house of his father-in-law Hoang Duong, Nguyen Sinh Sac received instruction in the Confucian classics. The room also served as a reception area for members of the Hoang clan during New Year's celebrations each year. After Duong's death in 1883, Sac used the room to give lessons in the Confucian classics to neighborhood children.

bottom: When Nguyen Sinh Sac took his family to live in Hué in 1895, it was still the imperial city of Vietnam. The imperial palace and its surrounding buildings, as shown in this aerial photograph, were protected by a series of extensive battlements designed after the style of the seventeenth-century French architect Vauban.

A view of the small apartment where Nguyen Sinh Sac and his family lived while he prepared to take the civil service examinations. It was in this house, located near the western wall of the imperial city, that Ho Chi Minh's mother died in 1901. It now contains a small museum.

The well-known scholar and revolutionary patriot Phan Boi Chau was a close acquaintance of Nguyen Sinh Sac and often visited Sac at his house in Kim Lien village. In the family room of the house, young Ho Chi Minh served tea or rice wine to his father and the illustrious visitor.

After his triumphant return home from Hué in 1901, Nguyen Sinh Sac received this house in Kim Lien from neighboring villagers who were proud of his scholarly achievements. The house was larger than the one in nearby Hoang Tru hamlet, with four rooms, one containing an altar for Sac's deceased wife Hoang Thi Loan. Ho Chi Minh lived in this house for five years.

above: In the fall of 1907, Nguyen Sinh Sac enrolled his two sons in the National Academy (Quoc Hoc), a prestigious school for aspiring bureaucrats located in Hué. The school is still in operation. Shown here is the massive gate, built in the Chinese style, at the street entrance to the school.

below: In June 1911, Ho Chi Minh sailed from Nha Rong Dragon Pier on a French passenger ship, the *Amiral Latouche–Treville*. Located on the river just east of the central district of Saigon, the building had been constructed on the wharf in the late nineteenth century. Carvings of dragons on the roof gave the building its name. Today it houses the municipal branch of the Ho Chi Minh Museum.

REVENDICATIONS
DU
Peuple Annamite

Depuis la victoire des Alliés, tous les peuples assujettis frémissent d'espoir devant la perspective de l'ère de droit et de justice qui doit s'ouvrir pour eux en vertu des engagements formels et solennels, pris devant le monde entier par les différentes puissances de l'Entente dans la lutte de la Civilisation contre la Barbarie.

En attendant que le principe des Nationalités passe du domaine de l'idéal dans celui de la réalité par la reconnaissance effective du droit sacré pour les peuples de disposer d'eux-mêmes, le Peuple de l'ancien Empire d'Annam, aujourd'hui Indo-Chine Française, présente aux Nobles Gouvernements de l'Entente en général et à l'honorable Gouvernement Français en particulier les humbles revendications suivantes:

1° Amnistie générale en faveur de tous les condamnés politiques indigènes.

2° Réforme de la justice indochinoise par l'octroi aux Indigènes des mêmes garanties judiciaires qu'aux Européens, et la suppression complète et définitive des Tribunaux d'exception qui sont des instruments de terrorisation et d'oppression contre la partie la plus honnête du peuple Annamite:

3° Liberté de Presse et d'Opinion;

4° Liberté d'association et de réunion;

5° Liberté d'émigration et de voyage à l'étranger;

6° Liberté d'enseignement et création dans toutes les provinces des écoles d'enseignements techniques et professionnels à l'usage des indigènes;

7° Remplacement du régime des décrets par le régime des lois;

8° Délégation permanente d'indigènes élus auprès du Parlement Français pour le tenir au courant des desiderata indigènes;

Le Peuple Annamite, en présentant les revendications ci-dessus formulées, compte sur la justice mondiale de toutes les Puissances et se recommande en particulier à la bienveillance du Noble Peuple Français qui tient son sort entre ses mains et qui, la France étant une République, est censée l'avoir pris sous sa protection. En se réclamant de la protection du Peuple Français, le Peuple Annamite: car il sait que le Peuple Français, bien loin de s'humilier, s'honore au contraire représente la liberté et la justice, et ne renoncera soumis à son sublime idéal de Fraternité jamais à la liberté et à la justice. En conséquence, en écoutant la voix des opprimés, le Peuple Français fera son devoir envers la France et envers l'Humanité.

Pour le Groupe des Patriotes Annamites:

NGUYEN AI QUÂC

above: The French steamship *Amiral Latouche–Treville* measured 400 feet in length, weighed 600 tons, and was staffed by 72 officers and ordinary seamen. Ho, known as "Ba," was hired in June 1911 as a kitchen helper, and sailed on the ship to Europe.

left: Shown here is a copy of the "demands of the Annamite people" that Ho Chi Minh, under the alias "Nguyen Ai Quoc," presented to the victorious Allied leaders meeting at Versailles in the summer of 1919. Ho not only helped to draft the petition, but also delivered it in person to delegations attending the conference at Versailles and to the homes of influential French politicians.

A fellow classmate of Nguyen Sinh Sac at the Imperial Academy, Phan Chu Trinh took up the cause of reform, and was eventually exiled to France, where he became a leading figure in the Vietnamese community. During his stay in Paris, Ho Chi Minh collaborated closely with Trinh, but eventually they drifted apart.

At the Villa des Gobelins on this quiet residential street on the right bank of Paris, Ho Chi Minh settled with Phan Chu Trinh and a number of other patriotic Vietnamese émigrés. Here, Ho cultivated his revolutionary rhetoric and made his decision to join the new French Communist Party.

top: A view of the main conference hall in Tours, France, where the French Socialist Party held its momentous congress in December 1920. Ho Chi Minh is seated at the middle table, fourth from the top on the left.

bottom: Under the suspicious eyes of the French police, who followed his every move with careful attention, Ho Chi Minh announced his allegiance to the principles of Lenin's new Communist International in this speech at the 1920 conference at Tours. To his immediate left is his patron Paul Vaillant-Couturier.

left: A view of Ho Chi Minh's apartment on the Impasse Compoint in a working-class district in northern Paris. Evicted from the Villa des Gobelins because of his radical ideas, Ho rented a small flat here in the summer of 1921. His one-room apartment was on the second floor, above a small shop where he supported himself as a photo retoucher and painter of curios.

below: A cartoon by Ho Chi Minh which appeared in the journal *Le Paria.* In the illustration, the European declares: "Hurry up, Incognito! Show your loyalty, in the name of God." Ho served as editor, graphic artist, and chief distributor for the magazine, which closed its doors after his departure for Moscow in the summer of 1923.

During his years in Paris, Ho Chi Minh was followed closely by agents of the Sûreté, who frequently took surreptitious photographs of him to try to ascertain his true identity. Here he is photographed near the fashionable Place de la Concorde. The photographer, a fellow Vietnamese living in France, was secretly serving as an agent for the French police.

Ho Chi Minh shortly after his arrival in the Soviet Union in 1923. This photograph, which clearly displays the unusual shape of his left ear, belies his later claim to an acquaintance that he had never worn a necktie in his entire life.

top: On his arrival in Moscow in the summer of 1923, Ho gradually emerged as a spokesman for the oppressed peoples of Asia, and he was frequently invited to attend ceremonial occasions as the token Asian revolutionary. Here he attends a rally in Red Square. To his immediate right on the Kremlin Wall is the old Bolshevik and Stalin intimate, Klementi Voroshilov. Next to Voroshilov is Evgeny Zinoviev, then serving as director of the Communist International.

bottom: In this building, the Comintern headquarters in downtown Moscow, Ho Chi Minh honed his revolutionary credentials during his stay in the Soviet Union from 1923 to the end of 1924. Ho worked at the Far Eastern Bureau, while attending classes in the Stalin School.

In the summer of 1924, Ho Chi Minh was selected as a delegate to the Fifth Congress of the Communist International, held in Moscow in July. Here he is seated in the front row, on the far left, with a number of other delegates and their families.

In December 1924, Ho Chi Minh left Moscow for south China, where he set up the first avowedly Marxist organization to promote revolution in Indochina. The origins of this picture are unknown, but Ho was later criticized by colleagues for allowing photographs of his comrades to fall into the hands of French agents in China.

Ho Chi Minh with students and faculty members at the Institute of Peasant Work in Canton. It is from this photograph, taken sometime early in 1925, that French security agents discovered the real identity of "Comrade Ly Thuy," then serving as an interpreter at Comintern headquarters in the city.

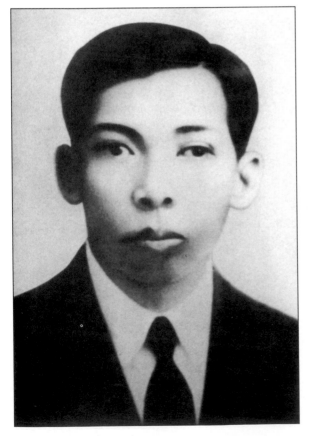

One of the brightest young stars in the Vietnamese revolutionary movement was Tran Phu, who joined the League in the late 1920s, and was then sent to Moscow to study at the Stalin School. In 1931, he died in French prison.

left: One of the first female members of the Indochinese Communist Party, Nguyen Thi Minh Khai came to the attention of Ho Chi Minh while serving as his assistant in Hong Kong in 1930. Plans for their marriage were apparently underway when she was arrested by the British police. She later married one of Ho's colleagues and was executed by the French in 1941.

below: In early June 1931, Hong Kong newspapers reported the arrest by British police of a man suspected of being the dangerous Vietnamese agitator Nguyen Ai Quoc. The suspect, who had been apprehended in an apartment on Kowloon peninsula, was described as the "supreme leader" of the Annamite revolutionary movement.

IMPORTANT H.K. ARREST.

COUP FOR FRENCH GOVERNMENT.

ANNAMITE LEADER IN CUSTODY.

POLICE RETICENT.

Nguyen Ai Quoc, the supreme leader of the Annamite revolutionists, has been arrested in Hongkong. His arrest constitutes a big political coup for the French administration of Indo-China, inasmuch as Nguyen has been the object of considerable attention for many years, and French political agents all over China had been striving to bring about his apprehension.

A most accomplished man, speaking half-a-dozen European languages, Nguyen, surnamed "The Patriot", by Frenchmen and Annamites, was a close associate of the late Dr. Sun Yat-sen. Espousing the cause of Annamite nationalism, he is a fearless speaker and writer, the author of a large number of books written in many languages on conditions in Indo-China, and an ardent supporter of constitutional reform.

Mainspring of Movement.

Over a decade ago, he made his way out of the country and immediately came into contact with the late Dr. Sun. The association was productive of the subsequent wave of nationalism, of which Nguyen is said to be the mainspring, which spread throughout Indo-China, leading to the many regrettable incidents of the last two years.

A firm believer in the axiom that the pen is mightier than the sword, Nguyen has sought to bring the cause of Annamite nationalism by constitutional means before such authorities as the League of Nations. Not finding his efforts very successful in that direction, he turned his attention to the development of Chinese politics with a view to finding therein an opportunity for furthering his cause.

Kuomintang Member.

He was a prominent speaker at the Pan-Asiatic Congress of Asiatic peoples at Canton in 1925, and as an honorary member of the Chinese Kuomintang he had appeared at sessional meetings at which he spoke on the identity of aims between the Chinese and Annamite peoples.

For a long time, the French Government, which accuses him of Communistic leanings, had sought his apprehension in China, but he had disappeared from public ken for a number of years, during which he is said to have travelled in Europe to study political affairs. Lately he reappeared in China, this synchronizing with the outbreak of the revolution in Indo-China, and a big reward was offered by the French Government for his apprehension.

Sudden Arrest.

What induced Nguyen to come to Hongkong is not known, but it appears that information regarding his movements was communicated to the Hongkong Police authorities, who appear to have arrested him in a lightning raid.

Beyond the information confirming advices received from Indo-China regarding his capture in the Colony, the local authorities are not disposed to disclose the details of his arrest.

The French Government, it is understood, has made a requisition for Nguyen's extradition.

proposed for sale of the railway

After his release from a Hong Kong prison in late December 1932, Ho made his way by a circuitous route back to Moscow, where he finally arrived in the late spring of 1934. This photograph, which was apparently taken in the Soviet Union, suggests that his prison experience must have been an arduous one.

In August 1945, Ho Chi Minh sent a letter of farewell to Charles Fenn in south China, expressing his belief that relations between their two countries would now undergo some difficult times. But he expressed his hopes that they might meet again in the future, hopes that were not to be realized.

Dear Mr. Bernard & Mr. Fenn.

I will be very much obliged to you of taking care of our boys. I wish they can learn radio & other things necessary in our common fight against the Japs.

I hope soon you will be able to visit us here, in our base. It will be great!

Permit me to send my respect to General Chenault.

Best greetings from

Yours Sincerely

May. 9   Hoo

Dear Mr. Fenn, I thank you very much for your active friendship. I'll try to send some one to meet you, Please send my greetings to our friends. I send you my kindest regards and remain ever sincerely yours.

HO CHI MINH

4/47   Hoo

sage containing advice to members of the Central Committee, along with his address in China, so that they could contact him. The message was an unabashed declaration of support for the united front policies adopted at the Seventh Comintern Congress.

1. For the time being, the Party should not be too ambitious in its demands (national independence, a parliament, etc.). To do so would be to play into the hands of the Japanese fascists. It should therefore only demand democratic rights, freedom of organization, freedom of assembly, freedom of press and freedom of speech, a general amnesty for all political prisoners, and struggle for the legalization of the Party.

2. To attain this objective, it must seek to organize a broad National Democratic Front. That Front should consist not only of the peoples of Indochina but also of all progressive French people living in Indochina, not only of working people but also of the national bourgeois class.

3. The Party must adopt a wise and flexible attitude toward the national bourgeoisie. It should seek to draw it into the Front, to rally the elements that can be rallied, and to neutralize those that can be neutralized. We must by all means avoid leaving them outside the Front, lest they should fall into the hands of the enemy of the revolution and increase the strength of the reactionaries.

4. We cannot make any alliance with or any concession to the Trotskyite group. We must do everything possible to lay bare their faces as the running dogs of the fascists and annihilate them politically.

5. To increase and consolidate its forces, to widen its influence, and to work effectively, the Indochinese Democratic Front must keep close contact with the Popular Front in France, because the latter also struggles for freedom and democracy, and can give us great help.

6. The Party should not demand that the Front acknowledge its leadership. It must instead show itself to be the organization that makes the greatest sacrifices, and is the most active and loyal. It is only through daily struggle and work that the masses of the people will acknowledge the correct policies and capability for leadership of the Party and that it can win the leading position.

7. To be able to carry out the above tasks, the Party must uncompromisingly fight against factionalism and must systematically

organize Marxist-Leninist cooperation to raise the cultural and political level of all Party members. It must assist all non-Party cadres to raise their level. It must maintain close contact with the French Communist Party.[8]

Nguyen Ai Quoc enclosed a copy of the message in a report that he sent to the Comintern. It was his first formal communication with his colleagues in Moscow since his departure the year before. Quoc apologized for his delay in reporting conditions in Asia, explaining that the present crisis had upset his plans. He explained that he had made some attempts to contact the ICP, but without result. In the meantime, he said that he had written a manuscript titled *Khu vuc dac biet* (The Special Region—this probably dealt with the CCP's liberated area in north China) and a number of newspaper articles.

Nguyen Ai Quoc also apologized for any theoretical shortcomings in his message of advice to the ICP Central Committee, explaining (perhaps disingenuously) that he had lost the notes on Comintern strategy that he had brought with him from Moscow and was forced to rely on memory. With what may have been a hint of sarcasm, he asked his comrades in the USSR to check carefully to see whether he had made any mistakes. He then concluded with a discussion of the current situation in Indochina, noting that the election of the Popular Front in France had resulted in a number of improvements since 1936, but adding that many of these reforms had been reversed with the appointment of the more conservative government of Prime Minister Edouard Daladier in late 1938. The government's lurch to the right had provoked a number of worker strikes, many of which were supported by other classes in Vietnam.[9]

In February 1939, CCP headquarters instructed commander Ye Jianying to set up a military training program at Hengyang, about 200 miles northeast of Guilin in Hunan province. The program was a cooperative venture by the CCP and the Nationalist government that had been planned the previous autumn. An institute was established in the nearby town of Nanywe to train Chinese Nationalist troops to carry on guerrilla war in enemy areas, and Chiang Kai-shek instructed Ye Jianying to select several Communist cadres to conduct classes there. The first class opened on February 15 and concluded in mid-May. A second class commenced shortly afterward. In June (still operating under the name Hu Guang, although now with the rank of major), Nguyen Ai Quoc was sent from Guilin to Hengyang to serve as an administrator at the institute. He also served as the unit's radio operator. He lived with other administrators in the manor house of a local landlord west of town.

After completing his assignment at the end of September, Nguyen Ai Quoc returned to Guilin. A few days later he left for Longzhou, the town in Guangxi province where Le Hong Phong had lived in 1932, in the hope of establishing contact with two cadres who had been sent by the ICP Central Committee specifically for that purpose. However, by the time Quoc arrived, the Vietnamese cadres had already run out of funds and returned to Indochina.[10]

Having failed at his first attempt to reestablish links with the Party leadership inside Indochina, Nguyen Ai Quoc returned to Guilin to make other arrangements. He now decided to go Chongqing, in the heart of Sichuan province, where Chiang Kai-shek had set up his wartime capital after the Japanese occupation of the Yangtze valley; Quoc's trip to Chongqing was apparently motivated by his desire to seek assistance from the CCP liaison office there. En route he stopped briefly at Guiyang, the capital of Guizhou province, and took temporary lodgings in a room on the upper floor of the local Eighth Route Army office. On November 7, he left Guiyang for Chongqing. Taking up residence at the CCP liaison office, he renewed his friendship with Zhou Enlai, whom he had known in Paris and later in Canton, where Zhou had served as Chiang Kai-shek's political commissar at the Whampoa Academy. Now Zhou was serving as the CCP liaison chief in Chongqing. A Chinese colleague later recalled that Quoc lived simply, dressed in a country manner, and spoke with a Cantonese accent, but always carried his typewriter with him. Few in the office knew his real identity.[11]

Ironically, Nguyen Ai Quoc's trip to Chongqing deprived him of an opportunity to restore contact with his comrades inside Vietnam. On November 11, Phung Chi Kien and Kien's colleague Dang Van Cap arrived in Guiyang to meet him. A member of the ICP Central Committee since the Macao conference in 1935, Kien had been living in south China and Hong Kong and had recently collaborated with two other Party veterans, Hoang Van Hoan and Vu Anh, to set up an "overseas party branch" in Kunming, the capital of Yunnan province, to handle Party affairs in south China. They were soon in bitter competition with local members of the VNQDD, the Revolutionary Youth League's old rival, led by the veteran nationalist Vu Hong Khanh. In late October 1939, the Central Committee had instructed Kien to get in touch with Nguyen Ai Quoc in Guiyang; upon learning he had just missed Quoc, Kien returned to Kunming, leaving Dang Van Cap behind to await Nguyen Ai Quoc's return. But plans once again went awry. Quoc returned to Guiyang on November 18, but owing to the heavy congestion in the crowded streets around the office, Cap was unable to establish contact with him.

By now, Nguyen Ai Quoc had become aware of the existence of the new overseas Party branch in Kunming, and in February 1940 he went there to contact Phung Chi Kien and his colleagues. Vu Anh, a cadre of worker background who was then employed under the pseudonym Trinh Dong Hai as a truck driver in a lumber factory, would later write:

> A man of middle age, dressed in the European manner with a collar and tie, arrived at the Yong An Thang factory and asked me in Chinese, "Is there an employee here by the name of Trinh Dong Hai?" I introduced myself. The visitor told me in a low voice in Vietnamese that his name was Tran, and he invited me to go to the town square to talk. En route, I was struck by his vivacious manner and his unusually brilliant eyes. I guessed that he was a cadre of some eminence, without doubting in the least that I was face to face with Nguyen Ai Quoc. I knew only that our Central Committee had asked the Chinese Communist Party to locate him, and here he was before me. This fact alone gave me confidence.[12]

Vu Anh informed his visitor that the Party had set up a clandestine network in Yunnan using the cover of a commercial firm and took him to meet Phung Chi Kien. They also met with Hoang Van Hoan, a graduate of the league's training institute in Canton who had spent several years in a Party branch in Siam and was now working as a tailor in Kunming. Quoc took up residence at a local bookstore, while advising his colleagues on how to carry out revolutionary operations in the area. As always, he had his typewriter with him, and hacked out numerous articles for the overseas Party branch newspaper *Dong Thanh* (United in Spirit). In April, he accompanied Phung Chi Kien in visits to the Party's bases along the railroad from Kunming to the Indochinese border. The French had built the rail line, using several thousand Vietnamese workers, to facilitate communications between Indochina and the southern Chinese provinces. Disguised as an old peasant dressed in faded khaki clothes, "Mr. Tran" stopped at several towns along the line over a period of several weeks, inspecting conditions and giving political advice, and then returned to Kunming in late May 1940.[13]

In the meantime, conditions for Party members were growing harsher inside Indochina. The Daladier government foreshadowed the end of the Popular Front in France; the colonial government had responded by placing tougher restrictions on Party activities in Indochina. Then, in late August, came the stunning announcement that Nazi Germany and the Soviet Union had signed a treaty of mutual nonaggression. A week later, German military forces crossed the Polish border, and Great Britain and France declared war on Berlin.

The news had a catastrophic impact on Party operations in Indochina. General Georges Catroux, the new governor-general, had ordered an immediate crackdown on all legal and semilegal activities by the ICP and other radical political organizations. Le Hong Phong, the ICP Comintern representative whose activities were under careful observation by the French, was rearrested in Saigon in late September. Ha Huy Tap, Nguyen Ai Quoc's harsh critic at the time of the Macao congress, was already in prison as the result of a police roundup during May Day rallies the previous year. In a desperate effort to prevent a disaster, General Secretary Nguyen Van Cu convened a meeting of the Central Committee at a safe location outside Saigon in early November. Because of heightened French surveillance, only four members attended, and none of the representatives from Tonkin (where the regional committee had just been forced to move its headquarters from Hanoi out into the suburbs) managed to show up for the meeting. The four tried to present a brave face. Although the government crackdown had forced the Party back into hiding, the increased likelihood of a general war in Europe created enticing prospects for a collapse of France or a Japanese invasion of Indochina, either of which heightened the chance for a popular uprising aimed at national liberation. After all, no less an authority than Lenin had declared that the best time to launch a revolution was during a world war. Concluding that the French crackdown rendered the Popular Front strategy null and void, the committee drew up a new policy calling for preparations to launch a general uprising to overthrow the colonial regime. For the first time since the collapse of the Revolutionary Youth League a decade earlier, the issue of Vietnamese national independence took the Party's immediate and direct attention. Two months later, Nguyen Van Cu and his colleague Le Duan, a young Central Committee member from central Vietnam who had attended the November conference, were arrested by the French and placed in a Saigon prison.[14]

Shortly after Quoc returned to Kunming in May 1940, two additional members of the Party arrived in the city, under orders from the Central Committee to seek further training in revolutionary operations: Pham Van Dong and Vo Nguyen Giap. Dong, a veteran Party member who had attended the Revolutionary Youth League Congress in Hong Kong in May 1929, had been born in Quang Ngai province, south of Da Nang, in 1908. The son of a mandarin who served as chief of staff for Emperor Duy Tan, Dong had graduated from the National Academy in Hué, but then joined the revolutionary movement and fled to Canton, where he studied at the Whampoa Academy. With his prominent cheekbones and deep-set eyes, Dong had a quiet and unassuming demeanor that disguised a fierce determination, and he soon came to the attention of his colleagues as a potential leader. Arrested during a government sweep operation in Saigon in April 1931, he spent several years in prison on the island of Poulo Condore in the South China Sea. After several years in the "tiger cages," the infamous jail cells that were used by the French to house dangerous political prisoners during the colonial era, he was granted amnesty in 1937 and served as a journalist during the Popular Front era.

His colleague Vo Nguyen Giap, was born in 1910 in Quang Binh province; Giap was also from a mandarin family, but his maternal grandfather had taken part in the resistance movement against the French in the 1880s. In 1924, Giap had entered the National Academy in Hué but, fiery and intense in character, soon became involved in radical activities after observing the funeral services for Phan Chu Trinh. Expelled from school in 1927, he joined the Tan Viet party but eventually shifted to the ICP and was arrested for taking part in student demonstrations in Hué during the Nghe Tinh revolt. Released from prison in 1933, he resumed his schooling and eventually received a law degree from the University of Hanoi. After graduation, he did not become a full-time revolutionary but accepted a position as a history instructor at a private school in Hanoi. It was there that he met Nguyen Thi Minh Giang, the younger sister of Nguyen Ai Quoc's wife, Nguyen Thi Minh Khai. They soon married and Minh Giang gave birth to a daughter, while Giap (known within the movement as Van) became a journalist for the Party newspaper, *Notre Voix;* he also collaborated with his colleague Truong Chinh on a pamphlet highlighting rural conditions in Indochina. Now under close police surveillance, Giap had become fascinated with military history and voraciously read books on the subject at the municipal library in Hanoi.

According to his own account, Vo Nguyen Giap had been instructed to leave Hanoi for China by Hoang Van Thu, a young Party member from the Tho minority group who had been named to the Central Committee in 1938 and was now secretary of the regional committee for Tonkin. Thu, who had often conversed with Giap about military matters, instructed him to consider carefully the potential of guerrilla warfare in a future struggle against the French (this was no great surprise to Giap, who was already familiar with Maoist tactics in China and the use of similar forms of warfare during the traditional era in Vietnam) and hinted that on his arrival in China, Giap was likely to meet Nguyen Ai Quoc for the first time.

After his discussion with Hoang Van Thu, Vo Nguyen Giap had launched preparations for his trip to China. In early May, after dismissing his last class at school, he walked to West Lake, in the northern suburbs of Hanoi, and said good-bye to his young wife and infant daughter. They agreed that she would join him in China once she could make arrangements for the care of their child. In fact, they would never meet again. Accompanied by Pham Van Dong, who was still recovering from illness incurred during his years in the Poulo Condore prison, Giap then left Hanoi for the Chinese border. Taking the train to Lao Cai, they crossed the frontier into China and continued on to Kunming. The train was so closely watched by the authorities that when inspectors came through the cars of the train to check identity cards, the two had to slip into the railcar that the inspectors had just exited.[15]

After arriving in early June, Vo Nguyen Giap and Pham Van Dong contacted Phung Chi Kien and Vu Anh, the local ICP representatives in Kunming, who told them to await a certain Mr. Vuong, who would assign them new duties. Vuong (who was Nguyen Ai Quoc) met them on the shores of Green Lake, a popular scenic area in downtown Kunming, and instructed them to proceed to CCP headquarters in Yan'an to enroll for a course in military science at the Party institute there. Giap and Dong left a few days later for Guiyang, where they were forced to wait at the CCP's Eighth Route Army liaison office for travel documents that would provide them with authorization to continue on to Yan'an. But just before their departure for the north, they suddenly received a cable from Nguyen Ai Quoc announcing his impending arrival in Guiyang; Quoc told them to wait there for him rather than proceeding on their journey.

Nguyen Ai Quoc's change of plans had been provoked by recent events in Europe, where the German offensive launched in May 1940 had resulted in the final surrender of France on June 22. As Quoc explained, the German occupation of France and the formation in the southern part of that country of a puppet Vichy regime meant that "new changes will undoubtedly take place in Indochina." A few days later, Phung Chi Kien and Vu Anh arrived in Guiyang as well, and Quoc joined them on a trip to Guilin, where he convened a meeting of the editorial board of the journal *D.T.*, the overseas party newspaper formerly known as *Dong Thanh*, to discuss the situation. "The French defeat," Quoc remarked, "represents a very favorable opportunity for the Vietnamese revolution. We must seek every means to return home to take advantage of it. To delay would be harmful to the revolution." When one of his colleagues pointed out the necessity of obtaining weapons, Quoc replied,

> We'll have the weapons when we launch our general uprising. That is one of the most important problems for the revolution. But if we had weapons now, who would bear them? So we must first find a way to return home and mobilize the masses. When the masses are aroused, they will have weapons.[16]

After conferring with his comrades, Nguyen Ai Quoc ordered Vu Anh and Phung Chi Kien to return to Guiyang to pick up Giap and Pham Van Dong and escort them back to Guilin; there they were instructed to make initial preparations for an eventual return of the external Party leadership to Indochina. Quoc instructed another colleague to get in touch with the CCP leadership at its headquarters in Yan'an, and then he made arrangements to fly to Chongqing to confer with Zhou Enlai and other Chinese Party leaders on strategy. He returned to Kunming by bus, arriving at the end of July.[17]

Although it was clear that conditions were ripe for the beginning of a new stage of the Vietnamese revolution, some important decisions had to be made. First, it had to be decided where to establish the external headquarters for the Party as it prepared for an eventual general insurrection. Nguyen Ai Quoc had already dispatched colleagues to the area of Yunnan bordering on Tonkin, but he eventually decided that conditions were unfavorable there because the Party lacked a mass following in Ha Giang and Lao Cai provinces across the frontier; in addition, both of them were covered with impenetrable mountains and were relatively remote from the Red River delta. A better site, in his view, was the region along the southern border of Guangxi province. There were a substantial number of Party sympathizers on both sides of the frontier, while there was a strong likelihood that Chinese officials in the border districts would be willing to cooperate with ICP leaders to train armed units to be used against the French government in Indochina.

After his return to Kunming from Chongqing, Quoc received a letter from Ho Hoc Lam, the Kuomintang military officer who had given sympathy and support to the Vietnamese revolution since the late 1920s, when Phan Boi Chau stayed at his home in Hangzhou. Lam informed Quoc that General Truong Boi Cong, an ethnic Vietnamese now serving in the Chinese Nationalist armed forces, had just been given instructions by his superiors to organize Vietnamese patriots in the border region north of Cao Bang province in preparation for eventual operations in Indochina. Since General Cong was known to harbor hostile feelings toward the Communists, Lam advised Quoc to dispatch some of his own followers to the area to make certain that the Party's interests were protected.

The sudden Chinese interest in conditions in French Indochina had been provoked by the appearance of Japanese armed forces in the region. By early in 1940, Japanese military activities had begun to spread southward from the Yangtze valley into the area around Canton, as well as Hainan Island, and the Paracel Islands in the South China Sea. In the late spring, Tokyo began to apply heavy pressure on French colonial authorities to prohibit the shipment of military equipment and supplies up the Red River into south China, where they were eventually to be used by Chinese Nationalist forces. Indochinese Governor-General Georges Catroux had been inclined to resist such pressure, but in the absence of any support from the beleaguered government in Paris, he had turned to the United States, requesting U.S. fighter planes from the Philippines. President Franklin Roosevelt, however, had rejected the plea on the grounds that any available military aircraft in the region would be needed to defend U.S. national interests there. Catroux thereupon agreed to Japanese demands to close the border, an act that led to his dismissal in July by the new puppet French government in Vichy.

Catroux's replacement, Admiral Jean Decoux, was immediately faced with a new set of Japanese demands for the use of airfields and permission to station several thousand Japanese troops in Tonkin. Decoux reluctantly gave his assent, but on September 22, even before they were in place, local Japanese military units along the Chinese border attempted to intimidate him by launching an attack across the frontier on French posts near the border town of Lang Son. They were accompanied by Vietnamese nationalist forces enrolled in a group called the Restoration Society, a newly formed pro-Japanese organization chaired by Phan Boi Chau's old colleague, the exiled prince Cuong De, who was now living in Tokyo.

The Japanese border attack soon caught the attention of ICP elements stationed in the area. During the 1930s, the Party had carefully built up a small base of popular support among the peoples living in the mountains around Lang Son. Much of the population in the region consisted of non-Vietnamese minority peoples, such as the Tay, the Nung, and the Tho. Most had practiced slash-and-burn agriculture in the area for centuries and had little contact with the lowland Vietnamese, or with the French colonial administration in the larger towns and cities. The first Party cells had been established near the town of Cao Bang in the spring of 1930, and in succeeding years a few cadres of minority extraction had been placed in important positions within the ICP. At the Macao conference in March 1935, the Tay leader Hoang Dinh Giong had been elected to the Central Committee, and Hoang Van Thu, the Tho who ordered Vo Nguyen Giap to China, had been elected a few years later. Organizational efforts were facilitated by the Party's political program, which—following the Leninist model—had promised self-determination for all minority peoples in a future revolutionary Vietnam. While it would undoubtedly be an overstatement to suggest that they had been converted en masse to communism, the Party had a strong base of sympathizers in the area.[18]

In the fall of 1940, such efforts began to bear fruit. On September 27, as the news of the Japanese invasion spread throughout the region, Party cadres took advantage of the disarray of the defending French colonial forces to order attacks by local minority tribal peoples under their command on villages in the mountains of Bac Son district, just west of Lang Son. At first, the rebels took advantage of the element of surprise, occupying a few villages and seizing weapons from government arsenals. But after colonial authorities reached agreement on a cease-fire with the Japanese military commanders, the French gradually went on the offensive and pacified the region. In late October, rebel forces broke up into small guerrilla units and fled into the mountains, while others crossed the Chinese frontier in the hope of receiving training and weapons from Truong Boi Cong's border command.

Nguyen Ai Quoc arrived in Guilin in early October, while the Bac Son uprising (as it was later called) was still under way. He took up lodgings in a small thatch hut in the countryside and discovered that in his absence, his colleagues had met with Li Jishen, chief of staff of the Nationalist government's Southwest Field Headquarters in the city, and the Kuomintang commander who had suppressed the Communist uprising in Canton in the spring of 1927. General Li, however, was quite amiable and asked his visitors to draw up a plan to provide local assistance for an anticipated Allied invasion of Indochina. On hearing the news from his colleagues, Quoc was cautious. We have only two real allies, he warned them: the Red Army in the Soviet Union and the PLA. Although Chiang Kai-shek's forces were now fighting against Japan, his government remained fundamentally reactionary. If the ICP were duped by them, "it would be very dangerous."[19]

Nguyen Ai Quoc's words of warning were well taken; conditions in Guilin were becoming more perilous, as government authorities were again beginning to harass Communists. Deciding that it would be better to establish a base of operations nearer the border, Quoc dispatched Hoang Van Hoan and Vo Nguyen Giap to Liuzhou to assess the situation and prepare a base area there. On arrival, they contacted Truong Boi Cong, who attempted to recruit them for his own purposes. But Giap was wary. Shortly after, Nguyen Ai Quoc traveled secretly to Liuzhou and changed his name, advising his colleagues there to return to Guilin to make it their temporary base of operations.

In the meantime, Quoc was giving some serious thought to the creation of a new united front appropriate to the new situation. Such a front must be susceptible to strong ICP influence and direction, but the Party's role would have to be carefully disguised in order to alleviate the concerns of non-Communist elements in Indochina and abroad as to the front's political leanings. Quoc proposed the formation of a broad organization that would unite all patriotic forces in a common struggle to evict the French colonial power. Suggesting three possible names for the new organization, Vietnamese Liberation Front (Viet Nam Giai phong Dong minh), Vietnamese Anti-Imperialist League (Viet Nam Phan De Dong minh), or League for the Independence of Vietnam (Viet Nam Doc lap Dong minh), he indicated his preference for the last one. Several years earlier, an organization by that name had been created by Ho Hoc Lam, serving briefly as a vehicle for cooperation between nationalist and Communist Vietnamese living in the Nanjing area; the hope was it might now serve a similar purpose during this reincarnation.[20]

After some discussion, it was agreed to accept Nguyen Ai Quoc's suggestion for the name of the new group, to be known as the Vietminh Front for short. To attract moderate elements, Ho Hoc Lam, now living in Guilin, was asked to chair the organization, while Pham Van Dong (identified only by his pseudonym, Lam Ba Kiet) was named vice chairman. Armed with their new cover, the group approached General Li Jishen once again to seek his assistance in mobilizing Vietnamese residents in south China for eventual military operations inside Indochina. Although some members of his staff were suspicious of the political goals of the organizers, Li Jishen was receptive, and the new front was granted formal recognition. He did warn his visitors, however, not to allow the Communists to achieve a dominant role in the organization.[21]

While Nguyen Ai Quoc and his colleagues were in Guilin attempting to obtain the support of Chinese Nationalist military leaders for future operations inside Indochina, their rival Truong Boi Cong had been active in his own recruiting efforts along the border. After receiving information that forty Vietnamese resistance fighters had crossed the frontier into Guangxi province to escape the French, Cong left Liuzhou for Jingxi, a small border town about thirty miles by mountain trails north of Cao Bang, with plans to recruit them.

By now the Central Committee, which had placed its headquarters in Saigon, was in almost total disarray. All of its members were in fact in jail, except for Phan Dang Luu, and links with the regional committees in central Vietnam and the north had been broken.

Lacking any contact with other regions or the external leadership in south China, ICP operatives in Cochin China were left to their own devices. Tran Van Giau, one of the leading Party members in the area, had been released from jail in May 1940, but was rearrested five days later. There had earlier been some discussion of launching a general uprising in Cochin China to take advantage of rising popular unrest in the region. Agricultural conditions were not as bad as in the other parts of the country, but taxes were higher, and as much as 30 percent of the population was sympathetic to the Communists. That spring, the situation grew increasingly tense when the colonial government began to conscript Vietnamese to serve in military units in Europe, or in Cambodia, where war with Siam was imminent over Bangkok's demand for the return of territories lost to the French in 1907. Party operatives played on discontent among the troops, popularizing slogans such as "don't die for the *colons* [French residents of Indochina] in Cambodia," and provoking popular demonstrations at recruiting centers in provincial towns in the Mekong delta. For many Vietnamese peasants in Cochin China, conscription brought not only the threat of death or injury on the battlefield, but also increased hardship for their families.

In July, the Cochin Chinese regional committee, under its general secretary, Ta Uyen, approved tentative plans to prepare for the insurrection that had been called for by the Sixth Plenum (i.e., the sixth formal session of the Central Committee since the First National Congress of the Party in March 1935) in November 1939. First, however, the insurrection leaders sent Phan Dang Luu to the north to consult with the Tonkin regional committee. During the next three months, thousands of Vietnamese soldiers rioted in Saigon and other cities in the region to protest plans to send them to the Siamese border. In haste, Ta Uyen gave the order to launch the uprising in late November, despite the fact that Phan Dang Luu had not yet returned from his mission to Tonkin.

Luu, in fact, had reached Hanoi, and had contacted members of the Tonkin regional committee just as they were assessing the overall situation at their headquarters outside the city in light of the failed Bac Son uprising along the Chinese border. Northern Party leaders, like Truong Chinh, Hoang Quoc Viet, and Hoang Van Thu, were opposed to Ta Uyen's plan, arguing that conditions throughout the country were not ripe for a successful insurrection. They did approve a recommendation to increase preparations to launch future local uprisings in areas where conditions were favorable, and sent Hoang Van Thu to assist the resistance groups who had fought at Bac Son to reorganize themselves into guerrilla units in the mountains near the border. Finally, to fill the vacuum left by the French arrests of Party leaders in Cochin China, the regional committee unilaterally transformed itself into a provisional central committee, with Truong Chinh serving temporarily as general secretary.[22]

Prior to adjourning the meeting, the committee instructed Phan Dang Luu to return to Cochin China and request a postponement of the uprising. When Luu arrived in Saigon on November 23, he was arrested by French police at the train station. In any event, he was too late, for the uprising had broken out the day before in rural areas southwest of Saigon, and several districts from My Tho to the Plain of Reeds were briefly seized by insurgent forces. Sympathy riots broke out in Saigon, but the authorities had been forewarned and were able to crush the urban insurrection with relative ease. Meanwhile, the rural unrest, lacking organization and cohesion, was suppressed after four days of bloody French counterattacks, during which more than one hundred insurgents were killed and several thousand participants were placed under arrest and led off to imprisonment. In Saigon, hundreds of Communist activists were rounded up, including Nguyen Ai Quoc's ex-wife Nguyen Thi Minh Khai. Several incriminating documents were found in her house. In

March 1941, Minh Khai, Nguyen Van Cu, and Ha Huy Tap were sentenced to death by a military court in Saigon; all were executed by firing squad shortly afterward. Ta Uyen had apparently been killed by the French during the uprising. Before her death, Nguyen Thi Minh Khai briefly met with her husband, Le Hong Phong, who had been in jail since June 1939. He died of torture or deprivation in the tiger cages at Poulo Condore prison in September 1942.[23]

In Guilin, Nguyen Ai Quoc had been kept informed about Truong Boi Cong's recruiting activities in Jingxi through letters from a Communist sympathizer within Cong's entourage. Quoc eventually ordered Vo Nguyen Giap and Vu Anh to go to the border area to evaluate the situation and decide how it could be turned to the Party's benefit. On arrival, they persuaded General Cong to invite Ho Hoc Lam, as chair of the new League for the Independence of Vietnam, to come to Jingxi to assist in the recruitment process. Quoc had just been informed about the suppression of the uprising in Cochin China and must have surmised that its impact on the Party apparatus in the South could be considerable. When Cong's invitation to Lam arrived at his headquarters in Guilin, Quoc remarked to his colleagues: "The world and the national situation are favorable to us, but the hour of insurrection has not yet arrived. However, because there has already been an explosion, it is necessary without delay to organize the retreat of patriots into hiding to preserve the movement."[24]

In fact, conditions on the international scene were rapidly evolving, with consequences that could not yet be foreseen. Nazi Germany had consolidated its occupation of France and the Low Countries and was now embarked on an effort to bring Great Britain to heel by means of air power. Although the Nazi-Soviet Pact of August 1939 was still in operation, German advances into the Balkans had strained relations between the two countries. In China, Japan was continuing its military advances into central China to defeat Chiang Kai-shek's government, while at the same time introducing military forces into Indochina with the reluctant acquiesence of French colonial authorities.

With preparations for future operations now virtually complete, Nguyen Ai Quoc left Guilin with Pham Van Dong, Phung Chi Kien, Hoang Van Hoan, and Dang Van Cap by automobile. From Nanning they went leisurely by boat westward along a branch of the Pearl River to Tiandong. To keep his identity secret, Nguyen Ai Quoc traveled as a Chinese journalist using a new name, Ho Chi Minh (He Who Enlightens). He spoke only in French, although on one occasion, he slipped. When a colleague dropped a cigarette ash on his clothing, Quoc inadvertently warned him in Vietnamese that his trousers were burning.[25]

Nguyen Ai Quoc remained briefly in Tiandong, while Pham Van Dong went on to Jingxi, near the frontier, to prepare conditions for the group's arrival. The final journey was made on foot over mountain trails sometime in December. On arrival in Jingxi, Quoc found accommodations in nearby Xinxu village, and then instructed Vu Anh to cross the border into Indochina to find a suitable location for the forthcoming meeting of the Central Committee. The spot, he directed, should be in an area where the local population was sympathetic to the revolution, and it should possess an escape route back into China if that should prove necessary.

The primary purpose of moving the Party's external headquarters from Guilin to Jingxi was to take advantage of the presence of the resistance fighters who were there receiving training and weapons for use against the Japanese and the French. After arriving, Nguyen Ai Quoc instructed Vo Nguyen Giap, Phung Chi Kien, and Pham Van Dong to establish a Party training program in Jingxi to provide political indoctrination and revolutionary training for young cadres. The first set of courses, taught over a two-week period in January 1941, consisted of courses in three major areas: the situation in the world and in Indochina; how to utilize mass organizations; and methods of propaganda, organization, training, and revolutionary struggle. Training materials were drawn up under Nguyen Ai Quoc's direction, and printed in lithograph in a pamphlet called *The Road to Liberation* (Con duong giai phong). The courses were taught in a shady grove on a hillside just outside of town. Nguyen Ai Quoc played an active role as a lecturer, tirelessly repeating to each class the importance of proper behavior to the local population, including an effort to learn the minority language and follow local customs, as well as the importance of dressing in local clothing to maintain secrecy. After completion of the program, the graduates took part in a ceremony in a jungle clearing, each stepping forward to kiss the future emblem of nationhood—a red flag with a gold star. Then they returned to Indochina.

Nguyen Ai Quoc also tried to cement the Party's fragile relationship with Truong Boi Cong. Quoc had sent already Hoang Van Hoan, Vo Nguyen Giap, and Pham Van Dong to talk with Cong about founding a new organization, to be called the Vietnamese National Liberation Committee to facilitate cooperation between Cong's followers, many of whom were members of the VNQDD, and members of his own Party.

The new organization was formally founded in December 1940 and Quoc, operating under the name of Hoang Quojun, served as chairman of its executive committee.[26]

But Nguyen Ai Quoc spent the bulk of his time preparing for the upcoming meeting of the Central Committee, later to be labeled in Party histories as the famous Eighth Plenum. In early January 1941, Hoang Van Thu, Truong Chinh, and Hoang Quoc Viet, all members of the provisional Central Committee that had been established in Tonkin two months earlier, arrived in Jingxi to report to him on conditions in the interior. Vu Anh had also returned from his brief reconnaissance trip across the border to Indochina, having located an appropriate spot to hold the conference; it would take place in a spacious cave not far from the small village of Pac Bo, in an area marked by massive limestone cliffs jutting out of the dense green jungle growth. Most of the local people were of Nung ethnic stock. On January 26, Nguyen Ai Quoc split his followers into two groups: one to accompany him back to Vietnam to settle at Pac Bo, the other to remain temporarily in Jingxi. Just before his group's departure, they all joined local villagers in celebrating the traditional New Year's holiday. In accordance with local custom, Quoc offered as a gift to every family a piece of red paper on which was written the Chinese characters for Happy New Year. On the twenty-eighth, accompanied by Vu Anh, Phung Chi Kien, the minority cadre Le Quang Ba, and a number of other comrades all attired in the dress of the local Nung people, Nguyen Ai Quoc left Jingxi and headed for the border.

The trip was only about forty miles, but it was physically difficult, as the trail wound over mountain streams and through rocky outcroppings and tangled jungle growth. In early February, they crossed the border into Vietnam at a spot marked by a small stone pillar. From there, a rocky path wound down through the jungle to the village of Pac Bo. With the aid of a local sympathizer, the group established their accommodations in a cave known to the locals as Coc Bo (the Source) and situated behind a rock in the side of one of the local cliffs. About 140 feet below the mouth of the cave was a stream that Nguyen Ai Quoc named for his hero Lenin. Overlooking the site was a massive outgrowth that he dubbed Karl Marx Peak. From the cave, a secret path wound straight to the Chinese border, less than half a mile away.

In later years, Nguyen Ai Quoc and his colleagues would remember their days at Pac Bo as among the most memorable in their lives. Yet conditions were harsh. They slept on a mat of branches, leaving them with bruised backs in the morning. The cave itself was cold and damp, so the occupants kept a small fire going all night. As was his habit,

Nguyen Ai Quoc rose early, bathed in the stream, did his morning exercises, and then went to work on a rock at the edge of Lenin Stream. As always, he spent much of his time editing, this time working on the Party's local newspaper, *Viet Nam Doc Lap* (Independent Vietnam), which was produced on a stone lithograph. Meals consisted of rice mixed with minced meat or with fish from the stream. In the evening, the group would gather at the edge of the cave, where Nguyen Ai Quoc lectured to his colleagues on world history and modern revolutions. "Hour after hour, seated around the fire" as Vo Nguyen Giap later recalled, "we listened to him, like children listening to a legend." Vigilance, however, was constantly necessary. Colonial border patrols from the nearby town of Soc Giang were frequent, and the local police came periodically to Pac Bo to search for criminals or illegal distillers of alcohol. On one occasion, the group was forced to avoid a local patrol by hiding under rocks. That night, it rained heavily, overflowing the local streams, and when they returned to Pac Bo, they discovered that snakes and rodents had entered their cave to seek refuge from the torrent. Nguyen Ai Quoc tolerated the discomfort with his unfailing good humor, but took the opportunity to warn his colleagues always to maintain secrecy and pay attention to the "three nothings" (when a Party member was accosted by a stranger, he was to say one of three things: I have seen nothing, I have heard nothing, or I know nothing). "Between the enemy and ourselves," Quoc warned, "it is a struggle to the death. We must be able to tolerate all hardships, surmount the worst difficulties, and struggle to the end."[27]

During the next three months, Nguyen Ai Quoc and his colleagues attempted to broaden their base of support in the border area by distributing copies of *Viet Nam Doc Lap*. To make it more understandable to the local population, it was written in simple prose. It was sold at a nominal price rather than given away to give the impression that it was something of value. Mass organizations, to be known, Chinese-style, as National Salvation Associations (Cuu quoc hoi), were created under Party leadership for peasants, youth, women, and soldiers, and a security network was established throughout the surrounding region to protect against spies.

The Eighth Plenum of the Indochinese Communist Party convened at Pac Bo on May 10, 1941, with Nguyen Ai Quoc serving as the representative of the Comintern. It was the first meeting of the Central Committee that he had chaired since the unity conference in Hong Kong in February 1930. In attendance were Vu Anh, Hoang Van Thu, Truong Chinh, Phung Chi Kien, and Hoang Quoc Viet, as well as a number of other delegates from other parts of Indochina and abroad. Other members like Vo Nguyen Giap, Hoang Van Hoan, and Pham Van Dong. were still assigned to maintain the Party's external headquarters in Jingxi, where the new Vietnamese National Liberation Committee established with the cooperation of Truong Boi Cong was also just beginning to launch its own operations. But Quoc and his colleagues now planned to create a rival organization, the National Liberation League, to win over non-Communist elements in the area to the Vietminh.[28]

The primary task of the Eighth Plenum was formally to establish the new Vietminh Front, which had initially been envisaged by Party leaders late the previous year. The program of the front symbolized the new stage in the Vietnamese revolution. According to the resolution drafted at the meeting, the immediate task for the Vietnamese people was to struggle for national liberation from the French colonial regime and the Japanese occupation forces. The conflict now sweeping the world was between two competing branches of global imperialism, and although many nations were attempting to stay neutral in the battle, it was inevitable that the entire world would be dragged into the struggle. In the end, just as World War I had led to the Bolshevik revolution in Russia, so the new global conflict would eventually lead to the emergence of several more socialist countries. The primary task of the front was thus to prepare to seize power at the appropriate moment.

The heavy emphasis on the issue of national independence in the front's program, of course, was a radical departure from the policies adopted at the Party's first national congress in Macao in March 1935, but it represented a logical culmination to the trend that had begun with the Seventh Comintern Congress in Moscow later that same year. The new focus on national themes was reflected in the front's formal name, the league for the Independence of Vietnam, which not only stressed the issue of independence but also replaced the term "Indochina" in the name of the Communist Party with the more emotive word "Vietnam," the use of which had for so long been forbidden by the French colonial regime. The name also appeared in appeals sent out to the general population after the close of the meeting. In a letter to the people dated June 6, 1941, that was published in both Chinese characters and romanized Vietnamese script, Nguyen Ai Quoc evoked the spirit of past heroes, as well as recent patriotic figures such as Phan Dinh Phung, to arouse his readers to defend their national heritage. In the letter he appealed to all patriotic elements, not simply the peasants and workers but also patriotic landlords and scholar gentry, to join together in the common endeavor.

In focusing the attention of the Party first and foremost on Vietnamese independence, Nguyen Ai Quoc and his colleagues had appeared to abandon the concept (first set forth at the Party's first plenary conference in October 1930) of a regional effort to liberate all of Indochina and to create a federation of separate independent Indochinese states that would then carry out later stages of the revolution. In fact, the cause of the non-Vietnamese peoples of Indochina was to be delayed, but not forgotten. In the resolution, the regional committees of Cochin China and Annam were instructed to establish Party bases in Cambodia and Laos, respectively, as well as among other minority nationalities, so that all could later be brought under the umbrella of what was still labeled the Indochinese revolution.[29]

Although the new front placed primary emphasis on the task of overthrowing imperialism, the issues of antifeudalism and social change were not entirely ignored, since Party leaders were aware that they needed to cultivate their natural constituency among workers and poor peasants to build a solid revolutionary base for the coming struggle. For the moment, however, the front's social program was to be relatively modest in order to avoid alienating progressive and patriotic elements among the landed gentry and the bourgeoisie. Slogans that had been used in the past advocating the confiscation of all land owned by landlords were replaced by calls for a reduction in land rents and the seizure of the property of French imperalists and their Vietnamese collaborators. As the Party resolution stated,

> The landlords, rich peasants, and a segment of the native bourgeois class have greatly changed their attitude. Before, they had an antipathy to revolution and wanted to destroy it or were indifferent. Now the situation has changed, and with the exception of a few "running dogs" who flatter and fawn on the Japanese enemy, the majority of such people have sympathy for the revolution or are at least neutral. . . . If previously the landlords and the native bourgeoisie were the reserve army of the antirevolutionary imperialists, they have now become the reserve of the revolution.

It was clear, however, that the policy was tactical only:

> This does not mean that our Party is ignoring the problem of class struggle in the Indochinese revolution. No, the problem of class

struggle will continue to exist. But at the present time, the nation has prime importance, and all demands that are of benefit to a specific class but are harmful to the national interest must be subordinated to the survival of the nation and the race. At this moment, if we do not resolve the problem of national liberation, and do not demand independence and freedom for the entire people, then not only will the entire people of our nation continue to live the life of beasts, but also the particular interests of individual social classes will not be achieved for thousands of years.[30]

The immediate goal was thus to build up a nationwide movement for national independence, one that could not only win the support of the mass of the Vietnamese population but even earn the sympathy of progressive peoples around the world. Victory would symbolize the triumph of the bourgeois democratic revolution and usher in the formation of a proletarian-peasant government dominated by the Communist Party. There would then be ample time to move toward the second, or proletarian socialist stage, of the revolution. In the meantime, the Party hoped that oppressed elements within the population would enthusiastically support the cause.

In setting up the Vietminh Front, Nguyen Ai Quoc had managed to re-create in slightly more advanced form the program that he had originally established with the formation of the Revolutionary Youth League in the mid-1920s. The two pillars of the front would be the issues of national independence and social justice, appeals that could be expected to earn wide support throughout much of the country. Almost two decades after Lenin's death, his strategy had been resurrected in far-off Indochina. Yet in establishing the new front inside Indochina, Quoc was gambling that conditions throughout the world would turn favorable to the cause of revolution in Vietnam. Would Japanese occupation lead to the weakening of the French colonial regime? Would the Japanese fascists themselves ultimately be defeated by an alliance of democratic forces around the world? Would the victorious Allies be sympathetic to the establishment of a new independent government of peasants and workers in Hanoi? All that remained to be seen.[31]

The ultimate goal of the Vietminh Front, of course, was to assist the Party in its struggle for power. The Sixth Plenum in November 1939 had set the stage by calling for an armed uprising to seize power and restore national independence. That objective was temporarily aborted with the arrest of Nguyen Van Cu and much of the remainder of the committee in the following months; now, with the outbreak of global conflict, it was resurrected by the Party's external leadership in a more concrete form. Where previously Party leaders had not been specific on how to carry out the future insurrection against the colonial regime, now they began to give closer attention to the forms of struggle that would be best suited to the occasion.

Central to this task was to undertake an examination of the strategy and tactics adopted by the CCP in its own conflict with Chiang Kai-shek's Nationalist government and later against the Japanese invaders. In the early 1930s, ICP leaders had faithfully followed strategic guidelines formulated in Moscow, which called for a future insurrection focused on control over the major cities. But by the end of the decade, dedicated young Party activists like Vo Nguyen Giap and Hoang Van Thu started to turn to the Chinese experience for inspiration. They read the works of Mao Zedong and began to express an interest in applying his strategy, which was based on the launching of guerrilla warfare in the countryside, inside Vietnam. During his period of residence in China in the late 1930s, Nguyen Ai Quoc had himself developed some familiarity with Mao's ideas on revolutionary warfare, and he undoubtedly found Mao's concept of a "people's war" suitable as a weapon to carve out a liberated base area in his own country. But for Quoc, it was not only a matter of what kind of revolutionary tactics to adopt; it was also important to decide when to put them into effect, and how to use them most effectively to seize power at the end of the war. As a small country now occupied by two powerful enemies, Vietnam did not possess the advantage of size that had enabled Mao and his colleagues to set up a large base area in north China. A premature uprising by the ICP could lead to severe repression and destroy the movement just as the promise of national liberation was about to brighten. Quoc would now need to caution his more headstrong colleagues that it was necessary to prepare the Party's tiny military forces for an eventual insurrection at the moment of maximum opportunity, when Japan was on the verge of defeat at the hands of its enemies. In the meantime, they should limit themselves to strengthening their political base by building a Vietminh network throughout the country, while creating a small military force that in due time would launch local insurrections in preparation for the final general uprising. With guerrilla units already beginning to form in the mountains of the Viet Bac, a potential liberated base in that area, isolated from the heart of French authority and close to the Chinese border, was already a strong possibility.

The final task of the Eighth Plenum was to choose a new central committee. When Nguyen Ai Quoc modestly refused the request of his colleagues to assume the position of general secretary, the choice fell on Truong Chinh, who had temporarily occupied that position since the fall of 1940. The choice appeared to be a sound one. Born in a family of scholars in North Vietnam in 1907, Chinh (real name Dang Xuan Khu) had received a baccalaureate degree at the prestigious Lycée Albert Sarraut in Hanoi. After joining the Revolutionary Youth League in the late 1920s, he was imprisoned for revolutionary activities. Released in 1936, he began a career as a journalist while serving simultaneously as an influential member of the ICP regional committee in Tonkin. Proud in his demeanor, cautious and thorough in his actions, didactic in relations with his colleagues, Chinh possessed a strong ideological bent and lacked the warm personality of Nguyen Ai Quoc, but he could be expected to add a mature voice to Party deliberations as it entered a fateful new stage in its career. Shortly after the conference adjourned on May 19, Chinh left for Hanoi to set up secret headquarters for the Central Committee. Other members returned to south China to seek assistance from abroad. For the moment, Nguyen Ai Quoc remained in the border region. But his spirits must have been high, for he was now back in Vietnam after thirty years abroad.

When Nguyen Ai Quoc slipped secretly out of Hong Kong for Xiamen in January 1933, his position as the leader of the Indochinese Communist Party had been a fragile one. The strategy that he had adopted at the moment of forming the Revolutionary Youth League in 1925 had been repudiated by Moscow and was actively under attack by younger members of the Party, many of whom had received ideological training at the Stalin School. Yet on his return to the area in the spring of 1940, Quoc's leading role over the movement was apparently accepted without demur by Party members inside the country. In part, this was a testimonial to the fact that his strategic views had been vindicated at the Seventh Comintern Congress, which recognized belatedly that Asian revolutions had their own dynamics and need not adhere to the Bolshevik model. He was also the unwitting beneficiary of the thoroughness of the Sûreté, which had systematically eliminated most of his potential rivals, including Tran Phu, Ha Huy Tap, and Le Hong Phong. For the moment, at any rate, no one in the Party was in a position to challenge him, and he took full advantage of his prestige and his already legendary career as a revolutionary to stake his claim to the hegemony of the Party.

Given these circumstances, it is not clear why Nguyen Ai Quoc decided to refuse the post of general secretary, which would have provided him with a firm hold over the levers of power within the Party. Perhaps he still viewed himself as an operator on the world stage, as an agent of the Comintern who would someday orchestrate the rise of a revolutionary wave that would sweep away the yoke of imperialism throughout the region of Southeast Asia. Perhaps, too, he already had begun to focus his eyes on a future time when, as president, he could hope to rise above the constraints of class struggle represented by the Communist Party to represent all the people in their struggle to build an independent and prosperous Vietnam.

IX | THE RISING TIDE

After the meeting of the Central Committee at Pac Bo in May 1941, the Party leadership began to disperse. General Secretary Truong Chinh, accompanied by Hoang Quoc Viet and Hoang Van Thu, returned to Hanoi to set up a new headquarters for the committee in the suburbs of the old imperial capital; other Party members were sent to nearby districts to organize guerrilla detachments and begin building a revolutionary base in the mountains of the Viet Bac. Others still crossed the border into China to receive training or to resume efforts to build up the fragile alliance with non-Communist nationalist groups in southern China. Nguyen Ai Quoc himself temporarily remained in Pac Bo to make preparations for future expansion to the south.

For the next few months, in a repetition of his earlier experience in Siam, he again became a teacher and the father of his flock. He organized a course to indoctrinate local cadres in Marxism-Leninism and provide them with the military training necessary to become both fighters and apostles of revolution. After four days of lectures, the students began to practice their skills as propagandists. Nguyen Ai Quoc observed their performance and then criticized their shortcomings. He also served as a regular instructor for the course, giving an opening lecture on the world situation, and then following up with a discussion of conditions inside the country and the forthcoming tasks for the revolutionary movement. Since the signing of the Nazi-Soviet Pact in August 1939, Party cadres had frequently encountered problems in explaining why Stalin had chosen to ally his country with Hitler's Germany, widely viewed as the archenemy of the world revolution. By late June 1941, however, word of the German attack on the USSR reached the border area and undoubtedly facilitated Nguyen Ai Quoc's effort to coordinate the activities of the ICP with the global struggle against world fascism. As he explained it on one occasion: "The fascists have attacked the Soviet Union, the fatherland of the world revolution, but the Soviet peoples will definitely be victorious. We Vietnamese also stand on the side of New Democracy, and support the Soviet Union against the fascists."[1]

Nguyen Ai Quoc also wrote a short pamphlet on the tactics of guerrilla warfare to serve as an instruction manual for the portion of the course that provided military training. The material was obviously culled from his experience observing the Communist forces in China, as well as from the guerrilla training course that he had attended in Hengyang two years previously. After an opening chapter devoted to a general description of guerrilla warfare, the remainder of the pamphlet consisted of a discussion of organizational techniques as well as the tactics of retreat, attack, and building a base area. It was eventually published for use in training programs in other areas of the Viet Bac.[2]

Nguyen Ai Quoc also found the time to write other things as well. He was an active contributor to *Viet Nam Doc Lap*, the journal which had been produced for the past year on a stone lithograph for the indoctrination of novice members of the movement. Printed on primitive paper made from bamboo pulp, the journal consisted of articles composed in a simple style to make them accessible to the local population. Very few of the local villagers were able to read, so he sponsored the creation of literacy programs, which taught not only *quoc ngu*, the romanized script, but also the rudiments of the history of the Party and the world revolution. Articles, many written by Nguyen Ai Quoc himself, dealt with a variety of subjects, but all had the purpose of spreading the message of the Vietminh and preparing the reader for the inevitable confrontation with the enemy. A typical piece was the short poem "Women," which appeared in issue 104:

Vietnamese women forever
Have sacrificed themselves for our country and our race
Ten thousand gathered in response to the call of the sisters Trung
Set out to save the country and the people forever.
Through the years of revolutionary struggle
Our sisters have often participated.
Many times struggle courageously
Hearts of gold, courage of iron, who could do less?
Like Nguyen Minh Khai
Convicted to death many times.
Now the opportunity is near,
Defeat the French, defeat the Japanese, save people and homes,
Women from young to old

Unite together to struggle
Gather together in the Vietminh Front
First save the country, then ourselves.
So that all the world will know
We are the sons of the Fairy and the Dragon.[3]

Since the early 1930s, the basic tool of the Party's outreach effort was the functional mass organization, representing the interests of specific social groups within Indochina. This means of recruiting followers at the base level, with the more advanced members then moving into higher-level organizations, was a technique originally devised by Lenin and then perfected by the CCP in China. In an article entitled "The World War and Our Duty," Nguyen Ai Quoc stressed the need for all patriotic groups in Vietnamese society—whether peasants, youth, women, children, workers, soldiers, or even the scholar-gentry—to join such organizations to fulfill the task of national liberation.

In his writings after the Pac Bo meeting, Nguyen Ai Quoc constantly referred to the sacred duty of liberating the fatherland. In a short pamphlet written in verse, which was titled *The History of Our Country* (Lich su nuoc ta), he opened with the statement that the Vietnamese people must learn the history of their own country; he then underscored the great historical lesson that "our people must learn the word 'unity': unity of spirit, unity of effort, unity of hearts, unity of action." At the end of the work he appended a list of important dates in the history of the Vietnamese people. The last date on the list was 1945, labeled as the year of Vietnamese independence. When colleagues asked him how he knew precisely when liberation would take place, he replied enigmatically, "We'll see."[4]

While Nguyen Ai Quoc was training cadres and inspiring his followers with the sacred cause of liberating the fatherland, colleagues were striving to build a liberated base zone in the Viet Bac as a springboard for an eventual leap to power. Shortly after the adjournment of the Pac Bo plenum, Quoc had instructed Phung Chi Kien to construct such a base for an eventual advance southward toward the Red River delta. Kien eventually set up a new military headquarters in the mountains between the villages of Nguyen Binh and Hoa An, just west of the provincial capital of Cao Bang. Cao Bang sat astride National Route 4, which meandered southeastward along the frontier and eventually connected with routes leading into the delta and the seat of the Central

Committee near Hanoi. The new command post was situated in a small basin surrounded by massive red boulders, inspiring Vo Nguyen Giap to dub it "the red blockhouse." The headquarters itself was located in a small hut on the side of a mountain and well protected by the surrounding deep forest. It was still primitive, but compared with the cave at Pac Bo, the new accommodations were almost luxurious, and during the next few months, cadres at the base set up their own training program in preparation for launching guerrilla operations.

Sometime in January 1942, dressed in faded clothes in the fashion of the local Nung people and clutching a small cloth bag with his few possessions (including his typewriter and exercise equipment), Nguyen Ai Quoc left Pac Bo with several colleagues and trekked to the new Vietminh base. When the group once lost its way en route, Nguyen Ai Quoc took the incident in stride. "What a *belle affaire*," he laughed. "In the future we must be better acquainted with these trails to learn how to escape."[5]

On arrival at his new command post (which he promptly dubbed Lam Son, in memory of a guerrilla base established by the fifteenth-century Vietnamese patriot Le Loi in his struggle against Chinese occupation forces), Nguyen Ai Quoc took part in the new political training course for local cadres. To preserve secrecy, the program was conducted at night in the open air, and with no training materials. Because the students were more advanced than those at Pac Bo, the subject material was more advanced as well, consisting of discussions of Marxist doctrine, Party regulations, and the history of the Communist Party of the Soviet Union. To build up the spirits of his colleagues, who occasionally despaired of victory in their seemingly endless struggle first against the French, and now also the Japanese, Nguyen Ai Quoc sometimes concluded his lecture by pointing out the necessity of a base area as a launching pad for the future general uprising. He also stressed the crucial importance of building up the strength of the movement through the recruitment of reliable followers. "A revolution," he pointed out, "is like the rising tide, and the reliable elements are like the pilings sunk in a riverbed; it is they who will maintain the soil at low tide."

One problem with the new location, however, was that it was more exposed than the border region near Pac Bo to enemy attack. On several occasions, Party cadres at the command post were forced to seek refuge among the local population in order to escape detention from French patrols in the area. On those occasions, they struck camp in the middle of the jungle, sometimes in areas where human beings rarely penetrated. To survive they were often forced to forage for food, such as corn, rice, or wild banana flowers. Despite the concerns of his colleagues, Nguyen Ai Quoc insisted on sharing the deprivations with the rest. When spirits flagged or enthusiasm grew to excess, he counseled them: "Patience, calmness, and vigilance, those are the things that a revolutionary must never forget."[6]

Under the circumstances, good relations with the minority peoples living in the area were essential. The Party had already begun to build support in the Viet Bac during the mid-1930s, and at the 1935 Macao conference it had promised self-determination for all ethnic groups in a future independent Indochinese federation. Now, with Quoc's encouragement, cadres attempted to win the support of local peoples by learning their languages and customs. Cadres participated in rituals celebrated by people in the nearby villages, and some even filed their teeth in the local fashion or took local wives and began to raise families.

On December 7, 1941, Japanese forces launched an air attack on Pearl Harbor. The following day, the United States declared war on Japan. In a brief editorial printed in *Viet Nam Doc Lap*, Nguyen Ai Quoc declared that the regional struggle in the Pacific had now been transformed into a world conflagration, making it increasingly urgent for the peoples of Indochina to mobilize their efforts to meet the challenges to come. Back in Pac Bo in July 1942, Quoc instructed his colleagues near Cao Bang to expand their operations in order to establish communications links with elements operating at Bac Son and Vo Nhai, farther to the south, and thus create a stable political corridor from Cao Bang southward toward the delta. The movement's "March to the South" (in Vietnamese, *"Nam tien,"* the same term as used for the historic migration of the Vietnamese peoples southward from the Red River delta after the recovery of independence from China in the tenth century), was about to get under way.

At Bac Son, Chu Van Tan, a Party cadre of Nung extraction, had managed to organize the remnants of the rebel forces who had fought against the French and the Japanese in the fall of 1940 into guerrilla detachments under the somewhat overblown title of the National Salvation Army (Cuu Quoc Quan). Because their base area was located close to the provincial capital of Lang Son, these units were dangerously exposed to attack from nearby French security forces, who frequently launched sweeps through the area, capturing suspects and torching villages. On one of these occasions, Phung Chi Kien, one of Nguyen Ai Quoc's most trusted colleagues and a member of the Party Central Committee since 1935, was killed in battle. It was Quoc himself who had sent Kien to Bac Son to set up training courses and expand guerrilla activities in the province, but Quoc may have found solace in the fact that his colleague's death was in a cause he felt was crucial. The task of communications, he frequently declared to his colleagues, was "the most important task" for their revolutionary work, since it was decisive for maintaining the principle of unified command and the proper deployment of forces, thus guaranteeing final success.

As the guerrillas increased their activities, the authorities stepped up their own efforts to suppress them, setting up a curfew throughout the lower provinces of the Viet Bac and sending out patrols to flush out dissident forces. It was to minimize the possibility of capture that Nguyen Ai Quoc left Lam Son in June 1942 and returned to Pac Bo. Posing as a local shaman, complete with a black robe and all the paraphernalia of the craft, including texts on black magic, incense sticks, and a live chicken (whose blood was thought to cure disease), he had several harrowing experiences until he and the small group that accompanied him managed to pass through enemy checkpoints to their final destination. On one occasion, the security officer at a local checkpoint asked the shaman to take a look at his wife, who was feeling unwell. One of Quoc's colleagues pleaded with the officer that the group had no time to waste, since the shaman's own mother-in-law was seriously ill. At that, the officer relented, asking that the shaman stop off on his way back through the village.[7]

With his internal program now in place, Nguyen Ai Quoc turned his attention to building up international support for the cause. On August 13, 1942, he headed back to China on foot with his colleague Le Quang Ba. To reduce the danger of being apprehended by a French patrol, they traveled at night and rested during the daytime; Quoc again carried the identity card of an overseas Chinese reporter by the name of Ho Chi Minh. At the small Chinese border town of Bamong on the twenty-fifth, he rested briefly at the home of Xu Weisan, a local farmer known to be sympathetic to the Vietnamese revolutionary cause. Two days later, he departed with a young Chinese guide, having informed his host that he wished to proceed on foot to the nearby market town of Binhma in order to catch a bus to the wartime capital of Chongqing; Le Quang Ba remained behind in Bamong. The two were arrested en route, however, by Chinese police in the village in Teyuan, not far from the district capital of Debao, about twenty miles northeast of Jingxi. The suspicion of the local authorities was aroused by the fact that, in addition to carrying papers identifying him as a representative of a group called "the Vietnamese branch of the Anti-Aggression League," Ho also carried a special card of the International Press Agency (Guoji Xinwenshe) and a military passport issued by the office of the commander of the Fourth Military Command. All these documents had been issued in 1940 and were no longer valid. Suspecting that anyone with so many false documents must be a Japanese agent, they took him and his young guide into custody.[8]

Ho Chi Minh's purpose in returning to China has long been a matter of debate. In his memoirs, he implied that his objective was to establish contact with Chinese President Chiang Kai-shek and other Nationalist authorities in order to solicit their assistance in evicting the Japanese from Indochina. Several other Vietnamese sources concur. But others have suggested that his actual purpose was to get in touch with representatives of the CCP at their liaison headquarters in Chongqing. In all likelihood, both are correct. There were certainly good reasons for him to establish closer ties with acquaintances in the CCP, many of whom he had not seen since his brief stopover in Yan'an nearly four years before. Still, although Ho Chi Minh undoubtedly intended to contact his old friend Zhou Enlai while in Chongqing, his main objective was probably to seek support from the Nationalist government and obtain its recognition of the Vietminh Front as the legitimate representative of Vietnamese nationalism. By now, news of the U.S. naval victory at Midway had reached continental Asia, and Allied support for Chiang Kai-shek's government made his survival at the end of the Pacific war increasingly likely. One logical contact was Sun Yat-sen's widow, Soong Qingling, who chaired the Chinese branch of the International Anti-Aggression League. With the Vietnamese revolutionary movement now badly in need of material support, it was essential that the Nationalist government tolerate Vietminh activities in south China and support the front's role in helping to defeat the Japanese.[9]

Convinced that anyone carrying so many false documents must be not only dangerous but also someone of considerable political importance, the local authorities decided to contact the military court in Guilin, the capital of Guangxi province; the court requested that Ho be sent to Guilin for interrogation and possible trial there. The route taken was via Debao and Jingxi, the site of Ho Chi Minh's activities just before the Pac Bo conference. He was incarcerated in a Kuomintang jail in Jingxi on August 29. By now, his friends in the border region had become aware of his predicament, and they immediately sent a messenger to the Jingxi district magistrate, who happened to be an acquaintance of Xu Weisan. But the official refused the request to release Ho and reported the arrest by telegram to higher authorities.[10]

Ho Chi Minh remained in Jingxi prison for several weeks while local authorities awaited directions from higher echelons on what to do with him. By his own account, conditions in the jail were primitive, and often inhumane. Prisoners were placed in a stock during the daytime, and at night were shackled to the wall in cells overrun with lice. Nourishment consisted of a single bowl of rice and half a basin of water, which had to be used for both washing and tea. Still, Ho Chi Minh was somehow able to obtain paper and pen, and in his free time he exercised his restless mind by writing poetry to describe his feelings and the conditions of his captivity. Many years later, these poems were published as his *Prison Diary*. The poems were originally written in Chinese in the quatrain style of the Tang dynasty:

> *Opening the Diary*
>
> I've never liked reciting poetry,
> But what else is there to do inside a prison cell?
> So I'll recite some verse to pass the time,
> Recite and wait til freedom returns.

The prisoner expressed indignation at his fate:

> *A Difficult Road*
>
> Although I've scaled the highest peaks,
> I've encountered problems in the plains.
> In the mountains I've faced tigers without incident,
> But in the plains I've been seized by my fellow men.
>
> I arrived as a representative of the Vietnamese people,
> Who came to China to consult with important leaders.
> Suddenly I encountered a storm of adversity
> And was placed as an "esteemed guest" in prison.
>
> I am loyal and clear of heart,
> But am suspected of being a traitor.
> Things have never been easy,
> But now they are even more difficult.

Yet Ho Chi Minh, with his inveterate optimism, never lost hope and infected his fellow prisoners with determination to survive:

Morning

As the sun rises over the prison wall,
It shines on the prison gate.
Inside the jail, all is still dark,
But outside the sun has spread across the land.

As we awake, all compete to catch the lice,
When the bell strikes eight, it's time for breakfast.
Brother, you'd better eat your fill,
For things soon will surely get better.[11]

On October 10, the thirty-first anniversary of the first Chinese revolution, Ho Chi Minh was transferred from Jingxi back to Debao. Travel clearly provided little relief from the monotony of prison life:

En Route

Those who walk the road know it is hard.
Scale one mountain and another appears.
But once you mount the highest peak,
10,000 miles appear before you eyes.

Arriving at Tianbao Prison

Today I trudged 53 kilometers,
My hat and clothes are soaked, my shoes tattered.
Throughout the night there's nowhere to lay my head.
Perched on the latrine, I await the break of day.

In Debao, he heard the news that Wendell Willkie, President Roosevelt's special envoy to the Chinese, had arrived in Chongqing for talks with Chiang Kai-shek. The news report of the visit provoked his frustration:

News Report: A Welcome Reception for Willkie

Both of us are friends of China,
Heading for Chongqing.
You're a guest of honor,
While I languish in a prison cell.

Both of us represent our country,
So why are we treated differently?
The ways of the world run hot and cold,
Just as water flows to the east.

From Debao, Ho was transferred via Tiandong and Lungan to Nanning, about 120 miles to the east, en route to Guilin. By now the strain of the long incarceration was beginning to get to him.

Night Chill

An autumn night, without a mattress or blanket.
You try to curl up, but still can't sleep.
Moonlight on the banana tree chills the atmosphere,
Through the window, the Big Dipper lies on its side.

Still, he did not lose the sense of humor and the gift of irony that had marked his writing since his early days as a revolutionary in Paris:

A Jest

The state provides your room and board,
Teams of soldiers serve as your escort.
You stroll through the countryside as you please,
To play the tourist is truly exciting!

In fact, his conditions were about to improve. On December 9, 1942, he was taken from Nanning by train to Liuzhou, the site of Chiang Kai-shek's Fourth Military Command headquarters. Ho Chi Minh undoubtedly hoped that his presence would be reported to the zone commander, Zhang Fakui, a veteran Kuomintang commander who did not share Chiang's visceral distrust of the CCP and was known to be sympathetic to the Vietnamese struggle for national liberation. To Ho's disappointment, however, he was kept waiting, and then finally transferred to Guilin the next day:

Detainment without Interrogation

As a cup of medicine is most bitter at the dregs,
A rough road seems most arduous at the end.
The magistrate's office is only about a mile away,
Why am I forced to wait here?

Four Months Later

"A day in jail is like a thousand years outside."
That old proverb is surely on the mark.
Four months of inhuman existence
Have aged me more than ten years.

By now his body was emaciated and covered with sores, his hair had begun to turn gray, and his teeth were falling out. Yet he refused to despair:

Luckily
I've persevered and endured.
Not taken a single step backward.
Although it's been physically difficult,
My spirit remains unshaken.

Seriously Ill

China's humid climate has made me feverish,
And makes me long for my homeland in Vietnam.
It's miserable to be ill in prison.
I should weep, but I'll sing instead.

After another delay of several weeks, the chief prosecuting officer of the military court in Guilin finally took up Ho Chi Minh's case. Under interrogation, Ho admitted to having connections with the Communist movement in Indochina, but denied that he had any ties with the CCP. Declaring him to be a political prisoner, the court ordered him transferred back to Fourth Military Command Headquarters in Liuzhou for trial. On his arrival there in early February 1943, Zhang Fakui turned the case over to the Political Department.[12]

Upon hearing of Ho Chi Minh's arrest, Le Quang Ba left Bamong immediately for Jingxi. Ho asked him to carry a letter to the Party Central Committee back in Vietnam. When news of Ho's incarceration arrived in Cao Bang in late October, Party leaders decided to mobilize a public protest against his arrest. They also decided to write to major news agencies such as UPI, Reuters, Tass, and Agence France Presse, alerting them to the situation and asking them to intercede with the Chinese government to obtain Ho's release. The cable to the Tass representative in Chongqing, dated November 15, simply identified Ho Chi

Minh as "one of the leading members of the Viet Nam Branch of the International Anti-Aggression League" who enjoyed "high prestige" among the people. The cable claimed that the league had a membership of 200,000 people. By the time similar alerts were received by all the foreign wire services in Chongqing, however, Ho Chi Minh was already in jail in Guilin.

In the meantime, the minority ICP cadre Hoang Dinh Giong had been sent to China to dispatch a telegram demanding Ho's release to Sun Ke, Sun Yat-sen's son and currently president of the Legislative Yuan in Chongqing, on behalf of the Vietnamese branch of the International Anti-Aggression League. Sun had already spoken publicly in favor of the liberation of colonial territories in Asia after the end of the Pacific War, and would presumably be sympathetic to the message:

President Sun
Our representative Hu K'o Ming was arrested in Jingxi on his way to Chongqing to present a banner and pay respects to Generalissimo Chiang. We entreat you to cable the local authorities to release him immediately.

Sun Ke, who presumably had no idea who Hu K'o Ming was, forwarded the cable to Wu Tiecheng, general secretary of the Kuomintang Central Executive Committee. On November 9, Wu cabled the provincial government in Guilin, as well as Zhang Fakui's Fourth Military Command headquarters in Liuzhou, asking them to investigate the matter and, if appropriate, to order Ho's release. Neither was able to act on the matter at that time, however, since Ho Chi Minh was still en route from Debao to Nanning and had not yet arrived in Liuzhou.[13]

While Party leaders inside Indochina were trying to obtain Ho Chi Minh's release, they heard shocking news. Sometime during the winter of 1942–1943, a young member of the Party who had been sent to south China to locate Ho and report back to Party leaders on his condition arrived at Cao Bang with a report that Ho Chi Minh was dead. He had learned while in Liuzhou that Ho had died in prison. After sending off a message to alert the Central Committee at its headquarters near Hanoi, the Party leaders in the Viet Bac charged Pham Van Dong with the task of organizing a funeral ceremony.

A few weeks later, however, a magazine arrived from China. In the margin were written a handful of Chinese characters in a familiar script: "To my dear friends—good health and courage in your work. Be in good health." A short verse was attached:

The clouds embrace the hills,
The hills clasp the clouds.
Like a mirror that nothing can dim,
the river drains its limpid waters.
On the crest of the Mountains of the Western Wind,
Solitary, I stroll, my heart moved.
Scanning the southern sky,
I think of my friends.

Overcome with joy, Party leaders summoned the cadre for an explanation. "I don't understand myself," he remarked. "The Chinese governor clearly told me that Uncle Ho was dead." When the cadre was asked to recall the governor's exact words, however, it suddenly became clear that he had misunderstood the Chinese words "okay, okay" (*shile, shile*), for "dead, dead" (*sile, sile*).[14]

At Liuzhou, Ho Chi Minh was detained in a military prison in the compound of the Political Department. By now—as he wrote in a poem at the time—he felt like a soccer ball, bouncing back and forth between Guilin and Liuzhou. During the last five months he had spent time in eighteen prisons in thirteen different districts in south China. Although Ho still chafed at being deprived of his freedom, as a political prisoner he was now given better treatment. The food was adequate, he was no longer shackled at night, and he was even permitted to read newspapers and books. Periodically he was allowed to leave his cell to stretch his limbs and relieve himself, and on one occasion he was even given a haircut and a hot bath. He was also in a better position to keep in touch with his colleagues back in Vietnam and inform them of his situation, so he frequently sent them copies of magazines and books with notes that had been written in disappearing ink composed of boiled rice foam in the margins. To his Chinese captors, he presented the image of an old scholar, courteous and quiet. To pass the time he translated Sun Yat-sen's famous *Three People's Principles* into Vietnamese.[15]

Sometime during the spring of 1943, General Zhang Fakui discovered the real identity of his troublesome prisoner, or at least confirmed that he was a Communist. Precisely how he learned is a matter of conjecture. Ho Chi Minh's colleague Hoang Van Hoan claimed that Ho's identity as a Comintern agent was revealed by Tran Bao, a longtime Vietnamese nationalist who resided in the area and hoped to have him executed. But General Liang Huasheng, then director of the Fourth Military Command Political Department, declared in an interview many years later that in his own conversations with Ho, he had become convinced of his prisoner's Communist leanings and recommended that he be eliminated. According to Liang, however, his proposal was rejected by the central government in Chongqing, which, although now itself in possession of information on Ho's actual political leanings, ordered that if possible he be "converted."[16]

The central government's decision on the matter may have initially been influenced by Zhou Enlai, who was still serving as head of the CCP liaison office in Chongqing. When Zhou became aware in the fall of 1942 that Ho Chi Minh had been arrested, he raised the issue with General Feng Yuxiang, the well-known Chinese warlord and one of Chiang Kai-shek's leading rivals during the 1920s and 1930s. Feng, who had periodically flirted with the Communists but was now an influential member of the Nationalist government leadership, took up the case with the Soviet adviser in Chongqing and then spoke with Chiang Kai-shek's vice president, Li Zongren. Together they approached Chiang and appealed for his release. By one Chinese account, Feng was forceful on Ho's behalf, arguing that even if Ho Chi Minh was a member of the Vietnamese Communist movement, the point was irrelevant. After all, he argued, Communist representatives from other foreign countries, including the Soviet Union, were not being detained. The key point, Feng insisted, was that the Vietnamese people supported the Chinese war of resistance against Japan. If Ho Chi Minh was a friend, he should not be treated as a criminal. That would simply cause China to lose international support and sympathy and make a sham of China's struggle against the Japanese. Li Zongren concurred with Feng's assessment, suggesting that the central government turn the matter over to the Guangxi authorities to resolve. Chiang reluctantly agreed, and cabled the Fourth Military Command headquarters to order Ho's release under surveillance while attempting to persuade him to cooperate with Chongqing's goals.[17]

What effect this cable had on General Zhang Fakui in Liuzhou is uncertain. In interviews held in the United States long after the war, Zhang denied that his own actions in the matter had been motivated by orders from higher echelons. As he explained it, once he discovered that his prisoner was really Nguyen Ai Quoc, an influential member of the Vietnamese Communist movement, he ordered the new director of his Political Department, General Hou Zhiming, to lure him into cooperating with the Fourth Military War Zone with a view to obtaining his eventual release. In conversations with him, Zhang became aware of Ho's considerable abilities and his fervent anti-French sentiments and was apparently convinced by Ho's remark that although he was a member of the Indochinese Communist Party, his immediate objective was freedom and independence for his country. Ho apparently offered to provide Zhang with assistance in reorganizing the Vietnamese resistance movement in south China and guaranteed to his captor that a Communist society would not be established in Vietnam for at least fifty years.[18]

Zhang's motives for deciding to liberate his prisoner were undoubtedly connected with his own long-term political objectives. A native of Guangdong and a veteran of the Northern Expedition in the mid-1920s, Zhang was a respected military commander who had held aloof from the political maneuverings of both Chiang Kai-shek and the CCP. He was hostile to both Japan and the French colonial regime in Indochina, and was probably sympathetic to the desire of the Vietnamese people for national independence. As commander of the Fourth Military War Zone in Liuzhou, he was responsible for preparing to launch an attack on Japanese forces in Indochina before the end of the war. It was towards that end that he had sought to organize Vietnamese nationalist forces in south China during the early 1940s and train them for future operations inside Indochina.

However, Zhang Fakui's plan to organize Vietnamese nationalist elements into an effective instrument had run into problems. Cooperation between nationalist groups and the ICP through the creation of the Vietnamese National Liberation Committee had come to an end by the end of 1941, when VNQDD leaders had discovered the true identity of their colleagues Pham Van Dong and Vo Nguyen Giap and evicted them from the organization. Shortly after, factionalism among leading nationalist figures such as Vu Hong Khanh, Nguyen Hai Than, and Nghiem Ke To led to the virtual collapse of the league. One of the Committee's sponsors, Truong Boi Cong, was himself arrested by local authorities on the charge of corruption.

In the summer of 1942, Zhang Fakui decided to try again, directing nationalist leaders to form a new organization, this time without any Communist participation, to be called the Vietnamese Revolutionary League (Viet Nam Cach menh Dong minh Hoi), popularly called the Dong Minh Hoi. Zhang's subordinate, General Hou Zhiming, was selected as Chinese adviser to the organization, which held its first meeting in Liuzhou in early October 1942. The Dong Minh Hoi, however, had no more success than its predecessor, as plans encouraged by General

Zhang to convene a national congress in early September 1943 foundered on the factional disputes among the leading members.

It was in the hope that Ho Chi Minh could provide the spark to energize the struggling Vietnamese nationalist movement in south China that Zhang decided to restore him his freedom. On September 10, Ho was released from jail but with limited freedom of movement. A member of the Fourth Military Command's Political Department at the time later recalled that one day that fall, the prisoner suddenly entered the department's dining hall and sat down with Hou Zhiming and other Chinese officials. From that point on, the ex-prisoner, who was addressed by his acquaintants as "Uncle Ho" (Hu Lao Bo), was no longer kept under lock and key, but was permitted to circulate freely within the compound and even to take a walk outside the area.[19]

During that fall of 1943, Ho Chi Minh gradually began to immerse himself in local political activities. As a means of urging the Vietnamese nationalist groups to revitalize their efforts to create an effective organization, Zhang announced that he intended to take a direct interest in the Dong Minh Hoi and replaced Hou Zhiming with his deputy, General Xiao Wen, as its Chinese adviser. Xiao, a native of Guangdong whose father was an overseas Chinese, was himself reputed to be sympathetic to the Communists. To broaden the base of the organization, Zhang directed that all graduates of the Vietnamese training class at Liuzhou become members.

Ho Chi Minh now began to play an active role in the Dong Minh Hoi; in November, at the request of General Zhang, he was appointed its vice chairman. The appointment undoubtedly created some uneasiness for Nguyen Hai Than, then chairman of the organization and Ho's bitter rival since their days in Canton during the 1920s. But Than was reluctant to anger his powerful sponsor and swallowed his uneasiness. In December, at a banquet hosted by General Hou Zhiming and attended by both Vietnamese, Nguyen Hai Than offered a toast: "Hou Zhiming, Ho Chi Minh, two comrades with a common commitment to enlightenment." Without losing a step, Ho Chi Minh quickly responded: "You are a revolutionary, I am a revolutionary, we are all revolutionaries, we will certainly transform our destinies."[20]

With Zhang's encouragement, by the late fall Ho was actively involved in reorganizing the Dong Minh Hoi. He had now moved out of the compound of the Political Department and was permitted to live at the league's headquarters. He gave regular lectures on local and national affairs to audiences throughout the city, as well as to the Vietnamese training class under the direction of the Fourth Military Command. He promised his rapt audiences that after the defeat of Japan, a united, peaceful, independent, and democratic Vietnam would certainly emerge in Southeast Asia. On one occasion, he lauded China as a great force for peace, and the elder brother of the Vietnamese people. He predicted that the Allies would complete their victory over Japan within a year or so, and China could then assist the Vietnamese to recover their complete independence by peaceful means and build a new society.[21]

Having grown increasingly dependent on Ho Chi Minh as his instrument to revitalize the Dong Minh Hoi, Zhang Fakui approached him about making a second attempt to convene a national congress. Ho agreed, and a preparatory conference was held in Liuzhou in late February 1944. At the conference, Ho suggested that the organization broaden its scope and include representatives from the Vietminh Front and its subsidiary mass organizations, as well as from other groups in Indochina identified with the antifascist cause. As for the fear that the alliance would be dominated by the ICP, he pointed out that of all the parties and organizations in the country, it was the Indochinese Communist Party that possessed the most influence and visibility. The Vietnamese people, he claimed, had nothing to fear from communism, which would gradually carry the idea of economic equality throughout the entire world, just as democracy had spread the concept of political equality throughout Europe after the French Revolution in 1789. The result would be a future state of great world unity. Ho added that in the past, all the Vietnamese political parties had been in competition. Now they would unify in order to struggle against oppression and achieve the sole objective that motivated them all—to liberate their country and their people. To do so would be to follow the general trend of humanity, since China with its three people's principles, imperialist England, Communist Russia, and capitalist America were now allies opposing the common enemy. General Zhang agreed with these grand sentiments and invited Ho to go ahead with plans to convene a congress of the Dong Minh Hoi at the end of March.[22]

But Ho Chi Minh's intention to include representatives of the Vietminh Front in the congress did not sit well with many of the non-Communist members of the Dong Minh Hoi, who were suspicious that Ho would try to dominate the meeting by padding it with his own followers. To allay their concerns, Ho suggested to Zhang that the meeting be simply labeled a conference of overseas representatives of the Dong Minh Hoi. Zhang concurred, and at a meeting of the organization's executive committee it was agreed to include representatives of all major

Vietnamese groups operating in south China. At a banquet held in mid-March, Zhang approved the plan, and those opposed to broad participation of all patriotic groups at the congress had no choice but to concede.

The conference of overseas representatives of the Dong Minh Hoi opened in Liuzhou on March 25, 1944. Fifteen delegates were in attendance, including representatives from the ICP, the VNQDD, and the strongly nationalist Dai Viet (Great Viet) party. Several delegates, including Pham Van Dong and Le Tong Son, attended in the name of the Vietminh or other organizations connected to the Party. Ho Chi Minh spoke at the conference, describing the current conditions inside Indochina and the activities of the Vietminh Front, and praising the close historical relationship between the Vietnamese and Chinese peoples. Zhang Fakui attended the opening and closing sessions and watched over the events like a mother hen to assure himself that the meeting succeeded. Before adjourning on the twenty-eighth, the congress passed two resolutions and elected a seven-member executive committee and a control commission. Ho Chi Minh was initially selected as an alternate member of the former, but soon became a full member. Zhang Fakui demonstrated his approval of the proceedings by providing the delegates with additional financial support.[23]

During the next several months, Ho Chi Minh threw himself into the effort to reenergize the Dong Minh Hoi and prepare for his own return to Vietnam. In July he traveled to Nanning to speak to a number of students who had been sent by his Vietminh colleagues to study at the training institute in south China. By now Zhang Fakui had decided that Ho Chi Minh was the best choice to lead the Vietnamese anti-Japanese resistance movement. He once said that while Ho was hard-working, the others were lazy and careless, and squabbled so much that they gave him a headache. In early August, despite complaints from non-Communists, he gave Ho Chi Minh total freedom of action and promised him that he would be able to return soon to Vietnam. In return, Ho drew up a plan of action to guide his activities on his return to his country. Among the elements in his plan were transmitting to the Vietnamese people the determination of China to promote the independence of their country, developing and promoting the Dong Minh Hoi, preparing conditions for the entry of the Chinese army into north Vietnam, and intensifying the struggle for national independence.

In promising to give his every effort to promote the growth of the Dong Minh Hoi, Ho listed those political parties and factions he hoped to attract to its banner: not only were the ICP and its various mass organizations included, but also the Party's longtime rivals, the VNQDD and even the Constitutionalist Party, the members of which Party propagandists had long dismissed as reactionaries and puppets of the French. Ho promised to open up two guerrilla base areas just south of the frontier, and requested that General Zhang provide him with weapons and a sufficient amount of money to assist him in that purpose, as well as a personal letter of introduction to various patriotic organizations in Vietnam and a military map of the country. Zhang agreed to provide Ho with a passport for multiple entries into China, as well as a supply of medicine and funds for his own personal use, but he indicated that additional financial support for anti-Japanese activities inside Indochina would require further consideration.[24]

Before his departure from Liuzhou, Ho Chi Minh made a final visit to General Xiao Wen, Zhang's adviser to the Dong Minh Hoi, who had been of considerable assistance to him in his final preparations for his return to Vietnam. "Ninety-nine percent of what I told you about Vietnam and the Vietnamese revolutionary movement is true," he assured his Chinese host. "There is only one percent that I didn't tell you." He had earlier promised General Zhang that communism would not be realized in Vietnam for fifty years.[25]

Sometime in late August, in the company of eighteen recent Vietnamese graduates from Zhang Fakui's training institute, Ho Chi Minh left Liuzhou and returned to Indochina by way of Longzhou and Jingxi. To reduce the likelihood that they would be accosted by local security authorities, they were all dressed in Kuomintang military uniforms. At the frontier, they changed into native garb, but still encountered difficulties with border guards, and Ho had to appeal to local officials in Longzhou to intervene and allow them to continue. On arriving at the frontier town of Pingmeng, he had to remain for several days in a grass hut outside the town to recover his health and prepare security arrangements to escort him back to Pac Bo, where he finally arrived on September 20.[26]

During Ho Chi Minh's extended absence in south China, the course of the war in the Pacific had been shifting inexorably in favor of the Allies. President Roosevelt's initial plan to focus the main military effort on the China-Burma-India theater—a plan based on the assumption that Nationalist Chinese military forces could play a major role in the war effort—had been discarded because Washington grew disillusioned with Chiang Kai-shek's unwillingness to use his troops in offensive operations against the Japanese. In 1943, a new U.S. strategy designed to advance toward the Japanese home islands across the Pacific had already begun to show signs of success. Allied forces had occupied a number of Japanese-held islands in the Pacific Ocean, while military units under the command of U.S. General Douglas MacArthur had engaged in their own island-hopping from New Guinea to the Philippines.

On the Southeast Asian mainland, Japanese military control over Indochina remained relatively secure, but the overthrow of the Vichy government in France after the Normandy invasion in June 1944 increased the temptation among French civilian and military officials in Indochina to shift their allegiance to the Free French movement under Charles de Gaulle, thus arousing doubts in Tokyo as to the future allegiance of the administration of Governor-General Jean Decoux to the alliance with Japan. Japanese occupation authorities inside Indochina increased their efforts to enlist the loyalty of the local population to their own regime.

In the meantime, Ho Chi Minh's colleagues were attempting to spread the base of the revolutionary movement throughout the northern portions of Indochina. During 1942 and into early 1943, Vietminh cadres began to build guerrilla bases and expand the front's political presence in the hilly provinces surrounding the Red River delta. In the meantime, the Central Committee directive creating the Vietminh Front had come into the hands of Party members further south sometime in 1942 or 1943, and they began to rebuild the movement painstakingly in various provinces along the central coast and in the Mekong River delta.

Other Party cadres attempted to build a small "security zone" for the Standing Committee (composed of Truong Chinh, Hoang Quoc Viet, and Hoang Van Thu), which was now located at Bac Ninh, about fifteen miles northeast of Hanoi. After the Bac Son uprising, the French had arrested most of the Party cadres in the area, but following its return to the delta, the committee had set up a small "technical unit" in Hanoi to initiate propaganda work within the labor movement there. By the end of 1942, more than one thousand workers had been enrolled in a local National Salvation Association; similar organizations had been founded for youth and women. A small guerrilla unit was established at Gia Lam Airport, just to the north of the city, as the first step in creating this security zone for the Party leadership in the area.

From its base in the Hanoi suburbs, the Standing Committee had been seeking to keep track of the overall situation in the region and the world beyond while also establishing and maintaining communications with all Party units throughout Indochina. Shortly after the Japanese attack on Pearl Harbor in December 1941, General Secretary Truong Chinh had issued a communiqué analyzing how the changed situation in the world might affect the fortunes of the Vietnamese people and how the Party should respond. In "The Pacific War and the Urgent Tasks of the Party," he declared that in case of an invasion of Indochina by Chinese nationalist troops, Vietminh forces should welcome them and provide them with assistance, while at the same time warning them that they should not come as conquerors. He thought it likely that the British and the Americans would also decide to invade Indochina, in which case the Party should be willing to make principled concessions to secure their support. "If they agree to aid the revolution in Indochina," he said, "we may accord them economic advantages." But if they were to seek to assist the Free French movement under Charles de Gaulle in restoring French control over the area, "we will energetically protest and carry on our struggle to win independence." If the time were to come when British and American troops began to arrive in each locality, he directed Party cadres to mobilize popular support to install a people's revolutionary administration, which would then enter into negotiations with the arriving Allied forces. "We should guard against the illusion that the Chiang Kai-shek and Anglo-American troops will bring us our freedom," he warned. "In our struggle for national liberation we must obviously seek allies—even if they are temporary, vacillating, or conditional—but the struggle must no less be the fruit of our own efforts."

Truong Chinh concluded by criticizing the proposals of impetuous "leftist" elements within the Party who advocated a nationwide uprising at the moment of Chinese invasion. "Conditions for an uprising in Indochina," he warned, "are not ripe yet." The movement in rural areas was more active than in the cities, and in Vietnam more than in neighboring Laos and Cambodia. Chinh did remark that in case conditions were ripe in one local area, a provisional people's authority could be established there in advance of the general insurrection.[27]

By early 1943, the likelihood of an invasion of Indochina by Allied forces was increasing. To prepare for the possibility, in late February Truong Chinh convened a meeting of the Standing Committee at Vong La, northwest of Hanoi. In the committee's view, although the revolutionary movement still suffered from a number of shortcomings, it was on the verge of great advances. It therefore decided to begin planning for the general insurrection; to intensify efforts in all areas to build up the political and military forces of the movement; and to broaden the workers' movement, because without the participation of the urban population, it would be difficult for the insurrection to succeed in areas vital to the enemy. The committee called for an expansion of labor organizations and the broadening of the democratic front to include French citizens sympathetic to the Free French movement and members of the overseas Chinese community, as well as all patriotic elements within the Vietnamese population.[28]

While the Standing Committee was making its own arrangements, Party leaders from the two base areas of Cao Bang and Bac Son–Vo Nhai were holding their own conference at Lung Hoang, in Hoa An district, just northwest of Cao Bang. To counter French efforts to suppress the movement, they decided to link up the two base areas and open a communications route toward the Red River delta as a first stage in integrating the Viet Bac with the revolutionary movement elsewhere in the country, as well as to establish reliable means of contact with the Standing Committee. After the conference adjourned, guerrilla units that had retreated toward the frontier to escape French sweeps were ordered to return to their original bases in Bac So–Vo Nhai, and they began to push south toward Tuyen Quang and Vinh Yen, the latter a market town on the fringe of the delta about twenty miles northwest of Hanoi. To facilitate the move southward, revolutionary units of Chu Van Tan's National Salvation Army in the area were now split up into two sections and advanced along both sides of the Cau River, which flowed into the Red River delta from the northern mountains.

In the meantime, guerrilla detachments in Cao Bang pushed south in the direction of Bac Can and Lang Son. In August 1944, small groups of shock troops commanded by Vo Nguyen Giap—advancing, he later remarked, "like a snowball"—created new base areas and carried on propaganda activities as far south as the mountainous area just north of Thai Nguyen, a provincial capital on the edge of the delta. In a ravine in the middle of the jungle near Lang Coc they established a linkage with detachments of Chu Van Tan's National Salvation Army pushing west from Bac Son–Vo Nhai. The first elements of the future liberated base area were finally coming into place.

As it turned out, the confidence reflected in such decisions was somewhat premature. By the summer of 1943, French colonial authorities had become increasingly concerned at reports of a possible future invasion of the area by Chinese Nationalist troops, and they were well aware of the growing level of cooperation between Chinese authorities and Vietnamese nationalist elements living in exile in south China. That fall, Governor-General Decoux launched a military campaign to clear resistance elements out of the Viet Bac and establish a stronger French presence in the area. French patrols intensified, and authorities offered large rewards for anyone who would provide information on the location of resistance leaders. To facilitate government control, officials sought to group the local population into surveillance zones. Several dozen Communists were caught in the net, while others were forced to flee to more isolated areas.[29]

Similar problems plagued the attempt to build up the movement in Hanoi. The Standing Committee's "technical unit" to promote revolutionary propaganda among the urban population had been suppressed in the spring of 1943. Party leaders tried to establish a municipal committee in the city, but that effort too was thwarted by the French security forces. Party operatives were now having difficulty recruiting in urban areas because of the reduction in the size of the labor movement in all cities, a consequence of declining economic activities during the war. Commerce had been badly hit by the war, while taxes and war requisitions by the authorities were at punitive levels. Although many Vietnamese workers chafed under stern Japanese discipline and sympathized with the cause of the revolution, some feared to take part in demonstrations and work stoppages. In August, Hoang Van Thu was betrayed to the French by a double agent; he was executed in May 1943. Truong Chinh managed to evade capture at a French checkpoint only by posing as a foreman directing labor in the nearby rice fields.

By mid-1944, however, the situation for the insurgents was beginning to improve. In the Viet Bac, French pacification efforts had some success in reducing the extent of Vietminh operations, but the end result was to bring about the concentration of guerrilla forces in resistance base areas, as activists began to create secret cells safe from the enemy; these cells later became the basis for rapid expansion of the movement. Similar growth was beginning to take place in rural areas in central and south Vietnam. At the same time, steadily worsening economic conditions throughout Indochina eventually led to a measurable increase in urban discontent and a rising incidence of strikes. Although the goals of the strikers were generally economic rather than political, the ferment facilitated the Party's recruitment efforts, while sympathy for the workers among students and middle-class citizens promoted the cause.[30]

In a burst of confidence, an ICP committee representing three provinces in the border region met in July 1944 to discuss a proposal by Vo Nguyen Giap to initiate guerrilla war with a view to create a liberated base area. Some in attendance had concerns about whether the area could be held against a possible concerted counterattack by the French. They also questioned whether guerrilla forces were prepared to carry on a protracted struggle against both the French and the Japanese. Eventually the conference tentatively agreed to Giap's proposal, while reserving judgment on whether guerrilla operations should be unleashed immediately or delayed until a later date. But the meeting failed to reach a consensus on whether to start building a liberation army. When Giap began to initiate the process on his own initiative, Vu Anh (who was a senior member of the Central Committee) countermanded the order.

When Vu Anh and Vo Nguyen Giap arrived in Jingxi in mid-September to greet Ho Chi Minh and accompany him back to Pac Bo, Giap reported on the decisions reached at the July conference and outlined the plan. Ho Chi Minh pointed out that the recommendation to launch an offensive campaign in the Viet Bac was based on local conditions only and took no account of the situation elsewhere in the country. He believed that to throw all of the forces into a large-scale insurrection would run the risk of a major setback greater than the one encountered at the end of 1943. Although the movement was growing in strength, in no region of the country were the Party's forces prepared to launch armed struggle in support of the uprising in the Viet Bac. The enemy could thus concentrate his forces against the fighters in the border region, whose forces in any case lacked sufficient regular armed units to serve as a pivot. "The phase of peaceful revolution has passed," he concluded, "but the hour of the general insurrection has not yet sounded." He felt that political struggle was no longer sufficient, but armed insurrection still too dangerous to undertake; that the struggle must begin to shift from the political to a violent stage, but for the moment, political activities must continue to have priority.[31]

Ho Chi Minh did offer some consolation to his young colleague. While rejecting Giap's proposal to begin the creation of a people's liberation army, he agreed to begin the formation of the first units of such a future army. "If we are not the strongest," he noted, "it is no reason for us to be destroyed without a response." The following day, Giap later recalled, Ho offered the suggestion that these new revolutionary units be temporarily labeled the "Army of Propaganda and Liberation of Vietnam," since they would be primarily engaged in the task of mobilizing the political force of the masses in preparation for the future insurrection.

Vo Nguyen Giap and Vu Anh remained one more day at Pac Bo to study the situation and draw up plans for the new armed propaganda brigades. Ho gave them some parting advice: "Secrecy, always secrecy. Let the enemy think you're to the west when you are in the east. Attack by surprise and retreat before the enemy can respond." On his return to the Bac Son–Vo Nhai base area, Giap proceeded to set up the first new units. The thirty-four members of the first brigade were specially selected by leading cadres and included a number of graduates from the training program in south China. From Ho Chi Minh in Pac Bo came a message of congratulations, written on a tiny piece of paper hidden in a pack of cigarettes:

> The propaganda brigade of the Vietnamese Liberation Army is called to be the elder brother for a numerous family. I hope that still other brigades will soon see the light of day. However modest in its beginnings, it will see open before it the most brilliant perspectives. It is the embryo of our future liberation army, and has for its field of battle the entire territory of Vietnam, from north to south.

With the formation of the first units of the armed propaganda brigades on December 22, 1944, the shape of the future revolutionary armed forces—to be known as the Vietnamese Liberation Army (Viet Nam Giai phong Quan, or VLA)—began to take form. The armed propaganda brigades represented the movement's first fledgling regular force units. They would supplement guerrilla forces organized and directed at the district level, as well as self-defense militia units recruited in local villages under Party control. Just two days after they saw the light of day, these new units won victories in assaults on French posts in the villages of Phai Khat and Na Ngan as enemy forces, taken by surprise by the intensity of the assault, were almost wiped out. The victors carried away not only the pride in their success, but also a number of weapons, while the defenders suffered more than seventy casualties. The news of the victories spread like wildfire throughout the Viet Bac.

Back in Pac Bo, Ho Chi Minh was continuing to promote the movement in his own way. In October, he wrote a "Letter to All Our Compatriots," in which he analyzed the current situation and said "the opportunity for our people's liberation is only in a year or a year and a half. The time approaches. We must act quickly!"[32]

On November 11, 1944, a U.S. reconnaissance plane piloted by Lieutenant Rudolph Shaw encountered engine trouble while flying over the rough mountainous terrain along the Sino-Vietnamese frontier. Shaw was able to parachute to safety, but the incident had been observed by French authorities stationed in the vicinity, and patrols were dispatched to locate him. Members of a local Vietminh unit were the first to reach him, however, and they decided to deliver him to Ho Chi Minh. For the next several days, the Vietminh troops led the American pilot over mountains and jungle trails toward Pac Bo, walking at night and resting during the day in caves to avoid the enemy. In the end, it took almost a month to cover a distance of only forty miles.

None of Shaw's escorts had been able to communicate with him (according to his own account, they communicated only when he said "Vietminh! Vietminh!" and the Vietnamese responded, "America! Roosevelt!"), but when he arrived at Pac Bo, Ho Chi Minh greeted him effusively in colloquial English: "How do you do, pilot! Where are you from?" Shaw was reportedly so excited that he hugged Ho and later said to him, "When I heard your voice, I felt as if I were hearing the voice of my father in the United States."[33]

To Ho Chi Minh, the arrival of the downed American pilot was equally fortuitous. Ever since the U.S. entrance into the War in December 1941, he had seen U.S. support for his movement as a possible trump card in his struggle against Japanese occupation forces and the French. After being released from prison in Liuzhou in the fall of 1943, he had spent considerable time at the library of the U.S. Office of War Information (OWI) there and had undoubtedly become aware of reports that President Roosevelt had no liking for European colonialism and was seeking to find the means of restoring to the colonies of Southeast Asia their independence after the end of the war. Roosevelt clearly had a particular animus against the French role in Indochina, and was quoted on one occasion as having remarked: "France has milked it for one hundred years. The people of Indochina are entitled to something better than that." Although Ho Chi Minh was well aware that the United States was a capitalist society, he had always expressed admiration for its commitment to democratic principles and may have felt that Roosevelt himself might lead the United States on the path of greater economic equality and social justice.[34]

For their part, U.S. officials stationed in China had already become aware of Ho Chi Minh long before his release from captivity. During the fall of 1942, news reports in the Chinese press (probably leaked by sources close to the ICP in China) mentioned the arrest of an Annamite named "Ho Chih-chi" who had an alleged connection with a pro-Allied "provisional government" of Indochina that was being formed in Liuzhou with support from the Chinese government. When U.S. Embassy officials contacted the local representative of the antifascist Free French movement, he discounted the truth of the story and denied that such a government existed. Nevertheless, U.S. Ambassador Clarence Gauss cabled the Department of State on December 31, 1942, to report the arrest and instructed embassy officers to look into the matter. Lacking cooperation from Chinese authorities, however, they had little success; when the following June Washington asked for an update on the situation, the embassy simply reported that so far as it could determine, the resistance movement in Indochina had no particular importance at that time.

But if the U.S. Embassy in Chongqing wanted nothing to do with an obscure "Annamite," other U.S. officials in China were of a different view. When, in the summer of 1943, the CCP liaison chief Zhou Enlai approached the local U.S. Office of Strategic Services (OSS) for assistance in securing Ho's release on the grounds that he could be of assistance to the Allied war effort, they, along with officials at the OWI (who might have been approached by Ho Chi Minh with an offer to serve as a translator), discussed the matter with U.S. Embassy officials, who apparently agreed to broach the issue with the Chinese government to seek his release and arrange for his collaboration.

Whether the U.S. approach ever took place, and if so, whether it had any impact on Zhang Fakui's decision to grant limited freedom for Ho Chi Minh is not clear. In any case, it did not lead to any immediate arrangements for Ho to collaborate with U.S. officials in south China. In November 1943, the Vietnamese branch of the International Anti-Aggression League, writing from Jingxi, appealed to the U.S. Embassy in Chongqing for U.S. assistance in obtaining full freedom of action for "Hu Chih-ming" to take part in anti-Japanese activities and, if necessary, to return to his own country.

Embassy officer Philip D. Sprouse recognized the name as "the person whose alleged arrest" had taken place the previous year. But Sprouse apparently had been persuaded by Free French representatives in Chongqing that the so-called provisional government of Indochina established in Liuzhou was simply a ploy by the Chinese government to promote its own interests in the area. Ambassador Gauss transmitted the appeal to Washington, with a cover letter indicating that since the French had denied the existence of such an organization, he would make "no reply" to the letter. Gauss's report was filed and forgotten in Washington.[35]

By the spring of 1944, the lure of potential U.S. support had piqued the interest of other Vietminh representatives living in south China. That April, Vietminh representatives in Kunming had met with officials at the Free French Consulate about arranging a meeting to discuss postwar French policies in Indochina, but after initial contacts their efforts had stalled. Rebuffed by the French, they turned to the United States, and met with local officials of the OSS and the OWI, to seek their assistance in writing a letter to U.S. Ambassador Gauss in Chongqing. The letter appealed for U.S. aid in the Vietnamese struggle for independence while offering to fight alongside the Allies against the Japanese occupation forces in Indochina. On August 18, an OSS officer delivered the letter to U.S. Consul General William Langdon in Kunming with the comment that there would be "considerable trouble in Indochina after the war if at least a substantial measure of self-government is not put into effect in that country at an early date." Langdon agreed to meet with the group on September 8. He promised to pass on the letter to the U.S. ambassador and expressed U.S. support for the aspirations of the Vietnamese people, noting that "the highest spokesmen of the American Government had in numerous declarations given assurances of the interest of their government in the political welfare and advancement of oppressed peoples in the Orient, among whom the Annamite people might believe themselves to be included." But Langdon was diplomatically cautious in responding to the request for U.S. sympathy, noting that "the Annamite people are citizens of France, who is fighting side by side with the United States . . . against the Axis. It would not make sense . . . if America with one hand at great expenditures of life and treasure rescued and delivered France from German slavery and with the other undermined her Empire."

Pham Viet Tu, the leader of the Vietnamese delegation, promised Langdon that the Vietminh had no intention of fighting the French, but only the Japanese, and asked for assistance for that purpose. But he added his hope that the United States would insist upon autonomy for the Annamite people after the close of the war. Langdon was noncommittal, noting that during Charles de Gaulle's visit to Washington, D.C., in July, the General had told the press that French policy was to introduce the peoples of the French empire to self-government, and that if the Vietnamese had any complaints against the French, they should deal directly with them.[36]

The stratagem by local representatives in Kunming to enlist U.S. support had thus once again failed. American officials still had little knowledge about Vietnamese nationalist groups operating in the area, and some were skeptical about their effectiveness because of the chronic factionalism that seemed to accompany their activities. Although the OSS office submitted a favorable report on the meeting, Langdon and the OWI representative were more doubtful. The latter noted that Vietnamese nationalist groups in south China appeared to have little experience in running a modern government (although he conceded that it was not their fault). Langdon was even more negative, reporting in a dispatch to Washington that Vietnamese groups in south China had "no real importance" in Indochina. That December, an OSS report, citing French sources, remarked that the League for the Independence of Indochina (as the Vietminh Front was known in English) "lacked any popular support" and was "largely a facade composed of a relatively small number of Indo-Chinese intellectuals and other dissatisfied elements in the colony."[37]

Ho Chi Minh was not directly involved in these events, but was presumably in contact with Pham Viet Tu and his colleagues, and may have suggested the meeting with U.S. officials in Kunming. In the months after his release from prison in September 1943, Ho had carefully cultivated the friendship and confidence of U.S. officers at the OWI branch in Liuzhou, who in August 1944, apparently sought to arrange for Ho Chi Minh to go to San Francisco. The U.S. Consulate General in Kunming requested guidance from the State Department on this request by OWI for a visa for a certain Ho Ting-ching (described as an Indochina-born Chinese) to travel to the United States to broadcast the news in Vietnamese. Philip Sprouse, who had now been transferred to Washington, took up the matter and wrote a memorandum on "Mr. Ho," describing his activities. Sprouse surmised that "Mr. Ho" was the same person who had been employed by the Kuomintang in Kunming to broadcast propaganda in the Vietnamese language into Indochina. The request was supported by the State Department's Far Eastern Division, but was opposed by Europeanists, who undoubtedly sensed that it would cause problems with the French. OWI argued on Ho's behalf that his activities in the United States would be tightly controlled and mainly mechanical, but the request was ultimately rejected.[38]

Why Ho Chi Minh would have wanted to go to the United States at that particular time is not clear. By the summer of 1944, the overall situation in the Pacific Theater was becoming increasingly favorable to the Allies and, as Ho had previously predicted, the end of the war beckoned sometime during the following year. Should that be the case, Ho would undoubtedly wish to be inside Vietnam directing the struggle against the French. Perhaps the most likely explanation is that the request was made at a time when Zhang Fakui still refused to approve his return to Indochina, and Ho saw the visa as an opportunity to influence the situation in the United States, perhaps through a direct appeal to the White House, in preparation for a return to his country at an opportune moment.

If U.S. support for the Vietminh Front was the ultimate prize, then Lieutenant Shaw's appearance on Ho Chi Minh's doorstep late in 1944 was his ticket to take part in the raffle. When Shaw asked for Ho's assistance in reaching the Chinese border, Ho agreed, remarking that he also intended to go to China on business. Shaw then invited Ho to join him in going to Kunming, then the headquarters of the U.S. Fourteenth Air Force. A few days later, Ho Chi Minh and two young colleagues escorted Shaw into China, Ho still wearing his threadbare Kuomintang military uniform and bearing the identity papers that Zhang Fakui had provided him before his departure from Liuzhou. Shortly after crossing the Chinese border, Shaw alerted the Air Ground Aid Services (AGAS) office in Kunming, a U.S. military agency responsible for assisting in the rescue of downed Allied airmen in the region, of his rescue and forthcoming arrival. Officials at AGAS wired back to Shaw, inviting him to bring Ho Chi Minh with him to Kunming. Local Chinese authorities decided to send Shaw on to Kunming by plane, leaving Ho to fend for himself, but Ho Chi Minh was determined to use the opportunity to meet with U.S. officials in Kunming, so he decided to continue the journey on foot, posing as an inspector along the French-built Hanoi-Kunming railroad.[39]

En route to Kunming, Ho and his two companions stopped at Yiliang, a small town on the rail line where Hoang Quang Binh, one of the comrades he had met four years previously during his stay in Kunming, was still working as a barber. In his reminiscences, Binh later recalled that Ho Chi Minh looked sickly and emaciated, and ate little. His uniform was patched and worn, and his thin canvas shoes were full of holes; the group had been walking for several days, spending the night with sympathizers, and often sleeping in the open or in pigsties. Ho had recently caught a fever from another traveler, and to his host he seemed uncharacteristically depressed. Yet his mind was still focused on the cause. When Binh remarked that he and his comrades were resisting appeals from the local office of the Dong Minh Hoi (many of whom were members of the VNQDD) to join their organization, Ho remonstrated with his host, advising him to join the Dong Minh Hoi and then steal away its followers to become members of the Party.[40]

After staying several days in Yiliang in order to allow Ho Chi Minh to recover, the little group continued on the last leg of their journey. Once they got to Kunming, sometime in the first weeks of 1945, however, they discovered that Lieutenant Shaw had already left for the United States by airplane. Ho Chi Minh took up lodgings with Tong Minh Phuong, one of the local Vietminh representatives who had written the letter to Ambassador Gauss the previous August. A former student at the University of Hanoi who had come to Kunming from Indochina in 1943, Phuong had set up a coffee shop near OSS headquarters which he used as a cover for the Party's clandestine activities; now he undoubtedly informed Ho of their abortive approach to the Americans.[41] Ho decided to contact the local AGAS office in the hope that officials there would, as an expression of gratitude for his bringing the downed U.S. airman to China, arrange for him an interview with General Claire Chennault, commander of the U.S. Fourteenth Air Force in Kunming. He also got in touch with the local headquarters of the OSS, since officials there had assisted Phuong and the other Vietminh representatives in drafting their letter to Gauss. Perhaps now, Ho Chi Minh hoped, his service to the Americans could be parlayed into official U.S. recognition of his movement and military assistance for Vietminh operations.

To his own good fortune, Ho Chi Minh had arrived in Kunming at a truly providential and opportune moment. For the last several months, the local AGAS office had been authorized to extend its activities beyond rescuing Allied airmen to obtaining intelligence information on Japanese activities inside French Indochina. Among its most valuable sources was a small group of Western civilians (known as GBT from the names of the individuals: a Canadian, L. L. Gordon; an American, Harry Bernard; and a Chinese-American, Frank Tan). All had formerly been employed by an oil company in Saigon and were able to use their local contacts to obtain valuable information about Japanese activities throughout Indochina. On March 9, 1945, however, that source suddenly dried up when the Japanese (doubting the loyalty of French officials in Indochina) abruptly announced the abolition of the Vichy French administration in Indochina and turned over control to a puppet administration under Bao Dai, the Vietnamese emperor. Most foreign citizens inside Indochina were now placed under arrest or removed from their positions, and the GBT group fled to south China.

Faced with the loss of their chief source of intelligence in Indochina, U.S. officials in Chongqing instructed intelligence units in south China to seek new channels of information, even from anti-French Vietnamese resistance groups. Previously, U.S. operatives had been ordered to refuse contacts with such groups as a result of orders from the White House that U.S. officials were not authorized to become involved in local Indochinese politics. Now, however, new orders arrived from Washington instructing them to work with whatever sources were available.

Sometime in mid-March, Marine Lieutenant Charles Fenn, who had recently been transferred from the local OSS office to AGAS to run the GBT operation, was informed by one of his colleagues that "an old Annamite" (at the time, Ho was actually only fifty-four years old, but looked older) who had arrived in Kunming after saving a downed U.S. flier apparently had connections with a patriotic group and might prove useful in carrying out intelligence operations in Indochina. A native of

Ireland and a former correspondent who had been assigned to Kunming because of his knowledge of Asia and the Chinese language, Fenn was eager to find a new source of intelligence information in Indochina to replace the GBT operation; he asked his contact to arrange a meeting for him with Ho Chi Minh, who had been spending his time at the local OWI office reading everything from *Time* magazine to the *Encyclopedia Americana*. Although Fenn had been warned about Ho's Communist connections, a meeting was arranged for March 17. As Fenn recorded in his diary at the time:

> Ho came along with a younger man named Fam. Ho wasn't what I expected. In the first place he isn't really "old": his silvery wisp of beard suggests age, but his face is vigorous and his eyes bright and gleaming. We spoke in French. It seems he has already met Hall, Blass, and de Sibour [OSS officers in Kunming], but got nowhere with any of them. I asked him what he had wanted of them. He said—only recognition of his group (called Vietminh League or League for Independence). I had vaguely heard of this as being communist, and asked him about it. Ho said that the French call all Annamites communists who want independence. I told him about our work and asked whether he'd like to help us. He said they might be able to but had no radio operators nor of course any equipment. We discussed taking in a radio and generator and an operator. Ho said a generator would make too much noise—the Japs were always around. Couldn't we use the type of set with battery, such as the Chinese use? I explained they were too weak for distant operation, especially when the batteries run down. I asked him what he'd want in return for helping us. Arms and medicines, he said. I told him the arms would be difficult, because of the French. We discussed the problem of the French. Ho insisted that the Independence League are only anti-Jap. I was impressed by his clear-cut talk; Buddha-like composure, except movements with wrinkled brown fingers. Fam made notes. It was agreed we should have a further meeting. They wrote their names down in Chinese characters which were romanized into Fam Fuc Pao and Ho Tchih Ming.

Fenn consulted with his colleagues at AGAS, and they all agreed to make preparations for sending "old man Ho" (he was formally given the code name of "Lucius," but the Americans called him "old man Ho" in private) back to Indochina with a Chinese radio operator. Three days later they met again:

Had a second meeting with the Annamites in the Indo-China cafe on Chin Pi Street. It seems that the proprietor is a friend of theirs. We sat upstairs and drank coffee filtered in the French style, strong and quite good. The room was empty but Ho said customers might come in. We agree to use certain terms: Chinese to be called "friends," Americans "brothers," French "neutrals," Japs "occupants," Annamites "natives." Ho said that in regard to taking down two Chinese, one of them American-Chinese, this might be difficult because the latter, certainly, would be easy to identify. Ho's group are inclined to be suspicious of the Chinese. Since there are no Annamite radio operators, the Chinese operator is of course inevitable. But instead of taking [Frank] Tan, he'd rather go with this one man and then later we could drop in an American officer. Would I go myself? I said I would. Ho said his group would give me every welcome. We then discussed supplies. Fam mentioned the "high explosives" that Hall had told him about. I tried to soft pedal this, but agreed we might later drop in light weapons, medicines and further radio sets. Our own operator could train some of Ho's men to use these. Ho also wants to meet Chennault. I agreed to arrange this if he would agree not to ask him for anything: neither supplies nor promises about support. Ho agreed. The old man wears Chinese-type cotton trousers and buttoned-to-the-neck jacket, sand-coloured, not blue. His sandals are the strap type they usually wear in Indo-China. His little beard is silvery, but his eyebrows are light-brown going grey at the top edge and his hair is still almost black but receding. The young man, Fam, wears a western-style suit and has enormous cheek-bones and a powerful chin. They both talk quietly but sometimes burst into chuckles. We seem to get on well together.[42]

After the meeting, Fenn checked with his colleagues about the Vietminh, and found that although the French labeled them as Communists, the Chinese simply considered them tricky. When Fenn asked general headquarters in Chongqing for advice, he received instructions: "Get a net regardless," but with a warning that intelligence operations were directed not to become involved in native-French politics.

A few days later, Fenn arranged for Ho Chi Minh to meet General Claire Chennault in his office at Fourteenth Air Force headquarters, but warned him once again not to submit a formal request for assistance. Ho arrived for the meeting dressed in his worn khaki-colored cotton tunic, although Fenn noticed that he had replaced a lost button on the collar. As was his custom, Chennault was immaculately dressed in his resplendent military uniform and sat behind a massive desk. The dapper Chennault, already famous for his role as the U.S. commander of the "Flying Tiger" detachment of volunteer pilots that had assisted Nationalist Chinese forces in fighting against the invading Japanese in the late 1930s, was widely reputed to be vain about his personal appearance. The general thanked Ho Chi Minh for rescuing Lieutenant Shaw; according to Fenn, there were no comments about political issues. Ho kept his promise not to request assistance and (at Fenn's advice) dutifully praised Chennault's efforts with the Flying Tigers, but at the end of the short visit he did ask his host for a signed photograph. As Fenn recalled:

> There's nothing Chennault likes more than giving his photograph. So he presses the bell and in comes Doreen [Chennault's secretary] again. In due course it's some other girl who produces a folder of eight-by-ten glossies. "Take your pick," says Chennault. Ho takes one and asks would the general be so kind as to sign it? Doreen produces a Parker 51 and Chennault writes across the bottom, "Yours Sincerely, Claire L. Chennault." And out we all troop into Kunming's sparkling air.[43]

Ho Chi Minh had thus established contacts with key U.S. military officials in Kunming. But he had yet to win formal recognition by the United States of the legitimacy of the Vietminh Front as the legal representative of the Vietnamese people or to obtain any more than a modicum of assistance for his movement. As he prepared for departure, he asked Charles Fenn for six new Colt .45 automatics in their original wrappers, which Fenn obtained from friends in the OSS.

At the end of March 1945, Ho Chi Minh flew in a small U.S. plane with his new radio operator to the town of Paise. Located about sixty miles north of Jingxi in Guangxi province, Paise was the new headquarters of Zhang Fakui's Fourth Military Command since the Japanese occupation of Liuzhou during their famous "Offensive Number One" in south China the previous November. Ho's objective at Paise was to reestablish contact with members of the Dong Minh Hoi in order to forge it into a weapon useful for the purposes of the Vietminh Front. After Ho's departure from Liuzhou the previous August, the Dong Minh Hoi had virtually disintegrated because of Chinese inattention and the decision of several of the leading non-Communist members to return to Yunnan province. With the aid of Vietminh representatives like Le Tong Son, who had followed the Fourth Military Command to Paise, Ho attempted to reorganize the Dong Minh Hoi by creating a new "action committee" dominated by his own followers. To allay the suspicions of leading members of other nationalist organizations, he showed them the signed photograph from Chennault and handed each of them a Colt automatic. A few days later, however, General Xiao Wen, who was himself becoming increasingly distrustful of the Vietminh, disbanded Ho's action committee and selected a new committee consisting of a mixture of Communist and non-Communist members, including Ho Chi Minh. Ho now departed for Jingxi en route to Pac Bo.[44]

While Ho Chi Minh was in Paise attempting to revitalize the Dong Minh Hoi, a U.S. military intelligence officer arrived in Kunming to join the OSS unit there. Captain Archimedes "Al" Patti had served in the European Theater until January 1944, when he was transferred to Washington, D.C., and appointed to the Indochina desk at OSS headquarters. A man of considerable swagger and self-confidence, Patti brought to his task a strong sense of history and an abiding distrust of the French and their legacy in colonial areas. It was from the files in Washington, D.C. that he first became aware of the activities of the Vietminh Front and its mysterious leader, Ho Chi Minh. In April 1945, he arrived in Kunming as deputy to the local OSS chief, Colonel Paul Helliwell, to direct OSS intelligence operations in French Indochina. As he quickly discovered, U.S. policy toward Indochina was in a state of flux, and there was considerable confusion among local U.S. officials over whether and how much to assist the Free French, and whether and to what degree such officials might be authorized to become involved with Vietnamese resistance groups inside the country. At a conference held shortly after Patti's arrival, the activities of the Vietminh movement came under discussion, and the representative from AGAS mentioned that an "old man" known as Ho Chi Minh had agreed to assist his office in organizing an intelligence network in Indochina. Another official added that Ho had been undertaking some psychological warfare work with the Chinese propaganda office in cooperation with OWI.[45]

To Patti, Ho Chi Minh's movement seemed a natural vehicle for his own operations in Indochina. Although any OSS effort to make active use of the Vietminh could encounter problems with both the Chinese and the French, Patti felt protected by recent directives from Washington to make use of whatever intelligence sources were offered to obtain information on Japanese activities in Indochina. What he now required was an opportunity to meet Ho Chi Minh, who had already left Kunming to return to his own country. Fortuitously, a few days after his arrival, Patti received a visit from Vuong Minh Phuong. After initial pleasantries, Phuong identified himself as a member of the Vietminh Front led by "General" Ho Chi Minh and delicately offered its support to the Allied cause in return for military assistance and recognition of the front as the sole political organization representing the interests of the Vietnamese people. When Patti asked how General Ho could be reached, Phuong remarked that he could be contacted at Jingxi, where he was stopping on his way back to Indochina.

Patti then consulted with his superior, Colonel Richard Heppner, chief OSS representative in Chongqing and, in peacetime, a prominent lawyer with high-level connections in the Roosevelt administration. Heppner at first was hesitant. Patrick Hurley, the veteran Oklahoma politician who had just replaced Clarence Gauss as U.S. ambassador to China, had become Chiang Kai-shek's advocate and was irritated with OSS officers in Yan'an for seeking to arrange a coalition between Chiang and the Chinese Communists; Hurley had also warned Heppner that both the French and the Chinese would be unhappy to discover U.S. intelligence contacts with the Vietminh, and especially with Ho Chi Minh, whom French intelligence sources had correctly identified as Nguyen Ai Quoc. On April 26, however, Heppner received a cable from General Albert C. Wedemeyer, commander of U.S. forces in the China Theater, authorizing him to introduce OSS operatives into Indochina to obtain intelligence and carry on demolition work against enemy installations in the area. Heppner informed Patti that the matter of enlisting Ho Chi Minh into the Allied effort remained open for consideration, while warning him not to alienate the French or the Chinese.

The next day, Patti arrived at Debao airport, just north of Jingxi, and after consultation with local AGAS representatives, drove into Jingxi, where he met a Vietminh contact at a local restaurant and was driven to see Ho Chi Minh in a small village about six miles out of town. After delicately feeling out his visitor about his identity and political views, Ho described conditions inside Indochina and pointed out that his movement could provide much useful assistance and information to the Allies if it were in possession of modern weapons, ammunition, and means of communication. At the moment, Ho conceded that the movement was dependent upon a limited amount of equipment captured from the enemy. Patti avoided any commitment, but promised to explore the matter. By his own account, Patti was elated.[46]

A week later, Ho Chi Minh was back at Pac Bo after a strenuous trek through the jungles along the border. The group accompanying him totaled about forty, and included U.S. Army radio operator Mac Shinn and Frank Tan, a member of the aborted GBT team. Both had been provided by Fenn in the hope that, as Asian Americans, they would attract less attention from prying eyes than another American might. From Pac Bo, Mac Shinn began reporting to Kunming, and the OSS began to air-drop additional supplies, including medicine, a second radio set, and more weapons, into the wilderness around Pac Bo. In return for the equipment, Ho and his colleagues provided the Americans with useful services, including weather reports, and rescued several U.S. airmen shot down over northern Indochina and returned them to China. Ho had finally established a linkage—however tenuous—with the Allied cause.

By now, an Allied victory in the Pacific War appeared only a matter of time. U.S. military forces were moving inexorably closer to the Japanese home islands, and air raids by B-29 bombers relentlessly laid waste to the major Japanese cities. Tentative plans were still under way for a possible Allied invasion of French Indochina, combined with Chinese Nationalist units moving south into the area; this idea had strong support from the White House.

Inside Indochina, the situation was evolving rapidly. Bad weather conditions over large parts of the country had led to a considerable shortfall in the fall 1944 harvest, resulting in hoarding and price speculation on the part of rice dealers. Japanese occupation authorities had compounded the problem by mandating shipments of rice to Japan and ordering peasants in agricultural districts throughout the northern part of Vietnam to shift from the cultivation of rice to oil seeds, peanuts, cotton, and jute. Now, as famine struck, the Japanese refused to open the state granaries or increase rice shipments from the fertile Mekong delta to hard-hit regions in central Vietnam and the Tonkin delta. Through indifference or incompetence, the Vichy regime under Jean Decoux had done little to help.

During the winter, the authorities had refused to reduce taxes or to increase the price of obligatory quotas of rice assigned to each farmer for sale to the government. Desperate farmers switched to the cultivation of other crops, such as sweet potatoes or manioc, but supplies quickly ran out. As prices for all staple commodities began rapidly to rise, the threat of famine loomed in urban areas as well. By midwinter, thousands were suffering from hunger, and deaths from starvation were rising rapidly. Peasants sought to ward off hunger by eating roots, weeds, and even the bark of trees, while city dwellers traded precious household items in exchange for rice and vegetables sold at inflated prices. As the number of dead mounted, bodies began to appear along the highways, and hungry peasants wandered aimlessly begging for food or gathered near granaries zealously guarded by Japanese troops.

However tragic its impact on the population of Vietnam, the crisis was a potential godsend to the Vietminh, who could now argue with little fear of contradiction that neither the French nor the Japanese authorities were capable of looking out for the interests of the Vietnamese people. During the winter, Vietminh activists urged local peasants to raid warehouses throughout the northern and central provinces, seizing the grain stored there and distributing it to the needy. In many cases, however, it was too late, and the number of deaths from hunger stretched into the hundreds of thousands. The bodies of the dead lay unattended by the roadside in rural areas, as family members were often too weak to help their kin.[47]

That winter, the French had made strenuous efforts to clean out Vietminh guerrilla bases in the mountains north of the delta. After their initial victories in the battles at Phai Khat and Na Ngan, Vo Nguyen Giap's armed propaganda units now marched northward toward the Sino-Vietnamese frontier, occupying villages inhabited by local minority peoples along the way. When the French sent out patrols, the rebels retreated to their base area (known as Hoang Hoa Tham) between Cao Bang and the village of Bac Can, where Giap and Vu Anh and Pham Van Dong, his colleagues on an interprovincial Party committee, began to draft plans to resume their March to the South to liberate Hanoi and the Red River delta from Japanese military occupation.

When, on March 9, 1945, the Japanese launched a coup d'état, they in a stroke of a pen brought to an end over half a century of French rule over Vietnam. By abolishing the colonial administration and replacing it with a puppet imperial government headed by Emperor Bao Dai but firmly under their domination, the Japanese had inadvertently opened up the entire region north of the delta to a revolutionary takeover. Party General Secretary Truong Chinh had anticipated the move, having called a meeting the previous day of available members of the Central Committee in Dinh Bang, a village twelve miles northeast of Hanoi, to discuss the implications. As the coup was taking place, the committee issued a directive ordering heightened preparations for an upcoming general uprising. Declaring that several factors favored the success of such an uprising, including the ongoing political crisis created by the coup, the intensifying famine, and the prospective Allied invasion, it concluded that military struggle should now receive the highest priority; the directive therefore called for the expansion of guerrilla bases, a broadening of the political base of the Vietminh Front, and a fusing of the various units of the revolutionary armed forces into a new VLA.

Nevertheless, the cautious Truong Chinh was concerned that the Party should not move until the internal and international conditions were ripe, for the revolutionary forces themselves were still not yet adequately prepared to launch a successful uprising. Only when those factors had ripened should his followers be prepared to act. The committee apparently assumed that an Allied invasion was likely, for the Party's forces were directed to strike behind the Japanese lines and wage a general insurrection once the Allied forces had landed in Indochina and begun their advance. But it noted that even if the Japanese government decided to surrender before such an invasion took place, "our general uprising could still break out and succeed."[48]

Prior to his departure from Kunming, Ho Chi Minh had provided his U.S. contacts with his interpretation of the March 9 coup. In a note signed "Luc" that is now in the U.S. archives, he declared that it had brought an end to the French domination in Indochina, a domination that had begun eighty-seven years previously. "Thus," he concluded, "the French imperialist wolf was finally devoured by the Japanese fascist hyena." Luc admitted that in the overall scheme of things in the world at war, this was only "a minute event," but he claimed that it would have "a serious bearing on the World War in general, on Indo-China, France, Japan, and China in particular." Ho's purpose in writing the report was clear—to persuade the Roosevelt administration to attack Japan in Indochina, which he called "Japan's only road of retreat." In characteristically colorful language, he stated that "from Japan to New Guinea, the Japan force lays [sic] like a long snake whose neck is Indo-China. If the Allies knock hard on its neck, the snake will cease to move."[49]

In the Cao Bang redoubt in northern Indochina, other Party leaders drew their own conclusions from the change of government in Indochina. On hearing the news of the coup, they ordered an intensification of guerrilla attacks throughout the frontier region near Cao Bang, while Giap's armed propaganda units began to move south, occupying villages and enrolling new recruits for the liberation armed forces along the way. Passing through Cho Chu, they finally arrived at Kim Lung, a tiny village located in the midst of tangled jungle midway between Thai Nguyen and Tuyen Quang. There they encountered military units of Chu Van Tan's National Salvation Army, who had been moving into the area from the east. With their meeting at Kim Lung, the junction of the revolutionary forces operating in the Viet Bac had been achieved and the road to the delta was open.

In early April 1945, the Central Committee convened a military conference at Hiep Hoa, a few miles northwest of Hanoi in Bac Giang province, to discuss how to carry out the directive issued at the Central Committee meeting held on the eve of the coup. This conference confirmed the conclusions reached in March, based on the assumption that Allied forces were likely to launch an invasion of Indochina prior to the end of the Pacific War. The conference formally ordered the creation of the VLA and instructed Vietminh cadres throughout the country to set up national liberation committees in preparation for the coming seizure of power. But the conference warned that the general insurrection must not take place until Japanese forces had become fully engaged in fighting against Allied troops—that is, unless Tokyo decided to surrender before an Allied invasion. In that event, when the Japanese regime in Indochina became "isolated and confused," the insurrection could be launched. At the meeting, Vo Nguyen Giap learned from a colleague that his wife had died in prison three years earlier.[50]

A few days after his return to Cao Bang from the conference, Vo Nguyen Giap received the news that Ho Chi Minh had just returned from China and was preparing to set out along the route newly occupied by Vietminh forces to join his colleagues. Giap immediately traveled north to greet him along the way. Ho had arrived back at Pac Bo at the end of April, and quickly sent off his first intelligence report to Archimedes Patti. Enclosed with his message were two pamphlets, one directed to the leaders of the Allies, the other to the newly created United Nations, both appealing for Allied recognition of Vietnamese independence. The documents were ostensibly authored by the "National Party of Indo-China (Annam)," described as one of five parties that had originally formed the Dong Minh Hoi in 1942 and later merged with the Vietminh Front. Patti passed the pamphlets on to U.S. authorities in Chongqing.[51]

On May 4, 1945, dressed in a dark blue jacket of Nung style, with a conical hat and a cane, Ho Chi Minh left Pac Bo and headed south toward Kim Lung, where revolutionary forces had linked up a few weeks previously. He was accompanied by bodyguards and the AGAS team. A few days later, fighting the hot sun, the rugged mountain trails, and the ever present leeches, the group arrived at the village of Lam Son, where they joined Hoang Quoc Viet, Vu Anh, and Pham Van Dong coming from Cao Bang. After sending off a short note to Charles Fenn in Kunming thanking him for agreeing to provide training in radio equipment for some of his colleagues, on May 9 Ho and the remainder of the group headed south toward Ngan Son. On the seventeenth, they reached Na

Kien, where they encountered Vo Nguyen Giap coming up from the south.[52]

Giap had not seen Ho Chi Minh since their meeting in Pac Bo the previous fall to plan for the creation of the armed propaganda brigades. He reported on current conditions in Indochina and on the results of the military conference at Hiep Hoa; Ho gave his colleague an account of the international situation. The two then discussed where to place the new military command post of the movement. Kim Lung's advantages proved decisive. It was strategically placed near the direct route from the Chinese border to the Red River delta, but because it was tucked away in the tortuous mountain range between Thai Nguyen and Tuyen Quang, it was sufficiently isolated from major arteries of communication to be reasonably secure from enemy attack. At the same time, the local minority population was fervently sympathetic toward the revolution and could be trusted not to disclose the location of the base. Sensing the historical importance of the village for the fortunes of the Vietnamese revolution, Ho ordered it renamed Tan Trao (New Tide).[53]

For the next few days the group resumed the journey southward. On May 21, they crossed the Day River and entered Tan Trao. To reduce the danger from potential enemy agents, Ho Chi Minh posed as an ordinary cadre and temporarily slept in the house of a local village sympathizer. The two U.S. radio operators set up their equipment in a well-camouflaged wooded area nearby. Then Ho and his host sought a new location for Ho to live, eventually selecting a spot about half a mile away in the midst of a small stand of bamboo adjacent to a small brook. In the meantime, villagers had begun to erect new buildings in the local style to serve as offices for the revolutionary leadership. Ho now turned his attention to plans for the general uprising, and called for a meeting of cadres in early June to discuss the situation. After hearing another report on the results of the Hiep Hoa conference, which had decreed the formation of a new liberated zone comprising seven provinces in the Viet Bac (Cao Bang, Bac Can, Lang Son, Ha Giang, Tuyen Quang, Thai Nguyen, and sections of adjacent provinces), he remarked that it would be too cumbersome to have the military forces in each province operate under separate orders, so he directed that all military units throughout the liberated zone be centered under the new VLA. The liberated zone itself, which contained more than one million people, was placed under the direction of a provisional executive committee. A resolution issued at the close of the meeting called for the holding of elections at all levels to create an administrative structure based on democratic principles, and for economic and social reforms to redistribute farmland, reduce taxes, and promote universal literacy. Ho hoped to convene a conference of cadres from throughout the country in the near future to carry out the directives of the meeting, but it soon became clear that under the circumstances such a meeting was impractical, so it was decided that Giap, after daily consultation with Ho Chi Minh, would coordinate the effort from his headquarters at Tan Trao.[54]

During the next two months, Ho Chi Minh and his colleagues scrambled to keep up with the rapidly evolving situation. There were now increasing indications that Allied forces were going to bypass Indochina and strike directly at the Japanese islands. The end of the war might be near. To win support from the local population, orders were issued to carry out the confiscation of the land of reactionary landlords within the liberated zone and to distribute communal village land to the needy. The practice of corvée was declared abolished, and people's revolutionary committees were created at the village level through elections based on universal suffrage. Ho attempted to oversee the entire operation, and messengers departed every day carrying dispatches from him or from Vo Nguyen Giap to revolutionary units throughout the region.

One of the tasks that required attention was easier communication with Ho Chi Minh's U.S. sponsors in south China. In a message to Kunming, Ho had offered the use of a thousand trained guerrillas located near Cho Chu for operations against the Japanese. Despite some reluctance among U.S. officers in Kunming and Chongqing over the possible political repercussions of a formal U.S. relationship with the Vietminh, after it became clear that French units under General Gabriel Sabbatier, who had fled to south China after the March coup, would be useless, Patti won the agreement of his superior, Colonel Helliwell, to pursue the matter. To facilitate the shipment of personnel and supplies, Patti radioed Ho Chi Minh, asking him to locate a small airfield that could be used to deliver personnel and equipment to the Vietminh headquarters at Tan Trao. Ho located a nearby site suitable for building a small airstrip. On June 30, he radioed Patti that he agreed to accept a team of Americans and asked for the date of their arrival. He warned, however, that no French personnel should take part in the operation. In the meantime, AGAS had air-dropped U.S. Army Lieutenant Dan Phelan into Tan Trao to set up a network to facilitate the rescue of downed Allied fliers and serve as U.S. representative until the arrival of the OSS team.

On July 16, Major Allison Thomas, head of the "Deer" team that had been assigned by OSS to establish contact with the Vietminh, parachuted with a small group into Tan Trao on a mission to evaluate the situation and assist the Vietminh in carrying out anti-Japanese operations. After two members of the team were helped down from the treetops where they had landed, they were all given a welcoming salute from two hundred guerrillas armed with a variety of captured weapons. Thomas was impressed:

> I was then escorted to Mr. Hoe, one of the big leaders of the VML (Viet Minh League) Party. He speaks excellent English but is very weak physically as he recently walked in from Tsingsi. He received us most cordially. We then were shown our quarters. They had built for us a special bamboo shelter, consisting of a bamboo floor a few feet off the ground and a roof of palm leaves. We then had supper consisting of Beer (recently captured), rice, bamboo sprouts and barbecued steak. They freshly slaughtered a cow in our honor.

Not all of the Deer team received an enthusiastic welcome, however. One of the new arrivals rescued from the trees was a French army officer, Lieutenant Montfort. When Thomas met with Ho on the morning of the seventeenth, Ho said that if the guards had known Montfort was French, they might have shot him. "I like the French, but many soldiers don't," he remarked. Although ten million Americans would be welcomed, he said, no French would be allowed. Montfort and two other French citizens were ordered out of the camp and eventually joined refugees en route to China. To make his new visitors comfortable, Ho instructed the local chef in how to prepare roast chicken the way Americans liked it and sent one of his followers to find bottles of champagne and Dubonnet for a welcoming banquet.[55]

Ho Chi Minh found accommodations for the Americans in a house next to his own. A day after their arrival, Ho asked Thomas to inform U.S. authorities that the "VML would be willing to talk to some High Ranking French officer (General Sebotier, eg) [sic] and see what the French would have to offer." In Kunming, Patti forwarded this message to Major Jean Sainteny, head of the Free French Military Mission that had recently arrived there to prepare for a resumption of French authority in postwar Indochina. A few days later, Ho indicated his willingness to talk with a French representative, either in Indochina or China, and forwarded an appeal for future reforms to take place after the end of the war. Among the points to be raised were the election of a parliament chosen by universal suffrage, the return of natural resources to the Vietnamese people, prohibition of the sale of opium, and commitments by

France that all freedoms outlined in the United Nations Charter would be granted to the Indochinese people and that independence would be restored to Vietnam in not less than five nor more than ten years.[56]

There was no immediate response from the French. But Ho Chi Minh had already begun to make an impression on his American visitors. Thomas was impressed with the quality of the Vietminh armed forces and, with approval from Kunming, his men began to provide local military units with instructions on how to use U.S. weapons (such as the M-1 rifle, the carbine, and the bazooka) and guerrilla tactics. One hundred of Ho's best troops were selected to take part in a training program that took place about two miles outside of Tan Trao village. As Henry Prunier, a U.S. member of the Deer team, recalled, they were quick learners.

Ho Chi Minh also set out to allay the possible suspicions of his visitors as to the ideological orientation of the movement. As Thomas remarked in a report to Kunming: "Forget the Communist Bogy. VML is not Communist. Stands for freedom and reforms from French harshness." Lieutenant Phelan of AGAS himself had initially been reluctant to take part in the operation because he felt that Ho Chi Minh probably had Communist leanings, but Ho soon put to rest the young American officer's suspicions. On one occasion he asked Phelan if he knew the opening words in the U.S. Declaration of Independence, which Ho intended to incorporate into the declaration for his own country. "But he actually seemed to know more about it than I did," Phelan reported. In one cable sent from Pac Bo to Kunming, Phelan described the Vietminh in telegraphese as "not anti-French merely patriots deserve full trust and support." Phelan apparently never changed his mind. Many years later he described Ho to the journalist Robert Shaplen as "an awfully sweet guy. If I had to pick out the one quality about that little old man sitting on his hill in the jungle, it was his gentleness."[57]

But the strain of the long journey from China now began to undermine Ho's already fragile physique. Although he was only fifty-four years old, he had contracted tuberculosis during his long months in Chinese prisons, and many observers remarked on his weakened condition after his release. He had apparently fallen ill once again on his journey into Indochina from Jingxi, but continued with his efforts in spite of that. As Vo Nguyen Giap tells the story:

> The strain had an effect on his health. He fell ill. For several days, in spite of the fatigue and the fever, he pushed himself and continued his work. Every day in coming to make my report, I worried about his condition. Invariably he responded: "It will pass. Come

on in and bring me up to date." But I clearly saw that he was weakening and had lost considerable weight. One day, I found him in a state of crisis, delirious with fever. We were terribly short of medicine, just had some aspirin and quinine tablets. He took them, but they had no effect. Ordinarily, except for his moments of repose, he never lay down. Now he lay on his cot for hours in a coma. Of all those who worked habitually by his side I was the only one who had stayed at Tan Trao. He was so tired one night that when I suggested that I stay the night with him, insisting that I was free, he opened his eyes and nodded his head slightly in agreement.

The black night and the jungle held our little hut on the mountainside in a vice. Each time that Uncle Ho recovered his lucidity, he returned to the current situation: "The circumstances are favorable to us. We must at all costs seize independence. We must be ready for any sacrifice, even if the entire chain of the Central Mountains must catch fire." When he could put a little order in his thoughts, he insisted on the points that preoccupied him: "In guerrilla war, when the movement rises, it is necessary to take advantage of it to push further, to expand and create solid bases, in preparation for critical times." At that moment I refused to believe that he had confided in me his last thoughts, but on later reflection, I told myself that he felt so weak that he was giving me his final recommendations. The moments of lucidity and agitation succeeded themselves all night. In the morning, I urgently informed the Party Central Committee of his condition. Then I asked the local villagers if they knew how to make some mixture of wild plants. They told me of a man who . . . was reputed for his medicinal preparations against fever. I sent a courier immediately to fetch him. The old man, who was of Tay origin, took his pulse, burned a root that he had just dug up in the forest, sprinkled the cinders in a bowl of rice soup and fed it to the patient. The miracle occurred. The medicine was efficacious. The President emerged from his coma. The next day the fever diminished, he took that mixture two or three times during the day. His condition continued to improve. After the fever subsided, he arose and resumed his daily work.[58]

American sources tell a different story. One of the OSS members who had been parachuted into the area was a nurse; he quickly diagnosed Ho Chi Minh's illness as a combination of malaria and dysentery, and injected him with quinine and sulfa drugs. Whether it was that treatment that cured him is unclear; Thomas later commented that although Ho was sick, he was "not sure that he would have died without us."[59]

One of the key tasks for Vietminh leaders at Tan Trao was to respond to a recent Central Committee directive that a Party plenum and a congress of Vietminh delegates from around the country should be convened as soon as possible. With Allied forces rapidly approaching the Japanese home islands, Ho urged his colleagues to make arrangements to hold the two events without delay. An effort to hold the congress in July proved abortive, however, because delegates were unable to arrive in time, and the meeting was postponed until mid-August.

By early August, Ho became ever more insistent. On hearing radio reports that an atomic bomb had been dropped on Hiroshima on the sixth, he directed all Vietminh organizations throughout the country to send delegates to Tan Trao as soon as possible. Four days later, he met with Truong Chinh and other members of the Central Committee who had just arrived from Hanoi. Some felt that the Party did not need to convene a congress of delegates and should simply seize power on its own initiative, but the majority eventually came around to Ho's view. When it proved difficult to agree on a date, Ho retorted: "We should hold the congress right away and shouldn't put it off. We must struggle to do it immediately. The situation is about to change very rapidly. We can't lose this opportunity." The meeting of the National People's Congress was finally scheduled for August 16. The Central Committee would hold its ninth plenum three days earlier.[60]

During the next few days, still weak from his recent illness, Ho Chi Minh continued to follow the world situation closely on Major Thomas's radio receiver. The creation of the United Nations in San Francisco, the entry of the Soviet Union into the war against Japan, and the dropping of the second atomic bomb on Nagasaki all came in rapid succession and made it clear that the end of the war was near. After some reluctance (possibly because of his illness), Ho had previously agreed to meet with a representative of the Free French Movement in Kunming; at one point in early August he went to the airstrip to await his flight, but the plane sent from China could not land because of the weather. When the news about Hiroshima arrived, Ho canceled his plans and decided to remain at Tan Trao. On August 12, Party leaders decided to move directly toward launching a general insurrection throughout the country, and (even though several delegates had not yet arrived) to hold their party conference, known to Vietnamese historians as the Ninth Plenum, the following day.

The Party conference was held in a small house in Tan Trao village. In attendance were about thirty delegates, including General Secretary Truong Chinh and Nguyen Luong Bang (representing north Vietnam), Nguyen Chi Thanh (representing central Vietnam), Ha Huy Tap's brother Ha Huy Giap (representing south Vietnam), Vo Nguyen Giap and Hoang Van Hoan (representing the Viet Bac), and additional delegates from Thailand and Laos, as well as Ho Chi Minh himself.

Because of illness, Ho Chi Minh did not attend the opening sessions, but he did present the main report at the Ninth Plenum. He opened with an overview of the international situation, noting the imminent surrender of Japanese forces throughout Asia, and predicting that Allied troops would soon arrive in Indochina. The presence of foreign occupation troops, whether British, French, or Nationalist Chinese, would be a complicating factor, he admitted, but the Party had no alternative but to be in contact with them. With that in view, it was important to be in a strong position to deal with them by seizing independence from the surrendering Japanese administration. As soon as Tokyo announced its surrender, he urged that the Party launch a general uprising to seize political power throughout the country.[61]

Debate over Ho Chi Minh's proposal was intense. Some Party leaders (probably including Truong Chinh) were reluctant to launch an early insurrection, citing the weakness of the revolutionary armed forces. Although the VLA had grown in size from about 500 in March to 5000 in mid-August, they argued that it was still no match for the Japanese forces inside Indochina, much less an Allied occupation force. If that were the case, the Party would be better to demand independence through negotiations with the Allied powers or the French. But Ho Chi Minh insisted that if the Party hoped to confront the Allies from a strong position, it had no alternative but to attempt to seize power on its own. Power was not beyond reach, he declared, since we have a mass following throughout the country. If it proved impossible to consolidate revolutionary authority, then it was vital to liberate areas prior to the arrival of the foreign troops and prepare for a protracted struggle while exploiting the contradictions among the Allies to obtain advantages for themselves.

In the end, Ho Chi Minh had his way. The conference called for the launching of a general insurrection to seize power throughout the country, and selected a national uprising committee (*uy ban khoi nghia toan quoc*) under Truong Chinh to provide central direction for the Party's military forces. The committee immediately issued an order to all troops:

> Soldiers and compatriots throughout the country. The hour of general insurrection has sounded. The unique opportunity has been given to all our troops and to the entire Vietnamese people to launch the reconquest of national independence. We must act promptly with our entire energies but also with extreme care. The country demands from us all great sacrifices. Total victory is in our hands![62]

On August 16, 1945, shortly after the news of the Japanese surrender had become known in Indochina, the leaders of the Vietminh Front (now becoming known as the Tong Bo, or General Bureau) convened a so-called National People's Congress in Tan Trao. Sixty delegates from all areas of the country and abroad attended, some having walked for weeks to get there. Many brought gifts of rice or meat. One delegate of the Tay minority even offered a live buffalo. The conference was held in a specially constructed three-room wood and thatch communal house situated on the banks of a small stream. The meeting itself took place in a room at one end. Portraits of Lenin, Mao Zedong, and General Claire Chennault were placed on the walls. The central room contained an altar and was festooned with captured Japanese weapons. At the other end was a library for revolutionary literature, which also doubled as the delegates' dining room. After an opening report by Truong Chinh, Ho Chi Minh took the floor. Astonishingly, few in attendance knew his real identity, for the organizational committee at the congress simply presented him as Ho Chi Minh, a veteran revolutionary. But some of the more sophisticated began to whisper among themselves that "the old man of Tan Trao," as he was familiarly named at the congress, was really Nguyen Ai Quoc.[63]

Ho Chi Minh repeated much of the message that he had given at the Ninth Plenum a few days previously about the overall situation in Indochina and abroad. He reiterated the importance of a rapid seizure of power in order to greet the arriving Allied occupation forces in a strong position. The Japanese had to be dealt with, by persuasion if possible. But he warned the delegates that the French might launch a massive invasion of Vietnam with the support of the Allied powers, and he added that if that happened, it might be necessary to hold talks with the French on a compromise solution that would lead to total independence within five years.

After Ho Chi Minh finished talking, the delegates approved a list of "ten great policies" drafted by the Vietminh leadership and calling for the creation of an independent Democratic Republic of Vietnam on the basis of democratic liberties and moderate policies designed to achieve economic and social justice. A five-man National Liberation Committee (*uy ban giai phong dan toc*), with Ho Chi Minh as chairman, was elected to lead the general insurrection and serve as a provisional government. After voting for a new national flag consisting of a gold star in a red field and a new national anthem, the congress adjourned. The following morning, Ho led delegates in a solemn ceremony held outside the communal hall on the banks of the nearby stream. The same day, an "appeal to the people" was issued. It said in part:

> The decisive hour in the destiny of our people has struck. Let us stand up with all our strength to liberate ourselves!
>
> Many oppressed peoples the world over are vying with one another in the march to win back their independence. We cannot allow ourselves to lag behind.
>
> Forward! Forward! Under the banner of the Vietminh Front, move forward courageously!

The appeal was signed, for the last time, Nguyen Ai Quoc.[64]

X | THE DAYS OF AUGUST

On August 14, 1945, the guns fell silent across Asia. With the announcement of the Japanese decision to surrender, U.S. General Douglas MacArthur headed for Tokyo Bay to present the Allied peace terms to representatives of the imperial government on board the battleship *U.S.S. Missouri.*

In their mountain fortress at Tan Trao, Vietminh leaders had already heard the news of Tokyo's impending surrender and had begun to react. On August 16, the day of the opening of the National People's Congress, units of Vo Nguyen Giap's Vietnamese Liberation Army, accompanied by Major Allison Thomas and his Deer team, had begun to move southward toward the Red River delta. On the same day, popular uprisings broke out in rural districts throughout North Vietnam. Some of the actions were essentially spontaneous in character; others were incited by local Vietminh units. In those areas where government power was successfully destroyed, local "people's liberation committees" were established. The seals of office were transferred to the new authorities, and hostile elements were beaten and in a few cases people were put to death.

The revolutionary forces were undoubtedly assisted by the famine in the northern and central part of the country that had continued since the previous winter. The government of Prime Minister Tran Trong Kim, which was appointed by Emperor Bao Dai after the Japanese coup in March, had attempted to end the crisis by stopping the forced sale of rice to Japanese authorities, placing a ceiling on prices, and seeking to increase grain shipments from the southern provinces by improving transportation facilities. Famine relief associations were established to provide grain to the needy. A good spring harvest had helped to reduce the famine, but heavy rains in midsummer caused the Red River and its tributaries to overflow. Many peasant families living in the low-lying regions of the delta were forced to abandon their homesteads and seek

refuge on the dikes above the swirling waters. Widespread hunger provided a golden opportunity for the Vietminh, who continued to encourage angry peasants in areas coming under their occupation to seize public
rice stocks for their own use. But at least in the short term, little could
be done to alleviate the suffering. Up to one million people, nearly 10
percent of the population of the northern half of the country, had died
of famine during the first half of the year.[1]

In a few instances, the insurgents encountered opposition from Japanese occupation forces. When units of Giap's VLA, carrying U.S. weapons and dressed in fatigues, entered the provincial capital of Thai Nguyen
on the morning of August 19, a massive popular demonstration broke
out in the center of town to welcome the new arrivals, and dispirited
soldiers of the Civil Guard turned their weapons over to the attackers.
The Vietnamese governor and other senior officials within the province
announced their surrender, but Japanese troops launched a vigorous defense of their own headquarters in the center of town. When news of
the stubborn Japanese resistance reached the Party Central Committee,
it ordered Giap to leave a portion of his troops in Thai Nguyen to block
the Japanese, while directing the remainder toward the capital of Hanoi.
A similar process took place in neighboring Tuyen Quang province.[2]

In Hanoi, rumors that Japan was about to surrender had begun to
circulate on August 11, after the dropping of the second atomic bomb,
on Nagasaki, two days earlier. Members of the Party regional committee
under Nguyen Khang began rapidly to prepare for an insurrection to
seize the city from the Japanese. In fact, they had been preparing for
that day for several months. Although there were only about fifty Party
members in the capital, several thousand people had reportedly joined the
Vietminh National Salvation Associations as disillusionment with the in-
effectual policies of the Tran Trong Kim government spread. By the end of
1944, the most dedicated activists were being enrolled in assault units
designed to seize government installations, or in so-called honorary units
to carry out terrorist operations against government officials and other
local residents sympathetic to the regime. In the surrounding villages,
armed propaganda units had been formed to prepare for the moment
when local villagers would be ordered to enter Hanoi to arouse the urban
population and assist urban forces to seize power.[3]

Economic conditions in all urban areas operated in favor of the insurgents. Industrial production had plummeted during the last two years
of the war, while inflation—brought on in part as a result of the issue

of banknotes by the Japanese military administration to meet its own needs—was rising rapidly. In a few months, the rate of exchange for the Indochinese piastre declined from about US$0.25 to less than US$0.10. By some estimates, the cost of living was up over thirty times what it had been at the beginning of the war. With living costs rising and the food shortage continuing, many middle-class residents in Hanoi and other major cities began to turn their eyes to the Vietminh, and some even began to buy Vietminh "revolutionary bonds" to curry favor with the potential new revolutionary authorities.

During the first two weeks of August, Party leaders based in Hanoi sought to infiltrate government military units stationed in the capital and established contact with Phan Ke Toai, the imperial delegate in Tonkin. Toai, who was reported to be secretly sympathetic to the revolutionary forces (his son was actively involved in the Vietminh Front), met with Nguyen Khang on August 13 and asked the Vietminh to join the Bao Dai government, which was now prepared to deal with the victorious Allies. But Khang refused and advised that the emperor abdicate and turn over power to a new republican government. Toai was noncommittal, but agreed to transmit the message to the imperial court in Hué. On the same day, Prime Minister Tran Trong Kim, conscious of the stain of illegitimacy on the current government and painfully aware of his own inexperience (prior to appointment as prime minister, he was a historian of moderate political views), resigned in Hué and turned over his authority to a committee designed to serve as a provisional government until the arrival of Allied forces. Non-Communist nationalists created their own Committee for National Salvation to serve as the representative of that government in Hanoi.[4]

Reports that Tokyo had accepted Allied peace terms the previous day arrived in Hanoi on August 15. Japanese occupation authorities immediately turned over power to the local Vietnamese government. That evening, members of the Indochinese Communist Party regional committee for Tonkin met in the suburb of Ha Dong to draw up their own response to the week's events. Although the committee had received no orders from Ho's headquarters in Tan Trao, the Party's March directive had emphasized the importance of local initiative in order to take maximum advantage of the vacuum that would be created at the moment of Japanese surrender. The regional committee ordered popular uprisings in the provinces throughout the Red River delta in preparation for an imminent attack on the capital. A five-man "Military Insurrection Committee" was created under Nguyen Khang to direct the operation. The next morning, Khang rode by bicycle into Hanoi, where he met with local leaders to coordinate their actions. But, lacking word from Tan Trao, they still made no final decision on how and when to seize power. [5]

On the night of August 16, the people of Hanoi lay in the dark awaiting their fate. The street lights in the center of the city had been dimmed and covered in black shades in preparation for possible air raids, and the occasional light emanating from local hotels and restaurants contrasted sharply with the prevailing blackness. Suddenly, the eerie quiet of the streets was punctuated by the sound of pistol shots. A Vietminh squad had entered a downtown movie house near Hoan Kiem Lake (known to the French as Le Petit Lac) and interrupted the film with a series of short speeches. When a Japanese military officer in the audience fled the theater, he was gunned down on the street. His body lay untouched for hours.

Hoping to devise a response to the rapidly evolving situation, leading members of the Tonkin Consultative Assembly, a deliberative body created two decades earlier by the French colonial regime, convened a meeting of the assembly at the imposing Governor-General's Palace in the fashionable northwest section of the city on the seventeenth. The meeting was dominated by pro-Japanese members of the Dai Viet party, who had formed the majority in the Committee for National Salvation created four days earlier. They called for popular demonstrations in support of the Bao Dai government. In the meantime, however, Vietminh units in the suburbs—responding to the order of the Military Insurrection Committee—had gone into action, seizing power from local authorities and establishing people's revolutionary committees in their place. Militia units, often armed with no more than sticks, sabers, and a handful of antiquated firearms, were created among the able-bodied, in preparation for an advance into the city the following morning. [6]

The stirring events taking place in the suburbs heightened the level of ferment inside the city. On the afternoon of August 17, while the Tonkin Consultative Assembly was still in session in the Governor-General's Palace, another meeting convened at the Municipal Theater, an ornate French-style opera house built at the beginning of the century in downtown Hanoi. This meeting had been called to bring together political parties and groups loyal to the provisional government just created by Tran Trong Kim; a large crowd, estimated at 20,000, gathered in the square in front of the theater to observe and perhaps influence the proceedings. But as the conference opened, pro-Vietminh demonstrators acting under the orders of the Party municipal committee began to chant slogans demanding national independence and power to the people. Soon, militant agitators entered the building and ascended to the second floor, where they ripped down the imperial flag on the balcony and raised the red and gold standard of the Vietminh Front. Nguyen Khang mounted the rostrum erected in front of the building, announced the Japanese surrender, and appealed to the assembled crowd to support the forthcoming uprising. The meeting ended in chaos when the crowd formed into a massive column that marched through a heavy summer rainstorm to the Palace of the Imperial Delegate, two blocks away. Others continued to the Governor-General's Palace or to the old commercial section of the city.

That evening, as the city lay tense in the heat of the hot summer night, the Party's local leaders met at a secret location in the suburbs, to map out plans for the following days. Spurred on by Nguyen Khang, the committee decided to use the next day to smuggle weapons into the city and place the Party's assault teams at strategic locations for an insurrection to be launched on August 19. Party leaders estimated that there were now over 100,000 Vietminh sympathizers in the city, or at least half the entire urban population. To bolster their strength, reinforcements were to be infiltrated from the suburbs, where militia units were awaiting the order to march. In the evening of the eighteenth, the members of the Military Insurrection Committee quietly entered Hanoi to direct the action.

A large crowd began to gather in the square before the Municipal Theater in the early morning hours. Many of those in attendance were peasants from the neighboring villages of Thanh Thi, Thuan Tin, and Phu Xuyen who had been mobilized by Vietminh armed propaganda teams and had begun streaming into the city before dawn. Others were townspeople, workers, students, merchants, and government officials simply curious to take part in the coming events. According to one participant, the men were dressed in brown shirts and rubber sandals, the women in brown blouses and kerchiefs and walking barefoot. The streets were a forest of red flags, each sporting the now familiar gold star in the middle. Because it was a Sunday, all the stores were shut, as were the local food markets.

A ceremony began in front of the Municipal Theater just before noon. After a moment of silence to commemorate those who had died in the struggle for independence, a band played the new national anthem as the flag was raised. Then a member of the Party's municipal committee appeared on the balcony and announced that the general insurrection was under way. Shortly after, the crowd branched out into several columns, each proceeding to a strategic point in the city: City Hall, the central police headquarters, and the Palace of the Imperial Delegate. Most were unopposed, but in a few instances they encountered temporary obstacles. When the group led by Nguyen Khang approached the palace, a unit of the local Civil Guard was deployed to offer resistance, but after a brief skirmish with a Vietminh assault team, the officer in charge surrendered. Members of the Vietminh unit scaled the wrought-iron fence in front of the palace and their Vietminh flag was soon hoisted in place of the imperial banner. Other columns marched to the headquarters of the Civil Guard, the city prison, and other municipal buildings, and occupied them as well.

Neither the provisional government nor the Japanese offered any resistance. After negotiations with Vietminh leaders, Japanese occupation authorities reached an agreement that Japanese troops would not intervene. The Committee for National Salvation established a few days earlier seemed powerless to act—and in fact, it disintegrated before the end of the day. By sundown, Hanoi was in the hands of the revolutionary forces in a bloodless takeover, and Vietminh authorities sent messages to units elsewhere announcing the victory and giving instructions for further action: "If possible act as in Hanoi. But where the Japanese resist, attack resolutely. It is necessary at all costs to seize power."

The events of the past few days had been an exhilarating experience for the population of Hanoi, which had suffered through several years of economic privation and Japanese military occupation. Unrestricted by Japanese police, crowds circulated through the streets, waving banners and shouting slogans demanding independence and the resignation of the puppet imperial government. Few of those wandering through the downtown streets had a clear idea of the nature of the Vietminh movement, which now claimed to represent the interests of all the Vietnamese people. But for the vast majority, the end of the Pacific War and the possible eviction of the French provided reason enough to celebrate.

News of the events in the capital spread quickly throughout Tonkin and undoubtedly facilitated the Vietminh takeover elsewhere in the region. Revolutionary forces brushed aside the halfhearted resistance offered by local authorities or the Japanese and in countless villages and market towns took power virtually unopposed. By August 22, the red flag with the gold star was flying throughout Tonkin and the upper districts of the panhandle. A cease-fire arranging for the surrender of all Japanese troops in the citadel at Thai Nguyen was negotiated the next day.

In the central provinces stretching south along the coast, the situation was somewhat more of a challenge. The revolutionary movement was not as well organized in the provinces of Annam, and lacked the advantage of a liberated base area within which to obtain recruits and provisions. Distance made communications with the Vietminh leadership in the north more difficult, and although Party units had received the March directive from the Standing Committee, it sometimes took several days to receive messages from Tan Trao, or even to obtain reliable news about the events taking place in Hanoi.

Under the circumstances, local Party leaders decided to act on their own initiative. Their main focus of attention was the imperial capital of Hué, where Party operatives had been preparing for the coming insurrection since receiving the March directive. The population mix in the region, however, was not as favorable to the revolution as it was farther to the north. As the old imperial capital, Hué was a city of administrators and court officials rather than factory workers or merchants. Although some residents—notably students, artisans, and petty functionaries—leaned toward the revolution, there were also a number of political parties or factions sympathetic to the old regime or even to the Japanese. As a consequence, cadres concentrated their efforts in neighboring rural villages, where support for the Vietminh was fairly strong.

On August 21, Emperor Bao Dai in Hué received a cable from the new government in Hanoi demanding his abdication. Local Party leaders seemed briefly uncertain what to do, but when the young revolutionary poet and Vietminh operative To Huu arrived in town, the ICP provincial committee became energized. Vietminh activists seized administrative power in surrounding villages and began to organize peasant militia units. Then, on August 22, more than 100,000 people gathered in the old imperial capital while the local uprising committee took power. As had been the case in Hanoi, there was virtually no resistance from the local government or the Japanese.

For the Vietminh, Cochin China was the toughest nut to crack. After the suppression of the 1940 uprising, the local ICP apparatus had been thrown into disarray. Most of the Party leadership in the region was either dead or in prison, and sympathizers were dispirited. In the meantime, non-Communist elements prospered under the Japanese occupation, which encouraged the growth of a nationalist movement directed against the West that reflected Tokyo's version of the Monroe Doctrine, one based on the slogan "Asia for the Asians." The Vichy French administration of Jean Decoux attempted to maintain its own influence by cultivating moderate elements connected with the relatively affluent middle class in Saigon and major market towns in the Mekong delta.

Faced with the threat of virtual extinction, Party elements painstakingly attempted to reconstruct the movement from scratch. Leading the effort was the veteran Stalin School graduate Tran Van Giau, who had been in prison at the time of the Cochin China insurrection in 1940 but had managed to escape the following summer. In the absence of any communication from the Party leadership in the north, local Party operatives decided to abide by the spirit of the Sixth Plenum of 1939, which had called for preparations for a future general uprising, while adapting it to conditions in Cochin China. Lacking a mountainous redoubt like the Viet Bac in the North, Giau decided to focus Party efforts on the city of Saigon-Cholon, while building up strength in rural areas for a general uprising at the end of the Pacific War. Although Party activists were unable to dominate their nationalist rivals as was the case elsewhere in the country, Giau attempted to boost the spirits of his colleagues by citing the example of the Bolshevik revolution to the effect that a trained and disciplined minority could seize power in a fluid situation. He thereupon began to plan for an urban uprising, with help from peasant elements infiltrated into the city from the suburbs.[7]

By early 1945 the Party had created a clandestine labor movement in the Saigon area with cells in more than seventy industrial establishments and a membership of 3000 workers. After the March coup, which toppled the Vichy French regime in Indochina, ICP activists took advantage of relaxed political restrictions by taking control over a youth organization established under Japanese sponsorship called the Vanguard Youth. Led by the covert Communist Pham Ngoc Thach (a son of the family friend Pham Ngoc Tho, who had sheltered Ho Chi Minh in Qui Nhon during his trek south after taking part in the peasant riots of 1908), the Vanguard Youth served as a cover for Party efforts to mobilize patriotic youth for future service in the revolutionary cause. Somewhat reminiscent of the Boy Scout movement in the West, with uniforms, songs, and an intense sense of mutual identity, it spread rapidly during the spring and summer of 1945 in schools, factories, and farm villages; by August the Vanguard Youth had a membership of over a million, in almost every province in Cochin China.[8]

After the March coup, the Japanese had decided to retain control over the administration of Cochin China for strategic reasons; only on August 14 did local occupation authorities permit Emperor Bao Dai to appoint the veteran nationalist Nguyen Van Sam as his imperial viceroy for the region. Non-Communist elements created a National United Front (Mat tran Quoc gia Thong nhat) to fill the vacuum that would be left by the departing Japanese. On August 16, the front's executive committee took power in Saigon in a bloodless coup, while awaiting the arrival of the imperial viceroy.

Faced with the dual danger of the prospective return of the French and the rise to power of a non-Communist Vietnamese administration in Saigon, Tran Van Giau attempted to improvise. On hearing of the Japanese surrender on August 14, he met with regional Party leaders to set up an uprising committee and prepare for an insurrection. But some of the members—undoubtedly recalling the debacle of 1940—expressed doubts that revolutionary forces were in a position to seize power. Not only did they lack sufficient numbers of weapons to arm the paramilitary forces that had been organized among progressive workers and the most militant elements in the Vanguard Youth, but Party leaders in Cochin China were unaware of the intentions of their colleagues in the north. Eventually the committee decided to delay the uprising until news had been received about the situation in Hanoi. In the meantime, they would launch a "test case" by attempting to seize power in a few select localities in the countryside while seeking to build up the base of the Vietminh movement among the general population throughout the southern provinces.

When news of the August Revolution in Hanoi reached Saigon, on August 20, Tran Van Giau requested a meeting with the executive committee of the National United Front. At the conference, held two days later, he argued that the Front, composed of many parties and groups that possessed damaging ties to the Japanese occupation regime, would certainly not be accepted by the Allied powers as the legitimate representative of Vietnamese national aspirations. Only the Vietminh Front—which, he argued, had full Allied support—could do that. During the meeting, word arrived that Emperor Bao Dai had called on the revolutionary authorities in Hanoi to form a new government to replace the defunct Tran Trong Kim administration. Reluctantly, nationalist representatives agreed then and there to cooperate with the Vietminh. The National United Front was disbanded and replaced by a new Committee for the South (Uy ban Nam Bo), with Giau as chairman.

In the meantime, Giau's "test case" uprising in Tan An, a town a few miles southwest of Saigon in the Mekong delta, had gone off without a hitch or any response from the Japanese. This success enabled Giau to persuade doubters on the Party regional committee to give their approval for a general insurrection to seize power in Saigon on August 25. That operation was to be followed by smaller local uprisings in rural areas. Success, he argued, was "ninety-percent certain," but action must be taken before the arrival of Allied troops. That night, the plan was finalized, and on the morning of the twenty-fifth assault teams seized key government installations and enterprises, while thousands of villagers who had gathered previously in the suburbs entered the city to mingle with townspeople in chanting "Down with the imperialists, down with the French colonialists," "Vietnam for the Vietnamese," and "All power to the Vietminh." By midmorning, most of the city was in the hands of the insurgents. Although revolutionary units were ordered to avoid confrontations with Japanese troops, there were a few violent clashes between Vietnamese and Europeans on the streets, and there were reports of scattered lynchings. Shortly after noon, the Committee for the South, six of whose members were from the Vietminh, was sworn in as the provisional government of Cochin China. The following day, Vietminh radio trumpeted the success of the revolution in "the city of Ho Chi Minh."[9]

While the wave of revolutionary fervor swept across the land, Ho Chi Minh was preparing to leave his guerrilla base in Tan Trao and travel to Hanoi. Although he must have shared the common jubilation over the stunning events taking place throughout the country, he was undoubtedly conscious of the intimidating challenges ahead, and quoted Lenin's famous words of warning to his own colleagues: "Seizing power is difficult, but keeping it is even harder." On the morning of August 22, he left for Thai Nguyen, traveling part of the way on foot and the remainder by auto and ferry, arriving there shortly after nightfall. The journey had been a difficult one—he was still suffering from the aftereffects of his illness, and had to be carried part of the way on a litter. The next day, accompanied by a local woman cadre, he continued south by automobile on Route 3 into the delta and crossed the Red River— still swollen by heavy summer rains—into the northern suburbs of Hanoi. The sight of the flooding, which had inundated rice paddies and villages throughout the area, inspired him to remark in sorrow, "What can we do to save the people from misery and famine?"

On the morning of August 25, Ho was met in the suburban hamlet of Ga by Vo Nguyen Giap and Tran Dang Ninh, who had come from Hanoi to greet him and give him an account of the situation in the capital. Shortly after, Truong Chinh arrived; that afternoon, he and Ho left by car for the city. Crossing the river over the Paul Doumer Bridge, they passed through streets now festooned with Vietminh flags and banners and went directly into the old Chinese section of town, where they stopped at a three-story row house on Hang Nhang Street owned by a Vietminh sympathizer. It was now used by a number of Party leaders as their temporary residence. Accommodations had been arranged for Ho Chi Minh on the top floor. It was the first time in his fifty-five years that Ho Chi Minh had been in Hanoi.[10]

That afternoon, Ho Chi Minh convened a meeting of the Party's Standing Committee at his new residence. While the conference was in session, the first detachments of the VLA began to arrive from Thai Nguyen and, after lengthy negotiations with the Japanese authorities, crossed the bridge into the city. The meeting took place on the second floor, where his colleagues Giap and Ninh had set up their own sleeping arrangements. As described by Vo Nguyen Giap, the room was used as both dining and sitting room, and had no desks. Ho worked at the dining table, with his familiar typewriter placed on a small square table covered with a green cloth in one corner. After the first night, he moved down from the third floor and slept on a collapsible canvas bed that was folded up during the day, while his roommates reposed on a davenport or two benches put together. To the servants and neighbors, Ho and his colleagues were simply "gentlemen coming from the village for a visit."[11]

The main topic at the meeting was the need to announce the formation of a provisional government. The Standing Committee had already confirmed that the National Liberation Committee created at Tan Trao, of which Ho was the chairman, would serve as a temporary government until a formal one could be elected. At the meeting, Ho suggested that the provisional government should be broadened to include a number of non-Party elements, and that the composition of the new government should be presented at a massive rally to announce the declaration of national independence. All this, he urged, must be accomplished before the arrival of Allied occupation forces.

It was none too soon, for even as Ho Chi Minh turned his attention to the formation of a new Vietnamese government, the first foreign troops were already beginning to arrive in Hanoi. At the Potsdam Conference, held in the suburbs of Berlin at the end of July and early August, the Allied powers had agreed to divide French Indochina into two separate zones in order to accomplish the surrender of Japanese forces and restore law and order in the country. Because U.S. forces were actively involved in accepting the surrender of the Japanese Imperial Army elsewhere in Asia, no U.S. troops were to be involved in the operation here.

North of the Sixteenth Parallel, the task was assigned to Nationalist China; to the south, it would be accomplished by Great Britain. At U.S. insistence, the French were not included in the operation.

Because the end of the Pacific War had come with such lightning swiftness, the main units of the occupation forces were not expected to arrive in Indochina for several weeks. But an advance party of American and French officers had already arrived at Gia Lam Airport and took up residence at Hanoi's stylish Metropole Hotel. A luxurious hotel built in French colonial style, the Metropole was located directly across from the Palace of the Imperial Delegate and a block east of Hoan Kiem Lake. Among the new arrivals was Captain Archimedes Patti, the OSS officer who had enlisted Ho Chi Minh's cooperation during their meeting at Jingxi four months previously.

Shortly after the Japanese surrender, Patti had been appointed to head a "Mercy" team to fly to Hanoi in order to obtain the release of Allied prisoners of war held in Japanese concentration camps, as well as to provide intelligence information on conditions in Indochina. Jean Sainteny, one-time head of the French military mission, and now the senior representative of General Charles de Gaulle's Free French government in China, had requested permission to join Patti on the trip, allegedly to ascertain the situation of the thousands of French residents there. Although both the Chinese and the U.S. governments were reluctant to authorize the French to play any formal role in the surrender of the Japanese, Sainteny was eventually given permission to accompany Patti's team to Hanoi, provided that he limit himself to taking part in humanitarian operations.

Once he was ensconced at the Metropole Hotel, Patti opened negotiations with the Japanese occupation authorities. He also established contact with local representatives of the victorious Vietminh Front, as well as groups representing French residents in the city, many of whom were fearful of possible attacks on Europeans. Around noon on August 26, he suddenly received an invitation to meet with Ho Chi Minh. He drove a circuitous route to Ho's residence on Hang Ngang Street. After opening pleasantries and a delightful meal of fish soup, braised chicken, and pork, followed by rice cakes and fruit, the two engaged in a lengthy conversation about the current situation. Ho complained about the presence of the French team in Hanoi, which, at Sainteny's instructions, had just taken up residence at the Governor-General's Palace—and warned Patti that its actual goals went well beyond its stated concern for the conditions of French citizens in Indochina. He expressed concern about the attitude of the Chinese and the British governments, remarking that the latter shared the French interest in retaining the Asian colonies, while the Chinese were likely to sell out the interests of the Vietnamese to obtain advantages of their own.

Ho also attempted to probe his visitor about the U.S. perspective on Indochina. Conscious of his reputation among politically knowledgeable observers as a veteran agent of the Comintern, Ho protested that he was only a "progressive-socialist-nationalist" who had turned to Moscow and the Chinese Communists because there were no alternatives. But Patti, according to his own account, was noncommittal, insisting that he was not authorized to engage in discussions of local politics. For Ho Chi Minh, there was one piece of good news. Just before Patti left, a messenger arrived with a report that Nguyen Van Sam, the imperial viceroy of Cochin China, had tendered his resignation to the court in Hué. Shortly after three-thirty in the afternoon, Patti took his leave and returned to his new residence at the Maison Gautier, a luxurious villa on a quiet tree-lined street close to Hoam Kiem Lake.

At the Maison Gautier Patti found a message from Jean Sainteny, who invited him for a conversation at the palace. Sainteny, who was undoubtedly aware that the American had been in contact with Ho Chi Minh, expressed an interest in holding discussions with the Vietnamese leader. Patti agreed to pass on the message; later in the day he was informed that Vo Nguyen Giap had agreed to meet with Sainteny and Patti the following morning. Clearly the Vietnamese hoped to use the American's presence to strengthen their case in this first meeting with a French official since the end of the war. Giap arrived at the palace in a white linen suit and a battered fedora, and was immediately subjected to a lecture from his host on the reckless behavior of the Vietminh authorities, which threatened law and order and the lives of innocent French citizens. Giap retorted that he had not come to defend the actions of the Vietnamese people, but to exchange views with a representative of the "new French government." Sainteny then became more conciliatory, promising his visitor that the French government would respond in a favorable manner to most of the requests of the "Annamite" people. But he refused to go into specifics and issued a veiled warning that without a French presence, the people of north Vietnam would be at the mercy of Chinese occupation forces. The meeting ended inconclusively.[12]

While Ho Chi Minh was beginning the long and tortuous process of negotiating with France over the postwar fate of the Vietnamese people, his government had also been exchanging messages with the imperial court in Hué over the potential abdication of Bao Dai. By August 20, the emperor had already hinted at a willingness to step down in response to a request from a group of patriots in Hanoi and he had formally appealed to the new authorities in Hanoi to form a government, but Ho and his colleagues had decided to forestall his action by sending a delegation to Hué to demand his abdication in favor of a new Vietnamese republic. The delegation, consisting of the veteran labor organizer Hoang Quoc Viet, Ho's old comrade Nguyen Luong Bang, and the journalist and Party propagandist Tran Huy Lieu, arrived in Hué on August 29. After attending a mass meeting before the townspeople to explain their intentions, they met with the emperor the next day in the imperial palace. The bespectacled intellectual Tran Huy Lieu, who had developed a reputation as one of the more militant members of the ICP, spoke for the delegation: "In the name of the people, the venerable Ho Chi Minh, president of the Liberation Committee, has honored us by sending us to Your Majesty to receive your authority." Bao Dai, who had never before heard the name Ho Chi Minh but suspected that the new president was indeed the veteran revolutionary Nguyen Ai Quoc, formally carried out the act of abdication. Then, at the delegation's request, he repeated it that afternoon before a hastily assembled audience in a brief ceremony on the terrace of the Moon Gate, at the entrance to the imperial city, where the flagstaff already flew the red banner with the gold star. After receiving the imperial seal, Tran Huy Lieu tendered an invitation to Bao Dai from President Ho Chi Minh to go to Hanoi to take part in the installation of the new government. Bao Dai agreed to attend, as an ordinary citizen of the republic. In general, the atmosphere surrounding the change of regime was festive rather than frightening, although some observers were visibly upset by the sight of the emperor abdicating the throne, even if the act appeared to be voluntary.

Not all of Bao Dai's subjects were treated with such elaborate courtesy. Two prominent opponents of the ICP, the conservative journalist and politician Pham Quynh and the court official Ngo Dinh Khoi, were quietly arrested by revolutionary activists in Hué and executed in early September. In Quang Ngai province, farther to the south, the veteran Trotskyite Ta Thu Thau, long one of the more outspoken critics of the ICP from the left, was arrested by Vietminh adherents and met the same fate.[13]

On August 27, Ho Chi Minh convened a meeting of the National Liberation Committee, soon to become the new provisional government, at the Palace of the Imperial Delegate, now to be renamed the Bac Bo Phu, or Northern Palace. In his now characteristic manner, Ho showed up at the meeting in his jungle clothing, with worn brown shorts, rubber sandals, and a khaki sun helmet. The agenda for the meeting was to formalize the membership of the new government and discuss the wording of the text for the Declaration of Independence. Ho had been at work in a dark small room at the back of the house on Hang Ngang Street, typing and retyping the draft document. Now he was ready to present it to his colleagues. As he told them later, these were "the happiest moments" in his life.[14]

At the meeting, Ho suggested that the new government be broadly based to reflect all progressive strata and political elements in the country, and that its policies be aimed at achieving broad unity within the population. His proposals were accepted unanimously, and several Vietminh members of the committee reportedly offered to resign to make room for members of other political parties. After Ho Chi Minh was elected chairman of the provisional government of a new Democratic Republic of Vietnam (DRV), he extended his welcome to each member of the new government, which decided to establish its headquarters at the Northern Palace.

Two days later, the names of the members of the new government were announced on the Hanoi radio. In addition to the presidency, Ho Chi Minh occupied the position of minister of foreign affairs. Vo Nguyen Giap, Pham Van Dong, Chu Van Tan, and Tran Huy Lieu occupied the ministries of Interior, Finance, National Defense, and Propaganda, respectively. Other high officials were from the Democratic Party, a puppet party representing progressive intellectuals that had been established under the aegis of the Vietminh Front in 1944, and among the appointees were a Catholic, and several individuals aligned with no party. About half of the ministries in the new administration were assigned to members of the Vietminh Front.[15]

During the next few days, Ho Chi Minh worked steadily at a small office in the Northern Palace, polishing his speech declaring national independence that was scheduled to take place on September 2. He had moved his residence to a more secluded villa on Rue Bonchamps, but continued to take his meals with his colleagues at Hang Ngang Street. Party leaders had decided that the ceremony would be held in the Place Puginier, a large square adjacent to the Governor-General's Palace. The city had returned to a semblance of normalcy, although popular demonstrations in support of the new government took place almost daily. Hastily produced flags bearing the gold star on a red background began to appear on the façades of homes and shops, while Vietminh self-defense units assumed sentry duty at public offices and buildings. With the war at an end, the black shades that had been placed over street lamps had been removed, and the downtown area took on a more festive atmosphere after dark. There were still relatively few foreigners in the streets, since most of the French who had been interned after the March coup had not yet been released from imprisonment and the bulk of Chinese troops had not yet arrived. Japanese troops generally stayed out of the public eye, although on several occasions a confrontation between Japanese and Vietminh military units was averted at the last minute through urgent negotiations.

Beginning in the morning hours of September 2, crowds began to gather in Place Puginier, soon to be renamed Ba Dinh Square. As described many years later by Vo Nguyen Giap:

> Hanoi was bedecked with red bunting. A world of flags, lanterns and flowers. Fluttering red flags adorned the roofs, the trees and the lakes.
>
> Streamers were hung across streets and roads, bearing slogans in Vietnamese, French, English, Chinese and Russia: "Viet Nam for the Vietnamese," "Down with French colonialism," "Independence or death," "Support the provisional government," "Support President Ho Chi Minh," "Welcome to the Allied mission," etc.
>
> Factories and shops, big and small, were closed down. Markets were deserted. . . . The whole city, old and young, men and women, took to the streets. . . . Multicolored streams of people flowed to Ba Dinh Square from all directions.
>
> Workers in white shirts and blue trousers came in ranks, full of strength and confidence. . . . Hundreds of thousands of peasants came from the city suburbs. People's militiamen carried quarter-staffs, swords or scimitars. Some even carried old-style bronze clubs and long-handles [sic] swords taken from the armories of temples. Among the women peasants in their festive dresses, some were clad in old-fashioned robes, yellow turbans and bright-green sashes. . . .
>
> Most lively were the children. . . . They marched in step with the whistle blows of their leaders, singing revolutionary songs.[16]

In the center of the square, a guard of honor stood at attention in the hot summer sun before a high wooden platform erected specially for the occasion. It was from this rostrum that the new president would introduce himself, present his new government, and read the Declaration of Independence. As the time for the ceremony approached, Ho Chi Minh uncharacteristically appeared concerned about the clothing he should wear, asking a colleague to find him a proper suit to wear for the occasion. Eventually someone loaned him a khaki suit with a high-collared jacket, the attire that he would wear along with a pair of white rubber sandals.

The program was scheduled to begin at 2:00 P.M., but because of the heavy foot traffic heading for the square, Ho Chi Minh and his cabinet arrived a few minutes late in their American automobiles. After they mounted the rostrum, Vo Nguyen Giap, the new minister of the interior, introduced the president to the crowd. Ho Chi Minh's speech was short but emotional:

> "All men are created equal. They are endowed by their creator with certain unalienable rights; among these are life, liberty, and the pursuit of happiness."
>
> This immortal statement appeared in the Declaration of Independence of the United States of America in 1776. In a broader sense, it means: All the peoples on the earth are equal from birth, all the peoples have a right to live and to be happy and free.
>
> The Declaration of the Rights of Man and the citizen, made at the time of the French Revolution, in 1791, also states: "All men are born free and with equal rights, and must always remain free and have equal rights."

Ho Chi Minh followed those words with a litany of crimes committed by the French colonial regime in Indochina, crimes that had finally driven the people of Vietnam to throw off the yoke of French colonialism and declare their national independence. He then concluded with a ringing affirmation of Vietnam's right to be free: "Viet Nam has the right to enjoy freedom and independence and in fact has become a free and independent country. The entire Vietnamese people are determined to mobilize all their physical and mental strength, to sacrifice their lives and property in order to safeguard their freedom and independence."

At one point in his speech, Ho Chi Minh looked out at the crowd and said simply: "My fellow countrymen, have you understood?" According to Vo Nguyen Giap, a million voices thundered in reply, "Yes!" The ceremony concluded with the introduction of the members of the new council of ministers, brief remarks by Giap and by Tran Huy Lieu, and a public recitation of the oath of independence. Then the dignitaries left the podium and the crowd dispersed, some of them excitedly point-ing out the squadron of U.S. P-38s that passed overhead. Ceremonies celebrating the transition to independence also took place at a Buddhist temple and the Catholic cathedral. That evening, the new president met with representatives from the provinces.

French citizens in the audience had undoubtedly reacted to the day's events with a mood of foreboding. There were about fifteen thousand French living in Hanoi at war's end, and many had taken the precaution of arming themselves in preparation for possible difficult days to come. There were nearly five thousand French prisoners being held at the cit-adel in the center of town, and Patti reported that they were making advance preparations to take up arms at the moment of landing by Free French forces in Indochina.[17]

On September 3, dressed in the same faded khaki uniform and pair of blue canvas shoes that he had often worn in the Viet Bac, Pres-ident Ho Chi Minh convened the first meeting of the new council of ministers in the downstairs conference room at the Northern Palace. The National People's Congress held at Tan Trao had already approved a series of measures—labeled the "ten great policies"—that had been drawn up earlier by the Executive Committee of the Vietminh Front. Some of them dealt with actions that needed to be taken to strengthen the armed forces in preparation for a possible future struggle with the French or the Allied occupation troops, others with the creation of a new political system and the adoption of measures to improve the national economy and to establish relations with other countries within the region and around the world.[18]

In his opening remarks, Ho Chi Minh explained that the most urgent topic was the terrible famine—specifically, how to alleviate its effects. Although the crisis may have abated somewhat during the early summer as the result of a good spring harvest, conditions had grown worse once again in August, when the Red River overflowed its banks and flooded low-lying rice fields throughout the lower reaches of the delta. Students at the local university organized teams to go out each morning to assist in removing the dead bodies that had accumulated on the streets of the city in the preceding twenty-four hours. At its meeting, the new gov-ernment adopted a series of emergency measures to fight the famine, including a campaign to encourage the population to conserve food by reducing consumption. To set an example, Ho announced that once every ten days he would go without food. The food that was saved was to be distributed to the poor. In subsequent weeks, the government approved a number of additional policies to conserve rice and increase production. Communal lands, which constituted more than 20 percent of all irrigated land in the northern and central provinces, were divided up among all villagers over eighteen years of age. The manufacture of noodles and the distillation of rice alcohol was prohibited, the agricultural tax was reduced and then suspended entirely, a farm credit bureau was opened to provide farmers with access to easy credit, and vacant lands throughout the north and center were ordered to be placed under cultivation.[19]

The council also turned its attention to several other issues. One of Ho Chi Minh's primary concerns, as expressed in his comments at the September 3 meeting, was the low rate of literacy in Vietnam. According to one source, 90 percent of the Vietnamese people were estimated to be illiterate in 1945, a damning indictment of French educational policies in a society where literacy rates had traditionally been among the highest in Asia. A decree was now issued requiring that all Vietnamese learn to read and write the national script (*quoc ngu*) within one year. The decree carried a strong Confucian flavor: "Let those who cannot yet read and write learn to do it. Let the wife learn from her husband. Let the younger brother learn from the elder. Let parents learn from their children. Let girls and women study harder." Mass education schools were to be opened to provide training for students ranging in age from young children to the elderly. Although teachers and school facilities were in short supply (in many instances, pagodas, hospitals, and markets were turned into schools), the program had a significant impact: by the fall of 1946 over two million Vietnamese had obtained a level of literacy.[20]

At the cabinet meeting, Ho Chi Minh also raised the question of how to prepare for general elections to create a formal government based on democratic liberties. On September 8, a decree announced that elections for a constituent assembly would be held in two months to draft a new constitution for the DRV. All citizens over the age of eighteen were declared eligible to vote. Later edicts declared the equality of all nationalities and freedom of religion. On October 13, a decree announced that the traditional mandarinate had been abolished, and authority in local areas was to be established through elections for people's councils and administrative committees at all localities throughout the northern provinces.[21]

The new government concentrated its economic efforts on lowering tax rates, improving working conditions, and distributing farmland to the poor. In addition to the abolition of the land tax that had been imposed by the French, the capitation tax, which provided three quarters of government tax revenue, taxes on the manufacture of salt and alcohol, and various other commercial taxes were immediately suspended, while the consumption of opium and the practice of corvée were officially prohibited. An eight-hour working day was promulgated, and employers were notified that they must provide employees with advance notice before dismissal. In the countryside, land rents were ordered reduced by 25 percent and all long-standing debts were abolished.

The government took no action, however, to nationalize industries or commercial establishments, nor did it embark on an ambitious land reform program to confiscate the farmlands of the affluent and redistribute them to the poor. For the moment, only the lands of French colonialists and Vietnamese traitors were to be seized. In his writings and statements during the Pacific War, Ho Chi Minh had made it clear that following a successful general insurrection at the end of the conflict, Vietnamese society would enter the first, national democratic stage of the Leninist revolutionary process. That stage would be characterized by the establishment of a broad united front government representing the vast bulk of the population and by moderate reformist policies in the social and economic arenas.

The decision by the provisional government to present a moderate face to the Vietnamese people was a calculated move by Ho Chi Minh and his senior colleagues to win the support of a broad cross-section of the people in order to focus on the key problem of containing the threat of foreign imperialism. Despite Ho's effort to avoid offending moderates, however, the government was not always able to control radical elements at the local level who wanted to settle personal scores or engage in class warfare. On some occasions village notables or mandarins were beaten, arrested, or even executed without trial. In some villages in central and northern Vietnam, newly elected councils abruptly declared the abolition of traditional religious rituals and confiscated the property of the affluent. To avoid complications, the government sent key Party members to reverse such measures and calm the ardent spirits of revolutionary elements.

While Ho Chi Minh was still putting the final touches on his speech in Ba Dinh Square, the first advance units of the Chinese occupation army had already crossed the border and were beginning to straggle into Hanoi. To many Vietnamese observers, they were a ragtag lot, their yellow uniforms tattered and worn, their belongings slung on poles over their shoulders, their legs swollen from beriberi. Many of them were accompanied by wives and children.

These were not among the best troops in the Kuomintang Army. For political reasons, Chiang Kai-shek had abandoned plans to use Zhang Fakui's crack Guangxi troops as the main force for his occupation of Indochina, and had directed Lu Han, a warlord of Yunnan province, to send units of his First Army down the Red River to Hanoi. In the meantime, General Xiao Wen, Ho Chi Minh's patron a few months earlier in Liuzhou, led units of Zhang Fakui's Guangxi army across the border at Lang Son. Lu Han was designated commander of the occupation force, which was expected to reach a strength of 180,000 men, while Xiao Wen was selected as his chief political adviser. In their baggage came Nguyen Hai Than, Vu Hong Khanh, and other members of the nationalist movement who had spent the war years living in exile in south China.

On September 9, the main body of General Lu Han's army entered Hanoi. Archimedes Patti described the scene:

> All through the night Lu Han's troops poured into the city; we could hear their traffic, the racing of motors, the shouted instructions. We awoke next morning to a scene of shocking contrast. The quality of the Chinese "army" had undergone a drastic change. Yesterday's elite corps was today a squatters' army. Crossing town I saw an almost incredible scene of confusion and aimlessly wandering Chinese. Sidewalks, doorways, and side streets were cluttered with solders and camp followers hovering over bundles of personal belongings, with household furnishings and military gear strewn everywhere. Many had staked claims in private gardens and courtyards and settled down to brew tea, do household chores and start the laundry.[22]

For Ho Chi Minh, the physical appearance of the newly arrived occupying army was less important than the question of its ultimate purpose. Ostensibly it had been dispatched to accept the surrender of Japanese troops and preserve law and order in Indochina until a new civilian administration could be established. But what kind of government did Chongqing foresee in Indochina, and what role would China play there in the postwar era? Although at the Cairo Conference in 1943 Chiang Kai-shek had promised President Roosevelt that China had no intention of attempting to seize the country itself, there seemed little doubt that his government was determined to manipulate the local situation in order to maintain a degree of influence over the area. Then again, how would Chinese occupation authorities react to French efforts to restore colonial rule in regions under their administration? Although some Chinese military officers, such as General Zhang Fakui, were clearly anti-French, others might be tempted to reach a compromise with the French in order to extend Chinese interests. This was the concern Ho Chi Minh had expressed to Patti during their August 26 meeting.

Even before the launching of the August Revolution, Party leaders had turned their attention to the question of how to deal with the victorious Allied powers. At the meeting of the Party Central Committee held at Tan Trao in mid-August, Ho Chi Minh had explained to his colleagues the complexity of the problem and the need for the future provisional government to exploit the contradictions among the Allies for its own advantage. In that report, he provided some key insights into his view of the world scene, and how it might affect the Vietnamese revolution. In Ho's view, the most dangerous of the Allied powers were the French and the Chinese—the former because of their desire to restore the colonial edifice, and the latter because of the plots of Chinese officials to wrest control over the territory or to support the aspirations of pro-Chinese nationalists to seize political power in Hanoi. He predicted that the contradictions among the Allies might evolve in two different ways: First, differences might emerge between the United States and China on the one hand and Great Britain and France on the other over France's desire to restore colonial rule. This was something, he said, that Vietnam might be able to exploit. On the other hand, if tensions developed between all of the other Allied powers and the USSR, it could lead the United States and Great Britain to support the French and enable them to return to Indochina.

Under those circumstances, Ho Chi Minh recommended dividing the Allied powers into separate camps and developing distinct tactics to deal with each. With regard to the French, he explained, "we must avoid military conflict, but when they arrive, we must direct the masses to demonstrate against French plots to restore their old power in Indochina." As for the British and the Chinese, it would be advisable to avoid clashes with their occupation forces and to develop friendly relations with both governments, but if they began to intrude on the provisional government's authority, it would be necessary to mobilize the masses and demand national independence. Above all, it was important to avoid fighting alone, which would play into the hands of the French and their "running dogs" within the collaborationist camp in Indochina.[23]

Based on that scenario, the new government sought to handle the Chinese occupation authorities with kid gloves. When Ho Chi Minh's onetime patron Xiao Wen arrived in Hanoi to serve as General Lu Han's political adviser, Ho was careful to stress the desire of his government to cooperate with the Chinese authorities. To minimize the danger of military clashes between Vietnamese and Chinese units, the VLA was renamed the National Defense Guard (Ve quoc Quan), and the bulk of Giap's troops were pulled out of Hanoi, while other Vietnamese units stationed in the capital were carefully placed to avoid confrontations. When General Lu Han himself arrived on September 14, the government made no objection when he took over the Governor-General's Palace from the French as his own residence. To their discomfiture, Sainteny and his entourage were forced to move to a villa downtown near the Bank of Indochina, which was still under the control of the Japanese.

One potential difficulty between the government and the Chinese occupational administration was how to deal with Vietnamese nationalist politicians who had arrived in Hanoi with the Chinese army. While still en route through the Viet Bac to Hanoi, some nationalist politicians had attempted to occupy the headquarters of the local people's revolutionary committees, compelling the government to send envoys to the border provinces instructing local military units and civilian officials to avoid a confrontation with the new arrivals. Once they were in Hanoi, Nguyen Hai Than and his colleagues settled downtown and attempted to set up an "autonomous zone," where they began to agitate against the new government.

Clearly, in Ho Chi Minh's mind, the United States could play a key role in fending off the challenges from other world powers, and he had sought to exact every advantage from the tenuous relationship he had established with the OSS in the spring of 1945. But Ho must have already sensed that his efforts had borne little fruit. Sometime in mid-August, he had written one final letter to Charles Fenn, his friend and associate with AGAS who was now preparing to return to the United States. It was good for everyone, he remarked, that the war was finished, but he felt badly that his American friends would be leaving him soon. "And their leaving," he said, "means that relations between you and us will be more difficult."[24]

Although in retrospect, his remarks appear prophetic, they were fully in character with his understanding of the nature of the world and the future policies of the United States. As the Pacific War came to an end,

Ho viewed the United States as a crucial but enigmatic factor in his country's struggle for national independence. As a capitalist country, it represented a potential opponent of the future world revolution. On the other hand, President Roosevelt had emerged during the Pacific War as one of the most powerful and vocal spokesmen for the liberation of the oppressed peoples of Asia and Africa from colonial rule, and Ho apparently held out the possibility that Roosevelt's policies would continue to shape U.S. attitudes after the close of the war.

Ho's dual vision of the United States as a beacon for human freedom and a bastion of global capitalism was graphically demonstrated in the resolution issued by the Party Central Committee at Tan Trao in mid-August. On the one hand, Ho felt that U.S. dislike of European colonialism might prove useful in the Party's struggle to prevent the return of the French to power in Indochina. On the other hand, if tensions rose between the capitalist powers and the USSR, Washington might decide to make concessions to Paris in order to enlist the French in an effort to prevent the spread of communism.

When Harry S. Truman assumed the presidency on the death of Roosevelt in April, he tacitly abandoned his predecessor's waning effort to prevent the restoration of the French to power in Indochina. At the conference in San Francisco creating the United Nations in May, U.S. officials had indicated that they would not oppose the return of the French to Indochina after the end of the war. That policy change had been opposed by Asian specialists within the State Department, many of whom sympathized with Vietnamese aspirations for national independence; but the Department's Division of European Affairs had argued that U.S. opposition to French sovereignty over Indochina could complicate relations with Paris after the war and—with tensions between Moscow and Washington on the rise in Europe—their views had prevailed. Free French leader Charles de Gaulle had tried to assuage U.S. concerns by promising in March that Indochina would receive "an autonomy proportionate to her progress and attainments," and at San Francisco U.S. delegates had responded with the announcement that Washington would not press for the transformation of Indochina into an international trusteeship. Still, in deference to the views expressed by Asianists in the State Department, the administration "insisted on the necessity of providing a progressive measure of self-government for all dependent peoples looking toward their eventual independence or incorporation in some form of federation according to circumstances and the ability of the peoples to assume these responsibilities."[25]

In late August, just as the Vietminh were consolidating their power in Hanoi, de Gaulle met with Truman at the White House. Although Truman urged his visitor to pledge the future independence of Indochina, de Gaulle demurred, remarking that any public statement to that effect would be just "fine words." He did assure his host that the French government would take appropriate steps that would eventually lead to self-government for the peoples in the area. A few days later, the State Department circulated a statement to the effect that the United States did not dispute the French claim of sovereignty in Indochina. Unfortunately, news of that decision did not arrive in Chongqing until October. As a result, Archimedes Patti and other Americans arriving in Indochina lacked formal instructions from the American Embassy there on future U.S. policies in the region.

Unaware that Patti was little better informed on current U.S. policies than he was, Ho Chi Minh concentrated his efforts on reassuring his visitor. In his meeting with Patti on August 26, Ho had already complained about Chinese intentions in Indochina, as well as those of the French. Then, on the day prior to the Independence Day ceremonies, Ho met with Patti again to complain that U.S. officials did not understand what the Chinese and the French were intending to do in Indochina. To relieve possible U.S. doubts about the ideological orientation of his government, he denied once again that the Vietminh Front was dominated by the ICP, and said that it was willing to accept a limited form of independence from the French (in his cable describing the meeting, Patti quoted Ho as demanding "limited independence, liberation from French rule, right to live as free people in family of nations and lastly right to deal directly with outside world"). As an additional inducement, he told Patti that his country badly needed U.S. investment and advice and implied a willingness to grant special concessions to U.S. commercial interests in Vietnam.

By his own account, Patti (like virtually every American who had met with Ho in the closing days of the war) was sympathetic to Ho Chi Minh and his new government, but he was operating under the restrictions relating to his assignment and the ambiguity of U.S. policy, and so refrained from making any promises. A short trip to Kunming in early September did not alleviate his concern. OSS chief Richard Heppner was angry at Patti's apparent willingness to mediate the Franco-Vietminh dispute and ordered him to refrain from future political activities. Left to his own devices, Ho Chi Minh decided to temporize with the Chinese. When General Xiao Wen met with him in early September and broadly hinted at the advisability of adding more non-Communist nationalist leaders to the provisional government, Ho replied that it was indeed his ultimate intention to "democratize" the government, but that elections could probably not take place until the end of the year.[26]

While Ho Chi Minh and his colleagues were trying to preserve their government's tenuous authority in Hanoi, the fragile position of their counterparts in south Vietnam was under a more immediate threat. After the tumultuous events in Saigon on August 25, the situation there had begun to stabilize, as the Committee for the South—under its Vietminh chairman, Tran Van Giau—attempted to consolidate its power in preparation for the imminent arrival of British occupation forces. A few days later, Hoang Quoc Viet arrived in Saigon as the representative of the Party Central Committee, and he undoubtedly advised Giau to avoid provocative actions or any confrontation with the British after they arrived. But Giau's position was a delicate one. He was forced to share power in the committee with representatives of rival parties, many of whom were not only deeply suspicious of the character and intentions of the Vietminh Front but were also ready to take advantage of any signs of Vietminh weakness toward the enemy, which would enable them to accuse Giau of selling out. To make it worse, despite the presence of Hoang Quoc Viet, Giau and his colleagues were still almost totally isolated from the Party leadership in Hanoi and forced to make decisions on their own. They had only just learned from Hoang Quoc Viet that the mysterious Ho Chi Minh was in reality Nguyen Ai Quoc. Long accustomed to taking action according to local circumstances, southern leaders did not respond with enthusiasm to Viet's suggestions (sometimes apparently phrased in the form of instructions). In return, Hoang Quoc Viet, a labor leader from a worker background with a strong bent toward ideological orthodoxy, apparently viewed Giau and his associates as petty bourgeois adventurers heavily tainted by the decadent character of life in capitalist Saigon. The mutual distrust between the northern and southern branches of the Party that had begun to emerge in the late 1930s was reinforced by the separate tracks followed by the two regions during and after the August Revolution.

On September 2, large crowds gathered in front of the Norodom Palace in the center of Saigon to celebrate Independence Day and listen to a radio broadcast of Ho Chi Minh's speech in Hanoi. But tensions ran high between Vietnamese and French residents within the city, and when demonstrators began to march down Rue Catinat, the affluent shopping street that led from the cathedral to the Saigon River, small-arms fire suddenly broke out in the square in front of the church. The crowd became agitated, and angry youths began to enter nearby build-ings searching for French snipers. In the tumult that followed, Father Tricoire, the curator of the cathedral, was struck by a bullet and killed as he observed the events while standing on the steps. Fanned by popular hysteria, the violence spread, as mobs raided homes, looted shops, and roamed the streets looking for Europeans to beat up. Before the day was over ("black Sunday," the French press labeled it), four were dead and hundreds injured.

Over the next few days, Tran Van Giau counseled his followers to maintain their discipline and pleaded with them to avoid unnecessary provocations, but rival elements within the nationalist camp and the local Trotskyite faction lurked in the wings, eager to profit from any Vietminh misstep. Also opposed to Vietminh authority were two growing religious sects, the Cao Dai and the Hoa Hao, both of which had recently flour-ished in the fluid and unstable atmosphere of the Mekong delta in the early twentieth century. Syncretic in nature and eager to maintain au-thority over their own flocks, the two sects had already attained follow-ings of several hundred thousand people and were determined to resist the infusion of outside authority.

On September 12, the first units of the British occupation force, most of them Gurkhas as well as a few French troops, arrived at Tan Son Nhut Airport. Their commander, British Major General Douglas Gracey, ar-rived the next day. Slim, mustachioed, and ramrod-straight, Gracey was every inch the image of a British general. He was the son of a colonial civil servant in India, and a graduate of Sandhurst. His own Twentieth Indian Division had just completed a long and successful stint fighting the Japanese in Burma, and Gracey had spent much of his own career in colonial areas, where he had earned the respect of his own troops, many of them Asians, for his courage and fair-mindedness. To many observers, he must have seemed an ideal appointment for the challenging task of accepting Japanese surrender and maintaining law and order in Indochina until a political settlement could be achieved.

Right from the start, however, problems arose. In the first place, Gracey was not suited by personal experience or political instinct for his delicate assignment. Long service in the British army had solidified in his mind the conviction that colonial rule over Asian territories was inevitable and correct. Second, his assignment was ambiguous. While in Rangoon, he had been assigned command of all Allied land forces in Indochina south of the Sixteenth Parallel, but en route to Saigon, his orders were amended by Lieutenant General William J. Slim, commander in chief of British land forces in the Southeast Asian Theater. Gracey was instructed to maintain law and order only in key areas of the country, unless requested by French authorities or by authority of General Louis Mountbatten, the Supreme Allied Commander for the Southeast Asia Command (SEAC), which, from its headquarters in Ceylon, had helped to direct Allied operations in much of the region during the Pacific War. By implication, General Slim was assigning the southern half of Indochina back to the French.

Conditions in Saigon on Gracey's arrival were also not optimal. With the surrender of the Japanese, the primary linchpin for maintaining law and order had been removed, and the city was now patrolled by Vietnamese police, who owed allegiance to no one. When, on September 8, Tran Van Giau had appealed to the local population for quiet and cooperation with the Committee for the South, he was severely criticized by militant nationalists, and even by some members of his own Party, who suspected him of being a "lackey" of the French. The next day, the committee was reorganized, and Giau resigned his chairmanship in favor of the nationalist Pham Van Bach. The composition of the committee was broadened, so that the Vietminh membership were only four out of thirteen. On September 12, French prisoners of war who had just been released from jail by newly arrived French troops in Gracey's detachment began to carouse through the streets, looting stores and attacking Vietnamese pedestrians. Appalled by the anarchic conditions that he found in the city, Gracey turned to the only stable element he could find, ordering Japanese troops to disarm all Vietnamese and evict the Committee for the South from the governor-general's residence in downtown Saigon. The British command headquarters then announced that British troops would maintain law and order until the restoration of French colonial authority.[27]

Under instructions from Hanoi to avoid providing the British with a pretext for further intervention, Tran Van Giau and other members of the committee sought to prevent an outbreak of outright conflict, but as a precaution Giau began to evacuate key Vietminh units from the city. During the next few days, Gracey's forces started to cleanse the metropolitan area of all rebellious elements. In the meantime, Tran Van Giau and other members of the Committee for the South sought a compromise with Jean Cédile, the senior French representative in Cochin China. Cédile, who had parachuted into Cochin China on August 22, was liberal-minded and a moderate in his political views, but the talks went nowhere. Cédile demanded that the political future of Indochina be discussed only after the restoration of French authority, while Giau insisted on a prior French recognition of Vietnamese national independence. Further negotiations, held in September at the instigation of U.S. Lieutenant Colonel A. Peter Dewey, Patti's OSS counterpart in the south, foundered on the same issue, as hard-line elements on each side prevented any tendency toward accommodation. It was, as the French diplomat Bernard de Folin noted, a dialogue of the deaf.

By mid-September, Pham Van Bach, the new chairman of the Committee for the South, had become convinced that a settlement with the French was impossible, so he called for a general strike on September 17. Gracey countered by declaring martial law, releasing and rearming the remaining French prisoners—many of them Legionnaires—and ordering them to restore order. Inevitably, clashes between French and Vietnamese troops took place, further inflaming the situation. On the night of the twenty-second, Cédile ordered French troops to take control of key installations in the city and evict the Committee for the South from its latest headquarters in the ornate Saigon City Hall. In the process, several Vietnamese soldiers were killed or taken prisoner. When they awoke the following morning, the 20,000 French residents of the city rejoiced to discover that once again Saigon was under French control. Many took to the streets, assaulting the Vietnamese they encountered— men, women, and children—at random. Hundreds, and perhaps thousands, were injured.

Colonel Dewey, the senior U.S. representative in Saigon, was appalled by Cédile's peremptory action. A Yale graduate and a onetime correspondent for the *Chicago Daily News* who had been recruited by the OSS in 1943 and served in the European Theater, the twenty-eight-year-old Dewey was the son of a former U.S. ambassador to Paris and spoke fluent French but shared the anticolonial predilections of Archimedes Patti in Hanoi. Dewey immediately went to British headquarters to complain to Gracey, but the general refused to receive him. Indeed, Gracey blamed much of the recent troubles in Saigon on the activities of the OSS detachment, which he labeled "blatantly subversive," and demanded that Dewey leave Indochina as soon as possible. But he did agree to order French troops off the streets and turned the task of maintaining law and order entirely over to the Japanese.[28]

Up until now, Vietminh representatives in Saigon had made it clear that radical actions, such as those that had occurred during "black Sunday" on September 2, were not part of the current stage of the Vietnamese revolution and would be severely punished, but such orders were widely ignored. On September 24, several hundred armed Vietnamese, many of them allegedly members of the Cao Dai or the Binh Xuyen, a local crime syndicate that ran vice operations in Saigon, ran rampant through the Cité Herault, a French residential section, calling out "death to the Europeans." Although the neighborhood was technically under Japanese guard, more than 150 Europeans were massacred, many of them women and children, while the Japanese troops stood by without intervening. One hundred hostages were led away, never to be seen again. The violence spread into the surrounding rural areas, where peasant riots destroyed many estates, seized and redistributed the land of the wealthy, and killed several landlords.

By now Tran Van Giau had lost confidence in his ability to bring about a compromise. Fearing that nationalist rivals would seize control over the movement, he called for a new general strike and ordered his followers to evacuate the city, which he now planned to place under siege. Barricades were erected to prevent French citizens from leaving Saigon, and to keep Vietnamese from entering from the outside. In a cable to Patti in Hanoi, Dewey (who had recently described the unrest in the south as a "popgun war") reported that "Cochin China is burning," and urged that the Americans "ought to clear out of Southeast Asia." The next afternoon, while Dewey was about to leave for the airport, he was fired upon in his Jeep at one of the Vietnamese barricades in the city, and he was instantly killed. Shortly after, the OSS headquarters nearby was placed under attack by Vietnamese units for several hours, until the area was cleared by Gracey's Gurkhas.[29]

The death of Colonel Dewey, the first American to die in the Vietnamese revolution, caused lengthy and bitter recriminations; accusations of blame were levied from all sides. An investigation of the incident by the local OSS team concluded that there was no evidence of a sinister plot against Dewey or the Americans by the Vietminh. In fact, Americans in Saigon at the time were convinced that the Vietnamese viewed them as separate from other Westerners, and more sympathetic to their aspirations for national independence. Partial responsibility for the incident was placed at the feet of General Gracey, since Gracey had refused Dewey's request to fly an American flag on his Jeep, arguing that as he was not an officer of flag rank he did not merit the privilege. There was indeed bad blood between Gracey and the U.S. military contingent in Saigon. Reports by OSS officers concluded that the incident was probably a case of mistaken identity, with the Vietnamese troops assuming that the Jeep was carrying French troops. When he heard the news from Patti, Ho Chi Minh was severely shaken, and later he wrote a personal letter to President Truman, expressing his regret for the incident.[30]

The incident also had repercussions at SEAC. Press reports of the situation in Saigon had damaged the reputation of the British role in the peace-keeping force in Indochina. Displeased by the events of late September, Lord Mountbatten met with Cédile and General Gracey in Singapore and instructed them to seek a cease-fire and a peaceful settlement of the spreading dispute. He criticized Gracey for attempting to apply law and order in an indiscriminate manner throughout Cochin China and for his refusal to deal with Vietnamese authorities. But Mountbatten's intervention had little effect in softening the positions adopted by either side. In early October, French troops under the command of General Henri Leclerc began to arrive in Saigon, and a few days later—with French residents in the city celebrating at the newly opened Cercle Sportif just behind the governor-general's residence—Gracey signed an agreement turning authority over from his occupation command to the French in all areas of Indochina south of the 16th parallel.[31]

On October 10, Tran Van Giau's forces attacked French and British troops at the Tan Son Nhut Airport and on roads at checkpoints entering the city. During the next few weeks, remnants of the military units of the Vietminh and other nationalist groups opposed to the French were driven inexorably out of the Saigon metropolitan area. Vietminh cadres operating under the command of Le Duan, who had spent the war years in prison, met secretly somewhere in the Mekong delta to begin preparations for war. But Vietminh forces lacked the strength and experience to deal with the French, who were methodically driving the Vietnamese away from the suburbs and into the swamps and jungles. In the meantime, Hoang Quoc Viet attempted to bring about the unification of the diverse political parties and the two millennarian religious sects for a concerted effort against the French.

As the situation in Cochin China deteriorated, the government in Hanoi did what it could to help. On September 26, Ho Chi Minh broadcast a radio message to his compatriots in the south, promising them that the entire nation would mobilize its strength to seek ultimate victory. In some provinces in central Vietnam, entire villages went south to fight the French. In private, however, Ho counseled patience to his colleagues, citing examples in Vietnamese history when ultimate victory required protracted war.[32]

Indeed, the new government was in no position to fight a war. The economic situation in the north was still dire, and although no French troops were stationed in the area, nationalist parties represented an increasingly vocal challenge. Behind them loomed the Chinese. Faced with threats from all sides, Ho Chi Minh maneuvered desperately to seek out allies and isolate adversaries. To placate Lu Han, the commander of the Chinese occupation troops, he ordered a subordinate to provide him with opium. To furnish an additional symbol of legitimacy for his fragile government, he asked former emperor Bao Dai, now citizen Vinh Thuy, to serve as his political adviser. Arriving from Hué on September 6, Vinh Thuy met immediately with Ho Chi Minh, who expressed his disapproval of the pressure that had been applied to persuade the emperor to abdicate. "Personally," Ho remarked, "I had envisaged that you would remain head of state and I would serve as the head of government." At a dinner held a few days later, Ho offered him the position of supreme counselor. Vinh Thuy accepted.[33]

Still, the most pressing immediate challenge came from the Vietminh's nationalist competitors. Ho Chi Minh's old rival Nguyen Hai Than, now a septuagenarian but still a leading member of the Dong Minh Hoi, had been attacking the government—which he described as "Ho and his gang of cutthroats"—for its willingness to compromise with the French. Dai Viet leaders also entered the city in September from south China and began to voice a similar message in their party newspaper. Despite Ho's efforts to present a friendly and moderate image to the population, there was little that he could do to diminish the hostility and suspicion of rival nationalist elements, many of whom had become convinced by their wartime experience in south China that long-term cooperation with Ho and his Vietminh colleagues was impossible. To nationalist leaders, the unilateral seizure of power by the Vietminh in Hanoi at the end of the war was ample proof of Ho's treachery and double-dealing. While such elements lacked the political and military strength to compete directly with the Vietminh—Patti noted later that none of the nationalist leaders appeared to have a socioeconomic program to deal with the situation and were "hopelessly disoriented politically"— they possessed a crucial trump card in their credibility with the Chinese occupation forces. Convinced that the Chinese would ultimately be forced to support them, nationalists like Vu Hong Khanh adopted a hard line in talks with the Vietminh. Khanh's party, the VNQDD, set up an opposition newspaper and a loudspeaker at its downtown headquarters, both of which began to denounce the "red terror."[34]

But Ho's rivals were divided, not only among themselves but also in their relations with the Chinese. Elements connected with the Dong Minh Hoi sided with General Xiao Wen, who was increasingly angry with Ho Chi Minh for his independent stance and now hoped for an early departure of both Japanese and Chinese troops to bring about the emergence of an independent government under nationalist leadership. Other groups, such as the VNQDD and the Dai Viet, supported Lu Han, who anticipated a lengthy Chinese occupation as a means of cementing Sino-Vietnamese relations.

Some observers claimed to see divisions within the Vietminh camp as well. According to the French journalist Philippe Devillers, who was then posted in Hanoi, there were at least three camps within the government: an old guard consisting of veteran Communists such as Hoang Quoc Viet, Tran Huy Lieu, and Ho Tung Mau; a group of more pragmatic members who had pursued legal careers during the 1930s, such as Vo Nguyen Giap, Hoang Minh Giam, and Giap's father-in-law, Dang Thai Mai; and a group of non-Communists who had rallied to the Vietminh cause for patriotic reasons. In Devillers's interpretation, Ho Chi Minh maneuvered skillfully among these factions, taking issue with colleagues who wanted to adopt a hard line with their nationalist rivals and arguing for a policy of conciliation. Ho's view can be seen in the comment of one Party publication, which said that nationalist parties should be neutralized gradually in order to wipe out their forces "step by step." When a member of his government expressed outrage at the behavior of nationalist elements, Ho counseled him to be patient, promising that such issues would be dealt with once the government was firmly in power. As the rhetoric on all sides became more inflamed, Ho Chi Minh was forced to take increasing precautions to guarantee his own safety, moving his residence frequently in order to avoid surprise attack.[35]

In Ho's view, the best way to deal with the Party's nationalist rivals was to placate the Chinese occupation authorities. There was as yet no indication as to when Chinese troops would leave Indochina. In late September, General Lu Han made it clear that there was no timetable for the departure of Chinese troops. By early October—after one of Chiang Kai-shek's favorite commanders, He Yingqin, arrived in Hanoi to urge Lu Han to devise a plan to keep the Vietnamese Communists from consolidating power—their immediate withdrawal appeared even less likely.

The French, of course, represented the main and greatest challenge. If the rest of the victorious Allies grouped together against the Soviets, the French could very well resume sovereignty in Indochina, and, however distasteful that might be, it would have to be at least temporarily accepted. In mid-September, in an attempt to placate the potential enemy, Ho Chi Minh began secret negotiations with French representatives General Marcel Alessandri and Léon Pignon (Jean Sainteny had left for consultations in India). In interviews with Western journalists, Ho indicated that the French would be welcomed back to Indochina as advisers, provided that they came as friends, not conquerors.[36]

With Chinese commanders supporting the nationalist parties in the north and the British operating hand in glove with the French in the south, the United States represented the last best hope for Ho Chi Minh as a possible patron for the government in Hanoi. During the late summer and early fall, Ho attempted to cultivate his American contacts, notably Archimedes Patti, who was obviously sympathetic to the cause of Vietnamese independence as well as the most senior U.S. representative in Hanoi. Despite the displeasure of his superiors in Chongqing, who were concerned at his increasingly favorable attitude toward the new Vietnamese government, Patti continued to report on conditions in Indochina, and in early September he cabled that although the new government was clearly leftist, it apparently was in full control of the situation and fully prepared to resist the return of the French. A few weeks later he reported on the goals of the Vietnamese leaders, indicating that they intended to seek national independence in ten years, with a French governor-general to serve until then as chief of state. Having observed the U.S. record in the Philippines, he reported, the Vietnamese would prefer to become a U.S. protectorate until the restoration of complete independence, but they recognized the unlikelihood of that and would be happy to accept temporary French administration, so long as it was under the watchful eye of the United Nations.[37]

But the U.S. attitude about the situation in Indochina was still ambiguous. One reason for that ambiguity was that policy differences between Europeanists and Asianists in the State Department had flared up again. Through cables from Patti and information from diplomatic missions elsewhere in Asia, Washington was well aware that the Vietminh government was Communist in orientation; close observers knew that Ho Chi Minh himself was in fact the veteran Comintern agent Nguyen Ai Quoc. Asianists were becoming increasingly concerned at the drift toward war in Indochina. On September 28, Assistant Secretary for Far East Affairs John Carter Vincent (later to become one of the prominent victims of Senator Joseph McCarthy's anti-Communist crusade) raised the issue with Under Secretary of State Dean Acheson, warning that the current "hands-off" policy of not opposing the restoration of French sovereignty in Indochina could result in a full-fledged crisis, since Paris appeared determined to restore its authority prior to opening negotiations with the Vietnamese government. Vincent proposed that the United

States join with Great Britain in establishing a commission to investigate the situation in Indochina. Pending the final report, he suggested that no additional French troops be authorized to land in Indochina. The commission report, he concluded, could become the basis for international discussions among concerned countries, including appropriate "Annamese" representatives. Vincent conceded that Paris might resent such initiatives, but he pointed out that this would be less dangerous than an explosion of Annamese nationalism.[38]

Europeanists in the State Department took issue with such reasoning. H. Freeman Mathews, chief of the Division of European Affairs, argued that it would be preferable to see if the British and the French could work out the problem themselves. A commission, Europeanists feared, could lead to only one result—the eventual eviction of the French from Indochina. It could also encourage Moscow to demand a role in the region for the USSR. This, said one, "would be bad for the French and the West, and generally be bad for the Indo-chinese themselves." Acheson, by instinct and training a Europeanist, agreed with Mathews, and he rejected action unless the situation deteriorated markedly. On October 20, Vincent issued an official statement reiterating U.S. policy and declaring that the United States did not question French and Dutch sovereignty over their Southeast Asian colonies, but that it expected the European colonial powers to prepare their subject peoples for the duties and responsibilities of self-government.[39]

The French clearly did not want any interference. In late October an official of the French Embassy in Washington, D.C., met with Far Eastern Division staff member Abbot Low Moffat to complain about a report that a representative from Ho Chi Minh's government was en route to Washington to discuss the situation with U.S. officials. Any such interference by the United States, the embassy official warned, "would be considered an unfriendly act" by the French government.[40]

Ho Chi Minh was not aware of such events in the United States, but he was clearly concerned at the trend in U.S. policy. On September 30, Patti's last day in Indochina, he invited Patti to the Northern Palace for a final conversation. In a tête-à-tête after dinner, Ho remarked that he could not reconcile the official U.S. position on self-determination that had been laid out at the Tehran, Quebec, and Potsdam conferences with the current policy of standing aside and permitting the British and the Chinese to assist in the return of the French to Indochina. Does not the Atlantic Charter, he asked, apply to Vietnam? Ho suggested the formation of a pan-Asian community including several of the colonial possessions in the region and assisted by political and economic programs for the common good. Patti expressed his personal sympathy for the Vietnamese struggle for independence, but reiterated official U.S. policy that neither questioned French sovereignty nor supported Paris's imperialist ambitions. At the close of the conversation, Ho recounted to his visitor some of the key events in his life as a revolutionary. Conceding that many Americans viewed him as a "Moscow puppet," Ho denied that he was a Communist in the American sense. Having repaid his debt to the Soviet Union with fifteen years of Party work, he now considered himself a free agent. In recent months, he pointed out, the DRV had received more support from the United States than from the USSR. Why should it be indebted to Moscow?

As they parted, Ho Chi Minh asked his visitor to carry back a message that the Vietnamese people would always be grateful for the assistance they received from the United States and would long recall it as a friend and ally, and that the American struggle for independence would always serve as an example for Vietnam. A few weeks later, a letter from Ho Chi Minh to President Truman was carried to Kunming by another departing U.S. military officer. But the likelihood of any U.S. assistance was rapidly dimming. Patti's activities had strengthened suspicions among U.S. officials in both China and the United States, and when his successor cabled Washington that Hanoi would welcome a U.S. effort to mediate the dispute, both Hanoi's offer and Ho's previous letters were ignored.[41]

B y the early fall of 1945, the immediate results of the August Revolution had clearly come into view. The DRV was in control of the north, but its support was based almost entirely on the euphoria brought on by the promise of independence and the popularity of its mysterious president, Ho Chi Minh. Moreover, the area was still under occupation by Chinese nationalist troops. In the south, where the Party's support had been weakened by the abortive 1940 insurrection and competition from nationalists was substantially greater, the French had managed to restore colonial authority, although Vietminh activists were struggling to build a resistance base in the countryside.

For Ho Chi Minh, the key to unraveling the knot was on the international scene, where he counted on assistance from progressive forces to prevent the French from seeking to restore their colonial empire. As a student of modern revolution, he was aware of the prospects for a postwar wave of revolutionary expansion similar to that which had brought the

Bolsheviks to power in 1917. But long experience warned him that Stalin had only a fitful interest in Asia and could not be counted on to throw the weight of the Soviet Union on the side of revolutionary forces there. The other potential source of support was the United States, where anticolonial sentiment remained strong. But prospects for assistance from Washington were decidedly uncertain. Should the wartime alliance between the United States and the Soviet Union come to an end under the stress of postwar conditions, the United States might be driven into the arms of the European colonial powers, and Vietnam could become a pawn in a new global conflict. In that case, Ho Chi Minh could have little doubt as to where his primary allegiance lay. At this stage in the Vietnamese revolution, the primary adversary was France. While Moscow could not be counted upon to provide firm support to the Vietnamese struggle for national independence, there was little risk that it would come to the assistance of France in seeking to restore colonial authority in Indochina. But for Washington, whose fear of world revolution he had clearly underscored in his remarks at the Tan Trao conference in August, the same could not be said.

Still, although the road ahead was strewn with obstacles, the first step had been taken, and a newly independent Vietnamese government held tenuous power in Hanoi. In later years, the August Revolution would become inflated to almost mythic proportions, as Party historians in Hanoi portrayed the events at the end of the Pacific War as a testimony to the genius of the Communist Party and its great leader. The strategy behind the uprising—described as a combination of political and military struggle to seize power in both urban and rural areas— became a prototype for future struggles of national liberation, not only in Vietnam but also in other parts of the Third World, such as Africa, Latin America, and other parts of Southeast Asia.

In recent years, that view has come under close scrutiny from a number of Western scholars, some of whom have argued that the element of planning was relatively limited in what was essentially a spontaneous popular uprising. Others contend that the events of August did not constitute a revolution, but a mere coup d'état. There is some truth in both observations, for there is an element of chance in all revolutions. Lenin once noted that revolution is much more complex in theory than in reality; despite all the careful planning that had gone into the Party's efforts in its mountain base at Tan Trao, there was a distinct aura of spontaneity and improvisation about the insurrection that erupted at the moment of Japanese surrender to Allied forces in Asia. In many areas,

Party activists were not even in touch with the Central Committee in the north and were compelled to take actions on their own. And, of course, the terrible famine that had swept the land during the last months of the war laid the groundwork for a swell of popular anger that thrust Ho Chi Minh and his comrades to victory.

Such observations, however, should not blind us to the fact that the August Revolution was an extraordinary achievement. Revolutions are not waged without revolutionaries. It is to the credit of the Party and its leadership that it was able to grasp the opportunity that beckoned so enticingly at the end of the Pacific War. Where other nationalist leaders were content to remain in south China and await the defeat of Japan by the Allies, Ho and his colleagues rose to the challenge and presented the world with a fait accompli.

By portraying the Vietminh Front as a broad-based movement armed with a program that could appeal to all progressive and patriotic forces, Ho not only managed to extend its appeal well beyond the normal constituency of the Communist Party, but he also put it into position to lobby for recognition by the victorious Allies as the legitimate voice of Vietnamese nationalism. Not all of his colleagues were comfortable with that moderate image. No less an observer than Truong Chinh later lamented that there had not been enough blood spilt during the August Revolution to rid the Party of its future enemies.[42]

That moderate face, it is clear, was that of Ho Chi Minh himself. In portraying himself as the avuncular figure from the countryside, the "simple patriot" in a worn khaki suit and blue cloth sandals, Ho won not only the hearts of millions of Vietnamese, but also the admiration and respect of close observers, such as U.S. military officers like Charles Fenn and Archimedes Patti, and French negotiators like Jean Sainteny and General Leclerc. There was, of course, an element of calculation in Ho Chi Minh's pose, and to some intimates he occasionally let slip that he was well aware of the artifice. But the tactic was an enormous success, and it is no surprise that he would adopt it as a crucial element in his strategical arsenal for the rest of his life.[43]

Yet there was also a risk in adopting the tactics of moderation, for in so doing Ho and his colleagues had come to power under false pretenses. The program of the Vietminh Front was not a blueprint for the future Vietnam, but only a starting point. If and when the Party decided to show its true face and objectives to the world, the risk of popular disillusion would be great. But Ho Chi Minh was above all a pragmatist. As he declared to the U.S. journalist Harold R. Isaacs during an interview in the fall of 1945, "Independence is the thing. What follows will follow.

But independence must come first if there is to be anything to follow at all later on." Whether independence could be maintained was another question. "We apparently stand alone," he remarked in a despondent moment to Isaacs. "We shall have to depend on ourselves." He would need all his guile to see clearly the road ahead.[44]

I n the two months following the close of the Pacific War, the situation in Hanoi slipped perilously closer to disaster. The trying conditions placed a severe strain on Ho Chi Minh, and on his position as a leader of the Party and the government. While hotbloods within the ICP called for vigorous action to suppress rival groups, Ho argued tirelessly for a policy of conciliation and negotiations with the eventual goal of dividing and isolating the Party's adversaries. Although many Vietnamese called for an attitude of uncompromising hostility to the return of the French in the north, he signaled a willingness to accept a French presence—provided that they came as friends, and not as conquerors.

At the same time that the Hanoi government was seeking a political solution, it began to prepare for war. Feverish efforts were undertaken to organize self-defense and guerrilla units throughout the northern and central provinces. During the autumn, militia units, praised by Ho Chi Minh as "the iron wall of the Fatherland," were organized in almost every village, hamlet, street, and factory throughout those areas under DRV administration. In some cases, the units consisted of just one or two platoons; in others, several platoons were organized into companies. In Hanoi, the self-defense militia comprised practically all the young men in the city and numbered in the tens of thousands. All such units were placed under the authority of local Party officials and provided with military training by the government, but they were designed to be self-reliant in terms of food and equipment. The core of the government's local forces was composed of shock troops selected from the ranks of the Youth National Salvation Association and consisted mainly of workers and students. They were armed by the Ministry of National Defense, quartered at specified locations, and underwent training at a newly established military academy called the Ho Chi Minh Self-Defense Training School.

But the heart of the government's defense effort focused on the National Defense Guard, the renamed Vietnamese Liberation Army. Under the direct command of the Party, the army was composed of battalions, companies, and platoons. To provide training, an anti-Japanese training institute that had been established in the Viet Bac before the August Revolution was now transformed into a Vietnamese Political-Military School, although it was disguised as a training program for cadres to placate the Chinese occupation command. In the months following the end of the war, the army was strengthened by the enlistment of former officers and soldiers from the Civil Guard. Its strength, including those units serving in the south, has been estimated at about 80,000 troops.[1]

One of the government's primary military problems was a shortage of weapons. The government had been able to lay its hands on a variety of firearms, some of them dating back to the previous century, and had obtained a few antitank mines and machine guns from surrendering Japanese forces. But many units were armed only with sticks, spears, or primitive flintlocks turned out by local blacksmiths. In a desperate effort to obtain new weapons, Ho Chi Minh reluctantly agreed to a plan to raise money from the general population for the purchase of weapons. During what was labeled "gold week" in the last part of September, the population of the northern provinces was encouraged to donate gold jewelry and other valuables to provide the government with precious funds to purchase weapons from the occupation forces.

According to Archimedes Patti, Ho Chi Minh was not particularly enthused about the plan to solicit funds from the general populace, believing that the poor would sacrifice out of patriotic duty while the rich would give just token amounts. His fears were apparently justified, since relatively little was provided by affluent residents in the north, and Ho "felt like a traitor" for letting "the whole farce" take place. Eventually the cabinet decided to levy a tax on food products. When one government official mentioned the possibility of taxing chicken, duck, and water buffalo, "Citizen" Vinh Thuy could not resist adding, "You've forgotten dog meat." The first to break out laughing was Ho Chi Minh.[2]

To supplement its meager resources, the government launched another drive to obtain or manufacture additional weapons. Village blacksmiths used their forges to produce spears and scimitars for village self-defense units. Children were mobilized to collect scrap iron, while adults contributed household utensils, such as copper trays and pans, or even articles for worship, such as incense burners and urns, all to be transformed into arms. Still, Ho Chi Minh tirelessly pointed out that the primary weapon of the new armed forces was the support of the people. In visits to training centers throughout the Hanoi region, he lectured his audience on the importance of behaving in a correct manner toward the general population, quoting the Chinese poet Lu Xun: "Glaring contemptuously at a thousand athletes, Bending gently to serve as a horse to the children."

Ho Chi Minh continued to insist that the key to guaranteeing the nation's survival was more political and diplomatic than military in nature. If the Chinese occupation forces could be placated, he expressed confidence that the threat from the rival nationalist parties could be deflected. And if that were to be the case, the Hanoi government might be able to present a united front in opposition to the possible return of the French to the north. The problem was that Chinese commanders Lu Han and Xiao Wen were not especially sympathetic to the Vietminh, but were inclined to support the nationalists. The pressure they applied to broaden the composition of the cabinet intensified with the visit of Chiang Kai-shek's chief of staff, General He Yingqin, to Hanoi in mid-October. The general's message to Chinese commanders was simple and direct: Reduce the influence of the Communists in Indochina.

In what may have been a signal of his government's willingness to work with nationalist elements—even those who were openly hostile to communism—Ho ordered the release from official custody of Ngo Dinh Diem, a politician who had been briefly incarcerated by Vietminh authorities. The son of a well-known patriotic court official in Hué, Diem had served as Minister of the Interior in Bao Dai's cabinet before World War II, but resigned in protest over the failure of the French to grant Bao Dai sufficient authority. A fervent Catholic, Diem openly detested the Communists, an attitude that was undoubtedly intensified when one of his five brothers, Ngo Dinh Khoi, was executed by the Vietminh during the August Revolution.

Ho's decision to release Diem (he had been detained in the Northern Palace rather than in prison) aroused concern among some of his colleagues, including an old friend from Paris days, Bui Lam. But when Lam complained, Ho replied that the execution of Diem would only tarnish the reputation of his illustrious father. In any event, he added, the French could always find someone else to replace Diem, so it made sense to seek the support of as many people as possible. Ho Chi Minh may have been motivated in part by a desire to win support from the Catholic community, many of whom were among the most educated and affluent people in the country. He had appointed a Catholic to his cabinet and on occasion attended Catholic ceremonies in Hanoi. But he also sent conciliatory signals to other groups as well, visiting with representatives of mountain peoples and taking part in the celebration of the birth of Confucius at the Temple of Literature.[3]

Ho Chi Minh also used his powers of persuasion and manipulation in his dealings with the Chinese, taking advantage of rivalries among the various Chinese military commanders in Indochina. Under pressure from General Xiao Wen, beginning in late October Ho opened secret talks with leaders of the various non-Communist nationalist parties, such as Nguyen Hai Than, the newly named "supreme leader" of the Dai Viet party, as well as with representatives of the VNQDD and the Dong Minh Hoi. But the negotiations were plagued with difficulties from the start, as the Dong Minh Hoi demanded the formation of an entire new government, which would include several non-Vietminh cabinet ministers, a change in the name of the Vietminh Front, and the adoption of a new national flag. Some of Ho Chi Minh's colleagues questioned the wisdom of negotiating with the Party's bitter rivals, but Ho reassured them that it was for tactical purposes only. As one of his followers put it:

> In our encounter with agents of the Viet Quoc [VNQDD] in the pay of Chiang Kai-shek, I was a partisan of their immediate liquidation. One day, in the course of an informational session, I asked him: "Respected Uncle, why do we allow this band of traitors and assassins to survive? At your order, we would exterminate them in the space of one night."
>
> Uncle smiled, and pointing to his office, asked us in turn: "Suppose that a mouse entered this room. Would you throw stones or try to trap it or evict it?"
>
> "If we threw stones we would risk destroying precious objects in the room."
>
> "It's the same with counterrevolutionary elements," said Uncle. "By themselves, they are nothing to fear, but they have masters. To accomplish a big task, we must know how to look ahead."[4]

Ho Chi Minh rejected most of the nationalist demands, but on November 11 the Indochinese Communist Party startled local observers by suddenly announcing its own dissolution and the formation in its place of a new Indochinese Marxist Study Society (Hoi nghi nghien cuu chu nghia Mac o Dong duong), which presumably would not actively promote the cause of world revolution. Party sources explained that the move was motivated by a desire to demonstrate its willingness to put the needs of the nation above those of class struggle, and the general interests of the people over those of the Party. As it turned out, the action did not reduce the antagonism among political organizations in the capital. The following day, a bitter clash between supporters of the Vietminh and nationalists in front of the Municipal Theater left a dozen killed.

The propaganda value of the decision among the Vietnamese people should not be underestimated, but undoubtedly the key desire was to placate Chinese occupation authorities and bring about a compromise agreement with the nationalist parties. As Party sources in Hanoi would confirm many years later, the ICP did not actually dissolve, but simply retreated into clandestinity, where it continued to dominate policy decisions for the next several years until its emergence under a new name in 1951. Nevertheless, internal sources confirm that the decision was a controversial one and aroused considerable opposition within the Party from those who placed class interests over those of the nation. It certainly inspired concern among other Communist parties. After the decision was announced, leading Party members were sent to various localities to explain it to the membership.[5]

Although the dissolution of the ICP had caused grumbling within the ranks and raised eyebrows in fraternal parties around the globe, the move did serve to lubricate the peace talks. On instructions from Zhang Fakui, on November 19 General Xiao Wen sponsored a meeting between representatives of the Hanoi government and members of the nationalist parties. The parties agreed in principle on the formation of a broad coalition government composed of members of several parties. They also agreed to issue a joint program, to unify all military units under government command, and to convene a military conference to discuss how best to aid their beleaguered compatriots in the south.

A few days later, the Party Central Committee met secretly to assess the general situation and explain the current policy. Exactly what took place at the meeting has never been divulged, but the decisions reached at the conference were contained in a resolution issued at its close. Titled "Resistance and Reconstruction," the resolution analyzed the many contradictions that were now emerging among the victorious Allies and charted a course to manipulate them to the advantage of the Vietnamese revolution. By now, the resolution concluded, both China and the United States were prepared to cooperate with France in returning Indochina to French sovereignty. Before agreeing to withdraw its forces, however, the

Nationalist government in Chongqing would undoubtedly seek to exact a number of concessions from the French. As far as the United States was concerned, its hostility to Vietnamese independence had now been unmasked:

> Although the United States is still talking of its neutrality in Indo-china, the United States already secretly helps the French to let the French borrow ships to send troops to Indochina. On the one hand, the United States wants to compete with Great Britain and France for advantages in Indochina and Southeast Asia; on the other hand, it also wants to cooperate with Great Britain and France in establishing an alliance to encircle the Soviet Union and therefore may be willing to sacrifice some of its interests in Southeast Asia."

Under these circumstances, the resolution concluded, in the domestic arena the Party must act so as to divide the opposition. In foreign affairs, it must minimize its enemies and maximize its friends, particularly the Chinese, who viewed the Hanoi government as the only force able to help them realize their own goals of evicting a European colonial regime from beyond their southern borders. France remained the main enemy, but it too could be manipulated. It was possible, for example, that the French might decide to concede national independence in order to save face in the international arena and preserve their economic rights in Indochina. If so, Party leaders concluded, they should be prepared to make the necessary concessions in the realm of economics in order to seek independence.[6]

The November 19 agreement had set out only the general outlines of a coalition government, with the details to be worked out in further talks. In the meantime, all groups were henceforth called upon to stop their mutual attacks upon each other and unite against the common adversary. But the negotiations dragged on for weeks with no result. At first the nationalists demanded the presidency and six seats in the cabinet. Ho Chi Minh rejected the proposal and offered three cabinet posts, in addition to forming a political advisory group to be directed by Nguyen Hai Than. That in turn was rebuffed by the nationalists. As the talks continued, tensions rose and the VNQDD journal *Viet Nam* accelerated its written attacks on the government. The government struck back. Vo Nguyen Giap later recalled that on one occasion he and a colleague mobilized militia units and members of a local National Salvation Association, ordered them to dress in plain clothes and armed them with weapons, and then took them to Hang Dau Street to disrupt nationalist activists who were passing out leaflets in the central market in the Chinese sector of the city. There was a brief scuffle before Giap's followers cast the leaflets to the ground and the nationalists fled. After another such incident, Ho Chi Minh was called to Chinese headquarters and given a stern lecture.[7]

One of the stumbling blocks in the negotiations was the fact that a government decree issued on September 8 had called for general elections in two months to choose a new national assembly. After the meeting on November 19, the government announced that the elections would be held on December 23, but representatives of the nationalist parties complained that this gave them inadequate time to prepare. General Xiao Wen, on Zhang Fakui's instructions, stepped in to break the deadlock, and on December 19 an agreement was hammered out, postponing elections for fifteen days, until early January, and setting out the terms for the creation of a new provisional coalition government to be established on January 1, 1946. According to a communiqué issued at the end of the meeting, the VNQDD was guaranteed fifty seats and the Dong Minh Hoi twenty seats in the future national assembly, regardless of the results of the voting. Ho Chi Minh was to be named president and Nguyen Hai Than vice president. The cabinet was to be composed of two members of the Vietminh Front, along with two each from the VNQDD, the Democratic Party, the Dong Minh Hoi, and two independents. The Vietminh and the nationalists then agreed to stop their mutual attacks and to settle differences by negotiations.

The decision to form a coalition government aroused a firestorm of debate within the Party and the Vietminh Front. On hearing that Nguyen Hai Than was to be assigned a senior position in the government, one cadre voiced his concern directly to Ho Chi Minh, whose relations with Than had been strained since the 1920s. "Manure is dirty, isn't it?" Ho replied. "But if it's good for the rice plants, would you refuse to use it?" When some of his colleagues questioned the decision to guarantee seventy seats to the opposition, pointing out that the difference between the Vietminh and their rivals was like that between fire and water, Ho (ever ready with a metaphor) concurred, but pointed out that if water was placed over fire, it would boil and could then be drunk safely."[8]

On January 1, the new government was presented to the people in a ceremony held at the Municipal Theater. In a speech delivered from the balcony, President Ho Chi Minh called for national unity and announced the program of the government, which called for national elections on democratic principles and the unification of the various armed forces under government command. In his own address, Nguyen Hai

Than accepted partial responsibility for the delay in achieving national union and promised to cooperate in resisting the French takeover of the south.

The national elections were held as scheduled on January 6, the first in the history of the country. Although there were a few minor incidents, for the most part they were peaceful. According to Vo Nguyen Giap, 90 percent of those eligible in the south voted, although the election was held only in areas controlled by Vietminh forces. Vietminh sources claimed victory after their candidates received a reported 97 percent of the popular vote. Such results would have given the Vietminh 300 seats in the assembly but, as promised, 70 seats were assigned to the opposition.[9]

Ho Chi Minh himself ran for office in a Hanoi constituency. Colleagues had suggested that as president he should be exempted from running for office in a single district, and simply be put forward as a single candidate for the whole country, but Ho refused. According to government statistics, he received 98.4 percent of the votes in the election that was held in his Hanoi constituency.

Ho Chi Minh had hoped that the formation of a new coalition government would enable him to present a united front to the French. As we have seen, in its meeting in late November the ICP Central Committee expressed the hope that Paris might be persuaded to offer national independence to the Vietnamese in return for economic concessions.

Whether Paris would be amenable to such a solution, however, was an open question. French President Charles de Gaulle was unwilling to negotiate until he had restored French authority in Indochina. In a letter to General Leclerc dated September 25, he stated in his characteristically imperious manner: "Your mission is to reestablish French sovereignty in Hanoi and I am astonished that you have not yet done so." But French representatives in Indochina appeared to be somewhat more realistic. After meeting with Ho in late September, Léon Pignon and General Alessandri had described him as "a strong and honorable personality," while Jean Cédile had cabled from Saigon that a moderate faction within the government was amenable to a settlement, and therefore it was worth talking to. On October 10, Paris cabled Alessandri to open talks with the Hanoi government "on all of Indochina."[10]

Jean Sainteny had returned to Hanoi two days previously. He had gone to India in September to see Admiral Thierry d'Argenlieu, de

Gaulle's high commissioner designate. Sainteny, whose position as the French plenipotentiary in negotiations over Indochina had never been formalized, had offered to resign, but d'Argenlieu asked him to return to Indochina with full powers to negotiate on his behalf. So Sainteny returned to Hanoi with the formal title of Commissioner of the Republic for Tonkin and North Annam, and took up residence at the Bank of Indochina.[11]

Sainteny met President Ho Chi Minh for the first time in mid-October. Although a tough negotiator and deeply imbued with a sense of French *amour propre* (he would later become prominent in international banking circles), the courtly Sainteny was genuinely fond of Ho Chi Minh and felt that, at heart, Ho was pro-French. He was accompanied by his political adviser, Pignon, a career colonial official who had served in Indochina before World War II and was irrevocably committed to the restoration of French sovereignty. Ho was joined by Minister of Culture Hoang Minh Giam. Sainteny's instructions were to obtain Ho's agreement for the return of French military forces to Tonkin, where about 30,000 French nationals still resided, in return for a French commitment to bring about the departure of Chinese occupation troops. General Leclerc already had in Cochin China a force of about 8,000 men, in the form of the prestigious Second Armored Division, which had played a major role in the seizure of Normandy from the Germans.

Sainteny's task was undoubtedly a delicate one. An outright invasion would encounter stiff resistance, not only from the Vietminh but also from Chinese occupation troops, who were carrying out the disarming of 30,000 Japanese with an alarming lack of urgency. Sainteny thus needed not only to reassure Ho Chi Minh about French intentions, but also to reach an accommodation with the Chinese occupation command. Given these realities, Sainteny strongly advised his government against the use of force: "If we attempt to reinstate the French government in Tonkin by force of arms," he warned, "we must be prepared to meet with powerful resistance."[12]

As he soon became aware, Sainteny had some advantages of his own. Vietminh military forces were still woefully weak, and Ho badly needed French assistance to get rid of the Chinese. At the same time, neither of the two major Allied powers, the Soviet Union and the United States, had shown interest in the proceedings. Moscow was preoccupied with the promising political situation in France, where the French Communist Party (FCP) appeared to be on the brink of coming to power, and had not bothered to send a representative or even an observer to Hanoi. Washington, increasingly concerned at the prospects of postwar Soviet domination over Eastern Europe, was fearful at the prospects of a leftist government in Paris and attempted to reassure the French that it had no thought of opposing their return to Indochina.

Ho Chi Minh took these factors into account in his talks with Sainteny. From the start, he was disarmingly frank in expressing the position that, although his long-term objective was to achieve full national independence for his country, he was willing to accept an arrangement that would not bring that about for several years. For the time being, he explained, his government was willing to accept a French presence in north Vietnam and membership in the French Union, so long as Paris agreed on the eventual goal of independence.

Still, the talks did not go easily. The problem was partly a question of semantics, although there were real issues at stake. Ho and his advisers insisted on the inclusion of the term "independence" (*doc lap*) in any final document, a term that was firmly resisted by the de Gaulle government back in Paris. On his return to Saigon after holding talks with SEAC Commander Mountbatten in Ceylon, General Leclerc attempted to bridge the gap by suggesting to Paris the possibility of offering a form of dominion status to postwar Indochina (the French term he suggested was *"autonomie"*). But de Gaulle was adamant: "If I listened to such nonsense, soon France would have no more empire. Please reread my declaration of March 24 and adhere faithfully to the text." When in October the U.S. Embassy in Chongqing asked for a new declaration of French intentions in Indochina, de Gaulle replied testily: "It is unacceptable that the French government should now issue a new declaration concerning Indochina. That of March is sufficient. A reiteration would just complicate the situation."[13]

A second major obstacle was the future status of Cochin China. Ho Chi Minh demanded that it be included in the negotiations with the other regions of Tonkin and Annam, but Sainteny, under orders from Paris, insisted that as a former colony, the status of Cochin China must be viewed as distinct from other areas. The people living there, he argued, should be allowed to determine their own destiny.

The talks proceeded for several weeks, as the two sides huddled in a smoke-filled room, arguing over the precise meaning of particular French words and phrases. While Sainteny smoked his pipe, Ho puffed incessantly on Chinese, American, or the acrid French Gauloise cigarettes. Occasionally, the talks were interrupted so that Ho Chi Minh could consult with his government, or with his supreme counselor, the former emperor Bao Dai. President Ho's relations with "Citizen" Vinh Thuy were indeed puzzling to Sainteny and other observers. Ho constantly referred to the ex-emperor in deferential terms, and on occasion even suggested that he might become the constitutional monarch of a future Vietnam. Once he reprimanded a subordinate for referring to Bao Dai simply as "counselor": "You might address him as 'My Lord,' as I do," he admonished.[14]

As supreme counselor to the Hanoi government, Bao Dai participated regularly in meetings of the cabinet, and was quickly made to feel at home, even by members of what he called the "old guard," a group of hard-liners such as Minister of Propaganda Tran Huy Lieu who had lived in the USSR and spent considerable time in prison. At a dinner held shortly after his appointment, Ho had assured Bao Dai that "we will work together for the independence of our country." At first, Bao Dai was smitten with the fragile physique and soft manners of the new president, who appeared more interested in Chinese literature and philosophy than in matters of politics, and looked and acted more like a Confucian scholar or a village ascetic than a Comintern agent or a head of state. He compared Ho favorably with non-Communist nationalists who were, in his words, "puppets in the hands of the Chinese"; Ho, in his own negotiations with Chinese commanders, managed to keep a cool head. Eventually, however, Bao Dai saw what he viewed as Ho's true visage and that of his government. When he heard of the arrest of Pham Quynh, his former prime minister, and the prominent Catholic official Ngo Dinh Khoi, brother of Ngo Dinh Diem, he had protested to Ho Chi Minh and asked for their release along with other political prisoners. But Ho demurred, explaining that the people wouldn't understand it. (As mentioned earlier, both were eventually executed.)

Bao Dai eventually began to suspect that he was being used as a pawn to provide the government with an aura of legitimacy with the Americans. In October, when tensions between the Vietminh and their nationalist rivals began to heighten, he was sent to Thanh Hoa province, allegedly for his own safety. Returning after the formation of the provisional coalition government in January, he was elected as a member of the new National Assembly. During the next few weeks, he joined Ho Chi Minh at Tết ceremonies and on several other state occasions "to reassure public opinion," as he put it regally, "of my presence."[15]

Armed with the imprimatur of a new coalition government, Ho Chi Minh resumed his negotiations with Sainteny in the first weeks of 1946. At first, it appeared that the gap might be too wide to bridge. Such at any rate was the concern of Kenneth Landon, a U.S. diplomat with extensive knowledge of Asian affairs in the State Department's Division of Southeast Asian Affairs. When Landon arrived in Hanoi on a fact-finding mission in mid-January 1946, Sainteny assured him that the French government would adopt a conciliatory tone in its talks with the Vietnamese. But in his conversations with Ho Chi Minh, Landon found that the Vietnamese president was less optimistic about prospects for a settlement. Ho questioned the sincerity of the French and pointed out the depth of Vietnamese determination to achieve total independence from colonial rule. At the end of the visit, Ho handed Landon a letter addressed to President Truman. Noting that the United States was in the process of granting total independence to the Philippines, Ho appealed for U.S. support in his own country's struggle for national liberation.

Ho Chi Minh's skepticism about French intentions appeared justified when the Foreign Ministry in Paris told U.S. Ambassador Jefferson Caffery that although France would adopt a "liberal and progressive" attitude toward Vietnamese demands, total independence was not under consideration. Caffery responded with the hope that Paris would adopt an enlightened position on the question, noting to Washington that some "old-line military leaders" had heretofore exerted an "unfortunate influence" on government policies toward Indochina.[16]

Despite such signs of French intransigence, pressures on Paris to reach a settlement were increasing as the result of reports that Sino-French discussions were under way in Chongqing to bring about the departure of Chinese troops and their replacement by the French. To lubricate those talks, official sources in Hanoi hinted at a willingness to consider concessions to bring about a satisfactory settlement. There were similar signs of compromise in Paris, where the resignation of Charles de Gaulle in mid-January resulted in the formation of a new and potentially more conciliatory coalition government led by Félix Gouin of the Socialist Party.

De Gaulle left no suggestions to his successor on how to handle the situation in Indochina, although he later chastised High Commissioner d'Argenlieu that order should have been restored prior to the opening of talks. D'Argenlieu returned to Paris in January to confer with the new government, while leaving instructions with General Leclerc not to use the word "independence" in talks with Ho Chi Minh. But Sainteny reported that Ho insisted on the phrase "independence within the French Union." Otherwise, he warned, there would be war. On February 14, Leclerc cabled Paris with the suggestion that if France agreed to include the word "independence," the preponderance of the problem could be resolved. "The moment is opportune," he proposed, "for a precise governmental declaration confirming the word independence." Independence, he said, could be accorded "on a limited basis, within the context of the French Union, to all of Indochina." But d'Argenlieu, an imperious former Jesuit priest whose conservative views once earned him the sobriquet "the most brilliant mind of the twelfth century," rejected the idea.[17]

Prior to his resignation, de Gaulle had dispatched Max André, a member of his cabinet, to Hanoi to sound out Ho Chi Minh's attitude on a settlement. According to a French source, Ho hinted to this visitor at a possible willingness to permit a return of French troops to the north under certain conditions. But Ho was also under pressure from within his own constituency not to give in to the French. Nationalist publications criticized him incessantly for engaging in discussions with the French and called for the dissolution of his "government of traitors," who would sell out the interests of Vietnamese independence in order to keep themselves in power.

Any tendency to compromise was becoming increasingly difficult because of the intensifying conflict in the south. In November 1945, French troops landed along the central coast and seized the resort city of Nha Trang. The city was then encircled by local Vietminh troops. A few weeks later, French units under General Alessandri crossed the Sino-Vietnamese frontier into Indochina at Lai Chau, in the far northwest, and began to seal off the border region to prevent the Vietminh from communicating with supporters in south China. Units of Hanoi's National Defense Guard were sent toward the area to halt or delay the French advance. In an interview, General Lu Han confirmed the entry of the French troops but denied reports that an agreement to permit them to enter Indochina had been reached at the Sino-French talks.

In mid-February 1946, however, French sources confirmed that an agreement with China to bring about the withdrawal of Chinese occupation troops from Indochina was about to be concluded, and warned authorities in Hanoi that a political settlement between France and the DRV must be achieved soon. Otherwise, they intimated, the consequences could be harmful. In a cable to Paris on February 18, Sainteny reported a decisive talk with Ho Chi Minh two days earlier during which Ho agreed to abandon his demand for inclusion of the word "independence" in the proposed peace settlement and agreed to his country's membership in the French Union. But Ho demanded in return that "the French government recognize in Vietnam the principle of self-government." In Paris, d'Argenlieu expressed his agreement in principle.

While these negotiations were under way, a Reuters dispatch on February 20 disclosed the provisions of the projected Sino-French agreement, whereby Chongqing agreed to permit the arrival of French troops in the north to replace departing Chinese forces. To punctuate hints that Paris would not hesitate to use force if Hanoi refused a compromise, General Leclerc began making preparations for a French military landing at Haiphong. When this news broke in Hanoi, the mood was somber. Nationalist activists, already galvanized about reports of Ho's willingness to compromise on the issue of independence, organized demonstrations on downtown streets and called for a general strike against the government. Some demanded the resignation of Ho Chi Minh and the formation of a new cabinet under "Citizen" Vinh Thuy. When crowds approached Hoan Kiem Lake, they encountered pro-government demonstrators, and clashes broke out between the two groups.

In an interview with journalists on February 22, Ho Chi Minh refused comment on the rumored Sino-French agreement, but subsequent events showed that Vietnamese leaders were concerned. During the next few days, the government intensified war preparations, organizing additional self-defense units and urging children and the elderly to leave the city. In the meantime, preparations were hastened to complete the formation of a new coalition government and convene the National Assembly, whose members had been elected in January. Sainteny had recently expressed his willingness to consider the possibility of Vietnamese autonomy (with no mention of independence), but he had raised a new hurdle by declaring his refusal to sign an agreement unless the Vietnamese government was broadened to include representatives of all groups in the population.[18]

Talks between Vietminh representatives and the nationalist parties had been tense, as the VNQDD, confident of Chinese support, still demanded a majority of cabinet posts in the new government. Ho may have momentarily lost hope that an accord could be reached. According to Bao Dai, on the morning of February 23 Ho suddenly asked to visit him and, on his arrival, appealed to him to take power. "Sire," Ho sighed, "I don't know what more to do. The situation is critical. I have well understood that the French will not treat with me. I have been unable to obtain the confidence of the Allies. The entire world finds me too 'red.' I urge you, my Lord, to make a second sacrifice, and resume power."

At first Bao Dai declined, but then agreed to discuss the matter with his advisers, who recommended that he accept. But now it was Ho's turn to change his mind. That afternoon, Ho asked Bao Dai to join him:

My Lord, please forget all that I told you this morning. I have no right to abandon my responsibilities just because the situation is difficult. To return power to you now would be an acт of treason on my part. I beg you to excuse this moment of weakness and to [forgive me for having] thought in such circumstances to discharge myself of my duties to you. I had planned to resign above all because of the opposition of nationalist parties to the accords that we are preparing with the French.

What had happened to change Ho's mind? It is significant that on the following day, government sources announced that the parties had agreed to form a new coalition government. Key ministries, such as Interior and National Defense, were to be assigned to independents, while the Vietminh, its puppet Democratic Party, the VNQDD, and the Dong Minh Hoi would share the remaining eight seats. According to Vo Nguyen Giap, Ho Chi Minh had consulted with Xiao Wen and emphasized the importance of forming a coalition government to resist the French. Xiao Wen, who had no liking for the French, apparently agreed to pressure the nationalists to compromise on their demands.[19]

D'Argenlieu returned to Saigon from Paris on February 27. That day, he accepted the broad outlines of the deal Sainteny was trying to work out for a "free state" in Vietnam, "with its own parliament, army and finances." But he refused the Vietnamese demand for autonomy in foreign affairs or for the political and territorial unity of the three regions, although he did agree in principle to the holding of a referendum on the latter question. As if to punctuate d'Argenlieu's views, on the same day French negotiators dropped their resistance to Chinese demands for an end to long-standing French extraterritorial rights (such as the French concessions in Canton and Shanghai) in China and agreed to sign the Sino-French accord. If an agreement with the DRV could be reached, the way was now clear for French troops to replace Chinese occupation forces in north Vietnam. Paris immediately sent word to Leclerc in Saigon: "Accord reached, the fleet can sail."[20]

With peace in the balance, it was now important for Ho Chi Minh to obtain the consent of his own government and people. At 7:00 A.M. on the morning of March 2, the new National Assembly convened for the first time at the Municipal Theater in downtown Hanoi. The building was bedecked with the now familiar red flag with the gold star, still the national emblem despite the protests of the nationalists.

Nearly 300 representatives, in addition to news reporters and other guests, jammed into the auditorium. Dressed in his rumpled khaki suit, Ho Chi Minh mounted the rostrum and appealed to the delegates to admit the 70 nonelected members of the VNQDD and the Dong Minh Hoi, who had been forced to wait in an anteroom until being invited into the meeting hall. After the assembly approved, they filed into the hall and took their seats, at which time Ho declared that the assembly now represented the entire country and must now set out to create a government to reflect and carry out national aspirations. At that point the National Assembly formally accepted the resignation of the provisional coalition government that had been appointed in January and unanimously elected Ho Chi Minh president of a new coalition government of resistance and reconstruction. Nguyen Hai Than, who did not attend the meeting on the pretext of illness, was elected vice president. Then Ho announced the formation of a National Resistance Committee (Uy ban Dan toc Khang chien) to carry on the struggle for full independence and appointed a National Advisory Group, to be chaired by former emperor Bao Dai. The session concluded shortly after noon. That same day the French fleet transporting General Leclerc was sailing up the coast from Saigon toward Haiphong.[21]

On March 5, Ho Chi Minh called a secret meeting of Party leaders at Huong Canh, a suburb of Hanoi. The Standing Committee had already met on February 24 to assess the situation and hammer out an appropriate strategy. There were widely disparate opinions on what to do. Some wanted to take up arms immediately, others recommended a request for Chinese military support against the French. But to Ho Chi Minh, given the current weakness of Vietminh forces, it was vitally important to reach an agreement if at all possible. At one point he remarked in exasperation: "Can't you understand what would happen if the Chinese stayed? You are forgetting our past history. Whenever the Chinese came, they stayed a thousand years. The French, on the other hand, can stay for only a short time. Eventually, they will have to leave." In a later comment to the French historian Paul Mus, he would use a more earthy remark: "It is better to sniff French shit for a while than to eat China's for the rest of our lives."[22]

In the end, the cool realism of Ho Chi Minh's argument held sway. As the resolution issued at the end of the meeting stated, "The problem now is not whether we wish to fight. The problem is to know ourselves and know others, to realize objectively all conditions which are favorable and unfavorable in the country and abroad, and then to advocate correctly." In fact, the problem was that the situation was considerably more complex than it had been during the August Revolution. Then, the political situation inside the country was favorable to the Party, and opposition parties had been unwilling or unable to oppose it in public. Now, nationalists felt emboldened to rely on the potential support of Chinese occupation forces and could afford to take a hard line against the government. During the August Revolution the Party had been able to manipulate the contradictions among the Allied powers to its advantage; now, the resolution noted, those contradictions had been at least temporarily harmonized, while at the same time, the progressive forces of the world led by the Soviet Union were unable to come to the aid of the Vietnamese revolution. Under those circumstances, a "fight to the end" would leave the Vietminh both weakened and isolated.

The resolution conceded that a conciliatory policy could make the Party vulnerable to charges of selling out the interests of the country, as well as of enabling the French to strengthen their own forces for a future attack on the north. On the other hand, it would eliminate or at least reduce the influence of the Chinese and their nationalist collaborators, and also give the Hanoi government time to prepare under more favorable circumstances for a struggle to seize full independence. In the end, it concluded, France must recognize the right of the Vietnamese people for full self-determination and national unity.[23]

On March 5, General Leclerc's fleet sailed into the Tonkin Gulf. That same day, Sainteny received a report from Saigon that the Chinese had abruptly reneged on their agreement with France and now refused to permit French troops to disembark on Indochinese territory without further concessions. Meanwhile, in Hanoi the newly established National Resistance Committee had issued an appeal to the people to prepare to rise up to defend the fatherland. If French forces should attempt to land in the absence of an agreement with Chongqing, they would be resisted by both the Chinese and the Vietnamese. For the safety of his troops, General Leclerc requested Sainteny to do everything in his power to reach an agreement within the shortest time possible, "even at the cost of initiatives that could eventually be disavowed."[24]

Later that day, negotiations resumed. Sainteny appeared anxious to reach an accord and Ho Chi Minh, who was undoubtedly aware of the recent difficulties in the Sino-French talks, may have decided to press his luck, insisting on inclusion of the word "independence" in the agreement, as well as French acceptance of the principle of Vietnamese territorial integrity. As the talks continued into the evening, Sainteny agreed to turn the latter issue over to a referendum to be held in all three regions of the country, but he categorically refused to include the word "independence." With the talks deadlocked, the French left, appealing to Ho Chi Minh to give further consideration to their proposals.

Early the following morning, the French fleet entered Haiphong harbor. At 8:30 A.M., as the first French landing craft was lowered onto the Cua Cam River, Chinese troops along the riverbank opened fire. After a delay of a quarter of an hour, the French responded. In the exchange, which lasted until 11:00 A.M., several French ships were slightly damaged, while a Chinese ammunition depot was set on fire. During the height of the battle, bullets were pelting the streets of downtown Haiphong like rain.[25]

While the French and the Chinese were exchanging fire in Haiphong, the talks in Hanoi were finally coming to a successful conclusion. Pressured by the Chinese occupation command not to be too adamant, Ho held final consultations with the Party Standing Committee late on the evening of March 5 and obtained its approval to make the needed concessions to reach an agreement. Shortly before dawn, Ho's emissary, Hoang Minh Giam, arrived at the Sainteny residence and announced that his government accepted French conditions and agreed to the French phrase recognizing Vietnam as a "free state." About four o'clock, Vietnamese delegates arrived at a villa on Ly Thai To Street, just across a park from the Northern Palace, where many of the talks had been taking place. Before an audience of French and Vietnamese representatives as well as several diplomatic observers, the agreement was first read aloud. It called for French recognition of the Democratic Republic of Vietnam as a free state, with "its own government, parliament, army and finances within the French Union." The French government agreed to the holding of a referendum to determine the possible unification of the three regions. In return, Vietnam agreed to allow 15,000 French troops to replace the departing Chinese in the north. Ho Chi Minh was the first to sign. He then handed the pen to his deputy commissioner of national defense, the VNQDD leader Vu Hong Khanh. After the ceremony, Sainteny expressed his satisfaction regarding the agreement, but Ho replied: "And I am sorry, because fundamentally you have won the contest. You were well aware that I wanted more than this. But I realize well that we cannot have everything at once." Then he recovered his good spirits and embraced Pignon and Sainteny. "My consolation," he remarked to Sainteny, "is our friendship."[26]

In asking Vu Hong Khanh to sign the agreement, Ho Chi Minh hoped to mute possible criticism of the agreement by nationalist elements. Shortly after the ceremony, he met with the ICP Standing Committee to determine how to present the agreement to the people and sent representatives to other parts of the country to explain the rationale behind the decision. Hoang Quoc Viet went to Saigon, Hoang Minh Giam to Da Nang, and Vo Nguyen Giap to Haiphong, where the French would soon be disembarking.

News of the agreement appeared in the Hanoi newspapers the following morning. According to reports, it was greeted with a combination of surprise, anger, and indifference. Despite the government's appeal to the populace to remain calm and avoid provocative actions against French residents, the tension in the capital was palpable. Nationalists charged that Ho Chi Minh had been duped by the French, and some even called him a traitor (*Viet gian*). To counter such charges, Party leaders planned a mass rally in front of the Municipal Theater at 4:00 P.M. to explain the decision. According to Jean Sainteny, nationalist elements circulated through the crowd to agitate the people to express their dissatisfaction. One activist threw a hand grenade, but forgot to pull the pin. Defense Minister Vo Nguyen Giap, who had arrived back from Haiphong just before the ceremony, spoke first, explaining the need for the accord and the importance of maintaining law and order. He compared the agreement to Lenin's decision in 1918 to accept a loss of Russian territory to Germany in the Treaty of Brest Litovsk, and promised that this development would eventually lead to full independence. After several other speakers, Ho Chi Minh appeared on the balcony and spoke a few brief words. "Our country," he said,

> became free in August 1945. However, to this day not a single great power has recognized our independence. The negotiations with France have opened the road to our international recognition, and toward strengthening the position of the Democratic Republic of Vietnam in the world arena. We have become a free nation. As is declared in the agreement, French troops will gradually be withdrawn from Vietnam. Our fellow countrymen must remain calm and disciplined, and must strengthen their unity and cohesion.

He concluded his remarks with a brief pledge: "I, Ho Chi Minh, have fought alongside my compatriots all my life for the independence of our Fatherland. I would rather die than betray my country."

The sincerity and emotion in his voice carried the day, and the ceremony ended with applause and cries of "Long live President Ho Chi Minh." But many Vietnamese, not least within the ranks of the Party, were skeptical of the agreement and would have preferred to face the issue directly. Two days later, the Standing Committee issued a directive titled "Conciliate to Advance" in an effort to allay distrust among Party cadres, while warning of the need for vigilance and preparation. "The fatherland," it concluded, "is facing a difficult time, but the revolutionary boat is gliding forward through the reefs. The agreement with France is to gain time, to preserve our force, and to maintain our position so as to advance quickly toward complete independence."[27]

On the evening of March 6, Vo Nguyen Giap returned to Haiphong to meet with General Leclerc and discuss the implementation of the preliminary agreement with regard to the military situation. Despite the agreement, armed clashes between French and Vietnamese units had taken place in several areas, and both sides kept their guard up. Ho Chi Minh remained in Hanoi, where he met with a delegation of civilian and military officials at City Hall. He also wrote a public letter to compatriots in the south, informing them of the cease-fire but asking them to maintain their preparations and their discipline. Nguyen Luong Bang, Ho's old colleague from his days in China and Hong Kong, was directed to undertake the task of reestablishing a base area near Thai Nguyen, while Hoang Van Hoan was sent to Thanh Hoa for the same purpose.

In Paris, press reports on the Ho-Sainteny agreement were generally optimistic. On March 9, Minister of Overseas Territories Marius Moutet submitted the accord to the Council of Ministers, where it was given tentative approval, and Foreign Minister Georges Bidault praised it as a potential model for application in other colonial areas under French administration. Still, the drumbeat of criticism from nationalists inside Vietnam continued. Some non-Communist leaders called on the government to seek support from China or the United States. Supreme Counselor Bao Dai offered to go to Chongqing to make a personal appeal to the Chiang Kai-shek regime. After some discussion, Ho Chi Minh agreed.

On March 18, 1200 French troops, transported in about 200 military vehicles—many of them American—crossed the Paul Doumer Bridge and then marched through Hanoi to the rejoicing of French residents in the city. Chinese occupation forces had been straggling out of town toward the border during the previous few days. According to a French source, one Vietnamese observer, on seeing the modern weapons and disciplined carriage of Leclerc's troops, remarked despondently, "We're lost, they're too strong."[28] But Leclerc was not so confident, expressing his fear that in case of a breakdown in the agreement, one division would not be sufficient to pacify the area. Many of the local French *colons*, however, were jubilant, arguing that the Vietnamese made poor soldiers.

That afternoon, Leclerc, Sainteny, Pignon, and other senior French officials went to the Northern Palace to meet Ho Chi Minh and members of his cabinet. Ho and Leclerc exchanged toasts to Franco-Vietnamese friendship, but the tension was as thick in the palace as it was on the streets of the city, where the presence of carousing French troops aroused among Vietnamese residents bitter memories of the past. The same evening, Ho Chi Minh invited U.S. Army Major Frank White, the new OSS representative in Hanoi, to attend a banquet in Leclerc's honor at the palace. When Ho met White for the first time earlier that day, he had pumped him for Washington's views on the situation in Indochina. Noting with some evident regret that the Soviet Union was too busy reconstructing its own war-damaged economy to provide much assistance to the fledgling Vietnamese government, Ho expressed the hope that the United States would provide "money and machines" to help the new country enter the path of national development. But even while making his pitch for a U.S. role in the future Vietnam, Ho expressed some skepticism that Washington would be willing to do much for this country, which was small and far away from North America.

After the conversation, Major White had returned to his residence, but suddenly received the invitation from Ho Chi Minh to attend the welcome dinner for French representatives just arrived in Hanoi. To his surprise, White was seated next to President Ho at the banquet that evening, which apparently irritated many of the others at the table, who were considerably senior in rank to the American army officer. When White remarked in some discomfort that the seating arrangement had displeased many of the guests, Ho remarked plaintively, "But who else would I have to talk to?" According to White's recollection, the atmosphere at the banquet was "glacial," with the French having little to say and the Chinese guests, headed by General Lu Han, "getting wildly drunk."[29]

Ho Chi Minh had been correct in lamenting to his American visitor that the United States was unlikely to intervene on behalf of the Vietnamese struggle for national independence, for the White House appeared to ignore the rapidly evolving situation in Indochina. In late February Ho had sent a telegram to President Truman appealing for U.S. support for Vietnamese independence, in keeping with the principles of the U.N. Charter. There had been no reply. When news of the Sino-French agreement arrived in Washington, Secretary of State James Byrnes told a French diplomat that the agreement "completes the reversion of all Indochina to French control." Now increasingly mesmerized by the rising danger of world communism (Winston Churchill had just given his famous "Iron Curtain" speech in Fulton, Missouri), the United States was not prepared to take action to support Hanoi's appeal for recognition of the DRV as a "free state" within the French Union.[30]

During the next few days, things did not improve. On March 22, a joint military parade took place near the Citadel of Hanoi in a gesture that was designed to provide a measure of warmth to the Franco-Vietnamese relationship, but most of the crowd limited themselves to applauding their own troops. Much of the mechanized equipment used by the French was of U.S. manufacture, and British Spitfires left smoke trails in the sky above. The next day, Leclerc left Hanoi, turning command over to his subordinate, General Jean-Etienne Valluy. Although no outright clashes took place, resentment ran high when the French occupied a number of official buildings, leading to a general strike, after which the French withdrew.[31]

In communications with Jean Sainteny, High Commissioner d'Argenlieu indicated that he wanted to hold an official meeting with Ho Chi Minh. Sainteny contacted Ho, who immediately agreed in the hope of arranging for formal negotations to ratify the preliminary agreement as soon as possible. On the morning of March 24, Ho Chi Minh, wearing a broad-brimmed hat as protection against the sun, accompanied Hoang Minh Giam and his new foreign minister, the non-Communist novelist Nguyen Tuong Tam, to Gia Lam Airport, where they were met by Sainteny and entered a Catalina flying boat. The seaplane alighted in Ha Long Bay, a scenic area of limestone formations along the coast east of Haiphong. They then boarded the French warship *Emile Bertin* and were greeted by d'Argenlieu and other French representatives.

After an exchange of toasts, Ho Chi Minh was invited to review the French fleet, which steamed slowly past Admiral d'Argenlieu's flagship. Later, in the admiral's cabin, the two sides exchanged views on when and where to hold further talks to implement the March 6 agreement. Ho wanted to hold them as soon as possible, but d'Argenlieu replied that a preparatory conference was needed to familiarize French representatives with the key issues, and suggested the mountain resort of Dalat as an appropriate site for formal talks later in the year. Ho agreed to hold preparatory talks in Dalat, but he feared that if the formal negotiations were to be held there, the high commissioner would try to control them, so he proposed France as the venue; in France, Ho would be able to bypass d'Argenlieu and use his own position as head of state to influence French public opinion, which had been in an unusually volatile state since the end of World War II. To the admiral's discomfiture, both

Leclerc and Sainteny agreed with Ho Chi Minh, on the grounds that a conference in France would remove Ho Chi Minh from militants within his own government and the influence of the Chinese. Eventually, d'Argenlieu gave in.

For Ho Chi Minh, the talks at Ha Long Bay had been a useful exercise. Although he was not able to gain French acceptance of his recommendation for an immediate resumption of peace negotiations, he had been able to take them out of the reach of the staunch colonialist Thierry d'Argenlieu. In the process, he had shown himself capable of standing up to the autocratic admiral. On the flight back to Hanoi, Ho commented to d'Argenlieu's subordinate, General Raoul Salan, who had participated in the meeting, "If the admiral thinks I was cowed by the might of his fleet, he is wrong. Your dreadnoughts will never be able to sail up our rivers."[32]

The preparatory talks at Dalat, which convened in mid-April 1946, did not go well. The Vietnamese delegates, Vo Nguyen Giap and Nguyen Tuong Tam, could not persuade d'Argenlieu to discuss the situation in Cochin China, where armed clashes continued despite the cease-fire. Serious disagreements also arose on the future arrangements for a free state. The Vietnamese envisaged their position in the French Union as one of an essentially sovereign state, but the French insisted that because the French Union was a federation, each free state must delegate much of its sovereignty to federal organisms and a high commissioner appointed in Paris. Faced with an impasse, the delegates decided to put off a decision on the future role of Vietnam in the French Union until the formal talks, which were now scheduled to convene in late May in France. On May 13, Giap returned to Hanoi disappointed. Ho Chi Minh tried to put a good face on the situation, claiming that both sides now understood each other better and had reached agreement on some key issues. He expressed the hope that the remaining differences, which he described as not irreconcilable, could be ironed out in France.

Five days later, d'Argenlieu made a short visit to Hanoi to discuss the peace talks. He asked his hosts to postpone the departure for Paris of the Vietnamese delegation, on the grounds that a national election campaign was under way in France, but Ho Chi Minh insisted on keeping the date as scheduled. More ominously, the high commissioner used the visit to forewarn the Vietnamese government of the imminent founding of a new autonomous state of Cochin China, an event that would undermine the Ho-Sainteny understanding reached in March.

On May 30, 1946, 50,000 people braved a torrential rainstorm to make their way to the campus of the University of Hanoi to attend a farewell rally for the Vietnamese delegates for the peace talks. Led by Pham Van Dong, the delegation arrived with Ho Chi Minh and General Raoul Salan, both of whom would join the group on its flight to Europe. Ho was not an official member of the delegation, but would attend the talks as an "honored guest" of France. In brief remarks to the crowd, he declared that his only aim was to serve the interests of his fatherland and the happiness of the Vietnamese people. He called on them to obey the government in his absence, and to treat foreigners with tolerance and respect.

When the delegation assembled at the Northern Palace early the following morning, they were all dressed in formal suits except for Ho Chi Minh, who wore his everyday khaki suit along with black leather shoes. On arrival at Gia Lam Airport, they boarded two military Dakota airplanes and took off in cloudy weather on their long journey.[33]

Following instructions from Paris, the planes were delayed on several occasions to make certain that the French elections were over before the delegation's arrival. After a brief stopover in Burma, because of bad weather, they arrived in Calcutta on June 1, where they were greeted by the French consul and a representative of the British government. They were then taken to the famous Great Eastern Hotel, and remained there for two days of sightseeing. On the fourth they landed in Agra and visited the Taj Mahal, then went on to Karachi, Iraq, and finally Cairo, on the seventh, for a three-day visit. Before leaving Egypt, they were informed that the French government had just recognized the Autonomous Republic of Cochin China, which High Commissioner d'Argenlieu had recently created in Saigon. Ho feigned surprise at the news, and urged General Salan not to make Cochin China "a new Alsace-Lorraine." If so, it could lead to a hundred years war.[34]

Meanwhile, a government crisis had erupted in France. In the parliamentary elections held on June 2, the conservative parties had won a striking victory, leading to the resignation of the government of Socialist Prime Minister Gouin. This, of course, posed potential difficulties for the upcoming negotiations, since a more conservative government in Paris would be less likely to accept the conciliatory verdict reached during the Ho-Sainteny negotiations in March. Of more immediate importance, it complicated the arrival plans for the DRV delegation. With negotiations on the formation of a new cabinet still in progress in Paris, there would be no French government to provide a formal reception to the visitors. So when the planes carrying the delegation left Cairo on the eleventh, they made a stopover in Algeria and were then rerouted to the French beach resort of Biarritz, on the Bay of Biscay, where they finally landed the next day. There they were met by local authorities and taken to hotels in the city. Ho Chi Minh was registered at the luxurious Carlton Hotel, just off the beach, while the remainder of the party stayed at a less prestigious hotel nearby.[35]

During the next few days, several members of the Vietnamese delegation continued on to Paris, but by mutual agreement Ho Chi Minh remained in Biarritz until a new government under Prime Minister Georges Bidault, head of the conservative Mouvement Républicain Populaire (MRP), could take office. Bidault delegated Jean Sainteny to fly to Biarritz to remain with Ho until the formal installation of the new government had taken place in Paris. During the next several days, Sainteny did his best to keep the president happy and occupied.

It was not always easy. According to Sainteny's account, Ho Chi Minh was uneasy about the situation in Paris, and even more about conditions in Indochina, where d'Argenlieu was patently doing everything in his power to undercut the preliminary arrangements reached in March; Ho even threatened to return to Hanoi. But Sainteny assured him that the French National Assembly would not formally ratify the new Autonomous Republic of Cochin China until obtaining the results of the referendum called for by the Ho-Sainteny agreement.

Under Sainteny's patient persuasion, Ho Chi Minh began to relax, and for the next several days submitted with good humor to Sainteny's tireless efforts to provide him with distractions. On several occasions, the two went to the nearby resort of Hendaye, where Sainteny's sister owned a villa, and Ho spent many enjoyable hours playing with Sainteny's nephews on the beach. They attended a bullfight across the border in Spain, and they visited the Catholic sanctuary at Lourdes. They went to the small fishing village of Biristou, where the two had lunch at a local restaurant. Afterward, Ho signed the visitor's book with the brief dedication, "Seas and oceans do not separate brothers who love each other." One day they embarked before dawn on a fishing trawler at St.-Jean-de-Luz. Although Sainteny remarked later that the day seemed long, Ho Chi Minh appeared to enjoy himself, catching several tuna and holding a friendly conversation with the captain. When the captain mentioned the Basque separatist movement that was active in the region, Ho replied, "In that field I am certainly more experienced than you are, sir, and I would emphatically urge the Basques to think it over very carefully before taking the plunge!" In later years, Ho Chi Minh occasionally commented that those were among the happiest days of his life.[36]

Ho Chi Minh also had the time to handle matters of state. Before leaving for Paris, he received several delegations from labor unions, Vietnamese émigré groups, and the FCP journal *L'Humanité*. On all occasions, he played the vintage "Uncle Ho," showing a genuine interest in everything and everyone and behaving with a simplicity of manner that was extraordinary in an individual of his stature. Yet, according to one French observer, there was always a toughness behind the amicable exterior. When he was informed by a French Socialist that the Trotskyite Ta Thu Thau had been assassinated by Vietminh forces in Saigon, Ho shed a brief tear for the "great patriot," but then added, "All those who do not follow the line that I have set out will be smashed."

On June 22, with the new Bidault government under formation in Paris, Ho Chi Minh left with Jean Sainteny for Paris, in preparation for the peace talks at Fontainebleau. Flying in splendid weather over the châteaux of the Loire River valley, they arrived over Paris in mid-afternoon. Later, Sainteny recalled that as the plane descended, Ho "was deathly pale. His eyes glittered, and when he tried to speak to me, his throat was so tight that he could not utter a word." As the plane came to a halt on the runway, he grasped Sainteny's arm and said: "Stay close to me. There's such a crowd."[37]

Le Bourget Airport was indeed crowded, and above the main terminal the flags of both France and Vietnam were fluttering in the breeze. After they disembarked from the plane, Ho was greeted by Marius Moutet, minister of overseas territories in the new government, and a friend from his days in Paris following World War I. After a few perfunctory welcoming remarks, Ho was taken to the Royal Monceau Hotel on Avenue Hoche, where he was assigned a suite of rooms. The image of the longtime guerrilla leader Ho Chi Minh trying to make himself comfortable in a soft bed at the sumptuous hotel struck Sainteny as incongruous. Sainteny suspected that Ho would probably sleep on the wall-to-wall carpeting rather than on the bed.

The new Bidault government did not formally take office until June 26 and the peace talks were not scheduled to begin until early July. For the next several days, Ho Chi Minh amused himself by revisiting many of the scenes of his earlier life in Paris. He spent an afternoon in the Bois de Boulogne and even returned to his old apartment on Impasse Compoint. At his request, he and Sainteny visited the beaches in Normandy, where Allied forces had landed two years earlier. They then spent the night at Sainteny's family estate nearby, where he rose at dawn to wander around the chicken coops and the stables, asking the resident farmer about French methods of breeding cattle.[38]

Not all was pleasure, of course. The news of Ho Chi Minh's arrival had circulated in Paris, and he was much in demand. A February article of the French newspaper *Le Figaro* had identified him as the Comintern agent Nguyen Ai Quoc, and some were eager to meet the old revolutionary. Ho Chi Minh allowed Jacques Dumaine, the director of protocol at the Ministry of Foreign Affairs, to guide him through the thickets of formal diplomatic behavior. But, characteristically, he kept it simple. To all those who requested an interview, he invited them to breakfast at 6:00 A.M., explaining that it was custom to rise early in the tropics. For all occasions, he wore his habitual attire. On July 4, he hosted a sumptuous dinner at his hotel in honor of incoming Prime Minister Bidault. Dress protocol was white tie, but Ho wore his familiar worn khaki suit, buttoned to the neck as a slight concession to the occasion, and canvas sandals.

Sainteny gave a reception for Ho Chi Minh at his own town house, and among the many politicians who attended was Ho's old adversary Albert Sarraut. "Well!" exclaimed the onetime minister of colonies. "Here you are, you old brigand. I have you within reach at last. What a good part of my life I've spent pursuing you!" Then he embraced the amused Ho warmly and praised him as a good friend, asking him just one question: Did the Lycée Albert Sarraut still exist in Hanoi?[39]

Ho Chi Minh had hoped to meet Charles de Gaulle, but was unable to, for "*le grand Charles*" had retired to his estate at Colombey and made it a rule not to intervene in affairs of state. Nor did he meet General Leclerc, who avoided him. Leclerc's aloof attitude puzzled many observers, since the two had gotten along well in Indochina. Sainteny speculated that because the general had been severely criticized in French military circles for his actions in Indochina, he was reluctant to meddle further in the issue. But he also noted that Leclerc might have felt that Ho Chi Minh had deceived him when he had denied that his government was making preparations for war.[40]

At eleven in the morning on July 2, Protocol Chief Dumaine picked up Ho Chi Minh at his hotel and escorted him in a fleet of fourteen automobiles to the Hotel Matignon for a diplomatic reception hosted by Prime Minister Bidault. In his welcoming speech, Bidault apologized for the delay in opening the peace talks and referred to the traditional friendship between two peoples. He described the new French Union as being "animated by a great humane spirit" and hoped that the two sides could work together with sincerity and mutual understanding. In his reply, Ho thanked his host for his warm welcome, noting that Paris was the cradle of the noble ideals of the 1789 Revolution. Warning that there would probably be difficult days ahead, he expressed the hope that sincerity and mutual confidence would clear away all obstacles, adding that both Eastern and Western philosophy extolled the idea that "you should not do to others what you do not want others to do to you."[41]

The next day, Ho Chi Minh walked up the Champs-Elysées to lay a wreath at the Tomb of the Unknown Soldier at the Arc de Triomphe. A reporter noted that he had drawn a large crowd. "Why, of course," he replied with a smile, "everyone wants to see the Vietnamese version of Charlie Chaplin." He also visited the Palace of Versailles, well known to all Vietnamese as a result of Ho's famous appeal to the Allied leaders at the peace conference after World War I. After stopping at Napoleon's tomb at Les Invalides, he visited Mount Valerian, in Montmartre, where a monument had been erected in memory of partisans executed by the Germans during the recent war.

Formal talks finally began on July 6 at the stately Palace of Fontainebleau, which still reflected much of the grandeur of the *ancien régime*. Leading the French delegation was Max André, who had visited Indochina at de Gaulle's request in January. (High Commissioner d'Argenlieu had flown to Paris from Saigon in the hope of chairing the French delegation, but the Bidault goverment feared an adverse reaction from the Vietnamese—or from the French public—and rejected his offer.) The French delegation was mixed in its political orientation, with members from the FCP and the Socialist Party as well as Bidault's MRP.

From the Vietnamese point of view, the circumstances surrounding the opening of peace talks were forbidding. In the weeks leading up to the conference, the situation in Indochina had deteriorated. On June 1, a provisional government of Cochin China under Nguyen Van Thinh had taken office in Saigon. That month, the issue of whether the Vietnamese or the French would occupy the Governor-General's Palace in Hanoi after the departure of Chinese occupation forces had been under discussion. On the twenty-fifth, French troops had suddenly occupied the building, the symbol of supreme power in all Indochina. After a vigorous protest from the Vietnamese government, General Valluy, d'Argenlieu's second-in-command, finally agreed that the palace would be guarded by a joint contingent of French and Vietnamese soldiers, pending a final decision on the matter in Paris.

After the French opened the first session with a general statement of welcome, Pham Van Dong, chair of the Vietnamese delegation, harshly criticized French actions in Indochina—actions, he charged, that could not facilitate the success of the negotiations. The two sides eventually managed to agree on an agenda, consisting of the status of Vietnam within the French Union, its relations with other countries, and the unity of the three regions. But on all of these issues, each side maintained the exact positions that it had held in April at Dalat. The French were evasive on the issue of Cochin China, demanding the withdrawal of all north Vietnamese troops from the region as a precondition for a cease-fire, and adopted a narrow interpretation of the concept of the Vietnamese "free state" within the French Union. As if to symbolize their arrogance, many French delegates began to absent themselves from committee meetings.

The Vietnamese delegation undoubtedly hoped that it would receive some support from their comrades in the FCP, and perhaps from the Socialists as well. Both party newspapers had praised and supported Ho Chi Minh since his arrival in Paris. A delegation of Vietnamese supporters from the DRV National Assembly had visited France earlier in the year and successfully restored contacts with the FCP, which had been broken since before World War II. But although individual Party members were sympathetic to the Vietnamese cause, many leading French Communists were suspicious of Ho because of the decision of the ICP to dissolve itself the previous November. At the same time, the FCP was now caught up in the wave of nationalist fervor that swept through French society in the immediate postwar era, as the French people tried to come to terms with their memories of collaborationist behavior during the war. Jean Sainteny had become aware of the equivocal position of the FCP on the issue of Indochina when he showed a copy of the March 6 agreement to Maurice Thorez, a coal miner who had become a leading Communist and a member of the Council of Ministers. Thorez expressed his approval of the terms of the agreement, but added that "if the Vietnamese do not respect these terms, we will take the necessary measures and let guns speak for us, if need be."[42]

Since he was not a formal member of the Vietnamese negotiating team, Ho did not attend the talks in Fontainebleau. Remaining in Paris, he used all the force of his long experience and charismatic personality ("operation charm," as one wag called it) to promote official and public support for his cause. He met with representatives of all the major political parties and organizations in France, as well as with a number of well-known journalists and intellectuals. He made prolific use of his contacts with the FCP and asked Maurice Thorez, currently the deputy prime minister, to use his influence to have Vietnamese concerns addressed by the French cabinet. What Thorez replied to this request is not known.[43]

Ho Chi Minh's contacts with members of local news organizations were especially crucial, since the talks were being carried on in relative secrecy, out of the glare of publicity. With the FCP and their allies vigorously supporting the Vietnamese, at least in public, and conservatives labeling as "treason" all public appeals to respond to Vietnamese demands, the atmosphere around the talks was tense and poisoned by political partisanship. Compromise was made more difficult by recent incidents in Indochina, where Vietnamese attacks on French civilians and military forces had begun to take place with increasing frequency. From Ho's point of view, it was in the Vietnamese interest that the true story of the negotiations be brought to public attention, and on July 12, he held a press conference in Paris to present his government's case. Pointing out that Vietnam insisted on national independence and would refuse to accept a federal solution to the problem, he added that Hanoi was willing to accept the concept of independence within the framework of the French Union—an arrangement, he said, that could be profitable to both sides. He further declared that the provinces of Cochin China were an integral part of the national territory and could not be dealt with separately. In return, he promised that all French property and other rights would be protected in the new Vietnam, and that if the DRV needed foreign advisers, French citizens would be given preference. When a U.S. reporter asked if it was true that he was a Communist, Ho replied that he was indeed a student of Karl Marx, but that communism required an advanced industrial and agricultural base, and Vietnam possessed neither of these conditions. Who knows, he remarked, when the dream of Karl Marx will be realized; two thousand years ago, Jesus Christ taught the importance of loving one's enemies, and that has yet to come true.[44]

In Saigon, Thierry d'Argenlieu was waging his own campaign to influence the talks. On July 23, word reached Paris that the high commissioner had announced his intention of convening a conference at Dalat on August 1. Its purpose would be to consider the creation of a federation of Indochinese states (Fédération Indochinoise) to include Cochin China, southern Annam and the Central Highlands, Cambodia, and Laos (Tonkin was not included, presumably because it was firmly under DRV control). Pham Van Dong strenuously protested the action and broke off negotiations, whereupon the French promised to take up the issue with the Bidault government.

Ho Chi Minh visited Fontainebleau on July 26 at the joint invitation of the two delegations. After a welcome banquet, he talked with members of his delegation as well as with French officials, returning that evening to Paris. Through this intervention, Ho was able to get the peace talks in France to resume—but only temporarily. On August 1, the day that the Dalat conference convened, the Vietnamese delegation formally protested French actions in Cochin China and, in the absence of a proper answer from the government, suspended the negotiations. Ho persisted in his efforts, and was eventually able to persuade his old friend Marius Moutet to seek a formula for renewing the talks. Moutet, who had argued that it was better to deal with Ho than with any alternative, wanted to continue the negotiations and abide by the spirit of the March 6 agreement. To do so, he said that both sides would need to lower the tone of violence, propaganda, and provocation. Unless law and order could be restored in Cochin China, he predicted, any elections would inevitably favor the Vietnamese.[45]

Whether peaceful conditions would return soon to the south, however, was doubtful. During the winter and spring of 1945–46, French troops under the command of General Henri Leclerc attempted to mop up resistance forces in the Mekong delta. Tran Van Giau attempted to counter French moves with a "scorched-earth" policy, which applied the tactics of brutality and terrorism on the local population to enforce allegiance to the movement. Areas under the control of the religious sects were attacked, and sect leaders who refused to place themselves under Vietminh command were sometimes assassinated. Leclerc responded by reverting to the "oil spot" technique (after pacifying individual districts, French forces would gradually extend their efforts to establish security into neighboring areas), which had been used successfully against rebel forces at the end of the nineteenth century. The insurgents were inexorably driven into the most isolated areas of the lower delta, including the heavily wooded Ca Mau Peninsula and the Plain of Reeds, and in the rubber plantation areas along the Cambodian border, where they sought to continue the struggle.

The negotiations at Fontainebleau resumed in late August, but when the French delegation refused to accept Vietnamese demands for the formal recognition of Vietnamese independence and a firm date for the projected referendum in Cochin China, Vietnamese delegates broke off talks once again, on September 10. Three days later, they left Paris—without Ho Chi Minh—to catch a ship to return to Indochina.

With the talks at an impasse, Jean Sainteny asked Ho to return to Hanoi in order to put an end to the anti-French climate in Indochina, but Ho decided to remain in Paris, declaring that he could not afford to return "empty-handed" and thus "discredited and consequently powerless." In an attempt to pressure him to leave, the government stopped picking up his bill at the Royal Monceau, but Ho thereupon moved to the suburb Soisy-sous-Montmorency, where he stayed at the house of Raymond Aubrac, a sympathetic acquaintance. While his living conditions were more spartan and less convenient, Ho was able to receive visitors and hold interviews, all the while keeping up his efforts to revive the peace process. "Don't let me leave France like this," he appealed to his old acquaintance Marius Moutet. "Arm me against those who are trying to outstrip me; you'll have no reason to regret it."

On September 11, Ho held a press conference in which he insisted on his desire to reach an agreement, and he compared the existing differences with those that normally occured within all families. He expressed optimism that an accord could be reached within six months and promised to do all in his power to end the violence in Indochina. That same day, he visited the U.S. Embassy to meet Ambassador Jefferson Caffery, who, in his account of their conversation, surmised that his visitor hoped to bring the United States into the game in order to play Washington off against Paris. Although Ho insisted that he was not a Communist, Caffery made no commitments (in a personal letter a few days later, he remarked that Ho had behaved "with dignity" and in a tactful manner during the negotiations). The next day Ho talked with George Abbott, then first secretary at the embassy and later to serve as U.S. consul general in Saigon. Ho mentioned his wartime collaboration with the United States and his admiration for President Roosevelt, and emphasized his country's desperate need for economic assistance, which the French were unable to provide. As a final inducement, he hinted at the possibility of future military cooperation between the two countries—including U.S. use of Cam Ranh Bay, on the central coast of Vietnam, as a naval base.[46]

But Washington took no action on the issue, despite concerns expressed by Asian specialists in the State Department. In a memo to Assistant Secretary for Far Eastern Affairs John Carter Vincent, Abbot Low Moffat of the Office of Southeast Asian Affairs warned that "a critical situation" was emerging in Indochina as a result of French actions in violation of the March 6 agreement. With tension increasing among

Vietnamese because of anger over French behavior, there were grounds to believe that the French were preparing to resort to force to secure their position throughout Indochina. Moffat suggested that the State Department might wish "to express to the French, in view of our interests in peace and orderly development of dependent peoples, our hope that they will abide by the spirit of the March 6 convention."

The Truman administration, however, was in no mood to irritate the French over the issue of Indochina at a crucial juncture in French politics. In fact, concern was rising within the State Department over allegations from intelligence sources that the government in Hanoi was a tool of the Kremlin in its plan to expand its influence in Asia. In August, a cable to Saigon had asked for clarification about "indications possible subservience to Party line by Ho and other leaders" and queried U.S. Consul Charles Reed about the relative strength of Communist and non-Communist elements in the Hanoi government.[47]

However, some American diplomats were becoming uneasy at growing indications of U.S. support for French policies in Indochina. From Saigon, Reed reported to Washington that many Vietnamese might logically assume that the United States was backing the French, since the latter were using Jeeps and trucks that they had purchased from surplus stocks in Manila which still bore U.S. markings. Officials in Washington had reported to the White House that the French were using U.S. surplus equipment in Indochina, but President Truman decided there was no point in removing matériel that was already there.

Ho Chi Minh's decision to remain in France after the departure of the DRV delegation inspired considerable debate. Some French observers predicted that Ho was trying to blackmail Paris into giving up what he could not win at the conference table. Others suspected that his appeal to Moutet for assistance was insincere, since in the end he would inevitably turn his government's weapons against the French. Even if Ho was sincere, there was growing doubt that he could control his own followers, that he would be anything but a "sorcerer's apprentice." In fact, Ho Chi Minh was already under heavy attack from many sources within the Vietnamese community, who feared that he was giving up too much in his desperate effort to avoid a war. Sentiment in Indochina (and even among Vietnamese émigrés in France) was running strongly against a compromise with the French. Sainteny himself believed that Ho was sincere, citing Ho's efforts to reduce hostility to the French in Indochina in recent months. But Prime Minister Georges Bidault claimed to have proof that Ho's pose of friendship was only a ruse, since

Ho had actually sent instructions to Hanoi to prepare for a renewal of hostilities in the north.[48]

Bidault may have had a point. In an interview with Ho on September 11, *New York Times* correspondent David Schoenbrun had asked whether war was inevitable. "Yes," Ho had replied, "we will have to fight. The French have signed a treaty and they wave flags for me, but it is a masquerade." When Schoenbrun noted that without an army or modern weapons, such a war would be hopeless, Ho disagreed:

> No, it would not be hopeless. It would be hard, desperate, but we could win. We have a weapon every bit as powerful as the most modern cannon: nationalism! Do not underestimate its power. You Americans above all ought to remember that a ragged band of barefooted farmers defeated the pride of Europe's best-armed professionals.

Schoenbrun countered that the advent of modern weapons of war made such an approach impossible in today's world, but Ho insisted that modern weapons could be obtained if necessary. In any case, he insisted, the heroism of the Yugoslav partisans against Nazi Germany showed that the spirit of man was more powerful than machines, which could not operate effectively in swamps and thick jungles. There were millions of straw huts that could serve as "Trojan horses" in the rear of an invading army. "It will be a war between an elephant and a tiger," he replied.

> If the tiger ever stands still the elephant will crush him with his mighty tusks. But the tiger does not stand still. He lurks in the jungle by day and emerges by night. He will leap upon the back of the elephant, tearing huge chunks from his hide, and then he will leap back into the dark jungle. And slowly the elephant will bleed to death. That will be the war of Indochina.[49]

There was always the possibility that national elections in France could bring the FCP into a new coalition government in Paris, and Maurice Thorez may have tried to persuade Ho to delay a decision to resort to hostilities on the chance that a diplomatic solution could still be achieved. On the evening of September 14, Ho met once again with Marius Moutet; shortly before, Ho had warned Sainteny that a failure to reach agreement would lead to war. "You will kill ten of my men while we will kill one of yours," he predicted. "but you will be the ones to end up exhausted." At the meeting, Ho asked that both sides take responsibility for solving the problem of Cochin China, but Moutet had refused, declaring that Vietnamese participation in a mixed commission to monitor the situation there would violate French sovereignty. Moutet then appealed to Ho Chi Minh to sign a modus vivendi (in diplomatic parlance, a temporary arrangement between parties pending a final agreement) to avoid a total breakdown of the talks. The draft document called for a cease-fire in Cochin China to take effect on October 30 and the resumption of negotiations in January 1947. Ho refused and left the meeting at 11:00 P.M., declaring his intention to leave for Indochina on Monday morning, September 16. Shortly after midnight, however, Ho contacted Moutet and asked to resume the talks. The two then agreed in principle that a Vietnamese representative would be authorized to cooperate with High Commissioner d'Argenlieu in bringing about an armistice in Indochina. Ho then consented to sign the modus vivendi.

This modus vivendi was precious little for Ho Chi Minh to have obtained after two months of talks at Fontainebleau. Sainteny later described it as a "pathetic" piece of paper that had been drawn up hastily in his own office and gave Ho "much less than he had hoped for when he came to France." In Indochina, French residents were delighted, but Vietnamese attitudes were ambivalent, with some convinced that it represented a national humiliation. Ho tacitly admitted as much, remarking to Sainteny as they left the meeting at three in the morning, "I have just signed my death warrant."[50]

E ven after signing the September 14 agreement, to the exasperation of his hosts Ho Chi Minh still seemed reluctant to return to Vietnam (in an extended biographical essay on Ho, David Halberstam noted that the French attitude toward Ho's visit could be marked by the steady shrinking of his protocolary red carpet). According to Sainteny, Ho had refused the plane that the French agreed to put at his disposal, citing reasons of health, and expressed a preference to go by ship. Sainteny was reluctant to approve the request, but Ho appealed directly to the Ministry of Marine and was assigned passage on the French cruiser *Dumont d'Urville*, which was then docked in the port of Toulon preparing to sail to Indochina. On September 16, Sainteny accompanied Ho Chi Minh on the train to Toulon. At Montélimar, Ho descended briefly from the train to address a number of Vietnamese students gathered at the station, explaining why he signed the modus vivendi and asking them to work hard at their studies. He did the same at Marseilles, where a few shouts of "traitor" (*Viet gian*) were heard in the audience. On the eighteenth, the train arrived at Toulon, and he boarded the *Dumont d'Urville*. (The Vietnamese delegation had departed on the warship *Pasteur* from Marseilles four days previously.)[51]

To make room for President Ho Chi Minh on his vessel, Captain Gerbaud had been instructed to remove the cargo and the passengers who had previously boarded the ship. In their place came Ho, his aides-de-camp, and four Vietnamese students who were returning independently to Indochina after completing their studies in France. On the morning of September 19, flying the red flag with the gold star of the government of Vietnam, the ship weighed anchor and sailed into the Mediterranean Sea. Ho Chi Minh had informed the Vietnamese government of the modus vivendi by telegraph before leaving Paris, sending a copy by airmail as well. From the ship he cabled Hanoi to explain the terms of the accord to the population and to order preparations to carry it out; he also asked for word on current conditions in Indochina. On his first day aboard ship, he sent a short message to Marius Moutet, thanking him for his assistance and asking for his cooperation in carrying out the agreement. A few days later he received a brief telegram from Prime Minister Georges Bidault. In his reply, Ho thanked Bidault for his courtesy, but remarked that the modus vivendi had not been received favorably by the Vietnamese people. The reaction, he noted, was human: "I will do my best and will succeed if French friends in Cochin China loyally apply democratic liberties, cessation of hostilities, liberation of prisoners, and avoid unfriendly words and acts. I count on your active assistance to carry through the work in the interests of both our countries."[52]

On September 22, the ship arrived at Port Said, the northern entrance into the Suez Canal. From there Ho sent a letter to a Frenchwoman who had recently written a brief appeal to him not to allow war to break out between the two countries. Ho used the occasion to make the point that the Vietnamese people hated bloodshed as much as did the French but that, like the French, they insisted on the independence and national unity of their fatherland. If France would agree to recognize Vietnamese independence, he concluded, it would win the hearts and love of all Vietnamese.[53]

The ship next stopped at the French port of Djibouti, where Ho left the ship for a short honorary visit with the governor-general. It then proceeded to Colombo, Ceylon, where envoys from the Indian nationalist leaders Mahatma Gandhi and Jawaharlal Nehru came to the ship to greet him. Throughout the journey, progress had been slow, for the ship had spent several days in port to undergo maintenance work, and at sea it carried out shelling exercises as part of its routine drill. On shipboard, Ho lived simply. He carried no luggage except for one change of clothes, and he did the washing himself. In spare moments he talked with the French sailors and Vietnamese students aboard, and as usual, got in his propaganda licks, giving the latter a study course on Vietnamese and world affairs. One of his shipmates later recalled his comments: "We lack everything," he said. "We have neither machines, nor primary materials, nor even skilled workers; our finances have been reduced to a minimum. But our country possesses mountains and forests, rivers and seas in abundance, and our compatriots are strong in resolution, in courage and creative spirit."[54]

Not all those onboard were seduced by his personality. Captain Gerbaud commented that although Ho Chi Minh was "intelligent and charming," he was "a passionate idealist entirely devoted to the cause he has espoused." In Gerbaud's view, the Vietnamese revolutionary had a naïve belief in the slogans of the day. When, at the captain's order, the ship tested its guns at sea, one of his compatriots asked Ho: "They're testing your nerves. Are you afraid?" Ho Chi Minh just laughed.[55]

The *Dumont d'Urville* finally sailed into beautiful Cam Ranh Bay on October 18. Here Ho was received by High Commissioner Thierry d'Argenlieu and General Louis Morlière, Sainteny's replacement as senior French representative to the Hanoi government, on the French cruiser *Suffren*. For the second time in seven months, the high commissioner welcomed the Vietnamese president in an official ceremony at sea. Then, after Ho Chi Minh had inspected the guard of honor, Ho, d'Argenlieu, and Morlière discussed the means of implementing the modus vivendi. Prime Minister Bidault had already forwarded a copy of Ho Chi Minh's cable about the Vietnamese reaction to d'Argenlieu, instructing him, as French plenipotentiary in Indochina, to respond as he saw fit. The two sides agreed on some points. D'Argenlieu consented to the appointment of a representative from the Vietnamese government to cooperate on the implementation of the cease-fire, while Ho Chi Minh disavowed any official support for terrorist incidents in Cochin China. But Ho adamantly refused the high commissioner's demand that all Vietnamese troops in the southern provinces be immediately repatriated to the north. Nevertheless, the meeting concluded in good spirits, and d'Argenlieu reported to Paris that success would depend on the actions of the Vietnamese government once Ho Chi Minh returned to Hanoi.

Two days later, the *Dumont d'Urville* entered the Cua Cam River and sailed into Haiphong harbor. The Vietnamese delegation had arrived two weeks earlier, and Pham Van Dong had reported on the results of the negotiations at Fontainebleau to his colleagues in Hanoi. As the ship docked in midafternoon, representatives from the government were on hand to welcome Ho Chi Minh home after four months abroad with a brief ceremony (Ho insisted that the crowd sing the "Marseillaise" as well as the Vietnamese national anthem). Then the group went to the headquarters of the Haiphong municipal committee, where they dined while Ho commented briefly on his voyage.

The next morning, Ho boarded a special train to the capital. In the towns and villages along the route, which were festooned with red and gold flags, crowds had gathered to wave at the president. As the train pulled into Hanoi railway station, Ho was met by French and Vietnamese representatives and then escorted by car through streets packed with onlookers to the Northern Palace. There he consulted with Truong Chinh and other members of the Party Standing Committee, while a crowd of nearly 100,000 gathered in the streets surrounding the palace to welcome him.[56]

Why did Ho Chi Minh take his time returning to Indochina? That question has inspired debate ever since, and it has not yet been satisfactorily resolved. Ho Chi Minh's own explanation to the French is hardly credible, since he had never before allowed his health to interfere with his political objectives. Some historians have suggested that he might have wanted to give his subordinate Vo Nguyen Giap sufficient time to eliminate opposition elements in Vietnam and thus strengthen the authority of the government in Hanoi in preparation for all-out war. Others have argued that he might have been concerned at the adverse reaction to the modus vivendi in Indochina and wanted to delay his return until passions had cooled. But Jean Sainteny later speculated that he might have feared an attempt on his life if he went by air, and in comments to colleagues in Hanoi many years later, Ho Chi Minh confirmed that this was his primary concern.[57]

There is no doubt that the intense Vo Nguyen Giap, who (like many of his colleagues) was increasingly skeptical of the prospects for a peaceful settlement, had taken advantage of Ho Chi Minh's lengthy absence to strengthen Party control over the apparatus of government. During the summer, tensions between Vietminh elements and non-Communist political parties had escalated, leading to armed clashes and the withdrawal of several nationalist figures—including Nguyen Hai Than, Vu Hong Khanh (who then left for China), and Foreign Minister

Nguyen Tuong Tam—from the government. Those who remained presented no threat to Vietminh control over the reins of power.

In Giap's view, the government's crackdown on rival groups was fully justified. Early in the summer, French military authorities had demanded the right to organize a march through Hanoi on July 14, Bastille Day. Vietnamese intelligence sources reported that nationalist elements were preparing a serious provocation against French troops during the celebration in the hope of provoking a breakdown of the peace talks. The government thereupon turned down the French request, citing security concerns, and on the following day police penetrated the VNQDD headquarters in Hanoi, where they reportedly discovered a torture chamber, the bodies of several victims, and a number of prisoners, along with incriminating evidence of a plan to kidnap French residents of the city. The operation crippled VNQDD efforts to discredit the government, but armed clashes and tension between Communist and non-Communist elements continued throughout the next months until Ho Chi Minh's return in October.[58]

The government's relations with the French also continued to be problematic. After he assumed Sainteny's post in the spring, General Morlière, an affable and conciliatory man, attempted to calm the situation, but with tensions inflamed by the failure of the peace talks at Fontainebleau, incidents between Vietnamese and French residents in Indochina became a frequent occurrence. On each occasion, Morlière felt obligated to issue an ultimatum to punish the perpetrators, leading sardonic Vietnamese to dub him the "general of ultimatums."

The ongoing conflict in Cochin China undoubtedly contributed to the problem. Widely criticized for his brutal tactics, Tran Van Giau had been replaced as commander of resistance forces by Nguyen Binh. Described by French sources as squat and ugly, with one blind eye hidden behind dark glasses, Binh was a native of Tonkin who had joined the VNQDD in the late 1920s. After many years in exile in China, he had suddenly reappeared after World War II in the Viet Bac and served with Vietminh forces there. Fanatically anti-French and totally lacking in scruples, Binh soon showed signs of military genius, and although he was apparently not a Party member, in January 1946 he was assigned to take charge of the struggling movement in Cochin China.

Party leaders may have hoped that Nguyen Binh would be more effective than Giau, whose scorched-earth tactics and pitiless elimination of rival elements had alienated many. But Binh was equally ruthless. (Some Vietnamese sources assert that Party leaders never trusted him, even when they sent him to lead the movement in Cochin China, because his methods were too brutal.) Energetic but pitiless in his disciplinary methods, Binh organized large guerrilla bases north of Saigon (in an area later to be known as Zone D), in the Plain of Reeds in the heart of the Mekong delta, and in the U Minh forest in the Ca Mau Peninsula, from which he harassed French installations and attempted to spread the revolution. However, Binh ignored an admonition by Ho Chi Minh to minimize violence and form a broad united front in the south, at the same time that he was raising the art of terrorism to a new level. One of those whom Binh ordered assassinated was Huynh Phu So, the religious mystic known popularly as the "mad bonze," who had founded the Hoa Hao sect just before the war.[59]

Ho must have had mixed feelings about the way his Party colleagues administered the country while he was away for four months. (He had repeatedly asked them to avoid provoking any problems until his return.) The consolidation of Vietminh authority and the suppression of rival elements would undoubtedly make it easier to adopt policies during the crucial months to come. But at the same time, the narrowing of the government's popular base—a base that Ho had so assiduously cultivated in the months following the August Revolution—could make it more difficult to mobilize national unity in the event of an armed confrontation with the French.

Ho Chi Minh may have also become increasingly aware that his efforts to secure a peace agreement in France had undercut his reputation and prestige with senior colleagues within his Party, many of whom were more skeptical than he that a compromise solution could be achieved, and more inclined to engage in a test of arms and wills with the French. Several of the leading members of the Party—including Vo Nguyen Giap, Pham Van Dong, Hoang Quoc Viet, and General Secretary Truong Chinh himself—may have had occasion to question Ho's judgment during his absence in Europe, and were now emboldened to take a more aggressive attitude in Party councils. In an article written to celebrate the first anniversary of the Declaration of Independence, Truong Chinh had set forth his own vision of the Vietnamese revolution. The article was critical of the tendency toward "unprincipled compromise," which demonstrated a lack of confidence in the masses, and added that revolutionaries should not fear the enemy but rather the "errors by our comrades." Although no criticism of Ho's leadership appeared in public, it was clear that from now on he would be compelled increasingly to take a collegial approach in arguing for the adoption of key policies.[60]

Whatever the reality of his relations with his senior colleagues, there seems little doubt that the vast majority of the people of north Vietnam were still devoted to him. Ho Chi Minh's fervent dedication to the cause of national independence, his personal simplicity, and his avuncular style had struck a responsive chord among the population, and he was already assuming an almost mythic role as bearer of the national destiny. Despite rising concerns about the prospects for peace, many accepted his decision to sign the modus vivendi in the conviction that if anyone could make it succeed, it would be President Ho Chi Minh. On October 23, he issued a public statement assuring the people that despite current difficulties, sooner or later Vietnam would be reunited and independent. To the population in the southern provinces he declared that all Vietnamese shared the same ancestors and belonged to one single country. "I solemnly declare to you," he promised, "that with your determination, with the determination of all the people in the country, our beloved south will certainly return to the bosom of the Fatherland."

Because Ho refused to talk about his past, continuing to insist that he was merely an "old patriot" who had long served his country, few Vietnamese realized at this point that their president was actually the Comintern agent Nguyen Ai Quoc. His own sister, Nguyen Thi Thanh, who had been living near Kim Lien since her release from prison prior to World War II, apparently realized his identity only by seeing his picture in the newspaper. She later traveled to Hanoi and visited him briefly in the Northern Palace. Later in the year, Ho's brother, Nguyen Sinh Khiem, now working as a schoolteacher in Kim Lien, also came to see him, and they met secretly in a house in the suburbs. His brother died in 1950, and his sister passed away four years later.[61]

During the first days after his return to Hanoi, Ho Chi Minh consulted with the Standing Committee to review the situation and plan future actions. Key issues that had to be resolved were whether to agree to the proposed October 30 date for a cease-fire in the south and how to deal with the growing tension with rival nationalist parties. Ho proposed convening the National Assembly to deliberate a draft constitution—this would lead to a new government replacing the coalition, which had been seriously weakened by the resignation of key figures like Vice President Nguyen Hai Than—and to approve new policies for the coming months.

When the National Assembly convened on October 28, it was a far cry from the atmosphere of carefully staged national unity at its last meeting seven months previously. In the preceding several days at least two hundred opposition figures had been arrested and placed in detention camps, while armed clashes in various areas of the north had resulted in several deaths, including those of two journalists. The mood in Hanoi was somber, with tensions running high between elements sympathetic to the government and those opposed. The session at the Municipal Theater was heavily guarded by a detachment of the National Defense Guard. Inside, 291 out of the 444 representatives who had originally been elected in January were in attendance. Of the 70 representatives of nationalist parties who had participated in March, only 37 took their seats. When one opposition deputy asked what had happened to the remaining delegates, he was informed that they had been arrested "with the approval of the standing committee of the assembly for crimes of common law."[62]

Unlike the previous session, the hall was now divided into three rather than two sections, with the far left (in the French manner) occupied by avowed members of the ICP as well as deputies from the newly formed Socialist Party, all wearing red neckties, as well as delegates from the ICP surrogate Democratic Party. In the center were non-party members participating in the Vietminh Front, while the VNQDD and Dong Minh Hoi delegates sat on the right. Also in the hall were a number of foreign guests.

At the opening session, the veteran Party member and Labor Minister Nguyen Van Tao, who had attended the Sixth Comintern Congress in 1928, proposed a message of confidence in "First Citizen" Ho Chi Minh. The proposal was adopted, to "prolonged applause." The government then submitted a report on its activities since the first session of the assembly in March. Ho Chi Minh defended the modus vivendi he had signed in Paris and assured his listeners that it would not prejudice the course of negotiations. Asked whether France would implement the agreement, he replied that it should be kept in mind that there were good people as well as bad in France, and the majority of the French people approved of the principle of Vietnamese independence and unity.

Before his departure from Paris, Ho Chi Minh had promised French officials that on his return to Hanoi he would broaden the government to make it more representative of the various groups within the population. On the second day of the session, the government submitted its resignation to the assembly, which thereupon asked Ho to form a new one. Three days later a new cabinet was submitted to the legislature, and given unanimous approval. But if French observers had hoped that Ho Chi Minh's promise would be fulfilled, they were now disappointed, because the new cabinet, far from being more moderate, actually moved significantly to the left. It was strongly Vietminh in composition, with militants in all key positions, including Vo Nguyen Giap remaining as minister of national defense and Pham Van Dong as under secretary for economic affairs. Ho Chi Minh retained the presidency, as well as the portfolio of foreign affairs. He also served as prime minister. Only two members of the new government were not attached to the Party or the Vietminh Front.

The move to the left reflected in part the collapse of the united front with nationalists that had been carefully constructed in the previous fall and winter. With rival parties now openly in opposition, Party leaders saw no need to compromise. But it also may have reflected the rising influence of radical leaders like Hoang Quoc Viet, Tran Huy Lieu, and Truong Chinh within the Party. In an article written a few weeks later, Chinh was publicly critical of the stage-by-stage approach adopted by Ho Chi Minh and indicated his preference for a more ideological approach to the Vietnamese revolution.

During the next few days, the assembly deliberated over the draft of the new constitution for the DRV. Despite the implicit criticisms by Truong Chinh, the new charter was essentially moderate in tone and designed to appeal to the majority of the population. The sections dealing with political organization stressed democratic freedoms and the need for a broad alliance of all patriotic groups to struggle against the restoration of French rule. Economic sections guaranteed the sanctity of private property and made no mention of the ultimate objective of creating a classless society. But French observers could not ignore that it also declared the total independence of Vietnam and made no reference to the Fédération Indochinoise, or to the French Union. The National Assembly approved the document, but left it to the government to decide when to implement it. On November 14, the assembly adjourned. By now there were only 242 delegates, with 2 belonging to the opposition.[63]

While the National Assembly was in session, the cease-fire that had been called for by the modus vivendi went into effect in Cochin China. At first, both sides made some effort to respect the truce, but inevitably clashes began to take place, and soon the war had heated up once again, as the French sent sweep operations into guerrilla-held areas and Nguyen Binh fought desperately to maintain his strongholds. By now, the French had lost faith in the peace process, and Thierry d'Argenlieu, fearing the possibility of a sudden Vietminh attack on his forces in the north or the center, began to consider organizing a coup to overthrow Ho Chi Minh and place a more compliant government in power in Hanoi. In September a French source contacted Bao Dai, the former emperor, who had settled in Hong Kong earlier in the year, to sound him out on the possibility of serving as head of a new government. D'Argenlieu instructed General Jean-Etienne Valluy in mid-November to strike quickly in the eventuality that negotiations broke down.

With the threat of war now imminent, Party leaders intensified their efforts to build up the readiness of their armed forces. One of their main needs was to obtain modern weapons; during the fall of 1946 the government began to smuggle guns into the country by sea from China, since the land border had been effectively sealed off by the French. Haiphong was one of the main ports of entry for smuggled matériel. As the major entry point for all goods imported into the DRV, the city had, in fact, been the focus of Franco-Vietnamese discussions for months. The French had raised the issue of customs several times during the talks at Fontainebleau, since the import tax constituted a high percentage of total revenue in colonial Indochina. But the issue had not been resolved, and the modus vivendi merely stated that the question would need further study. In Saigon, d'Argenlieu had been impatient at the failure to solve the problem, and on the very day that the temporary agreement was signed in Paris, he ordered Morlière to seize control of customs from the Vietnamese at his earliest opportunity.

In early November, French military forces finally did occupy the customs office in Haiphong and evict the Vietnamese administrators. Before it adjourned, the DRV National Assembly protested this action, asserting Vietnam's sovereign right to control all matters pertaining to custom house duties. For the moment, however, the most crucial issue remained the government's ability to use Haiphong as an entry point for weapons purchased abroad. On November 20, French naval craft seized a Chinese junk carrying a cargo of contraband gasoline presumably destined for the Vietnamese armed forces. While the junk was being towed into the harbor, local Vietnamese militia on shore fired on the French, who immediately responded; fighting spread rapidly throughout the city. A cease-fire was reached, but two days later Valluy ordered the commander of French forces in Haiphong to take total power over the city and restore law and order. On the twenty-third, French Colonel Dèbes issued an ultimatum to the Vietnamese to evacuate the Chinese quarter of the city and lay down their arms. When they did not respond, he ordered the shelling of this quarter of the city, killing hundreds of civilians. Then about two thousand French troops stormed the area, while their artillery pounded neighboring sectors of the city to neutralize the opposition. Still, the French came under heavy fire from defending Vietnamese forces, and the fighting in the city continued for several days, until the last Vietminh abandoned the battle on September 28.[64]

The incident at Haiphong shook the Truman administration from its lethargy regarding the situation in Indochina. In a cable from Hanoi on the same day, U.S. Consul James O'Sullivan reported that although the Vietnamese had fired first, the French had provoked the incident by their overbearing attitude. In Paris, Ambassador Caffery was instructed to register American unhappiness over the situation to French officials. But this irritation with the French was tempered by rising concern over the alleged Communist complexion of Ho Chi Minh's government. At the end of November the U.S. Embassy in Paris reported that the French had "positive proof" that Ho had received advice and instructions from Moscow. From Saigon, U.S. Consul Charles Reed warned that if Cochin China fell to the Vietminh, they would soon begin to unleash propaganda and terrorist operations in neighboring Cambodia and Laos, a danger that Reed suggested merited "closest attention." This was the first expression by a U.S. official of what would become known as the "domino theory."[65]

In late November, the State Department sent Abbot Low Moffat, chief of the Division of Southeast Asian Affairs, to Indochina to assess the overall situation and report on the underlying character of the Hanoi government. Moffat was an outspoken supporter within the State Department of the cause of Vietnamese independence, and he was instructed to assure Ho Chi Minh that the United States supported the terms of the March 6 agreement and was sympathetic to the effort of his government "to achieve greater autonomy within the framework of democratic institutions." But Moffat was also asked to warn Ho not to use force to seek his objectives, and to urge him to accept a compromise solution over the status of Cochin China. As a means of dissuading Vietnamese leaders from ill-advised actions, Moffat was to assure them that the French government had pledged to abide by the Ho-Sainteny agreement and had no intention of restoring colonial authority over Indochina.

Moffat arrived in Saigon on December 3, and after discussions with French officials, went on to Hanoi on the seventh. Consul O'Sullivan had just reported that Ho felt "desperately alone" and suggested that publicity for Moffat's impending visit might strengthen the president's position with his rivals. Although Ho was seriously ill (perhaps from a recurrence of his tuberculosis), he invited Moffat to the Northern Palace for a discussion. In conversation, Ho tried to reassure his visitor that his main objective was not Communism, but independence. As an inducement for U.S. support, he repeated his earlier offer of a U.S. naval base at Cam Ranh Bay. Moffat, however, had arrived without instructions on that point so, as he described it many years later in testimony before Congress, he "really couldn't say anything," and the conversation ended without any concrete result. Moffat did express his skepticism that the United States had any interest in Cam Ranh Bay and noted that it could not engage in diplomatic relations with Vietnam until its status had been decided in negotiations with the French.

After Moffat left for Indochina, the State Department had drawn up further instructions for him to evaluate the relative strength of Communist and non-Communist elements within the Vietnamese government. It sent a cable to Saigon indicating that the emergence in Hanoi of a government dominated by the Communists and oriented toward the Soviet Union would be the "least desirable eventuality." As it turned out, Moffat did not receive that cable until he was leaving Indochina, but in his report about his conversation with Ho Chi Minh, he did offer his own assessment on the current balance of forces in Hanoi. The Vietnamese government, he felt, was under control of the Communists and was probably in direct contact with both Moscow and the Chinese Communist Party. At the same time, he sensed a split between the relatively moderate and pragmatic elements around Ho Chi Minh and the hard-liners, like Vo Nguyen Giap, who bore a visceral hatred for the French. Moffat concluded that for the time being some sort of French presence was inevitable, not only as a means of limiting Soviet influence, but also to protect the region from a possible Chinese invasion. He therefore recommended U.S. support for a settlement before the prospects for a result satisfactory to the French deteriorated further.

Moffat's observation that the moderates and hard-liners within the government had severe differences was echoed in comments by other foreign observers in Hanoi. The French journalist Philippe Devillers also reported a division within the Vietminh leadership between Ho and more militant elements such as Giap and Hoang Quoc Viet, and Ho himself frequently appealed to French and other Western officials to support his efforts against his rivals. Skeptics derided such reports, claiming that Ho manipulated these rumors in order to pry concessions out of the French. Although the debate has not been resolved, available evidence suggests that while some members of the Party were clearly restive with their leader's willingness to reach a compromise, the nimble Ho Chi Minh adroitly used such differences to play on the fears of his adversaries. As for Moffat's remark about the likelihood of Soviet influence over the DRV, links between Moscow and the ICP had been virtually nonexistent since the beginning of World War II, and Ho and his colleagues were limited to learning about Soviet views only through their counterparts in the FCP.[66]

Concern over the alleged threat of communism in the region had suddenly emerged as a major force in U.S. foreign policy, as the civil war in China heated up. Like many Southeast Asian specialists, Moffat was increasingly concerned that the fear of communism was leading U.S. foreign policy away from its traditional support of national aspirations in the region, and he had voiced those concerns within the State Department. But, to Moffat's discomfiture, it was the fact that his report had referred to the Communist character of the government in Hanoi that had influence in Washington. In a circular sent to U.S. missions around the world on December 17, State reiterated Moffat's comments on the Communist character of the Vietnamese government and concluded that a French presence in the area was important, "not only as [an] antidote to Soviet influence, but to protect Vietnam and Southeast Asia from future Chinese imperialism."[67]

D'Argenlieu left for France on November 13 to seek additional forces for a possible preemptive campaign against Vietminh forces in the north, but as he discovered on his arrival in Paris, the French government was not yet ready to give up on a political solution. National elections had just returned a leftist majority and Georges Bidault was preparing to resign in favor of a government led by the Socialists. Bidault promised d'Argenlieu that reinforcements would eventually be made available, but he warned that Indochina could not be preserved by force alone. Further instructions, he said, must await the formation of a new government. To convey its message, Paris turned once again to Jean Sainteny as one of the few French officials who might still be able to avert the drift toward war. Appointed governor with plenipotentiary powers to replace General Morlière, Sainteny left Paris for Cochin China on November 23, a few hours after the Haiphong incident. After a few days in Saigon (at the request of Valluy, who wanted to spare him from responsibility for Haiphong), he arrived in Hanoi on December 2. In his pocket were instructions from d'Argenlieu, who was still in Paris:

> Military honor having been saved, French prestige restored and enhanced, it would be a mistaken policy to impose unduly harsh conditions.
>
> Henceforth it is essential not to go too far in forcing Ho Chi Minh and his government to take desperate measures. For this reason

I consider as premature and inopportune your installation in the palace of the general government, for it will be interpreted as a deliberate provocation signifying the return to forceful methods.

Those instructions had been reinforced by Valluy, who urged Sainteny to do his best to strengthen moderate forces to create conditions for negotiations. Perhaps, Valluy remarked, Ho did not want war.

Due to illness, Ho Chi Minh had not met Sainteny at the airport, but received him the following day. New French troops had just arrived in Da Nang harbor in contradiction to the agreement between France and Vietnam, thus arousing suspicions that the French were planning an attack. But Ho had been informed about the changing political situation in France by Hoang Minh Giam, who advised him to temporize in order to await the formation of a new government there. According to Sainteny, he and Ho did not engage in serious discussions, but limited themselves to discussing the Ho's health and his trip home from Paris. Sainteny had no further communication from Ho for the next several days, leading him to wonder whether the president still retained freedom of action in determining his government's policy. During this interval, Sainteny received no further instructions from Paris, and thus could not have engaged in serious negotiations even had Ho Chi Minh wanted him to. While Sainteny was waiting, a new government under the Socialist Party leader Léon Blum took office.[68]

One subject that Ho and Sainteny did apparently discuss was the composition of the new Vietnamese government. Sainteny demanded the removal of radicals from the cabinet, and he recorded his impression that Ho himself wanted to avoid a rupture. But, he said, it was hard to say how much influence Ho Chi Minh still wielded over his own colleagues. Sainteny told O'Sullivan that Paris had no objection to Ho's remaining in office, but that unless the radical elements resigned, the French were prepared to engage in a "police action" to get them out. But Sainteny admitted that the prospects of separating Ho from militants in the Party were slim. He expressed the hope that any French police action could be a rapid success, but O'Sullivan was skeptical, reporting to Washington that "Action to rid country [of] Vietminh will, I fear, greatly exceed police work and will take much longer than short time Sainteny foresees."[69]

In mid-December, Ho Chi Minh sent a message to Prime Minister Blum in which he proposed concrete ideas to reduce the growing tensions between the two countries. But Ho and his colleagues were by no means counting on a political solution. He had already consulted with Vo Nguyen Giap and other military leaders on the need to make preparations for war. In October, the ICP Central Committee, now operating entirely in secret, had established a new Central Military Committee to provide Party leadership over the armed forces. Party commissars were assigned to key positions in the army and Party committees were established in the various military zones. The entire operation was placed under the command of a promising officer named Van Tien Dung, later to be renowned as the commander of the final offensive on Saigon in the spring of 1975.

During the autumn, military preparations intensified. The army, now renamed the Vietnamese People's Army, was expanded. According to French sources, by the end of the summer the Vietminh had organized thirty-five infantry and three artillery regiments, with a total force of about 60,000 troops, in addition to 12,000 more fighting in Cochin China. Membership in the local militia and guerrilla units had reached almost one million. Villages under government control throughout the country were instructed to make preparations for self-defense as "combat villages." Weapons, however, were still in short supply (according to a French source, the Vietnamese had about 35,000 rifles, 1,000 automatic weapons, and 55 cannons), so a major effort was undertaken to establish weapons plants in secure areas of the Viet Bac. Informed by Vo Nguyen Giap that Hanoi could be held for only about a month, Ho ordered preparations for a new base area headquarters at Tan Trao, site of the jump-off point for the August Revolution.[70]

After the Haiphong incident, the situation became even more urgent, and a special Party committee began to plan for the defense of Hanoi, in order to allow time for the evacuation of the government into the nearby mountains. There were a few government troops at the Northern Palace and at an army camp nearby, but most of the Vietnamese military strength in the region was located in the outskirts of the capital. To compensate, there were nearly 10,000 combat militia and youth assault teams in the city itself. Composed of the most enthusiastic young supporters of the revolution, these groups were armed mainly with homemade weapons and wore square badges with a gold star in the middle. Arrayed against them as potential adversaries were several thousand French Legionnaires, mostly stationed in the Citadel; the rest were scattered at other locations, such as the Don Thuy Hospital, the former Governor-General's Palace, the railway station, the Bank of Indochina, the Paul Doumer Bridge, and, on the eastern side of the river, Gia Lam Airport.

As the defense of the city got under way (the Vietminh National Committee called for such preparations daily in the newspaper *Cuu Quoc*), government offices were surreptitiously transferred one by one to prepared locations outside the city. Inside the capital, government troops began to erect barricades, and French troops responded by strengthening their own defenses. On December 6, Ho Chi Minh appealed publicly to the French to withdraw their own troops to positions they held before November 20, but he received no answer. In an interview with a French journalist the following day, he insisted that the Vietnamese government hoped to avoid war, which could impose terrible suffering on both countries. "But if war is imposed on us," he said, "we will fight rather than renounce our liberties."[71]

By this time, however, General Valluy had concluded that Ho Chi Minh had no intention of removing radical elements from his government, and he appealed to Paris for a green light to take firm action as soon as reinforcements arrived, warning that delay beyond the end of the year could be disastrous for French fortunes in Indochina. But the new prime minister, Léon Blum, was reluctant to take military action; on December 12 he announced his intention to resolve the Indochina dispute in ways that would grant Vietnamese independence. Three days later, Ho Chi Minh gave Sainteny a message for the new French leader, with concrete suggestions on how to resolve the dispute. Sainteny sent it in a telegram to Saigon, requesting it to be forwarded to Paris.[72]

Whether Vietnamese leaders held out any hope that the formation of a Socialist government in Paris could lead to a political settlement is uncertain. In his own account, Vo Nguyen Giap declared categorically that although some of Blum's pronouncements were progressive in nature, he was actually a tool of the United States and of French business interests, and a dedicated opponent of the FCP. As if to confirm Giap's suspicions, Blum refused to select any Communists for his new cabinet, while reconfirming Thierry d'Argenlieu as high commissioner for Indochina. On the other hand, a cabinet meeting called to discuss d'Argenlieu's request for reinforcements and immediate military action against the Vietnamese reached no decision on either matter, and Bidault warned Valluy in a private message that he should not count on reinforcements and should try to deal with the situation without recourse to violence.

Valluy, who shared d'Argenlieu's determination to maintain a French presence in Indochina, had decided that it was necessary to provoke a break with Hanoi in order to initiate hostilities and present Paris with a fait accompli. On December 16, he ordered General Morlière (who continued to exercise military functions in North Vietnam after the return of Sainteny) to destroy the barricades erected by Vietminh units in the city. When Ho Chi Minh's message for Blum arrived in Saigon, Valluy appended his own acid commentary, warning that it would be dangerous to postpone military action until the new year. The cable did not arrive in Paris until the nineteenth. By then it was too late.[73]

On December 17, French armored cars ventured into the streets of Hanoi to demolish fieldworks erected by Vietminh units in the previous days, while Legionnaires lined the streets from the Citadel to the Paul Doumer Bridge, en route to the airport. The Vietnamese did not react, so the following morning the French issued an ultimatum that no further obstructions should be erected on the streets of the city. A second ultimatum issued that afternoon declared that, beginning on the twentieth, French military units would take charge of public security throughout the capital. In response, that evening Vietnamese units began to close all routes into the city from the outskirts. The next morning, a third ultimatum from the French demanded that the Vietnamese government cease all preparations for war, disband all militia units, and hand over security in the capital region to the French.

To the Vietnamese, the situation was ominously reminiscent of events the previous month, when Colonel Dèbes had issued similar demands before the bombing of Haiphong. On the morning of December 18, Ho Chi Minh issued a directive to launch preparations for an attack on French installations the following day. At the same time, fearful that his message might not have reached Prime Minister Blum, he sent a telegram directly to Paris. The next morning, he wrote a short letter to Jean Sainteny, and gave it to his foreign policy adviser, Hoang Minh Giam, to transmit: "The situation has become more tense these last few days. This is very regrettable. Pending the decision from Paris, I hope that you, together with Mr. Giam, will find a solution in order to improve the present atmosphere."[74]

Given the almost laconic tone of the letter, it seems highly doubtful that Ho Chi Minh expected a useful response. In fact, Sainteny had just sent Ho Chi Minh a more lengthy message the same morning, complaining about Vietnamese provocations that had led to the death or wounding of several French civilians and demanding that the perpetrators be immediately punished. Sainteny, who had apparently been apprised of Valluy's decision to provoke a conflict, refused to see Giam, saying that he would receive him the following morning.[75]

Informed by his secretary, Vu Ky, that Sainteny had declined to meet

Hoang Minh Giam, Ho drafted a directive calling for a meeting of the Party Standing Committee. Shortly after, Truong Chinh, Le Duc Tho, and Vo Nguyen Giap met with Ho Chi Minh, who declared that in present circumstances, it was impossible to make further concessions. His colleagues agreed on the necessity to mobilize the entire country to wage a war of protracted resistance against the French. Truong Chinh was assigned responsibility to draft a declaration calling for a war of "national resistance" (*toan dien khang chien*), while Giap was instructed to prepare an order to initiate hostilities. The group then examined an appeal to the populace that Ho Chi Minh had drafted that afternoon and suggested a few changes in wording. After setting a time for the attack at eight that evening, the meeting adjourned.[76]

Early the same evening, December 19, Jean Sainteny prepared to leave his office for his private residence. Like everyone else in the city, he was aware of the rising tensions, and expected hostilities to break out between the two sides at any moment. An agent had warned him that a Vietnamese attack was imminent. But when the clock at the Yersin Hospital struck eight, he remarked to a colleague, "Apparently it's not for tonight. I'm going home." Just as Sainteny entered his car, he heard a muffled explosion, and the streets were immediately plunged into darkness. Sainteny hurried to his home and climbed into an armored car that General Morlière had dispatched to transport him to the Citadel. En route, however, the vehicle struck a mine, and Sainteny was badly wounded. For the next two hours, he lay bleeding on the street, surrounded by dead and dying comrades.[77]

According to their plan, the Vietnamese had opened their campaign with a surprise attack on the municipal power station. Then militia units launched assaults on French installations throughout the city, while terrorist squads roamed through the European section attacking civilians. Giap had three divisions of regular forces near the race course in the suburbs southwest of the city and beside Le Grand Lac (now West Lake), but he decided not to use them just yet.

The French were taken by surprise by the scale of the attacks, but by late evening French troops had begun to establish their control over the central portions of Hanoi. One French unit attacked the Northern Palace, and Ho Chi Minh was reportedly barely able to escape. The First Indochina War had begun.

The events that took place in Hanoi on December 19 aroused outrage in France, where many viewed it as an unprovoked Vietnamese attack on French installations and civilians in Indochina. But a closer look at the evidence suggests that the French role in precipitating the conflict was substantial. Although the government in Paris had been reluctant to take decisive measures that might have led to war, French representatives in Indochina took matters into their own hands. General Valluy's decision to provoke a rupture was based at least partly on his assessment that Ho Chi Minh could not, or would not, take action to control radical elements in his government. If so, he calculated, war was inevitable and it was essential to act before French military capabilities in the region began to weaken. His ultimatum on December 17 demanding that the DRV turn over all security functions in the city to the French was obviously calculated to provoke a response.

Was Ho Chi Minh sincere in his effort to avoid conflict, or were his maneuvers designed simply to postpone the day of reckoning to enable Hanoi to make adequate preparations for a military struggle? It is not necessary to choose between these alternatives. As a disciple of the fourth-century Chinese military strategist Sun Tzu, Ho was convinced that the best victory was the one that could be won without the use of military force. To obtain an objective without violence, among the most effective methods were (again according to Sun Tzu) the use of diplomacy and propaganda techniques to divide the enemy and reduce his capabilities. By December 19, Ho and his colleagues had concluded that further compromise was impossible. It had become necessary to decide the issue on the battlefield.[78]

XII | THE TIGER AND THE ELEPHANT

In his interview with the *New York Times* correspondent David Schoenbrun during the summer of 1946, Ho Chi Minh had warned that if full-scale conflict broke out between the Vietnamese and the French, the Vietminh would crouch in the jungle like a tiger and then come out of its lair at night to tear the French elephant to pieces. That, he said, is what would characterize the war of Indochina.

Ho was as good as his word. As the French engaged in mopping-up operations in Hanoi and other major industrial centers in northern and central Vietnam, the old revolutionary and his colleagues abandoned their temporary headquarters in the grottoes of Ha Dong province, a few miles south of the capital, and took refuge at their old mountain base area at Tan Trao, in the heart of the Viet Bac, where they prepared for a lengthy conflict. With the encouragement of Ho Chi Minh, the Vietnamese had appropriated elements of the Chinese model of people's war into their own strategy as early as 1941. On December 22, only three days after the opening of hostilities in the capital, the Vietnamese government issued a public statement announcing that the coming conflict would take place in three stages. The announcement forecast a scenario straight out of the military doctrine of Mao Zedong. During the first stage, Vietnamese forces would remain on the defensive in order to build up their strength in their mountain redoubt; in the second, as the strength of the two sides became roughly equivalent, the revolutionary forces would begin to emerge from their lair for sudden attacks on exposed enemy installations; and the third phase would be a general offensive, when the Vietminh would launch the final assault to drive the enemy forces into the sea.[1]

Even as they withdrew, however, the Vietnamese sent a clear signal to the French that the struggle would be a bitter one. As government officials abandoned Hanoi and embarked on the route through the flatlands delta to the northwest, militia units remained entrenched in the narrow streets of the picturesque Chinese sector, home of more than thirty thousand residents of the city. Here they fiercely resisted French efforts to evict them. General Valluy proposed an aerial attack to wipe out the defenders, but Morlière opted instead for a street-by-street advance that would restore French control over the sector without incurring the risk of massive physical destruction. The operation was painstakingly slow and costly in terms of French casualties. Not until mid-January 1947 did French troops finally reach the market on the northern edge of the Chinese sector, while Vietminh units, accompanied by much of the local populace, abandoned the area and fled north across the Red River. Even as the troops left the city, Vietminh supporters scratched the words "We shall return" with charcoal or loose bricks on the walls of the old Citadel.[2]

In his account of the exodus, U.S. Consul O'Sullivan reported to Washington that the Vietnamese had fought with "unforeseen courage and stubbornness" reminiscent of the Japanese in the Pacific War. He estimated Vietnamese casualties in the hundreds. About one hundred French soldiers were listed as dead, and about forty-five European civilians lost their lives, with two hundred still missing. After clearing the suburbs, French troops began to move into the countryside, where they found that the Vietnamese had followed a scorched-earth approach to reduce the enemy's access to provisions. In other parts of the country, Vietminh militia units waged a delaying action in urban areas, while main-force units scattered to base areas in the countryside.

But Ho Chi Minh was apparently not yet ready to give up the search for a peaceful settlement. On the very day of the beginning of hostilities, Vietminh tracts appeared on the streets of Hanoi, informing "the people of France" of the willingness of his government to live peacefully within the French Union and blaming the outbreak of war on "reactionary colonialists who dishonor the name of France and who seek to separate us in provoking war." If France would only recognize Vietnamese independence and national unity, the tracts declared, an attitude of cooperation and mutual understanding between the two peoples could be immediately restored. The following day, Vietminh radio began to launch periodic appeals for a renewal of negotiations. On December 23, Ho wrote Marius Moutet, the minister of overseas territories, and General Henri Leclerc, proposing a meeting of representatives of the two sides. Moutet and Leclerc had just left Paris on a fact-finding mission to Indochina at the request of the new Blum government. A few days later, Ho formally proposed a cease-fire and the holding of a new peace conference in Paris within the framework of the Ho-Sainteny agreement of the previous March.[3]

But the French were not quite so eager to bring the hostilities to a close. In an address to the National Assembly on December 23, Prime Minister Léon Blum echoed the rising spirit of patriotism that affected all political factions in France in the aftermath of the Vietnamese attack on Hanoi: "We have been faced," he declared, "with the task of responding to violence. I declare that those who are fighting there, that French residents living in Indochina, and that friendly peoples can count without reserve on the vigilance and the resolution of the government." In closing, Blum left the door open to a peaceful settlement, affirming that once order had been restored, he would act "to take up again with loyalty the interrupted task, that is to say the organization of a free Vietnam in an Indochinese Union freely associated with the French Union. First of all, however, order must be restored."[4]

Marius Moutet was described by the French newspaper *Le Populaire* as "a messenger for peace." But although Moutet was well-known as a sympathetic observer of the Vietnamese struggle for independence, he too shared the common sense of French outrage at the surprise attack in Hanoi. Shortly after his arrival in Saigon on Christmas Day, he declared to the press that "before any negotiations, it is necessary today to achieve a military decision. I regret it, but one cannot commit with impunity such follies as those committed by the Vietminh." To press home his point, Moutet made no effort to contact his old socialist colleague Ho Chi Minh prior to his return to France in early January and spent much of his time in discussions with French officials in Laos and Cambodia. For his part, Ho Chi Minh had sent Moutet a letter on January 3 with a set of proposals for instituting a cease-fire based on antebellum conditions and a resumption of negotiations, but the package was seized by French colonial authorities before it reached the Minister and was returned.[5]

General Leclerc shared Moutet's conviction that a strong military response to the Vietminh attack was necessary prior to the opening of peace talks. But Leclerc was also convinced that the final solution to the crisis must be a political one, and Moutet's refusal to meet with Ho troubled him. On his departure from Indochina on January 9, he noted: "There are too many people here who imagine that a bridge between Vietnam and France can be built on a mound of cadavers." In his own report to the government in Paris, Leclerc noted that "the complex solution, which will probably not be realized for some time to come, cannot be but political." France, he concluded, could not use the force of arms to subdue a nation of 24 million inhabitants who are motivated by a strong sense of national identity. To Leclerc, the crucial question was how to replace the existing form of nationalism led by the Vietminh with a less virulent form represented by more moderate political parties. In the meantime, the stronger the French military position on the battlefield, the better the ultimate solution.[6]

Because Leclerc's views on the situation corresponded generally with Léon Blum's own, when the general arrived back in France in mid-January, the prime minister sounded him out on an offer to return to Indochina to serve as commander in chief and high commissioner, replacing Thierry d'Argenlieu, whose hard-line views were now widely viewed as having contributed to the impasse. But before Leclerc could make his decision, Blum was replaced in office by his fellow Socialist Paul Ramadier. Ramadier subscribed to the existing policy of restoring order by force, while making it clear that he was willing to consider the ultimate unification of the three regions of Vietnam into a single state within the French Union. But when the new prime minister would not commit himself to beefing up the strength of French forces in Indochina, Leclerc—on the advice of General de Gaulle—decided to decline the offer of the high commissionership. To fill the position, Ramadier turned to Emile Bollaert, a politician of liberal views and high repute who did not belong to any of the major factions in the National Assembly. Bollaert was described by one U.S. diplomat as "able and energetic but relatively unknown."[7]

Bollaert left for Indochina in early March. On his arrival in Saigon, he was immediately faced with a challenge from within his own camp. Under d'Argenlieu's sponsorship, a move was under way in colonial circles in Saigon to bypass the Vietminh and strike a deal with Bao Dai, the former emperor, who was currently in Hong Kong. Indolent and pleasure-seeking in nature, Bao Dai had stopped using the citizen's name Vinh Thuy, temporarily lost his zeal for national affairs, and was indulging in the joys of women and the gaming tables. Although the first French contacts with the now corpulent ex-emperor were fruitless, the prospect of a deal with him was gaining supporters, in both France and Indochina. For Bollaert, however, the plan posed a severe dilemma. The Vietminh still had considerable popularity in Vietnam, where Ho Chi Minh was widely respected as a nationalist leader. Before his departure from Paris, Leclerc had advised him to "negotiate at all costs." Many within Bollaert's entourage favored talks with the Vietminh, including his *chef de cabinet* Pierre Messmer and his personal adviser, the respected Indochina scholar Paul Mus. But there were already more than one thousand French troops dead or missing, and sentiment within the French community in Indochina was by now adamantly opposed to a deal with the Vietminh. Bao Dai was the only visible alternative, but could he serve as an alternative to the popular Ho Chi Minh? While the ex-emperor had some support among traditionalists, many Vietnamese were contemptuous of him because of his self-indulgent lifestyle. Others doubted his capacity to unite the chronically fractious nationalist groups, who were badly split on several key political issues.

Ho Chi Minh was still trying to preserve his fragile contacts with the French. On April 23, the non-Communist Hoang Minh Giam, who in March had been renamed DRV minister of foreign affairs, transmitted a message from Ho to Bollaert proposing an immediate cease-fire and the reopening of negotiations to achieve a peaceful settlement of the conflict. Suspicious of the enemy's intentions and reassured by his advisers that the military situation was now well in hand, Bollaert countered with a set of conditions that demanded the virtual surrender of Vietminh forces prior to the restoration of peace. To convey that message, he turned to Paul Mus, who had once known Ho Chi Minh. On the evening of May 12, Mus held secret meetings, first with Hoang Minh Giam at a location near Hanoi and then with Ho at a house in the provincial capital of Thai Nguyen. Ho listened politely to his visitor, but flatly rejected the French demands. "In the French Union there is no place for cowards," he remarked. "If I accepted these terms, I would be one."[8]

The contemptuous French reply to the Vietnamese proposal for peace talks was undoubtedly a disappointment to Ho Chi Minh, who had continued to express the hope that the French would ultimately reconcile themselves to the loss of their Indochinese colonies. For the moment, however, there was no alternative to the military option. Late that month, he launched a new appeal for national resistance, declaring that the French had posed unacceptable conditions for peace.

But Ho continued to pursue the possibility of an international solution to the problem. Admittedly, the climate of growing ideological hostility between the two global power blocs was not auspicious, and Moscow was still displaying little interest in the struggle in far-off Indochina. Still, there remained the chance that the United States might be induced to play a useful role in resolving the conflict. Indeed, the Truman administration had been observing French actions since the reopening of hostilities in Indochina with some discomfort (although Ho and his colleagues had no reason to be aware of this). A few days after the outbreak of fighting in Hanoi, Under Secretary of State Dean Acheson called French Ambassador Henri Bonnet to the State Department and warned him that the situation in Indochina was inflammatory and, in Washington's view, could not be resolved by force. Acheson assured Bonnet that the United States did not wish to interfere, but then offered Washington's good offices in reaching a solution. Paris bluntly rejected the offer, asserting that it would restore order before establishing contacts with the Vietnamese.

A few weeks later, General George C. Marshall, just returned from China, replaced James Byrnes as secretary of state. Since December 1945, Marshall had made periodic visits to Chongqing seeking to cobble together a peace settlement between the Nationalists and the CCP that would result in a coalition government under Chiang Kai-shek. Despite such efforts, however, civil war broke out at the end of 1946. After reviewing the situation in Indochina, Marshall sent a cable to U.S. Ambassador Caffery in Paris—a message that, as the first formal expression of Washington's views on the subject since the beginning of the Franco-Vietminh conflict, was a masterpiece of ambiguity. The United States has formally recognized French sovereignty in Indochina, Marshall pointed out, and does not wish to interfere in the area. At the same time, he added, "we cannot shut our eyes to fact that there are two sides [to] this problem and that our reports indicate both a lack [of] French understanding of other side (more in Saigon than in Paris) and continuing existence [of a] dangerous, outmoded colonial outlook and methods in area."

But Marshall immediately undermined the force of his own point by recognizing the nature of the French dilemma: "We do not lose sight [of the] fact that Ho Chi Minh has direct Communist connections and it should be obvious that we are not interested in seeing colonial empires and administrations supplanted by philosophy and political organizations emanating from and controlled by Kremlin." In the end, Marshall had no solution to offer, and contented himself with the suggestion that the French should keep the negotiations track open and "be generous" in seeking a solution. Marshall's patently agonizing indecision on how to approach the Indochina tangle set a tone that would last until Truman left office.[9]

At the end of February, Marshall instructed Consul James O'Sullivan in Hanoi to establish contact with Vietnamese leaders should the opportunity arise. It was not long in coming. In April, Pham Ngoc Thach, the onetime head of the Vanguard Youth in Saigon who had recently been named a deputy minister in Ho Chi Minh's government, contacted several American businessmen living in Thailand, as well as Lieutenant Colonel William Law, the assistant military attaché at the U.S. Embassy in Bangkok. After holding informal talks with Colonel Law, Thach agreed to respond to a series of questions posed in writing by Law and by Edwin F. Stanton, the American ambassador. In his reply, Thach emphasized the broad and nonpartisan character of the Vietnamese government, and its commitment to national goals rather than to those of social revolution. Its economic program, he insisted, would "favor the development of capitalist autonomy and call on foreign capital for the reconstruction of the country." Shortly after, Thach submitted an appeal to representatives of the U.S. business community in Thailand, offering economic concessions in return for various types of agricultural and industrial equipment as well as rehabilitation loans. In the absence of a peace settlement, Thach warned that the Vietnamese were prepared to wage a guerrilla war for six years. At about the same time, Ho gave an interview to an American reporter in which he denied that his government was inspired by Marxist principles and wondered aloud why a solution similar to that which had been achieved in the Philippines and India was not possible in Indochina.[10]

Initially, the Vietnamese gesture aroused a modicum of interest among State Department officials in Washington, who had already taken note of the appointment of the moderate Hoang Minh Giam as DRV foreign minister in March. In his own comments to Washington, Ambassador Stanton remarked that Pham Ngoc Thach—who had been viewed favorably by U.S. officials in Saigon in late 1945—was "a man of intelligence and very considerable energy." From Hanoi, O'Sullivan suggested that he meet directly with Thach in Bangkok. Although O'Sullivan voiced reservations about Ho—describing him as "a very shifty character"—he argued that an informal conversation with Thach might at least provide useful information on the nature of the Vietnamese government. Marshall cabled his approval, adding his hope that a meeting with Thach might reveal the extent of Communist control over the Vietnamese government and "the degree of subservience to Moscow to be expected of Communist leaders." But the meeting never took place. On May 7, Stanton informed the department that Thach had suddenly left Bangkok. Two days later, Marshall instructed O'Sullivan to abandon his plans to visit Bangkok, citing Thach's departure and U.S. concerns over a possible French reaction to the proposed meeting.

But the incident was not entirely at an end. On May 8, a message from Hoang Minh Giam formally appealed to the United States for diplomatic recognition of his government, declaring that such a move "would increase United States prestige and influence . . . and establish peace in Southeast Asia." Pham Ngoc Thach, now in Hanoi, followed up with a second message, asking for political, economic, and cultural assistance and requesting that Washington mediate the Franco-Vietminh conflict in order to bring about a settlement. When these new initiatives came to the attention of Secretary Marshall, he asked his diplomats in Paris, Saigon, and Hanoi for their evaluation of the Vietnamese government and the extent of Communist influence over its leadership. What, he asked, are Ho's real views? How much of a role would alleged militants like Truong Chinh and Hoang Quoc Viet have in an independent Vietnamese regime? What did non-Communist nationalists think of the Vietminh? Did they understand its Communist orientation? Could they cope with the Communists? Finally, could the DRV be persuaded to grant "reasonably free political expression"?

In his reply, O'Sullivan was cautious, asserting that although Communists had considerable influence in the government, it was not necessarily sufficient to put the country squarely in the Soviet camp, "although there would be a pull in that direction." He alluded to Ho Chi Minh's reluctance to admit he was really Nguyen Ai Quoc as an indication that Ho realized that he must deal with the West. O'Sullivan concluded that Ho was trying to obtain aid wherever he could get it and would tend to orient his policies toward whatever source the assistance came from.

Other replies were less sanguine. Charles Reed, O'Sullivan's counterpart in Saigon, described Ho as "a wily opportunist" who "could bring about the evolution of a Communist state even if the majority of the Vietnamese are not particularly interested in the Communist message." From Paris, Ambassador Jefferson Caffery weighed in with his own views. Although the Vietnamese people in general were not sympathetic to the Communists, he intoned, from Ho's past career "there can be little doubt but that he maintains close connections in Communist circles."[11]

The rejection of French peace terms by the Vietminh may have disappointed Bollaert, who was apparently sincere in his desire for a political settlement of the conflict, but it did not deter him from pursuing other options. French Minister of War Paul Coste-Floret, who had just completed an inspection tour of Indochina, declared, "There is no more military problem in Indochina. The success of our arms is complete." With the war situation apparently in hand, Bollaert now began to view the Vietminh not as the sole representative of the Vietnamese people, but as merely one among many groups that might be contacted in the search for peace. Bollaert's new approach was facilitated by the changing political scene in France, where the Communist Party was no longer in the governing coalition. Prime Minister Ramadier now needed moderate and conservative support to survive in office. With a political solution at least temporarily discredited, eyes now turned to General Valluy in Indochina, who had lost any lingering illusions about Ho Chi Minh's desire for peace and was convinced that the only solution to the problem was a military one.

In estimating that the military situation was favorable to the French, Coste-Floret was not entirely off the mark. In fact, Vietnamese efforts to maintain cohesion and strength in the opening stage of the war had been a disappointment, and Vietminh forces were frequently in a state of disarray as they faced the French. In some cases, main-force units had been overused or were overly aggressive, leading to heavy casualties. In others, Vietminh commanders displayed a poor grasp of the tactics of guerrilla war, re-sulting in confusion and widespread troop desertion on the battlefield. Adding to the problem was a continuing lack of firepower. For the most part, Vietnamese units were limited to locally manufactured weapons, or to those captured from the Japanese or the French. Vietminh leaders also tended to overestimate the importance of support from the rural gentry, many of whom refused to declare their allegiance to the cause. And by failing to establish stringent regulations calling for rent reductions, they lost an opportunity to mobilize support from poor peasants, who often dragged their feet when called upon to serve in the war effort.[12]

Confident in the ultimate success of French forces on the battlefield, General Valluy now proposed an assault on the Vietminh redoubt in the Viet Bac to seize Ho Chi Minh and disperse the rebel forces. Then and only then, in Valluy's view, would negotiations be appropriate. In the meantime, a concerted political offensive was under way to reduce pop-ular support for the Vietminh and dampen the ardor of those Vietnamese who wanted to drive the French out of Indochina.

One of the problems with Valluy's approach was that it would re-quire an increase in French force levels in Indochina to over 100,000 troops. So far, there was little public opposition in France to the conflict in Indochina, which must have seemed to most observers like a minor fracas in a far-off corner of the world. The French government, however, was temporarily preoccupied with a bitter anticolonial revolt on the is-land of Madagascar and was willing to give Valluy only a portion of what he had requested. Valluy was thus forced to draw up his plans with less than the minimum number of troops he considered necessary.

One of the keys to Valluy's strategy was to eliminate Vietminh activities in Cochin China. To achieve his objective, he assigned nearly half of the French Expeditionary Force (FEF) to that area. Opposing them would be about 18,000 Vietminh regulars under the command of Nguyen Binh. Throughout Indochina, the DRV now deployed nearly 60,000 troops, not counting an undetermined number of local militia and guerrillas. Weak in firepower but mobile in operation and possessing considerable local support, Vietminh battalions were now increasingly able to evade French sweep operations and engage the enemy at spots of their own choosing. The only real success for the French during the summer of 1947 was a political one, as Nguyen Binh's harsh tactics alienated many of his compatriots in Cochin China and drove the leadership of both religious sects—the Cao Dai and the Hoa Hao—into the arms of the French.[13]

In the meantime, Bollaert wanted to launch a new peace offensive. Ho Chi Minh had sent a signal of his own that August, dropping reputed hard-liners like the veteran war organizer Ton Duc Thang and Vo Nguyen Giap from the ministries of interior and national defense and replacing them with moderates. But Valluy vigorously disagreed with the timing of Bollaert's effort, and the two were recalled to Paris for consultations. The result was a compromise. In a speech given near Hanoi in September, Bollaert offered a united Vietnam within the French Union, but made no mention of full independence. He did not refer by name to his chief adversary and appealed instead to "all groups of Vietnamese." According to U.S. observers, many French residents in Indochina were pleased with the speech, but the Vietnamese were "stunned." On September 15, Hoang Minh Giam presented his government's response: No liberty without full independence. Three days later, Bao Dai publicly accepted a French offer to negotiate on behalf of his people. But he too insisted that he would accept nothing less than independence and national unity. A hastily formed National United Front composed of representatives of various non-Communist nationalist groups met in Hong Kong and rejected Bollaert's conditions. The Saigon rumor mill buzzed with unconfirmed reports of secret contacts between Bao Dai and Ho Chi Minh.

On October 7, 1947, the long-awaited French offensive into the Viet Bac was launched. Because he was forced to operate with fewer troops than he had anticipated, Valluy scaled down his plans. Instead of encircling the entire area and then attacking from the north as well as the south, he opted for a smaller operation aimed at seizing the heart of the Vietminh redoubt and then consolidating French control over the Red River valley from Hanoi to the border at Lao Cai. General Raoul Salan, who had been placed in charge of the operation, predicted that it would take three weeks to strike off the head of the Vietminh.

Operation Léa, as the campaign was labeled, opened with a parachute drop at Bac Can, on the northern edge of the Vietminh base zone. The area was heavily defended, with mines, barricades, and traps supplementing the tortuous mountain topography. Valluy had hoped to seize the Vietminh command post in the first stage of the operation, and then envelop the area in a pincers movement, with armored units marching westward into the area from Lang Son, while another group would move in from the north. The two groups were to make their juncture at Bac Can.

French troops advanced rapidly and soon located the Vietminh headquarters, but they were unable to capture Ho Chi Minh, who was chairing a meeting at his command post at the time of the attack. As soon as they learned that the French paratroops were so close, Ho, members of the Central Committee, and the general staff departed immediately. With Chu Van Tan, the ethnic Nung in the group, serving as guide, they marched all day over paths slippery with rain, each carrying over his shoulder a small satchel for clothes and necessities, and spent the night in a small corner of the forest. They departed the next morning to find a new headquarters. According to the scholar Bernard Fall, the attackers found burning cigarette butts and Ho Chi Minh's mail ready for signature on a table in the hut.

During the next few days, French units tried to eliminate any further resistance in the area, but their sweeps did not result in much direct contact with the Vietminh, who had faded quietly into the jungle and then began to harass French forces at locations of their own choosing. Still, Salan reported to his superiors that the operation had been a success, since the main route to China via Cao Bang on the northern border (the last remaining Vietminh contact with the outside world) was severed. Ho Chi Minh was now totally isolated. All that remained, the general averred, were "isolated bands of varying levels of importance, and susceptible to simple police operations." The Vietminh redoubt, he declared, had practically ceased to exist.[14]

Seldom in the annals of the Indochinese conflict has a prediction been so wrong, for in actuality the war was just beginning. Nevertheless, there is no doubt that Operation Léa had resulted in at least a temporary setback for the Vietminh, who were forced to dissolve their main-force units and divide them into armed propaganda units similar to those formed on the eve of the August Revolution. During the next few months, Vietnamese leaders made intensive efforts to prepare for the long road ahead. Vietminh commanders abandoned their unsuccessful efforts to engage in conventional tactics and embraced the techniques of guerrilla warfare. To centralize leadership at the local level, committees of resistance and administration (CRAs) were established in every village controlled by the resistance forces. Each village was given the responsibility not only to provide for its own defense, but also to furnish promising recruits for the guerrilla forces under central command.

With his return to the Viet Bac in late December 1946, Ho Chi Minh resumed the life that had appeared to come to an end with his election as president during the August Revolution of 1945. He arrived at the old base area with an entourage of eight men, comprising his personal bodyguard and those responsible for liaison with other units and for food preparation. The group erected a long hut built of bamboo and thatch that was divided into two rooms. One room was assigned for Ho's personal use, while the other served as dining hall, meeting room, and dormitory for his colleagues. To guard against wild animals, they obtained a shepherd dog, but it was soon killed and eaten by a tiger.

Ho and his companions led a simple life. Their meals consisted of a little rice garnished with sautéed wild vegetables. On occasion, they were able to supplement their meager fare with small chunks of salted meat, thinly sliced and served with peppers. Ho laughingly described it as "*conserves du Vietminh*." Sometimes food was short, and all suffered from hunger. Eventually the group began to grow its own food, planting vegetables on the more level plots of ground and manioc along the mountain slopes. By then, Ho had taken up lodging in a separate two-storied house. During the day he worked on the ground floor, but at night he slept on the upper floor as protection against wild beasts and the humidity. His bedding consisted solely of a mosquito net and his clothing. When the group was compelled to move (by the end of the decade, Ho would live in at least twenty different houses as he continually escaped detection by the French), they were able to pack up and leave in minutes. Ho carried a few books and documents in a small bag, while his companions took charge of his typewriter.

Whenever possible, Ho Chi Minh continued to perform his physical exercises, both morning and evening. He enjoyed volleyball and served with a sure hand, although his range was limited. When the opposing team fell behind, players often took advantage of his limited mobility and dunked the ball just over the net, at which time Ho laughingly cried, "You really got me there!" When they were forced to cross a river or a stream, the group stayed near him, especially if the current was strong; nonetheless, he was generally able to keep up, and one deserter claimed to French interviewers that Ho Chi Minh had more capacity to endure hardship than most of his younger colleagues, many of whom suffered periodically from malaria or other debilitating illnesses. On one occasion Ho remarked, "I'm like an old propeller-driven plane, while you are all jets."[15]

Eventually, their living conditions began to improve. Around Ho Chi Minh's residence there were now not only flower beds and vegetable trellises, but also a more formal volleyball court, and a fixed parallel bar for exercises. Ho and his colleagues purchased musical instruments from neighbors in the base area, and occasionally invited these villagers to join them for an evening of entertainment. Ho lectured his visitors about the culture of the lowland peoples and sometimes provided them with medicines to cure their illnesses. But then, in the fall of 1947, Operation Léa forced Ho and his allies to move on.

After the fall offensive, the conflict settled into what one French military observer described as a "war of stagnation." Lacking the means to continue offensive operations, Valluy limited himself to more modest efforts in the delta. This respite provided the Vietminh with an opportunity to create a liberated zone in central Vietnam, an area characterized by poor soil and considerable revolutionary potential that stretched more than 200 miles from Faifo to Cape Varella, thus dividing the country virtually in two. In the south, the French were in better shape, since Vietminh units there were a considerable distance from headquarters and almost totally deprived of contacts with their colleagues. With Nguyen Binh's forces driven ever deeper into the swamps and the mountains, French units tried to isolate their enemy by vigorous pacification operations.

The Vietminh also encountered active opposition in the south from nationalist groups who were becoming increasingly active in seeking to provide a "third force" for non-Communists as an alternative between the Vietminh and the French. In these conditions, the failure of Operation Léa to bring a definitive end to the resistance turned the attention of many nationalists to the political arena, and to Bao Dai. In December, the former emperor met with Emile Bollaert on a French cruiser in the stunning visual surroundings of Ha Long Bay, the site of Ho Chi Minh's first encounter with Thierry d'Argenlieu. But the results of the talks were meager, as Bollaert refused to be specific on the powers that would be assigned to a future Vietnamese state. At the close of the meeting, Bao Dai reluctantly agreed to sign a joint communiqué, but he quickly disavowed the action under criticism from militant nationalists in the recently formed National United Front. In March 1948, Bao Dai met with representatives of the front in Hong Kong and agreed to form a provisional government led by General Nguyen Van Xuan, a native of the south who had adopted French citizenship, as a ploy to strengthen himself in future talks with the French. After some hesitation, Bollaert agreed to recognize Bao Dai's new provisional government as a negotiating partner.

In June, talks resumed at Ha Long Bay and eventually the two sides reached agreement on the formation of a new Associated State of Vietnam based on the principle of Vietnamese independence and unity within the French Union. However, the precise meaning of the word "independence" and the specific powers to be allotted to the projected new government remained unsettled. In addition, there was no clear indication as to how the formation of this new non-Communist government could help to bring an end to the conflict with Ho Chi Minh's DRV. A solution to the Indochina tangle seemed as far away as ever.

For the French, however, one of the key motives for engaging in negotiations with Bao Dai was to lure the United States into providing military and economic assistance in the war against the Vietminh. Attitudes in Washington were indeed moving in a favorable direction, from Paris's point of view. Although the Truman administration had been exasperated at the French failure to solve the Indochinese problem, it was becoming increasingly concerned at the growing threat of communism in Asia, a concern that reflected not only Communist victories over Nationalist troops in north China but also deteriorating relations with Moscow. In the summer of 1948, Secretary of State George Marshall instructed U.S. diplomatic officials in Asia that nothing should be left undone in the effort to strengthen "truly nationalist groups" in Indochina at the expense of the Communists.

Although U.S. officials had little faith in Bao Dai (most viewed him as a playboy who lacked the stomach for political confrontation), they welcomed the signing of the Ha Long Bay agreement as a "forward step." When negotiations lagged, they warned Paris that it faced a grim choice between granting true unity and independence to the Vietnamese people within the French Union or losing Indochina altogether. Should France carry through on its tentative commitments, Washington intimated that it might reconsider its existing policy of withholding direct economic assistance to the French in Indochina.

With conditions there increasingly somber, in January 1949 the French finally acceded to Bao Dai's demand that the colony of Cochin China be included in the proposed Associated State of Vietnam. That concession broke the logjam, and on March 9, 1949, in a ceremony held at the Elysée Palace in Paris, representatives of the two sides signed an agreement whereby France recognized Vietnamese independence and unity within the French Union, subject to formal ratification of the agreement by the French National Assembly. The new state would be empowered to conduct its own foreign affairs, to control its finances, and to create a Vietnamese National Army. The only legal impediments to independence were those restrictions that were imposed by membership in the French Union and the current war situation in Indochina. As it turned out, these restrictions were major indeed.

In January 1948, the ICP Standing Committee, reflecting its confidence that conditions were shifting inexorably in favor of the revolution, formally decreed the end of the first stage of withdrawal and the opening of the second stage of equilibrium. Vietminh forces would now begin to initiate battles with the enemy. As part of their new approach, Party leaders now decreed that increased efforts should take place to organize the masses in neighboring Laos and Cambodia to contribute actively to the struggle for national liberation. By expanding the field of revolutionary operations throughout the territory of Indochina, Vietminh strategists hoped to divide French forces and make them increasingly vulnerable to attack. According to a Party document written in August 1948, if the Rhine River was viewed as Britain's first line of defense for Great Britain in World War II, the Mekong served the same purpose for the Vietnamese. As Truong Chinh put it in an article written in 1947, "If the enemy attacks us from above, we will attack him from below. If he attacks us in the north, we will respond in Central or South Vietnam, or in Cambodia or Laos. If the enemy penetrates one of our territorial bases, we will immediately strike hard at his belly or back . . . cut off his legs [and] destroy his roads."[16]

Party operatives had been active in neighboring Laos and Cambodia since 1935, when the ICP held its first national congress in Macao—

responding to Moscow's belief that the revolutions in all three Indochinese countries should be linked together—and called for the future creation of an Indochinese federation under Vietnamese guidance that would be similar to the Union of Soviet Socialist Republics. But efforts to build up ICP cells among urban workers (many of them of Vietnamese or Chinese extraction) in these two countries had achieved only minimum success until after World War II, when local nationalist forces created new organizations—known as the Lao Issara and the Khmer Issarak, respectively—to promote the struggle for national independence. As the Franco-Vietminh conflict got under way in early 1947, Party cadres in Laos and Cambodia were ordered to establish contact with these organizations and to place them firmly under Vietnamese guidance. Cadres were carefully instructed, however, to avoid condescension in their dealings with the Lao and Khmer peoples and to recognize their sensitivity to incipient signs of Vietnamese domination.[17]

The only cloud in this brightening sky was the growing danger of U.S. intervention in the Indochina conflict. Although the United States refused to consider an offer to provide direct assistance until Paris formally ratified the Elysée Accords, the pressure for U.S. entry into the war was growing. If that should take place, the Vietminh would be in dire need of a powerful patron. With Moscow seemingly indifferent to the plight of the Vietminh, Ho and his colleagues had only one option to counter the French gambit toward Washington. They would turn to China.

Since the end of World War II, ICP leaders had little contact with their counterparts in the Chinese Communist Party. In the spring of 1947, radio contact was established with Communist headquarters in Yan'an, and Zhou Enlai and Ho Chi Minh assumed the responsibility of exchanging information between the two parties and seeking ways of providing mutual assistance. Contacts also took place between Vietminh units and scattered CCP elements operating in the provinces adjacent to the border, and in a few cases the two sides were able to cooperate in joint operations against the French. According to one French source, sometime in 1946 Communists along the border created a joint Sino-Vietnamese unit (called the Doc Lap, or Independence, Regiment) to engage in guerrilla warfare against French administration in the area. This group operated especially among the local minority Nung and Tho populations on both sides of the frontier. At first, however, Vietminh leaders appear to have kept such relations limited to avoid complications in their relations with local nationalist elements.[18]

As the tide of the Chinese Civil War began to shift significantly toward the Communists in 1948, People's Liberation Army units became more active along the border and took part increasingly in local operations in cooperation with Vietminh units. The extension of Communist power into south China worried the French, and in March General Salan, who had recently replaced General Valluy as commander of the FEF, recommended aggressive action to restore French control over the border region before the anticipated victory of Communist forces in China.

To carry out new operations in the Viet Bac, Salan requested a substantial increase in the size of French forces. His recommendations, however, carried an implicit criticism of government inaction, and in April he was replaced by General Blaizot on the grounds that he was too young and lacked sufficient military experience. On his arrival in Indochina, Blaizot recommended a tactical retreat from the border to strengthen French forces in the northern delta in preparation for a major attack on the Viet Bac. High Commissioner Léon Pignon (Bollaert had also been replaced) agreed, but was less sanguine about Blaizot's planned military offensive.

To reconcile the two men's differences, Paris sent General Revers on an inspection trip in May 1949. Revers was critical of the existing strategy in both political and military areas, expressing doubt over the viability of the corrupt Bao Dai government and recommending that leadership over the French effort be placed in a high commissioner possessing both political and military powers. But he was also pessimistic about the possibility of a military solution, holding the view that the best that could be achieved was to improve the situation for a negotiated settlement. To promote such a result, he recommended an effort to strengthen the situation in Tonkin until the United States could be persuaded to introduce its own forces. For such a policy to be effective, the border needed to be secured, but French forces were inadequate to secure the entire area. As a stopgap, Revers recommended that defense of the border be based on the eastern region stretching from Mong Cai to That Khe. The remainder of the frontier would be evacuated.

With the weakening of the French position and the arrival of the first PLA units on the frontier, Vietnamese prospects began to improve. In early 1949, Vietminh guerrillas launched attacks along the border area. French intelligence sources reported that these operations had been coordinated with Chinese units on the northern side of the frontier. One report alleged that on one occasion in late March, PLA units briefly occupied the city of Mong Cai and then retreated back across the border.

Another declared that in April, Vo Nguyen Giap had signed a provisional agreement with Chinese Communist representatives at Jingxi calling for cooperation and a fusion of the two armies in the border area. According to a U.S. diplomatic source, that month Vietminh radio announced that units of the PLA had arrived in the frontier region and were already providing "important support" to the Vietminh.[19]

By the spring of 1949, Chinese Communist forces were crossing the Yangtze into south China and preparing to establish a new regime in Beijing. Chiang Kai-shek was preparing to evacuate his government to the island of Taiwan. For Vietminh leaders, the prospect of a friendly China on the northern frontier of Indochina created optimism that their long-awaited general offensive might be at hand. French intelligence reported that a major meeting of Vietminh leaders, including Ho Chi Minh, held in April near Vinh had evaluated the situation; Ho declared that although an increase in French forces would create problems, a general offensive was possible with Chinese assistance. In preparation for that eventuality, the meeting decided to initiate preparations to open up a battlefront along the frontier to facilitate contact with the PLA.[20]

All of this, of course, was good news to the Vietminh. But Ho Chi Minh was undoubtedly conscious that any open identification of his movement with the Chinese Communists could poison relations with Vietnamese moderates and provide an important incentive for a U.S. entry into the war on the French side. In a bid to defuse such suspicions, he periodically denied that his government was about to identify itself with the new regime in China. In March 1949, he reportedly denied the existence of an agreement with China as "a colonial rumor." The next month, he told an American journalist in an interview somewhere in the Viet Bac that independence would come through the DRV's own efforts and dismissed the accusation of "Communist domination" of the Vietminh as "pure French imperialist propaganda." In a statement in August, he admitted that there were some similarities between Mao Zedong's "new democracy" and the policies of his government, but, he added, "Chinese New Democracy is Chinese, ours is Vietnamese."[21]

The French decision to recognize Bao Dai's Associated State as the sole legal government in Vietnam represented an added challenge, since it could end Washington's doubts about French intentions and trigger a direct U.S. entry into the Franco/Vietminh war. In June 1949, in a bid to influence the course of events in Paris, Ho intimated in an interview with an Indonesian journalist that the Vietminh might be willing to negotiate with the French on the condition of national independence and unity. But the final Communist victory in China that summer undoubtedly persuaded many Party leaders that total victory might be achieved by military means, thus reducing the need to seek a negotiated settlement. On July 9, Pham Ngoc Thach, now serving as a DRV representative for south Vietnam, denounced Bao Dai as "a puppet in the pay of the invaders" and told a French journalist that the recent successes of the Chinese army presaged the end of hard times for the Vietminh. At the end of the month, French intelligence sources reported that Vo Nguyen Giap had ordered preparations for moving to the final stage of the general offensive.[22]

In mid-August, a secret meeting of the DRV Council of Ministers decided to make a formal request to the new Chinese government for aid in the war against the French. Ho Chi Minh selected two representatives to travel to Beijing to congratulate Mao Zedong on his victory over the forces of Chiang Kai-shek. That victory, Ho declared in a message to the Chinese leader, served to encourage other Asian peoples and especially his own compatriots in their efforts to free themselves from the yoke of colonial rule. Shortly after, Ho decided to make a personal visit to China to convey his request for a close relationship with the new leaders in Beijing.[23]

The two Vietnamese delegates reached Beijing in mid-October and conferred with Chinese officials. They had arrived at a delicate moment. The new Chinese government had just been established at a mass meeting held in Beijing's Tiananmen Square on October 1 and was in the process of determining its own future role in the world. Although Mao Zedong had already declared that the new China would "lean to one side" in its relations with the Soviet camp, the degree of tilt toward Moscow was still undetermined, as a direct meeting between Stalin and Mao had not yet taken place. While relations with the United States had been tense in recent months, U.S. diplomatic representatives remained in China, and there was still a hope among some officials in Washington—if not in Beijing—that a diplomatic rupture could be avoided.

The first public indication of the attitude of the new Chinese government toward the conflict in Indochina came in November, when Liu Shaoqi, Ho's acquaintance from Canton days who now ranked second to Mao Zedong in the Party hierarchy, delivered the keynote speech at an international trade union congress held in Beijing. In this widely reported address, Liu announced that the Chinese government would provide active assistance to national liberation movements elsewhere in Asia. He specifically mentioned the struggles in Indochina and in Malaya, where Communist guerrillas had launched a resistance movement against the British colonial administration. In a second speech later that month, Liu called on the Chinese people to give their active support to the oppressed peoples in colonial countries of Asia and Australasia. By that time, all other Communist governments around the world had granted diplomatic recognition to the new government in Beijing. In October, an article by Truong Chinh in the ICP newspaper *Su That* congratulated the new government of Mao Zedong. The author declared that the Communist victory in China represented a victory for all democratic and peace-loving peoples in the world, especially for peoples in the colonial world currently fighting against the forces of global imperialism. Beijing responded on November 25 with a brief and somewhat laconic declaration that China and Vietnam "are on the front lines in the vanguard of the struggle against imperialism."[24]

In December 1949, the DRV held its own first national conference of trade unions in the Viet Bac. In the course of the meeting, held in a conference hall under enormous portraits of Stalin, Mao, and Ho Chi Minh, two hundred assembled delegates listened as Truong Chinh proclaimed the political and ideological alignment of the DRV with the new regime in China. In a letter read aloud at the meeting, Ho Chi Minh pointed out that the working class must be the leading force in the nation. The final resolution of the conference celebrated the Chinese people, whose victory "shifts the balance of forces toward the democracies."[25]

In mid-December, Mao Zedong left for Moscow to work out a relationship with the Soviet Union. There had apparently not been enough time for Chinese leaders to decide on a response to the Vietminh request prior to Mao's departure for the USSR, but sometime in mid-December, Liu Shaoqi told Luo Guibo, a military officer assigned to the PLA general staff, that he was to be sent to Indochina to meet with Ho Chi Minh and other Vietnamese officials. His mission, Liu explained, would be threefold: to thank the Vietnamese for their assistance during the Chinese civil war; to restore regular contacts between the two parties; and to obtain information on the situation in Indochina. After a stay of three months, Luo was instructed to return to China to report his findings.[26]

On December 24, a week after Mao's departure for the USSR, Liu Shaoqi convened a meeting of the Politburo to analyze the situation in Indochina and formulate a policy. Any decision to provide assistance to the Vietminh would not be without cost, since the French government had not yet decided whether to grant diplomatic recognition to the new China and would obviously be offended should Beijing decide to recognize the Vietminh. The following day, acting in the name of Chairman Mao, Liu informed Vietnamese leaders by wire that the Chinese government was prepared to send a team to help the DRV assess its needs. He also invited the Vietnamese to dispatch a formal delegation to discuss the issue in Beijing.

A few days later, Liu received a reply from Indochina accepting the invitation. Ho Chi Minh had assessed the situation with his own cabinet in mid-December and had already concluded that the victory of Mao's forces opened up bright prospects for the Vietnamese revolution. Comparing the Communist victory on the mainland to a chess game in which the "red side" had won a convincing triumph, Ho predicted that the new China would provide significant assistance to the Vietminh and called for intensified preparations for the forthcoming general offensive.

By the time Beijing officials received the Vietnamese message, a delegation of Vietnamese officials had already left on foot for China. Unbeknownst to their hosts, who had been informed that the senior member of the delegation would be Tran Dang Ninh, commissar for supply on the Vietminh general staff, the actual leader of the DRV delegation was Ho Chi Minh himself. To avoid attracting the attention of the French security forces, Ho's participation was kept a secret; in fact, only two members of his own entourage were aware of his presence. After leaving the Vietminh redoubt in Tuyen Quang province on December 30, the team crossed the border on foot. Ho wore his familiar khaki suit, in the style of Sun Yat-sen, and traveled under the name of Ding. On January 16, 1950, the group reached Jingxi. Accompanied by a PLA escort, they continued on to Nanning, where they met with Chinese officials and were informed that the People's Republic of China (PRC) had just agreed to grant diplomatic recognition to the DRV. The Chinese announcement was made on January 18, four days after Vietminh sources in Bangkok had declared that the DRV was the sole legal government in Vietnam. After a brief rest, Ho and his comrades boarded a train for the Yangtze River port city of Wuhan.[27]

A few days later, the delegation reached Beijing, where Ho saw his old comrade Hoang Van Hoan, who had arrived from Europe too late to attend the trade union congress in November. The Chinese had tried to keep the arrival of the Vietnamese delegation secret, but Western intelligence sources had already learned about it. It was soon reported in the Western press. Liu Shaoqi had prepared for the upcoming talks by appointing a committee headed by General Zhu De, Mao's longtime comrade-at-arms and now vice chairman of the government and commander of the PLA, to deal with the military issues that would inevitably be raised in meetings with the Vietnamese. At the same time he informed Mao Zedong in Moscow of Ho's arrival. Mao cabled a reply asking Liu to pass on his warm regards to Ho Chi Minh and congratulating the DRV on joining the socialist camp.

In Beijing, Ho was given accommodations at Zhongnanhai, the sumptuous villa in the western section of the imperial palace where Mao Zedong had taken up his private residence. It also served as the seat of the Chinese Politburo. Liu formally informed his guest that China had decided to grant diplomatic recognition to the DRV, while noting pointedly that Chinese leaders expected to pay a price in their relations with France. At a banquet for the delegation attended by several Chinese leaders, Liu suggested to Soviet Ambassador Roshin that Ho Chi Minh go personally to Moscow to confer with Stalin and present him with an account of current conditions in Indochina. When Stalin signaled his approval by cable, Ho and his colleague Tran Dang Ninh left with Zhou Enlai for Moscow on February 3. Hoang Van Hoan remained in Beijing to make preparations to open a new Vietnamese embassy.[28]

Since the end of World War II, Soviet interest in the fate of the Vietnamese revolution had been at a low ebb. In a widely reported speech given in September 1947, Stalin's lieutenant, Andrey Zhdanov, had announced Soviet support for the struggle of oppressed colonial peoples against their imperialist exploiters, implying that bourgeois nationalist forces struggling for independence in colonial areas were viewed favorably in Moscow. But by early 1948, Soviet policy had hardened, as Communist parties in Asian societies were instructed to break their temporary alliances with local nationalist organizations and attempt to seize power on their own. That policy, apparently transmitted at a conference of youth organizations held in Calcutta, had been a disaster, resulting in the suppression of a Communist revolt in the Dutch East Indies and the eviction of Communist parties from united fronts by their nationalist rivals all over Southeast Asia.

Moscow's newly uncompromising hostility toward bourgeois nationalist parties—an attitude reminiscent of the sectarian mood of the early 1930s—was a reflection of Stalin's own views on the subject, an attitude sharpened by the failure of the CCP–Kuomintang united front during the 1920s. According to confidants, Stalin had harbored doubts about Ho Chi Minh's own ideological orthodoxy for many years and became especially suspicious when Ho sought to establish a relationship with the United States in the months immediately following the Pacific War. Stalin was also reportedly unhappy when the ICP formally abolished itself in November 1945. Two years later, when Moscow granted diplomatic recognition to Sukarno's struggling new Republic of Indonesia, it did not recognize the DRV, perhaps because of doubts that the Vietminh would be victorious in their struggle against the French.

In the early years of the Franco-Vietminh conflict, then, the Vietnamese apparently had no direct contacts with the USSR, although a French Communist Party delegation that traveled to Indochina in 1949 may have been sent on Moscow's orders to evaluate the situation. In any event, in late August of that year Ho addressed a letter to Stalin, thanking him for Soviet support to the CCP during the civil war and for its assistance to the World Federation of Trade Unions.[29]

Stalin's skepticism about Ho and the Vietminh's prospects was clearly on display during Ho's visit to Moscow. According to Nikita Khrushchev, Stalin treated the Vietnamese revolutionary with open contempt during the visit. On the second or third day after Ho's arrival, when Soviet officials arranged a meeting with Stalin, the latter's attitude toward his guest was, in Khrushchev's words, "offensive, infuriating." When Stalin and Mao Zedong finally signed their treaty of alliance on February 14, 1950, Ho Chi Minh was in attendance at the ceremony and proposed that Stalin should sign a similar agreement with his own country. Stalin replied that this was not possible, since Ho was in Moscow on a *secret* mission. When Ho—undoubtedly in jest—suggested that he be flown around Moscow in a helicopter and then land at the airport with suitable publicity, Stalin replied: "Oh, you orientals. You have such rich imaginations." Ho Chi Minh used all his familiar ruses to win the support of his gruff host. At the close of one meeting, he asked Stalin to autograph a copy of the magazine *The USSR Under Construction.* According to Khrushchev, Stalin reacted in his "typically sick, distrusting way," autographing the magazine but then later telling his personal bodyguards that he had been careless in signing it and instructing them to retrieve it. Later, after they got it back, Stalin joked with friends: "He is still looking for that magazine, but he can't find it."[30]

Stalin, however, did finally accede to one of Ho Chi Minh's requests. On January 30, 1950, Moscow officially announced diplomatic recognition of the DRV as the sole legal government of Vietnam. But the Soviet leader's doubts about Ho Chi Minh's unorthodox ideological views were not yet allayed. Vietnamese sources still tell the story (probably, but not certainly, apocryphal) that at a meeting between the two held in 1952, Stalin pointed to two chairs in the meeting room and remarked, "Comrade Ho Chi Minh, there are two chairs here, one for nationalists and one for internationalists. On which do you wish to sit?" Ho allegedly replied, "Comrade Stalin, I would like to sit on both chairs."[31]

Why did Stalin decide to grant diplomatic recognition to the DRV, despite his reservations about the ICP and its leader? According to Chinese sources, Stalin's motives may have been related to his ongoing talks with Mao Zedong. Mao had gone to Moscow determined to work out a new treaty with the USSR that removed some of the extraterritorial privileges that the Soviet Union possessed in China granted by the Allied Summit in Yalta in February 1945. Stalin wished to retain those rights for security reasons, but he was fearful that in retaliation China might decide to deal directly with the United States. It was therefore important for Stalin to guarantee that Chinese foreign policy in Asia would be sufficiently radical to ensure that the United States would be antagonized, thus preventing a possible Beijing-Washington alliance. At meetings between the three in Moscow, Stalin thus encouraged Mao to take the lead in promoting revolution in Asia. The USSR, he promised Ho Chi Minh, was willing to help Vietnam all it could, but China must play the prominent role in directing the struggle. "Toward Vietnam we feel equal concern as we do for China," he told Ho. "From now on, you can count on our assistance, especially now after the war of resistance, our surplus materials are plenty, and we will ship them to you through China. But because of limits of natural conditions, it will be mainly China that helps you. What China lacks, we will provide." Mao then assured Ho Chi Minh, "Whatever China has and Vietnam needs, we will provide."[32]

On February 17, Ho joined Mao Zedong and Zhou Enlai on the long train ride through Siberia back to Beijing. Like Ho Chi Minh, Mao had obtained at least part of what he had desired from Moscow. The new Sino-Soviet treaty removed some of the more humiliating elements in the Yalta agreement, and Moscow promised to provide economic assistance. But such gains were hard earned: Mao later informed colleagues that "getting something from Stalin is like taking meat from the mouth of a tiger."

The train pulled into Beijing on March 3. Mao hosted another banquet for Ho Chi Minh at Zhongnanhai, with all leading Chinese offficials in attendance. In formal negotiations, the PRC agreed to provide security at the border and to authorize the establishment of Vietnamese consulates in the southern cities of Nanning and Kunming. In return, Ho instructed Hoang Van Hoan—soon to be named the first Vietnamese ambassador to China—that the ICP's external headquarters were to be shifted from Thailand, where they had been located since the beginning of the Franco-Vietminh War, to China. According to the comments of a defector, Ho also agreed to provide guidance to fraternal Communist parties through-out the region, a return to the role that he had played as a Comintern agent during the early 1930s. On March 11, Ho and his colleagues left for Vietnam.

Ho Chi Minh must have been at least modestly pleased at the results of his trip. He had won diplomatic recognition from the two chief socialist states, and a promise of military and economic assistance—however limited—from each. The Vietminh would no longer fight alone. At the same time, China also benefited from the new relationship that had been established with the Vietnamese. According to Chinese sources, Mao Zedong had become increasingly convinced that war with the United States was eventually inevitable, and could break out at any ex-posed point along the Chinese border. For that reason, he believed that it was important to shore up Chinese defenses, not only in Korea, but in Indochina as well.[33]

If Ho Chi Minh, with his acute sensitivity to changes in the interna-tional climate, was concerned that the announcement of a closer re-lationship between his government and the new regime in China could provoke the United States into playing a greater role in the Indochina conflict, his fears were only too justified. In fact, Beijing's decision in mid-January to grant diplomatic recognition to the DRV, followed two weeks later by a similar announcement from Moscow, had a dramatic impact on Washington. The Truman administration had been observing with considerable discomfort the faltering French efforts to encourage non-Communist elements in Vietnam to participate in the struggle against the widely popular Vietminh Front. The decision by French lead-ers to select Bao Dai as their alternative to Ho Chi Minh as the legitimate representative of Vietnamese nationalism had aroused severe misgivings among many U.S. officials, who continued to view the former emperor as lacking the requisite degree of determination and popular support to serve as the focal point for a new independent state in Vietnam.

The signing of the Elysée Accords in March 1949 thus received only a lukewarm reaction in Washington. Dean Acheson, who had replaced George C. Marshall as secretary of state in early 1949, cabled U.S. Ambassador David Bruce in Paris that in his view, unless the French granted more autonomy to the young Vietnamese state, they were unlikely to succeed. There were rumors in the press that the White House was preparing to approach Ho Chi Minh about participating in a coalition government with Bao Dai. Other reports intimated that the two Vietnamese rivals were already in secret contact with each other. Ho Chi Minh, of course, was ever ready to take advantage of such reports as a means of disarming his adversaries. In an interview with the veteran U.S. journalist Harold Isaacs, he declared that he was not a Communist. As for the DRV, it was, he insisted, a broad-based government with legitimate nationalist credentials, and not a Soviet satellite.[34]

Reports that Washington was toying with the idea of a Ho–Bao Dai coalition regime, however, were far off the mark. Although Dean Acheson was skeptical of Bao Dai's ability to serve as an effective spokesman for the peoples of Indochina, he was even more suspicious of Ho Chi Minh's pose of being a "national Communist" along the lines of the Yugoslav leader Josip Broz Tito, who had recently been ejected from the Soviet bloc because of his independent views. Whether Ho was a nationalist or a Communist was purely academic, Acheson argued, because in colonial societies all Communists were nationalists as well. Once they had come to power, their Stalinist proclivities would clearly become evident.[35]

Throughout the last half of 1949, the White House rejected pleas from Paris for diplomatic recognition of the Bao Dai regime and refused to provide assistance to the French in carrying on the struggle in Indochina, while implying that aid would be forthcoming if France granted true independence to its new client state. But debate over the issue within the State Department was intense. Europeanists argued for recognition of the Bao Dai government as a means of appeasing the French, but Asianists argued that recognition would alienate nationalist forces in Vietnam and elsewhere. In June, Acheson tried halfheartedly to persuade Paris to grant further concessions, but after Ambasssador Bruce vigorously complained that such actions would undoubtedly antagonize the French, Acheson (who was a Europeanist by training and instinct) backed off, instructing Bruce simply to state to the French that future U.S. actions would be dependent upon implementation of the Elysée accords. Only a few U.S. officials continued to speak out against adopting a Bao Dai solution. Raymond Fosdick, the former president of the Rockefeller Foundation and a leading member of an ad hoc committee to advise the Truman administration on its Asian policy, warned that the Bao Dai experiment was doomed and that the Elysée Accords themselves were "a shabby business" and "a cheap substitute" for independence. Although Fosdick admitted that Ho Chi Minh was an unattractive alternative, he argued that Ho was an unpredictable factor because of the complex relations between China and Vietnam, which "in the end will be more favorable to us than now seems probable."[36]

Fosdick's views, however, had little resonance in a city where the issue of communism was now increasingly seen in the stark colors of the Cold War. The formation of the new People's Republic of China on October 1, 1949, added fuel to the fire of congressional criticism that the Truman administration had no policy to resist the further expansion of the "red tide" in Asia. During the last months of the year, Washington fretted and delayed a decision on the matter, resisting French pressure to commit itself to the struggle in Indochina and hoping forlornly that Paris would eventually grant more autonomy to the new Bao Dai regime.

However, the formal ratification of the Elysée Accords by the National Assembly in Paris on January 29, 1950, combined with reports (many of them provided by the French) of growing Chinese assistance to the Vietminh, changed the equation. In early February, the White House decided to grant diplomatic recognition to the Bao Dai government. The proposal was rapidly approved by the cabinet and signed by the president. Great Britain and a number of other nations followed suit shortly but, despite strenuous efforts by U.S. diplomats, most governments in Asia refused to follow their lead. Shortly thereafter, the White House approved an appeal from Paris for military assistance in the fight against the red tide in Asia. On March 10, Truman approved a grant of $15 million in military assistance for Indochina, and an additional $10 million for Thailand. Plans were launched to send advisory missions to Indochina to determine how best to administer the program.

The Chinese liaison team led by Luo Guibo arrived at the Vietnamese border on February 26, 1950. They were greeted by Vo Nguyen Giap and Hoang Van Thai, Giap's chief of staff, who led them to Vietminh headquarters in the heart of the Viet Bac. There, they were met by General Secretary Truong Chinh, who was in charge of the party in Ho Chi Minh's absence in China and the USSR.[37]

Three weeks after Ho's departure for China at the end of December 1949, Truong Chinh had convened a lengthy meeting of civilian and military leaders to discuss plans for the upcoming general offensive. Documents issued at the close of the meeting, known in Party histories as the Third National Conference (Hoi nghi toan quoc lan thu III) brimmed over with confidence in the prospects for ultimate victory. In the keynote speech to the conference, Truong Chinh had declared that, with the creation of the new China, "we are no longer encircled; a pathway to the world has been opened for Vietnam. We now have a large and powerful ally at our side." In preparation for the coming general offensive, on February 21 Party leaders called for a general mobilization of manpower under the slogan "All for the front, all for people's war, all for victory."

There is no doubt that the appearance of the PLA on the Sino-Vietnamese frontier changed the fundamental equation in the Franco-Vietminh conflict. At a minimum, China now provided a more secure sanctuary for Vietminh units in case they needed to flee from enemy attacks. Equally important, the presence of a powerful hostile force on the northern frontier of Indochina promised to act as a deterrent to the French in seeking to expand their efforts against rebel forces operating in the Viet Bac. At a maximum, the new situation opened up the exciting possibility of a shift to a more aggressive strategy to defeat the colonial forces and achieve victory throughout the entire country.

Still, in his report at the Third National Conference, Truong Chinh conceded that some within the Party were skeptical that conditions were ripe for an advance to the third stage, and even implied that he himself might be one of the doubters. Chinh cautioned that the campaign was unlikely to result in a quick victory, and warned that intervention by Great Britain or the United States might lead to increased French resistance or to the emergence of a more conservative government in Paris. At the same time, he alerted his comrades to the reality that Chinese assistance did not guarantee Vietminh success and counseled the Party that it must still rely primarily on its own efforts to bring about victory.[38]

The Party's internal debates at the conference were reflected in a lengthy analysis of the situation written by Defense Minister Vo Nguyen Giap. Giap admitted that the French still retained military superiority throughout Indochina as a whole, but he contended that the moral superiority and strategic leadership of the revolutionary forces, combined with the increasingly favorable international situation (a clear reference to diplomatic recognition and the promise of military support from the USSR and China), would all make contributions to a decisive victory. Giap explained that the offensive would not necessarily take the form of a single campaign, but might consist of a series of attacks launched in several areas of Indochina at the same time, thus resulting in a gradual shift of the balance of forces in favor of the Vietminh.[39]

During the next few months, China began to provide military equipment to the DRV, while a Chinese Military Advisory Group (CMAG)

In this building, located in the heart of the Viet Bac, leaders of the Vietminh Front held their fateful meeting, known as the Tan Trao Conference, to launch the August Revolution to restore Vietnamese independence from Japanese occupation and French colonial rule.

On August 19th, 1945, crowds began to gather in front of the Viceroy's Palace, in downtown Hanoi, to demonstrate their commitment to the creation of a free and independent Vietnam. Within two weeks, Ho Chi Minh would begin to use the palace as his administration building. Today it serves as a government guesthouse.

In late August, units of Vo Nguyen Giap's People's Liberation Army arrived in Hanoi to consolidate Vietminh power in north Vietnam. Shown here is a women's detachment, carrying weapons and bearing the flag of the new independent republic of Vietnam. Later, such units would become known as the "long-haired army."

On August 26, 1945, a Vietnamese delegation led by Vo Nguyen Giap visited the newly arrived U.S. OSS Mission in Hanoi. Here, Giap and Archimedes L. Patti salute Old Glory while a band plays the National Anthem. Other Americans in the picture were Robert Knapp and Ray Grelecki.

On his secret return to Hanoi in mid-August 1945, Ho Chi Minh settled in a typical three-story Chinese-style house in the old commercial district in the northern sector of the city. Here he wrote the Declaration of Independence for a new independent Vietnamese republic.

above: Built by the French at the beginning of the twentieth century, the baroque Municipal Theater played a crucial role in the Vietnamese revolution. Here Vietminh activists called on the populace to rise up against the French in mid-August 1945. Residents of Hanoi pictured here are preparing to march to Ba Dinh Square to hear President Ho Chi Minh declare national independence.

left: On September 2, 1945, on a hastily erected pavilion in a park in the northwestern sector of Hanoi, President Ho Chi Minh read the Declaration of Independence of the new Democratic Republic of Vietnam. Ho Chi Minh is standing fourth from the right behind the microphone.

Shortly after declaring Vietnamese national independence, Ho Chi Minh posed with members of his new government on the steps of the Municipal Theater. In the center of the photograph, Ho is clad in his now characteristic Sun Yat-Sen suit. Later the building would serve as the Vietnamese parliament.

left: President Ho Chi Minh and his chief advisers, taken sometime in the fall of 1945. In the foreground, standing left to right, are Phan Van Dong, Tran Huy Lieu, and Vo Nguyen Giap. In the background is the enigmatic Truong Chinh.

below: A view of President Ho Chi Minh at work on administrative matters in his office in the Northern Palace. In a playful mood, Ho would sometimes launch messages to subordinates by folding them into paper airplanes and tossing them from his window down into the courtyard.

left: Ho Chi Minh prior to his departure to take part in the delicate negotiations with the French government at Fontainebleau in the summer of 1946. The intensity of his demeanor suggests the seriousness of the purpose.

middle: En route to France to attend the Franco-Vietnamese conference at Fontainebleau, Ho Chi Minh remained briefly at the French resort of Biarritz to await the results of French national elections and the formation of a new government in Paris. The men with Ho Chi Minh strolling on the beach are members of his entourage.

bottom: In early June 1946, the French representative Jean Sainteny escorted Ho Chi Minh from Biarritz to Paris to attend the peace conference at Fontainebleau. Here Ho and Sainteny await the arrival of their plane at the airport in Paris. Sainteny, in his memoirs, noted that Ho Chi Minh appeared exceptionally nervous on the occasion.

above: During the days leading up to the opening of the Fontainebleau conference in the summer of 1946, President Ho Chi Minh was feted by French officials in the capital of Paris. Here he receives a wary welcome from the new French prime minister Georges Bidault, whose new government was about to adopt a tough stand in the negotiations.

right: During the summer and fall of 1945, a widespread famine caused the deaths of over a million Vietnamese living in the northern and central provinces. This letter from Ho Chi Minh to President Truman contained an appeal for U.S. assistance. There was no reply from Washington; officials at the State Department did not forward letters from Ho to the White House.

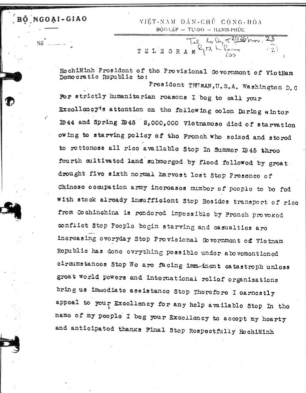

Via War Dept.

Mr. Ho Chi Minh, President Provisional government of Viet Nam Democratic Republic has requested the following be transmitted by radio:

"President Harry S. Truman;
"United States of America, Washington, D.C.;

"Mr. President, on behalf of Viet Nam people and government I wish to express to you our sincere gratitude for the declarations in twelve points you made on the US foreign policy. That declaration is enthusiastically welcomed by our people as the opening of a new era for the oppressed nations all over the world. It is the continuation of US liberal and humanitarian foreign policy as well as a personal stand of US President bringing about the materialization of ideals laid down in preceding charters of which the noble American republic was signatory power. Respectfully,
"Ho Chi Minh."

Received 11:00 a.m. November 2, 1945. OCB   NE Unit

711.00/11-245

NOV 27 1945
CS/AE
FILED

After the creation of the Provisional Republic of Vietnam in early September 1945, Ho Chi Minh sent several letters to President Harry Truman seeking U.S. support for his new government. Some, as in the case here, praised the United States for its humanitarian ideals.

Vietminh troops passed under the Long Bien bridge in mid-December 1946 to cross the Red River to flee from attacking French forces. A generation later, the bridge would be heavily bombed by U.S. B-52s during the Vietnam War.

In the fall of 1950, Vietminh forces confronted French units near the town of Dong Khe on the Sino-Vietnamese frontier. Ho Chi Minh, assisted by Chinese advisers, observed the battle from a command post in the mountains above the town.

After the outbreak of war in December 1946, Vietminh leaders retreated to the Viet Bac to carry on their struggle against the French. During the eight-year conflict, Ho Chi Minh changed his residence on at least twenty different occasions. Here he has taken temporary refuge in a cave.

In November 1953, Ho Chi Minh and other Vietminh leaders planned the pivotal campaign of Dien Bien Phu. Here the "four pillars" of the Party—Pham Van Dong, Ho, Truong Chinh, and Vo Nguyen Giap—map out their strategy at their command post.

The French fort at Dien Bien Phu, in the mountainous northwestern corner of Vietnam, fell to a final Vietminh assault on May 6, 1954, just a day before the peace conference on Indochina convened in Geneva, Switzerland.

HỒ CHỦ TỊCH MUÔN NĂM

above: After planning their spring 1954 campaign to attack Dien Bien Phu, Party leaders decided to strengthen the land reform program to win support from poor peasants. Here Ho Chi Minh addresses the land reform conference to describe the provisions of the new program.

right: With victory over the French in the summer of 1954, Ho Chi Minh and other Party leaders prepared to return to Hanoi. Ho Chi Minh, in his habitual jungle garb, was only occasionally able to savor a moment of relaxation.

top: The elaborate Presidential Palace, in a garden adjacent to Ba Dinh Square, was the scene of considerable bickering between the French and the DRV after World War II, with each claiming the right to occupy it. After Geneva, however, Ho Chi Minh refused to live in the palace, residing instead in a small gardener's cottage nearby.

bottom: In this small stilt house built in the style used by members of the mountain minoritie Ho Chi Minh spent most of his last years. Ho lived in a simple bedroom on the top floor, adj cent to a small study. In the bookcase were books by David Schoenbrunn, Benjamin Spo and Jack London.

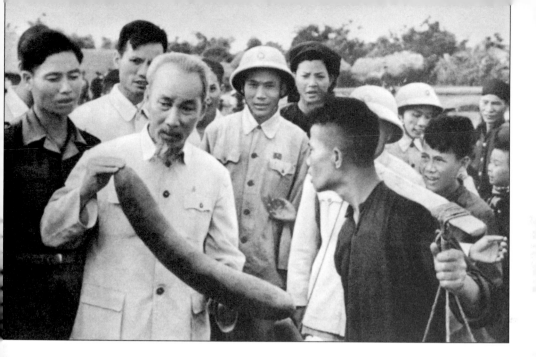

above: Ho Chi Minh inspecting one of the new collective farms in Hai Hung province in 1958. After the return of the DRV to Hanoi, Ho played a largely ceremonial role in the domestic arena, leaving executive duties to General Secretary Truong Chinh and other senior colleagues.

below: Ho Chi Minh presenting his political report to the Third National Party Congress in September 1960. To his right in the front row is the new general secretary Le Duan. To his left is Duan's predecessor Truong Chinh. At far left in the second row is General Vo Nguyen Giap. At the other end is Hoang Van Hoan.

top: Although relations between Ho Chi Minh and senior Party leader Truong Chinh were never close, each apparently respected the other, and Chinh treated the president with considerable reverence.

bottom: During the 1960s, Ho Chi Minh made several visits to Beijing to receive medical treatment. On some occasions, he was able to meet his colleague Mao Zedong. Here the two elderly leaders converse at Mao's residence in the imperial city.

top: On the grounds of the Presidential Palace and adjacent to the Stilt House was a small arbor where Ho Chi Minh often worked or hosted visiting delegations. Under towering shade trees, Ho found comfort here from the blistering heat of the sun.

above: During his last years in Hanoi, Ho Chi Minh drew considerable pleasure from feeding the goldfish in the pond adjacent to his Stilt House. Across the pond is the gardener's house occupied by Ho in the mid-1950s.

left: In the last years of his life, Ho Chi Minh continued to garden and perform exercises. Here he tends a small tree presented to him by a delegation of "liberation fighters" from South Vietnam.

The Ho Chi Minh Trail served as the main conduit for the shipment of personnel and provisions to the revolutionary movement in the South. Although at first the trail was limited to foot and bicycle traffic, by the end of the war it had been widened to accommodate well-camouflaged Soviet trucks.

When U.S. bombing raids approached the central district of Hanoi, a bomb shelter was constructed next to the Stilt House to protect the president from harm.

In 1976, this mausoleum was erected in Ba Dinh Square to hold Ho Chi Minh's mortal remains. Thousands visit the site yearly to view his embalmed body inside.

In the late 1980s the Ho Chi Minh Museum was built directly behind the mausoleum in northwest Hanoi. Shaped like a lotus leaf, the building serves as a testimonial to Ho's role in some of the most dramatic events of the twentieth century.

under General Wei Guoqing arrived at Vietminh headquarters to train cadres and provide advice on strategy and tactics. Before their departure from Beijing, members of the advisory group were given an audience with Chinese leaders, who informed them that their task in Vietnam had "global significance." If the enemy weren't driven out of Indochina and imperialism retained its toehold there, Liu Shaoqi warned his listeners, the situation for China could become more difficult and more complex.

The first Vietnamese main-force units left for training in Yunnan province in April. War matériel, much of it captured weapons of Japanese or U.S. manufacture, came by land or by sea from the port of Yulin, on the southern coast of Hainan Island. By mutual agreement, there was no provision for direct Chinese intervention in the conflict unless the very survival of the Vietminh should be threatened. At Beijing's request, all arrangements were to be kept secret to avoid aggravating China's relations with France. Such precautions turned out to be futile, however, as the French were fully briefed on Ho Chi Minh's trip and its consequences.[40]

By late spring, training institutes for Vietminh troops had been established at various locations in south China. Most of the programs lasted for three months and were administered by cadres of the PLA Second Army. By September 1950, about twenty thousand Vietminh soldiers had been armed and trained in south China; on return, many of them were integrated into a newly formed Vietminh 308 Division. Two schools for political cadres were opened at Nanning and at Kaiyuan in Yunnan province for a six-month training course. Senior Chinese advisers such as Luo Guibo and Wei Guoqing routinely attended important meetings of the Vietnamese Party leadership.[41]

The new relationship with China was destined to have enormous consequences for the future course of the Vietnamese revolution. Although there were now more than 160,000 troops serving under Vietminh command (a force numbering only slightly less than that of the adversary), they were poorly equipped and almost entirely lacking in logistical capabilities or artillery support. For the first time in its short history, the DRV now had a commitment of substantial assistance from a powerful outside donor. The promise of weapons, advisers, and other war matériel provided the basis for a shift in war strategy to the anticipated third stage of people's war—the general counteroffensive.

Vietnamese leaders made no secret of the importance of the new relationship. In an interview with the U.S. journalist Andrew Roth in August, Ho Chi Minh dropped his previous reticence about Chinese influence and remarked that the Vietnamese liberation movement had changed its tactics and was now prepared to adopt the Chinese model. As if to underline his point, a campaign was now launched throughout the Viet Bac to study the CCP's experience in the wars against Japan and Chiang Kai-shek; documents and training materials were translated into Vietnamese and distributed to cadres and troops throughout the area. Study sessions were held periodically to encourage those in attendance to internalize the Chinese model and put its precepts into practice in Indochina.

Public statements by Vietminh sources regarding the sudden relevance of the Chinese model were somewhat disingenuous, because, as we have seen, Party leaders had long since sought to draw useful lessons from the Chinese revolution. One of Ho Chi Minh's first official statements after the outbreak of war in December 1946 had been to announce that Vietminh leaders would follow the Maoist model of people's war in their struggle for victory. Early the following year, Truong Chinh had authored a pamphlet called *The Resistance Will Win*, which drew extensively from Mao Zedong's own writings on guerrilla warfare during the past two decades. Chinh had apparently written the pamphlet with the approval of the entire Party leadership, and the revolutionary pseudonym that he had chosen ("Long March") was a clear expression of his admiration for the Chinese revolution. Yet Chinh was careful to point out that some elements of the Chinese model did not cross national boundaries. Because Vietnam was smaller in territory and fully under colonial domination, the Vietminh could not hope to build a large liberated base area similar to that constructed by the CCP in north China during the war against Japan. Nor could they afford to neglect the importance of diplomatic initiatives, a tool that had played only a limited role in the Communist struggle for power in China. Still, Vietminh leaders clearly felt that the Chinese model had already been of significant value in their struggle against the French, and they were now willing to give the Chinese advisory team an opportunity to assist them in rendering their efforts more effective.

But it was soon clear that Chinese influence was not to be limited to the sphere of military activities, but would encompass domestic policies and the nature of the Party organization as well. Shortly after his arrival in the Viet Bac at the end of February, Luo Guibo had assumed leadership of a Chinese civilian advisory team to assist the Vietnamese in remodeling their party and government along Chinese lines. Since the Eighth Plenum, held at Pac Bo in May 1941, Party leaders had assigned a higher priority to the cause of national liberation against the forces of imperialism than to the struggle against feudal forces inside the country, thus returning to the Leninist model that Ho Chi Minh had brought back to Asia in the 1920s. Under this plan, the Vietnamese revolution had been divided into two stages, a first one to complete the task of national liberation, and a second to carry out the transformation to socialism. During the first stage, the central role of the ICP within the Vietnamese revolution was disguised in order to avoid alienating moderate elements inside the country and provoking intervention from reactionary forces abroad. It was this vision that had characterized DRV policy after the August Revolution of 1945, and during the first three years of the Franco-Vietminh conflict.

Now, with the triumph of Communist forces in mainland China and the heightened prospects for victory over the French, Party leaders shifted toward a new strategy based on the Chinese model, in which Party leadership over the movement was openly acknowledged, while the first stage of national liberation would evolve without a rigid dividing line into the second stage of social revolution. The process got under way at the Third National Conference in late January 1950, when Party leaders decided to place more emphasis on class issues in the united front and launch initial preparations to bring the Communist Party back into the open. Such actions would foster closer identification between the DRV and other members of the socialist community, including the new Chinese government and the "people's democracies" in Eastern Europe; but it would complicate efforts to achieve a negotiated settlement and to prevent the United States from entering the conflict on the side of the French. During the next few months, Party leaders inaugurated a major campaign to introduce their followers to the ideas and practices of the Chinese Communists and their leader, Chairman Mao Zedong.[42]

To what degree was this momentous shift in focus adopted with the approval of Ho Chi Minh? Ho had been clearly identified with the more gradualist two-stage formula since the mid-1920s, and was undoubtedly instrumental in bringing about its adoption at the Eighth Plenum in 1941. The new policy would not only restrict his capacity to manipulate the international situation to his advantage, but would also result in a degree of subservience to Chinese tutelage that Ho had successfully resisted in the past.

Moreover, it is curious that the fateful Third National Conference had been held in Ho's absence. There may have been growing doubts—both within the international Communist movement and among his senior colleagues—about his commitment to the principles of Marxist-Leninist orthodoxy as propagated by Moscow and Beijing at the end of the 1940s. During the winter of 1949–50, there was a flurry of press reports—many of them admittedly based on remarks by defectors—to the effect that Ho Chi Minh had been replaced by Truong Chinh as the leader of the Vietnamese Communist movement at Stalin's order, or even that he had been formally declared a heretic because he had refused to toe Moscow's line. When the French Communist Léo Figuères arrived in the Viet Bac for a visit in March 1950, it was widely rumored that he had been sent not only to restore party to party contacts with the ICP, but also to stress the importance of restoring the latter as the vanguard of the Vietnamese revolution.[43]

Still, although Ho Chi Minh may have accepted the new line with some reluctance, he undoubtedly recognized that growing U.S. support for the French could no longer be avoided, and that closer ties with Moscow and Beijing represented the best chance for a Vietminh victory in Indochina. In any event, he adjusted himself to the new realities and sought to use them to his advantage. In his messages to Chinese leaders during the remainder of the year, Ho was fulsome in his praise of the new government in Beijing and its wise leadership, suggesting strongly that his government and Party would follow the Chinese model. By now, of course, he had become a master at the art of flattering his benefactors by implying that their advice and experience would be taken to heart in the new Vietnam. For example, it was probably not by accident that in the fall of 1950, for the first time, he began to extol the benefits of collectivized agriculture for the future prosperity of an independent Vietnam.[44]

As Party strategists had concluded in the spring of 1949, one of the crucial prerequisites for a successful general offensive was to open up the border region to Vietminh control, thus enabling revolutionary forces to obtain easy access to material support from China. General Blaizot had already made Giap's task easier by calling for a French withdrawal from exposed locations along the border north of Lang Son, while basing future strategy on control of the region from Lang Son to the Tonkin Gulf. In the summer of 1950, however, Blaizot's plan had not yet been formally implemented, and a series of isolated French border posts was strung out along Route 4 from the coast at Mong Cai to the district capital of Cao Bang.

The French would soon have reason to regret their delay. In April 1949, Party leaders had first decided to focus their primary attention on the western portion of the frontier, where the French military presence was negligible. In July 1950, however, the Party Standing Committee decided to shift its focus to the eastern sector, which was more accessible to the Red River delta and to major transportation routes into China. As Ho remarked to his colleagues at the time, it was "easy to defend during a withdrawal, easy to attack during an offensive." Vo Nguyen Giap was put in charge of commanding the offensive, and General Chen Geng, a widely respected troubleshooter for PLA military operations during the Chinese Civil War, was ordered to travel to the Viet Bac to help Vietminh leaders plan the campaign. When Giap visited Ho Chi Minh, now settled once again at his old revolutionary base at Tan Trao, Ho alluded to the importance of victory. "The coming campaign," he said, "is extremely important. We must not lose!" Ho promised to travel to the frontier to observe the campaign in person. General Chen Geng was invited to accompany him.[45]

In mid-September, Vietminh units launched a series of sharp attacks on exposed French installations throughout the border region. When the French post at Dong Khe was attacked by eight thousand Vietminh troops, French intelligence sources reported ominously that the enemy now possessed bazookas, mortars, and recoilless rifles, and was able to concentrate its forces at regimental strength for the first time. Caught by surprise at the intensity of the attack, the French were thrown into disarray, and the retreating forces left behind hundreds of dead and wounded, as well as more than ten thousand tons of ammunition. A French reserve force sent north from Cao Bang to rescue their beleaguered comrades was likewise decimated. General Marcel Carpentier, commander of French troops in the region, suddenly ordered the abandonment of all other posts on the frontier, except for the coastal town of Mong Cai.

In Hanoi, High Commissioner Léon Pignon was growing increasingly skeptical of General Carpentier's judgment (Carpentier's attitude, remarked Pignon to a U.S. diplomat, was "so passive and defensive . . . that his qualifications for supreme military leadership must be questioned"), and at the end of the year the general was replaced.[46] But the change in command took place too late. By the end of the border campaign in late October, the offensive had opened up a vast area north of the Red River delta to virtually total Vietminh domination. Panicky French officials ordered the evacuation of French dependents from Hanoi, and warned Paris that more than half the population of the city now sympathized with the Vietminh. With the border region under enemy control, the French could no longer delude themselves that there was any possibility of a total victory in the war.

The sense of panic over the military situation was not limited to the

French. Donald Heath, who had just arrived in Saigon as chief U.S. envoy to the Associated State, warned that the situation in Tonkin was perilous. The entire northern region, except for the Hanoi–Haiphong corridor, must be written off, he reported, even in the absence of Chinese intervention, which he described as not unlikely. As for the new Vietnamese government in Saigon under Chief of State Bao Dai, Heath declared that it possessed neither dynamism nor the confidence of public opinion. Bao Dai himself lacked both energy and the know-how of leadership. The U.S. military attaché, however, weighed in with a note of sobriety, predicting that there would be no Chinese invasion unless the Vietminh met with serious reverses.[47]

Chinese advisers were intimately involved in the planning and execution of the border offensive, a role that would become subject to controversy between the two allies following the end of the Vietnam War. Vietnamese sources credit Vo Nguyen Giap and other Vietminh military strategists with coordinating the campaign. According to Hoang Van Hoan, however, it was General Chen Geng who counseled Ho Chi Minh to open the attack on Dong Khe rather than on Cao Bang, a strongpoint that was heavily defended by the French. Cao Bang, Chen reportedly advised the Vietnamese, should be placed under siege and occupied later. Ho Chi Minh agreed with the advice, and took charge of the campaign from a command post in the mountains above the town. With his consent, Chinese advisers were placed in all Vietminh units at battalion level and above. That claim has recently been countered by General Vo Nguyen Giap himself, who insists that he had reached the decision to attack Dong Khe rather than Cao Bang independently, and that both Ho Chi Minh and Chen Geng had given their approval to the plan.

Whatever the truth of the debate, after the campaign was over, Chen Geng returned to China and was assigned to command PLA units operating in Korea. Before his departure from the Viet Bac, he sent detailed criticisms of Vietminh battlefield performance to his superiors in China. As Chen reported to his Chinese superiors, Vietminh troops lacked discipline and battlefield experience and were not ready to engage in major operations, while their commanders did not have sufficient concern for the welfare of their troops and were reluctant to report bad news to their superiors.[48]

Vietminh strategists were pleased at the success of the 1950 border campaign (Ho Chi Minh reportedly said that it had been a greater triumph than he had expected), a result that encouraged some of them to argue that it could be used as a launching pad for the long anticipated general offensive in the heart of the Red River delta. Although some

Party leaders remained skeptical that revolutionary forces were prepared for a major confrontation with the enemy (Ho himself advised one of his headstrong commanders that a major offensive, like a woman's pregnancy, must await its proper time), a consensus emerged that in the more favorable conditions brought about by the successful border attack, a new offensive to bring about total victory had a reasonable chance for success. During the final two months of 1950, Vietminh planners, with the concurrence of their Chinese advisers, put their final touches on plans for the next year's campaign. At a joint conference held in December, Chinese representatives agreed to supply sufficient equipment to enable the Vietminh to reorganize their forces into larger units capable of carrying on a war of movement against their adversaries.

Giap's plan was to strike successively at three separate locations on the fringes of the Red River delta: at Vinh Yen, the market town northwest of the capital, just south of the forbidding Tam Dao Mountain; at Mao Khe, on the eastern edge of the delta not far from Haiphong; and finally at various points on the Day River directly south of Hanoi. If these localized attacks at exposed points in the French defenses should be successful, the next stage could begin, a major offensive to open up the route to the capital region. Vietminh Radio optimistically predicted that President Ho would be in Hanoi for the Têt holidays. If Party strategists were correct in their optimistic predictions, the end of the war was near.[49]

XIII | A PLACE CALLED DIEN BIEN PHU

The prediction that Ho Chi Minh would celebrate the Têt New Year's holiday of 1951 in Hanoi was premature. Although the early stage of the Vietminh offensive started out in a promising manner—with Vietminh units rushing out from the jungles at the foot of Tam Dao Mountain in a Chinese-style "human wave" offensive against enemy positions in Vinh Yen—their commanders had underestimated the determination of General Jean de Lattre de Tassigny, who had just arrived on December 19, 1950, as the new high commissioner and commander in chief of French Expeditionary Forces (FEF) in Indochina. De Lattre proved himself to be a worthy adversary for Vo Nguyen Giap. A war hero and a man of supreme self-confidence and military bearing, de Lattre immediately took action to shore up the French position. To bolster morale, he canceled his predecessor's order to evacuate dependents from the city of Hanoi. To blunt the Vietminh offensive, he brought in the strategic reserves from elsewhere in the country, while ordering French aircraft to use a shipment of napalm bombs recently received from the United States.

The results were stunning. Vietminh troops, who had never before encountered the effects of the burning gas, fled in disorder, and the town of Vinh Yen remained under French authority. As one member of the attacking force later wrote:

Our division had attacked since the morning. From a distance three *hirondelles* [swallows] grow larger. They are airplanes. They dive, and hell opens before my eyes. Hell in the form of a large egg container falling from the first plane, then a second, which lands to my right. . . . An intense flame which seems to spread for hundreds of meters, sows terror in the ranks of the fighters. It is napalm, the fire which falls from the sky.

Another plane approaches and spews more fire. The bomb falls behind us and I feel its fiery breath which passes over my entire body. Men flee, and I can no longer restrain them. There is no way to live under that torrent of fire which runs and burns all in its route.[1]

According to a U.S. intelligence report, the Vietminh forces suffered 3,500 to 4,000 casualties out of a total attacking force of 10,000. French losses were listed as 400 killed and 1,200 wounded. The later stages of the offensive at Mao Khe and on the Day River proved even less successful for the Vietminh troops, and eventually after suffering high casualties, they withdrew into the mountains. With the threat to Hanoi now at least temporarily relieved, de Lattre confessed that his decision to cancel the evacuation order had been just "whistling in the dark" and a grandstand play to restore public confidence.[2]

Far from opening the road to Hanoi, the general offensive had been a bruising setback for Vietminh forces, and an especially humiliating personal defeat for Ho Chi Minh's prize war strategist Vo Nguyen Giap. During the next few weeks, the high command began to rethink its approach. At a meeting of senior Party leaders held in mid-April, Ho Chi Minh called for a bout of self-criticism to learn from recent experience and prepare for the next battle. A broadcast by Vietminh Radio in May remarked that major military attacks should be launched only when victory was certain. Official sources stopped using the slogan "Prepare for the shift to the general offensive" and began to emphasize the importance of protracted war. In his writings and speeches throughout the remainder of 1951, Ho made the same point indirectly, alluding to the crucial importance of guerrilla techniques in carrying out a long-term struggle against the enemy. Chinese advisers extricated themselves from possible responsibility for the debacle by reporting to their superiors (after the fact) that Vietminh troops lacked the necessary experience to carry out such an ambitious military campaign. They too counseled a return to guerrilla war. Giap himself performed a mea culpa, conceding that it had been a mistake to confront better-armed French troops in a conventional battle with his still inexperienced forces, who sometimes failed to exhibit the required amount of aggressiveness and determination.[3]

While China's influence on Vietminh war strategy became increasingly apparent after 1950, its impact was equally visible in changes that were taking place in Vietminh internal policy. Beginning in mid-1950, Chinese cadres clad in Mao suits and spouting Chinese revolutionary slogans began to arrive in large numbers to advise their Vietnamese comrades on all aspects of administration and correct behavior. Prior to their departure from China, Liu Shaoqi had carefully instructed members of the advisory team not to force Chinese techniques on their hosts, but some ignored that counsel, arousing sharp resentment among rank-and-file Vietnamese officials and cadres, long sensitive to the condescending attitudes of their cousins to the north.

For many Vietnamese, the most onerous manifestation of growing Chinese influence was the establishment of an ideological training program for Party members. In conformity with Maoist theory, the goal of the program was to encourage the ideological reeducation of Party members, but it often degenerated into humiliation and punishment and was frequently marked by bitter class conflict, as cadres from poorer backgrounds exacted their revenge on colleagues from elite families. According to accounts by participants, the tactic of self-criticism that lay at the heart of the program terrorized many Vietminh cadres, most of whom had read few Marxist-Leninist writings and whose motives for joining the movement were often more patriotic than ideological.

The results of such ideological training were sometimes tragic. According to Georges Boudarel, a French Communist who served with a Vietminh unit in the early 1950s, some tortured souls had their razors confiscated in an effort to prevent them from attempting to commit suicide; the lights in the barracks at some training camps were left on at night, presumably for the same reason. Vietnamese political commissars were assigned to all units in the army to watch over the ideological motivation of the troops. In the event of a disagreement between a political commissar and the commanding officer of a unit, the former had the final say.[4]

Boudarel notes that such policies had a double negative effect. In the short run, they drove many patriotic intellectuals out of the movement and ruptured the solidarity that had previously existed between moderates and radicals within the Party. In the long term, the consequences were equally pernicious, as the fear of criticism and reprisal stifled the creativity of writers and artists. French intelligence sources obtained numerous captured documents that reported friction between Vietnamese cadres and their Chinese advisers; deserters from the Vietminh often cited excessive Maoist influence as a reason for their decision to leave the movement. Even Vietminh supporters who accepted the need for Chinese strategic advice sometimes balked at the virtual takeover of Vietnamese units by their foreign advisers. Defectors reported that a number of senior- and middle-level Vietminh officials had been purged as the result of Chinese pressure. According to French sources, it may have been as a result of Chinese pressure that Nguyen Binh, commander of Vietminh forces in the south and an alleged critic of growing Chinese influence in the movement, was relieved of his position in September 1951 and ordered north to undergo "orientation." Official DRV sources declare that he was killed in a skirmish with Cambodian royal troops while en route to the Viet Bac; unconfirmed reports said that he had been traveling under arrest and "happily met predestined death in combat rather than execution."[5]

Chinese influence also began to extend into rural villages, where the DRV gradually introduced more stringent land reform regulations that focused on eliminating the economic and political influence of the land-lord class at the village level. Since the outbreak of war in December 1946, the government's land policy had reflected Ho Chi Minh's decision to assign priority to the anti-imperialist struggle over the antifeudal revolution. The program therefore called for reduced land rents, but limited the confiscation of farmlands to the holdings of French citizens and Vietnamese collaborators with the Bao Dai regime. The land of patriotic landlords and rich peasants had not been seized, in the interest of enlisting their support for the movement.

By the early 1950s, however, there was growing criticism from militants that many of the provisions of the program were being widely ignored at the local level, where many landlords successfully evaded rent reduction regulations. Party leaders like Truong Chinh now contended that by failing to mobilize the fervent support of poorer elements in the countryside, the program was not adequately serving the interests of the revolution. Chinese advisers, fresh from their own experience with the more stringent land reform program still under way in the People's Republic of China (PRC), began to urge Vietnamese cadres to confront "feudal" elements in the countryside more directly. As a result, regulations calling for rent reductions and limitations on the participation of landlords in village councils began to be enforced more stringently.

The most significant event that underscored the government's decisive shift to the left occurred in mid-February 1951, when the Party held its Second National Congress—the first to be held since the conference at Macao in March 1935—at a secret location in Tuyen Quang province, deep in the heart of the Viet Bac. A total of 200 delegates, representing about half a million members, were in attendance.

There were persuasive reasons for holding a congress. In the first place, despite its formal abolition in November 1945, the ICP had grown rapidly during the late 1940s and many of its members—the vast majority of whom were peasants or petty bourgeois in origin—had little ideological training. Many cadres were infected with what Party documents labeled as "feudal attitudes" (comprising such alleged social ills as religious beliefs and superstitions, putting on airs, and male chauvinism), a "guerrilla mentality" (implying an attitude of secretiveness and a suspicion of outsiders), and a low level of political awareness. In his report to congress delegates, General Secretary Truong Chinh declared that it was crucially important to combat the high incidence of individualism, arrogance, bureaucratic attitudes and practices, and corruption and loose morals among Party members. Only a publicly visible and highly disciplined Communist Party, he insisted, could play an active role in combating such ills and play the vanguard role in guiding the Vietnamese revolution.

The growing influence of China in the forging of domestic policy was openly acknowledged at the congress. The future Vietnam, declared Truong Chinh, would adopt the Chinese label of a "people's democratic dictatorship," rather than following the Soviet-style Eastern European "dictatorship of the proletariat." Under the Chinese model, the immediate objective was to carry out the first stage of national democratic revolution in preparation for the later socialist revolution, but there would be no extended period of transition between the two stages. Rather, the national democratic revolution, in Leninist parlance, would "grow over" into a socialist stage. To win the support of the broad mass of the population, the Vietminh Front, the broad alliance of patriotic forces formed in 1941 that was now clearly identified in the public mind with its Communist leadership, was to be renamed the National United Front for Vietnam, or Lien Viet Front.[6]

To fulfill its task, the ICP was also to have a new name—the Vietnamese Workers' Party (Dang Lao dong Viet Nam, or VWP). In applying the emotive word "Vietnam" to the label of the Party, the leadership was giving explicit recognition to the crucial importance of the anti-imperialist struggle in winning the support of the general population, a view that Ho Chi Minh himself had held unswervingly since the mid-1920s. At the same time, the decision represented a tacit gesture to the rising spirit of nationalism in the neighboring associated states of Laos and Cambodia, where ICP members of Lao or Khmer extraction were growing restive under the sometimes suffocating guidance of their Vietnamese superiors and now demanded parties of their own. The Party now formally recognized that the revolutions in the three countries would proceed at different speeds, and that each would now have its own party to play the vanguard role in that process. While Vietnam was heading toward a national democratic revolution and then directly to socialism, Laos and Cambodia were moving in the direction of popular democracies; their socialist revolutions were to be delayed for several years.

The decision to divide the ICP into three separate parties did not mean, however, that Ho Chi Minh and his colleagues had lost interest in the rest of Indochina. To the contrary, although separate organizations—to be called People's Revolutionary Parties—were now to be set up in Laos and Cambodia, plans for a close alliance among the three groups were formally initiated shortly after the adjournment of the Second Congress. According to an official Party document issued at the conference and later seized by the French, the Vietnamese had no intention of relinquishing control over the movement throughout Indochina. "The Vietnamese Party," it declared, "reserves the right to supervise the activities of its brother parties in Cambodia and Laos." And although in later years Vietnamese sources claimed that the concept of the Indochinese federation (which had been first broached at the 1935 Macao Congress) had been explicitly abandoned at the 1951 conference, this captured document suggests the contrary, declaring that, although there were now three separate parties, "later, if conditions permit, the three revolutionary Parties of Vietnam, Cambodia, and Laos will be able to unite to form a single Party: the Party of the Vietnam-Khmer-Laotian Federation."[7]

The decision to maintain a close relationship among the three countries, now united in fact as associated states within the French Union, was a clear recognition that Party leaders had recognized the strategic importance of Indochina as a unified bloc. In a Vietminh training document seized by the French in 1950, the three countries were described as a single unit from a geographic, economic, political, and strategic point of view. The document stated that revolutionary movements in the three countries were directed to provide one another with mutual assistance in every field to carry on the joint struggle against the imperialist invader and in building the future "new democracies."[8]

The thumbprint of Ho Chi Minh could be found on various documents approved by the congress. Ho's colleagues deferred to his steady insistence on the need to place the anti-imperialist over the antifeudal struggle in Indochina, and they recognized the necessity of appealing to moderate elements in Vietnamese society. In emphasizing the importance of a two-stage revolution (however brief) and the need to adapt revolutionary ideology to concrete conditions in each country, they responded to the pragmatic bent that had marked his ideas since the early days of the movement.

Still, it is hard to avoid the conclusion that the major influence behind the decisions reached at the Second National Congress came from Beijing. In the decision to reestablish the Communist Party as the visible "guiding force" behind the Vietnamese revolution, the Vietnamese were responding to criticism from China, as well as the Soviet Union, that their struggle had heretofore lacked a sufficient Marxist coloration. The use of the term "new democracy" was a direct imitation of one recently adopted by the Chinese themselves, while in emphasizing the "growing over" of the revolution from a first to a second stage, they were stressing concerns expressed in Moscow and Beijing that the ICP was not sufficiently orthodox in its operations.

Ho Chi Minh's reaction to the decisions reached at the congress must have been mixed. As a longtime pragmatist, he understood the importance of placating Beijing in order to encourage Chinese assistance to the Vietnamese revolution, and few were his equal in kowtowing to Chairman Mao and his proud colleagues. Yet he must have been concerned at the danger of excessive Chinese influence and aware that some elements of the Chinese model—notably, the substantially enhanced role for the Party, the increased emphasis on ideological reeducation, and the harsh punishment meted out to those suspected of counterrevolutionary leanings—might not thrive in the tropical soil of French Indochina. His inclusionist instincts must have rebelled at the knowledge that many patriotic Vietnamese were about to be driven from the ranks of the Vietminh Front and into the hands of the enemy.

Ho's concerns did not escape contemporary observers, and rumors circulated that although Ho Chi Minh had been confirmed as chairman of the Party, the meeting marked a major defeat for Ho and his influence within the Vietnamese revolutionary movement. According to French intelligence sources, one result of the congress had been to replace the influence of moderates like Ho Chi Minh with hard-line elements led by Truong Chinh, who had been reelected to the key post of Party general secretary, and one source in the Saigon press even reported that Ho had been executed at the order of Vo Nguyen Giap. Knowledgeable sources in Hanoi today privately concede that the congress probably represented a defeat for Ho Chi Minh and a triumph for those, like Truong Chinh, who were determined to follow Chinese advice and apply a harsher approach to the Vietnamese revolution. A new central committee of twenty-nine members (consisting for the most part of veterans who had been active in the Party since before World War II) was elected. In its turn, the Central Committee created a new executive body (called, in imitation of Soviet practice, the Politburo), composed of seven leading

Party members and one alternate, that would direct the affairs of the Party and the government. The leading members of this organization— known popularly as the "four columns"—were Truong Chinh, Pham Van Dong, Vo Nguyen Giap, and Ho Chi Minh himself. In a biographical sketch published by the official Party newspaper *Nhan Dan* in March, Truong Chinh was described as the architect and the chief of the Vietnamese revolution, while Ho Chi Minh was its soul.[9]

After the failure of Giap's Red River delta offensive, the conflict gradually settled into a war of equilibrium. By 1951, most of the Vietminh effort was taking place in the north. After the end of Nguyen Binh's abortive offensive in the summer of 1950, Vietminh strategists placed the struggle in Cochin China on the back burner. As part of his strategy, Binh had organized vast demonstrations in Saigon to protest against the war and the social and economic difficulties that it had imposed. Popular participation in the demonstrations—known as the "red days"—had been heavy, especially on the part of workers and students who had been provoked by inflation and the introduction of military conscription, but many moderates were put off by the specter of incipient violence inspired by the demonstrations and refrained from giving their support to the movement. Bao Dai's newly appointed prime minister, Nguyen Van Tam—a former police chief known as "the Tiger of Mai Lai" because of his vigorous attempt to suppress rebel activities in the south—cracked down on the Vietminh apparatus in Saigon, and by August it had virtually ceased to exist. To run the revolutionary operation in the south, the Party set up the Central Office for South Vietnam (known in English as COSVN), and placed it directly under the VWP Central Committee.

With the Cochin China theater now essentially moribund, Giap and his associates began to put more effort into neighboring Laos and Cambodia, as well as on the mountainous northwestern part of Tonkin. Giap's objective was to tie down French military power and force its dispersal throughout all of Indochina. That would enable the Vietminh to select points of vulnerability, where it had the capacity to engage enemy forces in open combat, and then perhaps inflict on them a humiliating defeat.

Hoa Binh presented one such opportunity. The French had become convinced that this city, on the southern fringe of the Red River delta, was a key link between Vietminh headquarters in the Viet Bac and the central and southern parts of the country, now their prime source of recruits and supplies. "Rice fields," Ho Chi Minh remarked to his colleagues, "are battlefields." French units occupied the city after November 1951, and with the concurrence of Chinese advisers, the Vietminh launched heavy attacks on French positions there. Intense fighting—labeled by the historian Bernard Fall as a meat grinder—followed, and the French abandoned their position in February 1952, retreating to the delta. In the meantime, de Lattre had returned to France, where he died of cancer in January. By now, the optimism that had been engendered among pro-French elements in Indochina by his early show of dynamism had dissipated. The battle of Hoa Binh was widely viewed as a major reversal for the French; the U.S. Embassy in Saigon reported that non-Communist nationalists were discouraged and increasingly convinced that the Vietminh would occupy Hanoi by the summer.

At de Lattre's order, the French had built a string of defense posts (called blockhouses) in hopes of preventing the Vietminh from penetrating the delta, but the so-called de Lattre Line had been no more effective than its World War II equivalent in France, the Maginot Line. Vietminh forces simply bypassed the blockhouses or attacked and overran them one by one. By the end of 1952, Vietminh units were moving freely throughout the rice fields around Hanoi, and revolutionary organizations had been reestablished in half the villages of the delta. The victory at Hoa Binh opened prospects for more.

That fall, Vietminh strategists opened a new front in the far northwest. The French had held this extensive region of forbidding mountain ranges and narrow valleys since the beginning of the war. During the spring of 1952, at the suggestion of Chinese advisers, Vietminh strategists began to draw up plans for an attack on French posts in the region in preparation for a campaign in central and northern Laos. In so doing, they might succeed in diverting enemy forces to outlying areas, thus rendering them more vulnerable to attack. In September, Ho Chi Minh left secretly for Beijing to consult with Chinese leaders about the operation. He then continued on to Moscow, where he attended the Nineteenth Congress of the Communist Party of the Soviet Union. Final approval of a plan to attack the French base at Nghia Lo was reached in late September. Ho returned to Vietnam in December.[10]

In mid-October 1952, three Vietminh divisions attacked the French base at Nghia Lo. The French units there retreated to nearby posts at Na San and Lai Chau, while abandoning their base at Son La, about forty miles west of Nghia Lo. The Vietminh occupied Son La and concentrated their further efforts at Na San, where they waged an unsuccessful assault, suffering thousands of casualties in the process. But the failure to seize Na San was only a temporary setback. Early the following spring the

Vietminh regrouped and advanced across the border into northern Laos, occupying the provincial capital of Sam Neua and threatening the royal capital of Luang Prabang. Then, having forced the French to further disperse their forces, they returned to the Viet Bac.

Throughout this period, Ho Chi Minh remained invisible to the outside world, a shadowy figure who had not been seen by reliable sources from the West since the spring of 1947. Some pundits, noting that he had been in chronic ill health in Hanoi after World War II, speculated that he had died, or had even been sent into exile in China because of his resistance to the growing presence of the PLA. French intelligence sources obtained confirmation of his continued existence from a photograph in *L'Humanité* that was taken sometime in July 1952. Finally, Joseph Starobin of the *Daily Worker* met him at a secret location in the Viet Bac in March 1953 and reported the interview to the English-speaking world.[11]

In the liberated zone, however, Ho Chi Minh was highly visible, acting not only as a war strategist, but also as chief recruiter and cheerleader for the revolutionary cause. In February 1952, a released French POW reported that Ho was seen everywhere at the front, in the villages, in the rice fields, and at local cadre meetings. Dressed like a simple peasant, he moved tirelessly among his followers, cajoling his audiences and encouraging them to sacrifice all for the common objective. Although living conditions in the liberated zone were probably somewhat better than they had been during the final months of World War II, French bombing raids on the area were frequent and Ho continued to change his residence every three to five days to avoid detection or capture. Although he was now over sixty, Ho was still capable of walking thirty miles a day, a pack on his back, over twisting mountain trails. He arose early to do exercises. After the workday was over, he played volleyball or swam and read in the evening.[12]

According to scattered reports from defectors or released POWs, morale in the liberated zone was declining, and complaints about living conditions were on the rise. Vietminh leaders had been forced to reinstitute the hated corvée in areas under their control to carry out various types of public works projects, for which workers received no salary beyond a small amount of food for their subsistence. Intellectuals grew weary of the constant sessions of indoctrination and self-criticism, while high taxes, volunteer labor, and the incessant bombing raids by the French frayed nerves among the population as a whole. Nevertheless, most observers reported that the bulk of local citizens continued to support the Vietminh, if only because of its efforts to secure independence from the French.[13]

As the war escalated, recruitment and the supply of provisions posed increasing problems. By now, the source of manpower from urban areas had essentially dried up, as the Vietminh apparatus in the major cities had been virtually destroyed, and Party planners were forced to use more aggressive methods to obtain labor and conscripts in the countryside. There were unconfirmed reports that some peasants had migrated to other areas to avoid such duties. Whereas in the early years of the conflict, contributions of grain from peasants had been given, in principle, on a voluntary basis, now the regime felt compelled to levy an agricultural tax of 15 percent on the annual harvest.

One of the problems encountered in soliciting aid and support from the rural population was that many peasants were indifferent to the struggle, because they could not see how it affected them. Measures had been taken in the late 1940s to reduce land rents and interest rates on loans and to redistribute the land of collaborators to the poor, but they had achieved only limited results, and many landlords felt sufficiently secure to ignore Vietminh directives or to provide support to the French, in some cases even in areas controlled by the revolution.

By the time of the Second National Party Congress in early 1951, the problem had become serious enough to require action, and the Central Committee adopted some minor corrective measures. But decisive action continued to be impeded by the existing strategy of seeking the broadest possible united front against the common imperialist enemy. Although the approach was identified primarily with Ho Chi Minh, even Truong Chinh in his report to the congress had conceded that the primary task for the moment was to defeat imperialism. Although the anti-feudal mission was crucial and "must be carried out at the same time as the anti-imperialist mission," he said, it must take place "step by step" to maintain national unity in the common struggle. As a result, the government continued to refrain from a general confiscation and redistribution of land owned by the entire landlord class. By 1952, however, influential Party leaders began to argue that more radical measures were needed to win the allegiance of rural poor.

In January 1953, new directives were announced. Relying heavily on Chinese experience at the height of the Chinese Civil War, the plan called for drastic slashes in land rents and the seizure of all farmlands in the hands of landlords not actively cooperating in the war effort. Land reform tribunals composed of radical peasants were established at the village level to undertake a survey of village landholdings for future redistribution. Public criticism sessions reminiscent of the "speak bitterness" sessions organized in China were held in liberated villages to encourage the poor to criticize the allegedly tyrannical behavior of wealthy elements in the local community. In a few cases, Vietminh activists, urged on by their Chinese advisers, reportedly carried out the immediate execution of individuals judged guilty of "crimes against the people." As author Duong Van Mai Elliott has described the process in her gripping account of her own family's experience during the conflict, the land reform cadres would arrest landlords who were accused of having oppressed the poor. Then:

> they tried the landlords in a kangaroo court, carefully staged to make it look like it was the will of the people. About a dozen poor peasants who had suffered the most and who harbored the deepest hatred of the landlords were chosen and coached in advance to denounce them at this trial. While these peasants took turns denouncing the landlords in front of this tribunal, other poor peasants planted in the audience would shout "Down with the landlord!" to reinforce the atmosphere of hostility. If the sentence was death, the landlords would be executed on the spot. If the sentence was imprisonment, they would be led away. The property of landlords found guilty of crimes—including land, houses, draft animals, and tools—would be seized and distributed among the most needy peasants.[14]

Party leaders hoped that such measures would raise the enthusiasm of poor peasants and encourage their participation in the war effort. On June 4, 1953, Radio Vietminh broadcast a letter allegedly sent from a peasant woman to Ho Chi Minh:

> During the French domination, my children and I lacked rice to feed ourselves and clothes to clad us. My children had to rent out their services and I continued to live from day to day by collecting potatoes and by digging the ground for roots. . . . At the end of 1952, the peasants began the struggle against dishonest and nasty landlords. . . . It is thanks to you that we now have such an easy life and we shall never forget it.[15]

For militant elements, however, such measures were still inadequate, because the number of landless peasants in liberated areas, although steadily dropping, constituted up to 15 percent of the population. At a national conference on agriculture held in November, Truong Chinh proposed a tougher policy and submitted the draft of a new land reform law that would lead to the confiscation of the land and property of virtually the entire landlord class.

Ho Chi Minh's attitude toward the proposal has never been entirely clear, although it is likely that he had argued against any land reform program that would be so stringent that it would alienate moderate elements throughout the country. In any event, the manpower needs of the revolution ultimately prevailed. In a speech to the DRV National Assembly a few weeks after the November agriculture conference, Ho conceded that in past years government policies had been too solicitous of the views of the landlord class and not enough of the concerns of peasants. The next month, a new land reform law ordered the enforcement of rent reduction regulations, while extending the confiscation of landholdings to the entire landlord class. Landlords classified as politically progressive would be compensated for their loss by government bonds, but would still be compelled to give up all farmlands beyond the amount needed for their personal livelihood. Those convicted of tyrannical practices were to be punished. The objective of the new legislation was not only to win peasant support, but also to destroy the lingering power of the gentry in rural areas. While the program included provisions for the reeducation of landed elements not considered guilty of crimes against the people, in practice such provisions were often ignored by zealous cadres at the village level. For the first time since the Nghe Tinh revolt in 1930–31, the Party had decided to unleash the specter of class war in the countryside.[16]

In January 1953, Dwight D. Eisenhower entered the White House as the thirty-fourth president of the United States. Ike had campaigned on a platform that called for a "rollback of communism," and leading members of his Republican Party had been critical of the loss of China and the stalemate in Korea that represented the Asian legacy of his Democratic predecessor. In his State of the Union address delivered in early February, Eisenhower had little to say about Indochina, simply noting that the Korean War was "part of the same calculated assault that the aggressor is simultaneously pressing in Indochina and Malaya, and of the strategic situation that manifestly embraces the island of Formosa and the Chinese Nationalist forces there."[17] But during talks held with visiting French Prime Minister René Mayer at the White House in late March, the new chief executive indicated that he would be willing to increase U.S. military assistance to the French, but only if the latter demonstrated the will to adopt a more aggressive approach in seeking total victory in Indochina.

The French, however, had long since abandoned any such intention. As early as December 1949, General Carpentier had warned President Vincent Auriol that the best that could be hoped for was a political solution. The French withdrawal from the border region the following year reflected a tacit acceptance of Carpentier's gloomy outlook, and although the assignment of General de Lattre de Tassigny to command French forces in Indochina in late 1950 led to brief hopes for a triumph over the forces of communism in the region, after his departure and replacement by General Salan a year later French generals and politicians alike were reduced to seeking a political settlement.

To receive U.S. assistance in improving the French military position in advance of a negotiated settlement, however, it was necessary for the French to provide assurances that they would indeed adopt a more aggressive approach in Indochina. The task of persuading the White House to increase U.S. military aid fell to a newly appointed commander in chief of the FEF, General Henri Navarre. Then chief of staff of French NATO forces in Europe, Navarre was by no means Washington's first choice as a replacement for Salan, since he brought with him a reputation for caution and even indecisiveness. After his appointment, Navarre attempted to allay such suspicions by adopting an ambitious strategy (known popularly as the Navarre Plan) to seize the initiative in the fighting in Indochina.

Mayer's ploy of appearing to adopt an aggressive stance in Indochina had only limited success in Washington, where suspicion of French intentions was now chronic. In early August 1953, an article in *Life* magazine harshly criticized the French effort in Indochina and asserted that the war was "all but lost." But the new administration in Washington felt that it had little choice. Reluctantly, the Joint Chiefs of Staff gave their approval to the Navarre Plan, and in September the Eisenhower administration signed a new aid pact increasing U.S. aid to the FEF. The prognosis in Paris, however, was far from promising. Mayer's own defense minister, René Pleven, warned that Navarre's plan was unrealistic, and in July the U.S. Embassy in Paris reported that the French government had rejected the general's request for twelve battalions, which would have had to be transferred to Indochina from Europe. Public support in France for the war was now rapidly melting away, and when the news of the aid agreement was announced in Paris on September 29, critics charged that French blood was to be exchanged for American dollars.[18]

The Navarre Plan was not scheduled to take effect until the spring and summer of 1954. In the meantime, French forces would adopt a defensive policy, while shoring up their positions in the Red River delta and other key areas of the country. One of those areas was the far northwest, the area that had been occupied by Vietminh units in the fall of 1952 as a jumping-off point for their attacks in Laos. In November 1953, in response to an order from Paris to protect the Laotian capital of Luang Prabang from the enemy threat, Navarre decided to occupy the fort at Dien Bien Phu, a small district capital in a remote mountain valley of Vietnam near the Laotian border, as a means of disrupting Vietminh links with central and northern Laos. The town had previously been seized by the Vietminh during their offensive in the northwestern region. Now French paratroopers landed in the valley to take it back.

While General Navarre was attempting to put the first phases of his own strategy into effect, Vietminh strategists had drawn up their own plan of operations for the 1953 campaign. At a meeting of the Central Committee held early in the year, Party planners had decided to avoid an open confrontation with enemy forces for the foreseeable future, while continuing to seek to locate vulnerable points in the enemy's defensive shield, notably in Laos, Cambodia, and the far northwest. This strategy had not changed throughout the course of the year, even after it became clear that Navarre had decided to concentrate his own forces in the Red River delta to reduce the Vietminh threat to the region around Hanoi. Vo Nguyen Giap had proposed a major operation in the delta with the ultimate objective of seizing Hanoi and Haiphong, but Chinese advisers argued for a more cautious strategy focused on the mountainous northwest. Ho Chi Minh backed the Chinese suggestion, and the Politburo approved it in September. This plan was scheduled to be confirmed at a meeting of the VWP Central Military Committee held in November.[19]

News of the French occupation of Dien Bien Phu arrived at Vietminh headquarters just as military commanders were preparing to present to the Central Military Committee their plans for an attack on the French post at Lai Chau, the isolated French military post in the mountains about thirty miles directly to the north of Dien Bien Phu. To the Vietminh leadership, Navarre's gambit opened up promising possibilities, as well as risks. Although the French seizure of Dien Bien Phu posed a severe threat to their communications links with northern Laos, a Vietminh reoccupation of that base could have a significant impact on French morale and set the stage for further advances during the coming year. The area also offered a number of strategic advantages. Located more than two hundred miles from Hanoi, it would represent a severe problem for the French in their efforts to provide supplies and reinforcements.

On the other hand, if an attack at Dien Bien Phu were to be

launched, it would be the first time that the Vietminh had tried to wage a direct assault on a base strongly defended by French forces. Still, it was located in a mountain valley and was close enough to the Chinese border and to Vietminh headquarters in the Viet Bac to permit the shipment in substantial quantities of Chinese matériel. After a careful deliberation of the options and with apparent encouragement from Chinese advisers and their superiors in Beijing, on December 6 Party leaders decided to shift the focus of their efforts in the 1954 campaign to Dien Bien Phu. During the remainder of the year, Vietminh leaders began to infiltrate three newly organized main-force divisions into the mountains around the town, while other units advanced into northern Laos to provide a diversion and force the French to scatter their forces.[20]

Why had Chinese leaders suddenly decided to urge their Vietminh allies to engage in what promised to be a major confrontation with the French? After all, the decision to mount an assault on Dien Bien Phu would require a substantial increase in the quantity and quality of Chinese assistance; a key to success would be the ability of Vietminh artillery to reduce or even stop the French from bringing reinforcements and supplies into the area as the fighting intensified. Although Beijing had been providing assistance to the Vietminh in their struggle for power for three years and undoubtedly saw advantages in meeting China's international obligations as well as protecting its vulnerable southern border against imperialist control, in recent months Chinese leaders had begun to shift the focus of their thinking. In July, a cease-fire had taken effect on the Korean peninsula. The cost of intervention by the PLA in Korea had been high, and there were now signs that Chinese leaders had decided to seek improved relations with the West in order to reduce the threat of future conflicts and enable the government to shift scarce resources to a new five-year plan. In the new environment, Mao Zedong's apocalyptic vision of an inevitable war with imperialism in Asia lost its force. In an interview on August 24, Chinese Premier and Foreign Minister Zhou Enlai declared that "other questions" could be discussed in connection with a possible peace conference to bring a definitive end to the conflict in Korea. In December he had broached with members of an Indian delegation the idea of a mutual agreement based on what eventually came to be known as the "five principles of peaceful coexistence" among states. Washington had responded with its own subtle signal when Secretary of State John Foster Dulles, in a speech to the American Legion in early September, implied that the United States was willing to consider a negotiated agreement to bring an end to the conflict in Indochina.[21]

Interest in bringing an end to the Indochina conflict was also rising in Moscow. New Soviet Prime Minister Georgy Malenkov, who had emerged as the dominant figure on the scene after the death of Joseph Stalin in March, had strong reasons to seek improved relations with the West, including a burgeoning defense budget that diverted scarce funds from needed economic projects. In late September, the USSR suggested the convening of a five-power conference aimed at reducing international tensions. A few days later, China followed suit.

The French occupation of Dien Bien Phu, then, took place just as Chinese leaders (like their Soviet counterparts) were making the decision to launch a peace offensive to bring about a negotiated settlement in Indochina, and a reduction in tensions between the PRC and the United States. A Vietminh victory at Dien Bien Phu could lead to increased tensions in the area, tempting the United States to intervene directly. On the other hand, it could also stimulate antiwar sentiment in France and set the stage for a peace agreement that would be favorable to the Vietminh, and to the interests of China as well. For Beijing, the gamble was worth the risk.[22]

While Ho Chi Minh and his colleagues were undoubtedly grateful to China for offering increased assistance to their projected campaign in the northwest, the reaction in Vietminh headquarters to the flurry of interest expressed in major world capitals for a negotiated peace in Indochina must have been cautious. In the opening months of the war, when Vietminh forces were manifestly weaker than those of their opponents, Ho had tirelessly promoted the cause of a compromise settlement. As the conditions on the battlefield improved, and it became clear that the French no longer sought a total victory, however, it is likely that enthusiasm among Vietminh leaders for such a compromise declined. In remarks to the visiting French Communist Léo Figuères in March 1950, Ho stressed that although Party leaders were amenable to a negotiated settlement, they were not willing to make major concessions. Truong Chinh was even more hostile. In a speech on the sixth anniversary of the founding of the DRV given in September 1951, he warned that the DRV should not be lured into negotiations and insisted that it was necessary to "extirpate every opportunist's illusion of peace negotiations with the enemy." When Paris sent out feelers on a compromise agreement at the end of 1952, they were ignored by the DRV. As late as September 1953, the Soviet news agency Tass reported that in a speech on the eighth anniversary of the formation of the DRV, Ho Chi Minh had declared that peace could come about only as the result of victory.[23]

A few weeks later, however, Vietnamese Party leaders decided to go along with the proposal of Moscow and Beijing to seek a political settlement. In an interview held on October 20 with a correspondent from the Swedish journal *Expressen*, Ho declared that his government was willing to attend an international conference to bring about a peaceful settlement in Indochina. "If the French government wish to have an armistice and to resolve the question of Vietnam by means of negotiations," he declared, "the people and government of the Democratic Republic of Vietnam are ready to examine the French proposals." The interview was widely reported in the world press. Shortly after, Beijing made explicit its agreement in an editorial in *People's Daily*. According to a U.S. diplomatic source in Saigon, Ho's offer of peace talks caused "confusion, consternation, and outright fear" among Vietnamese non-Communists in Saigon.[24]

Ever the realist, Ho Chi Minh was aware that a negotiated settlement was one of the options for bringing about an end to the war. The decision by the United States in July 1953 to seek an end to the conflict in Korea was a comforting sign that the imperialists were willing to grant concessions when they faced major difficulties; the news had undoubtedly aroused hopes within the Vietminh movement that a similar result might be achieved in Indochina. But in a speech to a group of intellectuals in the Viet Bac a few weeks later, Ho had warned his audience that it should have no illusions that peace would come easily. Like the Americans, the French would not be willing to grant major concessions at the peace table unless they were defeated on the battlefield. The enemy, he warned, "is trying to trick us by dropping bait in the water; if we rush in like a school of fish and forget to be alert to defend ourselves, they will easily defeat us." It was therefore important to be vigilant and continue the struggle, even if the United States should decide to enter the conflict.[25]

Under the circumstances, even as he expressed his willingness to enter peace talks, Ho must have felt some misgivings for, as he pointed out to colleagues in a meeting held in November, conditions for a complete victory were not totally ripe. At the same time, the attitude of the USSR and China was a source for concern. Soviet support for the Vietnamese war of national liberation had always been lukewarm, and thus not much was probably expected from Moscow. But firm assistance from the PRC was a crucial component in the Vietminh strategy, and any indication that Beijing was preparing to compromise on the issue for the sake of its own national interests would have deepened the worry lines on the foreheads of Ho and his colleagues in the Viet Bac.[26]

On the other hand, Ho Chi Minh was aware that the Vietminh were in no position to continue their protracted struggle without the full backing of the Chinese. It would not be the first time that he had accepted the necessity of a compromise in order to fight again another day. For their part, Moscow and Beijing hardly needed Vietnamese concurrence to pursue their own national security needs. At a conference held in Berlin early in 1954, delegates for the major powers reached agreement that another international conference should be convened at Geneva in April to discuss issues relating to world peace. Much to the discomfiture of the Eisenhower administration, Indochina, along with the situation in Korea, was to be placed on the table for discussion. In March, a DRV delegation traveled to Beijing to consult with Chinese officials on hammering out a common strategy at Geneva. Shortly after, a Vietnamese delegation led by Ho Chi Minh visited Bejing and Moscow to formulate a joint negotiating strategy with Soviet and Chinese leaders. Basing their advice on experience derived from negotiations with the United States to bring an end to the conflict in Korea, the latter warned the Vietnamese to be "realistic" in their expectations at Geneva.[27]

Two days after the announcement of the upcoming conference at Geneva, French intelligence sources learned that Vietminh units in upper Laos were heading east in the direction of Dien Bien Phu. Although Vietnamese operations were under way in other areas—in Cochin China, in the Central Highlands, in Laos, and in the Hanoi–Haiphong corridor—by early March captured documents revealed to the French that a major Vietminh offensive in the northwest was imminent and that it would be synchronized with the upcoming negotiations in Geneva. There were additional indications that Chinese military assistance to the Vietminh had dramatically increased, thus improving the latter's prospects for victory.

On this occasion, French intelligence sources were correct. Beginning in December, Vietminh units gradually assembled in the mountains surrounding the French base at Dien Bien Phu, while thousands of civilian porters were mobilized to transport ammunition and heavy artillery pieces from the Chinese border into the area. As one participant later recounted it to an American journalist:

We had to cross mountains and jungles, marching at night and sleeping by day to avoid enemy bombing. We sometimes slept in foxholes, or just by the trail. We each carried a rifle, ammunition, and hand grenades, and our packs contained a blanket, a mosquito net, and a change of clothes. We each had a week's supply of rice, which we refilled at depots along the way. We ate greens and bamboo shoots that we picked in the jungle, and occasionally villagers would give us a bit of meat. I'd been in the Vietminh for nine years by then, and I was accustomed to it.[28]

To bring about favorable battlefield conditions necessary to realize a satisfactory peace settlement at the conference table, Chinese military assistance increased substantially over the next several months. According to Chinese sources, more than 200 trucks, 10,000 barrels of oil, over 100 cannons, 60,000 artillery shells, 3,000 guns, and about 1,700 tons of grain were shipped to the Vietnamese forces dug in around Dien Bien Phu. To encourage Chinese advisers in Indochina to seek a major victory, Zhou Enlai sent the following message: "In order to bring about a victory in the diplomatic field, we may need to consider whether we can achieve some dramatic victories in Vietnam such as took place prior to the armistice in Korea." Ho Chi Minh, for one, needed no persuading. In a letter to Vo Nguyen Giap in December, he declared: "This campaign is a very important one, not only militarily, but also politically, not only for domestic reasons, but for international ones as well. So all of our people, all of our armed forces, and the entire Party must entirely unite to get the job done."[29]

For Ho and his colleagues, the question had now become not whether, but how, to attack the French post. The newly cautious Vo Nguyen Giap argued for a plan that would wear down the enemy, using his artillery to destroy the small airstrip in the valley and cut off French sources of supply. Vietminh troops could then gradually neutralize French firepower and seize enemy strong points along the perimeter of the base one by one. According to Vietnamese sources, General Wei Guoqing, the senior Chinese adviser, argued for a different approach, advocating a lightning assault based on the "human wave" tactics that had been used with initial effectiveness by PLA units against United Nations troops in Korea.[30]

The first Vietminh assault on Dien Bien Phu was launched in mid-January. The Vietminh had managed to assemble a total of thirty-three battalions of regular troops, comprising nearly 50,000 combatants, in the mountains around the base. They confronted an enemy numbering about 16,000 men. In addition to their regular forces, the Vietminh had more than 55,000 support troops and nearly 100,000 transport workers. Many of the latter were women from the provinces of central Vietnam who had to pass through enemy-held areas in the Red River delta to reach their staging area near the Chinese border. This "long haired army" then carried artillery pieces and other war matériel over hundreds of miles through difficult terrain to the area around the base. Each transport worker carried an average of thirty pounds of provisions ten miles each night over rough mountain trails. Although most of the supplies consisted of petroleum and ammunition, there was also large artillery from the Soviet Union, carried piece by piece from the Chinese border at Lang Son, a distance of more than 200 miles.[31]

In the beginning stages of the battle, the attackers followed the Chinese advice to use "human wave" tactics, but the casualties suffered were so heavy that by the end of January, the Vietnamese high command (at the urging of Beijing) reevaluated the situation and decided to switch to a more cautious approach. In the course of the next several weeks, Vietminh troops dug a network of several hundred miles of shallow trenches to enable them to advance steadily but surely toward the outlying French defense works without being exposed to the enemy's firepower. In the meantime, a series of tunnels was dug into the mountain slopes surrounding the besieged fortress. Artillery brought piece by piece by porters from the Chinese border and then assembled on the spot was installed inside the tunnels; it could then be moved rapidly between locations, thus preventing French gunners in the fort below from zeroing in on the source of the shelling.[32]

At first, supplies and reinforcements were shipped to the defenders by airlift, but eventually the airfield on the outskirts of the base became virtually unusable because of heavy shelling by the enemy. Planes landing on the airstrip to unload their cargo were almost immediately destroyed by a Vietminh artillery barrage launched from the surrounding mountains. Soon, French pilots were reduced to making a hasty pass over the valley and dropping supplies and new troops by parachute. Eventually, Vietminh firepower became so concentrated that troop reinforcements coming in that way were often dead before they hit the ground.

As the situation became more perilous, the French turned in desperation to the United States for assistance. In mid-March, Paris sent General Paul Ely to Washington to request U.S. air strikes to relieve the French garrison and protect it from the threat of collapse. There was some support for the idea from Admiral Arthur Radford, chairman of the Joint Chiefs of Staff, and from Vice President Richard Nixon, who in a private conversation with French Ambassador Henri Bonnet on April 28 declared "that he entirely shared the point of view of Admiral Radford and that he favored a massive intervention by U.S. aircraft to save Dien Bien Phu." But President Eisenhower, whose appetite for engaging in land wars in Asia had been diminished by the inconclusive engagement on the Korean peninsula, was reluctant to introduce U.S. combat forces into Indochina without guarantees that the battle would henceforth be waged on a multinational basis, and on condition that the French would promise ultimately to grant full independence to all three states of Indochina. In a trip to London and Paris, Secretary of State John Foster Dulles found that neither the British nor the French would agree to U.S. conditions; Eisenhower thereupon refused the French request for air support and, while continuing to explore the possibility of U.S. intervention, reluctantly set his sights on achieving a satisfactory settlement at the peace table.[33]

In early May, the Vietminh penetrated the outer defenses of the fort at Dien Bien Phu and began to shell the French redoubt within. According to Chinese sources, at the last minute the confidence of Vietminh war planners began to waver as the result of heavy casualties and the threat of U.S. intervention, but with strong encouragement from Beijing they ultimately decided to storm the fort in a bid for total victory. The final assault took place on May 6 when, in Vo Nguyen Giap's somewhat laconic description, "our troops launched an offensive from all directions, occupied the enemy's headquarters and captured the whole enemy staff." The French defeat had been total. More than 1,500 of the defenders had died, 4,000 were wounded, and the remainder were taken prisoner or listed as missing. About 70 managed to escape and made their way back to the French lines. Vietminh losses were even heavier, with more than 25,000 casualites, of whom nearly 10,000 were killed in action.[34]

O n May 7, the day following the final surrender of the French base at Dien Bien Phu, peace talks on resolving the Indochina conflict opened as scheduled in Geneva. In attendance at the meeting were delegations from France, the DRV, Great Britain, the Soviet Union, China, and the United States, as well as representatives from the Bao Dai government and from the royal governments, now officially known as associated states, of Cambodia and Laos. DRV leaders, reflecting Ho Chi Minh's earlier warning that victory would not come easily, approached the conference warily, but felt that it offered an opportunity for a major advance in the struggle for complete national reunification.[35]

At the opening session of the conference, the French delegation stated its conditions for a settlement, calling for a regroupment of the armed forces of both sides under the supervision of an international control commission. Pham Van Dong, chairman of the DRV delegation (as he had been in Fontainebleau in 1946), accepted the French proposal for a cease-fire before a settlement of political issues, but in all other respects his demands (drawn up by the Politburo) differed markedly from those of the French. He demanded international recognition of the sovereignty and full independence of all three countries of Indochina, the withdrawal of all foreign troops (meaning, of course, the French), and the holding of free elections to be supervised by local authorities. In addition, he demanded that representatives of the revolutionary movements in Laos and Cambodia (known popularly as the Pathet Lao and the Khmer Rouge, respectively) be seated at the conference table as legitimate representatives of the people of both countries. In an almost contemptuous gesture, Dong agreed to examine possible future membership in the French Union, based on free will and a recognition of the economic and cultural interests of the French in the three Indochinese states.

Paris was in no position to drive a hard bargain. French intelligence sources openly predicted that, in the face of a vigorous Vietminh assault, Hanoi could fall. Opinion in Washington was equally pessimistic. At a briefing given at a meeting of the National Security Council on May 8, CIA Director Allen Dulles estimated that with five thousand trucks, the Vietminh should be able to move their troops from Dien Bien Phu to the Tonkin delta within two or three weeks' time. Although French armed forces in the delta numbered nearly 200,000, as compared with 76,000 Vietminh regulars, the French were plagued by low morale and enclosed in fixed strong points surrounded by a hostile or indifferent population. As for the Vietnamese National Army, created by the Bao Dai government after the signing of the Elysée Accords, General Navarre dismissed them as "rabble."[36]

However, the DRV faced a serious problem of its own at Geneva: the mood of its allies. Although Vietminh representatives had met with their Chinese and Soviet counterparts before the conference to formulate a common negotiating strategy, it had become clear that neither Moscow nor Beijing was eager to back the Vietminh in a continuation of the war, nor were they willing to give blanket support for Vietnamese demands. Both, in fact, had their own security interests in mind at Geneva, and were anxious to avoid a possible confrontation with the United States. After the preliminary skirmishing came to an end, it was obvious that both Soviet Foreign Minister Vyacheslav Molotov and China's chief delegate at Geneva, Zhou Enlai, favored a compromise based on the division of Vietnam into two separate regroupment zones, one occupied by the Vietminh and the other by the Bao Dai government and its supporters. Moreover, after initially supporting Vietminh views on Laos and Cambodia, Foreign Minister Zhou made it clear to Pham Van Dong that China did not support the DRV demand for the seating of Pathet Lao and Khmer Rouge delegates as the legitimate representatives of the Laotian and Cambodian peoples. That issue, Zhou warned, could scuttle prospects for a settlement and lead to direct U.S. intervention in the war. Better, he believed, to accept the neutralization of both states under their existing royal governments. As an inducement to bring about DRV acceptance, Zhou agreed to insist on the necessity of providing the Pathet Lao forces with a regroupment zone after the close of the conflict. With evident reluctance, Pham Van Dong agreed.[37]

Many years later, Vietnamese official sources would claim that Zhou Enlai's behavior at Geneva was motivated by China's desire to assimilate Laos and Cambodia into its own sphere of influence. Although there is little evidence to confirm this, it seems likely that Beijing viewed these two countries as crucial to its own security needs in the region and therefore may not have wished to see the Indochinese federation put into effect. Still, at the time, perhaps the main motivation was the more urgent objective of preventing the collapse of the peace talks and the future possibility of the establishment of U.S. bases in both countries. It was certainly in those terms that Zhou urged Dong to accept a compromise on the issue, a point of view that was strongly supported by the Soviet delegation.

With the issue of Laos and Cambodia resolved, the conference temporarily adjourned while the French and DRV delegations turned their attention to details connected with the settlement in Vietnam. In private military talks with the French, Vietminh delegates had made it clear that they wanted a contiguous territory for a regroupment zone for their troops and followers consisting, among other things, of the entire Red River delta, including Hanoi and Haiphong. ("We must have Hanoi, we must have outlets," said one senior Vietminh negotiator). The French were reluctant to concede the loss of Hanoi, but implied that if such were the case, they would want in return a free hand in the south and at least a temporary enclave in the north to complete the evacuation of troops and civilians from the delta.

The debate thus began to center on the dividing line between the two regroupment zones, and how the overall agreement would be enforced. At first Pham Van Dong demanded a line drawn at the Thirteenth Parallel, while the French held forth for a line just south of the Red River delta, much farther to the north. To police the agreement, DRV delegates wanted local supervision only, while the French (supported by the United States) called for the creation of an international control commission under the auspices of the United Nations.

While the French and DRV delegations at Geneva skirmished over these details, Zhou Enlai left by plane for Beijing to consult with Mao Zedong and other government leaders. En route he made a brief stop in India, where he solicited the support of Prime Minister Jawaharlal Nehru for the Chinese positions at the conference. To reassure Nehru, who was increasingly nervous about the possibility that all of Indochina might soon come under Communist rule (and thereby fall under the domination of China), Zhou promised that all Vietminh troops were to be withdrawn from Laos and Cambodia, and that both countries would be permitted to have independent governments of their own choosing. As for the situation in Vietnam, he assured the Indian leader that the DRV would respect any future division of Vietnam into two separate zones, declaring that communism was "not for export." In a communiqué issued after the series of meetings, the two leaders reaffirmed their support for the concept of the five principles of peaceful coexistence as the proper basis for international relations within Asia and throughout the world.[38]

After a short stop in Rangoon, where he exchanged similar views with Burmese Prime Minister U Nu, Zhou Enlai returned to Beijing, and then proceeded directly to Liuzhou, Zhang Fakui's onetime headquarters in south China, where he met with Ho Chi Minh and Vo Nguyen Giap. The meeting received little publicity. A press statement issued later by the New China News Agency said only that "the Prime Minister Zhou Enlai and President Ho Chi Minh had a complete exchange of views on the Geneva conference, the question of the restoration of peace in Indochina, and related questions." According to recently released Chinese sources, however, Zhou successfully persuaded Ho of the need to reach a compromise settlement at Geneva to avoid a direct U.S. intervention in the war. The two leaders agreed on the Sixteenth Parallel as an acceptable dividing line between the two regroupment zones. They further agreed on the acceptability of establishing non-Communist governments in Laos and Cambodia, provided that a small regroupment zone be set aside for the Pathet Lao. Ho also consented to issue a joint statement that future relations among the three countries of Indochina would be governed by the five principles of peaceful coexistence. In return, Zhou Enlai promised China's continued support and assistance for the DRV. In aid agreements signed in Beijing on July 7, China committed to a substantial increase in trade and economic assistance. Official sources in Vietnam were terse in reporting the results of the meeting. The Party newspaper *Nhan Dan* noted cryptically that "the restoration of peace in Indochina cannot be uniquely decided by one side."[39]

After brief consultations in Beijing, Zhou Enlai returned to Geneva, where the conferees wrapped up the remaining issues; the treaty was signed early in the morning of July 21, 1954. The agreement would be supervised by an International Control Commission, composed of India, Canada, and Poland. A nonbinding political declaration attached to the cease-fire called for consultations between the governments in the two regroupment zones, and national elections to unify the country to be held in two years. The final sticking point was an agreement to establish the dividing line between the two regroupment zones at the Seventeenth Parallel. When Pham Van Dong appeared reluctant to accept the compromise, Zhou argued that giving French Prime Minister Pierre Mendès-France a means of saving face was a small price to pay for obtaining the final departure of French troops. "With the final withdrawal of the French," Zhou promised, "all of Vietnam will be yours."[40]

From the point of view of Ho Chi Minh and his colleagues, however, there were some ominous developments shortly after the close of the conference. The Eisenhower administration had observed the course of the talks at Geneva with misgivings and had decided not to accept the terms of a settlement unless at least a part of the future Vietnam remained secure under a non-Communist government. Because the provision for the eventual unification of the entire country by national elections to be held in 1956 opened up the possibility of a total Communist victory, Washington indicated that it would not give its approval to the political declaration, nor would it commit itself to support the Geneva Accords themselves. The Bao Dai delegation followed suit and refused to assent to the political declaration, arguing that the decision to divide the country had been made by a colonial power and against the will of the Vietnamese people. A few days after the close of the conference, Secretary of State John Foster Dulles announced at a press conference that the United States would now begin to foster the development of the non-Communist states of South Vietnam, Laos, and Cambodia. It was hardly a good omen for the prospects of future national elections.

Many observers at the conference noted an attitude of bitterness within the DRV delegation over the alleged betrayal of Vietnamese interests by China and the Soviet Union. In his reminiscences, Chinese diplomat Wang Bingnan later remarked that some members of the delegation "hoped to unify the whole of Vietnam at one stroke."[41]

That bitterness was apparently not limited to Vietnamese delegates at Geneva, but was reflected inside Vietnam as well. The mood was apparently serious enough to seize Ho Chi Minh's attention. In a political report given to the VWP Central Committee a few days before the final signing of the Geneva Agreement, he pointed out that

> some people, intoxicated with our repeated victories, want to fight on at all costs, to a finish; they see only the trees, not the whole forest; with their attention focused on the withdrawal of the French they fail to detect their schemes; they see the French but not the Americans; they are partial to military action and make light of diplomacy. They are unaware that we are struggling in international conferences as well as on the battlefields in order to attain our goal.

Such people, he contended, "want quick results, unaware that the struggle for peace is a hard and complex one." What they fail to see is that the three countries have already made great advances in their struggle to obtain the complete independence of all countries of Indochina. Now, however, a new strategy was needed, because the United States was determined to sabotage the prospects for peace and justify its future intervention in the conflict in Indochina. Under the new circumstances, the old slogan of "Resistance to the end," must be replaced by a new one: "Peace, unity, independence, democracy." Such a policy would help to isolate the United States (which had now become the main and direct enemy of the Indochinese people) on the world's stage and help to defeat its nefarious schemes.

Ho Chi Minh conceded that the price for peace was the division of Vietnam. But the establishment of regroupment zones, he insisted, did not mean partition of the country, but was a temporary measure only:

> Owing to the delimitation and exchange of zones, some previously free areas will be temporarily occupied by the enemy; their inhabitants will be dissatisfied; some people might fall prey to discouragement and to enemy deception. We should make it clear to our compatriots that the trials they are going to endure for the sake of the interests of the whole country, for the sake of our long-range

interests, will be a cause for glory and will earn them the gratitude of the whole nation.

With the correct leadership of the Party and the support of the peoples of the world, Ho Chi Minh promised, full independence and national unity would surely be fulfilled.[42]

In calling on his colleagues in the Party to accept a negotiated settlement of the war that was substantially less than total victory, Ho Chi Minh was undoubtedly deferring to the advice of Zhou Enlai, who had urged such a step during their summit meeting in Liuzhou a few days before. Yet his willingness to accept a compromise peace en route to his final objective is reminiscent of his views on previous occasions, notably at the end of the Pacific War. Ho Chi Minh recognized that national independence and unity for the Vietnamese nation could not be achieved in isolation, but must be achieved in the context of the complex changes taking place on the world's stage.

XIV | BETWEEN TWO WARS

On October 9, 1954, French troops crossed the Paul Doumer Bridge, which stretched over the muddy waters of the Red River, and departed from the city of Hanoi. In a brief ceremony, Colonel Lefebre d'Argencé, commander of the last French detachment, turned the administration of the city over to Vo Nguyen Giap's capital regiment. During the previous two weeks, the city had appeared virtually empty, as thousands of refugees streamed southward along Route 5 to the port city of Haiphong. The streets of Hanoi were especially dead at night, as most restaurants, bars, and shops downtown were closed.

The following day, the city came back to life, as the local population celebrated the arrival of their new rulers. It was a festive occasion. The streets were plastered with flags and slogans welcoming the Party and the government; organized processions, composed of children and delegations representing a variety of social groups and associations, took place before large and enthusiastic crowds of onlookers gathered in front of the Governor-General's Palace and in the park next to the Northern Palace, which had once served as the administrative headquarters of the DRV. On October 11, Vietminh units bearing machine guns and light artillery pieces began to pour into the city, where they were greeted with shouts of "*doc lap*" (independence) from the assembled crowds. In their midst were members of the Ho Chi Minh's government, many of whom were setting foot in the capital for the first time in nearly eight years.

Ho Chi Minh himself arrived in the city quietly sometime on or after October 12, but there was no triumphal entry or celebration to mark the occasion, and his first public appearance did not take place until the arrival of Indian Prime Minister Jawaharlal Nehru, on the seventeenth. In an editorial appearing in a local newspaper the next day, Ho explained that he did not want to waste his countrymen's time in a public welcome. "Our mutual love," he remarked, "does not depend on appearance." The development of the economy and progress toward the unification of the country, he explained, were more important than ceremony.

But Ho Chi Minh had already met with a small group of municipal Party officials at a small ceremony on October 16. In brief remarks on that occasion he noted that there would be many difficulties to overcome, but that they could be gradually resolved if everyone cooperated and obeyed the laws of the new authorities. That new government, he declared, represented the will of the people, and it would subject itself to popular criticism. So in fact it seemed. Cadres were carefully instructed to behave properly to the local population, while students and teachers were urged to continue to attend their classes, and merchants to continue selling their wares in the liberated city. Foreigners were encouraged to remain and to continue in their occupations. Ho himself checked into a hospital for medical treatment. After his release, he refused an offer by his colleagues to live in the Governor-General's Palace, which he considered to be too pretentious for his tastes, and decided to take up residence in a small gardener's house on the palace grounds. Still, the main building was renamed the Presidential Palace (Phu Chu tich), in honor of its new role.[1]

In his customary manner, Ho Chi Minh adopted a conciliatory demeanor in his dealings with the outside world. In discussions with Nehru, he subscribed to the five principles of peaceful coexistence that Nehru and Chinese Prime Minister Zhou Enlai had recently affirmed at their meeting in June, and he assured his visitor that the new Vietnam would maintain correct relations with the royal governments in Laos and Cambodia. On October 18, he met with Jean Sainteny, recently returned to Hanoi at the request of Prime Minister Pierre Mendès-France to represent French interests in the DRV. Sainteny reported to Paris that Ho had expressed a willingness to retain a French cultural and economic presence in North Vietnam and to establish diplomatic contacts with other non-Communist countries. Ho further insisted that he was not a slave to hard-line elements in his Party. In an interview with a journalist in early November, however, Ho emphasized that hereafter Franco-DRV relations must be on a basis of equality.[2]

Still, despite Ho Chi Minh's reassurances, the small contingent of Europeans and Americans in Hanoi was closely watched, and their activities were severely restricted. In contrast to the generally relaxed and affable Ho, many of the cadres of the new regime were, in Jean Sainteny's appraisal, "meddlesome busybodies, organizing meetings, patriotic chorales, processions, indoctrination sessions, early morning calisthenics, and so on." Most closely watched was the small American community. The local press, now under firm Party control, was highly critical of the United States, and a statement by the local Vietminh committee that was running the government until the installation of a formal administration had announced that it did not recognize the legal status of the U.S. consulate in Hanoi. Anti-American attitudes among the local population were fanned by Ho Chi Minh himself, who continued to write occasional articles critical of the United States that were published in local newspapers under the initials C.B. During the next few weeks, a variety of petty restrictions were placed on the U.S. consulate's activities, and it was forced to close before the end of the year. Its last public event was a Thanksgiving party, attended by a handful of Western diplomats and members of the International Control Commission that had been established as the result of the Geneva Accords.[3]

On November 3, President Ho Chi Minh convened a meeting of his Council of Ministers to review government programs and appoint a new administrative committee for the capital region. The council faced some intimidating problems. What strategy should be adopted to help the northern provinces recover from eight years of war and several decades of foreign occupation? Should the DRV, under firm Party guidance, move rapidly to abolish the edifice of colonial authority and begin to lay the foundations of a future socialist society, or should it move forward slowly and gradually through a transitional phase in a bid to reassure moderates, spur economic growth, and raise the overall standard of living of the general population? Could the regime win the support of the rural and urban poor while at the same time placating affluent elements? Finally, how should it deal with the issue of reunification and the implementation of the Geneva Accords?

In a sense, the first question may have already been answered. For Ho Chi Minh and his colleagues, there was ample precedent for a policy of prudence. After the end of the Civil War in Soviet Russia in 1920, Lenin had encouraged a temporary continuation of private enterprise to promote rapid economic growth and technological modernization. That policy did not come to an end until 1928, when Stalin introduced a program calling for nationalization of industry and the collectivization of agriculture. China had followed a similar path after the rise to power of the CCP in 1949, launching its own program of "new democracy" to win the support of moderate elements and lay the economic basis for socialist transformation in the mid-1950s.

A few days prior to the signing of the Geneva Accords, the DRV from its liberated base in the Viet Bac had already published a decree elucidating its future strategy after the projected cease-fire. The announcement contained an eight-point program that was clearly designed to reassure merchants, professionals, bureaucrats, and foreigners that for the time being the new government would not attempt to interfere in their private activities. It called for a government takeover of business enterprises and public services previously owned and operated by the imperialists or by the "puppet authority" (i.e., the Bao Dai government). Private ownership of all other forms of property would be guaranteed. Civil servants employed by the previous regime would not be arrested unless they had taken up arms against the resistance or committed acts of sabotage against the people's property. All civilian officials were instructed to remain at their posts and obey orders while awaiting the installation of the people's authority. Former officers of the Vietnamese National Army were ordered to report to military committees established by the new revolutionary administration. Those who failed to do so would be "severely punished." Freedom of religion was guaranteed, as was the security of the persons and property of foreign nationals.[4]

In an appeal to the Vietnamese people circulated in September, prior to the return of the government to Hanoi, Ho Chi Minh had set the tone of conciliation. "We are ready," he said, "to unite with whomever from north to south approves peace, unity, independence and democracy, regardless of with whom they collaborated in the past." The rights of domestic and foreign capitalists to carry out their legitimate business activities were to be retained, and all those who had once been employed by the enemy who now wished to work for the people and the nation were welcomed.[5]

Party leaders had good reason to conciliate their former adversaries. During the autumn, refugees continued to stream southward out of Hanoi by the thousands. Eventually a total of over 800,000 Vietnamese left the North, many of them Roman Catholics who were warned by their priests, "the Virgin Mary has moved to the South. Shouldn't you?" A substantial number of Catholics had close ties with the French or the Bao Dai government, while those who did not feared that deep-seated suspicions of their loyalty on the part of DRV officials could result in persecution.

Although the exodus served to spare the new regime a potential source of opposition, it also deprived the northern provinces of a substantial proportion of their most affluent, creative, and industrious people, since Catholics made up a high percentage of the commercial, professional, and intellectual elite of the country. One observer estimated that in October 1954 the new government had within its ranks only fifty college graduates; no more than an additional two hundred possessed a high school diploma. Most factories were shut, and many of the owners had left the country. According to one report, twenty-nine of thirty factories owned by French in the port city of Haiphong had been closed. Transportation was a serious problem. Gasoline for motor vehicles was in short supply, and the railroads were not working.[6]

In addition, much of the irrigation network had been destroyed by the French, and nearly 10 percent of the cultivated land in the Red River delta had been abandoned because of the flight of the local population to urban areas in the closing months of the war (the French had declared much of the delta region to be a free fire zone, where their armed forces were authorized to shoot at anything in sight). Then, in December disastrous floods along the central coast raised the specter of a new famine, and the price of rice in the markets rapidly shot up.

As a result, when the DRV began to set up its central state apparatus in early November, it was compelled to fuse some of its existing departments and agencies while attempting to make use of remaining administrative personnel who had been employed by the Bao Dai regime. At the local level, the committees of resistance and administration that had been established during the Franco-Vietminh War continued to operate, although the reference to resistance in their title was dropped to conform to new conditions. Eventually, however, it was announced that elections for People's Councils would soon be held at local levels to provide a firm legal basis for the establishment of popular power.[7]

In the first few months after returning to Hanoi, the Party leadership limited itself to adopting measures to install a new revolutionary administration, to broaden the popular base of support for the DRV, and to establish a firm basis from which to engage in postwar economic reconstruction. Behind the scenes, however, there were signs that Party leaders had already begun to focus on the future. In early September, the Politburo had met to draft long-range policy. Once power was consolidated in the North, it concluded, preparations would begin for the future advance to socialism. Ho Chi Minh had already caught the attention of prescient observers in a speech on September 2, when he remarked enigmatically that the new regime would be bourgeois democratic in form, but people's democratic in content.[8]

O ne of the primary reasons for the decision to move slowly toward a socialist system in the North was the Party's desire to bring about the reunification of the two zones envisioned in the political declaration drafted at Geneva. Many members of the Vietminh movement—notably in the South—had been sorely disappointed with the results of the peace conference. Party leaders undoubtedly shared the dismay that years of sacrifice had resulted in only a partial victory, but they were able to console themselves with the conviction that, because of the overall popularity of Ho Chi Minh and the general ineptitude of the Bao Dai government, the provisions for future national elections at the Geneva conference obviously operated to their advantage. One way to ensure that the elections would be successful would be for the government in the North to present a moderate face to the world through its domestic policies, in order to avoid alienating non-Communist elements in South Vietnam as well as interested observers around the world.

According to one of his confidants, Ho Chi Minh was optimistic that scheduled elections would take place, and he may have felt that the pressure of world public opinion would force the regime in the South to adhere to the terms of the agreement. Still, although official sources in Hanoi publicly declared their confidence that the provisions of the political declaration would eventually be upheld, in private some of Ho's colleagues expressed their skepticism. Even Pham Van Dong, who had chaired the DRV delegation at Geneva and would be appointed prime minister in September 1955, reportedly remarked to an observer: "You know as well as I do that there won't be elections." If that should be the case, Hanoi would be forced to explore other options, including a possible return to the strategy of revolutionary war. In the meantime, Ho Chi Minh was compelled to use his formidable skills to persuade his colleagues to give the accords a chance to succeed.

For the time being, Party leaders attempted to prepare for either contingency. According to various estimates, somewhere between 50,000 and 90,000 Vietminh sympathizers (many of them sons and daughters of Party cadres living in the South) went north after the agreement, while approximately 10,000 to 15,000 others, mainly veterans of the revolutionary movement, remained in the South to take part in legal activities designed to promote the holding of national elections. Still others retreated underground to preserve and maintain the clandestine revolutionary apparatus, in the event that it needed to be reactivated.[9]

There were certainly many obstacles to holding elections, and among the most formidable was the attitude of the new government in the South. In June 1954, while the Geneva conference was still under way, Chief of State Bao Dai had named Ngo Dinh Diem, the veteran politician who had been briefly detained by Ho Chi Minh's provisional government in the fall of 1945, as his new prime minister. (Fearing for his own safety back then, Diem had gone into hiding briefly at the Canadian Embassy in Hanoi.) Diem had settled in the United States in the early 1950s, where he tirelessly sought to win the support of the Eisenhower administration for an eventual return to politics. A devout Catholic, he spent several months at a Catholic seminary in New Jersey and appeared to have an almost messianic sense of his own mission to save his compatriots from the threat of godless communism.

Support for Diem in Washington, however, was initially limited, since many U.S. officials viewed him as monkish and unrealistic, lacking in statesmanship, and altogether not a serious candidate for political leadership. One American observer dismissed him scornfully as a "messiah without a message." Undaunted, Diem continued to pester U.S. diplomats with advice and sought the sponsorship of prominent members of the Catholic hierarchy in the United States, including Francis Cardinal Spellman and Joseph Kennedy, the former ambassador to London.

By his own account, Bao Dai had been motivated to appoint Ngo Dinh Diem because of his belief that Diem's staunch anticommunism might appeal to cold warriors in Washington. Although it has often been assumed that the Eisenhower administration played a role in the decision, the news was apparently greeted in Washington with dismay as well as some reservations. It generated equally little enthusiasm in Saigon, where the Bao Dai government had established its capital. Having been brought up in a Catholic family with close ties to the imperial court in Hué, Diem was viewed with suspicion by many veteran political figures in the South. The new prime minister reciprocated the feeling, confiding to close members of his entourage that he found southerners too easygoing to resist effectively the Communists. Not surprisingly, his cabinet was composed for the most part of northerners and central Vietnamese.[10]

From his new post in Saigon, Diem had expressed his disapproval of the terms of the settlement reached at Geneva in July, and after the close of the conference he immediately made it clear that he had no intention of dealing with the Communists. The Saigon government's security forces began to harass Vietminh sympathizers in the South and closed the offices of committees that the Vietminh had established to promote national elections. Diem was equally adamant in suppressing the Cao Dai and Hoa Hao religious sects, whose leaders showed no more enthusiasm for the Saigon government than they did for the Vietminh. He also sought to cleanse his government of any members considered sympathetic to Chief of State Bao Dai, whom he despised as a collaborator of the colonial regime, or to the French themselves.

Diem's combative behavior during the winter of 1954–55 had aroused considerable anxiety among U.S. officials in Saigon and Washington. Still, with the Geneva conference at an end, the Eisenhower administration had already decided that the survival of an independent and viable non-Communist regime in South Vietnam was essential to preserve U.S. security interests in the region. In the fall of 1954, President Eisenhower dispatched his friend General J. Lawton Collins (known as "Lightning Joe" for his aggressive tactics as a corps commander in World War II) as his personal emissary to direct and coordinate U.S. activities in South Vietnam. From Saigon, Collins persistently advised that Diem be replaced by a more conciliatory figure who would be more acceptable to the French and to the South Vietnamese people themselves. In the early spring of 1955, the White House briefly gave serious consideration to heeding Collins's suggestion. By April of 1955, however, Diem had managed to suppress internal opposition to his rule, so Washington then decided to give him its firm backing. As Eisenhower remarked to General Collins, the odds of success in South Vietnam had just risen from 10 percent to 50 percent. Shortly after, Diem publicly rejected Hanoi's offer to hold consultations on future national elections.

In Washington, the news of Diem's refusal to discuss national elections aroused mixed feelings. A recent CIA report had flatly predicted a victory for the Vietminh, not only because of the nationwide popularity of Ho Chi Minh, but also because the DRV leadership in the North was much more experienced at political mobilization than the fledgling regime in the South; it would presumably make good use of classical Leninist techniques to guarantee a favorable vote in areas under its authority. With memories of the staged elections and purge trials that had been held in Soviet-occupied countries in Eastern Europe after the end of World War II still sharp, U.S. officials were convinced that a fair assessment of the popular will could not be held in Vietnam under current circumstances.

Then too, the public perception of Ho Chi Minh and his regime had shifted significantly in the United States in the years since the beginning of the Franco-Vietminh conflict. The earlier view that the Vietminh were selfless patriots struggling to throw off the yoke of an oppressive colonial regime had been replaced in the popular mind by a more somber image of Ho and his colleagues as committed agents of international communism. After the close of the Geneva conference in July 1954, this view seemingly had been confirmed by filmed scenes of thousands of desperate refugees fleeing south to avoid the terrors of a Stalinist-style regime about to take power in Hanoi.

Regardless of these developments, the administration was nervous about the political fallout from Saigon's flat refusal to hold consultations, which had been clearly called for at Geneva, and sought a tactical maneuver that would place the blame on Hanoi. In mid-spring of 1955, U.S. officials approached Saigon with the suggestion that Diem agree to hold consultations, and then demand stringent conditions, such as periodic inspections by teams of outside observers, to guarantee free elections. This would place Diem's government on a firm legal footing when such demands were inevitably rejected by the Communists (which is what had happened when the issue had been raised in preparation for similar elections in the occupied zones of Germany).

But despite a U.S. warning that in flatly rejecting national elections he would be open to criticism for violating the Geneva Accords, Diem refused this suggestion. Some U.S. officials approved the decision, and the Eisenhower administration was put in an awkward position. Although it had refused to commit itself to the provisions of the agreement, Washington had indicated at Geneva that "it would view any renewal of the aggression in violation of [the agreement] with grave concern and as seriously threatening international peace and security." But would the United States be justified, John Foster Dulles rhetorically wondered, in considering an invasion of the South as a violation of the Geneva Accords if Diem himself had refused to abide by their terms? In the end, however, Washington went along with Diem. At a press conference Dulles declared that the United States had no objections to free elections in Vietnam, but that it agreed with Ngo Dinh Diem that for the time being conditions were not ripe.

Ngo Dinh Diem's success in consolidating his rule in the South, along with Washington's subsequent decision to provide him with firm support, was a rude surprise to Party leaders in Hanoi, who were accustomed to viewing their nationalist rivals with a measure of disdain. In Politburo meetings held in late 1954, Ho Chi Minh urged his colleagues not be be pessimistic or to lose patience, but to reassess the situation and turn it to their advantage. To isolate the United States and its ally in Saigon, he recommended that cultural and economic concessions be made to the French with an eye toward winning them over. At its plenary session in March 1955, the Central Committee formally announced a new policy that would place the highest priority on nation building in the North, while using diplomacy to promote a peaceful solution in the South.[11]

Even though many DRV officials had been skeptical that the elections called for at Geneva would ever take place, Diem's refusal to hold consultations was undoubtedly maddening to Hanoi. Party leaders could only hope that pressure from their own allies would serve to change minds in Washington and Saigon. Late in June 1955, in the company of General Secretary Truong Chinh and other DRV officials, Ho Chi Minh made a state visit to Beijing. After two weeks in the PRC, during which he consulted with senior officials and visited the Great Wall, the delegation left via Outer Mongolia for Moscow.

Unfortunately for the DRV, conditions in China and the USSR were not especially conducive to a successful trip. In the months following the close of the Geneva conference, both Beijing and Moscow remained focused on improving relations with the United States and reducing the potential threat of a major ideological conflict with the capitalist nations. In Beijing, preparations were under way for a series of ambassadorial talks with U.S. diplomats at Geneva; the Chinese hoped these would lead eventually to an end to a U.S. embargo and a resolution of the conflict over Taiwan. In Moscow, the new Khrushchev leadership was actively promoting the new Soviet line of peaceful coexistence to stabilize the situation in Europe and reduce Cold War tensions with the United States. For Party leaders in both countries, any renewal of the dispute over Vietnam would be an obstacle to the realization of their larger objectives elsewhere in the world.

The reception in both capitals to Ho Chi Minh's appeal for support on the issue of national elections was thus decidedly cool. In a joint communiqué issued on the departure of the Vietnamese delegation from Beijing, however, China did promise to support Hanoi's position on consultations, and Prime Minister Zhou Enlai agreed to address a letter of protest to Great Britain and the USSR, co-chairs of the Geneva conference. Ho had less success in Moscow, where support for the DRV position was pro forma at best. Soviet leaders added insult to injury by implying that they still harbored lingering doubts about the orthodoxy of the brand of Marxism-Leninism practiced in Hanoi. Foreign Minister Molotov agreed to take up the issue of reconvening the Geneva conference with British Foreign Secretary Anthony Eden, but when Eden rejected the proposal, Molotov was surprisingly acquiescent. The issue was not formally raised at a meeting of Big Four leaders later in the year, although Molotov referred to the problem in a perfunctory manner in a statement declaring that "the execution of the

Geneva agreements on Indochina and other problems will not tolerate postponement."

As if to console the North Vietnamese for their disappointment, both China and the Soviet Union promised to provide substantial financial aid ($200 million from China and $100 million from the USSR) to assist the DRV in postwar reconstruction and advancing to a fully socialist society. Both countries also agreed to dispatch shipments of grain to reduce the growing danger of starvation in the North. In a speech at the municipal racecourse shortly after his return to Hanoi on July 22, 1955, Ho Chi Minh made an oblique reference to the mixed results from the trip, publicly thanking China and the USSR for their economic assistance, but warning his compatriots that they would have to rely above all on their own efforts to bring about national reunification. At its plenary session the next month, the Central Committee decided that for the time being Diem's decision should not be permitted to affect policy, and a communiqué issued after the meeting declared that the Party continued to prefer that unification take place by peaceful means.[12]

Hanoi's decision was of little solace to members of the revolutionary faithful who had remained in the South. That summer, Diem launched a "denounce the Communists" campaign to destroy the remnants of the Vietminh movement throughout the South. Thousands were arrested on suspicion of taking part in subversive activities. Some were sent to concentration camps—or incarcerated in the infamous "tiger cages" once used by the French colonial regime on Poulo Condore Island—while others were executed. A decree issued by the Saigon regime authorized "the arrest and detention of anyone deemed dangerous to the safety of the state and their incarceration in one of several concentration camps." As one account of the period written in Hanoi put it:

> From the end of 1955 to 1956, as Diem stepped up his "Denounce the Communists" campaign, the hunt for patriots and former resistance members became fiercer. Finding it impossible to live and carry on the political struggle in the countryside, the latter fled to former resistance bases such as the Plain of Reeds, the U Minh jungle or Resistance Zones D and C [west and northwest of Saigon].[13]

Nguyen Van Linh, a young veteran of the movement who had remained in the South after the Geneva conference to help direct the Party's activities there, called it "a ferocious time," with Vietminh cadres reduced to a virtual struggle for survival.[14]

Not surprisingly, Hanoi's decision to refrain, at least temporarily, from a return to revolutionary war led to vigorous debate among cadres in the South. Some decided to abandon the movement entirely, while others sought to organize armed resistance on their own initiative. In the jungles of Ca Mau or the marshy Plain of Reeds, they joined up with dissident members of the Cao Dai and the Hoa Hao sects who had been angered by Diem's heavy-handed efforts in 1955 to bring them under his control.

By the summer of 1955, then, any naïve hopes that unification with the South would be an easy matter had been replaced by a more sober realization. That message was reflected at the Central Committee's Eighth Plenum held in August by Ho Chi Minh. On the positive side, Ho declared, the world situation was less tense than it had been earlier in the decade. On the other hand, the situation within Asia was, if anything, more perilous. Recent events strongly indicated that the United States intended to transform the regroupment zone in the South into an advanced base to stem the tide of revolution in Southeast Asia.

The emergence of the United States as the primary supporter of the Saigon regime—and therefore the "main enemy" of the Vietnamese people—seriously complicated Hanoi's plans for an early reunification by peaceful means. Although Ho Chi Minh attempted to put a positive face on the situation, declaring in his report to the plenum that both China and the Soviet Union had given their verbal support for the Vietnamese struggle for independence, it was now obvious that the road to reunification would probably be a long one. The Central Committee approved a program of action that temporarily placed primary focus on the struggle to consolidate the political base of the VWP in the North, and to take initial actions to bring about postwar reconstruction and embark on the first steps toward laying the basis for a socialist society. The new slogan of the day reflected the new reality: "Build the North, look to the South."

One important question that needed to be answered in light of this decision was how to build a popular basis of support among the Vietnamese people. There were some initial signs that the regime intended to follow an inclusive policy that would embody Ho Chi Minh's promise in his appeal the previous September to seek the support of all those compatriots who shared the common objective of building a peaceful, democratic, independent, and unified Vietnam, regardless of what their political affiliations had been in the past. In September 1955, the Lien Viet Front, the 1951 successor of the Communist-dominated Vietminh

Front, was now replaced by a new broad front group labeled the Fatherland Front (Mat tran To quoc). The new front was aimed at encompassing a broad sector of the Vietnamese population in both zones, including all those who sincerely supported the goals of independence and national unity. In his closing address to the delegates at the founding congress, Ho emphasized that the purpose of the new organization was to bring about the creation of a broad national alliance to achieve peace, independence, and reunification for the entire country. The Fatherland Front, he said, was ready "to unite with all patriots whatever their political tendencies, religions, etc.," who were sincerely opposed to the U.S.–Diem scheme of dividing the country, and who sincerely stood for national reunification.[15]

The equivalent of such a pragmatic policy in the field of economics, of course, would be to continue the "new democracy" approach originally adopted after the Party's return to Hanoi in the fall of 1954. In urban areas, that was indeed the case. The regime continued to exhibit tolerance toward private enterprise activities, and it welcomed "bourgeois experts" willing to remain on the job to carry out functions within the government or throughout society as a whole that it was otherwise not capable of fulfilling itself. Most of the business firms that were taken over by the state were seized only because of the departure of management personnel and the danger of a shutdown, as was the case with mines, cement factories, and textile mills. According to one recent source, only 12 percent of manufactured goods produced in 1955, were made by the emerging state sector. In October, the government set up a National Planning Council, with the announced task of creating a one-year plan for 1956 aimed at restoring the national economy to the level achieved in 1939, the last year before the Pacific War. The government did become directly involved in establishing regulations to control prices and the availability of consumer goods, but primarily as a means of limiting inflationary pressures and the hoarding of scarce food products by private firms.[16]

The signs of moderation suggested by Ho Chi Minh's remarks and the creation of the new Fatherland Front were deceptive, however, for there were strong countervailing pressures within the Party pushing for the adoption of harsher policies, measures directed at punishing class enemies and laying the groundwork for a quick advance to a fully socialist society. Hints of incipient radicalization had begun to appear at the government's 1954 return to Hanoi. Haughty cadres voiced their suspicion of moderate intellectuals, many of whom were ordered to undergo reeducation to ascertain whether they had been seduced by the "sugar-coated bullets" of the enemy. In their suspicions, Vietnamese militants were actively incited by Chinese advisers, whose presence throughout the North, although less visible than it had been in liberated areas during the war, was nonetheless oppressive.

The weapon that radicals selected to wage their class war in the countryside was the issue of land reform. Ho Chi Minh had opposed harsh measures during the war against the French, but in 1953, at the behest of Chinese advisers, he had reluctantly agreed to more stringent regulations as a means of mobilizing the poor in preparation for the battle of Dien Bien Phu. With the war at an end, the Party now set out to complete the program and lay the groundwork for the future collectivization of all cultivable land in the country. In his appeal to the people in early September 1954, Ho Chi Minh had promised that a program of "land to the tiller" for newly occupied areas in the northern provinces was high on the government's agenda. Although Ho confided to intimates that he was personally "in no hurry" to carry out the program, he agreed to support it as a tactical measure to please Beijing, and possibly to placate such militant colleagues as Truong Chinh and Hoang Quoc Viet as well.[17]

In carrying out out the next stage of land reform, Party leaders had two objectives. One goal was economic in nature: to permit a more effective use of cultivated land through the transfer of "excess" land from wealthy villagers to the poor and landless peasants who made up the majority of the rural population. Following the model adopted in China a few years earlier, Party leaders hoped that land ownership would spur the peasants on to heightened efforts and an overall increase in grain production, thus laying the foundation for the building of collective farms in the near future. The second and perhaps more important objective was more political: to destroy the power of "feudal" elements at the village level (namely, the landlord class) and to create a new rural leadership composed of former peasants, who would then be grateful to the Party and loyally carry out its policies.

In emphasizing the political benefits of the land reform campaign, radicals within the Party leadership were following the dictum of Mao Zedong, who had adopted a similar program in China, remarking bluntly that "revolution is not a dinner party." Since the 1920s, Mao had been outspoken in his willingness to raise the specter of class conflict in winning the support of exploited elements within the rural population. Although that program had been put in abeyance during the war against Japan, during the last stages of the Civil War and during the land reform campaign in the early 1950s, Maoist cadres had deliberately organized "speak bitterness" sessions to encourage poorer villagers to speak out against their former oppressors—especially all those who owed "blood debts" to the people. At drumhead tribunals in villages throughout China, thousands were convicted of such crimes and summarily executed. Militant elements inside the Vietnamese Workers' Party (VWP) were quite willing to adopt similar measures in the DRV. As Le Duc Tho, then a leading Party cadre in the South, had remarked in 1952, "If one wishes to lead the peasants to take up arms, it is first necessary to arouse in them a hatred of the enemy," as well as to express a concern for their practical interests.[18]

The campaign was launched during the summer and early fall of 1954. Placed under the direction of the veteran Party member and labor organizer Hoang Quoc Viet, the early stages of the program reportedly won approval from some segments of the local populace, especially from poor peasants who had served as soldiers or transport workers during the battle of Dien Bien Phu and had been led by Vietminh propaganda to believe that they would be rewarded with land for their efforts. There were some complaints of coercion and brutality, however. When Ho Chi Minh was informed of such cases, he criticized cadres who belittled the people and behaved arrogantly.[19]

Although the first wave of the new program was modest—involving only about fifty villages in Thai Nguyen province, in the northwestern corner of the Red River delta—it set off shock waves throughout the country. It was a clear signal to moderate elements that the radical strain that had appeared in the Party in the early 1950s was still alive and well, and might undermine the program of inclusion that had been promised by Ho Chi Minh in the fall of 1954.

Successive waves of land reform were launched during the winter and early spring of 1955. Although an editorial in *Nhan Dan* in February warned against the danger of "leftist errors," militant cadres (many of whom were outsiders trained at land reform programs under the guidance of Chinese advisers and then sent to "work with, eat with, and live with" the peasants) incited the local populace to criticize those who had exploited them in the past. Many of those under attack were convicted of crimes against the people and were summarily executed. In some instances, villagers took advantage of the program to settle private feuds by accusing others of involvement in counterrevolutionary activities. In the process, several thousand people, many of whom had loyally supported the Vietminh movement, were accused of treason and punished. In some cases, revolutionary cadres drawn from poor peasant backgrounds attacked Vietminh veterans who had just been released from military service and their families. Even connections in high places were not always sufficient protection. In one incident, a former Vietminh official was shielded by Ho Chi Minh himself, who sent word to local administrators that the official was not to be exposed to a public tribunal. Nevertheless, the official and his family were exposed to public humiliation and persecution by their fellow villagers. The official's niece, Duong Van Mai Elliott, relates the story:

> Every time my uncle came out of his house, children would throw stones at him. Whenever anyone of any age insulted him or hit him, he had to bow his head and say, "Please, I beg you to spare me. . . ." Landlords were made the scapegoats for the harsh life of the poor peasants. In my uncle's village, people persecuted him with zeal to show how ardently they supported land reform and to be in the good graces of the militant peasants now holding power. Others who had envied his wealth and his influence now took pleasure in humiliating him.

In the end, the former official lost his house as well as his land and was forced to settle in a hut on a nearby hillside, where he and his family scratched out their subsistence on a few acres of poor soil assigned to them by local cadres.[20]

Undoubtedly, some of the violence associated with the land reform campaign was a natural and spontaneous consequence of the class anger emanating from the rice fields. As such, it was a familiar, albeit tragic, by-product of revolution. But there is ample evidence that much of it was deliberately inspired by Party leaders responsible for drafting and carrying out the program. Overall direction of the campaign was given to General Secretary Truong Chinh, an open admirer of agricultural policies in China who had publicly echoed the Maoist view that land reform should take the form of a "class war." Other leading members of the committee were, in addition to Hoang Quoc Viet, Vice Minister of Agriculture Ho Viet Thang and Le Van Luong, a militant Maoist and head of the influential Party secretariat who had been openly calling for a campaign to purge the VWP of its impure elements. Following the Chinese example, such leaders calculated that 4 to 5 percent of the local population must be declared to be class enemies, despite the fact that in many poor villages even the most well-off farmers did little better than survive.[21]

The violence of the campaign may have taken Ho Chi Minh by

surprise, although it seems clear that he shared the militants' view that one of the goals of the campaign was to remove hostile and counterrevolutionary elements at the village level. In remarks at a cadre conference in the town of Thai Nguyen at the end of 1954, he declared that land reform was a class struggle:

> In the village, the most important task is to remake rural organizations: the administrative committee, the guerrilla militia, the associations for peasants, youth, and women. . . . If bad elements are retained in these organizations, it will be impossible for us to carry through the reduction in agrarian rents. . . . In order to carry out that operation, bad elements must receive the appropriate sanctions: Whether it is necessary to exclude, to revoke, or to retrograde, let it be done. If they can be educated, let that be done. Here is the most important task that must be accomplished in the work groups.

Nevertheless, Ho Chi Minh expressed his opposition to indiscriminate punishment: "To apply the appropriate sanction," he directed, "it cannot be said of a group of people that they are all good or bad; to know who is good and who is bad, you must rely on the masses." In other words, cadres must learn how to discriminate between different types of landlords. Otherwise, he said, they will gang together to oppose the peasants.

Ho was also opposed to the use of torture. Certain cadres, he charged,

> are still committing the error of using torture. It is a savage method used by imperialists, capitalists and feudal elements to master the masses and the revolution. Why must we, who are in possession of a just program and a just rationale, make use of such brutal methods?[22]

Ho Chi Minh's remonstrances against the use of brutal techniques—which in any case appear highly unrealistic, given the circumstances—apparently had little effect. In one case, a landowner in Thai Nguyen province who had loyally supported the revolutionary movement for years (and had on occasion even sheltered Truong Chinh and Hoang Quoc Viet from colonial authorities) was accused by a Chinese land reform cadre of being a cruel landlord and sentenced to death. When local villagers came to her defense, they in turn were accused of being lackeys of the enemy. After Ho Chi Minh was informed about the case, he raised

the issue with Truong Chinh, and the severity of the sentence was reduced. That outcome, however, was apparently a rarity and, before the
campaign's end late in 1956, several thousand people would be executed
and countless others would be harassed, persecuted, and humiliated by
being labeled with the indelible stigma of "class enemy" of the people.
Although Ho Chi Minh may have been appalled at the indiscriminate
violence that accompanied the campaign, in the view of one Vietnamese
observer, he had been intimidated by Mao Zedong and was afraid to
contradict Chinese officials stationed in the DRV.[23]

In March 1955, the Central Committee convened in Hanoi. One of
the key topics for consideration was the implementation of the land
reform campaign. Although Ho Chi Minh was evidently concerned at
the growing level of violence in the countryside, the recent creation
under U.S. sponsorship of the Southeast Asia Treaty Organization in
Manila, as well as incidents of sabotage by guerrilla groups sponsored
by the CIA, had aroused much concern in Hanoi, and many Party leaders
increasingly viewed the land reform program as an essential tool in eliminating counterrevolutionary elements. Although the plenum called for
a carefully controlled program to guarantee that only guilty landlords
would be tried and convicted of crimes against the people, the conference
declared that "rightism" (expressing the view that completion of the task
of national reunification was a higher priority than beginning the process
of socialist transformation) was still a greater risk than "leftism" (excessive zeal in carrying out the program). In his address at the end of the
session, Ho implied his unhappiness at the decisions that had been
reached, complaining that the meeting had not been sufficiently well
prepared and appealing for greater efforts to achieve unity within the
Party—especially within the leading echelons.[24]

Throughout the remainder of 1955, successive land reform campaigns were launched throughout the countryside. More than twenty
thousand additional cadres were assigned to rural areas to carry out the
program. By midsummer, it was clear that the Diem regime in the South
had no intention of holding electoral consultations, thus undermining
the argument of those who wished to delay the consolidation of Party
power in the North until the process of national reunification had been
completed. In August, an editorial in *Nhan Dan* criticized "some comrades" for expressing the view that "it would be all right to carry out
land reform rather slowly, that it is necessary to concentrate all efforts
on unification and that consolidation of the North is in contradiction
with the struggle for unification."[25] At its eighth plenary session held in

Hanoi a few days later, the Central Committee called for heightened efforts to use the land reform program as a means of rooting out spies and counterrevolutionaries.

The final wave of the campaign was inaugurated at the end of 1955, at a time when enthusiasm for bringing to completion the class war in the countryside was at a fever pitch. Ho Chi Minh was still attempting to reduce the excesses of the program. In a speech to land reform cadres in Ha Bac province on December 17, he emphasized the importance of making a careful distinction between those who were guilty and those who were innocent of counterrevolutionary activities, and he repeated his warning not to use physical abuse against those charged with crimes against the people. At a luncheon following his address, he reminded his audience that land reform, like hot soup, is best to the taste when it is drunk slowly. But in the mood of the moment, Ho's words had little effect. A letter sent to land reform cadres by the National Peasant Liaison Committee the same month drew direct links between landlord elements at the village level and counterrevolutionary activities, while a directive from the Central Committee issued on December 14 instructed cadres to treat the land reform program as a "Dien Bien Phu against feudalism in the North."[26]

By the early spring of 1956, reports of the violence of the program in rural areas had become widespread in Hanoi, where many Party and government officials came from landed families that had been attacked during the campaign. When articles critical of the program began to appear in the press, Ho Chi Minh's erstwhile private secretary, Vu Dinh Huynh, was inspired to remonstrate with him: "The blood of our compatriots is being spilled, how can you rest easy?" Although Huynh had already provoked the suspicion of radicals for his lack of ideological militancy (Truong Chinh had dismissed him as a "running dog of the reactionaries"), Ho was sufficiently concerned about the situation to issue a new warning against the indiscriminate classification of all landlord elements as counterrevolutionary. In an April speech to cadres carrying out the program in coastal regions, he warned them not to adopt a mechanistic attitude in making judgments, pointing out that not all boat owners were dishonest and cruel. Only those guilty of tyrannical actions need to be punished. A boat, he reminded them, needs someone at the rudder as well as others manning the oars.

Ho Chi Minh had voiced such concerns before to little effect. But now, with anger rising throughout the countryside, his message was starting to find an audience. In mid-May, an article in *Nhan Dan* conceded that some land reform cadres had treated peasants as landlords and discriminated against the children of landlords. A few weeks later, another piece admitted that in some cases government officials had "overestimated the enemy" by assuming that a small number of cases of sabotage was representative of the general situation.[27]

In part, what happened to change the minds of Party leaders in Hanoi may have been the rising chorus of protest from Vietminh veterans, who, along with their families, had been victimized. But an event that took place several thousand miles away in Moscow may also have played a role. In a speech delivered at the Twentieth Congress of the Communist Party of the Soviet Union in February 1956, Party chief Nikita Khrushchev stunned his audience with his sharp criticism of the leadership style of his predecessor, Joseph Stalin. Stalin, he charged, had not only encouraged the emergence of a "cult of personality" that represented a betrayal of the Leninist principle of democratic centralism, he had also used his overwhelming power to carry out the brutal removal of loyal Bolsheviks from the Party and the government. Moreover, he had made a number of disastrous foreign policy decisions that had tragic consequences during the Second World War. Khrushchev called on the delegates at the congress to engage in the practice of "self-criticism" to ensure that such shortcomings would not be repeated.

Khrushchev's wide-ranging denunciation of Stalin aroused a good deal of anxiety in Beijing regarding the effect that such attacks, however justified in the Soviet context, could have on the prestige of the Chinese Communist Party, on Mao Zedong's leadership, and on the Marxist concept of the dictatorship of the proletariat. Reaction in Hanoi, however, was muted. A Vietnamese delegation headed by Truong Chinh and Le Duc Tho had attended the congress, but press commentary in Hanoi was sparse. *Nhan Dan* remarked laconically on February 28, 1956, that the VWP "would further endeavor to study Marxist-Leninist theory and to apply it creatively to the concrete situation in Vietnam, to combine this theory with the practice of Vietnam's revolution." Once the Vietnamese delegation returned from Moscow, the VWP Politburo met to consider the results of the congress and its impact on the situation in Vietnam. On March 31, Radio Hanoi broadcast a communiqué from the Politburo that referred to the "exaltation of individualism" and "the spirit of self-criticism" and concluded that the resolutions issued at the CPSU's Twentieth Congress would "strengthen our party in its theoretical aspects."[28]

In the official view, the issue of the cult of the personality was an affair for the Soviet Union and was not relevant in the Vietnamese context, where Ho Chi Minh ruled in a collegial style. Still, there may have been satisfaction among some Party leaders that the issue had been raised, especially among those who chafed under the weight of the progressive deification of Ho Chi Minh in the press. The president was now being rapidly metamorphosed into the avuncular "Uncle Ho" (Bac Ho) so familiar to the world during his final years. He was photographed greeting compatriots from every conceivable occupation and, despite his image of modesty, his picture appeared on postage stamps and even on the national currency. Truong Chinh, who may understandably have been privately jealous of Ho's towering reputation among the populace, was reportedly elated at the antideification campaign. "Socialism," he remarked, "can't survive with the glorification of the individual." The two, he pointed out, were as antithetical as fire and water: While socialism was democratic, the deification of the individual was antidemocratic.[29]

It probably struck many Vietnamese observers as fortuitous that Khrushchev's attack on Stalin's abuses had taken place at a time when decisions reached by the VWP in Hanoi were just beginning to come under serious scrutiny and debate. At an enlarged session of the VWP Central Committee held in late April, the issue of self-criticism came up for discussion, and the resolution issued at the close of the conference praised the CPSU for its courage in admitting errors, while noting that the VWP had not sufficiently engaged in examining its own practices in Vietnam. "It is through the development of criticism and self-criticism," the resolution noted, "that we can develop internal democracy, strengthen our relations with the masses, and curb bureaucratism." In his closing statement to the conference, Ho Chi Minh was more explicit, declaring that by engaging in self-criticism, the CPSU had displayed a degree of courage that should be imitated by all fraternal parties. The lesson was especially relevant to the VWP, he noted, because of the "feudal and colonial vestiges" that had not yet been eliminated in the country, thus enabling false and non-Communist influences to penetrate the organization. Although Ho focused his primary attention on the problems of bureaucratism and official arrogance, he admitted that a "cult of personality" existed to a certain extent in the DRV as well. While it had not yet led to any major damage, it nevertheless limited the zeal and spirit of initiative among Party members and the people as a whole. To resolve such shortcomings, he emphasized the importance of strengthening collective leadership at all echelons of the Party and government.[30]

To what degree the new "spirit of self-criticism" affected the debate over the land reform campaign is not clear. It seems likely that Ho Chi Minh's comments were intended to be received in such a light by the delegates, and by his colleagues within the Politburo. Indeed, there may have been some sense of irony in his concessions about the danger of the cult of the individual at the conference, since he must have felt that his own influence over the implementation of the program had been all too limited. In any event, Khrushchev's speech provided him with a tool to urge his colleagues to reevaluate their own decisions and make the necessary changes in the land reform program.

Whatever the impact of Khrushchev's de-Stalinization speech in Vietnam, during the next few months there was a serious reevaluation of the land reform program. Immediately following the close of the conference, cadre meetings were scheduled to discuss the decisions reached by the Central Committee. Oblique comments in the official press intimated that errors had been committed in implementing the program, and a number of those previously arrested for allegedly counterrevolutionary activities were released. An article in mid-May 1956 praised the overall results of the land reform campaign, but concluded with an admonition to all those involved to correct deficiencies in the program. In a letter of July 1, 1956, to a conference of cadres evaluating the latest wave of land reform, Ho Chi Minh described the program as a success in that "in the main" it had eliminated the landlord class at the village level, but he added that a number of serious errors had been committed that significantly limited its accomplishments. Many of those responsible for the tenor of the campaign, however, were still reluctant to admit the scope of the problem. In an article published in July, Le Van Luong conceded that errors had been committed in implementing the program, but insisted that action had been necessary because the local administrative organs in many newly liberated rural areas had been taken over entirely by counterrevolutionary elements.[31]

The tide, however, was now running strongly against Luong and his allies. In a report to rural cadres on the results of the land reform program on August 17, Ho Chi Minh declared that "some cadres do not yet grasp our policy and correctly cultivate the mass line. [This is] because the central leadership of the Party and the government have had significant shortcomings . . . therefore, land reform has suffered from numerous deficiences and errors in the task of bringing about unity in rural areas." He then promised that those who had wrongly suffered as the result of those errors would be released from prison or reinstated in their previous positions.[32]

The issue was the main topic for discussion at the Tenth Plenum of the Central Committee, which convened in September 1956. By now, proponents of the radical approach could no longer defend their positions, and the debate at the meeting must have been tempestuous. The communiqué issued after the close of the plenum was uncharacteristically blunt in its analysis of the problem and in assigning responsibility for the actions:

> Mistakes and shortcomings have been committed during the past period. In agrarian reform and the readjustment of organizations, grave mistakes have been committed. The 10th plenum of the Central Committee of the [Vietnamese] Workers' Party has analyzed the results of land reform and the readjustment of organizations and carried out a stern examination of the mistakes committed in these two tasks. It has found the causes of these mistakes and has adopted measures for correcting them.

For the first time, the Party sought to identify the source of the problem. Difficulties, the communiqué said, were caused by "leftist deviations":

> The 10th plenum of the Central Committee of the [Vietnamese] Workers' Party "recognizes that these mistakes are due to shortcomings in leadership." That is why the Central Committee of the Party bears responsibility for these mistakes. Those Central Committee members directly responsible for the mistakes committed in the guidance of the execution of the Party's policies have made a self-criticism of their mistakes and shortcomings before the Central Committee. The latter has taken appropriate disciplinary measures against these members.[33]

At the close of the conference, the Central Committee took the unprecedented step of relieving several leading members of the Party and the government of their positions. Among them were the four principals of the land reform committee: Truong Chinh was dismissed as general secretary of the VWP; Ho Viet Thang was dropped from the Central Committee; Le Van Luong was stripped of his influential positions in the Politburo and the Central Committee Secretariat; Hoang Quoc Viet was dropped from the Politburo. During the next few days, a series of decrees issued by the Council of Ministers directed that those people's tribunals that had been established at the village level to ferret out class enemies should be abolished, while agrarian reform committees that had previously been created at the central and regional levels were reduced in function to advisory bodies without executive powers. To undo the harm that had already been committed, those who had been unjustly imprisoned were to receive amnesties, and the improper seizure of private and church-held land was to be corrected.[34]

The dismissal of Truong Chinh, an almost unprecedented step for a party that had always sought to avoid the brutal factional struggles so characteristic of its fraternal parties in China and the USSR, forced his colleagues into a hurried decision to find a replacement. The natural successor would appear to have been General Vo Nguyen Giap. Ranked third in the hierarchy after Ho and Truong Chinh, Giap enjoyed high esteem among the people as hero of the battle of Dien Bien Phu. He and the army had avoided being tarnished by the failures of the land reform campaign. But Giap's very popularity may have worked against him among jealous colleagues. Moreover, there was a tradition within the leadership to avoid combining Party authority with military command. As a result, Giap was passed over, and Ho Chi Minh agreed temporarily to occupy the position.

Ho Chi Minh had not been directly involved in planning or implementing the land reform campaign and could thus play a key role in assessing the damage and assigning responsibility. But his prestige as an all-knowing and all-caring leader had been severely damaged in the campaign; many of his colleagues privately felt that, although he had criticized the excesses at the local level, he was not guilt-free, since he had approved of the program at its inception and defended its achievements "in the main" even after it became clear that serious errors had occurred. In private meetings with other Party leaders, Ho engaged in some self-criticism of his own, acknowledging that "because I lacked a spirit of democracy, I didn't listen and didn't see, so we must now promote democracy. I accept responsibility in this time of trial. All the top leadership [Truong uong] must listen, observe, think, and act accordingly. This grievous lesson must be a motivation for us."[35]

The fallout from the land reform campaign was a major setback for Truong Chinh. A distant and somewhat severe figure, respected but not loved by his colleagues and intimates, Chinh suffered less from a predilection for brutality than from a lack of warmth and humanity, and he undoubtedly believed that in carrying out the program at the suggestion of Chinese advisers he was acting properly according to the dictates of ideology. While he was certainly humiliated by the demotion, he was too proud to display his feelings in public, and reportedly never mentioned the issue to his colleagues. When occasion demanded, however, he was prepared to defend his decisions. A few weeks after the close of the Tenth Plenum, Truong Chinh argued that although some cadres had been guilty of committing grave errors during the campaign, land reform was "a revolution" and added that "a peaceful land reform equal to an exercise in offering up land is an illusion."[36]

The Party's attempt at a mea culpa came too late to prevent the outbreak of the first serious public protest against government policy since the end of the Franco-Vietminh War. To make it more embarrassing, the incident took place in a rural area not far from Ho Chi Minh's birthplace in Nghe An province, along the central coast. Quynh Luu district was distinctive in that the majority of the inhabitants were Catholics. Many inhabitants of Quynh Luu were highly patriotic and had supported the Vietminh against the French, but mistrust was prevalent on both sides. Vietminh cadres suspected that a significant number of local Catholics were loyal to the French or to Bao Dai, and hostile to the revolution. Catholics in turn were angered by periodic evidence of official hostility to them simply because of their faith.

Relations between the government and the Catholic community had been uneasy throughout the DRV since the end of the Pacific War. After the cease-fire in July 1954, nearly 600,000 Catholics fled to the South. Nevertheless, nearly 900,000 Catholics remained in North Vietnam after the Geneva Accords, and the DRV tried to reassure them that they would not be ill treated. A new liaison committee of patriotic and peaceful Catholics was created as a front group for the regime, and President Ho Chi Minh frequently spoke before Catholic audiences about his government's commitment to religious freedom. New bishops were nominated to replace those who had left for the South, seminaries to train Catholic priests were created in late 1954, and in June 1955 a government decree guaranteed religious freedom and recognized the authority of the Vatican in internal church affairs, although it forbade Catholics to disseminate propaganda against government policies.

With the inauguration of the land reform campaign, however, relations rapidly deteriorated, as militant cadres often displayed hostility to Catholics, many of whom were rounded up as suspected counterrevolutionaries. In some cases, there may have been grounds to question their commitment to the revolution, since many Catholics were among the more affluent members of the rural community and therefore opposed land reform. The Church itself, which held about 1.3 percent of the cultivated land in the country, was openly hostile to the government.

Problems in Quynh Luu district began to appear in 1955, when villagers protested that they had been prevented by government officials from emigrating to the South. During the summer of 1956, the land reform campaign swept through the area, and the resentment engendered by government abuses in carrying out the program was exacerbated by the complaint of religious discrimination. Party cadres frequently denounced local Catholic leaders as reactionaries and saboteurs. When an International Control Commission inspection team arrived in the area, tensions flared and a number of violent clashes between government security forces and villagers seeking to meet the inspectors broke out. On November 9, a group of villagers presented petitions to ICC members who were traveling through the district in a jeep. When a local police unit tried to disperse the crowd, violence broke out. On the thirteenth, several thousand people, armed with tools and rudimentary weapons, marched on the district capital of Quynh Luu. Their path was blocked by regular troops; a clash resulted, and several demonstrators were killed. The next day, an entire army division was sent to occupy the area and arrest the ringleaders who had provoked the disturbance. After an inspection team from Hanoi arrived to evaluate the situation, a number of persons who had been arrested during the land reform campaign were released, and their property was returned. But it was clear that the inner-Party debate over how to carry out the program had not been entirely resolved. Truong Chinh, who had retained chairmanship of the land reform committee, warned in his report on the incident that some "dangerous individuals" had been released without justification and that it was necessary to take care that "landlord elements" did not reemerge as influential forces at the village level.

Although the incident at Quynh Luu was unique in the sense that it involved sensitive relations between the regime and Catholics, it was a clear sign that the land reform program had seriously undermined the confidence of the population in the North in the character of the Party leadership, and undoubtedly strained the bonds of unity and collective leadership within the leading councils of the Party. When, in late October, hostile crowds composed primarily of family members of those who had suffered from the campaign gathered in front of Central Committee headquarters near Ba Dinh Square to complain that their demands for redress had not been addressed, General Vo Nguyen Giap agreed to address the public at a nearby sports stadium, where he admitted that mistakes had been made during the campaign. The Party leadership, he conceded, had overestimated the number of landlords in the country and had mechanistically regarded all members of that class as enemies of the people. It therefore failed to distinguish between friends and enemies and slighted the crucial importance of broadening the national united front for the period ahead. The Party, he added, also violated its policy of respecting religious freedom in carrying out land reform in areas inhabited by many Catholics and failed to recognize the revolutionary services of many demobilized soldiers and war veterans.

Ho Chi Minh, who for months had argued in meetings of senior leaders against the excesses of the campaign, kept a low public profile on the issue until February 1957, when at a session of the DRV National Assembly he, too, affirmed that "serious mistakes" had been been committed while carrying out the campaign. But once more he defended the program as a whole as fundamentally correct in its goal of removing the power of feudalist elements at the village level and liberating poor peasants from their cycle of poverty. Observers recall that he wept as he alluded to the sufferings that occurred during the campaign.[37]

In some respects, the land reform program could be viewed as a success by the regime. More than two million acres (800,000 hectares) of land were distributed to over two million farm families, a total of well over half the total number of agricultural workers in the DRV. The historic domination by the landed gentry at the village level was broken and a new leadership composed of poor and middle-level peasants emerged. But the tactics that had been applied left a bitter legacy. Although the actual number of people executed during the campaign is highly controversial, even sympathetic observers concede that a minimum of 3,000 to 5,000 may have died in the process, usually by firing squads immediately following conviction by a local tribunal. There are other estimates that 12,000 to 15,000 people were unjustly executed on false charges of sabotage or otherwise supporting counterrevolutionary activities. Countless others suffered in various ways because of their relationship to the victims. The consequences were a disaster for Party organizations at the local level. A study in the early 1980s showed that in some areas, 30 percent of the Communist cells had been disbanded as a result of losses of personnel to anger generated by the campaign. In seventy-six communes in Bac Ninh province, only twenty-one cell secretaries remained in place at the end of the final wave of the campaign.[38]

The social turmoil aroused by the land reform campaign was not limited to the countryside. It also exacerbated the Party's relations with urban intellectuals, who had been among the most fervent supporters of the Vietminh Front during the early stages of the resistance.

Many were highly patriotic and had responded enthusiastically to the Vietminh program, which combined the issue of national independence with moderate reform measures.

However, the Party's prestige among intellectuals was sorely tested when, beginning in 1951, the Chinese-inspired internal rectification campaign compelled them to engage in often painful bouts of self-criticism as they attempted to reconcile their patriotic instincts with the rigid requirements of the Maoist revolutionary ethic. Some responded by leaving the movement; others attempted to disguise their discomfort by adopting the rationalization that Party discipline and the sacrifice of personal goals were necessary during a time of struggle for national survival. As the writer and intellectual Phan Khoi remarked, the sweetness of patriotism, like sugar in coffee, offset the bitter taste of Party leadership and salvaged the dignity of the intellectuals.[39]

This dilemma was harder to evade after the Geneva conference, which, by temporarily shelving the issue of national independence, placed the Party's domestic agenda on center stage. The story of a young writer named Tran Dan illustrates the fix many intellectuals found themselves in. A veteran of Dien Bien Phu, Dan had just written a novel in the accustomed socialist realist style about his experiences on the battlefield, and shortly after the cease-fire, he was sent to China to seek professional assistance in writing a screenplay for a film based on his novel. While there, he met the writer Hu Feng, a vocal advocate of greater freedom for writers and artists in the new China. On his return to the DRV, Tran Dan revised his novel to tone down the obligatory references to heroism and self-sacrifice in the ranks that the first draft had contained and fashioned a more honest three-dimensional portrait of soldiers faced with the horrors of war. During the winter of 1954–55, with the collaboration of several like-minded colleagues within the army's propaganda section, he drew up a letter titled "propositions for a cultural politics" that he intended to submit to the Party Central Committee. The point of the project was to request greater freedoms for creative intellectuals to express the truth about the recent war as they saw it.

At first, there was apparently some support from senior military officers for the proposal, but eventually ideological militants got wind of the letter and brought about its official rejection. A leading spokesman for maintaining ideological purity was the poet To Huu, the Party veteran whose revolutionary poems had attained great popularity during the Franco-Vietminh conflict and who now served as the Party's cultural and intellectual watchdog. A leading advocate of "art for life's sake," he had made a major speech in September 1949 in the Viet Bac on how to eliminate the vestiges of reactionary feudalist and capitalist influence on the emerging revolutionary culture in Vietnam.

Tran Dan was soon under attack from the left, not only for his outspoken demand for an end to ideological controls over creative artists in the DRV, but also for allegedly leading a "bourgeois lifestyle." Expelled from the VWP, he was later incarcerated in the military prison at the Citadel in Hanoi. "I see nothing but rain," he remarked in sorrow, "falling on the red flag."[40] But the ferment caused by his letter, combined with the brutality of the land reform campaign and the literary "thaw" brought about in the USSR as a result of the impact of Khrushchev's de-Stalinization speech in February 1956, emboldened other intellectuals; and in the spring of that year a new literary journal called *Giai Pham* began to publish pieces that were at least implicitly critical of government policies. Despite official expressions of disapproval, additional issues of the journal appeared during the summer, encouraging the appearance of a second periodical, *Nhan Van*, in September. The editor of the new publication was the noted Vietnamese intellectual Phan Khoi, a participant in Phan Chu Trinh's reformist movement at the beginning of the century. By now, Vietnamese intellectuals had been encouraged by the appearance of the Hundred Flowers campaign in China, an officially sponsored but short-lived movement to encourage public criticism of the shortcomings of the CCP and the government. One article penned by the poet Hoang Cam lamented the official abuse meted out to Tran Dan and defended him from his critics. Other articles in the two journals described the sufferings of families whose members had been imprisoned during the land reform campaign, and the problem of bureaucratism.

Chastened by the uproar caused by the excesses of the land reform campaign and the calls for self-criticism emanating from Moscow and Beijing, ideological purists in the Party took no immediate action to suppress such criticism. In fact, the Tenth Plenum in September 1956 issued a communiqué calling for the extension of democratic freedoms, while in December a presidential decree guaranteed a limited freedom of the press. Truong Chinh appealed for the creation of a new Vietnamese culture which would be national in form and socialist in content. What he meant by that was uncertain. When one intellectual complained to Truong Chinh about the lack of freedom to speak out, Chinh replied in surprise, "but you have plenty of freedom to criticize imperialism!"

But the demonstrations at Quynh Luu aroused anxiety among Party leaders in Hanoi, and before the end of the year *Nhan Van* and *Giai Pham* were forced to close their doors. The official newspaper *Nhan Dan* called for strict Party control over intellectuals, and many were compelled to attend courses on Marxism-Leninism. The elderly Phan Khoi was expelled from the writer's association and eventually arrested. He died in prison before standing trial. Tran Dan resigned from the Party, but declared himself faithful to its utopian ideals, "a Communist without a party."[41]

It is not easy to discern to what degree Ho Chi Minh should bear responsibility for the persecution associated with the suppression of intellectual dissent and the land reform campaign. Apologists point out that Ho was not directly implicated in carrying out either program, and that he persistently urged senior colleagues and cadres alike to make a careful distinction between misguided elements who could be redirected onto the proper path and truly counterrevolutionary elements who had to be surgically removed like a cancer from the body politic of Vietnamese society. But critics retort that even if Ho did not wield the knife, he had nonetheless set the stage for those who did. It is significant that even after he was informed about excesses in the two campaigns, he made little effort to use his immense prestige to mitigate their effects.

While Ho demonstrated no personal predilection for the use of brutality against his adversaries or rivals, he was willing (in the pattern of ideologues throughout the ages) to condone such actions by his subordinates in the larger interests of the cause. Where he was personally acquainted with the victims—and Ho Chi Minh knew a number of the intellectuals who were attacked during the campaign—he sometimes intervened on their behalf, but often without effect. A family member of one intellectual who fell victim to the campaign informed me privately that Ho had attempted to alleviate his treatment in prison. Perhaps the most that can be said is that Ho Chi Minh had become a prisoner of his own creation, a fly in amber, unable in his state of declining influence to escape the inexorable logic of a system that sacrificed the fate of individuals to the "higher morality" of the master plan.[42]

While much of the attention accorded in Hanoi to the CPSU Twentieth Congress in early 1956 had been focused on Khrushchev's de-Stalinization speech, an equally significant product of the congress was Moscow's decision to pursue a policy of peaceful coexistence with the West. In justifying the new program, Khrushchev argued that the only alternative was a nuclear conflict, which could bring about the death of millions on both sides of the ideological divide.

For Hanoi, Moscow's adoption of the strategy of peaceful coexistence had disquieting implications, for it suggested that the Soviet Union might not look with favor on a possible resumption of revolutionary struggle to bring about the reunification of the two Vietnams. For the moment, the new approach did not run counter to policies adopted by the Party leadership in Hanoi, since in August 1955 the VWP Central Committee had reaffirmed its wish to seek reunification by peaceful means; and in early 1956, the DRV indicated its approval of a Chinese proposal to reconvene the Geneva conference to discuss the enforcement of the Geneva Accords. Still, the issue obviously remained under debate among senior leaders of the Party, and sometime during the late winter of 1956, a delegation led by Army Chief of Staff Van Tien Dung traveled secretly to the South to consult with ranking members of the local Vietminh apparatus. The chairman of the Party's Regional Committee for the South (the Party's leading organ in the South after the Central Office for South Vietnam, COSVN, was disbanded following the Geneva Accords) was Le Duan, the Party veteran who had directed operations there since the dismissal of Nguyen Binh in 1951. The stated objective of Dung's trip was to set up new revolutionary base areas and to consider the possible need for reinforcements, as well as to facilitate a formal alliance with dissident elements of the two religious sects.

The son of a carpenter in Quang Tri province, a rural area just north of the old imperial capital of Hué, Le Duan lacked the educational background and elite family credentials of many of the founding members of the Party, several of whom, like Ho Chi Minh himself, had come from the scholar-gentry class. Yet, although slight in physique and plainspoken and rustic in manner, Le Duan did not lack self-confidence, and he was viewed as an effective organizer and a vocal advocate for the interests of the movement in the South. On the other hand, some of his colleagues apparently found him to be arrogant and unwilling to consider ideas other than his own.[43]

Having served (with the code name of "Ba") as a senior representative of the Central Committee in the southern provinces since shortly after the end of the Pacific War, Le Duan was an appropriate choice for the assignment of commanding the movement in South Vietnam. He was totally devoted to the task of bringing about national reunification, but he was also a pragmatist, and in meetings of the Regional Committee he argued tirelessly for the adoption of a realistic strategy that took into account conditions not only in the South but also on the international scene. On the one hand, he sought to rein in the firebrands who wanted to return immediately to the strategy used against the French, arguing that the Party's armed forces were simply not yet up to the task. On the other hand, he was skeptical of a peaceful solution, feeling that some form of violence would ultimately be needed. Political activities in the South, he stated, "will sometimes have to be backed up with military action in order to show the strength of the forces which won at Dien Bien Phu."[44] In March 1956, Duan presented Van Tien Dung and his team with a plan to launch military preparations for a possible return to a policy of armed struggle. After their visitors left, Duan's Regional Committee for the South approved a limited increase in the Party's local military forces, including the formation of twenty main-force battalions and the mobilization of guerrilla squads in villages sympathetic to the revolution.

Le Duan's proposal to adopt a more aggressive approach in the South arrived in Hanoi at a time when Party leaders were actively discussing Moscow's new line of peaceful coexistence. In early April 1956, Soviet Deputy Prime Minister Anastas Mikoyan arrived in Hanoi to explain to Vietnamese comrades Moscow's view of the world situation. It was the first visit of a senior Soviet Party figure to the DRV, a gesture that was undoubtedly highly welcome to his hosts. Two weeks after his departure, the VWP Central Committee announced its formal approval of the resolutions of the CPSU Twentieth Congress at its Ninth Plenum. But Truong Chinh, who was still general secretary at the time, admitted that not all of his colleagues agreed with that view. "There are some people," he remarked, "who do not yet believe in the correctness of this political program and in the policy of peaceful reunification of the country, holding that these are illusory and reformist."[45]

Whether Truong Chinh was referring to Le Duan, the Party's chief representative in the South, is not known. In any event, such reservations were apparently held, among others, by Ho Chi Minh himself. Although he had publicly urged his colleagues to give the peace process a chance, he had never disguised his belief that the national issue must take precedence over other concerns, and he was not prepared to rule out a return to violence if it should prove necessary to bring about reunification. At a speech given on April 24, 1956, the final day of the Ninth Plenum, Ho declared that the Vietnamese people understood the "great significance" of the decisions reached in Moscow, and the growing strength of the powerful forces of world peace; however, he then qualified that statement by adding: "While recognizing that war may be averted, we must be vigilant to detect the warmongers' schemes; for as long as imperialism exists, the danger of war exists." Although in some cases the road to socialism may be a peaceful one, he pointed out, we should clearly recognize this fact: In those countries where the machinery of state, the armed forces, and the security police of the bourgeois class are still strong, the proletarian class must prepare for armed struggle. Therefore, while recognizing the possibility of reunifying the country by peaceful means, the Vietnamese people should not forget that their principal enemies are the American imperialists and their agents who still occupy half the country and are feverishly preparing for war. So, while we should firmly hold aloft the banner of peace, we must at the same time enhance our vigilance.[46]

Ho Chi Minh's views were incorporated into the resolution approved at the close of the conference, which stated that while some nations were capable of advancing to socialism by peaceful means, in some cases a fierce struggle might be unavoidable, so the working class must prepare for either contingency. Moscow was thus put on notice that although its ally was not yet prepared to confront Khrushchev directly on the issue of peaceful coexistence, it was willing, if necessary, to define its own strategy to bring to a successful resolution the struggle for national liberation and unification in Vietnam.

By approving the declaration of the CPSU Twentieth Congress on the new policy of peaceful coexistence, the Ninth Plenum rejected Le Duan's proposal to take the first steps toward adopting a more military strategy in the South. By so doing, however, it did not bring to an end the debate within the DRV over the proper path to follow in the South. A long editorial that appeared in *Nhan Dan* in mid-July noted that many people still harbored "complex ideas and illusions" about the question. Some, it said, had been "simple in their thoughts" and were sure elections would be held. Now they were disillusioned and pessimistic. Others were "reluctant to carry on a long and hard struggle" and continued to hope that unity could be achieved peacefully.

Among those who were undoubtedly the most upset were the southern cadres who had been shipped to the North after the Geneva conference to receive training and indoctrination in Marxist ideology and revolutionary tactics. In a bid to ease their discomfort, Ho Chi Minh tried to reassure them, via a public letter in June, by explaining the official policy of seeking reunification by peaceful means. The struggle, he warned, would be difficult and protracted, and could not succeed until the North had first been strengthened to serve as a powerful and reliable base of operations. The political struggle is just, he said, and would certainly be victorious. But "to build a good house, we must build a strong foundation." Ho's comments about the need for domestic construction must have resonated with many of his readers. That spring, North Vietnam was suffering from a severe food shortage, as well as a continuing lack of skilled personnel to help build the economy. Agreements were signed with China to provide technological assistance in building up a light industrial base in the DRV, but in the meantime, the people must be fed. In the words of a Vietnamese poet who had just visited rural provinces in the Red River delta:

> I have passed through
> Many villages of Kien-An and Hong-Quang
> Where the sea broke in and left its salt over wide plains
> Where, for two successive seasons, no grain of rice has grown
> And human excrement is red with peels of sweet potatoes.
> I have met
> Countless emaciated children
> Of five or six years old
> Eating less rice than bran.[47]

Party leaders had consulted with key members of the southern leadership on the issue of reunification just prior to the Ninth Plenum, and the southerners may have been chided by Truong Chinh for their impatience. But doubts about a peaceful solution to the problem certainly persisted in Hanoi as well. After holding a meeting on the subject in June 1956, the Politburo issued a resolution titled "The Situation and Missions of the Revolution in the South." This document noted that since South Vietnam had become a virtual colony of the United States, it was necessary to consider the adoption of a policy of armed struggle for self-defense. Still, the Politburo concluded that for the time being it was important to stay with the strategy of political struggle. In a letter to the Vietnamese people in July, Ho Chi Minh said that the DRV would continue the effort to pursue national unification by peaceful means through the mechanism of the Geneva Accords.[48]

As a member of the Politburo, Le Duan probably attended the June meeting. If so, he would have been instructed to carry Hanoi's views back to his colleagues in South Vietnam. Sometime that summer, he wrote a short pamphlet called *The Path of Revolution in the South* to present his own ideas on the subject. On the surface, his recommendations appeared to coincide with those of the advocates of a peaceful policy within the VWP Central Committee and the Politburo. At its present stage, the author declared, the Vietnamese revolution faced two major tasks, building socialism in the North and liberating the South. The existing policy of peaceful political struggle in the South conformed to existing realities, in light of the current weakness of the Party apparatus in South Vietnam, and it was also in line with decisions reached at the Twentieth Congress in Moscow and the prevailing situation around the world.

However, Le Duan's apparent emphasis on the need for a political approach was somewhat deceptive, for the central thrust of his argument focused on the need for a more vigorous approach to the revolution in the South. Although not formally deviating from the existing policy, he pointed out that there was a significant difference between a policy of reformism based on "legal and constitutional struggle" and one of political struggle adopted by a revolutionary movement that "takes the revolutionary political forces of the masses as its foundation." As the vanguard of the revolution, he argued, the Party must be ready to lead the masses (here he used the example of the August Revolution of 1945) to seize power. Otherwise, a favorable opportunity to overthrow the reactionary regime in Saigon might be wasted.

To Le Duan, the glaring lesson offered by the August Revolution was that it was necessary to prepare for a general uprising by building up the political and military strength of the revolutionary forces. Regrettably, Duan concluded, many cadres responsible for guiding the movement "had not yet firmly understood the strength of the revolutionary masses" and thus failed to lead them.[49]

At the beginning of 1956, China and the Soviet Union had appeared to be in agreement on the need for a period of international peace and stability as a backdrop for their efforts to engage in domestic construction. In February, both Moscow and Beijing had urged Hanoi to accept their proposal to reconvene the Geneva conference as a tactic to rescue the faltering peace process in Indochina. That overture proved abortive, because Great Britain, the co-chair with the USSR, was unwilling to reconvene the conference in light of Saigon's declaration that it was not a party to the agreement and would not be held accountable for its provisions. Moscow, which had essentially assigned responsibility for the Indochinese imbroglio to the Chinese, took no action. Beijing, still preoccupied with its own internal problems, followed suit.

By the autumn of 1956, however, differences between Beijing and Moscow had begun to appear over other issues. Chinese leaders were concerned at the implications of the recent Soviet intervention in Eastern Europe, where Soviet leaders had taken firm action to prevent social unrest in Poland and Hungary; this contradicted the Chinese view that differences among socialist nations should be dealt with by consultations based on the principle of equality and noninterference. In Beijing's view, the uprisings against Communist rule in Eastern Europe were a direct outgrowth of Khrushchev's de-Stalinization speech, which had undermined the prestige of the Communist Party as the vanguard of the socialist revolution.

It may have been at least partly for the purpose of exploring Chinese views on the issue of peaceful coexistence that the DRV invited Zhou Enlai to Hanoi. Zhou, who had long maintained good relations with Ho Chi Minh, arrived on November 18 on the first stop of a swing through several nations in Asia, and his hosts pressed him to provide concrete forms of support on the issue of Vietnamese reunification. Zhou agreed on the need for joint action to fulfill the provisions of the Geneva conference, but he avoided specifics on what could be done. When Vietnamese leaders pressed him to demand that the Geneva conference be reconvened, Zhou was studiously vague.

It eventually became clear to his hosts that Zhou Enlai's visit was motivated primarily by Beijing's desire to obtain Vietnamese support in connection with China's emerging dispute with the Soviet Union. Chinese leaders were particularly uneasy about the dispatch of Soviet military forces to overthrow the reformist government of Imre Nagy in Hungary. In public comments made in Hanoi, Zhou alluded briefly to the dangers of "great nation chauvinism," an oblique reference to Soviet actions in Europe, and to the importance of mutual relations based on the five principles of peaceful coexistence that had been publicized by China and India a couple of years earlier.

Beijing's discomfort with Moscow's tendency to dictate to other members of the socialist community was probably shared by many Party leaders in Hanoi; some also felt disdain for Khrushchev's policy of peaceful coexistence, which appeared to represent a capitulation to the class enemy, and argued for closer ties with China. But Ho Chi Minh insisted on the importance of maintaining cordial relations with both China and the Soviet Union, and the final communiqué from Zhou's state visit contained no direct or indirect criticism of the USSR.[50]

Zhou's stopover preceded the Eleventh Plenum of the VWP Central Committee, which convened the following month. Le Duan attended the conference, and he undoubtedly defended the ideas contained in his pamphlet, *The Path of Revolution in the South,* before the assembled delegates.

Since in recent years the pamphlet has frequently been described in Hanoi as a document of "pivotal importance" in the history of the Vietnamese revolutionary movement, it seems probable that Duan's proposals provoked lively discussion, but it seems clear that it did not result in an immediate shift in the general line of the Party. An editorial published in the Party's theoretical journal *Hoc Tap* a few days after the close of the plenum stated that consolidation of the North was still the primary task: "We must not allow the winning over of the South to detract from the requirements of consolidating the North." Ho Chi Minh's role in the debate is unknown. In a speech to the National Assembly early in 1957, he reiterated his view that for the time being domestic construction must take precedence, calling on the Vietnamese people to unite behind the task of consolidating the North in order to make it a solid rear base for national liberation, the struggle for which, although "long and difficult," would certainly be victorious.

The meeting did attempt to respond to Le Duan's appeal by approving a secret policy calling for the gradual buildup of the revolutionary organization in South Vietnam and the selective punishment there of reactionary elements (called *tru gian*, or "killing tyrants"). Although Ho Chi Minh had always criticized the indiscriminate use of terrorism as an inappropriate tool of revolutionary action, it had been applied selectively during the war of resistance against the French. Now the Central Committee approved a more concrete policy calling for a program of limited terrorism to protect the revolutionary apparatus in the South by throwing fear into the ranks of the enemy and creating confidence among the masses that the movement could take care of its own.[51]

The Eleventh Plenum in December 1956 had taken a cautious first step toward the approval of a more aggressive approach toward the unification of the two zones. The same month, Le Duan's regional committee had met to consider the June 1956 directive from the Politburo calling for preparations to strengthen the self-defense capabilities of the movement to supplement the political struggle against the Saigon regime. In the words of a document issued by the committee, "through Central's guidance" it had now become clear that revolutionary war was "the only correct way" to bring about national reunification. During the next few months, there was a marked rise in terrorist activities directed against government officials and other key personnel in South Vietnam. Official sources in Hanoi claimed that those targeted were corrupt officials, wicked landlords, and traitors. In fact, many victims were popular and honest officials and teachers who were seen as a threat to the revolutionary movement because they heightened the sense of legitimacy of the Saigon government in the eyes of the local population.

Perhaps the clearest signal that a new era was dawning came in early 1957, when Le Duan was suddenly selected to serve as acting general secretary of the DRV. After the dismissal of Truong Chinh at the Tenth Plenum the previous fall, Ho Chi Minh had formally taken over that post, but reluctantly. Ho had occupied the relatively ceremonial positions of chairman of the Party and president of the DRV since his return to Hanoi in October 1954. At the same time that he took an active interest in issues related to foreign policy and national reunification, he increasingly limited himself to an avuncular role in domestic and Party affairs, offering advice to colleagues at Politburo meetings while delegating executive authority to younger colleagues like Prime Minister Pham Van Dong and Truong Chinh.

The reasons for Le Duan's selection as acting general secretary have long inspired debate. Some believe it was a testimony to his organization, dedication, and strategic vision, qualities that had earned him the sobriquet of "Uncle Ho of the South" (Cu Ho mien Nam). Others see it as a gesture of recognition that the struggle to achieve national reunification was destined to play an increasingly major role in decision making in Hanoi. As a southerner, Le Duan could be expected to represent the vast constituency of Vietnamese living south of the demilitarized zone. Or perhaps it was because as an outsider, Le Duan represented no threat to Party leaders like Ho Chi Minh and Truong Chinh, who could be expected to retain their influence within the Politburo in a Le Duan era. Some have speculated that Le Duan was preferred over Vo Nguyen Giap because he had spent several years in prison during World War II. A stint in the famous "schools of bolshevism" was considered a necessary rite of passage among the leading Party faithful at the time, many of whom had paid their own blood debt by spending time in French prisons. Giap not only had avoided arrest, but had been tainted by having applied for a scholarship to study in France.[52]

The evidence on Le Duan's elevation is not yet clear. Whatever the case, the appointment appeared to have the blessing of Ho Chi Minh, who could rest assured that his successor would give high priority to the issue of national reunification. With Le Duan occupying the post of the Party's chief executive officer, Ho now had the time to focus on matters relating to diplomacy and relations with the socialist community, as well as to pen articles on a variety of subjects. After twelve years of disguising his real identity, at the age of sixty-seven, Ho now finally confessed that he was indeed the famous revolutionary Nguyen Ai Quoc, and official biographies suddenly appeared in print to praise his lifelong dedication to the cause of the fatherland. While the revelation was a complete surprise to many Vietnamese, close acquaintances had long been aware of his real identity. In June 1957, he made a ceremonial visit to Kim Lien, the childhood home that he had left half a century earlier.[53]

While North Vietnamese leaders were grappling with how to prevent the division of Vietnam from becoming permanent, Soviet officials appeared determined to make it a fait accompli. In early 1957 the USSR suddenly proposed that the two Vietnams be admitted as separate states in the United Nations. Hanoi, which had apparently not been briefed beforehand, was stunned and immediately issued a formal protest. Shorty afterward, the U.N. General Assembly, by a large majority, voted for the admission of the Republic of Vietnam, or RVN (as the non-Communist government in South Vietnam now formally called itself) into the United Nations. Pham Van Dong wrote a letter of protest to the Soviet Union and Great Britain, co-chairs of the Geneva conference, and the question was referred to the U.N. Security Council. The issue had not yet been resolved when in mid-May, Kliment Voroshilov, chairman of the presidium of the Supreme Soviet in the USSR and one of Stalin's longtime cronies, arrived in Hanoi on a state visit.

There has been some speculation about the purpose of the trip, which was announced at the last minute and came after relatively leisurely stops in China and Indonesia. Vietnamese officials probably wanted to ascertain Soviet thinking on the issue of national reunification, while Moscow's objective may have been to persuade the DRV to avoid hostile acts that might provoke a renewal of war in Indochina. On several occasions, Voroshilov publicly called on his hosts to maintain their policy of promoting the "peaceful reunification" of the two zones.

Such appeals for a moderate approach to the issue could not have been welcome to all of his Vietnamese listeners. To soothe the growing sense of irritation in Hanoi, Voroshilov also announced an increase in Soviet economic assistance to the DRV, and assured Vietnamese leaders that the USSR would not permit the RVN to be admitted to the U.N. (In September, the Soviets would use their Security Council to kill a proposal for the admission of both Vietnams into the U.N., and the question of membership was indefinitely postponed. The official press in Hanoi laconically declared its approval of Moscow's "correct attitude."[54])

Voroshilov's trip to Hanoi may have been intended to paper over the strains brought about by Moscow's maladroit proposal to admit both Vietnams to the United Nations, but the potential for a rift between the two countries over the issue of Vietnamese reunification still remained. According to one foreign observer living in Hanoi, sentiment against the Soviet Union was looming so large within the Party leadership that a number of events on the agenda during Voroshilov's visit were canceled or took place with a minimum of ceremony in order to avoid the likelihood of bringing the disagreement before the public eye.[55]

For Hanoi, any serious breach in relations with Moscow could be catastrophic, since the DRV relied on the USSR not only for financial aid to build up the domestic economy and modernize the Vietnamese armed forces, but also for diplomatic support. In July 1957, Ho Chi Minh left for Moscow to seek a closer understanding with Soviet leaders on key issues. En route he stopped off in Beijing, where Mao Zedong reiterated the current Chinese view that the reunification of the two Vietnams might have to be postponed until a more appropriate time. The trip lasted almost two months and included stops in several Eastern European countries, as well as North Korea. On his return to Hanoi in September, Ho announced in a speech to the Vietnamese people that he had achieved "unity of views" with the nations of the Soviet bloc.[56]

This was hardly the case. A few weeks later, Ho set off again in the company of a delegation including Politburo members Le Duan and Pham Hung to attend the November meeting of world Communist parties in Moscow. The composition of the delegation was significant, since both Duan and Hung were southerners by birth and upbringing, and Hung had served as Le Duan's deputy in the southern apparatus after the Geneva conference. Clearly, the issue of national reunification would figure prominently in Vietnamese concerns in Moscow.

One of the underlying objectives of the November conference was to hammer out an agreement among the socialist nations on the issue of a peaceful transition to socialism. Among those opposing the Soviet view were the Chinese, who had become increasingly concerned about resolving the problem of Taiwan since the recent breakdown of Sino-U.S. talks on that issue and were increasingly suspicious that the new leadership in Moscow was prepared to betray the interests of world revolution on the altar of peaceful coexistence. In a bid to thwart the Soviets, Mao Zedong himself headed the Chinese delegation, the first time since the winter of 1949–50 that he had left the country. In Mao's view, recent achievements in the Soviet Union demonstrated the technological superiority of the socialist over the capitalist camp (the "east wind," he said, now prevailed over the "west wind"), and Moscow should use its superior might to play a more aggressive role in leading the struggle against imperialism throughout the world. A major debate on the subject at the meeting resulted in a compromise. According to a Chinese source, the first Soviet draft had said nothing about a nonpeaceful transition to socialism, but after discussion among the delegates it was amended, and in the end the final communiqué noted that "in conditions in which the exploiting classes resort to violence against the people, it is necessary to bear in mind another possibility—the nonpeaceful transition to socialism. Lenin teaches and history confirms that the ruling classes never relinquish power voluntarily."[57]

The precise role played by Ho Chi Minh and the Vietnamese delegation in the drafting and final approval of the declaration is unknown. German and Italian reports claimed that the declaration was drawn up as the result of discussion between the Soviets and Chinese, with little input from representatives of other parties. But the phraseology quoted above is so close to what Ho Chi Minh had used in his speech to the Ninth Plenum in April 1956 that it seems likely that he played a crucial role in bringing about the final compromise. In any event, Vietnamese sources indicate that the DRV delegation made clear to Moscow its view that although a peaceful transition to socialism may sometimes take place, a policy of "revolutionary violence" was the general rule.[58]

After the conference, Le Duan returned to Hanoi with the remainder of the delegates, but Ho Chi Minh remained in Moscow for additional talks with Soviet leaders. The topic of his discussions is unknown, but it seems probable that they dealt with the ominous split that was beginning to emerge between Soviet and Chinese leaders over the issue of peaceful coexistence and the leadership of the socialist community. For the Vietnamese, a split could obviously have disastrous consequences, since it would enable the United States to play off one Communist giant against the other. To prevent such a development, during his swing through Eastern Europe in September Ho had expressed his opinion that unity of views among Communist states was in the best interests of the revolutionary camp. In an article published in *Pravda* in November, he called for a commitment from all socialist nations to unify around the leadership of the USSR, a view that he repeated in a speech before the Supreme Soviet in Moscow. But his article did stress the need to adapt revolutionary tactics to local conditions.[59]

Once Le Duan and his asssociates arrived back in Hanoi in late November, they conferred with the Politburo. On December 1, the Vietnam News Agency announced that Party leaders were elated at the results achieved in Moscow and expressed confidence in the maintenance of solidarity among the nations within the socialist community. Whether such solidarity actually existed within the socialist camp is doubtful. It certainly did not exist in Hanoi, where growing differences were beginning to emerge within the Party leadership over the relative priority to be assigned to domestic concerns and advancing the cause of reunification with the South. For three years, Party leaders had maintained a fragile consensus on the advisability of delaying initial moves toward the construction of a socialist system until the consolidation of the North had been completed and the question of reunification clarified. Now, with plans for reunification placed on hold for an indefinite period, some senior Party leaders—chief among them Truong Chinh, who had managed to retain his influence within the Politburo despite his demotion—began to press for immediate steps to begin a socialist transformation in both urban and rural areas of the DRV before the end of the decade.

This issue was hotly debated at an enlarged thirteenth plenary session of the Central Committee in early December 1957. Although one of the stated reasons for the meeting was to report on the results of the Moscow conference, the key topic for discussion was a new three-year plan drafted by the Politburo to begin the transformation to a socialist society in the North. Press reports indicated that the decision to approve the plan was by no means unanimous. In the weeks following the close of the meeting, Party leaders launched a campaign to explain the decision and put an end to "confused ideas concerning the close relationship between the task of the socialist revolution in the North and that of national liberation in the South."[60]

The debate at the Thirteenth Plenum was undoubtedly complicated by the emergence of Le Duan as acting general secretary of the Party. The sudden elevation of a relatively junior member of the ruling clique could not avoid irritating some senior Party leaders. To his predecessor Truong Chinh, Le Duan was a cheeky upstart who had usurped his own rightful role as Ho Chi Minh's chief lieutenant and the senior ideological mentor of the Party. Moreover, Duan's obvious interest in the struggle in South Vietnam threatened to derail Chinh's plans to begin the installation of socialist institutions in the DRV. It may well be that Truong Chinh had managed to rally his supporters within the Politburo and the Central Committee to bring about approval of the three-year plan as a way of thwarting Le Duan. To the intense Vo Nguyen Giap, who had been passed over in the recent contest for Party leadership, Le Duan's brash recommendations on how to wage the struggle in the South undercut Giap's position as the chief military strategist within the Vietnamese revolutionary movement. Moreover, Duan's burning desire to intensify revolutionary activities in the South threatened to involve the People's Army of Vietnam (as it was now known), or PAVN, in a conflict for which (in Giap's view) it was not yet prepared. The comment in *Nhan Dan* in early November that "some comrades" had to learn that Party control over the army must be complete may well have been directed by Le Duan at Giap.[61]

Ho Chi Minh played no role in the debate, and in fact was not even present at the meeting. After his visit to Moscow for the Communist party summit, he had continued on to Beijing, where he remained "for a rest." His long and unexplained absence fueled speculation in Hanoi that he may have been marginalized by recent events or had even died in the USSR. Some suggested that he may have deliberately stayed away in order to force his colleagues to accept his advice. As yet there is no adequate explanation for his absence from Hanoi at such a critical time. While it is possible that he had gone to China for medical treatment, it is indeed curious that he did not attend the Thirteenth Plenum, which was destined to have a momentous impact on the DRV.

Whatever the reason for his not being present, on his return to Hanoi on December 24, Ho Chi Minh appeared to approve the decision to place a new priority on building a socialist society in the North. One week after his return, he greeted the new year with a speech announcing that the period of economic reconstruction had come to an end, giving way to a new era of planned economic development. It was, he said, "a new advance in the revolutionary work of our people." Five days later, *Nhan Dan* announced that there were now to be two revolutions—a socialist one in the North and a national democratic one in the South. A conference of senior cadres was convened to map out procedures for the transition to the socialist stage of the revolution. But doubts lingered. In March 1958, Truong Chinh complained that "some people" still failed to understand the importance of achieving socialism in the North as preparation for the liberation of the South. In a talk to representatives of the Fatherland Front, Chinh called for a cultural revolution to train new intellectuals to serve society in the new era. Explaining the reasoning behind the decision to launch the program, Prime Minister Pham Van Dong—who apparently was one of Truong Chinh's allies at this juncture—declared that "a stronger North" made the Vietnamese nation stronger in the struggle for national reunification, while "the road to a stronger North is the socialist road."[62]

By this time, Ho Chi Minh's dominant role within the Party was on the decline. The process may have begun with the rise of Chinese influence over the movement in the early 1950s, and it accelerated after Geneva, when many of his colleagues grew restive at the failure to achieve the peaceful reunification of the country. With the emergence of Le Duan as the most important figure on the political scene, it was about to decrease further.

Although he may have been outmaneuvered by Truong Chinh in the policy debate at the Thirteenth Plenum, Le Duan wasted no time in putting his own stamp on the Party apparatus. During the next few months, followers of Truong Chinh and Ho Chi Minh were dismissed from influential positions and replaced by new members. As his instrument in cleansing the organization of potential opposition, Le Duan selected his old colleague Le Duc Tho. Born near Hanoi in 1911 in a scholar-gentry family, Tho (real name Phan Dinh Khai) had joined the revolutionary movement in the late 1920s, but was soon arrested and spent most of the next two decades in prison. Released in 1945, he was sent to the South and served (under the revolutionary code name "Sau") as Le Duan's deputy during the Franco-Vietminh conflict. Narrow-minded in outlook, devious in manner, and dour in his public image, Tho soon became known as "Sau Bua" (Sau the Hammer) for his toughness in dealing with his colleagues. Although Tho may have envied Le Duan for his more senior position within the Party, the two collaborated effectively, and when Duan was elevated to leadership, Tho joined him in Hanoi as head of the Central Committee's Organization Department, a position that he quickly transformed into an effective apparatus to investigate and control the activities of Party members.

If Le Duc Tho had a rival in his ability to inspire fear and loathing in Hanoi, it was the Party apparatchik Tran Quoc Hoan. Born about 1910 in Quang Ngai province south of Da Nang, Hoan rose in the Party hierarchy during the Franco-Vietminh War, and was named DRV minister of public security in 1953. Secretive and resentful of his superiors, he lacked both culture and intellect, and became known as "the Vietnamese Beria" for his thoroughness and brutality in ferreting out alleged counterrevolutionaries within the ranks. Le Duc Tho was quick to see his promise as an ally and an instrument of power.

It was Tran Quoc Hoan who became the central figure in one of the most bizarre incidents in the history of the DRV. In 1955, a young woman from the border province of Cao Bang arrived in Hanoi. Winsome in appearance, Miss Xuan soon came to the attention of the aging president, who arranged to have her serve as his private nurse. Eventually she gave birth to his son, who was subsequently adopted by Ho's private secretary, Vu Ky. One day in 1957, Miss Xuan's body was discovered beside a road in the suburbs, the apparent victim of an automobile accident. Two female roommates in the Hanoi apartment where she had been assigned to live died under mysterious circumstances shortly after.

At first, the incident received little publicity, but several years later, the fiancé of one of the deceased young women charged in a letter to the National Assembly that Miss Xuan had been raped by Tran Quoc Hoan, and was then killed at Hoan's order to cover up his crime. The other two women were similarly disposed of, the fiancé claimed, to prevent them from disclosing what had happened. Although the story was quicked hushed up and Hoan was never charged, reports of the incident circulated among knowledgeable Party members in Hanoi. Whether Ho Chi Minh was aware of the details of the pathetic story is unknown, and he never referred to it.[63]

In December 1957, the Thirteenth Plenum gave tentative approval to a plan to lay the foundation for an advance to socialism throughout the DRV. By then, the process was already under way. While most agricultural production remained in private hands (a few experimental collective farms had been created in the mid-1950s), about 40 percent of all manufacturing and retail trade and almost half of the transportation sector were under state or collective ownership. Work exchange teams—a rudimentary form of socialism based on cooperative seasonal labor, which had been adopted in China in the early 1950s—had begun to appear.[64]

The initial moves coincided with the inauguration of the Great Leap Forward in China, and the new Chinese program provided Vietnamese officials with an opportunity to study the consequences of a similar possible application in the DRV. China had collectivized agriculture over a three-year period beginning in 1955, but the results in terms of food production had been somewhat disappointing, and in 1958 the government suddenly encouraged the building of massive "people's communes" throughout the countryside. These communes, of more than thirty thousand people each, included all forms of economic and administrative organization and common ownership and represented in principle the highest form of organization in the Marxist-Leninist lexicon—a stage that not even the Soviet Union had yet attempted.

At first, there were indications, including comments in the official press, that the Vietnamese would base their own program on the Chinese model. During his brief stay in Beijing in December 1957, Ho Chi Minh offered his own praise of the Great Leap Forward, writing admiringly in several articles (under the pseudonym T.L.) of the Chinese strategy of self-reliance and its policy (known as "to the village") of encouraging urban cadres to spend part of their time engaging in manual labor with the masses. But it is likely that Ho Chi Minh was engaging in his old game of flattering potential benefactors in order to win their support, for in March 1958, he advised the Politburo to be cautious and avoid haste in collectivizing the countryside. In an article that appeared in *Nhan Dan* that July, he warned that the experiences of fraternal socialist countries must be studied carefully and applied not "blindly," but in a creative manner. On the other hand, he appeared to approve of China's "to the village" movement, suggesting in September that senior Vietnamese officials should engage in manual labor one day a week to raise their own consciousness.[65]

In his doubts about the relevance of the Great Leap Forward to conditions in North Vietnam, Ho Chi Minh was in good company. Le Duan, who presumably viewed any radical program to change society in the North as an obstacle to his own objectives in the South, warned against an adventurist approach. Use ripples, not waves, to bring about changes, he quoted Mao's cautious colleague Liu Shaoqi. For his part, Prime Minister Pham Van Dong emphasized that the purpose of the three-year plan was to increase food production and raise the standard of living (rejecting, by implication, the Maoist view that its primary objective was to raise ideological consciousness in the villages), while even Truong Chinh announced that the process should be carried out "step by step." Vietnamese leaders had learned by bitter past experience that the Chinese model could not be imported lock, stock, and barrel into the DRV.[66]

In November 1958, the Central Committee held its Fourteenth Plenum and formally laid down the basic path for socialist transformation, which consisted of replacing private with collective or public ownership in both urban and rural areas. The Three-Year Plan for Economic Transformation and Cultural Development (1958–1960) was approved by the National Assembly the next month. The plan called for an acceleration of both agricultural and industrial production but stressed agriculture as the key link.

To some, the adoption of a rural strategy suggested that the Party was following recent practice in China. In fact, however, Ho Chi Minh had argued for years that underdeveloped countries such as Vietnam should begin their growth process in the countryside. The central objective of the program was to strengthen the national economy—which at that time was still overwhelmingly agricultural—in order to create the foundations for a future industrial revolution. In an article in December, Ho (writing under the name Tran Luc) recommended imitation of the Chinese strategy of maintaining "very tight" Party control from the capital to local areas, but emphasized that the formation of cooperatives must be carried out with caution and on the basis of "the principle of voluntarity." Ho Chi Minh, at least, had learned his lesson from the disaster of the land reform program.[67]

During most of 1958, the issue of national unification attracted little attention from Party leaders in Hanoi. Although a key reason for the neglect was the need to pay attention to domestic needs in the North, certainly another factor was the attitude of the regime's patrons in Moscow and Beijing. Khrushchev's views were well known. In private conversations with North Vietnamese officials, Mao Zedong had offered similar advice. The problem of a divided Vietnam could not be resolved in a brief period, but would require a protracted struggle lasting many years. "If ten years is not enough," he warned, "it may take one hundred."[68] Although some senior leaders in Hanoi may not have agreed, they kept their own counsel.

For the time being, then, Party leaders focused on issues of domestic reconstruction, while limiting their efforts on national reunification to seeking support in the diplomatic arena for carrying out the provisions of the Geneva Accords. In February 1958 Ho Chi Minh led a North Vietnamese delegation on a tour to India and Burma, two countries with neutralist governments that had expressed some support for the DRV. The visit to New Delhi was designed in part to counterbalance India's recent decision to grant diplomatic recognition to the Republic of Vietnam. In talks with Prime Minister Nehru, Ho successfully solicited his host's support for the principle of Vietnamese reunification, but Nehru refused to issue a public condemnation of the RVN or of the United States for their role in frustrating the holding of nationwide elections. He received a similar response in Rangoon.[69]

By now, Ho Chi Minh's role was increasingly limited to that of senior diplomat and foreign policy adviser, as well as to fulfilling his growing image as the spiritual father of all the Vietnamese people and the soul of the Vietnamese revolution. Ho played his part as the kindly Uncle Ho to perfection. He continued to shun the more ornate trappings of his presidential role. In 1958, he moved into a new small stilt house on the grounds of the presidential palace, just a few yards away from the gardener's cottage he had occupied. Built at the Party's order in the simple style of the houses of the mountain minorities settled in the Viet Bac, it served as his main office and residence for the remainder of his life.

Shortly after the close of the Fourteenth Plenum, Le Duan embarked on a secret inspection trip to South Vietnam to assess the situation there in preparation for a major policy review by the Central Committee. On his return in mid-January 1959, he presented a report to the Politburo, which had been called urgently into session to discuss the situation. Conditions in the South, Duan declared, were perilous. The enemy's determination to drown the revolution in blood had placed the lives of the masses in serious danger and heightened popular hostility to the Saigon government.

Although the tone of Le Duan's report was obviously colored by his political objectives, his description of the situation in the South was fairly accurate. When revolutionary activists launched their terrorist campaign in 1957, Ngo Dinh Diem had responded with a desperate effort to destroy the movement. To extend its control over the countryside, Saigon established a new program to fortify and defend villages from being infiltrated and controlled by Vietminh elements. Known as "agrovilles," these new fortified hamlets were strengthened with barbed wire, mud walls, and moats to enable residents to defend their village from enemy attack. Within each agroville, villagers were organized into militia units to protect the community against infiltration from the outside, while government agents and informers sought to identify Vietminh sympathizers, some of whom had surfaced as such after the Geneva Accords.

As an internal Party document later conceded, the Saigon regime was initially quite successful in stabilizing the situation in South Vietnam and limiting the effectiveness of the revolutionary forces:

> The enemy at this time had completed the establishment of his ruling machinery from top to bottom, being able to build a tight espionage network and to form popular force units in every village. He was able to control each and every family by means of the house-block system [a Saigon-run security network in which families throughout the RVN were organized into units of five and made jointly responsible for the loyalty of all of their members]. The movement's influence was so low that even the people's low-level struggles, such as the requests for relief or for loans to grow crops, were labeled as "Viet Cong activities," and the enemy participants were intimidated and terrorized. At the same time, the enemy kept on systematically building his agrovilles, concentrating people in centers and hamlets away from remote areas and to zones near com-

mercial centers, wide roads and waterways. He carried out a tight system of oppression in the rural areas. . . .

During this period, the people were somewhat perturbed and shaken even though they strongly hated the enemy and believed that the revolution would be victorious in spite of everything. Doubt in our struggle method and old views from the past were now revived and voiced more vigorously. People said that the struggles for "democratic and civil rights only lead to the prisons and to the tombs," and that "such struggle will end with everyone's death." In many localities people requested the Party to take up arms and fight back against the enemy.[70]

Between 1957 and 1959, more than two thousand suspected Communists were executed, often by guillotine after being convicted by roving tribunals that circulated throughout rural regions of the RVN; thousands more who were suspected of sympathy with the revolutionary cause were arrested and placed in prison. South Vietnamese military units launched raids into Vietminh base areas in the Ca Mau Peninsula and in Zone D, where the population had long harbored sympathies with the revolutionary movement. According to sources in the DRV, Party membership in the South plummeted from over five thousand members at the beginning of 1957 to less than one third that level by the end of the year. According to Tran Van Giau, who had emerged as a prominent historian in the DRV, it was "the darkest hour" for the revolutionary cause.[71]

But subversive activity undertaken by Vietminh elements who had remained in South Vietnam after the Geneva conference was not the only threat to the stability of the Saigon regime, for in many respects Ngo Dinh Diem was his own worst enemy. At the instigation of the United States, in 1956 Diem agreed to promulgate a constitution to create an aura of legitimacy for his new government. The constitution of the RVN called for a combination of the presidential and parliamentary forms of government and included provisions to protect individual human rights. However, Diem lacked the instincts of a democratic politician. Stiff in demeanor and uncomfortable in large crowds, he found it difficult to mingle with his constituents. Distrustful of southerners, he surrounded himself with his fellow Catholics, many of whom were recent refugees from the North and shared his deep distrust of communism. Sensitive to criticism, he was quick to suppress any potential opposition to his rule. A government-sponsored political party, known as the Personalist Labor Party, was created under the leadership of his younger brother,

Minister of the Interior Ngo Dinh Nhu. Opposition parties were declared illegal and critics of the regime were routinely silenced or put in prison.

Perhaps Diem's worst failing was his inability to comprehend the needs of the peasants, who made up more than 80 percent of the population of the RVN. At U.S. urging, the Saigon regime launched a land reform program of its own to rectify the vast inequalities in the distribution of land (about 1 percent of the population owned half the cultivated acreage in the country and poor peasants often paid up to one third of their annual harvest in rent to absentee landlords). Wealthy landowners or the affluent bourgeoisie in the large cities, who could be expected to oppose a land reform program as inimical to their own interests, were among the government's most fervent supporters. As a consequence, the land reform legislation was written with loopholes large enough to make it easy for landlords to evade its provisions, and after several years of operation, only about 10 percent of eligible tenant farmers had received any land. In many instances, families living in previously Vietminh-held areas were now forced to return land they had received during the Franco-Vietminh conflict to its previous owners, often at gunpoint. For them, as for many of their compatriots throughout the country, the Diem regime represented little improvement over the colonial era. By the end of the 1950s, much of the countryside in South Vietnam was increasingly receptive to the demand for radical change.

Shortly after Le Duan reported to the Politburo in January 1959, the Central Committee convened its Fifteenth Plenum. Some of the delegates at the meeting were southern cadres, who were undoubtedly eager to add their personal accounts to help dramatize the recent course of events in the RVN. Others were supporters of the movement who had left the South after the Geneva Accords and had grown increasingly restive at the failure of the Party leadership to take sufficient action to protect their compatriots in South Vietnam. Such delegates undoubtedly had a powerful spokesman in Le Duan, who argued before the Central Committee that if the insurgent forces in the South were not allowed to build up their size and firepower, the revolutionary movement might be extinguished. The rising chorus of dissent against the Diem regime, he declared, represented a golden opportunity to take a giant step toward the future reunification of the country.

For the Party leadership the decision was not easy. According to one document captured by South Vietnamese military forces a few years later, there were "many opinions and hesitancies" among the delegates over how to respond to the rapidly evolving situation. Some argued that the Party had no choice but to come to the aid of the movement in the

South, which had been reduced to a struggle for survival. Popular resentment throughout the country against the Diem regime, they declared, had reached a boiling point. But others pointed out that a resumption of armed struggle could anger Hanoi's allies in Moscow and Beijing, and might even provoke active U.S. intervention. Still others, such as Truong Chinh and his allies, feared that an escalation of the fighting in the South would divert precious resources from the North at a time when the DRV was making a major attempt to lay the initial foundations of an advanced socialist society.[72]

Ho Chi Minh remained one of the strongest voices stressing the need for caution. He warned his colleagues not to rely simply on armed violence, for that would create a pretext for U.S. intervention. He pointed out the importance of placing the Vietnamese revolution in a global context. With the strength of American imperialism steadily weakening throughout the world, Ho argued that a gradual approach was preferable. He promised that when opportunity struck, Vietminh forces in the South would be in a position to achieve a swift and decisive victory. In the meantime, he urged that they be satisfied with small victories.[73]

Perhaps in response to Ho Chi Minh's pleas, the plenum reached a compromise. The decision to resort to a strategy of revolutionary war to bring about the reunification of the two zones of the country was approved, but the relative degree of political and military struggle to be applied was left unresolved. As the resolution, which was not released until many years later, stated:

> The fundamental path of development for the revolution in South Vietnam is that of violent struggle. Based on the concrete conditions and existing requirements of revolution, then, the road of violent struggle is: to use the strength of the masses, with political strength as the main factor, in combination with military strength to a greater or lesser degree depending on the situation, in order to overthrow the ruling power of the imperialist and feudalist forces and build the revolutionary power of the people.[74]

The Central Committee conceded that the struggle would be arduous and complicated, but it expressed the hope that although it might be necessary to adopt methods of self-defense and armed propaganda, it would still be possible to achieve victory primarily through political struggle.

In recent years, some Western scholars have argued that the debate in Hanoi essentially turned into a contest between cautious northerners fearful of the implications of escalation and militant southerners deter-mined to topple a tyrannical regime. Although there is undoubtedly some truth in that hypothesis—many southerners tried to make a strong case for a policy of armed violence and encountered resistance from cau-tious delegates from the North—the image of a North-South divide should probably not be overstated. A number of prominent Party leaders in Hanoi, including General Vo Nguyen Giap and Ho Chi Minh himself, had been convinced for years that a strategy of revolutionary violence might eventually be needed to bring about national reunification. Ho and his colleagues had argued strongly to that effect in Moscow in the fall of 1957 and had probably repeated those arguments in discussions with Chinese officials. The debate at the Fifteenth Plenum, then, was more a matter of timing. All—or almost all—Party leaders agreed that armed struggle might be needed and would be fully justified if all other avenues had failed. But whether it was now appropriate for such a strat-egy to be adopted, and what mix of military and political tactics should be applied, was a matter for careful discussion and calibration. In Ho Chi Minh's view, it was not yet time to abandon the hope for a political solution.

The scholarly debate over the decisions reached at the Fifteenth Ple-num is not simply an academic one. If, as some argue, the stimulus for the escalation of revolutionary violence came primarily from southerners, then the evolving revolutionary struggle can be described essentially as an internal resistance movement against a corrupt and despotic regime. North Vietnam in turn can be portrayed as a somewhat passive observer and eventually a reluctant participant in the process. But if Party leaders in the North played a crucial role in the decision, then the resulting events in the South can be described, as some insist, as a consequence of the determination of Hanoi to consolidate its control over the entire country. The evidence suggests that the truth is in between these two extremes, with Ho Chi Minh and his colleagues seeking to bring orga-nization and discipline to a vocal but unfocused chorus of discontent against political and economic conditions in South Vietnam.[75]

The decision by the Central Committee to resort to a strategy of revolutionary war, known in Party histories as Resolution 15, was not immediately circulated to all echelons. For the next four months, Vo Nguyen Giap was assigned responsibility for assessing all aspects of the problem, while current reports on the situation in the South were gath-ered. In the meantime, Ho Chi Minh was sent abroad by the Party to consult with Hanoi's chief allies and seek their support. Now almost seventy years old, he was still tirelessly pursuing his final dream of bringing about the reunification of his country under socialism. Ho visited Beijing in mid-January, and then proceeded to Moscow to attend the Twenty-first Congress of the CPSU. He returned to Hanoi after a few days in China on February 14, 1959. The details of Ho's conversations with Chinese and Soviet leaders about the situation in South Vietnam have never been divulged, but in May, Resolution 15 was formally approved by the Central Committee.[76]

W ith the decision reached at the Fifteenth Plenum in January
1959, the Party leadership had made a formal commitment
to abandon its policy of watchful waiting and now placed
reunification with the South as a matter of highest priority. But there
was as yet no consensus on exactly what the new policy would entail.
Some sought victory through a combined strategy of political and military struggle such as had been adopted during the August Revolution
of 1945. Others predicted that it might be necessary to return to the
style of direct military conflict that had been adopted during the later
war against the French.

For the moment, there were too many unresolved questions to draft
a concrete strategy. Whether the Diem regime would collapse under the
weight of its own incompetence and corruption; whether the United
States would react to the weakening of its ally in Saigon by escalating
its own role; whether Hanoi's sponsors would prove willing to support
a new round of conflict in Indochina—all these remained to be determined. Until such questions could be answered, Party leaders postponed
an internal debate over specifics and compromised with an approach that
for the time being was simply called "revolutionary war." As Le Duan,
who was now emerging as the leading strategist in the Politburo, described it, the revolutionary forces in the South should for the moment
continue to rely primarily on the techniques of political struggle, while
gradually enlarging their base areas and building up their military
strength in order to push the movement forward.[1]

Hanoi's decision to limit the role of armed violence in the South was
motivated in part by the desire to avoid excessive loss of lives and vital
resources. But there were other factors as well, including the urgings of
its allies not to endanger world peace. During the summer of 1958, Ho
Chi Minh had consulted with Mao Zedong at Mao's summer beach re-

treat at Beidaihe about how the DRV should proceed in its struggle to unify the two Vietnams. Mao had responded that in his view the "most urgent task" at the moment was to complete the socialist revolution in the North. To Beijing, the South was not yet ripe for revolutionary change. In the meantime, Mao believed that dissident forces there should build up their political and military strength in preparation for a future opportunity to achieve a great leap forward.[2]

But the decision reached at the Fifteenth Plenum in January 1959 also reflected Hanoi's growing concern over the threat of direct U.S. intervention in the South. Since replacing the French as the primary sponsor of the regime in Saigon, the Eisenhower administration had shown no indication that it was ready to abandon its effort to prevent the unification of the two zones. Not only had Washington followed up on the threat to build a firm anti-Communist base in the South (announced by Secretary of State Dulles shortly after the Geneva conference), but it had also indicated that the new states in Indochina would be covered in the new SEATO agreements created in Manila in 1954. Although the Republic of Vietnam was not a member of the organization, a clause in the founding charter declared that in case of an armed attack on South Vietnam, Laos, or Cambodia, each member of SEATO would "act to meet the common danger in accordance with its constitutional processes."

For the time being, then, there were persuasive reasons for Party leaders to be cautious in their approach to the South. Even Le Duan, probably the most militant member of the Politburo, had privately expressed his view that the strategy applied against the French had focused excessively on military operations and should not be repeated. During the remainder of 1959, cautious preparations got under way to advance to the next stage of the struggle. Small clusters of "regroupees"—young Vietnamese who had been born and raised in the South but then were transported to the North after the Geneva conference for training in the techniques of revolutionary warfare—were now ordered back to the South to provide the insurgency there with a solid nucleus of experienced and loyal cadres. Of the approximately 90,000 refugees who had gone north in 1954, many of the most dedicated had received training at the Xuan Mai Training School near Hanoi in preparation for a possible return to revolutionary war in the South. As one trainee later commented:

> It was a very interesting time for us in the northern part of Vietnam. We had always been strong fighters for the Viet Minh, and we always admired Ho Chi Minh and the other Viet Minh leaders.

The trip to North Vietnam was very difficult and very long, but we did not ever complain, because we knew the difficulties were for the revolution.

Our training in North Vietnam was also difficult. Sometimes the food was not good. Sometimes we were very lonely and wanted to go home and see our family and friends. But we learned after a while not to be lonely, and learned to find strength in our revolutionary struggle. We learned not to think much about our families any more. We learned not to miss our families any more—like Ho Chi Minh.[3]

The regroupees were infiltrated back into South Vietnam, usually in groups of forty to fifty, traveling by truck into the mountains of southern Laos and then continuing on foot over jungle trails that bypassed the demilitarized zone to the east. On their arrival in South Vietnam, they were assigned to leading positions within the Party's southern apparatus. A unit labeled Group 559 (the name came from May 1959, the date of its creation) was directed to construct a system of trails to transport troops, weapons, and supplies from north to south. The trails—many of which had previously been hacked out of the jungle during the war against the French—would eventually be known to the world as the Ho Chi Minh Trail. A second unit, called Group 759, was ordered to facilitate the shipment of goods and personnel by ship down the long and relatively undefended South China Sea coast. Supplies were carried by special units called the Bo doi Truong son (Central Mountains Troops). At first they carried equipment on foot or on bicycles; later the trails were expanded to handle truck traffic. It was often hard going. As one commented, "The farther south we got, the worse our situation became. Finally we were down to a few kilos of rice, which we decided to save for the last extremity. For two months we ate what we could find in the jungle—leaves, roots, animals, jungle birds."

According to another account:

At first we would walk about eight hours a day. But with the climbing and the jungles, it was slow going. When and where we rested depended on the guide and our leader. Any place that was clear and safe would do. But even the way stations were not like some stopover in the city. There was nothing to shelter you from the rain, no beds. You just put up your hammock and slept in it.

The way stations had been established by our predecessors on the trail. They were supposed to supply us with food and water. But they were often short. So each individual learned to save his own food and water. The farther along we got, the worse the hunger we faced. As food grew scarcer, comradeship broke down. People became more and more intent on saving their own lives.[4]

Information about the decisions reached at the Fifteenth Plenum in January 1959 and confirmed by the passing of Resolution 15 in May did not reach insurgent commanders in the South until late summer. To many, the news was undoubtedly welcome, since the Diem regime had just begun to intensify its effort to suppress the revolutionary movement by means of a set of new directives known as Law 10/59, which gave Saigon's security forces increased authority to apprehend and punish the opposition. During the remainder of the year, roving tribunals circulated throughout the country, charging, convicting, and sometimes executing individuals suspected of political connections with Hanoi. Because peasant families in the densely populated Mekong delta were now increasingly herded into the heavily defended agrovilles, guerrillas had much less access to the rural population.

Driven to desperate measures, insurgent leaders tried to respond. In late August, crowds of villagers in the hardscrabble piedmont areas of Quang Ngai province gathered to protest upcoming elections for a National Assembly of the RVN, which, in the view of Party leaders in Hanoi, was an illegal government. The demonstrators, who were supported by Vietminh forces operating in the area, temporarily seized sixteen villages in Tra Bong district, a hilly region on the eastern slope of the Central Highlands, and briefly carved out a liberated zone consisting of about fifty villages with a population of more than one thousand people.

Five months later, a second uprising erupted, this time in Kien Hoa province (known to Vietminh supporters by its previous name of Ben Tre) in the heart of the Mekong delta. The local population had been sympathetic to the revolutionary cause since the war against the French, when Vietminh activists had seized the farms of pro-French landowners and distributed them to the poor. After the Geneva Accords, the landlords had returned, and with the support of government troops took back their lands, sometimes after harsh reprisals (including arrest and imprisonment) against the previous occupiers. In January 1960, local self-defense forces under Vietminh command suddenly attacked government outposts and with the aid of local residents occupied dozens of villages. Party cadres had carefully planned the operation, arming sympathizers with spears or wooden rifles to frighten the enemy and dispatching units disguised as South Vietnamese troops to various villages to seize administrative authority. Then, as one participant described,

> Sometime after 9:00 P.M., I had just arrived in the permanent office [headquarters] when I heard the sound of drums and wooden blocks echoing from one village to another and resounding everywhere, followed by the happy shouts of the people. . . . As the night advanced, the sound of drums and wooden bells intensifed and became insistent as though urging everyone to rise up. This was the people's signal for combat being transmitted everywhere. . . . Suddenly there was a shout: "The post is on fire, and it's burning rapidly!"
>
> The forces encircling the posts had been ordered to burn down any posts they captured. The people immediately tore up the flags, and burned the plaques bearing their house numbers and family registers. On the roads, the villagers cut down trees to erect barriers and block the movement of the enemy. . . . All the posts were surrounded by the people who made appeals to the soldiers through bullhorns. It was a night of terrifying thunder and lightning striking the enemy on their heads. Attacked by surprise, they were scared out of their wits and stayed put in the posts.[5]

The rising tempo of armed resistance in South Vietnam created problems for the Party leadership in Hanoi, which was still concerned about the ramifications of a wider conflict. In an obvious effort to reassure Hanoi's allies, Le Duan declared in an April speech that it was important to restrict the revolutionary violence to the South. Duan conceded that the need to keep peace in the world and carry out the socialist revolution in the DRV created "complications" for the revolution in South Vietnam, but he maintained that in the long run these factors would work to the advantage of the cause of national unity.[6]

In the meantime, Ho Chi Minh played his usual role as the DRV's chief diplomat by taking a prominent part in the effort to win support from Hanoi's allies for the reunification effort. It was a time of increasing tension within the Soviet bloc because of the widening split between China and the USSR over global strategy. As an indication of its displeasure with Beijing's uncooperative attitude, Moscow had just refused a formal request from China for a sample atomic bomb, as had been promised in a mutual agreement a few years previously. In the future, the North Vietnamese would learn how to play one ally against the other, but in these early stages of the dispute they were reduced to pleading with their allies for fraternal unity. In early July 1959, Ho Chi Minh traveled to Moscow for talks with Soviet leaders. Before his departure from Hanoi he warned the Politburo that the struggle in the South would be fierce and complicated. He warned against an attitude of blind adventurism.[7]

It was not an auspicious time for discussions in Moscow about the resumption of revolutionary war in South Vietnam; Nikita Khrushchev was making preparations for a September trip to the United States and was reluctant to risk antagonizing Washington over an issue of peripheral concern to Moscow. The Soviet Union announced a long-term aid pact to bolster the DRV economy, but on the issue of national reunification its leaders were less forthcoming. Speeches by Khrushchev and Kliment Voroshilov during Ho's visit emphasized the importance of implementing peacefully the provisions of the Geneva Accords.

After Ho's meeting with Soviet leaders, he remained briefly in Moscow for a medical checkup (he was told he was in better health than the previous year) and then embarked on a leisurely tour through the European republics of the USSR, passing through the Ukraine, Crimea, and Caucasus. In late July he traveled by train through Central Asia to Alma-Ata, capital of the Soviet republic of Kazakhstan. On August 1, he flew from there to Ürümqi, in China's Xinjiang province.

Ho had extended his sojourn in the USSR because the Central Committee of the Chinese Communist Party was gathering for a critical conference, and thus would not be able to meet Ho until later. The meeting was convened at Lushan, a mountain resort in south China, to address growing discord within the Party leadership, sparked in part by the disastrous Great Leap Forward. Launched the previous year with the objective of increasing food production and hastening the socialization of the countryside, that campaign had encountered widespread resistance from peasants and resulted in mass starvation in rural areas. At the Lushan conference, Defense Minister Peng Dehuai, commander of People's Liberation Army forces in the Korean conflict, angered Mao Zedong by criticizing the Great Leap Forward for its tragic impact on the Chinese economy. He also defended China's military relationship with the USSR against those who would replace it with a policy of self-reliance. For his temerity, Peng was dismissed from his post and replaced by Marshal Lin Biao, a senior military officer who had commanded Chinese troops during the Civil War and was now one of Mao Zedong's closest allies.

Ho Chi Minh remained in Ürümqi a few days and then made his way slowly eastward by train to Xian where, as in the fall of 1938, he once again played the role of a tourist. He finally arrived in Beijing on

August 13. Because Mao had still not returned to the capital, Ho met with Zhou Enlai and Liu Shaoqi, who informed him that there had been no change in the Chinese view that resistance operations in South Vietnam should be limited to political and low-level forms of paramilitary struggle, although they did approve the DRV's decision to resort to the strategy of revolutionary war. Ho returned to Hanoi on the twenty-sixth.[8]

Ho Chi Minh could not have been pleased at the meager results of his lengthy trip abroad. Neither Moscow nor Beijing had expressed more than polite sympathy at the breakdown of the Geneva Accords, nor had they indicated any firm support for Hanoi's decision to resort to a policy of revolutionary violence to complete the task of national reunification. He must have been particularly incensed at his treatment in China, where Mao Zedong had not even bothered to return to the capital to greet him. But Ho was accustomed to condescension on the part of Chinese comrades, and in remarks to his colleagues he occasionally referred sarcastically to Mao Zedong as the "Celestial Emperor." In any case, the slight was soon patched up. That autumn, he led an official delegation to Beijing to commemorate the tenth anniversary of the founding of the PRC. After meeting with his old friend and benefactor Madame Soong Qingling, Ho conferred with Mao on October 3 and returned home the following day. In an article printed in *Nhan Dan* that month, Ho urged his compatriots to study the Chinese experience and to be eternally grateful for Chinese support in the Vietnamese war of national liberation.[9]

While Ho Chi Minh was consulting with Hanoi's allies about foreign policy, his colleagues were preoccupied with domestic concerns. The three-year plan aimed at building the foundations of a socialist society in the North was well under way and in general had proceeded without the violence and discord of the land reform program. The relative absence of class violence that accompanied the collectivization campaign was undoubtedly gratifying to Ho Chi Minh, who urged his colleagues to avoid coercion and to use "democratic methods" to indoctrinate the rural population in the superiority of the socialist system. Ho was similarly insistent that persuasion rather than force be used in urban areas, where the industrial and commercial sector was being steadily placed under state or collective ownership. In a meeting devoted to Party rectification, Ho took issue with the view expressed by some militants that the bourgeois class was the natural adversary of social revolution in North Vietnam, arguing that the bourgeoisie had joined the ranks of the masses and could be transformed peacefully and voluntarily into useful members of the working class. How much weight Ho's words carried within Party councils, however, is difficult to ascertain. His influence over decisions relating to domestic affairs had waned considerably, and senior Party leaders had decided that he would devote the bulk of his time to foreign policy concerns and the issue of national reunification.[10]

By the end of 1959, most of the urban and rural economy in the DRV had been transformed along socialist lines, and Party leaders began to turn their attention to the next step—a five-year plan, Soviet-style, to begin the process of socialist industrialization. Not only would the plan require a major effort, it would take place in conjunction with an escalation of the struggle in the South, so Party leaders decided that a national Party congress should be convened to provide a platform for public discussion of the plan and a means to secure its approval. In October 1959, preparations for the congress, to take place sometime in the late summer or fall of 1960, got under way.

Meanwhile, tensions between Hanoi's chief allies escalated. At a congress of the Romanian Communist Party in June 1960, the Sino-Soviet dispute for the first time broke out into the open to a stunned world, sparked by bitter attacks uttered by delegates on both sides. After the congress, Moscow ordered many of its advisers in China to return home. Vietnamese representatives in Bucharest had probably not been advised of Khrushchev's intentions at the congress, and remained largely silent in the face of Soviet attacks on Chinese views regarding imperialism and global war; Le Duan, the senior VWP delegate at the conference, issued a brief statement supporting the Chinese line that the U.S. imperialists were attempting to foment a new world war. But Hanoi was not ready yet to take sides in the dispute, which reflected the growing chasm between Moscow and Beijing over the strategy to be adopted by socialist countries in the Cold War. A *Nhan Dan* editorial published after the conference adjourned ignored the issues raised there and warned that the lack of Communist unity could badly hurt the Party and the cause of Vietnamese reunification.

Hanoi tried desperately to keep the dispute from damaging its own security interests, and Ho Chi Minh himself took every opportunity to appear evenhanded in dealings with Moscow and Beijing. That May, he had flown to south China to celebrate his seventieth birthday and rest for a few days. Shortly after his return, an article supporting Moscow's "correct policies" appeared under his name in *Nhan Dan*. In August, he made a quiet visit to Moscow and Beijing, where he undoubtedly tried to reassure both his hosts regarding DRV intentions in South Vietnam, while at the same time urging them to make every effort to reconcile their differences.

The Third National Congress of the VWP, the first to be held since the resistance congress in the Viet Bac in early 1951, convened in Hanoi on September 5, 1960. In attendance were 576 delegates representing more than half a million Party members in both zones. As Party chairman, Ho gave the opening speech, in which he made a brief reference to past mistakes (the Party, he pointed out, had actively corrected its shortcomings and was not "dizzy with success"), but he devoted the bulk of his address to the future, declaring that the major task for the next few years was to lead the North onward to socialism. The best guarantee of victory for the Vietnamese revolution, he emphasized, was "to steep ourselves in Marxism-Leninism, to remain loyal to the interests of the working class and the people, and to preserve solidarity and unity within the Party, between all Communist parties, and all countries of the big socialist family." He had relatively little to say about the South—which he described as the "brass wall of the fatherland"—except to note that the Party hoped to achieve reunification by peaceful means.[11]

Ho's speech set the tone at the congress; the bulk of attention was devoted to giving formal approval to the new five-year plan to lay the basis for a technologically advanced and fully socialist society. The struggle for national reunification was by no means ignored; in the resolution issued at the close of the meeting, it was assigned equal billing with the Party's domestic objectives over the next five years. But it was clear that Party leaders had still not reached a consensus on how to proceed in the South. In his political report to the congress, Le Duan made a number of references to the situation, but he avoided specifics, noting only that it would be "a long and arduous struggle, not simple but complex, combining many forms of struggle," requiring flexibility and a move from legal to illegal forms of activity. The primary tool, he declared, would be the revolutionary power of the masses. He did not refer to the possibility of active involvement by the DRV. That the Party leadership did not expect that it would be required, at least for the immediate future, was suggested by the fact that the congress approved without much debate the Politburo's ambitious proposal to adopt a five-year plan for socialist industrialization in the North. Still, there were indications that the debate over strategy in the South had not entirely abated. In his address before the delegates, Vo Nguyen Giap remarked that some comrades were not fully aware of the plots of the United States and their lackeys in Saigon, pointing out that they "don't understand that while our policy is to preserve peace and achieve peaceful reunification, we should always be prepared to cope with any maneuver of the enemy."

Finally, the Third Congress ratified the shift in Party leadership that had been under way for several years. Le Duan was formally elected first secretary (replacing the old title of general secretary, in imitation of a decision taken by the Soviet Party) of the VWP. Ho Chi Minh remained Party chairman. Duan's promotion to a ranking in the Party second only to that of Ho himself left no doubt that the issue of national reunification would receive ample attention during the next decade. As a further indication of its growing importance, there were now three native South Vietnamese in the new Politburo—Le Duan, Pham Hung, and a senior military officer of rising prominence, Nguyen Chi Thanh. Charismatic and ambitious, Thanh had been promoted to the highest grade of General of the Army in the late 1950s, thus equaling in rank his rival Vo Nguyen Giap. Unlike Giap, Thanh was a political creature, having previously served as head of the army's Political Department, which was charged with maintaining ideological purity among the troops. A fourth new member of the Party's ruling body, Le Duc Tho, was not a southerner, but had served there as Le Duan's deputy during the war of resistance against the French.[12]

The Third National Congress took no official position on the Sino-Soviet dispute, and (with delegates from both countries present) the issue apparently did not spark debate at public sessions. Statements issued after the meeting continued to describe the USSR as the leader of the socialist camp, but with militant new leaders under Le Duan coming to the fore, Ho's long effort to maintain a balance in relations with the DRV's two socialist patrons was now increasingly in jeopardy. Ho did his part in minimizing tensions by acting as interpreter in discussions between Soviet and Chinese representatives at the congress. But neither ally was prepared to give its approval to a possible escalation of the ferment in South Vietnam. Moscow refused to give Ho a blank check in South Vietnam and rejected Ho's appeal to lower tensions within the socialist camp. During a short visit to Hanoi in July, Zhou Enlai had urged the Vietnamese to be flexible and to make maximum use of political struggle in seeking victory in the South.[13]

Party leaders continued to grapple with the problem of how to bring about the collapse of the Diem regime without running the risk of provoking direct intervention by the United States. Past experience suggested that a new political organization in the South was needed that could occupy a role similar to that played by the Vietminh Front in the early years of the struggle against the French. In effect, Hanoi required a national front that would serve as a magnet for all dissident elements opposed to the Saigon regime, while remaining subject to the will of the VWP. It would need a program that would appeal to patriots dedicated to Vietnamese reunification without alienating separatist elements in the South who were suspicious of northern domination. It would need to appeal to moderates who distrusted communism in ideology and practice, while still eliciting the enthusiastic support of workers and peasants. It would also need to hold the promise of liberating South Vietnam from the clutches of Diem's authoritarian rule without embodying the threat of an immediate takover of the southern provinces by the Communist regime in the North.

The first public reference to the projected new front appeared at the Third National Congress, when it was briefly described in an address by the Party elder statesman Ton Duc Thang. According to Thang, the onetime labor organizer who had promoted the formation of dockworkers' unions in colonial Saigon, the front would be based on the familiar Leninist concept of the four-class alliance, but in deference to the complexity of South Vietnamese society, it should also encompass the various religious and ethnic minorities. Its aim was to be general in nature in order to appeal to a wide range of the population. It should emphasize nationalist and reformist themes and set forth as a final goal the creation of a peaceful, unified, democratic, and prosperous Vietnam. The interim step would be the formation of a government composed of all progressive elements in southern society, a coalition that would eventually discuss peaceful reunification with the North. This new southern front, like its famous predecessor, the Vietminh Front, would need to be organized at various echelons, from a central committee down to cells at the village level. There would be no mention of communism.

The National Front for the Liberation of South Vietnam (commonly known as the National Liberation Front, or NLF), was formally established on December 20, 1960, at a secret conference of representatives of various strata of South Vietnamese society "somewhere [as Party histories described it] in the liberated area of South Vietnam." In fact, the meeting took place in a collection of small buildings in a densely forested area of rubber plantations along the Cambodian border, an area that would later serve as the headquarters of the Party's military command in the South. For the sixty delegates, it was a moving experience. According to Truong Nhu Tang, a South Vietnamese intellectual who participated in the congress, "each individual in the hall was conscious that he was participating in a historic event." After the conference adjourned, Tang returned by bus to Saigon, nourishing "sublime hopes." A few weeks later, a new president, John Fitzgerald Kennedy, took office in the United States. In briefing his successor, President Eisenhower made no mention of the rising tempo of insurgent activity in South Vietnam.[14]

In fact, although Dwight Eisenhower was unaware of it, anger against Ngo Dinh Diem and his influential younger brother Ngo Dinh Nhu was on the rise in many sectors of South Vietnamese society: among farmers suffering from official corruption and high rents charged by absentee landlords; among Buddhists outraged at the alleged favoritism shown by the government to Catholics; and among national minorities such as the overseas Chinese, the sects, and the mountain peoples, from the regime's efforts to consolidate control over all aspects of society. Most vocal were dissident intellectuals in Saigon and other cities, who criticized Diem's dictatorial tendencies and his intolerance of any form of opposition to his rule. The constitution, drafted in 1956 with the assistance of U.S. advisers, appeared to many to be a dead letter.

The rapid growth of the resistance movement in South Vietnam convinced Party leaders in Hanoi that a reorganization of the existing revolutionary apparatus there was vital. In mid-January 1961, shortly after an abortive putsch by disgruntled military officers against the Diem regime in Saigon, the Politburo met to reevaluate the situation and issue directives for future operations. Concluding that the period of stability in the South was now at an end, Party leaders called for an intensification of both political and military struggle in preparation for a general uprising that, in their view, could come at any time. There was no longer any possibility, they concluded, of a peaceful resolution of the problem. Although Ho Chi Minh agreed with these conclusions in general terms, he continued to caution his colleagues against launching a premature uprising or placing an overemphasis on military activities; careful preparations, he advised, should be adopted for any opportunity that should arise.[15]

To handle military operations, Party strategists decided to return to the operational arrangements that had been used in the war against the French. The Central Office for South Vietnam (COSVN), the old southern branch of the Central Committee that had operated in the South during the Franco-Vietminh War and then was abolished after the Geneva conference, was secretly reestablished, with Nguyen Van Linh, a quiet-spoken Party veteran, as chairman. Beneath COSVN were five regional committees, along with a range of Party branches at the provincial, district, and local levels. At a secret conference held in February 1961 in Zone D, paramilitary units in the Mekong delta and the Central Highlands were merged into a new People's Liberation Armed Forces (PLAF) and placed under unified command. Before the end of the month, some of these new units, operating in coordination with the military forces of the dissident religious sects, had begun to engage with the enemy. The PLAF would now become the military arm of the National Liberation Front. The Saigon regime had already begun to call them the Viet Cong, or Vietnamese Communists.

While resistance leaders were at work creating a new infrastructure for the insurgent movement in South Vietnam, Ho Chi Minh remained focused on the diplomatic front. With the Sino-Soviet dispute now out in the open, the question of bloc support for wars of national liberation became a major issue for debate at all gatherings of world Communist leaders. The first to take place after the close of the Third Congress of the VWP was the conference of 81 Communist and workers' parties, held in Moscow in November 1960. Ho Chi Minh led a delegation that included Le Duan and General Nguyen Chi Thanh.

Nikita Khrushchev may have hoped to use the conference as a forum to compel the Chinese to conform to Soviet policies, but other delegations at the meeting intervened to avoid an irrevocable split. The Vietnamese said relatively little at the conference, but they were active behind the scenes in bringing about a settlement that reaffirmed the 1957 declaration on the different forms of transition of various countries from capitalism to socialism. The document declared that if the exploiting classes resorted to the use of force against the people, it was necessary to bear in mind the possibility of a nonpeaceful transition to socialism. Ho Chi Minh's role was crucial. When PRC Vice Chairman Liu Shaoqi refused to attend one of the sessions where Soviet speakers were upbraiding their Chinese colleagues and returned angrily to his embassy, Khrushchev appealed to Ho to persuade Liu to return. Through Ho's efforts, a public rupture was avoided. But according to intimates, Ho was deeply saddened by the Sino-Soviet dispute over global strategy, a split that, in his view, severely undermined the prestige of the socialist community in the Third World and played to the advantage of its imperialist adversaries. While many Vietnamese delegates favored the Chinese view, Ho Chi Minh harbored deep suspicions of Mao Zedong's ambitions and his willingness to "stand on the mountaintop while the tigers fight" (presumably a reference to the relationship between Moscow and Washington). He therefore supported the Soviet position on key occasions at the conference. Because of the tradition of deferring to Uncle Ho's views ("whatever Uncle says is okay"), Le Duan and Nguyen Chi Thanh kept their own counsel. But on their return to Hanoi, their grumbling to colleagues undoubtedly contributed to rising dissatisfaction within the Politburo about Ho Chi Minh's refusal to take sides in the dispute.[16]

The debate was resumed at the Twenty-second Congress of the Soviet Party, held the following autumn. Once again, Ho Chi Minh led the DRV delegation at the meeting and sought to avoid the necessity of adopting controversial positions on the issues; but when Zhou Enlai walked out of the conference and returned to Beijing, the Vietnamese were forced to take a stand. Ho Chi Minh and Le Duan also left Moscow, but instead of returning immediately to Hanoi, they signaled their neutrality by embarking on a tour of the western regions of the Soviet Union.

The creation of the NLF and its military arm, the PLAF, gave a major boost to the fortunes of the anti-Diem resistance movement in South Vietnam. By the end of 1961, the PLAF had grown to about fifteen thousand troops, five times the size of the insurgent forces in the spring of 1959. Taking advantage of their increased size and mobility, Viet Cong units began to attack South Vietnamese military installations, convoys, and administrative offices; they also carved out a liberated base area in the Central Highlands, which they hoped to use as a launching pad for an eventual offensive against the densely populated lowlands.

One reason for the rapid growth of the Viet Cong was the steady increase in the numbers infiltrated down the Ho Chi Minh Trail, doubling between 1959 and 1961 and topping five thousand the following year. But the key factor was probably the expansion of the NLF, which benefited from growing popular hostility to the Diem regime and began to sink roots in villages and towns throughout the RVN. As the political apparatus grew in size and strength, the most enthusiastic and capable of the new members were recruited into the PLAF.

The growth in the insurgent movement caused anxiety in Washington. During the final months of the Eisenhower administration, concern among U.S. policy makers had centered on neighboring Laos, where Pathet Lao forces supported by Hanoi had reacted to the overthrow of the fragile coalition government by right-wing elements in Vientiane by intensifying their own military operations. But when Kennedy entered the White House in January 1961, he was greeted with a somber report that conditions were rapidly deteriorating in South Vietnam as well. The new president established an interagency task force to make recommendations for action, and at the end of the year approved an ambitious program to bring about a dramatic increase of the number of American advisers in the RVN. The objective was to train the South Vietnamese armed forces in counterinsurgency techniques in the hope that they could defend themselves without active U.S. intervention. At the same time, Kennedy decided to seek a negotiated settlement to the spreading conflict in Laos, where, because of its isolation and mountainous terrain, any American presence based on the defense of Free World security interests would be more difficult to justify.

The rising tempo of revolutionary violence in South Vietnam was a testimony to the validity of Ho Chi Minh's judgment that the Diem regime had fatal flaws and would ultimately fall under the weight of its weaknesses. At the same time, Ho cautioned his colleagues against excessive optimism. Ngo Dinh Diem, for all his faults, was a determined leader with a core following, and prudent Party leaders knew that it would be a serious error to underestimate him or to predict the imminent collapse of his government. Hanoi also kept an eye on Washington, which now appeared convinced that South Vietnam was vital to U.S. national security and was fearful of the repercussions of a humiliating defeat in Southeast Asia. Party leaders debated their strategic options at a meeting of the Politburo held in October 1961. Ho Chi Minh pointed out that the United States was much stronger militarily than the French had been during the Franco-Vietminh conflict. Therefore, he warned, to apply force against force, "tit for tat," would not succeed. The weakness of the imperialists, and the strength of the revolutionary forces, he argued, was in the realm of politics. Ho recommended a strategy based on guerrilla warfare, the mobilization of the support of the masses, and winning the battle of public opinion in the world arena. With conditions in South Vietnam evolving rapidly in favor of the revolution, Ho Chi Minh's recommendations for caution and tactical flexibility were persuasive, and they were embodied in directives sent to the Southern leadership in succeeding months. There was as yet no revolutionary high tide, Party directives pointed out, and final victory could only be realized gradually, "bit by bit."[17]

In July 1962, the Kennedy administration signed an agreement creating a neutralized Laos based on the formation of a national union government including neutralist, rightist, and Pathet Lao elements in a tripartite coalition regime. In letters to senior Party cadres in the South, Le Duan speculated that the United States might be willing to use this as a model for a similar agreement in South Vietnam. After all, he pointed out, Washington had previously pulled out of China and North Korea without a military victory. Such a solution was particularly appealing to Ho. In an interview with a reporter from the London *Daily Express* in March 1962, he had laid out conditions for a settlement of the conflict in South Vietnam on the basis of the Geneva Accords. Hanoi now began actively to approach neutralist elements in the RVN and in France to seek their private support in case a tripartite government was to be created in Saigon.[18]

Washington's willingness to accept a neutralist coalition government in Laos was based on the assumption that the DRV, under Soviet pressure, would honor a provision in the agreement to cease infiltrating troops and supplies down the Ho Chi Minh Trail, key parts of which ran through Laos. But when it became clear from intelligence reports that Hanoi had no intention of honoring that provision, the White House lost interest in pursuing a similar settlement in South Vietnam. Ho Chi Minh did not lose hope. At a meeting of the Politburo in February 1963, he argued the importance of intensifying political efforts in the South in order to promote a negotiated settlement and the formation of a neutral government, with strong participation by the NLF. Washington, he pointed out, was confused and was trying not to win, but to save face.[19]

Skeptical members of the Politburo might have begun to question President Ho's confidence that reunification could be achieved without an escalation in the level of revolutionary violence. There were indeed ominous signs that Washington was still seeking victory in the South. One such indication was the strategic hamlet program. A modified version of the agrovilles established in the late 1950s, the strategic hamlets were designed to be self-defense communities established to enable the RVN to deprive the Viet Cong of access to recruits and provisions. The idea, successfully applied by British officials in Malaya a few years previously, attracted favorable attention in both Saigon and Washington; in 1962 President Diem gave his approval to apply the concept in South Vietnam. Within months, thousands of strategic hamlets were hastily constructed throughout the country.

Hanoi quickly recognized that the program represented a serious threat to the revolutionary movement. Urgent instructions were sent to southern commanders on how to infiltrate or destroy the hamlets. Ho Chi Minh weighed in with his own ideas, recommending that a combination of political and military tactics be adopted to defeat them, including the use of counterespionage, terrorism, and an expansion of guerrilla warfare. "We must figure out a way to destroy them," he remarked at a Politburo meeting in November 1962. "If so, our victory is assured." Although the strategic hamlets were initially a serious challenge to the movement's control over the countryside, Saigon's program was hampered by government inefficiency and bureaucratic meddling; in the end, more than one half of the hamlets were infiltrated or destroyed by the Viet Cong.[20]

In the meantime, Ho Chi Minh pleaded with his colleagues to make a maximum effort to maintain the sympathy and support of both Moscow and Beijing. During the early 1960s, Hanoi's effort to balance relations with the Soviet Union and China came under increasing strain. Although Khrushchev was anxious not to offend the North Vietnamese by appearing unwilling to support the cause of wars of national liberation, he also hoped to avoid a direct confrontation with the United States and was increasingly uneasy at the trend toward violence in Southeast Asia. Khrushchev's discomfort gladdened hearts in Beijing. While Chinese leaders were hardly eager for a confrontation of their own with Washington, they were determined to replace Moscow as the natural leader of the oppressed peoples of the world. To Chairman Mao, the increasing American military presence in South Vietnam would ultimately weaken its overall position in Asia, thus creating a "hangman's noose" to strangle U.S. imperialism by its own overcommitment abroad.

It was undoubtedly with a view to gain an advantage over Moscow, as well as to ingratiate themselves with Hanoi, that Chinese leaders promised to increase military assistance to the DRV during the early 1960s. As Beijing had discovered during the Franco-Vietminh conflict, military aid as such ran little risk of provoking a direct conflict with the United States, while at the same time it enhanced Hanoi's reliance on the PRC. When, in the summer of 1962, a Vietnamese delegation led by Ho Chi Minh and General Nguyen Chi Thanh visited Beijing to ask for increased support to balance the growing U.S. presence in the RVN, China was quick to oblige.[21]

Chinese leaders hoped that their generosity would earn plaudits in Hanoi, and in May 1963, Liu Shaoqi, now the head of state, visited the DRV to test the waters. In his remarks, Liu emphasized the historically close relations between the two countries and openly criticized "modern revisionists" (i.e., the USSR) by charging that on matters of principle a "middle course" was not appropriate. In talks with Ho Chi Minh, Liu promised that if the war in South Vietnam escalated, the DRV could count on China as its "strategic rear." Nevertheless, Liu warned his hosts that the struggle for national reunification would be a long one, and that Chinese assistance would necessarily be limited in scope.

The Vietnamese, however, were not yet ready to place themselves firmly on the Chinese side in the Sino-Soviet dispute. Although their response to Liu was warm, Party leaders had given equal treatment to a Soviet trade delegation a few days earlier; speeches by DRV leaders carefully thanked both allies for their support, while adopting a neutral position. In his own speech at a banquet honoring Liu, Ho Chi Minh expressed gratitude for Chinese assistance, but took no position on key issues that divided the two Communist powers, emphasizing the importance of unity within the socialist camp.[22]

In the spring of 1963, the Diem regime entered its final period of crisis, as unrest within the Buddhist community at alleged favoritism to Vietnamese Catholics led to riots in cities throughout South Vietnam. On June 11, a Buddhist monk immolated himself on a downtown street in Saigon. The photograph of the incident, which appeared on television screens around the globe, electrified the world. When the Kennedy administration publicly criticized Saigon for crushing the demonstrations, Diem's brother and political counselor Ngo Dinh Nhu angrily retorted that he was engaged in peace talks with representatives of the NLF on the imminent removal of U.S. advisers and the neutralization of South Vietnam. According to one report, sometime in late summer Ho Chi Minh sent a private letter to Ngo Dinh Diem offering to negotiate. Whether Diem responded is unknown, but when Mieczyslaw Maneli, Poland's International Control Commission representative in the DRV, asked Pham Van Dong what Hanoi's conditions for peace would be, the prime minister reportedly responded that "the Americans have to leave. On this political basis, we can negotiate about everything." Asked whether a coalition government between North and South was feasible, Dong replied, "Everything is negotiable on the basis of the independence and sovereignty of Vietnam. The Geneva Accords supply the legal and political basis for this: no foreign bases or troops on our territory. We can come to an agreement with any Vietnamese." According to Maneli, Ho Chi Minh had been present during his conversation with Pham Van Dong, but made no comment.[23]

Whether Ho was serious about his offer to negotiate with Diem, and on what terms, is uncertain. Hanoi had appeared sincere in its 1962 offer to engage in peace talks with the United States, but its conditions for peace—the total withdrawal of U.S. military forces and the formation of a tripartite coalition government in South Vietnam, which would tacitly be dominated by the NLF—were too stiff to win Washington's acceptance. A year later, conditions in the South had measurably improved from Hanoi's point of view; still, although Diem's government was shaky, Ho Chi Minh recognized him as a formidable opponent who possessed a substantial constituency of fervent supporters in the RVN. Any settlement satisfactory to Party leaders would have left Diem with no semblance of authority and little room to maneuver. Ho urged that insurgent commanders in the South make every effort to win sympathy and support from all strata of the local population, while waiting for Washington to come to its senses. In an interview with a Japanese journalist in July, Ho noted that in his experience, despite the attitude of their leaders, the American people loved peace and justice. The only answer to the problem, he said, was for the United States to withdraw so that the Vietnamese people could resolve the issue in accordance with the Geneva Accords.

Ho Chi Minh's cautious optimism over the prospects for a negotiated settlement, however, was not universally shared in Hanoi. At a Politburo meeting in December 1962, Party leaders had concluded that the struggle in the South had become an anti-imperialist war, a conflict that called for an intensification of both political and military struggle. A secret directive sent to the South shortly after stressed that the problem would inevitably have to be resolved by force, and would gradually escalate from a small-scale to a high-level military conflict. Although this document did not openly disparage the importance of political activities and specifically rejected a return to the military approach used against the French, it said that the revolutionary tide in the South had begun to crest, and the only immediate question was when and in what manner armed force should be applied. It predicted that the war would close with a combined general popular uprising and a counteroffensive launched by the PLAF—a synthesis of the August Revolution and the Maoist model of three-stage people's war.

While the author of this directive is not identified, it appears to reflect the views of Le Duan, who had now clearly become the leading war strategist in Hanoi and whose predilection for a clear-cut military victory had grown increasingly pronounced since the escalation of the revolutionary movement. Le Duan, in fact, had ridiculed Ho Chi Minh for his reluctance to turn to the military option, and his reliance on diplomacy, which Duan apparently viewed as naïve. "Uncle [Ho] wavers," he remarked on one occasion, "but when I left South Vietnam

I had already prepared everything. I have only one goal—just final victory."[24]

In early November 1963, a military coup launched with the quiet approval of the Kennedy administration overthrew the Diem regime. The White House quietly signaled to the plotters its support for the new leadership in Saigon. To Kennedy's dismay, however, both Diem and his brother Ngo Dinh Nhu were executed after having surrendered to the leaders of the coup.

The creation of a new military government in Saigon substantially changed the perspective of Party strategists in North Vietnam. On the one hand, they could no longer count on the widespread unpopularity of Ngo Dinh Diem as a stimulant to recruitment for the NLF and the Viet Cong. In fact, the new ruling clique, under the popular southern General Duong Van "Big" Minh, had come to power on a wave of enthusiasm, especially in the cities, where hostility to Diem and his family had reached virulent proportions. On the other hand, policy makers in Hanoi anticipated correctly that the new regime would lack Diem's single-mindedness and vigor in suppressing the resistance movement. Conscious of the endemic factionalism that had marked the Vietnamese nationalist movement since the colonial era, Party leaders anticipated a rapid weakening of the Saigon military government, thus opening the door to a revolutionary triumph. At a Politburo meeting in early December, Ho Chi Minh predicted—correctly, as it turned out—that it would probably not be the last coup in Saigon.

However, even though it was easy to assess the new situation, hard questions remained before any conclusions could be reached about what to do next. Should insurgent forces in the South escalate the level of conflict in the hope of bringing a quick collapse to the new regime? Or should they refrain from increasing military pressure in the hope that it might be amenable to a negotiated settlement? Should the North play a more direct role in the war? What if the United States reacted to the impending collapse of its puppet in Saigon by escalating its own role in the conflict? Barely three weeks after the death of Ngo Dinh Diem in Saigon, John F. Kennedy was assassinated in Dallas. What if his successor, Lyndon B. Johnson, turned out to be even more warlike than the slain young president?

Such concerns were on the minds of Party leaders as they convened the Ninth Plenum of the Third Congress of the VWP in early December 1963. Based on the scattered evidence available, it must have been one of the most explosive meetings in the history of the Party, as delegates argued bitterly over what course to pursue. For once, the committee did not act simply as a rubber stamp for decisions already reached by the Politburo. Some members apparently urged the immediate introduction of conventional military units from the North with the objective of bringing Saigon to its knees before the United States could react. Others worried that a visible northern presence in the South could trigger a harsh response from Washington and lead to direct U.S. intervention in the war. Such an eventuality, of course, would not sit well with the Soviet Union and would necessitate a policy of increased reliance on China. Although the PRC had increased the level of its military assistance to the DRV following Liu Shaoqi's state visit in May 1963, many Party leaders shared Ho Chi Minh's discomfort with the growing pressure from Beijing to toe the Chinese line in the Sino-Soviet dispute.

After lengthy debate, the Central Committee reached a compromise; the level of military assistance from the DRV was to be increased, but combat units from the North were not to be sent south to take a direct part in the fighting. Party strategists had decided to gamble that the Saigon regime could be brought to the point of collapse without running the risk of a U.S. entry into the war. Southern insurgents were instructed to push toward final victory in the shortest possible time, but without the promise of vastly increased assistance from the rear base in the North. It was now formally recognized that armed struggle would play a crucial and decisive role in the revolutionary process, although political agitation would continue to be of importance.

Ho Chi Minh's role in the policy debate is not clear, but it is probable that he urged caution before adopting any decision that could alienate Moscow and Beijing or bring the United States directly into the war. Still, Ho recognized the opportunity posed by the situation and the need to react. At a Politburo meeting on December 10, he urged his colleagues to take advantage of the "disorder" in the South by escalating both military and political pressure on the Saigon regime. Even if the United States should escalate the struggle tenfold, he declared, "we shall still be victorious."[25]

The decision to escalate at a moderate rate remained fraught with risks, not only of a possible confrontation with the United States, but also of serious problems with Moscow. For years, Party leaders had carefully sought to avoid antagonizing either of their chief allies, but there had recently been warning signs that some Party leaders were getting restive. In an article written during the summer of 1963, General Nguyen Chi Thanh declared that he and his colleagues had no illusions about the United States and did not underestimate it as an opponent. But, he contended, they were not afraid. If "one is afraid of the U.S. and thinks that to offend it would court failure, and [believes] that firm opposition to United States imperialism would touch off a nuclear war, then the only course left would be to compromise with and surrender to United States imperialism." Nguyen Chi Thanh's message would not have been lost on the Kremlin.[26]

General Thanh's views were shared by Le Duan and his protégés within the Politburo, who now dominated that policy-making body. With the connivance of Public Security Minister Tran Quoc Hoan and his close ally Le Duc Tho, Le Duan had successfully marginalized potential rivals within the Party leadership. Prime Minister Pham Van Dong presented no problem. Although an efficient administrator and a veteran with a revolutionary pedigree that stretched back to Revolutionary Youth League days in Canton, the self-effacing Dong lacked the stomach for Party infighting and often lamented to intimates about his lack of influence. The fifty-six-year-old Truong Chinh represented a greater potential danger. Prouder than Dong and more assertive in his demeanor within the Party, he undoubtedly resented Le Duan for taking over his position as general secretary and for expressing a preference for the liberation of the South over the task of socialist construction in the North. Still, he too appeared reluctant to raise a challenge to the growing power of his rival. Perhaps to ingratiate himself with the new leadership, Chinh agreed to draft the political report at the Ninth Plenum, thus in effect aligning himself with Le Duan in decisions to come.

Another potential threat was Vo Nguyen Giap. Possessing a degree of prestige and personal popularity exceeded only by Ho Chi Minh himself, General Giap held different views than either Le Duan or Nguyen Chi Thanh on how to conduct the struggle in the South. He rejected Duan's preference for intensified guerrilla war in favor of a more conventional military approach, but, unlike Thanh, he was reluctant to challenge the Americans until the PAVN had been successfully trained and equipped with modern weapons. To Giap, it would be suicidal to irritate Moscow, since only the Soviet Union could provide the right kind of training and weapons. Yet, like Pham Van Dong, Giap was curiously silent in the face of Le Duan's arrogant challenge; in Politburo meetings he failed to speak out forcefully against proponents of the new strategy.

The most dangerous potential opponent of the Le Duan faction may have been Ho Chi Minh himself, but by now, Le Duan and his allies clearly harbored a condescending and even contemptuous attitude toward the president, who, in their view, had in recent years lost his acute grasp of politics and was now increasingly muddled in his thinking. Rumors even circulated in Hanoi that Le Duan planned to replace Ho Chi Minh as president with Nguyen Chi Thanh, while relegating the veteran revolutionary to an innocuous position as director of Marxist-Leninist studies. Le Duan, of course, would retain control over the Party.[27]

Whether or not Ho Chi Minh resented the personal slight of being shunted to the sidelines, he must have had serious reservations about the new strategy to be adopted in South Vietnam. He had clearly expressed his preference for a war of stratagem over one of direct confrontation, and could not have welcomed an approach that could result in a direct conflict with the United States. Similarly, he had always argued in favor of balancing relations with Moscow and Beijing and rejected a policy of exclusive reliance on China. When General Le Liem, a Dien Bien Phu veteran, warned him privately that the draft resolution to be issued at the close of the plenum would contain direct attacks on Moscow, Ho agreed that it would be unseemly for the DRV to slap its primary benefactor directly in the face and encouraged Liem to speak up against the proposal. But when Liem did so, Ho Chi Minh (like Vo Nguyen Giap) sat silently, not uttering a word. As the anti-Soviet tone in the speeches reached a climax, Ho left the conference hall quietly to smoke a cigarette. Ten members of the Central Committee voted against the final report. When a friend asked Ho how he had voted, he said nothing. Had Ho Chi Minh been intimidated into silence by the new leadership?[28]

Once the new strategy had been approved, the most important question remaining at the plenum was how to placate the Soviet Union. The draft of the resolution issued at the close of the meeting had originally included a direct attack on Khrushchev, but, at Le Duan's request, the reference was eventually removed. Duan, who, like many of his colleagues, harbored deep-seated suspicions of the Chinese, did not want to burn his bridges with Moscow. In fact, the resolution made a tacit gesture to Soviet leaders by declaring that the basic objective of the new strategy was "to restrict the war within the framework of South Vietnam and to defeat the enemy on the main battlefield." Even if Washington decided to intervene, "the possibility that a limited war in the South would turn into a world war is almost non-existent because the purpose and significance of this war cannot generate conditions leading to a world war." In a bid to reassure nervous allies, the Politburo drew up a circular letter to fraternal Communist parties to explain the decision and seek their support and understanding. The letter attempted to assuage fears of a wider war and pleaded for bloc support for wars of national liberation throughout the Third World. Declaring that the concept of peaceful coexistence was a tactic that applied between different world systems, and not between oppressors and oppressed in a particular society, it argued that the concepts of peaceful coexistence and revolutionary struggle were interdependent, not contradictory. A peaceful ascent to power in a repressive society, it concluded, was an illusion.[29]

Although Party leaders had made a belated effort to placate Moscow, sentiment against the Soviet Union and its Vietnamese defenders was hardening in Hanoi. After the plenum adjourned in mid-December, a secret tribunal was established under the authority of the Politburo to remove "revisionists" from the Party; many senior political figures who were considered sympathetic to the Soviet point of view or suspected of opposing the official line were dismissed from their posts or even placed under arrest. Among those suspected of harboring such views was Defense Minister Vo Nguyen Giap himself. Although Giap was too popular to attack directly, a number of his protégés, including Le Liem, were purged because of their allegedly pro-Soviet views. A few months later, Giap was accused by some Politburo members of having exchanged private correspondence with Nikita Khrushchev, but that charge was dropped when Ho Chi Minh stepped in to remark that he was aware of the exchange and had fully approved of it.[30]

Despite its growing animus to the Soviet leadership, the dominant faction in the Politburo was conscious of the need to avoid a complete break with Moscow. After the Ninth Plenum adjourned, Le Duan, Le Duc Tho, and their ally, the revolutionary poet To Huu, visited the USSR to present Hanoi's views. The presence of To Huu was significant. Born in 1920 near Hué, he made his debut as a major political figure when he publicly attacked Soviet revisionism at the Ninth Plenum. Ho Chi Minh, who must have anticipated the results of the talks in Moscow with foreboding, remained in Hanoi.

En route to the USSR, the delegation stopped briefly in Beijing for discussions with Chinese leaders. In Moscow, the talks with Soviet officials apparently had little success. The final communiqué was vague and suggested that disagreement over the situation in the South continued. After the delegation returned to Hanoi, editorials in the official press praised China's role in leading the global revolution and continued their scathing attacks on revisionism.[31]

Ho Chi Minh must have viewed the events surrounding the Ninth Plenum and its aftermath with some discomfort. Washington's decision to approve the coup that overthrew the Diem regime had raised serious questions about its desire to avoid a direct conflict in South Vietnam. Although Ho had endorsed the decision to escalate the struggle in the

South, the readiness of his more headstrong colleagues to offend the Soviet Union and persecute its friends in Hanoi, which ran counter to his conciliatory instincts, were undoubtedly worrisome. After a lengthy silence following the December plenum, Ho finally surfaced in late March 1964, when he presided over a "special political conference" that had been convened hastily to paper over the growing policy split within the Party leadership. In his remarks to the delegates, Ho repeated his appeal for the reunification of the two zones peacefully in accordance with the provisions of the Geneva Accords, but declared that the people of the North "wholeheartedly support the patriotic struggle of our southern compatriots." Appealing over the head of the U.S. government to the American people, he declared that the unjust war in Vietnam was staining the honor of the United States and called upon them to bring an end to the dirty war and rebuild friendship between the peoples of the two countries. Lastly, he called for unity of purpose within the DRV and among the countries of the socialist community as a whole.[32]

During the next few months, the resistance forces in South Vietnam intensified their efforts to bring down the Saigon regime; as Ho Chi Minh had predicted, the regime was mired in factional struggles and seemed incapable of focusing on the growing threat in the countryside. Although the Party's strategy in the South had now shifted perceptibly in the direction of an armed conflict, the role of political struggle remained central to the equation, notably because it was here that the revolutionary forces were seen to operate at a decisive advantage. Although the PLAF did not possess the firepower or the numerical strength of its adversary, it benefited from the inherent political weaknesses of the Saigon government. The goal of the resistance was now to wage a combined "general offensive and uprising," based on the Party's plan to launch military attacks on rural areas in conjunction with a popular uprising against the government in the major cities and towns. The anticipated result was the collapse of the Saigon regime and the formation, through negotiations, of a tripartite coalition government consisting of a mixture of officials from the Saigon regime, neutralists, and members of the NLF. Because the Party had already managed to win the secret allegiance of a number of prominent neutralists in South Vietnam and abroad, it was confident that this coalition government would serve as a springboard for the gradual takeover of the South by political forces loyal to the Party.

Ho Chi Minh shared his colleagues' view that it was vital to persuade

Washington that the Vietnamese people were determined to unify their country and were willing to endure enormous sacrifices to achieve that end. At a Politburo meeting in December 1963, he stressed the importance of launching attacks on the U.S. aggressors in Vietnam. "Americans greatly fear death," he told his colleagues, so it was important that they should not feel immune from the consequences of the struggle. In articles published under a pseudonym in *Nhan Dan* (several were titled "Beautiful, but Not Handsome," a reference to the official Vietnamese term for the United States, "Beautiful Country"), he lambasted the United States for its aggressive policies all over the world and its domestic problems at home. Citing articles in the U.S. press (some of them connected to Lyndon Johnson's highly publicized War on Poverty program), Ho pointed out that, far from being a "beautiful" society, America suffered from such major problems as high crime rates, increasing unemployment, rampant poverty, and racial divisions.[33]

Throughout the spring and early summer of 1964, Party strategists continued to hope that their formula for a general offensive and uprising could succeed without a substantial input of regular forces from the North. The presence of the PAVN in the South could trigger a retaliation from the United States and bring it directly into the war, something Party leaders fervently wished to avoid. Unknown to Hanoi, however, the Johnson administration was increasingly determined to remain in South Vietnam. In early August, North Vietnamese naval vessels attacked U.S. warships operating in the Tonkin Gulf. When a second attack allegedly took place a few hours later, the White House, which had been searching for a pretext to demonstrate its resolve to Hanoi, immediately launched retaliatory air strikes against military installations in the nearby North Vietnamese panhandle. Although Defense Secretary Robert S. McNamara announced that the American vessels had been on "routine patrol," it soon became clear that they were engaged in reconnaissance operations close to the North Vietnamese coast and may have been testing the ability of enemy radar to monitor U.S. maneuvers in the area. To make matters doubly suspicious, a South Vietnamese guerrilla operation was taking place nearby. DRV military commanders in the area were probably convinced that the two operations were related, and had ordered the attack on U.S. warships on the spot.

The Tonkin Gulf incident convinced Party leaders that Washington was preparing to escalate its role in the war. A few days after the incident, the Politburo decided to make preparations to send the first regular units of the PAVN down the Ho Chi Minh Trail. Once in the South, they would be expected to bolster the strength of the PLAF for a final push to victory in the spring of 1965. Party leaders still hoped that they could bring about the collapse of the Saigon regime before the United States decided to intervene in the conflict. After the Politburo meeting adjourned, Le Duan flew to Beijing to inform Chinese leaders of Hanoi's decision and to consult on future strategy.[34]

In Beijing, Mao Zedong encouraged his visitor to pursue an aggressive strategy in South Vietnam, expressing his confidence that the United States, despite the recent passage by Congress of the Tonkin Gulf Resolution, did not wish to become directly involved in the conflict in South Vietnam, since it was overextended in the world and lacked available troops to send to Southeast Asia. The Americans, he told Le Duan, "do not want to fight a war" in Indochina; therefore, because neither Hanoi nor Beijing wished the conflict to spread, "there will be no war." In the meantime, Mao did not believe that a negotiated settlement was appropriate, since conditions in South Vietnam were not yet sufficiently favorable to the DRV. As he remarked to Pham Van Dong in a conversation in Beijing a few weeks later: "The more thoroughly you defeat them, the more comfortable they feel. For example, you beat the French, and they became willing to negotiate with you. . . ."

Mao conceded that the United States, contrary to expectations, might decide to increase its military presence in South Vietnam, or even to invade the North. After all, the Tonkin Gulf Resolution had authorized President Johnson to take actions he deemed necessary to protect U.S. security interests in Southeast Asia. In such conditions, he advised the Vietnamese not to confront U.S. troops on the coast, but to avoid direct battle and withdraw into the interior, where they could wage guerrilla warfare against invading forces. In that protracted struggle, which might last one hundred years, Mao promised Chinese assistance, remarking metaphorically, "So long as the green mountain is there, how can you ever lack firewood?"[35]

During the next few weeks, Beijing acted to back up its promises. Army and air force units stationed in south China were placed in a state of military readiness, and additional forces were dispatched to the area. Anti-U.S. rallies carefully orchestrated by Beijing broke out all over the country, and China's official press promised firm support for its beleaguered ally. Still, Vietnamese leaders were determined to resist an over-reliance on Chinese assistance and refused an offer by Vice Prime Minister Deng Xiaoping to provide major assistance on the condition that the DRV reject any further relationship with Moscow.

The Tonkin Gulf incident had served to strengthen Hanoi's relations with Beijing, but it led to a further deterioration in its ties with Moscow.

Soviet officials had reacted to the news with equivocation, simply condemning the U.S. attacks and renewing their appeal for peaceful reunification. When Le Duan arrived in Moscow after his visit to Beijing in mid-August, Soviet officials emphasized the need for a negotiated settlement to end the Vietnam conflict, but then compounded the problem by procrastinating on a request by the NLF for formal diplomatic recognition as the sole legal government of South Vietnam.

The situation was to change, however, when, in the autumn, Nikita Khrushchev was overthrown by a cabal led by Leonid Brezhnev. On October 16, shortly after the news reached Hanoi, Ho Chi Minh and Le Duan sent a brief letter of congratulations to Brezhnev on his election to the position of Party first secretary. This note was carefully balanced by a message to Beijing a day later congratulating the Chinese on the explosion of their first nuclear device.

The emergence of a new leadership in Moscow was a welcome development to Ho Chi Minh, not only because it brightened prospects for an increase in Soviet military assistance, but also because it raised the possibility that the DRV could resume its previous evenhanded approach in relations with its two major allies. Even for Le Duan, the decision to favor Beijing reached at the Ninth Plenum had been a tactical rather than a strategic move. In November, Pham Van Dong was sent to Moscow to evaluate the attitude of the new Soviet leadership. For once, the visit went well. Soviet leaders promised to increase their assistance to the DRV and pledged further support in case the United States decided to extend the battle to North Vietnam. As a testament to their sincerity, they agreed to permit the opening of an NLF office in Moscow. In return, Hanoi vowed to refrain from further public attacks on Soviet policies and to make every effort to contain the war within the borders of South Vietnam. Hanoi now had firm promises of support from both its chief allies.[36]

By the autumn of 1964, instability continued in Saigon, as South Vietnamese politicians and military officers jockeyed for power under the exasperated eye of the United States. In the meantime, the military situation in the South grew ever more perilous. Lacking direction from above, commanders of the Army of the Republic of Vietnam refrained from adopting an aggressive posture on the battlefield and even made their own private arrangements with Viet Cong forces operating within their jurisdictions. U.S. intelligence sources predicted that without decisive action on the part of the United States, the Saigon government would fall to the Communists within three to six months. Such views were shared in Hanoi, where Party leaders ordered southern commanders to increase their efforts to obtain final victory. Terrorist attacks were ordered on U.S. installations in South Vietnam as a means of warning Washington that escalation could lead to increased American casualties. The directive resulted in a Viet Cong attack on the U.S. air base at Bien Hoa on October 31, 1964, killing four American soldiers and wounding thirty more. Further terrorist bombings took place in downtown Saigon: at the Caravelle Hotel, a favorite watering hole of Western journalists, and at the Brink's BOQ (Bachelor Officers' Quarters) across the street, on Christmas Eve, killing two Americans.[37]

COSVN commanders in the South were not quite as optimistic as their superiors in the North. In a year-end assessment, they lamented that the PLAF was still unprepared to inflict a direct defeat on the enemy. But when, in December, Viet Cong forces mauled South Vietnamese units near the village of Binh Gia, about twenty miles east of Saigon, strategists in Hanoi boasted that the battle demonstrated the ability of the PLAF to defeat Saigon's regular forces. Even the normally cautious Ho Chi Minh exulted that Binh Gia had been a "little Dien Bien Phu." In a February letter to Nguyen Chi Thanh, newly appointed as commander of all insurgent forces in the South, Le Duan urged the general to make every effort to bring about the collapse of the Saigon regime before the United States could decide whether to send in ground troops. If that should be the case, he believed, the White House would have no alternative but negotiations and a final U.S. withdrawal. Le Duan admitted that success was not guaranteed, but—citing Lenin—he remarked, "Let's act and then see." Even if the campaign did not totally succeed, they would be in an excellent position to recoup and try again.[38]

For once, Hanoi was too late. On February 7, 1965, Viet Cong forces attacked a U.S. Special Forces camp at Pleiku, a provincial capital in the Central Highlands, killing eight Americans and wounding one hundred others. Six days later, President Johnson ordered retaliatory air strikes over North Vietnam. At first limited in scope, the attacks were eventually extended into an intensive series of regular bombing raids over much of the DRV, including some of its major cities. In March, Johnson ordered two Marine battalions to South Vietnam to protect U.S. military facilities at Da Nang air base. Two additional Marine battalions soon followed, as General William C. Westmoreland, the commander of U.S. forces in South Vietnam, argued that without a substantial American combat presence, "a VC takeover of the country" was likely within a year.

In the meantime, relations between the Soviet Union and the DRV continued to improve. In early February, Alexei Kosygin, the new Soviet prime minister, visited Hanoi. In talks with Ho Chi Minh and other Vietnamese leaders, Kosygin promised "all necessary support and assistance" to his hosts and conveyed Moscow's commitment of increased military aid, including advanced surface-to-air missiles and anti-aircraft equipment. In return, the Vietnamese promised to make every effort to prevent the war in the South from spreading and to give serious consideration to a negotiated solution to the conflict.

Meetings with Chinese officials did not go as well. Beijing had just refused Kosygin's offer to join with Moscow in a joint statement of support for the Vietnamese cause, arousing anger among Party officials in Hanoi. During a visit to the DRV in early March, Zhou Enlai explained that China had refused the offer because the new Soviet foreign policy was just "Khrushchevism" in disguise. Zhou also sought to persuade his hosts to refuse Soviet military assistance, warning bluntly that an increased Soviet presence in the DRV could endanger Sino-Vietnamese relations.[39]

By the time the VWP Central Committee convened its eleventh plenum on March 26, the scope of Washington's response to deteriorating conditions in South Vietnam was becoming clear, even if its ultimate objective was not. Perhaps, some Party leaders speculated, the United States was only widening the war in order to negotiate from strength. If that was the case, there was no urgent necessity to change the existing strategy of seeking victory without the large-scale introduction of North Vietnamese regular forces. To Ho Chi Minh, however, the situation appeared more dangerous; U.S. air strikes after the Tonkin Gulf incident had convinced him that the Johnson administration had made a strategic decision to take a stand in South Vietnam. At a Politburo meeting in late February, he warned his colleagues not to underestimate the United States. In his view, it was vitally important to keep the conflict at the level of a "special war" (i.e., without the massive introduction of American combat forces), rather than advancing to the next stage of "limited war," with U.S. troops involved in the fighting.[40]

Uncertain about Washington's intentions, the Eleventh Plenum opted to continue existing policy, while seeking to determine whether the White House was willing to negotiate a U.S. withdrawal. During the fall and winter of 1964–65, Hanoi had rejected peace inquiries from Washington on the assumption that the United States was not yet sufficiently discouraged, nor was final victory yet in sight. Now Party leaders were prepared to test the diplomatic waters again. The NLF, through its Liberation Radio, set out its own conditions for a peace settlement on March 22, in a five-point statement that declared that talks could not begin until U.S. forces had been withdrawn from South Vietnam. Radio Hanoi rebroadcast the NLF declaration a few days later, but in a slightly modified version, implying that a full American withdrawal need not take place before the opening of talks so long as Washington pledged to do so. Then, on April 8, Pham Van Dong issued Hanoi's "four points" declaration, which called for the departure of all foreign troops from Vietnam, a return to the provisions of the Geneva Accords, the resolution of the internal affairs of the South in accordance with the program of the NLF, and the eventual reunification of the two zones peacefully. The statement was vague on the timing of the U.S. withdrawal, and Ho Chi Minh served to muddy the waters when he told a Japanese journalist that Washington must withdraw its troops to create the proper conditions for a peace conference.[41]

As always, Ho Chi Minh played an active role in orchestrating Hanoi's peace campaign. In Politburo meetings he urged his colleagues to prepare for the possible reconvening of the Geneva conference, so that whenever Washington indicated a willingness to withdraw, the DRV would be ready to facilitate the move. In the meantime, he argued that antiwar opinion in the United States and throughout the world should be stimulated, and Hanoi's allies carefully consulted. The peace campaign, he advised, must express firmness and determination, but also be carried out with subtlety and flexibility.

If there were any hopes in Hanoi that the White House was ready to negotiate, they soon dissipated. In early April, just as Pham Van Dong was preparing to issue his "four points" proposal, President Johnson ordered two U.S. Army divisions to Vietnam to strengthen South Vietnamese positions in the Central Highlands. Then on April 7, he presented his own offer of "unconditional" peace talks in a speech at Johns Hopkins University, although he gave no hint of major U.S. concessions in order to bring them about. At the same time the Party leaders quickly concluded that the White House was not yet ready to consider a peace agreement on Hanoi's terms and lost interest in pursuing negotiations.

Washington's obdurate attitude undoubtedly confirmed in the minds of militants like Le Duan that victory would come only on the battlefield and not, as Ho Chi Minh had hoped, at the peace table. In a letter to General Nguyen Chi Thanh in May, Duan concluded that the introduction of U.S. combat troops indicated that conditions were not ripe for negotiations. "Only when the insurrection [in South Vietnam] is successful," he wrote, "will the problem of establishing a 'neutral central administration' be posed again." Although the "four points" remained on the table, they were only "intended to pave the way for a U.S. withdrawal with a lesser loss of face."[42]

As the war escalated in early 1965, the role of China became increasingly crucial to the DRV. While Soviet assistance could provide Hanoi with advanced weaponry to defend North Vietnamese air space against U.S. air strikes, China was important both as a source of military and economic assistance and as a deterrent to Washington's taking the war directly to the North. In both public and private statements, Chinese leaders had promised that the PRC would serve as Vietnam's "great rear," providing various forms of support for the cause of Vietnamese national reunification. Equally important to Hanoi, however, was Beijing's implied threat that should the United States decide to extend its operations north of the demilitarized zone, China would intervene in the war directly on the side of the DRV.

For Mao Zedong, now on the verge of embarking on a major struggle with his more pragmatic rivals within the CCP leadership, the spreading conflict in Vietnam served as a useful means of mobilizing revolutionary zeal in China in favor of his domestic policies, while at the same time bogging down the United States in an unwinnable war in Southeast Asia. When Le Duan and Vo Nguyen Giap went to Beijing in April to request military equipment and fighter pilots to protect North Vietnamese airspace, Liu Shaoqi (soon to be purged in the Cultural Revolution) appeared amenable to the request as a means of raising morale in the DRV and protecting North Vietnamese airspace above the Twentieth Parallel, just south of the Red River delta. During a visit by Ho Chi Minh to China the next month, Mao agreed to provide "whatever support was needed by the Vietnamese." Mao would send road-building crews to assist his allies in improving the transportation network, including the Ho Chi Minh Trail and roads from the Chinese border into the DRV, and to construct routes from northern Laos toward Thailand. The latter, Mao remarked, would be especially useful for "large scale battles in the future." In return, Ho expressed his country's gratitude for the firm support of "brotherly comrades" in China and promised that the Vietnamese would be able to wage the war themselves with the assistance of units that would now be sent from the DRV to the South.[43]

Beijing, nonetheless, was wary of a direct confrontation with Washington, and thus more circumspect in its references to possible greater involvement in the Indochina conflict. In a highly publicized interview with the U.S. journalist Edgar Snow in January, Mao declared that China would not enter the war unless directly attacked—a subtle signal that Washington could escalate the level of its presence in the South so long as it did not invade the DRV. In April, Zhou Enlai sent a private message to Washington via Pakistani President Ayub Khan that China would not provoke a war with the United States, but would perform its international duty in supporting the DRV; if the Johnson administration decided to expand the war beyond South Vietnam, Zhou remarked, the flames of war would spread and China would have to extinguish them. In that case it would be difficult to prevent the outbreak of a world war. Even if the war does not spread to China, Zhou concluded, "Still China will support Vietnam, so long as the DRV requests, so long as the NLF in South Vietnam requests it."[44]

The following month, General Van Tien Dung went to China to complete the Sino-Vietnamese military agreement and work out the details. If the situation remained unchanged, the Vietnamese would fight the war by themselves, with military support provided by the PRC. If the United States provided air and naval support for a South Vietnamese invasion of the North, China would send its own air and naval forces to support PAVN units in self-defense. If U.S. troops invaded the North, China would provide its land forces as a strategic reserve and carry out operational tasks when necessary.

China had thus agreed to provide substantial assistance to the DRV in its struggle with the United States. But there were already signs of discord between China, the USSR, and the DRV. Mao Zedong's January interview with Edgar Snow had caused anxiety among Vietnamese Party leaders, who feared that his comments would simply encourage Washington to believe that it could escalate the conflict inside the South with impunity. Then, in July, Beijing rejected Hanoi's request for Chinese combat pilots to take part in the defense of DRV airspace. In an article that served as an elliptical message to Hanoi, Marshal Lin Biao called on the Vietnamese to practice "self-reliance," as China had done during its own civil war with Chiang Kai-shek. Le Duan reacted angrily and went off to Moscow, where he praised the USSR as a "second motherland."[45]

China's backpedaling on its offer of combat pilots to the DRV may have been a product of the changing mood in Beijing. During the spring and summer of 1965, when Moscow publicized its proposal for the co-ordination of Sino-Soviet assistance to the DRV, bitter debates erupted in Beijing over the degree to which China should become involved in the conflict. While some Chinese leaders argued that it was their "internationalist" obligation to help a fraternal country in distress, anti-

Soviet elements retorted that Moscow's proposal was an insidious plot to engage China in a direct conflict with the United States. In the end, Beijing turned down the Soviet offer of united action, while warning the North Vietnamese of the perfidy of the Soviet Union. Soviet assistance to the DRV, Zhou Enlai cautioned Ho Chi Minh during Ho's visit to Canton in November, was motivated by Moscow's desire to isolate China and improve U.S.-Soviet relations; it would be better for Hanoi to refuse it.[46]

The number of U.S. military forces in the RVN increased steadily throughout 1965, topping 200,000 by the end of the year. Recognizing that American strategy in South Vietnam had escalated from a "special war" to a "limited war" with full participation by American combat troops, the VWP Central Committee approved a plan in December to introduce North Vietnamese regular forces in significant amounts to match the U.S. escalation. Under the aggressive command of General Thanh, PAVN units sought to engage the United States in selective locations throughout South Vietnam to demonstrate their capacity to match their adversary on the battlefield. While some leading Party strategists in Hanoi, including Vo Nguyen Giap, argued against Thanh's strategy, the general received crucial support for his "seething" approach from Le Duan, who derided Giap as a "scared rabbit" who was afraid to take on the enemy directly.

By now, Ho Chi Minh found physical activity increasingly tiring, and was no longer taking an active role in mapping war strategy; still, when his health permitted, he contributed to discussions on the subject in Politburo meetings. Although he had argued persistently in favor of measures to minimize the risk of U.S. intervention, he now firmly supported the decision to escalate the role of the North in the conflict, on the grounds that the United States must be convinced that the Vietnamese people were absolutely determined to bring about reunification, whatever the cost. The people of North Vietnam, he argued, had every right to assist their brothers in defending themselves against the American "war of aggression" in the South. He warned his colleagues that the war would continue to escalate, since the United States now recognized that a defeat would have catastrophic effects on its global objectives and was determined to negotiate from strength; but he concluded that "we will fight whichever way the enemy wants, and we will still win."

Ho now shared the view that conditions were not yet ripe for a negotiated settlement. He believed that revolutionary forces must both fight and negotiate, but for the time being fighting must have priority, with diplomacy serving the needs of the battlefield. Negotiations should not get under way until the United States agreed unconditionally to a halt on bombing of the North, and recognized Hanoi's "four points" as a road map for a solution of the conflict. In the meantime, the DRV must present its position clearly, so that the deceptive character of the U.S. negotiating position would appear obvious to the world. Ho Chi Minh and his colleagues were well aware of the rising chorus of antiwar sentiment that was beginning to emerge within the United States. He stressed the importance of attacking American forces in South Vietnam as well as those of the Saigon regime; this would not only weaken their position on the battlefield but also strengthen the position of dovish elements in Congress and the U.S. public.[47]

The intensification of the war in South Vietnam and Hanoi's growing reliance on Soviet military assistance continued to place a severe strain on Sino-Vietnamese relations. Chinese admonitions to Vietnamese leaders to be wary of Soviet perfidy rankled. Beijing's advice on how to wage revolutionary war and when to open peace talks with the United States—Zhou Enlai liked to point out that the Chinese had more experience in dealing with Washington than the Vietnamese—aroused bitter memories in Hanoi of Chinese arrogance and condescension. Chinese Red Guards (many of whom went to the DRV voluntarily during the early years of the Cultural Revolution to "make revolution") irritated local citizens, who were reminded of an earlier generation of Chinese advisers who had mindlessly spouted Maoist slogans during the land reform campaign. As Zhou Enlai later confessed to a colleague, the Cultural Revolution did not always travel well.

By the spring of 1966, tensions between Hanoi and Beijing had reached a dangerous level. In a speech delivered in May, Le Duan responded obliquely to Lin Biao's article about the virtues of self-reliance published the previous September. Duan declared that Hanoi paid close attention to the experiences of fraternal parties in the practice of revolutionary war, but sought to apply them creatively, and not in a mechanical manner. "It is not fortuitous that in the history of our country," he declared, "each time we rose up to oppose foreign aggression, we took the offensive and not the defensive." As an additional signal that Hanoi's patience was running thin, articles in the Vietnamese press began to refer to the "threat from the North" that had been posed by the Chinese empire during the feudal era.

Beijing was quick to take notice of the tension. In a meeting in mid-April with Pham Van Dong in Beijing, Mao Zedong apologized for the behavior of unruly Red Guards residing in the DRV. Mao conceded that they did not always respect the rules that guide the relations between the two countries and thus inevitably caused complications. If that happened, he concluded, Hanoi should "just hand them to us." Zhou Enlai followed up by confronting Le Duan over the oblique criticism of China that was appearing in the DRV press, asking whether Vietnamese comrades were concerned that China was trying to impose its historical domination over its ally. If so, he replied, Beijing was willing to withdraw its troops from North Vietnam (now numbering more than 100,000), as well as those additional units that were stationed in the Chinese provinces along the border.

Reluctant to offend China, Le Duan adopted a conciliatory tone. He indicated gratitude for the assistance as an important guarantee of the DRV's survival and future success in bringing about national reunification. But Duan argued the importance of Hanoi's relationship with Moscow, partly as a matter of pragmatism, a posture that (he pointedly observed) the Chinese Communists had themselves adopted at various moments in their history. As for the alleged Soviet betrayal of revolutionary doctrine, Duan noted that it was important to adopt a conciliatory attitude to "reformist" (i.e., revisionist) countries within the socialist community as a means of persuading them to return to their revolutionary principles.

Eventually, Ho Chi Minh himself became embroiled in the debate. When the Vietnamese president met with Chinese leaders, Zhou Enlai bluntly charged that "you are threatening us." Zhou repeated his offer to remove all Chinese troops from the border provinces if they gave the impression in Hanoi that they were being used to intimidate the DRV. Deng Xiaoping interrupted, saying that the forces were there solely to guard against the possibility of a U.S. invasion. Ho immediately protested that his government had no intention of threatening its Chinese ally and declared that it welcomed the comforting presence of People's Liberation Army units located north of the frontier. As a consequence of these and other discussions, the tension in Sino-Vietnamese relations that had marked recent months began to decline, but the seeds for future irritation and mutual distrust had been sown.[48]

Throughout 1966, the conflict in South Vietnam increased in intensity. Determined to avoid a humiliating defeat in Southeast Asia, the Johnson administration steadily poured more combat troops into the war effort. By now, U.S. units had begun to engage in "search and destroy" operations to weaken the resistance movement and drive the insurgent forces out of the lowland villages back into the Central Highlands and across the Cambodian border, thus depriving the revolution of access to recruits and provisions. South Vietnamese forces were assigned primary responsibility for undertaking pacification operations to secure local areas and clean out pockets of resistance in the heavily populated provinces in the Mekong delta and along the central coast. Joint U.S.–South Vietnamese operations were launched into Viet Cong–held areas in Zone D and other areas near the capital.

General Nguyen Chi Thanh attempted to meet the challenge head-on, ordering a series of attacks on enemy-held areas throughout the South. In his view, and that of his supporters in Hanoi, to back down not only would undermine morale in the revolutionary camp, but would also reduce the pressure on Washington to seek a negotiated settlement. For the time being, Party leaders decided to maintain the pressure on the battlefield in order to maximize American casualties and promote the growth of antiwar sentiment throughout the United States. Newly introduced combat forces from North Vietnam bore the brunt of the fighting in the Central Highlands and in the northern provinces of the country, but PLAF units continued to play an active role in combating Saigon's pacification operations in the Mekong delta.

The strategy was an extremely costly one, since Hanoi could not hope to match the enemy in terms of firepower, but would have to rely on the force of numbers and the advantage of surprise. For several months, General Thanh attempted to maintain the initiative on the battlefield. Although U.S. "head count" figures of more than 300,000 enemy casualties a year were no doubt exaggerated, there is little doubt that Hanoi's losses were high. To maintain force levels, it was necessary to increase the level of infiltration from the North, which now reportedly reached well over 50,000 annually.

By the summer of 1966, there was growing debate in Hanoi over Nguyen Chi Thanh's aggressive strategy in the South, an approach that had so far resulted in few concrete benefits. The South Vietnamese government remained unstable, but the prospects for its collapse had declined since the summer of 1965, when a new military leadership under "young turk" leaders Nguyen Cao Ky and Nguyen Van Thieu had brought an end to the series of coups and countercoups that had shaken the capital in previous months. Under U.S. pressure, preparations were now under way in Saigon to draft a new constitution and hold elections to choose a new president. The peace movement in the United States was increasingly vocal and apparently winning broader support among the American people, but there were no indications of a change of mood in the White House. Thanh's critics in Hanoi, including his longtime rival Vo Nguyen Giap, began to question his "heaven-storming" strategy and to propose a more cautious approach.

In Politburo debates on the subject, Ho Chi Minh took the side of the moderates, expressing his preference for a protracted war strategy that applied a mixture of political struggle, propaganda, and guerrilla warfare to wear down the enemy on a gradual, step-by-step basis. To colleagues who expressed a sense of urgency about winning the final victory, Ho compared the situation to preparing rice for a meal. If you remove the rice from the fire too soon, it is inadequately cooked; if removed too late, it will be burned. Yet Ho continued to express optimism about the prospects for final victory, pointing out that internal contradictions in the United States were growing and would reach a climax in the next presidential campaign. In December 1966, he attempted to bypass the White House, writing a public letter to the American people that pointed out the damage that the U.S. military presence was inflicting on the people of Vietnam, as well as to the reputation of the United States. Ho's letter may have helped to persuade some Americans of the sincerity of Hanoi's desire for peace, but it had little effect on the Johnson administration. At the time he wrote the letter, secret peace initiatives from Washington were already under way through the Italian ambassador in Saigon; however, they came to nothing after a series of U.S. bombing raids in the vicinity of Hanoi, which led the DRV to cancel a scheduled meeting between the two sides in Warsaw.[49]

It was that message of toughness that Ho expressed to Jean Sainteny when his old friend and adversary arrived in Hanoi in July 1966 to explore the prospects for French mediation of the conflict. Like French President Charles de Gaulle, old Indochina hand Sainteny had concluded that Washington could not reach its goals in South Vietnam. The best that could be achieved, in his view, was a negotiated settlement to create a neutral government in Saigon. In their discussions, Ho remarked to Sainteny that he was well aware that the United States had the capacity to destroy every city in the DRV, but he insisted that he and his compatriots were prepared to fight to the end, regardless of the sacrifice required, and would not give in before final victory. Ho expressed a willingness to seek a face-saving method to bring about a U.S. withdrawal, but he insisted that in the end the only solution was for them to get out. If so, he proclaimed, all things could be resolved.[50]

I n May 1965, Ho Chi Minh had turned seventy-five. For the previous decade, he had played a largely ceremonial role in the affairs of his country, presiding over meetings of the DRV Council of Ministers, as well as the Politburo and Central Committee, but increasingly delegating his authority to his senior colleagues in the Party and the government. Although they continued to defer to his experience in world affairs and in the strategy of revolutionary war, his influence had declined in other areas and his primary function during the mid-1960s was to serve as the beloved "Uncle Ho," visiting schools, factories, and collective farms to promote the cause of socialism and national reunification.

The mid- and late-1960s were exceedingly difficult years. As the war intensified, the need for manpower to serve in the cause of liberating the South increased drastically. Between 1965 and the end of the decade, the North Vietnamese army grew from about 250,000 to over 400,000 soldiers. Eventually all males between the ages of sixteen and forty-five were subject to the draft. The infiltration of North Vietnamese troops into the South likewise grew rapidly. The vast majority who embarked on the journey each year were men, but women were sometimes permitted to volunteer, often serving as entertainers, intelligence agents, or transportation workers. While most northerners serving in the South were ethnic Vietnamese, some units composed of overseas Chinese or mountain peoples also took part. Most of the northerners who went south were replaced on the farm and in the factory by women. Some women also served in the village militia or in anti-aircraft and bomb-defusing units created throughout the DRV.

Casualty rates for North Vietnamese combatants serving in the South, as well as for the PLAF and civilian members of the NLF, were alarmingly high, with the number of dead and seriously wounded eventually numbering in the hundreds of thousands; but conditions in the North during the height of the war were difficult as well. Because of the departure of much of the rural population for military service in the South, food production dropped precipitously, and mass starvation was avoided only by generous shipments of rice from China. The availability of other consumer goods was severely reduced by bombing and by the government's decision to devote all productive efforts to the war in the South. U.S. air raids left many cities in ruins, including the old provincial capital of Vinh. While the heaviest bombing took place in the panhandle, the raids eventually intensified above the Twentieth Parallel and extended to the outskirts of the capital. To protect the population, the government evacuated many people to the countryside and ordered the construction of bomb shelters in the cities, as well as in frequently targeted rural areas. According to official statistics, more than 30,000 miles of trenches and 20 million bomb shelters, most of the latter only large enough for one individual, were constructed. Although an accurate count of civilian casualties in the North is not available, for many these were not protection enough. While over 55,000 Americans were killed in Vietnam, more than 1 million Vietnamese were estimated to have died in the northern and southern parts of the country in the course of the war. Uncle Ho's compatriots indeed paid a high price for his determination to realize his dream.

Ho Chi Minh wanted to carry his share of the burden. Much to the concern of his younger colleagues, Ho insisted on remaining in his stilt house on the grounds of the Presidential Palace near Ba Dinh Square. The house evidently reminded Ho of the romantic early years of the liberation struggle and demonstrated his determination to live simply during a time of extreme hardship for his people. It served as his office and residence for the remainder of his life.[51]

Ho Chi Minh was clearly beginning to show his age. Foreign acquaintances noticed that he had difficulty breathing and moving and experienced occasional lapses in mental acuity. Sometimes in the course of a discussion with foreign visitors, his attention would lapse and he would appear to have fallen asleep. On reaching his seventy-fifth birthday, Ho had produced the first draft of a testament that he intended to leave to the Vietnamese people at his death. Soviet leaders had expressed some concern about his health as early as 1959, when he had visited Moscow to consult with them about the expanding conflict in South Vietnam. When Ho rejected suggestions that he undergo a medical examination ("I don't think about my health," he remarked), Kliment Voroshilov had insisted, declaring that "the Central Committee has already decided."[52]

In May 1965, Ho left for a three-week trip to China, partly to consult with Mao Zedong on providing additional assistance to the DRV, but also to receive medical treatment and perhaps to take him out of harm's way as the U.S. bombing campaign inexorably approached the capital. He was accompanied by his aide Vu Ky, who continued to serve as his private secretary. After meeting with Mao Zedong in Changsha, Ho went on to Beijing for talks with other Chinese leaders. As in Moscow, his hosts were solicitous of his health. Asked whether he had slept well, Ho responded: "Ask Vu Ky." Despite his protests, Chinese leaders also arranged for an elaborate birthday celebration for their guest, with a number of young women included as guests (because, as Vu Ky remarked enigmatically in his recollections of the incident, Ho Chi Minh "respects them").

After his political discussions were concluded, Ho proceeded to the birthplace of Confucius in nearby Shandong province; he professed himself to be a lifelong admirer of the Old Master. At a temple in the ancient philosopher's hometown, Ho recited classical Chinese phrases that demonstrated Confucius' deep commitment to humanitarian principles and noted that the philosopher's famous principle of Great Unity was an ancient equivalent of the modern concept of an egalitarian society. Real peace, he concluded, could appear only when an era of Great Unity had spread throughout the globe. On the plane that carried him back to Hanoi, Ho Chi Minh wrote a brief poem that recorded his deep emotions on visiting the birthplace of China's most famous son.[53]

After this trip, Ho Chi Minh grew steadily weaker, although he still showed flashes of his earlier vitality. During an official visit by the Chinese Party leader Tao Zhu to Hanoi a few months later, Ho suddenly requested that his old friend provide him with a young woman from the Chinese province of Guangdong to serve as his companion. When Tao asked why Ho did not seek someone to serve his needs in the DRV, his host said simply, "Everyone calls me Uncle Ho." On his return to China, Tao Zhu reported the request to Zhou Enlai; because of the delicate relationship between the two parties, Zhou decided to consult with North Vietnamese leaders. Eventually the matter was quietly dropped.[54]

In May 1966, Ho Chi Minh returned to China to celebrate his seventy-sixth birthday. While he was in Beijing, Chinese leaders reassured him of the firmness of their support for the Vietnamese revolutionary cause; Ho wrote a letter to his colleagues in the VWP Politburo, assuring them that China intended to help its ally realize final victory, even at the risk of a direct U.S. attack on the PRC. He then left for a few days of rest at resort areas in central China, continuing on to Shandong and Manchuria before returning home in June. On July 17, he addressed a message to the entire Vietnamese people, thanking them for their sacrifices and declaring that "nothing is more important than independence and freedom." In Beijing, a rally attended by hundreds of thousands of people had taken place at Tiananmen Square to honor Ho Chi Minh and demonstrate Chinese support for the Vietnamese struggle for national liberation.[55]

By now, Ho was finding movement increasingly difficult. Always a stickler for physical conditioning, he continued his calisthenics on a daily basis. He left his stilt house on the palace grounds regularly to eat meals, tend his garden, and feed the carp in the nearby pond, as well as to greet visitors—from Western journalists, foreign dignitaries, and NLF representatives, to delegations of ordinary people from various walks of life—in a leafy arbor next to his private residence. Politburo meetings were held at a table on the ground floor of his house, open to the air. But when U.S. bombing attacks began to focus on the outskirts of Hanoi, Ho took up residence in a bomb shelter that had been constructed on the palace grounds. By then, he apparently did not regularly attend meetings, and some observers noted that he often appeared "muddled." When important issues came up, Le Duan sometimes observed to colleagues, "Spare Uncle the worry. We should not bother our supreme leader."

Party leaders were becoming more and more concerned about Ho's declining condition; shortly after his seventy-seventh birthday, Le Duan convened a Politburo meeting, while Ho was receiving medical treatment in Canton, to discuss how to preserve his health. It was decided to keep the meeting strictly secret in order to avoid incurring his anger or worrying the Vietnamese people. The government assigned Ho's old friend Nguyen Luong Bang to monitor his health and dispatched a delegation of specialists led by the Party veteran Le Thanh Nghi to Moscow for advice and training in how to preserve his remains after death.[56]

Ho Chi Minh returned from south China at the end of June and was brought up to date on conditions in the South. He was still occasionally involved in matters of diplomatic importance; in early 1967, he had met with U.S. peace activists Harry Ashmore and William Baggs and hinted that peace talks could begin only after Washington declared an end to its bombing raids on North Vietnam. After the two reported to the State Department on the results of the trip upon their return to the United States, President Johnson sent a letter to Ho Chi Minh expressing a willingness to terminate the bombing campaign, but only when infiltration from North Vietnam into the South had stopped. To Party leaders, who were counting on an end to the bombing as a means of increasing the shipment of personnel and matériel to the South, Washington's proposal was unaccepable. In his March response to Johnson's letter, Ho Chi Minh insisted on a halt to the bombing campaign on the DRV without conditions. That position was reiterated to Raymond Aubrac, his old friend from Paris, in July. Aubrac had arrived on a brief visit to test Hanoi's receptivity to the opening of peace talks. The DRV response, as it was provided by Ho Chi Minh himself, was that negotiations could not start until the United States had unconditionally stopped its bombing of the north. In September, Ho went to China for a lengthy convalescence in the mountains near Beijing.[57]

I n his absence, the Politburo had engaged in a momentous debate on whether to launch the long-awaited "general offensive and uprising" that had been under consideration since the beginning of the decade. Party leaders recognized the need to restore momentum to the revolution in the South, recovering ground lost as a result of the growing U.S. military presence there since the summer of 1965. Although Viet Cong forces in South Vietnam (now bolstered by the participation of more than 100,000 compatriots from the North) continued to operate at relatively high levels of effectiveness throughout the country, casualty rates were alarming and morale problems had begun to surface within the resistance movement. Recruitment was down and the number of desertions was on the rise, as Washington's refusal to concede defeat raised doubts about the inevitability of a victory by the revolutionary forces. As a result of visits to Hanoi by U.S. peace activists, the Politburo took heart from the fact that the antiwar movement was on the rise in the United States; still, there were no signs that the Johnson administration was preparing to withdraw. In fact, the number of U.S. military personnel stationed in South Vietnam had risen to almost half a million, with the prospect of more to come.

For years, Ho Chi Minh had insisted that the best time to launch such a campaign was during a U.S. presidential election year, when Hanoi could exert the maximum pressure on the American political scene. Attacks by PLAF units in the countryside were to be coordinated with a popular general uprising in the major cities. At a minimum, this would destabilize the South and force the United States to negotiate in a position of weakness, but the ultimate goal was to bring about the collapse of the Saigon regime. The decision to launch the general offensive and uprising during the Têt New Year's holidays in early February was just being finalized by the Politburo in December, when Ho Chi Minh returned from China. Ho gave his approval to the plan and then immediately went back to Beijing for additional treatment.

The Têt offensive began on January 31, 1968. Insurgent forces assaulted major cities, provincial and district capitals, and rural villages in a nationwide campaign. Highly publicized attacks took place in Saigon, where sapper units and suicide squads assaulted government installations and briefly occupied the ground floor of the new U.S. Embassy, and in the old imperial capital of Hué, which was occupied by North Vietnamese troops for almost three weeks before they were evicted from the city by American ground troops in bloody hand-to-hand fighting. The results were somewhat disappointing in military terms: insurgent units taking part in the offensive suffered more than 30,000 casualties. Because the vast majority were local Viet Cong forces, these losses would weaken the movement for years to come. And it did not bring about the anticipated collapse of the Nguyen Van Thieu regime. However, the political consequences in the United States were more encouraging, because U.S. casualties during the offensive had been high. Nearly 2,000 Americans had been killed in the month of the Tết campaign, with an additional 3,000 seriously wounded. Antiwar fever among the American people reached new heights and compelled the White House to offer new concessions to bring about a peaceful settlement of the war. In late March, Lyndon Johnson offered a partial halt to the bombing below the Twentieth Parallel in a bid to jump-start negotiations.

As the White House was pondering its dilemma, Politburo member Le Duc Tho visited Ho Chi Minh, who was still in Beijing, to brief him on the results of the Tết offensive. Although Tho (soon to be selected as Hanoi's chief negotiator in the upcoming peace talks) would later concede that Tết was only a qualified success, he undoubtedly presented it to President Ho as a great victory, and Ho was delighted. When Tho informed him of his own upcoming trip to the South to evaluate post-Tết conditions, Ho expressed a fervent wish to accompany him. Tho attempted to dissuade him, explaining that Ho would need a visa to pass through the Cambodian port of Sihanoukville (the route most senior Party officials now took to reach the South) and thus would be recognized because of his famous beard. Ho replied that he would shave it off. But then, Tho quickly replied, our southern compatriots won't recognize you! Ho was persistent, suggesting that he could pose as a sailor or hide in a ship's hold. To pacify the old revolutionary, Tho promised to look into the matter; when Tho rose to leave, Ho Chi Minh hugged him and wept. Tho later informed acquaintances that when they parted he feared he might never see his old colleague again.

Ho Chi Minh had anticipated that this request would be rejected by Party leaders because of his poor health. In a letter to Le Duan in Hanoi, he argued that a change of air would do him good. He also explained that his trip to the South would build up the spirits of the thousands of his compatriots who were sacrificing their lives for the cause. On March 19, he wrote a note to Prime Minister Zhou Enlai asking for his assistance in gaining approval for his request. In Hanoi, the request was quietly shelved.[58]

After he returned to North Vietnam on April 21, Ho Chi Minh was invited to attend a meeting of the Politburo to evaluate the results of the Têt offensive. Ho's health was fragile, but he insisted on being kept abreast of the situation in the South and expressed his delight that the strains of the war had forced the resignation of U.S. Defense Secretary Robert McNamara. He was also pleased with President Johnson's decision, announced during his March 30 speech declaring a partial bombing halt, that he would not run for reelection in 1968. After the June assassination of Senator Robert F. Kennedy, one of the most prominent politicians opposed to the war in the United States, Ho lamented in a brief article published in *Nhan Dan* that because of the war increasing numbers of ordinary Americans would be killed in Vietnam as well.[59]

In early May, Ho Chi Minh was informed that President Johnson had put into effect a partial bombing halt below the Twentieth Parallel and had agreed to engage in peace talks in Paris. Ho had apparently not been consulted on whether to accept the offer, but he was delighted. Nevertheless, he warned his colleagues that after victory was achieved, it would be vitally important to heal the wounds of the Vietnamese nation, a task that "would be complicated and difficult." To prevent serious mistakes, he recommended that a concrete plan be drawn up to reorganize the Party, so that each member would recognize the sacred task of serving the people. Important tasks included healing the wounds of war among the population and successfully transforming the "dregs" of southern society—thieves, prostitutes, drug addicts—into useful citizens through indoctrination and, if possible, other legal means.[60]

Ho also sought to provide advice to his colleagues on how to conduct future negotiations with the United States. The issue was indeed becoming complicated; not only had Washington resisted Hanoi's demand for a written and unconditional promise not to resume bombing the DRV, but Beijing—now mired in the throes of the Cultural Revolution—had criticized its North Vietnamese comrades for being too eager to establish contact with the United States. In April, Zhou Enlai advised Prime Minister Pham Van Dong to insist on fulfillment of his famous "four points" before opening negotiations. Zhou told him he should negotiate only from a strong position. Dong retorted that Hanoi would not compromise on its basic principles and would never engage in peace talks under disadvantageous conditions. In any case, he remarked, it was the Vietnamese who were doing the fighting.[61]

Ho Chi Minh did not take an active part in the deliberations, but in his comments he adopted a pragmatic attitude, counseling the Politburo in July that it should decide carefully what could be gained or lost once negotiations began. In meetings held in succeeding weeks, he warned his colleagues that, at the same time they were grasping at any opportunity for a diplomatic breakthrough, they must also focus their efforts on enhancing military preparations. He warned them to be wary of a U.S. trap, which could lead to a cease-fire in the South while enabling Washington to resume bombing the North at some time in the future.

In early November, peace talks convened in Paris after Washington agreed to a complete halt to bombing, even though Lyndon Johnson refused to put the promise in writing. There was no cease-fire in the South, although Hanoi promised not to launch a major attack similar to the Têt offensive. But the breakthrough on peace talks came too late to help Hubert Humphrey, the Democratic presidential candidate. Humphrey, who had won the nomination during a tumultuous national convention held in Chicago in August, had become a silent critic of the war, but had been forced by his position as Johnson's vice president to keep his reservations to himself. Growing public sentiment against the war hurt his own candidacy, while the Republican nominee, Richard M. Nixon, promised that he had a "secret plan" to bring an end to the war. In the November election, Nixon brought the Republicans back into the White House for the first time in eight years.

During the late 1960s, Ho Chi Minh periodically revised his testament, but each draft contained his wish to be cremated. The last version indicated that he wanted to have his ashes deposited at three unnamed locations in the northern, central, and southern sections of the country, a symbolic act designed to express his lifelong devotion to the cause of national reunification. Then, he wrote, he would embark on his way to meet Karl Marx, Vladimir Lenin, and other venerable revolutionaries. Ho also expressed the desire that after the restoration of peace, agricultural taxes should be canceled for one year to reduce the hardship that the war had imposed on the Vietnamese people and to express the Party's gratitude for their labors and sacrifices during the long, bloody conflict.[62]

During the 1969 Têt holidays, Ho Chi Minh took his last brief trip out of Hanoi, visiting the nearby district capital of Son Tay. After his return, his health appeared normal; he attended meetings of the Politburo in April, advising his colleagues that if the new administration decided to withdraw U.S. troops from South Vietnam, it was important to allow them to do so with honor. But in a speech at the Sixteenth Plenum of the Central Committee in mid-May, he warned Party leaders not to be hasty in their judgment, since although the U.S. position in

South Vietnam was weakening (President Nixon had announced his new policy of "Vietnamization," which called for a gradual withdrawal of U.S. forces from the RVN), it remained dangerous.

Ho continued to be concerned about the welfare of the troops in the South. In response to his long-standing request, he was finally able to meet with a delegation of southern resistance fighters at West Lake, in the northern suburbs of Hanoi. At the seventy-ninth birthday celebration held at his house, his close colleagues promised to bring about the final victory and reward him with his long-awaited visit to South Vietnam. That same month, he wrote the last draft of his testament, jotting down notes in the margins of an earlier draft. But Ho was growing increasingly feeble, and doctors decided to monitor his heart rate on a regular basis. Although the U.S. bombing halt permitted him to return to the stilt house (a location that was surrounded by several shade trees), he began to weaken during the hot, muggy summer. Party leaders urgently requested Soviet and Chinese doctors to provide assistance. Ho attempted to maintain his regular morning schedule of physical exercises; he watered his plants and fed the fish daily. Close colleagues Truong Chinh and Nguyen Luong Bang ate with him regularly.[63]

One day in mid-August, Ho's condition suddenly worsened, and his lungs became heavily congested. Although doctors administered penicillin, the next day he remarked of feeling a pain in his chest; on the twenty-eighth he developed an irregular heartbeat. When Politburo members arrived to report on the situation in the South, Ho told them that his physical condition had improved. Two days later, Ho asked Pham Van Dong, who had come to visit, whether preparations were complete for National Day celebrations, scheduled for September 2. After rising the following morning, he ate a bowl of rice gruel and met with a group of military veterans. At 9:45 A.M. on September 2, the twenty-fourth anniversary of the restoration of Vietnamese national independence, Ho Chi Minh's heart stopped.[64]

EPILOGUE | FROM MAN TO MYTH

The news of Ho Chi Minh's death was greeted with an outpouring of comment from around the globe. Eulogies flowed in from major world capitals, and Hanoi received more than twenty-two thousand messages from 121 countries offering the Vietnamese people condolences for the death of their leader. A number of socialist states held memorial services of their own and editorial comments were predictably favorable. An official statement from Moscow lauded Ho as a "great son of the heroic Vietnamese people, the outstanding leader of the international Communist and national liberation movement, and a great friend of the Soviet Union." From Third World countries came praise for his role as a defender of the oppressed. An article published in India described him as the essence of "the people, the embodiment of the ardent aspiration for freedom, of their endurance and struggle." Others referred to his simplicity of manner and high moral standing. Remarked an editorial in a Uruguayan newspaper: "He had a heart as immense as the universe and a boundless love for the children. He is a model of simplicity in all fields."[1]

Reaction from Western capitals was more muted. The White House refrained from comment, and senior Nixon administration officials followed suit. But attention to Ho's death in the Western news media was intense. Newspapers that supported the antiwar cause tended to describe him in favorable terms as a worthy adversary and a defender of the weak and oppressed. Even those who had adamantly opposed the Hanoi regime accorded him a measure of respect as one who had dedicated himself first and foremost to the independence and unification of his country, as well as a prominent spokesperson for the exploited peoples of the world.

One key question in the minds of many commentators was the effect that his passing would have on the course of the war in Indochina. For all his reputation as a dedicated revolutionary and veteran Communist agent, Ho Chi Minh was viewed in many quarters as a pragmatist, a man of the world who grasped the complexities of international politics and acted accordingly. Even Lyndon Johnson, perhaps his staunchest adversary during the 1960s, occasionally remarked in exasperation that if he could only sit down with "Old Ho," the two veteran political figures could somehow manage to reach an accommodation.

Toward Ho Chi Minh's successors in Hanoi, there was no such sense of familiarity. Few of Ho's colleagues were well-known in the outside world. Except for Ho, no senior Party official had ever lived or traveled extensively in France, much less in other Western countries. Of those who had been abroad, most had received their training in China or in the Soviet Union, and their worldview was bounded by the blinkered certainties of Marxist-Leninist orthodoxy. First Secretary Le Duan, who had been quick to establish his credentials as Ho's legitimate successor in Hanoi, was a virtual unknown in the West. Even in Moscow and Beijing, Duan was somewhat of an unknown quantity.

In his final testament, as in his life, Ho Chi Minh had sought to balance his commitment to Vietnamese national independence with a similar dedication to the world revolution. In this document, which he first drafted in 1965 and then amended by hand in 1968 and 1969, Ho reaffirmed the dual importance of nationalism and socialism, although he emphasized that the immediate priority was to heal the wounds of war and improve the living standards of the Vietnamese people. He paid particular attention to the importance of realizing equality of the sexes. He praised the Party for having played the leading role in the Vietnamese revolution, but called for a campaign of rectification and self-criticism to democratize the organization and raise the level of morality among Party cadres after the end of the war. Finally, he included a fervent plea to restore the unity of the world Communist movement on the basis of the principle of proletarian internationalism.

Funeral ceremonies for Ho Chi Minh were held at Ba Dinh Square in Hanoi on September 8, 1969, with more than 100,000 people in attendance, including representatives from the socialist countries. In a speech before the National Assembly, Le Duan pledged that Party leaders would seek to fulfill Ho Chi Minh's fervent request to defeat the U.S. aggressors, liberate the South, and reunify the country. Then, he promised, the Party would devote all its efforts to bring about the creation of a socialist society in Vietnam and restore the spirit of unity within the socialist camp.[2]

In some respects, Le Duan was as good as his word. Under his firm leadership, in the years following Ho Chi Minh's death the DRV continued to pursue final victory in the South. Hanoi's immediate objective was to strengthen its forces in the South in preparation for the launching of a new military offensive during the U.S. presidential campaign in 1972. North Vietnamese representatives held talks with their U.S. counterparts in Paris, but with little result, as both sides sought to bring about a military breakthrough in South Vietnam as a means of gaining an advantage at the conference table. Although Hanoi's war casualties remained high, Party leaders were optimistic, since rising antiwar sentiment in the United States had compelled President Nixon to announce a program calling for the progressive withdrawal of U.S. combat troops by the end of his first term.

During the Easter holidays of 1972, with fewer than 50,000 U.S. troops remaining in South Vietnam, Hanoi launched a new military campaign in South Vietnam. Like its more famous predecessor in 1968, the Easter offensive did not result in total victory, but it set in motion forces on both sides that hastened the peace process. In January 1973, Hanoi and Washington finally reached a compromise agreement. The Paris peace treaty called for a cease-fire in place and the removal of remaining U.S. combat units. Nothing was said about the presence of North Vietnamese troops in South Vietnam. The division of territory under the control of the NLF and the Saigon government was to be decided in negotiations between the two sides, through the formation of a subgovernmental administrative structure (known as the National Council for Reconciliation and Concord) including representatives of both sides, as well as neutralists. The council would then turn to the issue of holding new national elections.

As with the Geneva Accords two decades previously, the Paris treaty did not end the Vietnam War. It simply facilitated the final departure of U.S. troops and returned the situation in South Vietnam to what it had been in the early 1960s. When neither side appeared willing to honor the Paris provisions, conflict in the countryside resumed. In early 1975, Hanoi launched a new offensive with the objective of completing a takeover of the South by the following year. The United States had been weakened by the resignation of Richard Nixon the previous summer, and his successor, Gerald Ford, was reluctant to reintroduce American combat troops into South Vietnam. Flushed with success, North Vietnamese troops advanced out of the Central Highlands in March and poured south toward Saigon, while others occupied Da Nang and the northern half of the country. By the last week of April, Communist forces were poised on the edge of victory, as Saigon's resistance crumbled and the remaining Americans were evacuated by helicopter from the rooftop of the U.S. Embassy to aircraft carriers waiting offshore. After a bitter struggle that had lasted fifteen years and left more than 1 million Vietnamese dead, it was, in President Ford's phrase, "a war that is finished." Meanwhile, the Khmer Rouge had seized power in Phnom Penh two weeks previously; a revolutionary government would take office in Laos before the end of the year.

In early July 1976, the two zones of Vietnam were reunified into a single Socialist Republic of Vietnam (SRV), thus fulfilling Le Duan's pledge to carry out one of Ho Chi Minh's wishes. But Duan's success in carrying out Ho Chi Minh's testament was not as impressive in other areas. In 1968, a Soviet specialist had secretly arrived in Hanoi to advise the Vietnamese on embalming procedures. The following March, a team of Vietnamese traveled to Moscow to hold further consultations and report on their progress in mastering the technique. According to one account, however, the issue remained a sensitive one within the Party leadership, since Ho Chi Minh himself would have vigorously objected to any plans that contradicted his desire to be cremated. At the moment of Ho Chi Minh's death, the Politburo had not yet reached a final decision on how to deal with the matter. After urgent consultations with Moscow, a second Soviet specialist arrived in Hanoi in mid-September to assist Vietnamese medical personnel in preserving Ho's body.[3]

On November 29, 1969, the Politburo formally approved plans to erect a mausoleum to display Ho Chi Minh's embalmed body for the edification of future generations. A committee composed of representatives from the Ministries of Construction and National Defense was appointed to oversee the project with the assistance of Soviet advisers. In its final report to Party leaders, the committee concluded that the mausoleum should be contemporary in style but imbued with a national flavor. In conformity with the president's character, it should be solemn and simple in appearance, and placed in a convenient, accessible location. In drawing up its recommendations for the design for the building, the committee had studied a number of other commemorative structures, including the Pyramids in Egypt, the Monument to Victor Emmanuel in Rome, the Lincoln Memorial in Washington, D.C., and Lenin's Tomb in Moscow. After additional suggestions from the Politburo, models of the projected structure were then displayed throughout the country to solicit public comment. Over thirty thousand suggestions were eventually submitted to the committee.

In December 1971, the Politburo gave its final approval, and construction began shortly after the signing of the Paris peace treaty. The site chosen for the mausoleum was one of the most sacred precincts of the Vietnamese revolution—at Ba Dinh Square in Hanoi, adjacent to the Presidential Palace and Ho's stilt house. When it was finally opened to the public on August 29, 1975, the mausoleum was reminiscent above all of the Lenin mausoleum in Red Square. The facing was of gray marble, much of it quarried at Marble Mountain, a limestone outcropping south of Da Nang, where Viet Cong troops housed in a cave inside the mountain could watch American GIs swimming at famous China Beach, one of the most popular resorts in the area. The mausoleum was intended to reflect the shape of a lotus flower rising from the primeval mud, thus providing a modern counterpoint to an eleventh-century Buddhist pagoda in a nearby park. Many observers, however, found the style of the mausoleum to be heavy and ponderous, in total contrast to the whimsical humor and unpretentious character of its occupant who was lying in state inside, hands crossed, and dressed in a simple Sun Yat-sen tunic. As the historian Hue-Tam Ho Tai observed, the overall effect was to portray Ho Chi Minh as the international Communist leader rather than the more approachable Uncle Ho beloved by millions of Vietnamese. The results have apparently not deterred his compatriots, however—more than fifteen thousand visit the mausoleum each week.[4]

In proceeding with their plans to preserve Ho Chi Minh's body in a mausoleum, Party leaders had clearly ignored Ho's requests for a simple funeral ceremony and cremation. He had always disdained the luxurious trappings of high office, and in 1959, shortly after disclosing his real identity as the famous revolutionary Nguyen Ai Quoc, he had even vetoed a proposal to construct a small museum at Kim Lien village to commemorate his life, arguing that scarce funds could be better used to build a school. To avoid the possibility of public criticism for their decision to contravene his request, Party leaders deleted those sections in his testament that dealt with the disposal of his body. The version of the testament published in 1969 also omitted Ho's request for a one-year reduction in the agricultural tax and his warning to his compatriots that the war in the South could last for several more years. The Party also announced that Ho had died on September 3, one day later than its actual occurrence, in order to preserve the mood of the national holiday of independence, which celebrated the anniversary of September 2, 1945, when Ho Chi Minh had read the Declaration of Independence in Ba Dinh Square.[5]

After the Fourth Party Congress in December 1976, Party leaders announced that socialism should be achieved "in the main" throughout the country before the end of the decade. To symbolize the new stage of the revolution, the VWP was renamed the Vietnamese Communist Party (Dang Cong san Viet Nam, or VCP). Ho Chi Minh's successors attempted to make liberal use of his image to mobilize popular support for their ambitious program. Portraits of the late president appeared on postage stamps, the national currency, and the walls of buildings throughout the country, while books and pamphlets in profusion were published about his life, his ideas, and his revolutionary morality. Party leaders like Truong Chinh, Pham Van Dong, and Vo Nguyen Giap recounted their memories of Uncle Ho, and stressed the importance of "Ho Chi Minh thought" (tu tuong Ho Chi Minh) as a crucial tool for building the future Vietnam. Young people were urged to follow the path of Ho Chi Minh in guiding their everyday actions, and youth organizations were established throughout the country in his name. Several other socialist countries attempted to appropriate his reputation for their own purposes, naming schools, factories, streets, and squares after him and holding seminars to study his testament and his career achievements.[6]

The putative values of Ho Chi Minh thought were embodied in the new Ho Chi Minh Museum, which was completed in the fall of 1990, on the centenary of his birth. Placed just behind the mausoleum near Ba Dinh Square, the museum was imposing in size, but not as heavy in style as its neighbor. With a facing of white marble, it too was designed to resemble a lotus flower, although to some observers the four-sided structure with the entryway at one corner was more reminiscent of the prow of a ship.[7]

Despite the Party's monumental effort to enshrine Ho Chi Minh thought as the very embodiment of the new Vietnam, many observers found significant differences between the style of Le Duan and that of his illustrious predecessor. Where Ho had persistently urged a gradual approach to carrying out the Vietnamese revolution in order to maximize popular support across a broad spectrum of society, Le Duan frequently adopted more ambitious tactics that accentuated divisions within the Party leadership and alienated significant segments of the population. And where Ho Chi Minh had always sought to calibrate his own strategy with due regard to the realities of the international situation, his successors adopted an aggressive approach in the realm of foreign affairs that not only antagonized Hanoi's neighbors in Southeast Asia but also irritated China, once Hanoi's closest ally and strongest supporter. Those who objected to Le Duan's policies were dismissed from the Party leadership (a prominent example was Vo Nguyen Giap) or chose to go into exile abroad (as in the case of Hoang Van Hoan).[8]

The results were tragic for a country just emerging from a generation of war. When the regime suddenly announced the nationalization of industry and commerce in March 1978, thousands fled to seek refuge overseas. A program to begin the collectivization of agriculture antagonized much of the rural population in the South. By the close of the 1970s, the Vietnamese economy, shaken by the Party's ill-advised effort to lay the foundations of a fully socialist society before the decade ended, was in a shambles.

The country's internal problems were exacerbated by crises abroad. When the fanatical and genocidal Pol Pot regime that had come into power in Cambodia rejected Vietnamese overtures to form the projected militant alliance of the three Indochinese states, in December 1978, Hanoi launched an invasion of Cambodia and installed a puppet regime in Phnom Penh. In retaliation, Chinese forces crossed the Vietnamese border in a campaign that, however brief, forced the SRV to devote precious resources to the cause of military defense. By the mid-1980s, popular resentment of the Party leadership—a group who had singularly failed to follow Ho Chi Minh's advice to provide the people with the fruits of victory—had reached alarming levels.

After the death of Le Duan in the summer of 1986, Party leaders belatedly recognized their error (described by one as "triumphalism") and embarked upon a new path. Guided by a new general secretary, a former southern militant named Nguyen Van Linh, the Politburo approved plans to stimulate the stagnant economy by adopting market socialism and opening the country to foreign investment, while encouraging a more tolerant attitude toward the expression of ideas among the populace. Known as *doi moi* ("renovation"), the new program was highly reminiscent of Mikhail Gorbachev's policy of perestroika in the USSR, although sources in Hanoi insisted that the strategy was Vietnamese in inspiration.

Before the end of the decade, however, conservative forces within the Party had second thoughts. Although the introduction of foreign ideas had stimulated the growth of the Vietnamese economy, it also led (at least in the view of ideological conservatives) to the increased presence of drugs, prostitution, AIDS, and hedonistic attitudes among young people, as well as to heightened criticism of the Party's dominance over all aspects of national affairs. Alarmed at the collapse of Communist systems in Eastern Europe and increasingly concerned at the corrosive impact of

Western culture on socialist institutions in Vietnam, the Party began to crack down on political dissent and what conservative elements labeled the "poisonous weeds of bourgeois capitalism." Under Nguyen Van Linh's successor, the veteran apparatchik Do Muoi, Hanoi followed the lead of post-Tiananmen China and cracked down on dissident activities under a policy of "economic reform, political stability." While economic liberalization continued at a modest pace, the Party reasserted its traditional role as the only political force in the country.[9]

Vietnamese advocates of reform were quick to appropriate the legacy of Ho Chi Minh in promoting their own cause. Citing Ho's reputation as a pragmatist, they argued that he would have recognized the need to raise the standard of living before embarking on the road to a fully socialist society. Pointing to his image as a humanist with a broad tolerance for opposing ideas, they asserted that he would have prevented the split that had developed within the Party leadership and adopted a more inclusive approach to winning the support of the people. In the late 1980s, the reformist case was strengthened when Ho Chi Minh's last private secretary, Vu Ky, revealed that Le Duan and some of his colleagues had tampered with Ho's testament by deleting his plea for a tax reduction and a simple funeral ceremony. A chastised Politburo was forced to admit its culpability, but rationalized its own actions as being ultimately in the best interests of the Vietnamese people and in accordance with Ho Chi Minh's own lifetime objectives.[10]

The confusion about Ho Chi Minh's true character and legacy exists not only in Vietnam but abroad, where he is viewed variously as a saint dedicated to the liberation of the oppressed masses from the yoke of Western imperialism, a sinner committed to the spread of Communist totalitarianism throughout the world, or (perhaps most damaging of all) an unprincipled opportunist who exploited his reputation for integrity and simplicity of character in order to secure his own self-glorification. When UNESCO sponsored a conference in Hanoi in 1990 to celebrate the centennial of his birth, praise of Uncle Ho at the conference was countered by a spate of criticisms from those around the world who objected to the deification of a man they felt bore ultimate responsibility for the deaths of so many of his compatriots.

To many observers, the crux of the debate over Ho Chi Minh has centered on the issue of whether he should be identified as a Communist or a nationalist. Many of his foreign acquaintances insist that Ho was more a patriot than a Marxist revolutionary. Ho appeared to confirm this view in 1961, when he publicly declared that it was the desire to save his compatriots that initially led him to Leninism. While he voiced such sentiments on numerous other occasions, there is perhaps no clearer exposition than his remark to the U.S. intelligence officer Charles Fenn in 1945 that he viewed communism as the means to reach a nationalist end. When asked to explain himself, Ho replied:

> First, you must understand that to gain independence from a great power like France is a formidable task that cannot be achieved without some outside help, not necessarily in things like arms, but in the nature of advice and contacts. One doesn't in fact gain independence by throwing bombs and such. That was the mistake the early revolutionaries all too often made. One must gain it through organization, propaganda, training and discipline. One also needs . . . a set of beliefs, a gospel, a practical analysis, you might even say a bible. Marxism-Leninism gave me that framework.

Fenn asked Ho why he did not select democracy or some other form of political system, rather than an ideology that so clearly would forfeit the goodwill of the United States, a country he claimed to admire so much? Ho Chi Minh replied that it was only when he arrived in Moscow that he received any practical support. The Soviet Union alone of the major powers was "a friend in need and a friend in deed." Its loyalty won his loyalty.[11]

There seems little doubt that for Ho Chi Minh the survival of his country was first and always his primary concern. Indeed, such views aroused the suspicion of other senior Party leaders in Hanoi, Beijing, and Moscow, who sometimes questioned whether Ho was a genuine Marxist. Nevertheless, there is ample evidence that, whether or not he was an orthodox Marxist, under his patriotic exterior beat the heart of a dedicated revolutionary. The revolutionary strain in his outlook was probably triggered by his shipboard experience before World War I, when he discovered that the sufferings of his compatriots were shared by peoples elsewhere in Asia and Africa living under the yoke of world imperialism. It was undoubtedly accentuated by his period of residence in Paris, when he discovered the hypocrisy of the French, who failed to apply their own ideals to their colonial peoples. Two years in Moscow during the early heady days of the Soviet experiment appear to have aroused his naïve enthusiasm for a future Communist society. In Ho's brave new world, patriotism would be replaced by the Leninist concept of a future global federation of Communist societies.

Later events undoubtedly had a sobering effect on his attitude. The purge trials in Moscow—which apparently came perilously close to endangering his own safety—must have undermined his faith in the Soviet experiment. Moscow's failure to live up to its own commitment to give active support to the liberation of colonial peoples must have aroused doubts in his mind as to the relevance of proletarian internationalism in a world of power politics. But nothing appeared to shake his faith in the ultimate superiority of the socialist system. To the end of his life, he held tenaciously to the view that the capitalist model had brought untold suffering to millions of oppressed peoples throughout Asia, Africa, and Latin America.

The issue is thus not whether he was a nationalist or a Communist—in his own way, he was both. It is more a question of his tactics. Ho Chi Minh was a believer in the art of the possible, of adjusting his ideals to the conditions of the moment. To many, even within his own party, his behavior often appeared as an absence of principle, but in his own mind progress could often be most effectively realized by infinitesimal steps. To Ho Chi Minh, in the apt phrase of the British social scientist Walter Bagehot, the best was sometimes the enemy of the good. Ho applied this pragmatic attitude in foreign policy: when, for example, he accepted compromise solutions in 1946 and 1954 rather than fight under disadvantageous conditions. He was also pragmatic in domestic affairs, always believing that the transition to a socialist society should be undertaken gradually in a bid to win broad popular support.

Like U.S. President Lyndon B. Johnson, Ho Chi Minh saw himself as a Great Communicator, a leader who, given the opportunity, could achieve his objectives not by force, but by reason. In some instances, he succeeded. On several occasions, his willingness to compromise disarmed his adversaries and enabled him to turn military weakness into political advantage. At the same time, his image of simplicity, goodness, and selflessness exerted an enormous appeal, thus contributing significantly to the widespread approval at home and abroad for the Vietnamese revolution and struggle for independence. It is difficult to imagine the global outpouring of support for the Vietnamese war of national liberation during the 1960s had it been identified with the face of Le Duan or Truong Chinh rather than that of Ho Chi Minh.

Was Ho Chi Minh's image genuine? There is probably no easy answer to that question. There seems little doubt that he was genuinely uncomfortable in an atmosphere of luxury and preferred to live in simple, unpretentious surroundings. Still, many of Ho's more discerning acquaintances have observed that there was often an element of artifice in his pose as the simple ascetic, the Confucian scholar turned Marxist revolutionary. While in France after the end of World War II he told his private secretary, Vu Dinh Huynh, that sometimes fake tears were useful in getting a point across in a speech. Many years later the Polish ICC representative in Hanoi observed that, despite his public protests, Ho appeared to enjoy the adulation that he received from his compatriots. Ego was undoubtedly involved when, during the 1940s and 1950s, he wrote two self-congratulatory autobiographies under assumed names. Ho Chi Minh's image of saintliness was not just a trait ascribed to him by others, but was carefully cultivated by the man himself.

There were, of course, sound political reasons for him to encourage this cult of personality. When in 1947 an American correspondent asked Ho why he was the object of so much adulation, he replied that it was partly because the people viewed him as a symbol for realizing their own aspirations. Or perhaps, he added, it was because he loved all Vietnamese children as if they were his own nephews, and in return they had a special love for "Uncle Ho." Early in life, when his nation and its culture appeared to be on the verge of extinction, he had observed the reverence that young Vietnamese bestowed on the rustic village scholars who sought in their lives and their teachings to carry out the timeless principles of Confucian humanism. To the end of his days, Ho adopted that persona as a means to bring about the salvation of his people and the resurrection of their nation.[12]

Whatever the political benefits that accrued from that decision, Ho Chi Minh sometimes paid a price for his image of selflessness and pragmatism. By nature a conciliator who believed in the power of persuasion rather than intimidation, in directing the Indochinese Communist Party he relied from the outset on the tactic of collective leadership rather than on the assertion of personal dominance in the manner of a Lenin, a Stalin, or a Mao Zedong. During the 1930s and 1940s, his powers of persuasion—bolstered by his immense prestige and long experience as a Comintern agent—were generally successful. But they began to fail him in the 1950s, when senior colleagues started to question the aptness of his recommendations and assert their own claim to a major role in formulating strategy. In the end, Ho Chi Minh was virtually reduced to a figure of impotence. His ideas were greeted with consideration by his colleagues, but were increasingly rejected as inappropriate.

Was Ho Chi Minh naïve in believing Sun Tzu's aphorism that the most successful victories are those that are achieved without violence? In retrospect, it might be said that he had been somewhat credulous in his expectation that the French could be persuaded to withdraw from Vietnam peacefully after World War II. Several years later, Ho similarly miscalculated when he argued that the United States might decide to accept a Communist-dominated government in Vietnam, if it could be achieved without U.S. humiliation. Yet the evidence suggests that Ho's assessment of the international situation was usually clear-sighted, and he was cognizant of the need for flexible policies to take account of varying possibilities. Although he sought to achieve his objectives without recourse to violence, he was prepared to resort to military force when the occasion demanded. The same could not be said about some of his colleagues, who lacked the subtlety and the patience to pursue a solution by diplomatic means.

It has often been said that the United States lost a golden opportunity to avoid a future conflict in Indochina when it failed to respond to Ho Chi Minh's overtures at the end of World War II. After all, as a pragmatist, Ho must have recognized that his country had more to gain in the postwar environment in terms of practical assistance from Washington than from Moscow. He was also a professed admirer of American civilization and had incorporated its ideals in the Vietnamese Declaration of Independence. By viewing Indochina in the context of growing ideological competition with Moscow, many critics contend, the Truman administration set the stage for the Vietnam War.

Although there is some plausibility to this argument, it may be partly a case of Americans having their own myths about Ho Chi Minh. In the first place, the evidence suggests that Ho's oft expressed admiration for the United States was more a matter of calculation than of ideological conviction. Ho lavished praises on American civilization, as he praised many of his country's allies and potential adversaries, primarily in order to gain tactical advantage. Although he always entertained the possibility that U.S. leaders might eventually recognize the futility of intervention in Indochina, he was also convinced that those same leaders were representatives of an exploitative capitalist system that at some point might enter into mortal conflict with the member states of the socialist community. Ho left little doubt as to his own allegiance in that potential confrontation.[13]

The question assumes that Ho Chi Minh had carte blanche to formulate strategy in Hanoi, much as Stalin dominated the scene in Moscow. In fact, many of Ho's colleagues did not share his confidence in the possibility of a nonviolent road to national liberation and might well have resisted what they viewed as his unprincipled compromises with the class enemy. As U.S. presidents have to consider domestic matters when they formulate their own foreign policy objectives, so Ho Chi Minh had to contend with his own constituency—notably his restless colleagues in the Politburo—many of whom, like Truong Chinh and Le Duan, did not share his credulous faith in the powers of reason.

There is good reason for skepticism, then, that a conciliatory gesture from the White House in 1945 or 1946 would have been sufficient to lure Ho Chi Minh and his colleagues onto the capitalist road. While U.S. recognition of the DRV would undoubtedly have been welcome in Hanoi, it would not have been enough to wean the Indochinese Communist Party from its primary allegiance to Moscow or its dedication to the doctrine of Marx and Lenin. As Hanoi in later years artfully played off Moscow against Beijing, so Ho and his colleagues would have attempted to manipulate Washington in the interests of achieving their own objectives. Some of those objectives, as we have seen, involved other countries. Southeast Asia at the end of the Pacific War went through a period of considerable political and social instability. Whether U.S. policy makers would have been willing to sit by while Hanoi sought to promote the budding revolutionary movements in neighboring Laos and Cambodia is highly doubtful.

Still, the failure of policy makers in Paris and Washington to grasp the hand offered to them by Ho Chi Minh after World War II had tragic consequences for the Vietnamese people, and for the world as a whole. While there were risks involved in granting legitimacy to the new government in Hanoi, it seems clear in retrospect that they were preferable to the alternative. While the political and moral superiority of Ho Chi Minh's ideological principles over those of his rivals is a legitimate matter for debate, it is hard to dispute the contention that in the conditions of the time, Vietminh leaders were the best prepared to deal with the multitude of problems afflicting their compatriots. The depth of popular support for the DRV, at least in the north, seems amply demonstrated by its ability to maintain that allegiance in a generation of struggle against the concerted efforts of France and later the United States.

Today, three decades after his death, the state cult of Ho Chi Minh is still in existence in Hanoi, where it serves primarily as a prop for a regime desperately seeking to maintain its relevance in changing times. For many Vietnamese (especially in the north, where reverence for Uncle Ho is still quite strong), the image still succeeds. It is less successful in the south, where the central government is often viewed suspiciously, its representatives deemed carpetbaggers from Hanoi. In any event, Ho's dying vision of a Party motivated by revolutionary purity and concern for the people lies today in tatters. Little has been done in recent years to curtail the endemic level of official corruption that threatens to swamp the revolution in a rising tide of popular anger and resentment.

Future prospects for maintaining the Ho cult are equally dim. There are clear signs that while most younger Vietnamese respect Ho Chi Minh for his contribution to the cause of national independence and reunification, many no longer see him as a figure of central importance in their lives. As one young Vietnamese remarked to me recently, "We respect Ho, but we are not interested in politics." To the new generation raised in the shadow of the next millennium, Ho Chi Minh probably has no more relevance than does Abraham Lincoln to the average American.

Even among those who see the value of the Ho Chi Minh cult, many view it as an opiate for the people. As one Vietnamese intellectual has remarked: All people at war must have their founding myths. And many feel today that the official view of Uncle Ho as the unsullied paragon of revolutionary virtue should be replaced by a more realistic image that portrays him as a fallible human being. In recent years, unconfirmed rumors about his past marriages and love affairs—and even his reputed illegitimate children—have circulated widely, despite vigorous denials of their accuracy from official sources. One recent Vietnamese film, for example, has speculated about a liaison that allegedly took place before his initial departure for Europe.[14]

On the world scene as well, the image of Ho Chi Minh as a seminal twentieth-century figure no longer has the emotive power that it possessed a generation ago, although the appearance of his portrait in a shop run by a Vietnamese émigré in California recently was sufficient to provoke anger among fellow Vietnamese-Americans. A generation ago, wars of national liberation were breaking out all over the Third World, and the United States seemed to be a civilization in decline. In those conditions, Ho Chi Minh appeared to be the voice of the future. With communism widely discredited and capitalism ascendant at the turn of the millennium, Ho's distinctive amalgam of patriotism and socialism appears almost quaint, like Mao Zedong's Cultural Revolution or the spiritual ideas of Mahatma Gandhi. Today, Ho Chi Minh is often viewed as a clever tactician of revolution and no more; his writings are dismissed as pedestrian in style and devoid of ideological content. His vision of a world revolution appears as distant in time as the Marxist vision of an angry proletariat beating at the door of its capitalist oppressors.

Such attitudes, however, fail to do justice to Ho Chi Minh's legitimate importance to our times. While his vision of a future world community of Communist societies was flawed (at least, so it appears from today's perspective), it still cannot be denied that the cause that he promoted and directed provided a defining moment of the twentieth century, representing both the culmination of an era of national liberation in the Third World and the first clear recognition of the limits of the U.S. policy of containment of communism. After Vietnam, the world would never be the same.

It is difficult to imagine the Vietnamese revolution without the active participation of Ho Chi Minh. Although the current historical fashion emphasizes the importance of great underlying social forces in unleashing the major events of our time, it remains clear that in many instances, such as the Bolshevik revolution and the Chinese Civil War, the role of the individual can sometimes be paramount. Such was the case in Vietnam. Not only was Ho the founder of his party and later the president of the country, but he was its chief strategist and its most inspiring symbol. A talented organizer as well as an astute strategist and a charismatic leader, Ho Chi Minh was half Lenin and half Gandhi. It was a dynamic combination. While the Vietnamese war of national liberation is an ineluctable fact that transcends the fate of individual human beings, without his presence it would have been a far different affair, with far different consequences.

For many observers, the tragedy of Ho Chi Minh is that such a wondrous talent for exercising the art of leadership should have been applied to the benefit of a flawed ideology—indeed, one that has now been abandoned even by many of its most sincere adherents around the world, although not yet in Ho's own country. Whether under different conditions the young Nguyen Tat Thanh might have decided to adopt the ideals and practices of contemporary Western civilization is a question that cannot be answered. Like many other Asian leaders of the day, his experience with capitalism was not a happy one, and the brutalities perpetrated by Western colonialism that he observed during his early years deeply offended his sensibilities. However, many of his philosophical beliefs appear to be more compatible with Western ideals than with those of Karl Marx and Vladimir Lenin. Although he sought to portray himself to colleagues as an orthodox Marxist, it seems clear that he had little interest in doctrinal matters and frequently made sincere efforts to soften communism's hard edges when applied in Vietnam. Nonetheless, as the founder of his party and the president of his country, Ho Chi Minh must bear full responsibility for the consequences of his actions, for good or ill. In the light of the conditions that prevail in Vietnam today, even many of his more ardent defenders must admit that his legacy is a mixed one.

Ho Chi Minh, then, was (in the American philosopher Sidney Hook's memorable phrases) an "event-making man," a "child of crisis" who combined in his own person two of the central forces in the history of modern Vietnam: the desire for national independence and the quest for social and economic justice. Because these forces transcended the borders of his own country, Ho was able to project his message to colonial peoples all over the world and speak to their demand for dignity and freedom from imperialist oppression. Whatever the final judgment on his legacy to his own people, he has taken his place in the pantheon of revolutionary heroes who have struggled mightily to give the pariahs of the world their true voice.[15]

A NOTE ON SOURCES

There are a number of bibliographic problems that afflict any prospective biographer of Ho Chi Minh. Not the least among them is the fact that Ho wrote two brief autobiographies, as well as numerous articles in newspapers and magazines, under assumed names. One of the autobiographies, *Vua di duong vua ke chuyen*, authored by T. Lan, has apparently never been translated into a foreign language. The other, *Nhung mau chuyen ve doi hoat dong cua Ho Chu tich*, by the fictitious historian Tran Dan Tien, was written by Ho in the late 1940s and has been translated into several foreign languages. An abridged English-language version, known as *Glimpses of the Life of Ho Chi Minh: President of the Democratic Republic of Vietnam*, was published in Hanoi by the Foreign Languages Press in 1958. A somewhat longer French-language translation appeared in *Souvenirs sur Ho Chi Minh* (Hanoi: Foreign Languages Press, 1967) under the title "Nguyen Ai Quoc," by Tran Dan Tien. A Chinese-language version, published in Shanghai by the August Publishing House in 1949 under the title *Hu Zhih-ming Zhuan* [A Biography of Ho Chi Minh], is apparently the most complete, but is difficult to obtain. Because the English- and French-language versions are the most readily available for the use of most readers, I have decided to cite them in the endnotes.

A second problem lies in the similarity in the titles of many Vietnamese-language books about Ho Chi Minh as well as about other aspects of the Vietnamese revolution. I have done my best to be precise when citing such sources, but readers interested in tracing them should take care to note the exact information contained in the endnotes. On other occasions, such as in the case of *Ho Chi Minh Toan tap*, editions I and II, the second editions often contain material not included in the first edition. Because the first edition of *Ho Chi Minh Toan tap* is probably more available in libraries in the United States, I have cited that version whenever possible.

A third issue concerns the use of the Vietnamese language. The written language, known as *quoc ngu* (national language), contains diacritical marks to indicate the proper tone to be adopted when pronouncing each individual word. Some recent books on various aspects of Vietnamese society use such marks for Vietnamese words incorporated in the text. I have decided not to do so in this biography, since they would undoubtedly represent an unnecessary distraction to readers not conversant in Vietnamese. Readers familiar with the Vietnamese language will, in any case, be acquainted with most of the Vietnamese words and phrases appearing in the text or the endnotes.

Finally, a word on the question of proper names might be appropriate. The Vietnamese people, like the Chinese, place their proper name first, while given names follow. In recent decades, however, it has become usual to refer to individuals by the last word appearing in their name. Ngo Dinh Diem, the one-time president of South Vietnam, was thus known as President Diem. Ho Chi Minh however, was known as President Ho, or Chairman Ho, perhaps because the name Ho Chi Minh was a pseudonym adopted from the Chinese language. Other individuals appearing in the text, such as Vo Nguyen Giap and Pham Van Dong, are usually referred to by their last name, as in Giap and Dong.

NOTES

The following abbreviations are used for frequently cited sources:

BNTS

Ho Chi Minh bien nien tieu su [A chronological history of Ho Chi Minh]. 10 vols. Hanoi: Thong tin Ly luan. 1992.

CAOM

Centre des Archives d'Outre-Mer, Aix-en-Provence, France.

CO

Colonial Office. Documents contained in the Public Record Office, London and Hong Kong.

Glimpses/Childhood

Nhung mau chuyen ve thoi nien thieu cua Bac Ho [Glimpses of the childhood of Uncle Ho]. Hanoi: Su that, 1985.

Glimpses/Life

Tran Dan Tien [Ho Chi Minh]. *Glimpses of the Life of Ho Chi Minh.* Hanoi: Foreign Languages Press, 1958. An abridged English-language translation of a Vietnamese publication entitled *Nhung mau chuyen ve doi hoat dong cua Ho Chu tich.*

HZYZ

Hoang Zheng. *Hu Zhiming yu Zhongguo* [Ho Chi Minh and China] Beijing: Jiefang Zhun, 1987.

JPRS

Joint Publications Research Service (Washington, D.C.)

Kobelev

Yevgeny Kobelev. *Ho Chi Minh.* Moscow: Progress Publishers, 1989.

NCLS

Nghien cuu Lich su [Historical Research] (Hanoi).

SLOTFOM

Service de Liaison avec les Originaires de Territoires de la France d'Outre-Mer.

Souvenirs

Souvenirs sur Ho Chi Minh. Hanoi: Foreign Languages Press, 1967. A collection of articles and memoirs by colleagues of Ho Chi Minh.

SPCE — Service de Protection du Corps Expéditionnaire. This archive is located at CAOM, Aix-en-Provence, France.

Toan Tap I — *Ho Chi Minh Toan tap* [The complete writings of Ho Chi Minh]. 1st ed. 10 vols. Hanoi: Su that, 1980-1989.

Toan Tap II — *Ho Chi Minh Toan tap* [The complete writings of Ho Chi Minh]. 2nd ed. 12 vols. Hanoi: Chinh tri Quoc gia, 1995-1996.

USNA — U.S. National Archives (College Park, Md.).

UPA — University Publications of America. These microfilms reproduce the central files of the Department of State, now held in USNA.

ZYG — Guo Ming, ed. *Zhong-Ywe guanxi yan bian ssu shi nien* [Forty years of Sino-Vietnamese relations]. Nanning: Guangxi Renmin, 1992.

Introduction

1. See Vo Nguyen Giap, "Tu tuong Ho Chi Minh qua trinh hinh thanh va noi dung co ban" [The process of formation and inner content of Ho Chi Minh Thought], in *Nghien cuu tu tuong Ho Chi Minh* [Studying Ho Chi Minh Thought] (Hanoi: Ho Chi Minh Institute, 1993), p. 17. Some critics of the current regime contend that the quotation is not complete and originally contained the additional phrase "and without freedom there is no independence."

2. Some estimates of his pseudonyms exceed seventy-five. For two efforts to amass the names used by Ho Chi Minh over his lifetime, see A. A. Sokolov, "Psevdonimyi Ho Shi Mina kak opyt izucheniya politicheskoi biografii" [The pseudonyms of Ho Chi Minh as an experience in the study of political biography], in *Traditsionnyi V'ietnam: Sbornik Statei* [Traditional Vietnam: A collection of articles], vol. 2 (Moscow: Vietnamese Center, 1993), pp. 187–218; and "His Many Names and Travels," in *Vietnam Courier* (May 1981).

3. The most widely known of his autobiographies was published in Vietnamese under the title *Nhung mau chuyen ve doi hoat dong cua Ho Chu tich*, authored by the fictitious Tran Dan Tien, one of Ho Chi Minh's many pseudonyms. An abbreviated English-language version, *Glimpses of the Life of Ho Chi Minh*, appeared several years later. The earliest and most complete version of this autobiography, entitled *Hu Zhi Ming Zhuan* [A biography of Ho Chi Minh], was published in Chinese by the Ba Ywe publishing house in Shanghai in 1949. Curiously, this Chinese version, unlike later translations into other languages, identified the name Ho Chi Minh as the pseudonym of the onetime Comintern agent Nguyen Ai Quoc—see p. 4. Ho's other autobiographical work, which has not been translated into Western languages, is T. Lan, *Vua di duong, vua ke chuyen* [Walking and talking] (Hanoi: Su That, 1976).

4. The most complete collection of his writings is *Toan Tap I*. *Toan Tap II*, just published, is also an excellent source.

5. The best known biography of Ho Chi Minh in English is Jean Lacouture's *Ho*

Chi Minh: A Political Biography (New York: Vintage, 1968). Originally published in France, it was translated by Peter Wiles. Also see Nguyen Khac Huyen, *Vision Accomplished?* (New York: Collier, 1971), and David Halberstam's short *Ho* (New York: Random House, 1971).

6. Bernard B. Fall, "A Talk with Ho Chi Minh," in Bernard B. Fall, ed., *Ho Chi Minh on Revolution: Selected Writings, 1920–1966* (New York: Praeger, 1967), p. 321.

I | *In a Lost Land*

1. Cited in Truong Buu Lam, *Vietnamese Resistance Against the French, 1858–1900* (New Haven: Yale University Press, 1967), pp. 127–28.

2. Information on Nguyen Sinh Sac is relatively scarce. I have relied here on my interview with staff members of the branch office of the Ho Chi Minh Museum in Kim Lien village and two recent studies published by the Research Institute of Nghe Tinh province in Vietnam, *Glimpses/Childhood* and *Bac Ho thoi nien thieu* [The childhood of Uncle Ho] (Hanoi: Su that, 1989). According to Trinh Quang Phu, *Tu Lang Sen den ben Nha Rong* [From Lang Sen to the Nha Rong pier] (Ho Chi Minh City: Van Hoc, 1998), the family traced its heritage in the area back to a certain Nguyen Ba Pho, who arrived in Kim Lien in the sixteenth century (p. 13).

3. Ho Chi Minh's date of birth has often inspired controversy. As an adult, he claimed a number of different birthdates, probably to confuse the authorities. For example, in one autobiographical statement written in Moscow, he claimed that he was born in 1903; in another, he gave the date 1894. Official sources in Hanoi now assert that he was born in 1890, and although some researchers are skeptical, evidence relating to his childhood, such as his long trek to the imperial city of Hué with his family in 1895 and other childhood activities, makes the date seem plausible. See *BNTS*, vol. 1, p. 17.

There has also been skepticism over the actual day of his birth. Some maintain that it was selected to coincide with the formation of the Vietminh Front in 1941, or to provide a pretext for a national celebration on the arrival of a French delegation in Hanoi in the spring of 1946. See Huynh Kim Khanh, *Vietnamese Communism, 1925–1945* (Ithaca, N.Y.: Cornell University Press, 1982), p. 58, and interview with Vu Thu Hien, *Politique Internationale* (fall 1997). Given the fact that, at the time of his birth, rural Vietnamese normally employed the lunar calendar, it is not unlikely that Ho Chi Minh was never certain of the exact date of his birth.

4. For one personal account of the incident, see Son Tung, "An Episode of Uncle Ho's Childhood in Hué," *Vietnam Courier* (April 1976), pp. 25–29. Also see Trinh Quang Phu, *Tu Lang Sen*, pp. 39–40. According to Phu, neighbors admonished young Cung not to weep in public after his mother's death on the grounds that public displays of grief were not permitted in the vicinity of the imperial city.

This narrative of Ho Chi Minh's childhood is based on several sources, including *Glimpses/Childhood*; *Bac Ho thoi nien thieu* (Hanoi: Su that, n.d.); Duc Vuong, *Qua trinh hinh thanh tu tuong yeu nuoc cua Ho Chi Minh* [The process of formation of Ho Chi Minh's patriotic thought] (Hanoi: Chinh tri Quoc gia, 1993); Nguyen Dac Xuan, *Bac Ho thoi thanh nien o Hué* [Uncle Ho's youth in Hué] (Ho Chi Minh City: Tre, 1999); and *Di tich Kim Lien que huong Bac Ho* [Traces of the Ho Chi Minh's home village of Kim Lien]

(Nghe Tinh: n.p., 1985); as well as interviews with personnel at the Ho Chi Minh Museum branch in Kim Lien village.

5. According to local tradition, at one point he joked to a visitor, in wordplay on the names of his two sons, that their names were "*khong com*" or "no rice"—see *Glimpses/ Childhood*, p. 29. Also see *Di tich Kim Lien*, pp. 36–40. Sac's pessimism about the current political situation had apparently affected his answers in the metropolitan examination, and it was only at the intervention of an influential friend at court that he was awarded his degree—see Nguyen Dac Xuan, *Bac Ho thoi*, pp. 46–47.

6. Quoted in *Nash Prezident Ho Shi Minh* [Our president Ho Chi Minh] (Hanoi: Foreign Languages Press, 1967), p. 26. For a similar comment, see Trinh Quang Phu, *Tu Lang Sen*, pp. 21, 36.

7. Nguyen Dac Xuan, *Bac Ho thoi*, pp. 34–35.

8. Once, while under the influence of a cup of Nguyen Sinh Sac's rice wine, Phan Boi Chau remarked that he had never liked to study the old classical texts and recited a poem he recalled from his youth that ridiculed the classical writings as worthless. When they met twenty years later in south China, Nguyen Tat Thanh was still able to recite the verse to his older compatriot. See *Glimpses/Childhood*, p. 35, citing Phan Boi Chau, *Phan Boi Chau nien bieu* [A chronological autobiography of Phan Boi Chau] (Hanoi: Van su dia, 1955), p. 55. Also see Trinh Quang Phu, *Tu Lang Sen*, pp. 22–23, and Nguyen Dac Xuan, *Bac Ho thoi*, pp. 51–52.

9. Information on Phan Boi Chau's revolutionary career can be found in his two autobiographies, *Phan Boi Chau nien bieu* and *Nguc trung thu* [A letter from prison] (Saigon: n.p., n.d.). For analysis, see David G. Marr, *Vietnamese Anticolonialism, 1885– 1925* (Berkeley, Calif.: University of California Press, 1971); William J. Duiker, *The Rise of Nationalism in Vietnam, 1900–1941* (Ithaca, N.Y.: Cornell University Press, 1976); and Vinh Sinh, ed., *Phan Boi Chau and the Dong Du Movement* (New Haven: Yale Center for International and Area Studies, 1988).

10. For the first version, see Truong Chinh, *President Ho Chi Minh: Beloved Leader of the Vietnamese People* (Hanoi: Foreign Languages Publishing House, 1966), pp. 10–11. For the second, see Nguyen Dac Xuan, *Bac Ho thoi*, p. 51. According to Xuan, the meeting with Phan Boi Chau took place on a ferryboat. The Russian scholar Yevgeny Kobelev says Thanh used the need to seek his father's permission as an excuse to refuse the offer—see Kobelev, p. 18. According to Hong Ha, *Thoi thanh nien cua Bac Ho* [The Childhood of Uncle Ho] (Hanoi: Thanh nien?, 1994), Chau sent a friend to Kim Lien and did not meet with Thanh himself; see p. 11. Also see *Avec l'Oncle Ho* (Hanoi: Foreign Languages Publishing House, 1972), pp. 15–16, the first chapter of which is a lengthy passage from the early sections of *Glimpses/Childhood*.

11. *Bac Ho thoi nien thieu*, p. 53; BNTS, vol. 1, p. 35; *Glimpses/Childhood*, p. 51.

12. Nguyen Dac Xuan, "Thoi nien cua Bac o Hué" [Uncle's childhood in Hué], in *NCLS*, no. 186 (May-June 1979). Also see Trinh Quang Phu, *Tu Lang Sen*, p. 45. The apartment was on Mai Thuc Loan Street, not far from their last residence in Hué.

13. At that time, the imperial civil service was divided into nine ranks, with two grades within each rank. Nguyen Sinh Sac was given an appointment at rank seven, grade two. BNTS, vol. 1, p. 35, fn 11. According to Nguyen Dac Xuan, in *Bac Ho thoi*, pp. 54–55, it was Cao Xuan Duc who persuaded Sac to accept a post at the Board of Rites as the only way his friend could remain in Hué and provide an education for his children. At Sac's age, Duc said, if one did not accept a post at court, the only recourse

was to become a rebel. Sac agreed to accept an assignment, but only in a menial position, so he would not be serving a corrupt system.

14. The original French version is printed in the *Bulletin de l'Ecole Française d'Extrême Orient* (March–June 1907), pp. 166–75. For a discussion, see The Nguyen, *Phan Chu Trinh* (Saigon: n.p., 1956).

15. *Bac Ho thoi nien thieu*, p. 60. In letter to a nephew in his home village, Sac wrote an enigmatic poem: "The life of a man is like a dream,/life is like a cloud;/skill can be dangerous./Be aware! Be aware!"—*Glimpses/Childhood*, p. 58.

16. *Glimpses/Childhood*, p. 61; Nguyen Dac Xuan, *Bac Ho thoi*, pp. 57–58.

17. Hong Ha, *Thoi thanh nien*, p. 11. Tormentors called young Thanh a "fish and wood man," akin to a hillbilly—see Nguyen Dac Xuan, *Bac Ho thoi*, p. 64. According to Xuan (pp. 66–67), when he was scolded by the school superintendent, Thanh replied that he was only voicing complaints that had already been raised by Phan Chu Trinh and other reformers. The superintendent replied that they too had been punished, and asked why Thanh was unhappy with a system that had provided him with a grant to study at the school. In the end, he warned Thanh's instructors that if they could not control his behavior, the police would be called in and they themselves would be dismissed. There is some documentary confirmation of this incident: a French police report dated February 23, 1920, reported that Thanh and his brother showed an attitude of "clear resistance" to authority, prompting school officials to discipline them severely. A copy of the document is located at the Ho Chi Minh Museum in Ho Chi Minh City.

18. Hong Ho, *Thoi thanh nien,* p. 68.

19. "Thoi nien cua Bac o Hué," p. 80; *Glimpses/Childhood*, p. 70; *Bac Ho thoi nien thieu,* 74. Some Vietnamese historians have sought to link Nguyen Tat Thanh directly with the protest movement—see Nguyen Dac Xuan, *Bac Ho thoi*, p. 65. According to Nguyen Dac Xuan, (pp. 72–73), Thanh was quite liberal in his translation of the representative's remarks, and his comments to Levecque may have inflamed the situation. When Levecque argued that agricultural taxes could not be reduced, since they must be used to pay for flood control efforts undertaken earlier in the year, Thanh replied that those efforts had only exacerbated the situation, since the levies that had been constructed had only retained the flood waters in the rice fields, thus damaging the harvest even further. Why, he asked further, did the French build a bridge over the Perfume River that brought little benefit to the peasants. Levecque retorted angrily that violence was not the way to resolve the situation. Xuan's version of the conversation seems highly speculative, but plausible. After the events of May 9, Hoang Thong was arrested, and police found a few patriotic statements among his writings, but he claimed that he was drunk at the time and couldn't remember writing the material in question, so he was given 100 strokes of the cane and released. His students were outraged at his treatment by the authorities. "Thoi nien cua Bac," p. 81; Nguyen Dac Xuan, *Bac Ho thoi*, p. 68.

20. A French intelligence report written in December 1920 recounted that Sac had recently told a friend that his son had once visited him at Binh Khe, but that he had sent him away after giving him a beating. According to Sac, he no longer wished to have any contact with his children. See Note, December 27, 1920, in SPCE, Carton 364, CAOM. For another reference to the beating, see Nguyen Khac Huyen, *Vision Accomplished?* (New York: Collier, 1971), p. 9. Sac's comment that he no longer had any desire to see his son seems unlikely, in light of other evidence to be cited later. Perhaps the remark was made in a fit of pique. Still, there is additional support for the contention that he was sometimes abusive to his children. French police sources reported

in 1920 that Sac's daughter had declared under interrogation that she had left Hué for her home village in 1906 because she could no longer tolerate the brutality of her father, who beat her frequently—see Daniel Hémery, *Ho Chi Minh: De l'Indochine au Vietnam* (Paris: Gallimard, 1990), pp. 132–33.

21. *Bac Ho thoi nien thieu*, pp. 85–86. Pham Ngoc Tho was the father of Pham Ngoc Thach, who would later became a prominent member of the Indochinese Communist Party and a close associate of Ho Chi Minh. Thach later recalled family remarks that Thanh had arrived in Qui Nhon shortly after he was born. According to Ho Chi Minh's longtime colleague Ha Huy Giap, Ho once told the American journalist Anna Louise Strong that he wandered along the coast in an effort to find a port from which to sail to Europe—see Trinh Quang Phu, *Tu Lang Sen*, p. 51.

22. The principal of the school was Nguyen Gui Anh, a teacher from Nghe An province. The sponsor was the Lien Than Thuong Quan, a manufacturer of *nuoc mam*, the famous Vietnamese fermented fish sauce. See *Bac Ho thoi nien thieu*, pp. 90–91, and Nguyen Dinh Soan, "Uncle Ho's Former Student," *To Quoc* , no. 5 (May 1970), translated in *Vietnam Documents and Research Notes* (U.S. Mission in Vietnam, Saigon), document 100, pp. 28–32. Trinh Quang Phu discusses the origins of the school in *Tu Lang Sen*, pp. 53–55.

23. Cited in Kobelev, p. 23. For additional information, see Nguyen Dinh Soan, "Uncle Ho's Former Student."

24. Ho Chi Minh, *Hu Zhi Ming zhuan* [A biography of Ho Chi Minh] (Shanghai: Ba Ywe, 1949), p. 10; *Bac Ho thoi nien thieu*, p. 86; Ton Quang Duyet, "From the Nha Rong pier to Pac Bo Cave," *Tap chi Cong san* (February 1980); *BNTS*, vol. 1, p. 44; Kobelev, p. 23.

25. For Sac's request to travel to Cochin China, see dossier labeled "1920," in SPCE, Carton 364, COAM. Also see *Bac Ho thoi nien thieu*, pp. 82–85; *Glimpses/Childhood*, p. 97. The French intelligence report is Document no. 3780, dated March 8, 1911, in the Ho Chi Minh Museum.

26. According to the *résident supérieur* of Annam, Sac had bypassed French authorities to obtain from a local mandarin permission to travel to Tourane.

27. *BNTS*, vol. 1, p. 43; Trinh Quang Phu, *Tu Lang Sen*, pp. 79–82. That Thanh feared that French authorities were aware of his presence at the Duc Thanh school is suggested by a letter he wrote to a friend there after his departure for Europe in June 1911. In the letter he declared that he could not tell his friend when he had left the country, since it must be kept a secret. See Ton Quang Duyet, "From the Nha Rong pier," p. 33. According to a French report, Thanh left the school in anger after being chastised for a minor infraction. See Annex 475, February 4, 1928, Sûreté Générale, Saigon, in SPCE, Carton 368, CAOM.

28. *Avec l'Oncle Ho*, pp. 15–16. The Chasseloup-Laubat school was a prestigious lycée established by the French for children of the elite.

29. For information on his stay in Saigon, see Ton Quang Duyet, "From the Nha Rong pier . . ."; *Bac Ho thoi nien thieu*, p. 95; *BNTS*, vol. 1, p. 44; and Kobelev, p. 24. The latter says he gave his name as Van Ba, or "Van the third." Presumably Thanh was identifying himself as the third oldest child in his family. Van is a familiar name for males in Vietnam, meaning "literature." The French captain's skepticism is understandable. According to contemporary accounts, Thanh may have weighed less than 100 pounds.

30. Both comments are quoted in *BNTS*, vol. 1, pp. 47–48. According to the

historian Trinh Quang Phu (see *Tu Lang Sen*, pp. 82, 97–98), Nguyen Sinh Sac played an important role in encouraging his son's desire to go abroad to serve his country, but Phu's tendency to dramatize events during this period in Ho Chi Minh's life and to fabricate conversations raises questions about his credibility. I have therefore treated his evidence with extreme caution.

II | *The Fiery Stallion*

1. *Glimpses/Life*, p. 6. In this source, Ho claimed that the ship held 700 to 800 passengers and crew, which seems very unlikely for such a small vessel. In fact, it held 40 first-class passengers and 72 officers and seamen.

2. Report of Paul Arnoux September 21, 1922, in SPCE, Carton 365, CAOM. Also see Daniel Hémery, *Ho Chi Minh: De l'Indochine au Vietnam* (Paris: Gallimard, 1990), p. 37.

3. *Glimpses/Life*, p. 8.

4. See Hémery, *Ho Chi Minh*, p. 40, for a copy of the letter to the president. He apparently sent an identical message to the minister of colonies in Paris. See Nguyen The Anh and Vu Ngu Chieu, "Tu mong lam quan den duong cach menh, Ho Chi Minh va Truong Thuoc dia" [From mandarinal dream to road to revolution, Ho Chi Minh and the Colonial School], *Duong Moi*, no. 1 (June 1983), p. 14. A copy of the letter is also available in the Ho Chi Minh Museum in Hanoi. For a critical interpretation of Thanh's motives, see ibid. For a more favorable one, see the article by Daniel Hémery titled "La bureaucratie comme processus historique," in Georges Boudarel, ed., *La bureaucratie au Vietnam* (Paris: L'Harmattan, 1983), pp. 26–30, and Thu Trang Gaspard, *Ho Chi Minh à Paris* (Paris: L'Harmattan, 1992), pp. 55–56. It is also possible that he hoped to gain entry into the school to help his father regain his position in the bureaucracy. It is worthy of note that he specifically mentioned his father in the letter. Thanh's letter to his sister is mentioned in Police de l'Indochine, Note Confidentielle no. 711, May 7, 1920, in dossier labeled "1920," in SPCE, Carton 364, CAOM.

5. Thanh evidently left Saigon shortly after writing the letter, for he gave a return address of *Amiral Latouche-Tréville*, Colombo. The letter is included in Note Confidentielle, April 28, 1920, SPCE, Carton 364, CAOM. Also see *Glimpses/Childhood*, p. 97. On his father, see "Père de Ho Chi Minh," undated note, in dossier labeled "Ho-Chi-Minh année 1949," in SPCE, Carton 370, CAOM. According to one recent source, Sac had now begun to establish contact with patriotic elements in Cochin China, partly out of a desire to obtain news of his son. See Trinh Quong Phu, *Tu Lang Sen den Nha Rong* [From Lang Sen to the Nha Rong pier] (Ho Chi Minh City: NXB Van Hoc, 1998), pp. 98–99.

6. Many years later, Ho Chi Minh told a French acquaintance that he had first visited Paris at the age of twenty. See Thu Trang, *Nguyen Ai Quoc tai Pari (1917–1923)* [Nguyen Ai Quoc in Paris] (Hanoi: Thong tin ly luan, 1989), p. 20. With regard to his application to the Colonial School, under interrogation by a French official many years later, Thanh's older brother (then known as Nguyen Tat Dat) recalled that his brother had written him that any application for entry into the school had to be countersigned by the authorities in Indochina. Dat thereupon wrote a letter to Governor-General Albert Sarraut on Thanh's behalf, but apparently without result. Dat was himself under suspicion for taking part in rebel activities; see Note Confidentielle, April

28, 1920, SPCE, Carton 364, CAOM. For the rejection letter from the Ministry of Colonies, also see Nguyen The Anh and Vu Ngu Chien, "Tu mong", p. 15. On his stay in Le Havre, see Nguyen Thanh, *Chu tich Ho Chi Minh o Phap* [Chairman Ho Chi Minh in France] (Hanoi: Thong tin ly luan, 1988), p. 23, and Hong Ha, *Thoi Thanh Nien* [The Childhood of Uncle Ho] (Hanoi: Thanh nien, 1994), p. 28. He himself recounted his experiences in Le Havre in *Glimpses/Life*, pp. 7–8. Also see Tran Ngoc Danh, *Tieu su Ho Chu tich* [A short biography of Chairman Ho] (Lien Viet, 1949), in SPCE, Carton 370, CAOM. According to the author, a member of the Indochinese Communist Party who knew him in France, Thanh lived in Sainte-Adresse for about six months. Several sources state that he left the ship in Le Havre after his first arrival in Marseilles in 1911. This seems very unlikely, since it is clear that he remained on the ship and returned to Saigon at that time. It is more likely that his stayover in Le Havre came during his second visit to France the following year. Also see *BNTS*, vol. 1, p. 52.

7. *Glimpses/Life*, pp. 8–9; A biography of Ho Chi Minh (Shanghai: Ba Ywe, 1949). According to both sources, the ship was carrying wine from Algeria and Bordeaux to the French colonies. Many of the seamen were able to attach rubber hoses to the barrels and drink to their heart's content. Thanh apparently did not imbibe and advised his colleagues (presumably with little success) to abstain as well.

8. Information in this paragraph comes from a variety of sources, including Charles Fenn, *Ho Chi Minh. A Biographical Introduction* (New York: Scribner's, 1973); Tran Thanh, ed., "Bien nien Chu tich Ho Chi Minh voi nuoc My" [A chronicle of Chairman Ho Chi Minh's relations with the United States] (Hanoi: 1994, mimeographed); an article by David Dellinger (title unknown) in *Libération* (October 1969); an excerpt from Anna Louise Strong, *Letter from China* (reported in *Nhan Dan*, May 18, 1965); and an oral interview of Robert F. Williams by Archimedes L. Patti, contained in the Patti archives at the University of Central Florida in Orlando. Williams was a member of the peace delegation that visited Hanoi in November and December 1964. In remarks to Williams at that time, Ho recommended that "black Americans become more serious about the liberation of their race." In Ho's view, blacks in the United States had become seduced by material possessions and avoided personal sacrifice.

9. Thanh's letter to Annam dated December 15, 1912, contained a moving appeal to the *résident supérieur* to provide Nguyen Sinh Sac with meaningful employment, or at least to send Sac's address so that his son could provide him with material support. The letter is contained in SPCE, Carton 367, CAOM. Henry Prunier, who served in Indochina with the OSS at the end of World War II, recalls that Ho Chi Minh told him briefly about his experiences in Boston. See Raymond P. Girard, "City Man Helped to Train Guerrillas of Ho Chi Minh," *Worcester (Mass.) Gazette* (May 14, 1968). Recent inquiries to the management of the Omni Parker House Hotel have turned up no concrete information on Ho's alleged employment there. There is also no information in the records of the U.S. Immigration and Naturalization Service on Ho Chi Minh's presence in the United States. I am grateful to A. Thomas Grunfeld, who researched this issue in connection with a Ford Foundation project on "Ho Chi Minh in America" in 1993, for providing me with this information. See Grunfeld, "On Ho Chi Minh's Trail," untitled report dated May 1, 1994.

10. For a French-language version of the letters, see Gaspard, *Ho Chi Minh à Paris*, pp. 57–60. Also see Alain Ruscio, ed., *Ho Chi Minh: Textes, 1914–1969* (Paris: L'Harmattan, n.d.), p. 21. For a Vietnamese version of both letters, see *Toan Tap*, vol. 1, pp. 477–78. Another indication that Thanh left the United States in 1913 is the

fact that his letter to the *résident supérieur* from New York City in December 1912 gave the address 1 Rue Amiral Courbet in Le Havre as *poste restante,* suggesting an imminent return to France. Under interrogation many years later, his sister mentioned that in 1915 she received a letter from a Vietnamese court official stating that his son had gone to London with Thanh. She could not remember the name of the official, nor her brother's address in London: Police de l'Indochine, Note Confidentielle no. 711, May 7, 1920, in SPCE, Carton 364, CAOM.

11. *Glimpses/Life,* pp. 10–12. Escoffier did not mention the incident in his memoirs. Ho Chi Minh may have suffered some physical damage from his experience as a laborer in London. Many years later, a member of the French Socialist Party recalled that when he first met Ho in Paris after World War I, his hands were disfigured because of their exposure to the cold. See Gaspard, *Ho Chi Minh à Paris,* p. 72.

12. *Avec l'Oncle Ho,* pp. 26–27; Grunfeld report, "On Ho Chi Minh's Trail," pp. 16, 21; Hémery, *Ho Chi Minh,* p. 41; Gaspard, *Ho Chi Minh à Paris,* p. 73. The latter cites a remark by one of Ho's later acquaintances in France that he had been involved in a labor disturbance on board the French ship *La Tamise.* A search of labor union records in Great Britain provides no information on any organization called the Overseas Workers' Association. Vietnamese sources cite unconfirmed reports that Thanh may have visited Scotland and the city of Liverpool. Many years later, Ho Chi Minh remarked to young colleagues that it took him six months to learn the English language in Great Britain—see Mai Van Bo, *Chung toi Hoc Lam Ngoai giao voi Bac Ho* [I studied diplomacy with Uncle Ho] (Ho Chi Minh City: Tre, 1998), p. 15.

13. *Toan Tap I,* vol. 1, p. 479.

14. The reports from London are contained in the Public Record Office, Foreign Office records (FO) in London. For the original inquiry, see FO 83562, June 23, 1915 and June 24, 1915. The results of the surveillance are contained in FO 372/668, September 8, 1915. For the reference to Thanh's promise to carry out Trinh's work, see "Nguyen A. Quoc den Pa-ri nam nao" [When did Nguyen A. Quoc arrive in Paris], unidentified news report, Patti archive. A number of researchers have apparently concluded that one of the two men under surveillance was Nguyen Tat Thanh, noting that Tat Thanh had been apprenticed to the Igranic Electric Co. in Bedford and was on friendly terms with the daughter of his landlord. Despite the coincidence in names, however, there is nothing specific to link the Tat Thanh under surveillance with Ho Chi Minh. For example, see Hémery, *Ho Chi Minh,* p. 41.

15. Even his harshest critics concede that he probably visited England at one time or another, although some maintain that he may have made only short visits while at sea—see Nguyen The Anh, "La prolétarisation de Ho Chi Minh: Mythe ou réalité," *Duong Moi* (July 1984); and Huy Phong and Yen Anh, *Nhan dien Ho Chi Minh: thuc chat gian manh cua huyen thoai anh hung* [partly translated into English as *Exploding the Ho Myth*] (San José, Calif.: Van Nghe, 1988), pp. 18–19. His sister, who had been arrested in 1918 on the charge of smuggling weapons and sentenced to nine years of hard labor, recounted under interrogation in 1920 that she had received a letter indicating that he had gone to Great Britain sometime before the war and settled in London—see Note Confidentielle no. 711, May 7, 1920, in Police de l'Indochine, Dossier labeled "1920," in SPCE, Carton 364, CAOM. That same year, French authorities reported that sometime in 1917 he had sent a letter to Governor-General Sarraut through the British consul in Saigon asking for a message to be sent to his father. The Sûreté were unable to locate him. The fact that he wrote through the British consul suggests that he might

have sent the message from Great Britain. See Note, December 27, 1920, in GGI, Feuillet no. 116, S.G. Minute 1, in ibid. I am grateful to researcher Bob O'Hara for making exhaustive researches into the Public Record Office in an effort to locate materials related to Ho's life in Great Britain.

16. Note Confidentielle no. 1967, May 29, 1931, in SPCE, Carton 365, CAOM; *Avec l'Oncle Ho*, pp. 31–32; Gaspard, *Ho Chi Minh à Paris*, pp. 61–63; *BNTS*, vol. 1, p. 59; *Toan Tap, I*, vol. 1, p. 545; Hémery, *Ho Chi Minh* p. 42. Christiane Pasquel Rageau, author of *Ho Chi Minh* (Paris: Editions Universitaires, 1970), declares (p. 30) that she has located an advertisement in a French newspaper placed by a photo retoucher by the name of Nguyen Ai Quoc—Thanh's pseudonym in Paris—sometime in 1918.

17. Rageau, *Ho Chi Minh*, p. 27, speculates that he may have decided to return to France after an abortive mutiny broke out in the French army in 1917. Also consult Dennis Duncanson, "The Legacy of Ho Chi Minh," *Asian Affairs* 23, part 1 (February 1992). There is a brief and enigmatic reference in the French archives to someone who remembered meeting him in a hospital for wounded soldiers in Limoges where both were undergoing treatment and taking a course in dictation. See Note of Secretary General A. S. de Drujon, in SPCE, Carton 364, CAOM. Also see "Man Behind a War: Ho Chi Minh," in *Esquire*, 1967, which alleges that at the end of World War I he traveled through France visiting barracks and housing developments for Vietnamese workers.

18. Boris Souvarine, "De Nguyen Ai Quac en Ho Chi Minh," *Est et Ouest* (Paris), March 1–15, 1976, pp. 567–568. Souvarine, who first joined and later left the Communist movement, eventually became one of Ho Chi Minh's most bitter critics.

19. Karnow describes his interview with Léo Poldès in *Paris in the Fifties* (New York: Random House, 1997), pp. 216–17. He also mentions Thanh's interest in mysticism and other topics, noting on one occasion that he challenged the psychologist Emile Coue, "whose formula for self-perfection lay in repeating the mantra, 'Every day in every way I am getting better and better.' " See Hong Ha, *Thoi thanh nien*, p. 78, and Karnow, p. 217. Apparently Thanh also wrote for a movie magazine and made an application to join the Freemasons.

20. Gaspard, *Ho Chi Minh à Paris*, p. 76. It is difficult to trace his movements during the early stages of his return to France. According to various reports he lived in a residence on the Rue de Charonne, near the Place de la Bastille, and later shared a flat with a Tunisian, but soon moved out because the latter was under surveillance. So far as I can determine, his first verifiable address was at a hotel for transients (now known as the President Wilson Hotel) at 10 Rue de Stockholm sometime in early June 1919. Its location adjacent to the Gare St. Lazare suggests that he may have just arrived from a trip out of the city. See *BNTS*, vol. 1, p. 65, citing an unnamed French police report. For other sources, see Nguyen Thanh, *Chu tich Ho Chi Minh*, p. 34; *Toan Tap I*, vol. 1, p. 545; and Gaspard, *Ho Chi Minh à Paris*, pp. 71–73.

21. The French authorities originally felt that Phan Van Truong was the mastermind behind the Association of Annamite Patriots, with Nguyen Tat Thanh as his tool, but eventually began to focus the bulk of their attention on the latter. See Ministre des Colonies à Gouvernement générale, no. 1735, December 5, 1919, in SPCE, Carton 364, CAOM. The Vietnamese title for the organization was the Hoi nhung nguoi Viet Nam yeu nuoc.

22. Gaspard, *Ho Chi Minh à Paris*, pp. 64–65; *Avec l'Oncle Ho*, p. 33; Hémery, *Ho Chi Minh*, p. 44. The building on rue Monsieur-le-Prince is today the fashionable Hotel

Le Clos Médicis. The management has no record of his residence there, although it confirms that the building was a hotel at that time. Perhaps it served as temporary lodgings for students at the Sorbonne. In the petition, Thanh used the spelling "Quac," but soon changed it to the more common usage "Quoc."

23. Kobelev, p. 31, tells the story of Thanh ringing the doorbell at the home of Jules Cambon, a member of the French delegation at Versailles. Also see Hong Ha, *Thoi thanh nien*, pp. 70–71. The latter source contends that Phan Chu Trinh and Phan Van Truong had just returned from a trip to Germany when the petition was delivered and were angry with Thanh for promoting his radical views. For the charge that Thanh was not the original Nguyen Ai Quoc, see, among others, Huy Phong and Yen Anh, *Nhan dien Ho Chi Minh*, p. 22. One fact that suggests that Thanh was indeed the author is that advertisements had appeared in local French newspapers such as *La Vie Ouvrière* since 1918 publicizing the work of a certain photo retoucher by the name of Nguyen Ai Quoc (see note 16, above); I have not seen a copy of this ad.

24. Vietnamese-language versions of both letters are in *BNTS*, vol. 1, p. 67. Also see Hong Ha, *Thoi thanh nien*, pp. 65–68.

25. Jean Lacouture, *Ho Chi Minh: A Political Biography*, trans. Peter Wiles (New York: Vintage, 1968), p. 23. The sequence of events whereby French authorities were able to identify him conclusively as Nguyen Tat Thanh is not clear from available documents in the French archives. Police reports were vague and sometimes contradictory—for example, on the date of his arrival in France—and reports periodically surfaced that he had spent the latter part of the war in France. The Sûreté still could not confirm his activities in Great Britain during the war. See GGI [Governor-general of Indochine] à Minister of Colonies, October 20, 1919, in SPCE, Carton 364, CAOM. For communications between Paris and the office of the governor-general in French Indochina seeking the identity of the author, see the relevant cables in SPCE, Carton 364, CAOM.

26. Cited in Gaspard, *Ho Chi Minh à Paris*, pp. 68–69. According to one agent—code-named "Edouard"—who was well acquainted with him, Nguyen Ai Quoc generally approved of Albert Sarraut. See Note Confidentielle, December 20, 1919, in SPCE, Carton 364, CAOM. For the comment about Woodrow Wilson, see his March 5, 1930, report to the Comintern contained in *Van kien dang toan tap* [Complete Party Documents], vol. 2, *1930* (Hanoi: Chinh tri quoc gia, 1998), p. 31.

27. Nguyen Ai Quoc to Albert Sarraut, governor-general of Indochina, September 7, 1919, in SPCE, Carton 364, CAOM.

28. Several researchers have attempted to determine the precise date of his entrance into the FSP. According to Gaspard, *Ho Chi Minh à Paris*, p. 73, and Nguyen Thanh, *Chu tich Ho Chi Minh*, p. 43, there were no Vietnamese in the party in 1918. The latter declares that eighty Vietnamese joined the following year. Kobelev, p. 31, claims he joined the FSP in 1918. The quote at the beginning of the paragraph is from Ho Chi Minh, "The Path Which Led Me to Leninism," an article originally written in April 1960 for the Soviet journal *Problemyi Vostoka*, reproduced in Bernard B. Fall, ed., *Ho Chi Minh on Revolution: Selected Writings, 1920–1966* (New York: Praeger, 1967), pp. 23–25.

29. I have discussed this issue at greater length in *The Communist Road to Power in Vietnam*, 2d ed. (Boulder, Colo.: Westview Press, 1996), pp. 26–29. Also see the interesting treatment of the question in Nguyen Khac Vien, ed., *Tradition and Revolution in Vietnam* (Berkeley, Calif., and Washington, D.C.: n.p., 1974), pp. 15–74.

30. Kobelev, p. 44. The quotation is from Fall, *On Revolution*, p. 24. For the earlier remark to Jacques Duclos, see Hong Ha, *Thoi thanh nien*, p. 84. For his early support

for Bolshevism, see "Renseignements divers" in SPCE, Carton 365, CAOM. For comments on his ideological naïveté, see Gaspard, *Ho Chi Minh à Paris*, pp. 113–15, and Nguyen Thanh, *Chu tich Ho Chi Minh*, p. 52.

31. The article was reprinted in *Tap chi Cong san* [Communist Review] (Hanoi), April 1984, pp. 69–72.

32. The article, written in Biarritz on October 16, 1919, is located in Ruscio, *Textes*, pp. 24–28. The author remarks that "Mr. Albert Sarraut is not unknown to me," thus informing readers that Nguyen Ai Quoc had indeed met Sarraut briefly in the ministry on Rue Oudinot during his interview in early September. According to Gaspard, *Ho Chi Minh à Paris*, pp. 84–85, some of these early articles were written in collaboration with Phan Chu Trinh, so it should not be assumed they were all his work. On the other hand, there is no reason to doubt that they represented his views at that time.

33. Agent reports and other analyses of *Les opprimés* can be found in Gaspard, pp. 94–110; Kobelev, pp. 38–39; and Hémery, *Ho Chi Minh*, pp. 45–46. A copy of *Le procès de la colonisation française* is available in English translation in Fall, *On Revolution*, pp. 73–126.

34. Report of Edouard, December 20, 1919, in F7–13405, SPCE, Carton 364, CAOM, cited in Nguyen Phan Quang, "Nguyen Ai Quoc va Phan Chau Trinh o Phap (1917–1923)," an undated clipping in my possession.

35. See Report of August 10, 1920, in SPCE, Carton 364, CAOM. As for Quoc's role in the 1908 demonstrations in central Vietnam, see "Note de Jean," December 8, 1919 in SPCE, Carton 364, CAOM.

36. Quoted in Gaspard, *Ho Chi Minh à Paris*, pp. 131–32. I have assumed that this incident took place on September 17, when, according to material in the French archives, Nguyen Ai Quoc was called into the Ministry for a conversation—see Report on surveillance of Nguyen Ai Quoc, September 18, 1920, in SPCE, Carton 364, CAOM. In a declaration that he filled out before leaving the ministry, Quoc declared that he had arrived in Paris in June–July 1919, and that he had come on a Chargeurs Réunis liner from Saigon to Marseilles. He did not recall the name of the ship. On arrival he lived first at no. 5 or 7 Rue Monsieur-le-Prince, then moved to 6 Villa des Gobelins. See Nguyen Ai Quoc, declaration, September 17, 1920, in ibid.

37. Gaspard, *Ho Chi Minh à Paris*, pp. 107–8.

38. Kobelev, pp. 46–47, Hong Ha, *Thoi thanh nien*, p. 88.

39. Tran Thanh, "Bien nien Chu tich," p. 67. Gaspard, p. 157, implies that Nguyen Ai Quoc may have attended this congress. That seems very unlikely, given the fact that he was called to the ministry in mid-September.

40. Tran Thanh, "Bien nien Chu tich," pp. 70–72 The quote is in *Avec l'Oncle Ho*, pp. 45–46. According to Ho Chi Minh, who recounted the story, his listeners responded with condescending sympathy toward a colleague who was too young and naïve to grasp the complexity of the problem.

41. See Ho Chi Minh's reminiscences in *Avec l'Oncle Ho*, p. 46. Also see Kobelev, p. 46.

42. For the original French version of the speech, see Ruscio, *Textes*, pp. 31–33. An English-language version is in Fall, *On Revolution*, pp. 21–22. On one other occasion in the speech, Nguyen Ai Quoc was interrupted by a delegate from Turkey. For a reference, see Gaspard, *Ho Chi Minh à Paris*, pp. 114–123, and Tran Thanh, "Bien nien Chu tich," p. 73.

43. See Dang Hoa, *Bac Ho: Nhung nam thang o nuoc ngoai* [Uncle Ho: the Months and Years Abroad] (Hanoi: Thong tin, 1990), p. 33. In his reminiscences, Ho Chi Minh recounted a conversation with a certain Rose, the stenographer at the conference who had attempted to explain the theoretical issues discussed at the conference to the naïve young Vietnamese. When she heard that Quoc had voted in favor of the motion, she asked why. "It's simple," he replied. "I didn't understand you when you talked of strategy of proletarian tactics, and still other points. But there is one thing that I understand clearly: the Third International is directly interested in the problem of emancipating the colonies, it has declared that it would assist the oppressed peoples to reconquer their liberty and their independence. As for the Second International, it has never made the least reference to the fate of the colonies. What I want is liberty for my compatriots, independence for my country. That's why I voted for the Third International. That's what I understood. Do you agree?" "Comrade," Rose replied, "you've made some progress." See *Avec l'Oncle Ho*, p. 47.

44. Gaspard, *Ho Chi Minh à Paris*, p. 128, citing Charles Fourniau and Léo Figuères, eds., *Ho Chi Minh: Notre Camarade* (Paris: Editions Sociales, 1970), pp. 203–4.

45. For other excerpts from the original French version, see Gaspard, *Ho Chi Minh à Paris*, pp. 138–39.

46. The text of the article is in Ruscio, *Textes*, pp. 34–37.

47. For the text, see ibid., pp. 38–39. For the September article, see Gaspard, *Ho Chi Minh à Paris*, pp. 164–65.

48. Gaspard, *Ho Chi Minh à Paris*, p. 132. The date of the interview is not certain. According to *BNTS*, vol. 1, p. 107, Nguyen Ai Quoc was called to the ministry sometime in February. According to other archival evidence, he was in Cochin Hospital from January to early March and a police informant reported a conversation with Quoc while he was in the hospital in which Quoc mentioned his interview with Sarraut. See Note, February 26, 1921, in SPCE, Carton 364, CAOM.

49. Note by Devèze, December 27, 1920 in SPCE, Carton 364, CAOM; also see *BNTS*, vol. 1, p. 108. The woman involved was a Mlle. Brière, believed by police to be Nguyen Ai Quoc's former mistress.

50. Kobelev, p. 37; BNTS, vol. 1, p. 119; Report of Devèze, July 16, 1921, in SPCE, Carton 364, CAOM. According to police files, the previous October Nguyen Ai Quoc had been responsible for the breakup of Vo Van Toan and his fiancée, Mlle. Germaine Lambert. An agent reported that Quoc had demanded that she give up her entire salary to the cause, do the family washing on Sunday, and obey her husband blindly. She refused and broke off the relationship. According to the agent, she probably did not like the Communist Party. See Note, October 12, 1920, in SPCE, Carton 364, CAOM.

51. *Avec l'Oncle Ho*, p. 39; Dang Hoa, *Bac Ho*, p. 34. Vietnamese émigré circles declare that he had a wife and child, but I have seen no evidence to confirm this. See the article in the magazine. *Thuc Tinh* (Paris), no. 3, p. 19.

52. Note by Devèze, July 29, 1921, in SPCE, Carton 364, CAOM; "Renseignements divers" in SPCE, Carton 365, CAOM. Nguyen Ai Quoc, declaration, September 17, 1920, in SPCE, Carton 364, CAOM. It may have been at this time that someone in the Party, perhaps Paul Vaillant-Couturier, obtained him a work permit. See Gaspard, *Ho Chi Minh à Paris*, p. 76.

53. The police reported that six strangers had visited Phan Van Truong at the

apartment on the day before the debate. See Notes by Devèze, July 9 and 13, 1921, in SPCE, Carton 364, CAOM.

54. For a copy of the manifesto, dated May 1922, see Ruscio, *Textes*, pp. 42–43.

55. At a meeting held on February 14, 1923, at a bookshop on Rue St. Severin, a European in attendance complained about the membership requirement, which stated that one had to be a colonial subject or born of such parents to join. Why, he asked, not open membership to all regardless of origin? Quoc asked why the speaker had come, and added that if he came to spy, he could just leave. The European retorted that socialists had no frontiers, since they were all exploited. The question of membership was turned over to the Executive Committee for study. See Series III, Note by Agent de Villier, June 15, 1923, in SLOTFOM, Carton 109, CAOM. The agent also reported that Phan Van Truong wanted to revive the purely Vietnamese group, because the Intercolonial Union was too broad and the Vietnamese wanted to speak their own language. Nguyen Ai Quoc had apparently taken the headquarters of the Association of Annamite Patriots with him when he moved to Impasse Compoint, and it had apparently been disbanded with the formation of the union. Now he said that he had no objection to reconstituting the organization, but apparently little was done before his departure from Paris. See Note sur les Associations des Indochinois à Paris, in ibid.

56. Gaspard, *Ho Chi Minh à Paris*, p. 180.

57. For a comprehensive survey of the background of the journal, see The Tap, "Le Paria," *Hoc Tap* (April 1972). An English-language version of this article is located in JPRS, no. 56,396, Translations on North Vietnam, no. 1186.

58. Gaspard, *Ho Chi Minh à Paris*, pp. 207–9. In his reminiscences, Ho Chi Minh claims that many Vietnamese students were afraid to read it out of fear that they might be apprehended by the authorities. See *Avec l'Oncle Ho*, p. 44.

59. For excerpts, see Gaspard, *Ho Chi Minh à Paris*, pp. 200–201. Also see *Toan Tap I*, vol. 1, pp. 505–6. Unfortunately, no version of the play appears to be extant. Kobelev (p. 53) says it was published in Paris and performed at a festival sponsored by the newspaper *L'Humanité*. Nguyen Thanh, *Chu tich Ho Chi Minh*, p. 130, says it was organized by the Club du Faubourg. His father's remark was quoted in "Nguyen Ai Quoc," Sûreté note, January 1, 1928, in dossier labeled "Correspondance 1927 à 1930," in SPCE, Carton 368, CAOM.

60. A French-language version of the letter is in Gaspard, *Ho Chi Minh à Paris*, pp. 183–87. Gaspard notes that although Trinh refused to join the Communist Party, he continued to admire many of its humanitarian ideas and principles (see pp. 188–89). But Trinh's inadequate grasp of recent history is shown in his comment that "even Marx and Lenin, whom you evidently admire, did not stay abroad but went home to fight for their ideas."

61. The question of his employment, like so much about his years in Paris, is often confusing. Police sources seem firm that he was dismissed from his job at 7 Impasse Compoint in November 1921. Various reasons are advanced, including the charge that he was a poor worker or that fellow workers complained about his tubercular condition. See undated note by Devèze in SPCE, Carton 364, CAOM. After that he was briefly unemployed, but returned to the job in mid-1922—see BNTS, vol. 1, p. 138, 147. Kobelev (pp. 56–57) implies that he was dismissed in December 1921 as a result of his political activities, leading the authorities to threaten his employer and revoke his work permit. Kobelev's date, however, is in error, and as usual he gives no source.

62. Kobelev, p. 56. Although there is no proof to that effect, it seems likely that this conversation took place during the meeting at the ministry in June 1922. Also see Nguyen Thanh, *Chu tich Ho Chi Minh*, p. 133.

63. "An Open Letter to M. Albert Sarraut, Minister of Colonies," in *Ho Chi Minh: Selected Works*, vol. 1, (Hanoi: Foreign Languages Publishing House, 1960), pp. 28–29. Also see Nguyen Thanh, *Chu tich Ho Chi Minh*, p. 133.

64. Hong Ha, *Thoi thanh nien*, pp. 114–15; Kobelev, p. 55.

65. Nguyen Ai Quoc, "Some considerations on the Colonial Question," in *L'Humanité*, May 25, 1922, cited in Fall, *On Revolution*, pp. 25–27.

66. Cited in Gaspard, *Ho Chi Minh à Paris*, p. 75. Doriot later left the FCP and became a supporter of Nazi Germany.

67. BNTS, vol. 1, p. 175; Dang Hoa, *Bac Ho*, p. 40.

68. Dang Hoa, *Bac Ho*, p. 47; Kobelev, p. 57. Gaspard, *Ho Chi Minh à Paris*, p. 243, surmises that it was now too dangerous for Quoc to remain in Paris.

69. The date of his departure for Moscow has long been a matter of dispute. Ruth Fischer, a German Communist, claimed that he had attended the Comintern Congress in Moscow in 1922. A similar claim is made by the Indian Communist M. N. Roy. Other sources stated that he did not leave France until the fall of 1923. Archival sources in France now confirm the date and the circumstances as described here. See Series III, Carton 103, Note on Nguyen Ai Quoc, SLOTFOM, CAOM. Ruth Fischer, "Ho Chi Minh: Disciplined Communist," in *Foreign Affairs*, vol. no. 1 (October 1954), p. 88, and *M.N. Roy's memoirs* (Bombay: Allied Publishers, n.d.), p. 511.

70. *Avec l'Oncle Ho*, pp. 51–52; BNTS, vol. 1, p. 184; *Glimpses/Life*, p. 28; Kobelev, pp. 58–59.

71. Trinh à Monsieur Ai, in dossier labeled "1923," in SPCE, Carton 365, CAOM. Nguyen Van Ai had become one of Nguyen Ai Quoc's most vocal critics.

III | *Apprentice Revolutionary*

1. Kobelev, p. 62; BNTS, vol. 1, pp. 190, 192; Dang Hoa, *Bac Ho: Nhung nam thang o nuoc ngoai* [Uncle Ho: The Months and Years Abroad] (Hanoi: Thong tin, 1990), pp. 51–52. In his reminiscences, Ho Chi Minh presented what may have been a somewhat fanciful account of his arrival in Petrograd. According to this source, Nguyen Ai Quoc wrote to Marcel Cachin and Paul Vaillant-Couturier, who were both in Moscow at the time, to verify his identity. He said that his first words to the immigration official in Petrograd were that he wanted to see the great Lenin, but was informed that Lenin had just died, an obvious untruth. While awaiting permission to leave Petrograd he stayed at the Hotel International. See the excerpt from *Glimpses/Life* in *Avec l'Oncle Ho*, pp. 52–54.

2. Charles B. McLane, *Soviet Strategies in Southeast Asia* (Princeton, N.J.: Princeton University Press, 1966), p. 19; Nguyen Thanh, "The Communist International and the Indochinese Revolution," in *Tap chi Cong san* [Communist Review] (February 1983), pp. 53–59, translated in JPRS, no. 83,452. In 1919, Leon Trotsky had already called for vigorous efforts to promote revolution in East Asia—see Anotoly A. Sokolov, *Komintern i V'ietnam* (Moscow: Iv Ran, 1998), p. 5.

3. Nguyen Thanh, "Communist International," p. 69.

4. A copy of Quoc's letter is located in the Ho Chi Minh Museum in Hanoi. Also

see Alain Ruscio, ed., *Ho Chi Minh: Textes, 1914–1969* (Paris: L'Harmattan, n.d.), pp. 50–53.

5. A Vietnamese-language version of this undated report, titled "Bao cao hui Quoc te Cong San" [Report to the Comintern], is reproduced in *Toan Tap II*, vol. 1, pp. 203–5. Notes by "Nguyen Ai Quoc" in preparation for a meeting of the French delegation at the Dalburo on September 21, 1923, are located at the Ho Chi Minh Museum in Hanoi and probably formed the basis of the document. The term "national revolutionary" was adopted by the Comintern as a compromise at the behest of the Indian Communist M. N. Roy.

6. *Toan Tap II*, vol. 1, p. 204; Hong Ha, *Ho Shi Min v Strane Sovetov* [Ho Chi Minh in the Land of the Soviets] (Moscow: n.p., 1986), p. 59. This book is a Russian translation of the Vietnamese original. I have not been able to locate a copy of the latter. For the origins of the Peasant International, see George D. Jackson Jr., *Comintern and Peasant in Eastern Europe, 1919–1930* (New York: Columbia University Press, 1966), chapter 3. On Nguyen Ai Quoc's initial selection, see Kobelev, p. 61.

7. Hong Ha, *V Strane Sovetov*, p. 59. According to *BNTS*, vol. 1, pp. 197–98, he had been invited to make a few remarks on the opening day of the conference. In the speech, he compared Russian and Indochinese peasants. The Russian *muzhik*, he said, is like a man seated uncomfortably in a chair, while the Indochinese peasant is like a person attached to a post with his head at the bottom. The French-language version of the speech is located in the November 1923 report on the activities of Nguyen Ai Quoc in Russia; Series III, Carton 103, SLOTFOM, CAOM. For a translation into Vietnamese, see *Toan Tap I*, vol. 1, pp. 153–58. A more easily available indication of his views is his article entitled "Annamese Peasant Conditions," in *La Vie Ouvrière*, January 4, 1924, which is contained in Bernard B. Fall, ed., *Ho Chi Minh on Revolution: Selected Writings, 1920–1966* (New York: Praeger, 1967), pp. 24–26. Note his continuing use of the word "Annamese" to describe his compatriots. Not until the early 1940s would he begin systematically to use the emotive term "Vietnamese."

8. Note on Krestintern meeting of 1923, SLOTFOM, Series III, Carton 112, CAOM. According to George D. Jackson, *Comintern and Peasant*, p. 74, Smirnov later tried to revive a right opposition to Stalin in 1932 and was purged.

9. For information on the Stalin School, see series III, Carton 44, SLOTFOM, CAOM. Also see Sokolov (p. 29), *Komintern*, pp. 15–20, 48–50. Some Vietnamese researchers believe that he did not enter the school until the summer of 1924. According to Sokolov (p. 29), there are no documents in the Russian archives to confirm his presence at the school. In an interview with an Italian newspaper in March 1924, Nguyen Ai Quoc claimed to be a student at the school—see *Toan Tap II*, vol. 1, p. 480.

10. Nguyen Ai Quoc, "The USSR and the Colonial Peoples," cited in Fall, *On Revolution*, p. 45. The article was originally printed in *Inprecor*, no. 46, 1924. Nguyen Ai Quoc also commented on the school in an interview with the Italian Communist Giovanni Germanetto. For the interview, see below, note 17, and *Toan Tap I*, vol. 1, pp. 194–98. Also see Sokolov, *Komintern*, pp. 32–40.

11. Cited in Kobelev, p. 70; Hong Ha, *V Strane Sovetov*, p. 66; also see *BNTS*, vol. 1, pp. 219–20. The letter to Petrov was dated May 20, 1924. Copies are in the Comintern files and the Ho Chi Minh Museum in Hanoi.

12. *BNTS*, vol. 1, pp. 227–28. At the labor meeting he commented on the lack of a working class in Indochina and proposed efforts by the FCP to assist the workers

in the colony to struggle against imperialism. For the invitation to take part in May Day festivities, see ibid., pp. 216–17. The meeting with Nadezhda Krupskaya is described in Kobelev, pp. 73–74. For information on the school curriculum, see Sokolov, *Komintern*, pp. 14, 42–43. Sokolov declares that the long program consisted of three to four years, with the short program lasting one or one and one half years. According to him, it is possible that Quoc did not attend the school as a full-time student, but simply audited classes in his spare time (p. 31).

13. Boris Souvarine, "De Nguyen Ai Quac en Ho Chi Minh," *Est et Ouest*, March 1–15, 1976, p. 99. Interview with Ossip Mandelstam, in Ruscio, *Textes*, pp. 54–57. In this interview, Nguyen Ai Quoc commented that he had left Indochina at age nineteen, leading the editor to suggest that this indicated he was born in 1892, rather than the official date of 1890. It should be kept in mind, however, that on many occasions, even in official biographical statements in Moscow, he gave a variety of different birth dates. In this interview, he stated that he came from a privileged Confucian family, a long distance from the poor peasant background he always claimed when talking to the authorities in France. He also talked of the young Vietnamese monarch Duy Tan, who had been deposed for his patriotic leanings by the French, and declared that such progressive leaders could sometimes play a positive force in liberating their countries. It is a curious statement. See Georges Boudarel, "Ho Chi Minh," in Georges S. Fischer, ed., *Hommes d'état d'Asie et leur politique* (Université René Descartes, 1980), p. 120.

14. Roy had vigorously argued for the correctness of his approach at the Second Comintern Congress and on several subsequent occasions. Quoc did disagree with him on the uses of bourgeois nationalist parties to the revolutionary process. While Roy argued that they would eventually betray the proletariat, Quoc felt that they could be effectively utilized in the common struggle, and had already so argued in his letter to the Comintern Executive Committee.

15. The pamphlet on Chinese youth was recently located by Vietnamese researchers in the Soviet archives. Other articles written in Moscow are printed in *Toan Tap* and various other collections of Nguyen Ai Quoc's writings. The manuscript on the history of Indochina is reprinted in *Toan Tap II*, vol. 1, pp. 345–422. For a discussion of his works on China, see Sokolov, *Komintern*, pp. 30–31.

16. In his biography of Ho Chi Minh, Jean Lacouture speculates that Quoc's friend Nguyen The Truyen may have written it, but in a letter to a friend at the time, Quoc expressed relief that the project was finally out of the way. For the English-language version, see Fall, *On Revolution*, pp. 73–128.

17. Cited in Kobelev, pp. 65–66. Germanetto's story also appears in Dang Hoa Bac Ho, p. 51. The funeral ceremony at Red Square left him with black marks on his ears and toes for the remainder of his life. Kobelev states that henceforth Nguyen Ai Quoc set out to read everything that the Soviet leader had ever written, and that his notebooks were packed with extracts from Lenin's works. The essay he wrote was printed in the Soviet newspaper *Pravda* on January 27, 1924.

18. The letter is available in *Toan Tap II*, vol. 1, p. 248, and the Ho Chi Minh Museum in Hanoi.

19. For these letters, see *BNTS*, vol. 1, pp. 212–13, and *Toan Tap II*, vol. 1, pp. 241–42. In the first letter he explained that he had not been able to come to work at Comintern headquarters since the funeral of Lenin because of frostbite on his fingers.

20. For an English-language version of the article, see Fall, *On Revolution*, pp. 40–43. It is also in *Toan Tap I*, vol. 1, pp. 241–48.

21. The speech is available in a Russian version in the Ho Chi Minh Museum in Hanoi. For the comment, see A. Neuberg, ed., *Armed Insurrection* (London: NLB, 1970), p. 22.

22. Hong Ha, *V Strane Sovetov*, p. 74. According to *BNTS*, vol. 1, p. 222, he attended as an observer.

23. According to *BNTS*, vol. 1, pp. 222–23, the congress was held in the Andreyevskiy Palace in the Kremlin. Researchers in Hanoi may have mistaken the Fifth Congress for the founding meeting of the Peasant International.

24. Quoted in Helmut Gruber, ed., *Soviet Russia Masters the Comintern* (Garden City, N.Y.: Anchor/Doubleday, 1974), pp. 308–9; also see *Toan Tap II*, vol. 1, pp. 272–75.

25. For an English-language version of the speech, see Fall, *On Revolution*, pp. 63–72. A Vietnamese version is in *Toan Tap I*, vol. 1, pp. 215–31. The latter half of the address was apparently given on July 3—see *Toan Tap II*, vol. 1, pp. 276–89.

26. Hong Ha, *V Strane Sovetov*, p. 74; Kobelev, pp. 71–73.

27. Quoc translated the appeal into Vietnamese. Xenia J. Eudin and Robert C. North, *Soviet Russia and the East, 1920–1927* (Stanford, Calif.: Stanford University Press, 1957), p. 341. Circular dated November 18, 1924, series III, Carton 103, SLOTFOM, CAOM. A later report (dated February 28, 1925) declared that in July 1924, fifteen hundred tracts written in *quoc ngu* and published by the Executive Committee of the Comintern in Moscow appeared in Indochina.

28. Nguyen Ai Quoc had been telling his friends that he hoped to return to Asia as soon as the Fifth Comintern Congress came to a conclusion. This letter, dated April 11, 1924, is located in the Comintern archives. The capitalization is in the original text. See *Toan Tap II*, vol. 1, pp. 251–52.

29. Hong Ha, *V Strane Sovetov*, pp. 77–78.

30. Ibid., pp. 81–82. The Far Eastern Secretariat had been established in Irkutsk in 1920. It is quite possible that this conversation is apocryphal, although the meeting may have taken place. In Hong Ha's account, Manuilsky suggested that Quoc meet with Borodin before his departure for China. Borodin, however, was already in Canton.

31. Both the letter to Voitinsky and the report of September 25, 1924, are located in the Ho Chi Minh Museum in Hanoi. According to one source, Quoc's trip to China might have been delayed for health reasons. On September 5, he had been ordered to spend a few days at a sanatorium in the Crimea for treatment of tuberculosis. This may have been a ruse to disguise his movements. See Hong Ha, *V Strane Sovetov*, pp. 83–84.

32. Letter to Treint, September 19, 1924, in *Toan Tap II*, vol. 1, p. 305; also see *BNTS*, vol. 1, pp. 231–34.

33. Report of Agent Désiré, April 10, 1925, in dossier labeled "1925," in SPCE, Carton 365, CAOM; *BNTS*, vol. 1, pp. 237–38; Hong Ha, *V Strane Sovetov*, p. 85.

34. Hong Ha, *V Strane Sovetov*, p. 85.

IV | *Sons of the Dragon*

1. Some CCP members argued that the Kuomintang represented the bourgeois class in China and would eventually betray the revolution. Maring, who had recently created a similar "bloc within" among anticolonial groups in the Dutch East Indies, countered that Sun's party consisted of a "four-class alliance" between the nationalist bourgeoisie (a Marxist term for the more prosperous members of the urban middle class),

the petty bourgeoisie, the proletariat, and the peasants. Such a definition opened the way for efforts by the CCP to strengthen revolutionary elements in the Kuomintang and move it to the left. See James Pinckney Harrison, *The Long March to Power: A History of the Chinese Communist Party, 1921–1972* (New York: Praeger, 1972), pp. 49–51.

2. Information on Chau's later career can be found in David G. Marr, *Vietnamese Anticolonialism, 1885–1925* (Berkeley, Calif.: University of California Press, 1971), and William J. Duiker, *The Rise of Nationalism in Vietnam, 1900–1941* (Ithaca, N.Y.: Cornell University Press, 1976). Sun's promise to provide assistance is contained in S. L. Tikhvinskii, *Sun Yat-sen: Vneshnepoliticheskie vozzreniya i praktika* [Sun Yat-sen: Foreign policy views and practice] (Moscow: International Relations, 1964), p. 101.

3. By one Vietnamese estimate, less than 10 percent of Chau's followers were peasants, in a land overwhelmingly rural. See Chuong Thau, "Moi quan he giua Ton Trong-son va Phan Boi Chau" [Relations between Sun Yat-sen and Phan Boi Chau], in *NCLS*, no. 88 (October 1966), p. 23.

4. See Paul Monet, *Français et Annamites: Entre deux feux* (Paris: Rieder, 1928), p. 40.

5. Quoted in Louis Roubaud, *Vietnam: La tragédie indochinoise* (Paris: Librairie Valois, 1931), p. 261.

6. Of the 40,000 Europeans living in Indochina in the 1920s, about half were dependents. One quarter were in the armed forces, and the remainder were government officials, professional people, or members of the mercantile class. See David G. Marr, *Vietnamese Tradition on Trial* (Berkeley, Calif.: University of California Press, 1981), p. 24. Poincaré's comment is in Roubaud, *Vietnam*, p. 268.

7. For a reference to the early years of Chieu's party, see Megan Cook, *The Constitutionalist Party in Cochinchina: The Years of Decline, 1930–1942* (Clayton, Australia: Monash University Papers on Southeast Asia, 1977), chapter 1.

8. Léon Werth, *Cochinchine* (Paris: Rieder, 1926), pp. 160–61.

9. Hong Ha, *Ho Shi Min v Strane Sovetov* [Ho Chi Minh in the Land of the Soviets] (Moscow: n.p., 1986), p. 89; *HZY*, p. 18. On disembarking in Canton, Nguyen Ai Quoc immediately wrote three letters to Moscow announcing his arrival. In a message to an unnamed acquaintance, he said that he was now living in a house with Borodin and two or three Chinese comrades. In a letter to Dombal, now general secretary of the Peasant International, he asked that the news of his departure be withheld from his colleagues, since he was in China illegally. He added a few remarks about the state of revolutionary work among the peasantry in south China, many of whom, he said, had already been organized by the Communists. He asked that propaganda materials be sent to Canton to enable him to intensify efforts to mobilize them for the revolutionary cause. In the third letter, to the editor of *Rabotnitsa*, he volunteered to continue writing articles for that journal, but asked that they be published as "letters from China" under a woman's name. That, he said, would facilitate his effort to keep his identity and his location a secret. For copies of the three letters, all of which were recently discovered in the Comintern archives, see *BNTS*, vol. 1, pp. 237–39, and *Toan Tap II*, vol. 2, pp. 2–7. Kobelev, p. 86, states without attribution that Nguyen Ai Quoc got the job with the Comintern by applying to a want ad in a local newspaper. Given their acquaintance in Moscow and his comment in the letters cited above that he had immediately moved in with Borodin, it seems much more likely that Quoc had gone directly to Comintern headquarters on his arrival.

10. The Indian Communist M. N. Roy had argued against Lenin's policy of seek-

ing limited cooperation with bourgeois nationalist groups in the colonial and semicolonial areas, arguing that such parties would inevitably betray the revolution in the end. But Manuilsky had defended the tactic, arguing that since there were no revolutionaries in many of these countries, there was no choice. A compromise was reached, which authorized Communist support and cooperation with "national revolutionary" elements. In practice, the terms "bourgeois nationalist" and "national revolutionary" were often used interchangeably during these years. See Charles B. McLane, *Soviet Strategies in Southeast Asia* (Princeton, N.J.: Princeton University Press, 1966), pp. 36–40. Manuilsky's comment to Nguyen Ai Quoc is reported in Xenia J. Eudin and Robert C. North, *Soviet Russia and the East, 1920–1927* (Stanford, Calif.: Stanford University Press, 1957), pp. 326–28. For Nguyen Ai Quoc's proposals to seek to establish cooperative relations with other anticolonial groups, see *Toan Tap II*, vol. 1, pp. 203–4, 251–52.

11. Both quotes are from Tran Van Giau, "The first influences of the Russian October revolution on Vietnamese politics," *Hoc Tap* (August 1957), pp. 51, 64. In a report to Moscow on March 5, 1930, Nguyen Ai Quoc said much the same thing—see his "Bao cao gai Quoc Te ve Phong trao Cach Mang o An-nam" [A report to the Comintern on the revolutionary movement in Annam], in *Van kien Dang Toan Tap* [Complete Party Documents], vol. 2 (Hanoi: Chinh tri Quoc gia, 1997), p. 32.

12. Ho Chi Minh, "Some considerations on the colonial question, in *L'Humanité*, May 25, 1922. This article is reprinted in Bernard B. Fall, ed., *Ho Chi Minh on Revolution: Selected Writings, 1920–1966* (New York: Praeger, 1967), pp. 8–10.

13. Accounts of their trips to China and their reasons for doing so can be found in police interrogations contained in the French archives. For example, see the interrogation of Le Hong Son, October 24, 1932, in SPCE, Carton 367, CAOM. In 1922, Le Hong Son had reportedly assassinated Phan Ba Ngoc, a son of the famous Can Vuong rebel Phan Dinh Phung, for urging Phan Boi Chau to follow a course of reconciliation with the French—see Agathe Larcher, "La voie étroite des réformes coloniales et la collaboration franco-annamite (1917–1928)," in *Revue Française d'Histoire d'Outre-Mer* vol. 82, no. 309 (December 1995) (Paris: Société Française d'Histoire d'Outre-Mer, 1995), p. 411. For the accounts of Truong Van Lenh and Le Quang Dat, see the interrogations dated February 3, 1932, and November 6, 1931, in SPCE, Carton 367, CAOM.

14. Dang Hoa, *Bac Ho: Nhung nam thang o nuoc ngoai* [Uncle Ho: The months and years abroad] (Hanoi: Thong tin, 1990), p. 64; *HZYZ*, p. 23. The name of the organization was reportedly adapted from the phrase "tam tam tu'ong ai" (hearts beating in mutual love)—see Tran Van Giau, *Giai cap cong nhan Viet Nam* [The Vietnamese working class], vol. 2 (Hanoi: Su That, 1961), pp. 367–68. According to the French historian Georges Boudarel, leading members of the Tam Tam Xa were influenced by the ideas of Liu Shifu and other anarchist Chinese intellectuals after their arrival in south China— see Boudarel, "L'extrême gauche asiatique et le mouvement national vietnamien (1905– 1925)," in Pierre Brocheux, ed., *Histoire de l'Asie du Sud-est: Révoltes, réformes, révolutions* (Lille: Presses Universitaires de Lille, 1981), p. 190.

15. The news account is from the *South China Morning Post*, cited in Boudarel, "L'Extrême gauche asiatique," p. 185. For biographical information on Pham Hong Thai, see To Nguyet Dinh, *Pham Hong Thai*: (Saigon: Song Mai, 1957), and Tran Huy Lieu, *Tai lieu tham khao lich su cach mang can dai Viet Nam* [Historical research materials concerning the revolution in modern Vietnam], 12 vols. (Hanoi: n.p., 1958), vol. 4. On the initial choice of Le Hong Son as assassin, see To Nguyet Dinh, *Pham Hong Thai*,

pp. 64–65, and the interrogation of Le Hong Son, October 24, 1932, in SPCE, Carton 367, CAOM.

16. For Le Quang Dat's suspicions, see his interrogation of November 6, 1935, in SPCE, Carton 367, CAOM. According to To Nguyet Dinh, *Pham Hong Thai*, Thu had indeed informed the French about the plot, and had also informed them of the whereabouts of other members of the organization who, for the moment, were able to avoid French arrest. Dinh also claims that Le Hong Son did suspect Thu and attempted unsuccessfully to assassinate him—however, this seems unlikely, since Thu remained his colleague for the next several years (see pp. 118–19). For such suspicions, see *Nguyen Ai Quoc o Quang Chau* [Nguyen Ai Quoc in Canton] (Hanoi: NXB Chinh tri Quoc gia, 1998), p. 53.

17. In taking credit for the attempt, Chau was at least partly correct, for the Tam Tam Xa had maintained loose ties with his own organization, but he was apparently not directly involved. For references and a comment on Chau's *Truyen Pham Hong Thai* [The story of Pham Hong Thai], see Duiker, *Rise of Nationalism*, pp. 83–84. Chau declared that Thai had been motivated to carry out the plot after a conversation with Nguyen Ai Quoc, but that seems obviously fabricated, since the latter did not arrive in Canton until several months after Thai's death.

18. The original February 19 report, written in French, is in the Revolutionary Museum in Hanoi. The letter dated December 18, 1924, is in the Ho Chi Minh Museum in the same city. Vietnamese translations are available in *Toan Tap II*, vol. 2, pp. 7–9 and *Toan Tap I*, vol. 1, pp. 314–16, respectively. References to the Indochinese Nationalist Party are in his "Gui doan chu tich Quoc te Cong san" [Report to the chairman of the Comintern], dated January 1, 1925, in *Toan Tap II*, vol. 2, pp. 5–6, and "Van de Dong Duong" [The problem of Indochina], n.d., in *Toan Tap II*, vol. 2, pp. 16–17. Nguyen Ai Quoc may have temporarily decided to use the name in deference to Phan Boi Chau's recently created Vietnamese Nationalist Party.

Precisely how Quoc came in contact with members of the Tam Tam Xa is not clear. By the time he arrived, two of them were studying at the Whampoa Academy, and he might have learned of their names through colleagues at Comintern headquarters. Le Hong Son later told French interrogators, however, that he had been introduced to Nguyen Ai Quoc by Lam Duc Thu. See his interrogation in SPCE, Carton 365, CAOM. Thu confirmed that supposition—see Letter of Pinot to Noel, January 23, 1925, in ibid.

19. *Phan Boi Chau nien bieu* [A chronological biography of Phan Boi Chau] (Hanoi: Van su dia, 1955), p. 189; Huong Pho, "Gop phan danh gia tu tuong cua Phan Boi Chau" [A contribution to an analysis of the thought of Phan Boi Chau], in *NCLS*, no. 94 (September 1967), p. 24. Also see Anatoly A. Sokolov, *Komintern i V'ietnam* (Moscow: Iv Ran, 1998), pp. 22–26. Chau once confided to a friend that he was "too old" to understand many of the new doctrines.

20. Phan Boi Chau's letter to Nguyen Ai Quoc is reported in Annex 6, note by Noel, no. 144, in SPCE, Carton 365, CAOM. On February 3, 1925, Quoc reported to the Comintern on a meeting with a veteran patriot, but did not mention the individual's name or the date of the meeting. Phan Boi Chau's account is in *Phan Boi Chau nien bieu*, pp. 201–2. The problem is complicated by the fact that many Vietnamese used the lunar calendar at that time. See Note by Noel, no. 158, May 24, 1925, in SPCE, Carton 365, CAOM, and Pinot's letter to Noel, January 23, 1925, in SPCE, Carton 364, CAOM.

21. For Nguyen Ai Quoc's report to the Comintern itemizing these plans, see his letter dated February 19, 1925, in the Revolutionary Museum.

22. It has long been suspected that Lam Duc Thu was a French agent, but until recently, proof has been lacking. Now Thu's identity as the "Pinot" in Sûreté files is convincingly established in materials contained in the French archives at CAOM. French official efforts to identity Ly Thuy are recorded in a series of cables between Canton, Hanoi, and Paris during the first six months of 1925 and contained in SPCE, Carton 364, CAOM. The *Sûreté* was apparently able to prevent Nguyen Ai Quoc from discovering that he had been identified. The snapshot is still in the French archives.

23. The proclamation is contained in "Proclamation de la Ligue des Peuples Opprimés à l'occasion de sa formation," Envoi no. 190, July 18, 1925, in dossier labeled "1950", in SPCE, Carton 366, ibid. For a detailed analysis of the various names for the Revolutionary Youth League, see Huynh Kim Khanh, *Vietnamese Communism, 1925–1945* (Ithaca, N.Y.: Cornell University Press, 1982), pp. 63–64. As Khanh pointed out, there were a number of variations in the title of the organization, even within the movement. For convenience I have chosen to stick with the customary title.

24. *Komsomolskaya Pravda*, May 1, 1969. A copy is located in the Indochina Archives at Texas Tech University, Lubbock, Texas.

25. This letter, addressed to Petrov and dated May 21, 1924, is located in the Ho Chi Minh Museum in Hanoi and in the Comintern archives in Moscow. Also see Kobelev, p. 70.

26. Throughout the report, the author uses the term "Annam" as opposed to Vietnam or Indochina. A copy is located in Alain Ruscio, ed., *Ho Chi Minh: Textes, 1914–1969* (Paris: L'Harmattam, n.d.), pp. 76–78. I agree with Ruscio that from the context, Nguyen Ai Quoc was probably the author of this report. Not only was he the only Comintern official in Moscow knowledgeable about conditions in Indochina, but a number of remarks in the report relating to the need to end the Eurocentric attitude in the FCP and within the Comintern itself, as well as suggestions for future initiatives, appear to match his own ideas on the subject. Researchers in Hanoi agree—the report is included in *Toan Tap, II*, vol. 2, pp. 464–69.

27. See Ruscio, *Textes*, p. 76.

28. The text of Nguyen Ai Quoc's letter, written in early April, is contained in SPCE, Carton 364, CAOM. For another discussion, see Hue-Tam Ho Tai, *Radicalism and the Origins of the Vietnamese Revolution* (Cambridge, Mass.: Harvard University Press, 1992), pp. 172–75. The French were apparently quite anxious to obtain a copy of the tract, which they thought Huyen might have written in cooperation with Phan Boi Chau. Their agent Pinot (Lam Duc Thu) explained that he had not been able to distract Quoc long enough to steal it, and his camera broke. See Note by Noel, no. 153, May 22, 1925, in SPCE, Carton 365, CAOM.

29. For Phan Boi Chau's complaint that Nguyen Ai Quoc was ignoring him, see Annex 196, July 24, 1925, in SPCE, Carton 365, CAOM. Some sources claim that the funds for Chau's trip were provided by the Revolutionary Youth League. Chau's letters to Quoc and Ho Tung Mao are contained in Annexes 6 and 7 to Note by Noel, no. 144, in ibid. In the letter to Quoc, Chau reminisced about reciting drunken verses to the younger man two decades earlier and said that even then he knew Quoc would be a savant. For the exchange between Phan Boi Chau and Nguyen Ai Quoc, also see *HZYZ*, p. 24.

30. Suspicions by league members that the guilty party was Nguyen Thuong Huyen are contained in Envoi no. 210, September 6, 1925, in SPCE, Carton 365, CAOM. For Phan Boi Chau's own conclusions on the matter, see *Phan Boi Chau Nien*

bieu, pp. 202–3. Lam Duc Thu was charged with responsibility for the act in an article by Dao Trinh Nhat in the October 30, 1948, issue of the Vietnamese-language journal *Cai Tao*. The author cited the remarks of Phan Boi Chau's old associate Prince Cuong De, who in his own memoirs claimed that in later years Lam Duc Thu had often bragged that he had initiated the plot on the grounds that Chau's arrest would make good propaganda for the revolution. This is probably the key source for the suspicion that he was the responsible party. See *Cuoc doi cach mang Cuong De* [The revolutionary life of Cuong De] (Saigon: Nam Viet, 1957), pp. 120–21. At least one member of the league agreed—see "Déclarations de Le Quang Dat et Ly Phuong Duc," in Saigon report, July 28, 1931, in SPCE, Carton 367, CAOM. Also see Joseph Buttinger, *Viet-Nam: A Dragon Embattled* (New York: Praeger, 1967), vol. I, p. 80. For the assertion that the decision was Nguyen Ai Quoc's, see Huy Phong and Yen Auh, *Nhan Dien Ho Chi Minh* [Exploring the Ho myth] (San Jose, Calif: Van Nghe, 1988), pp. 32–37. For Hanoi's rebuttal, see Vietnamese historian Chuong Thau's "Phan Boi Chau qua mot so sach bao mien nam hien nay" [Phan Boi Chau in a recent book published in South Vietnam], in *NCLS*, no. 67 (October 1964).

31. A message from the Sûreté Générale in Hanoi to the French concession in Shanghai, dated September 26, 1931, refers to the fact that the latter had introduced an informer into Ho Hoc Lam's household in Hangzhou prior to Phan Boi Chau's arrest—see SPCE, Carton 369, CAOM.

32. In his report to the Comintern in March 1930 (cited in note 11, above), Quoc conceded that Chau's arrest had spurred the growth of the nationalist movement in Indochina—see *Van kien Dang Toan Tap*, vol. 2, p. 33. Also see *Nguyen Ai Quoc o Quang Chau*, pp. 66–67.

33. The informer was Lam Duc Thu. See Report of Agent Pinot, April 12, 1926, annex to Note by Noel, no. 300 of May 8, 1926, in SPCE, Carton 368, CAOM, cited in Larcher, "La voie étroite," p. 413.

34. Nguyen Ai Quoc may have also feared that such actions would only result in putting French authorities on guard against league activities in Canton. See Note 273, "Renseignements de l'informateur habituel à Canton," April 22, 1926, in dossier labeled "Nguyen Ai Quoc 1926–1927," in SPCE, Carton 368, CAOM.

35. *HZYZ*, pp. 24–27. Interview with Le Xien Heng, director of the Canton Revolutionary Museum. Also see Thep Moi, "Uncle Ho in Canton," *Vietnam Courier*, no. 48 (May 1976), p. 29. Sometimes the neighboring building was used as well. There is some confusion in the evidence on the date when the institute was moved to Wen Ming Street, since memoirs by or interrogations of ex-students are not consistent. For sources, see the interrogation of Le Hong Son, October 24, 1932, in SPCE, Carton 367, CAOM, and Le Manh Trinh's recollections, "Dans le Kouang Toung et au Siam," in *Souvenirs sur Ho Chi Minh*, p. 99. When classes became too large, they were moved to a CCP-owned building nearby—see *ZYG*, p. 11.

36. Thep Moi, "Uncle Ho," p. 26.

37. Ibid, p. 28.

38. Hoang Zheng says in *HZYZ*, p. 25, that the institute had three terms, each lasting three to four months. The first class opened with ten students in early 1926, and classes continued until the spring of 1927. By the third term, there were over fifty students enrolled. For statistics on enrollment, see *Nguyen Ai Quoc o Quang Chau*, pp. 56–59. Nguyen Ai Quoc wrote a letter to the Comintern seeking permission to send students to Moscow (dated January 5, 1925; see *BNTS*, vol. I, p. 250).

39. *Nguyen Ai Quoc o Quang Chau*, p. 86; Vu Tho, "Qua trinh thanh lap dang vo san o Viet Nam da duoc dien ra nhu the nao?" [How did the process of forming the proletarian party in Vietnam take place?], in *NCLS*, no. 71 (February 1965), p. 18, citing Hong The Cong, *Essai d'histoire du mouvement communiste en Indochine*. Also see Tran Huy Lieu, *Tai lieu tham khao*, vol. 4, pp. 132–33. Each branch was composed of cells consisting of five members.

40. Nguyen Ai Quoc, "Indochine," in *Ho Chi Minh: Ecrits* (Hanoi: Foreign Languages Press, 1977), p. 14. The article originally appeared in *Cahiers du Communisme*, no. 15 (May 1921).

41. Huynh Kim Khanh corrected earlier misconceptions about the journal *Thanh Nien*. See his *Vietnamese Communism*, p. 67.

42. *Nguyen Ai Quoc o Quang Chau*, p. 102. Copies of almost all issues of *Thanh Nien* are available in SLOTFOM, Series V, Carton 16, CAOM.

43. The pamphlet was printed in linotype by the Propaganda Bureau of the Association of Oppressed Peoples of Asia. According to the memoirs of some party veterans who had attended the school, it was a compilation of the lectures that Nguyen Ai Quoc presented to students during the training program. Many of the ideas bore a strong resemblance to those published in the journal *Thanh Nien*, but in a more coherent form. A complete version is available in *Toan Tap II*, vol. 2, pp. 177–254. The spelling of "*kach menh*" in the Vietnamese title conforms to contemporary usage in Quoc's home province of Nghe An.

44. Ibid., p. 186. It is interesting to note that the term Quoc uses for "global unity"—*thien ha da dong*—is taken from the Chinese *tian xia da tong*, the traditional Confucian term for a final era of eternal peace and unity. The author was obviously assuming that his audience would be familiar with the concept.

45. For example, in his 1924 report on conditions in Indochina written in Moscow, Nguyen Ai Quoc had assumed that when Vietnam launched its own armed revolt against the French, that uprising would take place simultaneously with a proletarian revolution in France and would be supported by Soviet economic and military assistance, while a Soviet flotilla would sit offshore to prevent assistance to the French by any foreign power. See Ruscio, *Textes*, pp. 73–74. While describing the process in *The Revolutionary Path*, Quoc may have been hoping that an uprising in Indochina would be supported by Chinese Nationalist troops crossing the border from south China—see the dossier labeled "Nguyen Ai Quoc 1926–1927," in SPCE, Carton 368, CAOM. It is noteworthy that he always viewed the liberation of his country in conjunction with events abroad.

46. *Toan Tap II*, vol. 2, p. 187.

47. Ibid., pp. 197, 203.

48. Ibid., pp. 178–79.

49. This perhaps is one reason that the Democratic Republic of Vietnam (DRV) did not publish the pamphlet during his lifetime, and that only excerpts appeared in scattered works written by historians in Hanoi. The complete version was not republished until 1981 in *Toan Tap I*; in a December 3, 1990, interview the chief editor of the collection, Nguyen Thanh, told me that some factual errors had been corrected in the text. Thanh remarked that Ho Chi Minh did not originally want the pamphlet to be published in the DRV. See Vu Tho, "From 'The Revolutionary Path' to the 'Political Program' of the Indochinese Communist Party," in *NCLS*, no. 72 (March 1965).

50. Cited in Georges Garros, *Forceries humaines* (Paris: André Delpeuch, 1926), p. 241.

51. Ruscio, *Textes*, p. 71.

52. See Report by Noel, annex no. 228, November 28, 1925, in SPCE, Carton 365, CAOM. In a report to the Comintern on December 19, 1924, Nguyen Ai Quoc remarked that whether the Constitutionalist Party could be "used" depended upon "the attitude of the French government and our cleverness"—see *Toan Tap II*, vol. 2, p. 14.

53. Comintern archives in Moscow, Carton 495, series 154, file 555, cited in Sophie Quinn-Judge, "Ho Chi Minh: New Perspectives from the Comintern Files," *The Vietnam Forum*, no. 14 (1994), p. 65. The quote from the Second Congress is from "The Report of the Commission on the National and Colonial Questions," in V. I. Lenin, *Collected Works*, vol. 31 (Moscow: Gospolitizdat, 1950).

54. A flagrant example of this tactic is located in "Déclarations dernières de Nguyen Dinh Tu—dit provisoirement Phan Van Cam, dit Van Cam dit Nguyen Van Cam—sur sa vie depuis juin 1925 jusqu'à son arrestation en date du 5 août 1929 à Ha Tinh," an intelligence report in Dossier 2690, Carton 335, CAOM. It is not clear, however, whether such tactics in luring new candidates into the Revolutionary Youth League took place while Nguyen Ai Quoc was in Canton, or after his departure. For his report on the Constitutionalists, see *BNTS*, vol. 1, p. 242; a full copy is located in the Revolutionary Museum in Hanoi.

55. In his courses at the institute, Quoc regularly criticized Nguyen Hai Than's Vietnamese Nationalist Party, comparing it with the Second International in Europe. See Tran Van Giau, *Giai cap cong nhan Viet Nam* [The Vietnamese working class], vol. 1 (Hanoi: Su That, 1957), p. 392.

56. *BNTS*, vol. 1, pp. 260, 265; King C. Chen, *Vietnam and China, 1938–1954* (Princeton, N.J.: Princeton University Press, 1969), p. 22; Hong Ha, *V Strane Sovetov*, p. 109; *Nguyen Ai Quoc o Quang Chau*, pp. 127–29, 155. Peng Pai died in the service of the revolution in 1929.

57. See *HZYZ*, p. 33, and *Nguyen Ai Quoc o Quang Chau*, p. 145. Quoc spoke in French under the name Wang Hai-jen. A Vietnamese translation is available in *Toan Tap II*, vol. 2, pp. 213–17.

58. The source of much of this information was the French agent Lam Duc Thu himself. See the Hanoi report, October 28, 1931, in SPCE, Carton 367, CAOM, and "La conversation entre Pinot et Noel," July 4, 1926, in dossier labeled "Nguyen Ai Quoc 1926–1927," in SPCE, Carton 368, CAOM. See also "Lam Duc à M. D.," January 29, 1927, in dossier labeled "Nguyen Ai Quoc 1926–1927," in ibid. For Tuyet Minh's physical characteristics, see the interrogation of Lesquiendieu [Le Quang Dat], October 28, 1931, in SPCE, Carton 367, CAOM. For the rumor that Quoc had a daughter from this marriage, see Nguyen Khac Huyen, *Vision Accomplished* (New York: Collier, 1971), p. 8.

59. *ZYG*, p. 11; Dang Ho, *Bac Ho*, p. 75; T. Lan, *Vua di duong, vua ke chuyen* [Walking and talking] (Hanoi: Su that, 1976), p. 32; interrogation of Truong Van Lenh, February 7, 1932, in SPCE, Carton 367, CAOM.

60. See Envoi 354, January 1, 1927, and Noel reports of April 10, 1926, December 27, 1926, and June 1, 1927 in SPCE, Carton 368, CAOM. The French became aware of the feud through Lam Duc Thu. The latter and Nguyen Hai Than themselves eventually had a falling out. See "Lettres de Pinot," April 8 and 14, 1927, in the dossier labeled "Nguyen Ai Quoc, 1926–1927," in ibid.

61. See Pinot's agent report dated May 7–9, 1928, in SPCE, Carton 365, CAOM.

V | *The Magic Sword*

1. Several sources have asserted that he took a different route, joining a group of Soviet refugees traveling from Shanghai directly across China through the Gobi Desert, following the route taken earlier by Mikhail Borodin and his party. See Kobelev, pp. 90–91; *ZYG*, p. 11; Dang Hoa, *Bac Ho: Nhung nam thang o nuoc ngoai* [Uncle Ho: The months and years abroad] (Hanoi: Thong tin, 1990), p. 75. There is some plausibility to this assumption, since "Pinot" reported to his control "Noel" that he had received letters from Nguyen Ai Quoc mailed from Hankou in June 1927. But Quoc's own letter to the Dalburo, written after his arrival in Moscow, makes it clear that he went through Vladivostok. Perhaps he wrote the message to Thu to throw possible pursuers off the scent. The letter to the Dalburo is contained in the Ho Chi Minh Museum in Hanoi. Also see a Vietnamese translation in *Toan Tap II*, vol. 2, pp. 241–244.

2. He argued that "other comrades" could replace him in Shanghai, but not in Siam. Letter to the Dalburo, in *BNTS*, I, 285–86.

3. For Quoc's request that the Stalin school set up a Vietnamese section, see *Toan Tap II*, vol. 2, pp. 255–56. Also consult Hong Ha, *Ho Shi Min v Strane Sovetov* [Ho Chi Minh in the land of the Soviets] (Moscow 1986), pp. 115–18. For information on Tran Phu, see Ton Quang Duyet, "Mot vai y kien bo sung ve lich su hai dong chi Tran Phu va Nguyen Thi Minh Khai" [Some opinions on the history of comrades Tran Phu and Nguyen Thi Minh Khai], in *NCLS*, no. 139 (July–August 1971). Other Vietnamese students at the Stalin School were Nguyen The Ruc, Ngo Duc Tri, Bui Cong Trung, and Bui Lam. Quoc's colleague Le Hong Phong was temporarily enrolled in an aviation school in Leningrad. See *BNTS*, vol. 1, pp. 284–87.

4. The letter is available in a Vietnamese version in *Toan Tap II*, vol 2., pp. 167–68. For a contemporary Comintern report on revolutionary tasks in Indochina, see "Directives pour le travail en Indochine," in the Russian Center for the Preservation and Study of Contemporary Historical Documents], Moscow, Carton 495, Series 154, file 556.

5. The conference had been convened to oppose the rise in international tensions and the growing danger of a new world war. See "His Many Names and Travels, *Vietnam Courier* (May 1981), p. 9. Also see Charles Fenn, *Ho Chi Minh: A Historical Introduction* (New York: Scribner, 1973), p. 51; *BNTS*, vol. 1, p. 290; *Avec l'Oncle Ho*, p. 61; Charles Fourniau and Léo Figuères, eds., *Ho Chi Minh: Notre Camarade* (Paris: Editions Sociales, 1970), p. 43, and Hong Ha, *V Strane Sovetov*, pp. 124–25.

6. The letters are contained in a Vietnamese version in *Toan Tap II*, vol 2., p. 265 and *BNTS*, vol. 1, pp, 292–94.

7. *BNTS*, vol. 1, p. 296. In another letter sent at the same time, he told a friend: "You can understand how I am in my spiritual and material state. There is much work to do but I can do nothing, I have nothing to eat, and no money. Today is April 12, can I expect to hear in twenty-four hours?" Ibid., p. 297.

8. According to a letter dated April 28, 1928, the costs were to be borne by the Dalburo. See *BNTS*, vol. 1, p. 300. Funds for the Comintern and all its subordinate organizations were provided by the Soviet state. For his letter to the Dalburo, see ibid., p. 302.

9. T. Lan, *Vua di duong, vua ke chuyen* [Walking and talking] (Hanoi: Su that,

1976), pp. 35–36. A contact with the Italian Communist Party had suggested taking a French ship to Siam, but Quoc rejected the idea as too risky—see Hong Ha, *V Strane Sovetov*, pp. 127–28.

10. Le Manh Trinh, "Dans le Kouang Toung et au Siam," in *Souvenirs*, p. 102.

11. Ibid.

12. Ibid., p. 104; Thep Moi, "Uncle Ho in Canton," *Vietnam Courier*, no. 48 (May 1976), p. 24.

13. *Nash Prezident Ho Shi Minh* [Our President Ho Chi Minh] (Hanoi: Foreign Language Press, 1967), p. 142.

14. Le Manh Trinh, "Dans le Kouang Toung," p. 110.

15. *Glimpses/Life*, p. 36; Nguyen Viet Hong, "Nguyen Ai Quoc co hay khong ve nuoc nam 1929?) [Did Nguyen Ai Quoc return to his country or not in 1929?"], in *Tap chi Xua va Nay* [Yesterday and Today] (Hanoi), no. 4 (July 1994), p. 15. Also see Hoang Van Hoan, *A Drop in the Ocean: Hoang Van Hoan's Revolutionary Reminiscences* (Beijing: Foreign Languages Press, 1988), p. 47, and Tran Lam, "De la fable à la réalité," in *Souvenirs*, pp. 122–23.

16. Li Xianheng, "Ywe Nan Geming jen canjia Guangzhou qiyi de jingguo" [The case of Vietnamese revolutionaries taking part in the Canton uprising], unidentified article in my possession, p. 333.

17. Information on the competition between the various groups is contained in *Contribution à l'histoire des mouvements politiques de l'Indochine Française*, 6 vols. (Hanoi: Imprimerie de l'Extrême Orient, 1933).

18. See "Déclarations dernières de Nguyen Dinh Tu—dit provisoirement Pham Van Cam, dit Van Cam dit Nguyen Van Cam—sur sa vie depuis Juin 1925 jusqu'à son arrestation en date du 5 août 1929 à Ha Tinh," pp. 44–49, in Dossier 2690, Carton 335, CAOM. According to this source, Lam Duc Thu was elected president at that meeting. Also see William J. Duiker, *The Comintern and Vietnamese Communism* (Athens, Ohio: Ohio University Center for International Studies, 1975), p. 14.

19. Tran Van Cung has given his version of the issue in his memoirs, *Buoc ngoat vi dai cua lich su cach mang Viet Nam* [A great step for the history of the Vietnamese revolution] (Hanoi: Ban nghien cuu lich su Dang, n.d.), pp. 105–19.

20. See Phan Than Son, "Le Mouvement Ouvrier de 1920 à 1930," in Jean Chesneaux, ed., *Tradition et Révolution au Vietnam* (Paris: n.p., 1971), pp. 169–70. For information on Thang, see Christophe Giebel, "Telling Life: An Approach to the Official Biography of Ton Duc Thang," in K. W. Taylor and John K. Whitmore, eds., *Essays into Vietnamese Pasts* (Ithaca, N.Y.: Cornell University Southeast Asia Program, 1995), pp. 246–71.

21. For a trenchant discussion of the impact of the Sixth Congress on the league, see Gareth Porter, "Proletariat and peasantry in Early Vietnamese Communism," *Asian Thought and Society* 1, no. 3 (December 1976).

22. I. N. Ognetov, "Komintern i revoliutsionnoe dvizhenie vo V'ietname" [The Comintern and the revolutionary movement in Vietnam], in *Komintern i Vostok* [The Comintern and the East] (Moscow: n.p., 1969), p. 428. Nguyen Van Tao may have been selected as an FCP delegate at the suggestion of Nguyen Ai Quoc—see Hong Ha, *V Strane Sovetov*, p.128. At one time, many observers in Vietnam thought that An was Nguyen Ai Quoc; see, for example, Nguyen Kien Giang, *Viet Nam nam dau tien sau cach mang thang tam* [Vietnam in the first years following the August Revolution] (Hanoi: Su that, 1961), p. 215. Nguyen Van Tao has since discussed his attendance at the Sixth

Congress in his memoirs. His topic was evidently picked on the instructions of his superiors. See "Recalling the days spent attending the Sixth Congress of the Communist International," in *Tap chi Cong san* [Communist Review], no. 7 (July 1983), translated in JPRS, no. 84,288. One of the delegates at the congress, Nguyen The Binh, did not like Tao and, when he was later seized by the French, provided information about the congress. See "note concernant Ngo Duc Tri et Nguyen The Binh," in dossier labeled "Les élèves Annamites a l'école Staline et le Pacte Franco-Sovietique du 29 novembre 1932," in SLOTFOM, Series III, Carton 44, CAOM.

23. Whether Le Hong Son's fear of Chinese retaliation was justified must remain a matter of speculation. There is some evidence that Chinese officials tolerated the activities of the league so long as it was restricted to the Vietnamese community and directed specifically at the colonial regime in Indochina, toward which Chiang Kai-shek harbored a deep distrust. The creation of a formal Communist Party, though, would obviously stretch Chinese official tolerance to its limits. It is also possible, in the light of events that will be discussed below, that by this point Le Hong Son had strong suspicions that Lam Duc Thu was actively betraying the league to its enemies. For a list of the delegates present at the congress, see "Les Associations anti-Françaises en Indochina et le propagande communiste: Historique," in SLOTFOM, Series III, Carton 48, CAOM. This source, a series of classified reports known as "Notes Périodiques," was issued periodically by the Sûreté Générale in Hanoi from 1929 until the eve of World War II; they provide a valuable insight into Vietnamese nationalist activities and the French attempts to control them. The Sûreté reported that Le Hong Son himself had initially wanted to change the name of the organization to the Vietnamese Communist Party when he had moved the headquarters of the organization briefly to Guangxi in 1928. See "Note Périodique: Historique," p. 62, in ibid.

24. For this statement, see Tran Huy Lieu, *Tai lieu tham khao Lich su cach mang Can dai Viet Nam* [Historical research materials concerning the revolution in modern Vietnam], vol. 4 (Hanoi: n.p., 1958), pp. 170–73. For references to the meeting in Hong Kong, see Tran Van Cung *Buoc ngoat*, and Quang Hung and Quoc Anh (Tran Van Cung), "Le Hong Son: Nguoi chien si xuat sac thuoc the he nhung nguoi cong san dau tien o Viet-nam" [Le Hong Son: The most outstanding fighter of his generation among the first communists in Vietnam], in *NCLS*, no. 184 (Jan–Feb 1979), pp. 11–16. A French intelligence report on the conference, "Note Périodique," no. 4, January 1930, is located in SLOTFOM, Series III, Carton 48, CAOM.

25. The letter of request is contained in appendix no. 3, *Contribution à l'histoire*, vol. 4. Moscow's negative reply came in December 1929—see appendix 7, ibid.

26. This information is from the dossier on Duong Hac Dinh, undated, in SPCE, Carton 367, CAOM. Duong Hac Dinh, the only member of the Tonkin regional committee not to leave the congress in May, later became a French agent.

27. Quang Hung and Quoc Anh, "Le Hong Son," p. 19.

28. The decision to send Le Duy Diem (code name Le Loi) to find Nguyen Ai Quoc was reported in the dossier on Duong Hac Dinh, in SPCE, Carton 367, CAOM. Diem had once been a member of the Tan Viet. For the transformation of the Tan Viet Party into the Indochinese Communist League, see Tran Huu Chuong, "Memoirs concerning the Indochinese Communist League," in *Tap chi Cong san*, no. 2 (February 1983), translated in JPRS, no. 83,452.

29. The Comintern directive of October 27, 1929, titled "On the Problem of Forming an Indochinese Communist Party," is contained in a Vietnamese version in

Tran Van Cung, *Buoc ngoat*, pp. 68–74 and in *Van kien Dang (1930–1945)* [Party documents, (1930–1945)], vol. 1 (Hanoi: Ban nghien cuu lich su dang truong uong, 1977) pp. 9–17. For an English translation, see *Vietnam Documents and Research Notes* (U.S. Mission in Vietnam, Saigon), document no. 100, part II, pp. 247–52.

30. Correspondence between the two parties contained in the Annex to the report of the governor-general to the ministry of colonies, February 12, 1930, in SLOTFOM, Series III, Carton 129, CAOM.

31. Do Ngoc Dzu provided information on his trip during an interrogation by the French. See "Dossier on déclaration de Do Ngoc Du," August 10, 1931, in SPCE, Carton 367, CAOM. Do Ngoc Dzu, also known as Phiem Chu, was born in Hai Duong province in 1907. Born in an educated family, he attended the Collège du Protectorat and was expelled in 1928 for taking part in school strikes. He then joined the league and attended its training class in Canton during its second term, from October 1926 to January 1927. Then he attended the Whampoa Academy and was sent back to Vietnam to work in Hanoi with Duong Hac Dinh. See Huynh Kim Khanh, *Vietnamese Communism, 1925–1945* (Ithaca, N.Y.: Cornell University Press, 1982), p. 124.

32. The formation of the Federation of Communist Groups of Insulinde and the visit of the "Chinese inspector" in November were noted by the French in a report titled "L'Action déterminante de Nguyen Ai Quoc dans la création du Parti National Communiste Annamite," undated, in SPCE, Carton 367, CAOM. According to French sources, Le Hong Son and his colleagues were also unhappy at being placed under Chinese supervision as the result of reports that the CCP was making its followers work in factories or mass associations to weed out weaker members. See the Note Périodique dated November 1929 in ibid. For information on the formation of the Shanghai branch of the Far Eastern Bureau, see Gunther Nollau, *International Communism and World Revolution* (New York: Praeger, 1961), p. 141. Also see Frederick S. Litten, "The Noulens Affair," *China Quarterly*, no. 138 (June 1994), p. 503. According to Nollau, the first head of the Shanghai branch was the American Communist Earl Browder. He was succeeded by the German Gerhard Eisler sometime in 1929.

33. Note Périodique, January 1930, p. 6, in SLOTFOM, Series III, Carton 48, CAOM; Note Confidentielle, no. 1725/SG, March 17, 1930, in SPCE, Carton 368, CAOM. Some observers have speculated that the Comintern representative might have been Nguyen Ai Quoc. In fact, it is probable that the visitor was a Ukrainian going by the name of Hilaire Noulens, who had arrived in Shanghai to work at the Bureau in 1928 and was reportedly out of the city on a tour of the region during the winter of 1929–30. As we shall see, he returned to Shanghai in February or March 1930. See Litten, "Noulens Affair," pp. 502–3.

34. Quoc's letter to the CPI is in Letter of Nguyen Ai Quoc to leaders of DDCSD [Dong duong Cong san Dang, or CPI], contained in report of Sûreté Générale, December 31, 1929, in SPCE, Carton 368, CAOM. Nguyen Ai Quoc's account of his trip is contained in his letter to the FEB, February 18, 1930, in the Ho Chi Minh Museum in Hanoi. For a French account, see "L'Action déterminante . . . ," in SPCE, Carton 367, CAOM. Also see Kobelev, p. 96, and Hong Ha, *V Strane Sovetov*, p. 135.

35. Presumably Nguyen Ai Quoc was traveling on a false passport. For one account of his trip, see "Interrogation of Hong Son," October 24, 1932, in SPCE, Carton 367, CAOM. Nguyen Ai Quoc's own account is contained in his letter to the FEB, February 18, 1930, in the Ho Chi Minh Museum in Hanoi. For a French version compiled by the Sûreté, see "L'Action déterminante . . . ," in SPCE, Carton 367, CAOM. In his letter,

Quoc gave December 23 as the date of his arrival, but that date was based on the lunar calendar—see Huynh Kim Khanh, *Vietnamese Communism*, p. 125n. According to *Contribution à l'histoire*, vol. 4, p. 24, he arrived in Hong Kong in January. In his interrogation by the French, Le Hong Son declared that Quoc arrived in February, and that the unity conference took place in March.

36. Dossier on Duong Hac Dinh, in SPCE, Carton 367, CAOM. For Kobelev's version, see p. 94. Nguyen Ai Quoc apologized for not coming sooner, and explained that he had tried without success to enter Vietnam via Siam. Nguyen Ai Quoc's meeting with members of the CCP is described briefly in *HZYZ*, p. 43. The invitation to various cadres to come to Hong Kong for a unity conference was sent by Ho Tung Mau on November 29, 1929. On January 15, 1930, CPI responded that it would sent two representatives. See *Contribution à l'histoire*, vol. 4, p. 24.

37. The representatives from the ACP were Chau Van Liem and Nguyen Thieu. Trinh Dinh Cu and Nguyen Duc Canh represented the CPI. For the mishaps of the Indochinese Communist League delegates, see T.C., "Cac co so bi mat cua co quan lanh dao Dang Cong san Dong duong" [The clandestine foundations of the leading organs of the Indochinese Communist Party], in *NCLS*, no. 37 (April 1962), p. 20.

38. Huynh Kim Khanh, *Vietnamese Communism*, p. 125, stated that there were a few days of invective before agreement to unite was reached. But Le Hong Son said the program was accepted by unanimous vote in one day. See his interrogation, October 24, 1932, in SPCE, Carton 367, CAOM.

39. The note of January 6, 1930, is contained in the Ho Chi Minh Museum in Hanoi and is reproduced in *Van kien Dang toan tap* [Complete Party Documents], vol. 2 (Hanoi: Chinh tri Quoc gia, 1998), Huynh Kim Khanh, *Vietnamese Communism*, p. 125n, noted that with the new name of the Party, they adopted the Vietnamese form, putting the word "party" first, instead of in Chinese fashion, with "party" last. Also see *Van kien Dang*, vol. 1, p. 191.

40. This is not the same document that had been sent by the Comintern from Moscow in October—see 29, above. For a reference to the arrival of the December report in Saigon, see Nguyen Nghia, "To chuc va phat dong phong trao dau tranh o Nam ky sau khi Dang ta vua moi thong nhat ra doi" [The organization and mobilization of the struggle movement in the South after our newly united Party was formed], in *NCLS*, no. 67 (October 1964), p. 59. Since Nghia makes no mention of being aware of the report's existence during the meeting in Hong Kong, presumably Nguyen Ai Quoc had not seen a copy at that time.

41. For a French-language version, see *Contribution à l'histoire*, vol. 4, appendix 7. A Vietnamese-language version exists in Hanoi. Excerpts are cited in the report titled "L'Action déterminante . . ." in SPCE, Carton 367, CAOM. It was also cited in Note Périodique of December 1929, p. 4, in SLOTFOM, Series III, Carton 48, in ibid.

42. A Vietnamese version of the appeal is in *Toan Tap II*, vol 2., pp. 307–8. An abridged English-language version is contained in *Viet Nam Social Sciences* (January 1985), pp. 170–71.

43. For this strategy document, see *Toan Tap II*, vol 2., pp. 297–98.

44. The letter to Noulens is in the Ho Chi Minh Museum in Hanoi. It is printed in a Vietnamese language version in *Van kien Dang Toan tap*, vol. 2, pp. 18–25. In a report to Moscow on the results of the conference, Nguyen Ai Quoc remarked that it was a mistake to have abolished the league—see "Bao cao tom tat hoi nghi" [Summary report on the conference] in ibid., pp. 10–13.

VI | *Red Nghe Tinh*

1. Copies of both letters are contained in the Ho Chi Minh Museum in Hanoi. For a Vietnamese version of the letter to the Dalburo, see *Toan Tap I*, vol. 3, pp. 9–11. Also see Pierre Rousset, *Communisme et Nationalisme Vietnamien* (Paris: Editions Galilée, 1978), p. 199.

2. Information on Nguyen Ai Quoc's stay in Thailand is contained in Hoang Van Hoan, *A Drop in the Ocean: Hoang Van Hoan's Revolutionary Reminiscences* (Beijing: Foreign Languages Press), pp. 52–54. The Comintern had decided to abolish the South Seas Communist Party on the grounds that the Chinese Communist Party had neglected its responsibilities in the area. The South Seas Party, which was composed primarily of ethnic Chinese residing in Malaya and Singapore, had decided to cultivate the overseas Chinese community there because the Malay peoples were allegedly "lazy and contented." See Note Périodique, no. 5 (February-March 1930) in SLOT-FOM, Series III, Carton 48, CAOM; also see Charles B. McLane, *Soviet Strategies in Southeast Asia* (Princeton, N.J.: Princeton University Press, 1966), pp.131–36. McLane cites British government sources to the effect that Nguyen Ai Quoc felt that the failure of the South Seas party was a consequence of its inability to resolve the racial question.

3. French official reports on the uprising are contained in dossier 2614, SPCE, Carton 322, CAOM. For a succinct account of the mutiny, see Thomas Hodgkin, *Vietnam: The Revolutionary Path* (New York: St. Martin's, 1981), pp. 240–42. For a Vietnamese point of view, see Hoang Van Dieu, *Viet Nam Quoc Dan Dang* [Vietnamese Nationalist Party] (Saigon, Khai Tri, 1970), pp. 89–104.

4. Diep Lien Anh, *Mau trang—mau dao: Doi song doa-day cua phu cao-su mien dat-do* [Latex and blood: The wretched life of the rubber plantation workers in the red-earth districts] (Saigon: Lao Dong Moi, 1965), pp. 35–40, cited in Ngo Vinh Long, *Before the Revolution: The Vietnamese Peasants Under the French* (New York: Columbia University Press, 1991), pp. 109–12.

5. Nguyen Ai Quoc, *Le procès de la colonisation française* is included in English in Bernard B. Fall, ed., *Ho Chi Minh on Revolution: Selected Writings, 1920–1966*, p. 81. Also see Report of M. Favre, special commissioner of the Sûreté at Vinh, June 27, 1931, in dossier 2686, Carton 333, SPCE, CAOM.

6. See the report of M. Billet, June 27, 1931, in SPCE, dossier 2686, Carton 333, CAOM. For an analysis of the impact of French policies on rural income, see Robert L. Sansom, *The Economics of Insurgency in the Mekong Delta of Vietnam* (Cambridge, Mass.: MIT Press, 1970), and Truong Chinh and Vo Nguyen Giap, *The Peasant Question (1937–1938)*, (Ithaca, N.Y.: Cornell University Southeast Asia Program, 1974), data paper no. 94, pp. 35–37. For Nguyen Ai Quoc's report on the seizure of land, see "Annamese Peasant Conditions," in Fall, *On Revolution*, p. 37.

7. Interrogation of Thai Van Giai, June 28, 1931, in SPCE, dossier 2686, Carton 333, CAOM. Giai, a native of Ha Tinh province, was a graduate of the National Academy at Hué and a former school teacher. Other official accounts of these incidents are contained in dossier 2628, Carton 323; dossier 2641, Carton 327; and dossier 2684, Carton 332, all in CAOM. Also see Tran Huy Lieu, *Les Soviets du Nghe Tinh* (Hanoi: Foreign Languages Press, 1960), pp. 19–21.

8. Interrogation of Thai Van Gai, June 28, 1931 in SPCE, dossier 2686, Carton 333, CAOM.

9. See Nguyen Luong Bang's article in *Souvenirs*, p. 63, and "Bao Cao gui Quoc te Cong San," in *Van kien Dang Toan tap* [Complete Party Documents], vol. 2 (Hanoi: NXB Chinh tri Quoc gia, 1998), p. 34. For Nguyen Ai Quoc's comment in Siam, see Le Manh Trinh, "Dans le Koung Tung et au Siam," in *Souvenirs*, p. 117. The French intelligence report is in Note Périodique, February–March 1930, in SLOTFOM, Series III, Carton 48, CAOM. One Party history described the VNQDD mutiny as a glorious "clap of thunder," but according to the VNQDD historian Hoang Van Dao, Communist agitators actually distributed leaflets to alert the French to the pending attack.

10. The provincial committee directive is contained in Tran Huy Lieu, *Lich su tam muoi nam chong Phap* [A history of eighty years of struggle against the French], vol. 2 (Hanoi: Van su dia, 1958), pp. 66–67.

11. An official French report on the incident, dated December 31, 1930, is contained in SPCE, dossier 2634, Carton 325, CAOM.

12. Details on the formation of the members of the provisional central committee can be found in T.C., "Cac co so bi mat cua co quan lanh dao Dang Cong san Dong duong" [The clandestine foundations of the leading organs of the Indochinese Communist Party], in *NCLS*, no. 37 (April 1962); Nguyen Nghia, "Gop them mot it tai lieu ve cong cuoc hop nhat cac to chuc cong san dau tien o Viet Nam va vai tro cua dong chi Nguyen Ai Quoc" [Some additional materials on the unification of the first Communist organizations in Vietnam and the role of comrade Nguyen Ai Quoc], in ibid., no. 59 (February 1964); and Nguyen Nghia, "Cong cuoc hop nhat cac to chuc cong san o trong nuoc sau hoi nghi Huong Cang va viec to chuc ban trung uong lam thoi dau tien" [The unification of the Communist organizations in the country after the Hong Kong meeting and the organization of the first provisional central committee] in ibid, no. 62 (May 1964). These sources do not explain the reasons that the conference did not take place in April, as originally scheduled. In all likelihood, local branches of the VCP had been unable to select their delegates by then.

13. Quoc's undated report to the Comintern Executive Committee was probably written in late September. A copy is contained in *Toan Tap I*, vol. 3, pp. 27–28.

14. The article is published in A. Neuberg, ed., *Armed Insurrection* (London: NLB, 1970), pp. 255–71 (emphasis in original). According to Pierre Rousset, the article had been ordered by Ossip Piatnitsky, the new head of the Comintern, later to be purged by Stalin. Erich Wollenberg helped to edit the article and later remarked that Nguyen Ai Quoc opposed the decision by the CCP leadership to launch the Canton uprising and said that it was doomed to failure—see Rousset, *Communisme*, pp. 62–63. Rousset raises doubts that Quoc wrote the article, since it did not mention Vietnam, but the latter had specifically mentioned to acquaintances that he was writing an article on the subject of the Chinese revolution. For a brief discussion of Quoc's views, see *Nguyen Ai Quoc o Quang Chau* [Nguyen Ai Quoc in Canton] (Hanoi: Chinh tri Quoc gia, 1998), pp. 159–61.

15. For Nguyen Ai Quoc's comments in these discussions and his colleagues' response, see the Declaration of Ngo Duc Tri, in SPCE, Carton 367, CAOM. In his March 1930 report to the Comintern, Quoc criticized Party cadres for prematurely forming "soviet" organizations in villages not under their firm control—see "Bao cao gui Quoc te Cong san," pp. 35–36.

16. The document is contained in *Van kien Dang (1920–1945)* [Party Documents

(1930–1945)], vol. 1 (Hanoi: Ban nghien cuu lich su Dang truong uong, 1977), pp. 58–60. The author of this directive is not indicated. The only copy available was evidently located in the Comintern archives and bore the notation "Lettre du CC Comité région en Annam Concernant les Soviets, septembre 1930." The directive was signed Trung uong (Central). Because there was no formal central committee inside the country at the time, I have concluded that it was probably drafted by Nguyen Ai Quoc, with the possible assistance of Tran Phu and any other members of the provisional central committee who had already arrived in Hong Kong for the first plenum. Trung uong became the common term within the Party to refer to the central leadership.

17. Cited in Trung Chinh, "Tinh chat tu phat cua xo viet Nghe Tinh" [The spontaneous character of the Nghe Tinh soviets], in *NCLS*, no. 31 (October 1961), p. 4. Where the journal was published in unclear.

18. A French-language translation of this circular is contained in SPCE, dossier 2637, Carton 326, CAOM. It seems likely that this message was issued before the regional committee's admonishment had been received. The provincial committee did concede that the movement had suffered severe losses in recent weeks as the result of a lack of discipline and poor planning. I have been unable to locate any accurate information regarding the number of assassinations that took place at the time.

19. Declaration of Ngo Duc Tri, in SPCE, Carton 367, CAOM. There is some discrepancy on dates in the recollections of various participants, perhaps because some of them were referring to the lunar calendar. Also see Bui Lam's memoirs of the meeting in *Tap chi Cong san* [Communist Review], no. 9 (September 1982), and the Declaration of Nguyen Van Sau in SPCE, Carton 365, CAOM.

20. Declaration of Nguyen Van Sau, in SPCE, Carton 365, CAOM. The sequence of events during this period is somewhat confusing, and it is possible that the trip to Shanghai was undertaken prior to the final decision to hold the conference.

21. Declaration of Ngo Duc Tri in SPCE, Carton 367, CAOM; *Van kien Dang Toan tap*, vol. 2, p. 268. Others in attendance were Tran Phu (Ly Quy), Le Mao (Cat), Nguyen Trong Nghia (Nhat), and Ngo Duc Tri (Van) representing Cochin China, Ho Tung Mau (Ich), Bui Cong Trung, and Bui Lam. Tran Van Lam (Giap) was the delegate who got lost in Hong Kong. See Bui Lam, "Nguyen Ai Quoc and the First Plenum of the Party Central Committee (October)," in *Tap chi Cong san*, no. 9 (September 1982), translated in JPRS, no. 82,610.

22. Report titled "L'Action déterminante de Nguyen Ai Quoc dans la création du Parti National Communiste Annamite," appendix 1 ("Critique du travail") in SPCE, Carton 367, CAOM.

23. "Tho cua trung uong gui cho cac cap dang bo" [Letter by the Center to all Party branches], in *Van kien Dang (1930–1945)*, vol. 1, pp. 189–200. For a French-language version, see "Lettre du CC au sections différentes," December 9, 1930, in SPCE, Carton 367, CAOM. For an interesting discussion of the issue of the "growing over" of the revolution, see Rousset, *Communisme*, p. 108.

24. Tran Van Cung, *Buoc ngoat vi dai cua lich su cach mang Viet Nam* [A great step for the history of the Vietnamese revolution] (Hanoi: Ban Nghien cuu lich su Dang, n.d.), pp. 78–79. The program is reproduced in *Van kien Dang (1930–1945)*, vol. 1, pp. 61–77. Nguyen Ai Quoc, of course, had criticized the Tam Tam Xa on his arrival in Canton in late 1924 for precisely those tendencies.

25. See "Truyen don giai thiec viec doi ten Dang" [Announcement on the decision to change the name of the Party], in *Van kien Dang (1930–1945)*, vol. 1, pp. 177–78.

Also see "Thong cao cho cac xu uy" [A directive to all regional committees], in ibid., pp. 182–86.

26. "An nghi quyet cua trung uong toan the hoi nghi ve tinh hinh hien tai o Dong duong va nhiem vu cap kip cua Dang" [Resolution by the Central Committee on the current situation in Indochina and the urgent tasks of the Party], report dated October 1930, in ibid., pp. 78–92. These views were passed on to Party members inside Indochina in an undated report titled "Thu gui cho Dang Cong san Dong duong" [Letter to the Indochinese Communist Party], in *Van kien Dang Toan tap*, vol. 2, pp. 284–314. I surmise that the author was Tran Phu.

27. "Thong cao cho dong chi" [Directive to Comrades], in *Van kien Dang (1930–1945)*, vol. 1, pp. 169–71.

28. Declaration of Ngo Duc Tri in SPCE, Carton 367, CAOM. Names of other members of the Central Committee, as well as key members of the various regional committees, are located in T.C., "Cac co so," pp. 21–23; and dossier 18, Note Périodique (April–May 1931), in SLOTFOM, Series III, Carton 48, CAOM.

29. See Declaration of Ngo Duc Tri in SPCE, Carton 367, CAOM. Also Bui Lam, "Nguyen Ai Quoc." Some observers in Vietnam and abroad maintain that Nguyen Ai Quoc did not attend the October plenum. From the evidence, it seems clear that he did.

30. *Van kien Dang (1930–1945)*, vol. 1, pp. 175–81. This decree is puzzling, since it implicitly contradicts many of the views expressed by the Tran Phu faction in October. Some scholars in Hanoi speculate that the November circular might have been written by Nguyen Ai Quoc himself, but it is specifically indicated that it had been issued by the Standing Committee. See I. N. Ognetov, "Kominterni revoliutsionnoe dvizhenie vo V'ietname" [The Comintern and the Revolutionary Movement in Vietnam], in *Komintern i Vostok* [The Comintern and the East] (Moscow: n.p., 1969), p. 435.

31. "Tho cua Trung uong ghi," pp. 189–200. For similar comments on the re-actionary character of the bourgeoisie, see "Thu gui cho Dang Cong," pp. 284–314. In so defining the united front, the Standing Committee was only carrying out Comintern directives—see Noulens' letter of November 13, 1930, to the ICP in *Van kien Dang Toan tap*, vol. 2, p. 274–83.

32. "Thong cao cac xu uy" [Directive to all regional committees], in *Van kien Dang (1930–1945)*, pp. 201–11. For a version in French, see "Lettre du sécretariat aux organes régionaux," in SPCE, Carton 367, CAOM.

33. *Toan Tap I*, vol. 3, pp. 29–31.

34. Letter from Nguyen Ai Quoc to FEB, January 29, 1931, in SPCE, Carton 367, CAOM.

35. Undated letter in ibid. The context suggests that the letter may have been written on February 12 and sent with a copy of Tran Phu's previous letter.

36. Dossier 127, Series III, in SLOTFOM, Carton 44, CAOM. Also see SPCE, Carton 368, CAOM.

37. Letter from Lefranc to Far Eastern Bureau in Shanghai, March 7, 1931, in SPCE, Carton 364, CAOM.

38. Information from "Nga" (Ngo Duc Tri) in Note Confidentielle no. 1967, May 29, 1931, in SPCE, Carton 365, CAOM. Lefranc's postcard to Quoc in Hong Kong in ibid. read: "My old friend, Here I am well established in the good city of Saigon where it is quite hot. I met your two cousins and I am happy to be able to tell you that they are doing famously. On Sunday I went to the races but didn't win anything. Everything

goes well here and I think that my affairs will be soon completed. I plan to return to Hong Kong at the anticipated date. Thus, I will see you soon. I will inform you of my arrival. Best wishes, Ferrand."

39. Letter of executive committee of the regional committee of Annam to the regional committee of Tonkin, March 3, 1931, and decisions of the provincial committee of Ha Tinh, March 25–31, 1931, both in Note Périodique, May 1931, in Series III, SLOTFOM, Carton 49, CAOM. Nguyen Duc Canh was executed by the French in July 1932.

40. The resolution is contained in *Van kien Dang (1930–1945)*, vol. 1, pp. 227–49.

41. According to dossier 3, Note Périodique, May 1931, in SLOTFOM, Series III, Carton 115, Tri was seized on April 2. Under interrogation, he was given the name "Nga." Several other leaders, including Ho Tung Mau and Nguyen Phong Sac, were arrested in succeeeding weeks (the former British police in Hong Kong). Ho Tung Mau was later released but Sac, who had directed the movement in the central provinces for several months, was executed.

42. "Pis'mo TsK Indo-Kitaya," dated April 17, 1931, in Comintern archives, Carton 495, folder 154, file 462. Nguyen Ai Quoc shared many of these views, although he placed the responsibility elsewhere. Writing as "Viktor" to Noulens on April 28, Quoc complained that many Party members of worker or peasant extraction were illiterate. Despite their courage, they worked poorly and their ideological awareness was low. As a result, they depended entirely on intellectuals and had strong tendencies toward terrorism and "putschism." See letter by Viktor in ibid., Carton 495, Folder 154, File 462. In this letter he reported Tran Phu's escape from the French in early April.

43. The letter, stamped April 2, 1931, is in the Comintern archives, Carton 495, folder 154, file 462. Noulens had become aware that part of the problem within the ICP was rooted in the personality conflict between Nguyen Ai Quoc and Tran Phu. In a letter to Serge Lefranc dated May 20, 1931, he remarked that relations between Quoc and the ICP Central Committee were not especially good, but that the former should eventually be able to resolve the difficulties with his colleagues. See letter from Shanghai to Ducroux, May 20, 1931, in SPCE, Carton 364, CAOM.

44. Letters by Viktor, April 20 and 24, 1931, in SPCE, Carton 365, CAOM.

45. On the death of Tran Phu, see the Letter to Minister of Colonies, March 22, 1933, in SPCE, dossier 640, Carton 55, CAOM, and Ton Quang Duyet, "Mot vai y kien bo sung ve lich su hai dong chi Tran Phu va Nguyen Thi Minh Khai" [Some additional opinions on the biographies of Tran Phu and Nguyen Thi Minh Khai], in *NCLS*, no. 139 (July–August 1971).

46. Tran Huy Lieu, *Les Soviets*, p. 40. Reports of the decline of the movement are in SLOTFOM, Series III, Carton 49, CAOM.

47. The information on the drought is in Report of M. Favre, June 27, 1931, in SPCE, dossier 2686, Carton 333, CAOM.

48. Comintern archives, letter of May 12, 1931, Carton 495, folder 154, file 569.

49. Ton Quang Duyet, "Mot vai y kien."

50. Lam Duc Thu's comments about Tuyet Minh's feelings toward Nguyen Ai Quoc appear in the interrogation of Lesquendieu (Le Quang Dat), October 28, 1931, in SPCE, Carton 367, CAOM. For rumors of her alleged encounter with Quoc in Hong Kong, see ibid. According to Lam Duc Thu, by that time she had already remarried.

The letter from Nguyen Ai Quoc to Tuyet Minh expressing sorrow over their separation is in the French archives—see Daniel Hémery, *Ho Chi Minh: De l'Indochine au Vietnam* (Paris: Gallimard, 1990), p. 145.

51. Both letters, undated, are located in the Comintern archives, Carton 495, Folder 154, File 469. Information on Minh Khai's arrest in Hong Kong (under the name of Duy) is contained in Declaration of Nguyen Van Sau, September 3, 1931, SPCE, Carton 367, CAOM.

52. Letter of Nguyen Ai Quoc to CC/CPM [Central Committee, Communist Party of Malaya], May 9, 1931. Letter from Ly Phat [Nguyen Ai Quoc] to Joseph Ducroux, May 15, 1931. See SPCE, Carton 364, CAOM. In the latter, written in disappearing ink, Quoc reported that links with Indochina were still broken, as were those with the Siamese Communist Party. "The other route" to Malaya has also been destroyed, since we lost our "Chinese friend." The author asked Ducroux to work with the Siamese Communist Party as it had "been neglected too long." In his letter to Lefranc on May 20, Noulens asked him to pass on information on the activities of the Malayan Party since he had lost contact with them. "Is there a Center? Is there any mass work being carried out?" He asked Lefranc to find someone to work in the Dutch East Indies, preferably a Hindu. See ibid.

53. Telegram from Singapore, June 2, 1931, and letter, consulat de France, Hong Kong, June 10, 1931, both in SPCE, Carton 365, CAOM. Also see Jean Onraet, *Singapore: A Police Background* (London: Dorothy Crisp, 1941), pp. 110–15.

54. The French had already discovered that Quoc was in Hong Kong when they captured his last letter to Tran Phu on a courier in April—see Dang Hoa, *Bac Ho: Nhung Nam Thang o Nuoc Ngoai* [Uncle Ho: The months and years abroad] (Hanoi: Thong tin, 1990), p. 91. The French consul reported that his address in Hong Kong was 104 Tan Truong Road. Onraet gave his address as 49 Kai Yee Street, which may have been the location of his office. In his memoirs, Ho Chi Minh declared that he had been arrested at 186 Tam Lung Road in Kowloon—see T. Lan, *Vua di duong, Vua ke chuyen* [Walking and Talking] (Hanoi: Su that, 1976), p. 40. On the circumstances of his arrest, see Telegram, Sûreté in Saigon to Dirsurge [Director, Sûreté Générale], Hanoi, June 2, 1931, and letter, Consulat de France, Hong Kong, June 10, 1931, both in SPCE, Carton 365, CAOM; cable, Sûreté Générale in Hanoi to French concession in Shanghai, September 26, 1931, in SPCE, Carton 368, CAOM.

VII | *Into the Wilderness*

1. International Red Aid was an organization set up to assist revolutionary activitists in need throughout the world. According to Frederick S. Litten, the police found Noulens's telegraph address among Lefranc's possessions. After investigation, the Shanghai authorities discovered that Noulens operated out of several addresses, but eventually they located a key for his office in the Central Arcade Building on Nanjing Road, in the heart of Shanghai's business district. It was here that they found incriminating documents relating to his activities as a Comintern agent. See Litten, "The Noulens Affair," in *China Quarterly*, no. 138 (June 1994), p. 494. Hilaire Noulens has sometimes been identified as Paul Ruegge, but Babette Gross, the wife of the German Communist Willi Munzenberg, maintained that the Ruegges, a Swiss couple involved in radical causes, were actually in Moscow at that time. According to information available to the

British scholar Dennis Duncanson, Soviet authorities at the time regularly relieved visiting delegates of their passports and copied them or lent them to fellow agents serving abroad. See Babette Gross, *Willi Munzenberg* (Stuttgart: n.p., 1967), p. 235, cited in Dennis Duncanson, "Ho Chi Minh in Hong Kong, 1931–1932," in *China Quarterly*, no. 57 (January-March 1974), fn 25. It is now believed that Noulens was a Ukrainian named either Luft or Jakov Rudnik. See Litten, "Noulens Affair," and Frederick Wakeman, Jr., *Policing Shanghai, 1927–1937* (Berkeley: University of California Press, 1995), pp. 149–150. According to Wakeman, Noulens and his wife were probably eliminated during the Stalin purges of the late 1930s. The *South China Morning Post*, on July 4, 1931, reported the denial of the Belgian consulate that Noulens and his wife, Mrs. Van der Cruysen, were Belgian—see SPCE, Carton 365, CAOM.

2. Gov Tel 124, July 1, 1931, and Gov Tel 142, July 24, 1931, both in CO 129/535/3. The best single published source for information on Nguyen Ai Quoc's arrest is Duncanson's "Ho Chi Minh in Hong Kong."

3. Duncanson, "Ho Chi Minh in Hong Kong," p. 92. In T. Lan, *Vua di duong, vua ke chuyen* [Walking and talking] (Hanoi: Su that, 1976), p. 41, Ho Chi Minh later explained that when Ho Tung Mau heard of his arrest, he told Loseby, who obviously had connections with Communist elements operating in the colony.

4. Duncanson, "Ho Chi Minh in Hong Kong," pp. 91–94.

5. Letter from Howard Smith of the Foreign Office to the undersecretary in the Colonial Office, July 28, 1931, in CO 129/539/2, PRO. Also see Duncanson, "Ho Chi Minh in Hong Kong," p. 93.

6. Notes by Calder, August 14 and 17, 1931, and Ransom, August 4, 1931, in dossier titled "Arrest of Nguyen Ai Quoc," in CO 129/535/3, PRO.

7. *Hong Kong Weekly Press*, August 28, 1931. Nguyen Ai Quoc was awarded HK $7,500 in damages as compensation for the irregularities in the banishment inquiry. See Duncanson, "Ho Chi Minh in Hong Kong," pp. 93–95. The young woman, who had been identified by French intelligence sources as Le Ung Thuan, was freed on August 20 from Victoria Prison. In September she arrived in Nanjing, where she stayed at the home of Ho Hoc Lam, her husband's father and a Kuomintang military officer with close ties to the ICP (see chapter 8). It was at Lam's house in Hangzhou that Phan Boi Chau had stayed prior to his arrest by the French. Hanoi telegram, Sûreté Générale to French Concession Shanghai, September 26, 1931, in SPCE, Carton 368, CAOM. Before her departure she met with Nguyen Ai Quoc in prison at his request and told him that she would go to Shanghai to carry out his instructions. See Pinot report, Envoi no. 624, September 8, 1931, marginal note in report of September 9, 1931, signed by S. G. Néron, in ibid.

8. T. Lan, *Vua di duong*, p. 49. A literal translation of Ho's comment to the nurse is "so that employees with blue collars [Chinese nurses] would not have to take orders from superiors with red collars [English chief nurses]." For other comments about how he passed the time, see *Glimpses/Life*, pp. 37–38, and report of Pinot in Envoi no. 624, September 8, 1931, in dossier labeled "Rapports d'agents 1931," in SPCE, Carton 369, CAOM. Also see Ly Ung Thuan letter to Lam Duc Thu, Envoi no. 633, October 24, 1931, in ibid.

9. Letter to Phac Chan (Lam Duc Thu), June 6, 1931, and letter to Lam Duc Thu, in Envoi no. 640, November 30, 1931, in SPCE, Carton 367, CAOM. French sources claim that Quoc attempted to secure assistance from Chinese Communist elements operating in Hong Kong to make arrangements to leave the country (see Néron letter to

Mr. Perdue, September 15, 1931, in SPCE, Carton 368, CAOM), but they were apparently unable to come to his aid.

10. For further information on Nguyen Ai Quoc's family, see *Glimpses/Childhood*, pp. 101–11. According to this source, the imperial authorities had intended to burn down the village of Kim Lien after the Nghe-Tinh uprising, but Nguyen Thi Thanh's vigorous protests led them to abandon the idea. There have been conflicting reports about the activities of Tang Tuyet Minh, Quoc's first wife, during this period. Le Quang Dat (Lesquendieu), Quoc's colleague in Shanghai, stated under interrogation by the French that Quoc had informed him that she had not come to see her husband in Hong Kong during the winter of 1929–30. Lam Duc Thu, however, told Noel that she had indeed visited Hong Kong to see Quoc and further declared that, after his arrest, she asked Loseby about him. See Noel report, Envoi no. 660. May 23, 1932, in SPCE, Carton 369, CAOM; the dossier labeled "Mission Laurent," in ibid; dossier labeled "Arrestation," in SPCE, Carton 365, CAOM; and Hanoi report, October 28, 1931, in SPCE, Carton 367, CAOM. For a report that Quoc sent fifty Chinese dollars to his brother, Khiem, in January 1926, see Police de l'Indochine Annam (Sogny) à DirAfPol [Directeur des Affaires Politiques] et de SurGe [Sûreté Général], note confidentielle no. 45, Hué, September 1, 1926, in the dossier labeled "Nguyen Ai Quoc 1926–1927," in SPCE, Carton 368, CAOM. For his father's death, see Annexe à la transmission no. 777/ SG du 2 juin 1930, in dossier labeled "Correspondances 1927 à 1930," in ibid. Nguyen Thi Thanh obtained permission from the authorities to visit her father during his last illness and took his remains back to Kim Lien: *Glimpses/Childhood*, p. 105.

11. Burton to Bushe, October 6, 1931; letter by Cowell, December 30, 1931; C. Howard Smith (Foreign Office) to Shuckburgh (Colonial Office), October 15, 1931; all in CO. The governor in Hong Kong was evidently reluctant to hold Nguyen Ai Quoc indefinitely, in the conviction that if the Privy Council should rule against the government it would place him in an awkward position. See letter by Cowell, December 31, 1931, CO, PRO.

12. Letter by Jacques Truelle, December 22, 1931, in CO, PRO.

13. Memoir by D. N. Pritt, in the Ho Chi Minh Museum in Hanoi. For the claim that Stafford Cripps had followed his political tendencies, see Duncanson, "Ho Chi Minh in Hong Kong," p. 98. Cripps later became a prominent Labour Party politician and British ambassador to the USSR. The charge that Quoc agreed to become a British agent appears in Hoang Van Chi *From Colonialism to Communism* (New York: Praeger, 1964), p. 50. The author may have picked up the rumor from the French, who apparently believed it. See "Fiche pour l'inspection évolution générale des forces communistes en Indochine, début 1950," in dossier: CAEO/2b, VI. Viet minh, I, Renseignements généraux, Service Historique de l'Armée de l'Air (Paris).

14. Secretary of State (124) to Governor Hong Kong, October 8, 1932, Hong Kong to Cunliffe-Lister, October 27, 1932, and Governor Hong Kong to Sir P. Cunliffe-Lister, date January 31, 1933, CO.

15. The decision to release Nguyen Ai Quoc for political reasons angered some British police officials in Hong Kong and Singapore, who argued that it would make it more difficult to maintain public security throughout the region. See Note sur Nguyen Ai Quoc, signé Tessier, February 12, 1933, in dossier labeled "Hong Kong," and Handwritten note, signed Ballereau, on a copy of Consul de France à Singapour "Ballereau," GouGen Indochine, no. 16, March 14, 1933, in dossier labeled "Singapore," in SPCE, Carton 369, CAOM. Mrs. Loseby described her own role in these events in an article

printed in the *New York Times*, September 14, 1969. Also see Duncanson, "Ho Chi Minh in Hong Kong," p. 99.

16. Why Nguyen Ai Quoc left the ship, the S.S. *Anhui*, at Xiamen is not clear, but it may have been to avoid the possibility of capture in its final destination of Shanghai. In fact, the French consul in Hong Kong had established good relations with the British police and in late January informed French authorities in Shanghai of Quoc's departure from Hong Kong. That is probably why the French police in Shanghai were convinced that he might be hiding in the city. See Consulat de France Hong Kong à Gougal, no. 8, January 22, 1933, in dossier labeled "Projet d 'échange . . . ," and DirSurGe (Marty) à Consulat de France Shanghai, no. 979, January 10, 1933, in dossier labeled "Correspondance 1932," in SPCE, Carton 369, CAOM. According to Vietnamese sources, Quoc did not leave Amoy until July. See BNTS, II, p. 42. Also see T. Lan, p. 43. In his own memoirs, Quoc's colleague Nguyen Luong Bang said that he was in Xiamen for six months.

17. For the quote, see T. Lan, Vua di duong, p. 51. According to this source, Quoc handed the note to a servant at the door. For other versions, see Charles Fourniou and Leo Figuerès, *Ho Chi Minh: Notre Camarade*, (Paris: Editions Sociales, 1970), pp. 115–116, and Nguyen Luong Bang article in *Nash Prezident Ho Shi Minh*, [Our President Ho Chi Minh] (Hanoi: Foreign Languages Press, 1967), p. 102. Kobelev, p. 110, claims that he lived the life of a rich Chinese on vacation while in Shanghai.

18. T. Lan, *Vua di duong*, pp. 55–56.

19. Nguyen Khanh Toan, "En URSS avec 'Oncle Ho,' " in *Souvenirs*, p. 145; information on the funeral ceremony is on p. 143. Also see Kobelev, p. 114.

20. Kobelev, p. 115. According to Anatoly A. Sokolov, Quoc enrolled at Lenin University in October 1934. For information on his circumstances in Moscow, see Sokolev's *Komintern i V'ietnam* (Moscow: Iv Ran, 1998), pp. 85–86. The timing of Nguyen Ai Quoc's arrival in Moscow is difficult to pinpoint. Nguyen Khanh Toan reported that he saw him there in early 1933, which is almost certainly mistaken. A brief autobiography written by Nguyen Ai Quoc himself at the time stated that he arrived in Moscow in July 1934 and then spent several months in the Crimea, enrolling in the Lenin School at the end of the year. Other dates in his account, however, are so inaccurate that it is difficult to know how much credence to give to it. See his "Avtobiografiya," of April 17, 1938, in the Comintern files, Carton 495, Folder 201, File 132.

21. Jean Lacouture, *Ho Chi Minh: A Political Biography*, trans. Peter Wiles (New York: Vintage, 1968), trans. Peter Wiles (New York: Vintage, 1968), p. 69.

22. I am grateful to Mr. Do Quang Hung of the Institute of History in Hanoi for providing me with speculation about Quoc's trial. Sophie Quinn-Judge has also heard reports in Moscow about the trial and speculates about the reasons—see her "Ho Chi Minh: New Perspectives from the Comintern Files," *The Vietnam Forum*, no. 14 (1994), p. 73. Sokolov has little to say about the matter, except that while Quoc was in Moscow during the mid-1930s he met with Dmitri Manuilsky and Vera Vasilieva.

23. Quoted in ibid., citing Moscow, Carton 495, Folder 154, File 586. Vasilieva's daughter recalls that Nguyen Ai Quoc often visited their home during this period, and took part in a number of "national evenings"—see Sokolov, *Komintern*, p. 87. According to Quinn-Judge (p. 80, fn 34), although Vasilieva's husband, Mark Zorkii, had come under accusation during the 1930s, she herself often courageously sought to protect the wives of arrested colleagues. This coincides with reports from other sources.

24. Le Hong Phong's arrival in China was reported in Note Périodique, second

quarter 1935, dossier 35, in SLOTFOM, Series III, Carton 54, CAOM. Also see Nguyen Van Khoan and Trieu Hien, "Le Hong Phong tim bat lien lac voi Dang" [Le Hong Phong seeks to establish ties with the Party], in *Xua Nay*, September 1997, pp. 9–11, and Pham Xanh, "Su no luc cua Quoc te Cong san trong viec khoi phuc phong trao cach mang Viet Nam" [The efforts of the Comintern to revive the Vietnamese Revolutionary Movement], in *Tap chi Lich su Dang* (Hanoi), no. 25, 1989, p. 31. On the Overseas Executive Committee, see Notes Périodiques of November and December 1932, SLOTFOM, Series III, Carton 52, CAOM.

25. An article in Giau's *Tap chi Cong san* [The Communist Review] noted that revolutionary work among the workers was more difficult than among peasants in Cochin China at that time, partly because it was difficult to penetrate the factories. See Note Périodique, first quarter 1934, annex 9, SLOTFOM, Series III, Carton 52, CAOM.

26. On Le Hong Son, see Note Périodique, first quarter 1933, SLOTFOM, Series III, Carton 52, CAOM. Also see "Interrogation of Hong Son," October 24, 1932, in SPCE, Carton 367, CAOM. For French reports on ICP activities during this period, see Note Périodique, second quarter 1933, in SLOTFOM, Series III, Carton 52, CAOM. The quote on police frustration is from Note Périodique, report of third quarter 1933, in ibid.

27. Note Périodique, second quarter, 1933, in SLOTFOM, Series III, annex 9, Carton 52, CAOM. For a discussion, see William J. Duiker, *The Comintern and Vietnamese Communism* (Athens, Ohio: Ohio University Center for International Studies, 1975), p. 28. For operations in Tonkin, see Note Périodique, second quarter, 1934, in SLOTFOM, Series III, annex 9, Carton 52, CAOM. According to this source, a provisional regional committee was established in Hanoi sometime in early 1934. That same day, however, the organizers and much of their network were arrested by the French. This source also mentions that a provisional regional committee was set up in Vinh. The reference to those released from prison is from SLOTFOM, Series III, Note Périodique, third quarter 1934, annex 9, Carton 52, CAOM.

28. All these are quotations from *Bolshevik* Note Périodique, no. 34, fourth quarter, 1934, annex 9, in SLOTFOM, Series III, Carton 52, CAOM. For information on the drawing up of the program of action, see Nguyen Van Khoan and Trieu Hien, "Le Hong Phong." A Vietnamese-language version of the program is contained in *Van kien Dang (1930–1945)* [Party Documents (1930–1945)], vol. 1 (Hanoi: Ban nghien cuu Lich su Dang Troung uong, 1977), pp. 292–324; for a discussion, see Pierre Rousset, *Communisme et nationalisme vietnamien* (Paris: Editions Galilée, 1978), pp. 125–126. Historians in Vietnam today agree that the program was too leftist to meet the needs of the times. See for example, Tran Huy Lieu, *Lich su tam muoi nam chong Phap* [A history of eighty years of struggle against the French] (Hanoi: Van su dia, 1958). I.N. Ognetov says that the ECCI meeting in March 1932 had called upon the ICP to fight petty bourgeois ideas in its ranks, while also criticizing "left deviationism" and "adventurism," such as addiction to the idea of a premature general uprising. According to Ognetov, it was as a result of rising petty bourgeois influence in the Party that the program of action was issued—see his "Komintern i revoliutsionnoe dvizhenie vo V'ietnam" [The Comintern and the Revolutionary Movement in Vietnam], in *Komintern i Vostok* [The Comintern and the East] (Moscow: n.p., 1969), pp. 435–37.

29. See Daniel Hémery, *Revolutionnaires vietnamiens et pouvoir colonial en Indochine* (Paris, 1975), pp. 53–54. The quote comes from *Bolshevik*, no. 5, December 1934, in Note Périodique, first quarter 1935, annex in SLOTFOM, Series III, Carton 54, CAOM. Ha Huy Tap wrote under the pseudonym Hong The Cong [Redness Will Bring About

Communism]. Many years later, I interviewed Tap's brother Ha Huy Giap in Hanoi. He conceded that in wanting to combine the anti-imperialist and antifeudal task Nguyen Ai Quoc had been correct, rather than focusing exclusively on antifeudalism, as his brother Tap had wanted.

30. The resolution is contained in Note Périodique, second quarter, 1935, annex 1, p. 6, in SLOTFOM, Series III, Carton 54, CAOM. The inclusion of Nguyen An Ninh in the list of national reformists is especially surprising, since he had already begun to cooperate with ICP leaders in Saigon. According to one French security services report, also in attendance at this conference were Nguyen Van Dut, Tran Van Chan, and Nguyen Van Than—see Note Périodique, second quarter, 1935, in SLOTFOM, Series III, Carton 54, CAOM.

31. See Orgwald note in SLOTFOM, Series III, Carton 54, CAOM. There have long been disagreements over the identity of the author. Charles B. McLane, in his *Soviet Strategies in Southeast Asia* (Princeton, N.J.: Princeton University Press, 1966), assumed that it was written by Nguyen Ai Quoc, which is almost certainly an error, since Quoc did not arrive in Moscow until early in 1934 (pp. 163–64). The Sûreté was convinced that the author was the Ukrainian Comintern official Dmitri Manuilsky, who had for years played an advisory role to the ICP. Sophie Quinn-Judge, based on material available to her in the Moscow archives, is of the same opinion. The Vietnamese historian Do Quang Hung, who has done extensive research in the archives in Moscow, believes that there was an actual Orgwald, who was a member of George Dimitrov's faction in Moscow (interview with Do Quang Hung, December 15, 1990). For a recent discussion of the issue, see Anatoly A. Sokolov, "Psevdonimyi Ho Shi Mina kak opyt izucheniya politicheskoi biografii" [The pseudonyms of Ho Chi Minh as an experience in the study of political biography] in *Traditsionnyi V'ietnam: Sbornik statei* [Traditional Vietnam: A collection of articles] (Moscow: Vietnamese Center, 1993), pp. 216–17, fn 39. Sokolov suggests that the name might have been used by more than one person. I am inclined to accept the French view that Orgwald was Manuilsky.

32. The original was published in *Communist International* on August 5, 1934, and was later reprinted by the Trotskyite journal *Partisans*, no. 48 (June–August 1969). It appears in a French version in Note Périodique, third quarter, 1934, annex, in dossier 32, in SLOTFOM, Series III, Carton 52, CAOM. The quotes are taken from Pierre Rousset, *Le Parti Communiste Vietnamien* (Paris: François Maspero, 1975), pp. 69–70. The identity of the author of the letter is a matter of debate. Rousset speculated that it might have been written by a Soviet official in the Comintern. Sophie Quinn-Judge suggests that it might have been Kang Sheng or Wang Ming, both of whom were then serving as representatives of the CCP Central Committee in Moscow and were highly sectarian in their views of the Asian revolution.

33. Note Périodique, second quarter, 1935, (March), pp. 21, 58, in dossier 35, in SLOTFOM, Series III, Carton 54, CAOM. The ICP congress was scheduled to take place in Ha Huy Tap's three-room apartment in Macao, and the delegate from the Comintern was to receive the only bed (ibid., p. 62). Also see Nguyen Van Khoan and Trieu Hien, "Le Hong Phong," p. 10.

34. For French coverage of Tran Van Giau's travels, see Note Périodique, second quarter 1935 (March), in dossier 35, in SLOTFOM, Series III, Carton 54, CAOM. Ha Huy Tap's suspicions were reported in a letter to the Comintern. Vera Vasilieva in a letter dated March 17, 1931, advised Tap that in case of suspicions of disloyalty, he should immediately remove the suspect from any position of responsibility within the Party, change the

location of its headquarters, and then seek to verify his suspicions. Tap's later admission that Giau was apparently not a provocateur was contained in a report to Moscow dated April 4, 1935, filed in Carton 495, Folder 154, File 586, in the Comintern archives. In that letter, Tap said that "two hours before his [Giau's] departure for the Party congress, eight automobiles of the Sûreté came to fetch him at his residence." It is difficult to reconcile this with other information that Giau left Macao in mid-March, several days before the congress, and was not arrested in Saigon until May. Perhaps he was apprehended in Macao en route to the supposed March 18 congress.

35. Ha Huy Tap's complaints are contained in his letters to Moscow dated April 4 and April 20, 1935, Carton 495, Folder 154, File 586, in the Comintern archives. Also see SLOTFOM, Series III, Carton 52, CAOM, and the dossier on the Seventh Comintern Congress, in SLOTFOM, Series III, Carton 113, CAOM. Nguyen Huu Can claimed to his colleagues that he had gone to the consulate to lead the French astray about plans for the congress. Tap did not accept his explanation, but French reports indicate that the Sûreté did not trust him either—see Note Périodique, second quarter 1935, pp. 62–65, in dossier 35, in SLOTFOM, Series III, Carton 52, CAOM. According to ICP sources, the cook Nguyen Van Tram had raped a female Party colleague shortly before taking flight. She later died from her wounds.

36. Documents from the congress indicate that the Overseas Executive Committee was considered to be superior in rank to the Central Committee, and was to consist of from five to seven members, with a three-member Standing Committee. See Note Périodique, fourth quarter 1935, in dossier 37, in SLOTFOM, Series II, Carton 54, CAOM. On the reasons for the postponement of the Macao congress, see the letter from Ha Huy Tap of the Overseas Executive Committee to the Comintern dated March 31, 1935, in the Comintern archives and at the Ho Chi Minh Museum in Hanoi.

37. Letter of April 20, 1935, to Moscow, in Comintern archives, Carton 495, Folder 154, File 586. What comes across most forcefully in Tap's reports to Moscow is his almost pathological fear of "*provocateurs*." The extent of Tap's suspicion of Nguyen Ai Quoc is indicated by his asking in his letter of March 31 that, in translating the documents of the congress for the use of Comintern officials in Moscow, Quoc be held entirely responsible for political errors resulting from "false translation."

38. Quoc's letter, dated January 16, 1935, is contained in the Ho Chi Minh Museum in Hanoi and was written in French. A Vietnamese-language translation is available in *Toan Tap I*, vol. 3, pp. 55–59.

39. Le Hong Phong's speech, as well as those of the other Vietnamese delegates, is reproduced in a Vietnamese-language translation in *Van kien Dang* (1930–1945), vol. 2, pp. 7–41. A number of writers, as well as the Sûreté itself, have mistakenly assumed that the speaker was Nguyen Ai Quoc. It is now clear that "Chayan"—a corruption of Hai An—was in fact Le Hong Phong. See Rousset, *Le Parti Communiste*, p. 70, and Note Périodique, fourth quarter 1935, in dossier 37, in SLOTFOM, Series II, Carton 52, CAOM.

40. There is a questionnaire confirming Quoc's participation in the Seventh Congress in the Ho Chi Minh Museum in Hanoi. It is reproduced in *BNTS*, vol. 2, pp. 51–52. The banquet is mentioned in ibid., p. 50.

41. The date of Minh Khai's return to Asia has been a matter of disagreement. Sophie Quinn-Judge places Minh Khai's date of departure from Moscow as February 1937. According to Ton Quang Duyet, she returned in 1936—see "Mot vai y kien bo sung ve lich su hai dong chi Tran Phu va Nguyen Thi Minh Khai" [Some opinions on

the history of comrades Tran Phu and Nguyen Thi Minh Khai], in *NCLS*, no. 139 (July-August 1971). For the wedding, see Kobelev, pp. 116, 118. There has been supposition that she may have identified herself as Quoc's wife during the Comintern Congress to divert suspicions over her identity, but the argument is not convincing. Vera Vasilieva's daughter recalls that Nguyen Ai Quoc occasionally visited her mother's apartment in the company of a young woman called Phan Lan—see Quinn-Judge, "Ho Chi Minh," p. 76. For reports of Quoc's "temporary wife" and child in the USSR, see Hoang Van Chi, *From Colonialism*, p. 51; Bao Dai, *Le Dragon d'Annam* (Paris: Plon, 1980), p. 134; and *China News Analysis*, December 12, 1969. Sources in Moscow today add credence to the rumor.

42. Kobelev, pp. 118–19. For Quoc's role at the Congress, see Tu Huu, *Di hop Quoc te Cong san* [At a meeting of the Comintern] (Viet Bac: NXB Dan toc, 1964), and Hong Ha, *Bac Ho tren dat nuoc Lenin* [Uncle Ho in the country of Lenin] (Hanoi: NXB Thanh nien, 1980), pp. 313–15.

43. *BNTS*, vol. 2, pp. 56–59; also see Sokolov, *Komintern*, pp. 85–89.

44. Letter dated June 6, 1938, quoted in Sokolov, *Komintern*, pp. 89–90. According to Sokolov, the official to whom he had written was probably Manuilsky. Also see *BNTS*, vol. 2, pp. 56–59.

VIII | *A Cave at Pac Bo*

1. Wu Xiuquan, *Wodi Licheng* [My historical journey] (Beijing: Liberation Army Press, 1984), p. 61. In 1950, Wu met Ho Chi Minh again during Ho's visit to China and for the first time realized who his "important Asian" really was.

2. Sources in Hanoi report that Ho Chi Minh did not meet Mao Zedong during his short visit to Yan'an, explaining only that Mao Zedong was not there at the time. According to one Vietnamese source, during a visit to the People's Republic of China after the Geneva Conference of 1954 Ho Chi Minh remarked that he had visited Yan'an before Mao Zedong's arrival, and that he had closest contact at that time with Ye Jianying. For his brief visit, see Nguyen Khanh Toan, "En URSS avec 'Uncle Ho,' " in *Souvenirs*, p. 134, and *BNTS*, vol. 2, p. 63. For Ho's recollections, see T. Lan, *Vua di duong, vua ke chuyen* [Walking and talking] (Hanoi: Su that, 1976), pp. 65–66.

3. Kobelev, p. 125; Nguyen Khanh Toan, "Avec 'Uncle Ho,' " p. 132; T. Lan, *Vua di duong*, p. 66.

4. Quotations in *HZYZ*, pp. 53–55.

5. These articles appear in Vietnamese in *Toan Tap I*. See "Nguoi Nhat-Ban muon khai hoa Trung-Quoc nhu the nao" [How the Japanese hope to civilize China], and two letters, all titled "Thu tu Trung-Quoc" [Letter from China], in vol. 3, pp. 60–96.

6. In attendance at this July 1936 meeting were Le Hong Phong, Phung Chi Kien, Vo Van Ngan, Hoang Dinh Giong, and General Secretary Ha Huy Tap. There are apparently no documents still existing from the meeting, so reports on the results are based on memoirs of participants and documents issued by the Party after the close of the plenum. For information on the meeting, see Vu Thu, "Mot so van de lich su Dang thoi ky 1936–1939" [Some problems in Party history in the period 1936–1939], in *NCLS*, no. 85 (April 1966), and Tran Huy Lieu, *Tai lieu tham khao lich su cach mang Can dai Viet Nam* [Historical research materials concerning the revolution in modern Vietnam] (Hanoi: n.p., 1958), vol. 7, p. 57.

7. Others in attendance at the meeting were Nguyen Chi Dieu, Phan Dang Luu, Hoang Quoc Viet, and a rising young party cadre named Le Duan. Interview with Nguyen Thanh, Hanoi, December 3, 1990; interview with Pham Xanh, Hanoi, December 12, 1990. Sometime in early 1939, Nguyen Van Cu, known to the Sûreté as "one eye" (*le borgne*), wrote a piece titled "Tu chi trich" [A self-criticism], which indirectly criticized Le Hong Phong for adopting an overly trusting attitude toward counterrevolutionary elements in Indochina. See *Van kien Dang (1930–1945)* [Party Documents (1930–1945)], vol. 2, (Hanoi: Ban nghien cuu lich su Dang trung uong, 1977), pp. 402–31.

8. *Toan Tap II*, vol. 3, pp. 114–16. I have slightly revised the familiar translation by Bernard Fall in *Ho Chi Minh on Revolution: Selected Writings, 1920–1966* (New York: Praeger, 1967), pp. 30–31. According to Vo Nguyen Giap, who was then a reporter with *Notre Voix*, the group at the newspaper were indeed convinced that P. C. Line was Nguyen Ai Quoc—see Giap's "Ho Chi Minh: Père de l'armée révolutionnaire du Vietnam," in *Souvenirs*, p. 179.

9. "Tinh hinh chinh tri o Dong duong tu 1936 den 1939" [The political situation in Indochina from 1936 to 1939], in *Toan Tap II*, vol. 3, pp. 117–44. Nguyen Ai Quoc received much of his information about conditions in Indochina from copies of *Notre Voix* and other newspapers sent to him by the editor of *Notre Voix*. See his letter to a friend in the Comintern, dated April 20, 1939, in *BNTS*, vol. 2, pp. 72–76.

10. According to Li Beiguan, who served as his CCP escort on the journey, the envoys from inside Indochina had been been cheated out of their money in Longzhou. See "Li Beiguan Huiyi" [The recollections of Li Beiguan], cited in *HZYZ*, p. 58. Also see Vu Anh, "De Kunming à Pac Bo," in *Souvenirs*, pp. 152–53. For Quoc's activities in Hengyang, see T. Lan, pp. 67–68, where Ho recounts that he had never operated a shortwave radio before, and stayed up five nights before he located the London channel. Also see *HZYZ*, p. 55, and *BNTS*, vol. 2, p. 69. The latter appears to be in error in stating that he took part in both classes.

11. There has been some confusion as to when and why he went to Chongqing. Vietnamese sources place the visit earlier in the year. I have concluded from the evidence that it took place at this time and that Quoc's purpose was to seek Chinese assistance in restoring contact with the ICP Central Committee. See interview with Liu Ang in *HZYZ*, pp. 59–60. Also see *BNTS*, vol. 2, pp. 70, 86–87. In his *Vietnam and China, 1938–1954* (Princeton, N.J.: Princeton University Press, 1969), p. 34, King C. Chen reports that while in Chongqing Quoc made the acquaintance of an American professor named Franklin Lien Ho. In a letter to Chen, Professor Ho declared that he had met Quoc (wearing a Sun Yat-sen suit and using the name Hu, a comrade visiting from Vietnam) on several occasions at Zhou Enlai's residence.

12. Vu Anh, "Kunming," p. 154. For this comedy of errors, see Dang Van Cap, "Con duong dan toi den voi Bac" [The road that led me to Uncle], in *Bac Ho ve nuoc* [Uncle Ho returns home] (Cao Bang: n.p., 1986), p. 48, cited in *BNTS*, vol. 2, p. 87; and Hoang Van Hoan, *A Drop in the Ocean: Hoang Van Hoan's Revolutionary Reminiscences* (Beijing: Foreign Languages Press, 1988), p. 108.

13. Hoang Van Hoan notes that "Mr. Tran" was very helpful in improving his comrades' journalistic work, lecturing them on the need to use simple language (write so that Hai—i.e., Vu Anh, who was from a working-class family—can understand, he said) and suggesting that the name of the journal be changed to *D.T.*, which could stand for several things, including Dang Ta [Our Party], Dau Tranh [Struggle], Dan

Tay [Defeat the Westerners], as well as Dong Thanh, its existing name. For an account of Nguyen Ai Quoc's activities along the Kunming rail line, see Hoang Quang Binh, "Au Yunnan," in *Souvenirs*, pp. 135–52. Binh, in whose house Quoc stayed, repeats the by now familiar stories of Quoc's rigid daily regimen and modest behavior. He paid rent to his host and took part in household chores, but he also lectured Binh on one occasion for striking his wife. According to *BNTS*, vol. 2, p. 91, in Kunming Quoc lived at the house of a Tong Minh Phuong, an overseas Vietnamese from a family that had taken part in leftist causes for a decade. The house was located on Kim Bich Road.

14. The policy statement is contained in *Van kien Dang (1930–1945)*, vol. 3, pp. 26–88. Besides Nguyen Van Cu and Le Duan, the other attendees were Phan Dang Luu and Vo Van Tan.

15. Giap recounts the story in his "Ho Chi Minh," pp. 173–74. Also see his *Tu nhan dan ma ra* [From the people] (Hanoi: Quan doi Nhan dan, 1964), p. 28.

16. *BNTS*, vol. 2, p.98, citing Vu Anh, "Nhung ngay gan Bac" [Days near Uncle], in *Bac Ho ve nuoc*, p. 15.

17. According to a Chinese acquaintance who was living with him at a bookstore at 67 Huashan Nan Lu at the time, Nguyen Ai Quoc received a telegram from Zhou Enlai—just returned from a conference in Yan'an—to come to Chongqing for consultations. According to this source, Quoc often met with students at Southwest United University to discuss world affairs—see *HZYZ*, p. 66. Also see *BNTS*, vol. 2, pp. 98–100. The information on the mission to Yan'an is from Chen, *Vietnam and China*, p. 41. I have been unable to confirm the existence of this mission, although it was reported in a cable from the U.S. Embassy in Tokyo to the State Department on June 14, 1954. The envoy's name was Tran Van Hinh.

18. The Party's nationality policy had first been adopted at the plenum in October 1930. For a discussion, see Le Van Lo, "Ba muoi nam thuc hien chinh sach dan toc cua Dang" [Thirty years of creating a nationality policy for the Party], in *NCLS*, no. 10 (January 1960), pp. 69–71. Also see Phan Ngoc Lien, "Cong tac van dong giao duc quan chung cua Ho Chu Tich trong thoi gian Nguoi o Pac Bo" [The Agitprop work of Ho Chi Minh during his stay at Pac Bo], in *NCLS*, no. 149 (March–April 1973), p. 20.

19. Giap, "Ho Chi Minh," pp. 180–81; Hoang Van Hoan, *Drop in the Ocean*, pp. 110–11.

20. See Hoang Van Hoan, *Drop in the Ocean*, p. 86. For the discussion over the selection of a name for the new front, see Vo Nguyen Giap, "Ho Chi Minh," pp. 182–83.

21. Hoang Van Hoan, *Drop in the Ocean*, pp. 113–15. While in Guilin, Nguyen Ai Quoc wrote a number of articles, under the alias of Binh Son, for the CCP newspaper *Jiuwong Daily*. See *BNTS*, vol. 2, p. 105.

22. In Party histories, this meeting is labeled the Seventh Plenum of the ICP, but sources in Hanoi confirm the fact that it had originally been a meeting of the regional committee. For a description of the meeting, see Hoang Tung, *Dong chi Truong Chinh* [Comrade Truong Chinh], vol. 1 (Hanoi: Su that, 1990), pp. 27–44.

23. See the accounts of the insurrection in René Bauchar, *Rafales sur l'Indochine* (Paris: n.p., 1946), and Phillippe Devillers, *Histoire du Viet Nam de 1940 à 1952* (Paris: Editions du Seuil, 1952). For an official report, see telegram Bombay to Department of State, February 18, 1946, in U.S. Department of State, Central Files, RG 59, UPA. The cable contained information from a Sûreté report titled "Le Parti Communiste Indochinois," which had been obtained by a U.S. journalist in Indochina.

24. Vo Nguyen Giap, "Ho Chi Minh," p. 182.

25. Vu Anh, "Kunming," p. 160.

26. See Chiang Yung-ching, *Hu Chih-ming tsai Chung-kuo* [Ho Chi Minh in China] (Taipei: Nan T'ien Publishing Co., 1972), pp. 119–22. For the stated objectives of the new organization, known as Vietnam as the Viet Nam Dan toc Giai phong Uy vien Hoi, see *HZYZ*, p. 75. Also see *BNTS*, vol. 2, p. 121.

27. Vo Nguyen Giap, "Ho Chi Minh," p. 188. Giap joined other Party members at Pac Bo after the Eighth Plenum of the ICP in May.

28. Vu Anh, "Kunming," pp. 163–65; *BNTS*, vol. 2, p. 128, n. 2. Whether the plenum was held in the cave is unclear. According to a French source, a two-story thatch hut was constructed for the occasion, with the Central Committee meeting on the upper floor, and the regional committee for Tonkin convening on the floor below—see Service de la Sûreté au Tonkin à Résident Supérieur Tonkin, no. 12234–S, June 10, 1941, in dossier labeled "lll6 Nguyen Ai Quoc," in SPCE, Carton 369, CAOM.

29. The document is contained in *Lich su Dang Cong san Viet Nam: Trich van kien Dang* [History of the Vietnamese Communist Party: A Selection of Party Documents], vol. 1 (Hanoi: Marxist-Leninist Institute, 1979), p. 358. Also see *Van kien Dang (1930–1945)*, vol. 3, pp. 177–221. There is also a tantalizing but unconfirmed report that Nguyen Ai Quoc may have linked the Vietnamese struggle for independence with the prospect of a global revolutionary wave led by the Soviet Union that would take place at the end of the war—see the report of R. Perroche, May 30, 1941, in Archnote/ 410530–410531 and 410612, in CAOM. According to this source, in his speech at the Eighth Plenum, Quoc criticized the internal Party leadership for its failure to adapt itself to the rapidly evolving events. I am grateful to Stein Tonnesson for providing this information.

30. See *Van kien Dang (1930–1945)*, vol. 3, pp. 199–200.

31. As David Marr points out, not all of Ho Chi Minh's predictions were destined to come true. Workers in Germany and Japan did not rise up against their rulers, nor did the Soviet Union play a major role in the defeat of Japan. For his comments, see David G. Marr, *Vietnam 1945: The Quest for Power* (Berkeley, Calif.: University of California Press, 1995), p. 168, fn 54.

IX | *The Rising Tide*

1. Quang Trung, "Dom lua chien khu," in *Pac Bo que toi* [My village of Pac Bo] (Hanoi: Quan doi Nhan dan, 1967), pp. 69–78, cited in *BNTS*, vol. 2, p. 130. Vu Anh, "De Kunming à Pac Bo," in *Souvenirs*, pp. 129–31.

2. The pamphlet is contained in *Toan Tap I*, vol. 3, pp. 163–209.

3. See ibid., p. 156. Also see Vo Nguyen Giap, "Ho Chi Minh: Père de l'armée révolutionnaire du Vietnam," in *Souvenirs*, pp. 188–89. During Têt celebrations, Nguyen Ai Quoc would often provide villagers with a gift of a few pennies, and then ask them to use it to purchase the journal. Some of the articles were signed Ho Chi Minh. See Stein Tonnesson, *The Vietnamese Revolution of 1945: Roosevelt, Ho Chi Minh, and de Gaulle in a World at War* (London: Sage, 1991), p. 34.

4. *Toan Tap I*, vol. 3, pp. 214–24. Originally written sometime in 1941, the pamphlet was published in 1942. For "The World War and Our Duty," see ibid., pp. 160–61. Also see Vu Anh, "Kunming," p. 167.

5. Vu Anh, in "Kunming," p. 169.

6. Vo Nguyen Giap, "Ho Chi Minh," p. 192. For the quote on revolution, see ibid., p. 195, and Bang Giang, *Bac Ho o Viet Bac* [Uncle Ho in the Viet Bac], cited in *BNTS*, vol. 2, p. 147.

7. Le Quang Ba, "Bac ve tham lai Pac Bo," in *Uong nuoc ngo nguon* (Hanoi: Quan doi Nhan dan, 1973), p. 153, cited in *BNTS*, vol. 2, p. 157. Also see Vo Nguyen Giap, "Mot manh dat tu do" [A fragile slice of freedom], in *Bac Ho ve nuoc* [Uncle Ho returns home] (Cao Bang, 1986), p. 78, cited in *BNTS*, vol. 2, p. 153. On Phung Chi Kien, see Giap's "Ho Chi Minh," p. 193. For Ho Chi Minh's instructions to undertake the March to the South and related movements to the east and west, see also *Nhung su kien lich su Dang* [Events in the history of the Party], vol. 1 (Hanoi: Su that, 1976), pp. 552–53.

8. Report by General Zhang Fakui, January 23, 1944, cited in *HZYZ*, pp. 82–83. According to this report, Ho was arrested in Jiezhang village in the district of Debao. See also Zhang Fakui Oral History, held in the Columbia University Library, New York City. Additional information on Ho's trip is contained in *BNTS*, vol. 2, pp. 161–65, and *Glimpses/Life*, p. 47.

9. In his memoirs, Hoang Van Hoan stated that Ho intended to solicit an audience with Chiang Kai-shek and Soong Qingling—see *A Drop in the Ocean: Hoang Van Hoan's Revolutionary Reminiscences* (Beijing: Foreign Languages Press, 1988), p. 193. Christiane Pasquel Rageau, however, speculates that his real purpose was to get in touch with comrades of the CCP—see her *Ho Chi Minh* (Paris: Editions Universitaires, 1970), p. 103. Vu Anh agreed—see "Kunming," p. 168. One reason to stress the point that he intended to contact Chiang Kai-shek, of course, was to emphasize his wish to establish a good relationship with Chongqing. Ho Chi Minh's own comment on the issue is in *Glimpses/Life*, p. 47.

10. On the road from Debao to Jingxi with a squad of Chinese soldiers, Ho had accidently encountered Xu Weisan's sister, who returned home to report the news to her family—interview of Wang Xiji dated June 24, 1981, in *HZYZ*, pp. 83–84.

11. Translation by the author, from "Nhat Ky trong Tu" [Prison Diary], from *Toan Tap* I, vol. 3, pp. 242–371. Ho may have benefited from the fact that one of the prison guards was acquainted with members of Xu Weisan's family and tried to make things easier for him—see Wang Xiji interview, in *HZYZ*, pp. 83–84.

12. The complexity of Ho Chi Minh's case is indicated by a report from Zhang Fakui's headquarters dated January 23, 1944. As described in this document, the case was originally sent from the local authorities at Teyuan to the district office in Debao, and thence to the provincial government in Guilin, which then forwarded it to the special commissioner's office in the same city. The latter bumped it up to the local branch of the National Military Council, which thereupon forwarded it to Zhang's Fourth Military Command in Liuzhou for disposition. Zhang Fakui Oral History, p. 684. Also see Chiang Yung-ching, *Hu Chih-ming tsai Chung-kuo* [Ho Chi Minh in China] (Taipei: Nan t'ien Publishing Co., 1972), p. 148, and *HZYZ*, p. 84. *BNTS*, vol. 2, p. 180, implies that Ho arrived in Guilin in early January—that appears to be an error. See the report by Chang Fa-k'uei [Zhang Fakui] to Wu T'ieh-ch'eng, December 27, 1942, cited in Chiang Yung-ching, *Hu Chih-ming*, p. 146.

13. Chiang Yung-ching, *Hu Chih-ming*, pp. 147–49. Ho was identified in Chinese as Hu Tzu-ming in the November 9 cable. Also see Hoang Van Hoan, *Drop in the Ocean*,

pp. 193–97; Also cf. *Chu tich Ho Chi Minh voi cong tac ngoai giao* [Chairman Ho Chi Minh and foreign relations] (Hanoi: Su that, 1990), p. 28; the Cao Bang group included a book titled *Doc lap Dac san* in their messages to the press agencies; the book stated that "representative Ho is a great leader of the Vietnamese revolution and a representative of the Anti-Aggression League."

14. The cadre was apparently Dang Van Cap. See Vo Nguyen Giap, in "Ho Chi Minh," pp. 196–97. Vu Anh recounts a slightly different version: after hearing the news of Ho's death, Party leaders dispatched a second emissary to confirm the news, who returned with the report that Ho was still alive—the misunderstanding had been caused by Cap's mistaking "the prisoner's companion is dead" for "the prisoner is dead."

15. For an account of his accommodations, see the interview with Peng De, in *HZYZ*, p. 93. On his means of communicating with colleagues, see Vu Anh, in "Kunming," pp. 168–69. In one case he said simply, "keep on working hard, I'm okay"—see Chiang Yung-ching, *Hu Chih-ming*, p. 147.

16. Zhang Fakui Oral History, p. 685; Hoang Van Hoan, *Drop in the Ocean*, p. 198. Chiang Yung-ching (*Hu Chih-ming*, p. 150) claims that Chongqing was not immediately aware that he was actually the veteran revolutionary Nguyen Ai Quoc.

17. *HZYZ*, p. 95. The information on Feng Yuxiang is from Feng Hongda and Xu Huaxin, "General Feng Yuxiang, Soul of China," published by the Historical Reference Materials Publishing House, 1981, cited in ibid, p. 94. Chiang Yung-ching makes no reference to the role of Feng Yuxiang and declares that Chiang Kai-shek took an interest in the case as a result of a request from General Hou Zhiming—see *Hu Chih-ming*, p. 150. In his unpublished memoirs, OSS veteran Charles Fenn recalls a conversation with the Kuomintang leader Chen Lifu, who said that when General Zhang suggested cooperating with Ho, Chiang Kai-shek rejected the idea. He has "a big sales talk," Chiang remarked, but he has "nothing to sell." See Charles Fenn, "Trial Run to Doomsday," p. 87 (manuscript provided by Charles Fenn).

18. Zhang said that he merely informed the central government of his decision, and they approved. He further commented that Ho Chi Minh was "very good. He talked cautiously, stroking his beard. He seemed very 'deep.' He had a cool head and was hardworking." It probably didn't hurt that Ho spoke passable mandarin Chinese. See Zhang Fakui Oral History, p. 687.

19. Chiang Yung-ching, *Hu Chih-ming*, p. 151; draft history presented in honor of visit of North Vietnamese delegation to Liuzhou, July 1964, cited in *HZYZ*, pp. 95–96.

20. Ho Chi Minh's toast was an adroit play on words in the classical Chinese tradition. The names of Hou Zhiming and Ho Chi Minh both had the same meaning in the Chinese language—the will to enlighten. At the same time, the word for "revolution" in Chinese (*geming*), incorporated a different character with the same pronunciation. By deftly switching characters, Ho got his point across. For a discussion, see *BNTS*, vol. 2, p. 193, note 1.

21. *HZYZ*, pp. 101–2, citing two manuscripts: "Recollections of Chairman Ho Chi Minh's Leadership over the Vietnamese Revolution in China," April 11, 1979, and Ye Ruiting, "A Vignette from the Activity of the Vietnamese Revolutionary League in Liuzhou at the End of the Resistance War," August 23, 1980.

22. Ho Chi Minh, "Bao cao cua Phan hoi Viet Nam thuoc Dai hoi Quoc te chong

xam luoc" [Report of the congress of the International Anti-Aggression League], March 1944. Unpublished report in my possession.

23. Hoang Van Hoan, *Drop in the Ocean*, p. 200. In past years, a number of Western scholars reported that the conference had established a provisional government for a future Vietnamese republic, but this appears not to be the case. The issue was discussed among members of the Dong Minh Hoi, but rejected for a variety of reasons. For a discussion, see Chiang Yung-ching, *Hu Chih-ming*, pp. 167–68 (see especially note 95). According to Chiang (p. 169), after the conference some "Vietnamese Communists" allegedly pressed for a government, but it was rejected by Chongqing, partly on the grounds that it might antagonize the Allies. I have seen no evidence that Ho Chi Minh was involved in such proposals. Ho's speech at the conference is mentioned briefly in *HZYZ*, p. 103.

24. Hoang Van Hoan, *Drop in the Ocean*, pp. 201–2; Zhang Fakui Oral History, pp. 691–92.

25. Zhang Fakui Oral History, p. 692. Also see Liu San, "When President Ho Chi Minh was in South China," *Wen Hui Bao* (Hong Kong), September 7, 1953.

26. *HZYZ*, p. 106. Hoang Van Hoan, *Drop in the Ocean*, p. 202. King Chen states that only sixteen men accompanied Ho from Liuzhou—see his *Vietnam and China, 1938–1954* (Princeton, N.J.: Princeton University Press, 1969), p. 85. If that is so, the additional two members of the group who returned to Vietnam may have been Vu Anh and Vo Nguyen Giap, who met him near Jingxi and joined him en route to Pac Bo.

27. The communiqué is contained in *Van kien Dang (1930–1945)* [Party Documents (1930–1945)], vol. 3 (Hanoi: Ban nghien cuu lich su Dang Truong uong, 1977), pp. 289–99. For a summary, see *Histoire de la révolution d'août* (Hanoi: Foreign Languages Press, 1972), pp. 37–38. Also see Hoang Tung, *Dong chi Truong Chinh* [Comrade Truong Chinh] (Hanoi: Su that, 1991), pp. 123–24.

28. The conference resolution is contained in *Van kien Dang (1930–1945)*, pp. 313–362.

29. Vo Nguyen Giap, in "Ho Chi Minh," pp. 198–99; Philippe Devillers, *Histoire du Vietnam, 1940–1952* (Paris: Editions du Seuil, 1952), pp. 107–8; Chiang Yung-ching, *Hu Chih-ming*, pp. 184–85.

30. Tran Van Giau, *Giai cap cong nhan Viet Nam* [The Vietnamese working class (1939–1945)], vol. 3 (Hanoi: Su that, 1963), pp. 143–71.

31. Vo Nguyen Giap, in "Ho Chi Minh," pp. 201–2. Ho's critical comments about Giap's plans for an insurrection are contained in Hoang Van Hoan, *Drop in the Ocean*, pp. 187–88.

32. The quotations are from *Toan Tap I*, vol. 3, pp. 375–76. Also see Hoang Van Hoan, *Drop in the Ocean*, pp. 203–4. King Chen cites a Chinese report that the Vietminh forces had disguised themselves as Vietnamese soldiers in the French army and were thus able to use the element of surprise; Giap had informed Ho Chi Minh that it was important that the new units obtain a victory in their first battle—see Chen, *Vietnam and China*, p. 89. Also see *BNTS*, vol. 2, p. 212.

33. Shaw's own account is given in an unpublished paper titled "The Real Indochina," and apparently submitted on his return to the United States. Also see Hoang Van Hoan, *Drop in the Ocean*, p. 203, and "Nguyen Ai Quoc," a French-language abridgement of *Glimpses/Life* in *Souvenirs*, pp. 93–94. According to this source—Ho Chi Minh himself—the Japanese arrived at the crash site shortly after the French patrol and accused

the French of assisting the pilot to escape. The Japanese offered a cash reward to anyone who turned him in and threatened severe punishment for those who might assist him. Shaw adds that the local French agreed to cooperate with the Japanese and put a price on his head.

34. Roosevelt's comment about Indochina, along with his overall views on the situation there, are discussed in William Duiker, *U.S. Containment Policy and the Conflict in Indochina* (Stanford, Calif.: Stanford University Press, 1994), chapter 1.

35. Letter by U.S. Ambassador Clarence Gauss to Secretary of State, December 23, 1943, with enclosure in the Patti collection. The cable dated December 30, 1942, mentioning the arrest of "Ho Chi-chi" is in ibid. For a discussion and other sources, see Archimedes L.A. Patti, *Why Viet Nam? Prelude to America's Albatross* (Berkeley: University of California Press, 1980), pp. 46–50. Also see *Chu tich Ho Chi Minh*, p. 29. According to Patti (p. 56), Pham Van Dong had sent the petitions to the U.S. Embassy.

36. Letter by U.S. Ambassador Gauss dated August 18, 1944, in the Patti collection. Patti, *Why Viet Nam?*, p. 53.

37. Patti, *Why Viet Nam?*, p. 53–54. For a report by Langdon that dismissed Vietnamese nationalist leaders living in south China as "naive politically," see "Political Conditions in Indochina, August 1944," enclosure to despatch no. 2945, dated September 9, 1944, from U.S. Embassy Chongqing, in the Patti collection. Also see Tonnesson, *Vietnamese Revolution*, p. 137, fns 129 and 130.

38. Telegram from Langdon to the Department, October 9, 1944, in the Patti collection. Memorandum by Philip D. Sprouse titled "Activities at Kunming of a Mr. Ho in connection with Kuomintang broadcasts to Indochina," dated December 11, 1944, in ibid. The issue remains a bit puzzling. Patti declared that Ho was approached in mid-1944 by the OSS (presumably in Liuzhou) in a vain attempt to organize an intelligence network in Indochina, but provided no source for the information. The visa request submitted by Langdon came from the OWI office in Kunming. There is some circumstantial evidence to support the hypothesis that U.S. officials were interested in him, since General Zhang Fakui later recalled that a U.S. adviser had informed him that U.S. officials wanted to invite Ho to Kunming for training. See Zhang's comments in his Oral History, p. 696.

39. Hoang Van Hoan, *Drop in the Ocean*, p. 203. Whether AGAS or any other U.S. agency in Kunming had actually invited Ho Chi Minh to China to thank him for his efforts is uncertain. Vietnamese sources mention that Shaw contacted Kunming and that U.S. officials had invited him to come, but evidence suggests that this is unlikely, for other accounts suggest that neither General Claire Chennault nor the local office of the OSS was aware of his existence. If any U.S. office in Kunming knew of him, it would most likely have been AGAS, but Charles Fenn states flatly that he was not aware of Ho's identity until his arrival in Kunming. In his autobiography, Ho only noted briefly that the Americans came to see him in order to thank him for rescuing Lieutenant Shaw. If Zhang Fakui's remark that the Americans wanted Ho to go to Kunming for training (Oral History, p. 696) is accurate, OSS officials there appeared unaware of it. It is possible that the conversation referred to by Zhang Fakui had taken place after Ho left Kunming to return to Indochina, and during his brief stopover in Paise, where he probably met Zhang Fakui again.

40. Hoang Quang Binh, "Au Yunnan," in *Avec l'Oncle Ho* (Hanoi: Foreign Languages Press, 1972), pp. 239–40.

41. The coffee shop was called the Quang Lac Restaurant on 39 Tai Ho Gai.

42. Charles Fenn, *Ho Chi Minh: A Biographical Introduction* (New York: Scribner, 1973), pp. 76–77. "Fam" is not identified but, from his description as a man with "enormous cheekbones and a powerful chin" was probably Pham Van Dong. Patti agrees—see *Why Viet Nam?*, p. 544, note 52. Also see Fenn, "Trial Run to Doomsday," p. 211. The reference to the brush-off of Ho Chi Minh by the local office of the OSS seems puzzling, since they had originally expressed an interest in using his services. Perhaps they were responding to the recent prohibition against contacts with resistance groups in Indochina. According to Charles Fenn, the new senior officials in the Chongqing office tended to be pro-French (interview with Fenn, September 22, 1997).

43. Fenn, *Ho Chi Minh*, pp. 78–79. Also see "Trial Run to Doomsday," p. 233. According to the journalist Robert Shaplen, Chennault had been warned by Kuomintang acquaintances to stay away from Ho Chi Minh—see Shaplen's *The Lost Revolution* (New York: Harper & Row, 1966), p. 34.

44. For Xiao Wen's distrust of the Vietminh, see Mai Van Bo, *Chung toi hoc lam ngoai giao voi Bac Ho* [I studied diplomacy with Uncle Ho] (Ho Chi Minh City: Tre, 1998), p. 41. Also see Chen, *Vietnam and China*, pp. 95–96. Ho Chi Minh's movements are not well documented during this period. According to Hoang Van Hoan, Ho stopped in Bose (Paise), before returning to Pac Bo; if that is the case, he must have stopped by en route to Jingxi (see his *Drop in the Ocean*, p. 207). If King Chen's information is correct, Ho was still in Paise as late as April 12. Charles Fenn's account makes no reference to a stopover in Paise, and declares that Ho was back in Pac Bo a week after his arrival in Jingxi. But he also cites a conversation that he had with one of Ho Chi Minh's couriers after the latter's return to Indochina. The courier said that Ho had met with a group of rival nationalist leaders who expressed doubt about his links with the Americans. Although the courier seems to imply that the meeting took place inside Vietnam, it seems more likely that it refers to his meeting with the Dong Minh Hoi in Paise. Interview with Fenn, September 22, 1997.

45. The plan was labeled Operation Quail, and was prepared by the Special Intelligence Branch of OSS in China. See "The Quail Project," report dated February 26, 1945, in OSS Entry 154, Box 202, Folder 3431, RG 226, USNA. Also see Heppner to Bird, April 19, 1945, in Field Station Files, Entry 154, Box 199, Folder 3373, RG 226, USNA. Although Patti appears to imply that the decision to recruit Ho was his own, Fenn recalls being told by an acquaintance that OSS Director William Donovan had heard about Ho and wanted to make use of him for OSS operations in Indochina. If that is the case, Patti was probably under orders to seek him out on his arrival. See Patti, *Viet Nam*, p. 67 and Fenn, "Trial Run to Doomsday," p. 265.

46. Patti, *Why Viet Nam?*, pp. 69–71, 79–88. For Wedemeyer's instructions, see HQ OSS China, from Wedemeyer to Heppner, April 26, 1945, in NR CFBX 36313, RG 226, USNA.

47. Patti (*Why Viet Nam?*, p. 86) says that Ho Chi Minh gave him a "black book" composed of photographs displaying the evidence of the catastrophe; Patti sent the book to the U.S. Embassy, but after the war could not find a copy in State Department files. According to Vietnamese sources, the average fall grain harvest was about 1.1 million metric tons. In 1944 it was only slightly over 800,000 tons, of which the French and Japanese requisitioned about 125,000 tons, leaving only about 700,000 tons for local consumption. For a description, see Marr, *Vietnam 1945*, pp. 96–107, and Nguyen Kien

Giang, *Viet Nam nam dau tien sau cach mang thang tam* [Vietnam in the first years after the August Revolution] (Hanoi: Su that, 1961), pp. 138–50.

48. "Nhat, Phap ban nhau va hanh dong cua chung ta" [The Japanese-French conflict and our actions] in *Van kien Dang (1930–1945)*, vol. 3, pp. 383–93. Communist historians often describe the March 8 conference as a meeting of the Standing Committee, but several other members of the Central Committee attended as well, including Nguyen Luong Bang, Le Duc Tho, Le Thanh Nghi, and Nguyen Van Tran—see Tonnesson, *Vietnamese Revolution*, p. 356, and *Nhung su kien*, vol. 1, pp. 601–2.

49. Tonnesson, *Vietnamese Revolution*, pp. 238, 337, citing "Franco-Jap Squabble in Indo-China," unsigned note dated March 19, 1945, OSS Records, Soc. 124840, RG 226, USNA. Tonnesson feels that the English in the report was too colloquial to have been written by Ho Chi Minh alone, and that he may have had help in writing it (p. 356, fn 17). In fact, by this time Ho's command of English was fairly good.

50. Tonnesson, *Vietnamese Revolution*, p. 345; Marr, *Vietnam 1945*, p. 226; Vo Nguyen Giap, *Tu nhan dan ma ra* [From the people] (Hanoi: Quan doi Nhan dan, 1964), p. 207. Attending the meeting were Truong Chinh, Giap, Tran Dang Ninh, Van Tien Dung, Chu Van Tan, and Le Thanh Nghi.

51. Patti, *Why Viet Nam?*, p. 102. The pamphlets were sent on to Washington, with a note from the U.S. Embassy official Langdon that the authors were members of the same group that had sent an appeal to Ambassador Gauss in August 1944 under the name of the League for the Independence of Indochina. Langdon commented that the pamphlets reflected a "hatred of France." Langdon report to Department of State, undated, in RG 59, UPA.

52. Comments by Kim Hien and Mac Shinn at OSS–Vietminh Conference at Hampton Bays, Long Island, September 22, 1997. Ho Chi Minh's route southward is chronicled in *BNTS*, vol. 2, pp. 229–39. The letter to Fenn is reproduced in Fenn, *Ho Chi Minh*, p. 80. According to King C. Chen, the entire group eventually comprised over fifty people—see his *Vietnam and China*, p. 102.

53. Giap, in "Ho Chi Minh," p. 207.

54. There is some confusion over this conference. A detailed resolution appears in *Van kien Dang (1930–1945)*, vol. 3, pp. 545–49, and the conference is mentioned in *Histoire de la révolution*, pp. 101–2, which states that it was called at the order of the Vietminh. In *Tu nhan dan ma ra*, p. 201, Vo Nguyen Giap mentions that he and Ho Chi Minh met with Hoang Quoc Viet and Nguyen Luong Bang to draft a plan to set up the liberated zone and decided to hold a conference of cadres, which took place on June 4. See also *BNTS*, vol. 2, p. 244. But in another place, Giap ("Ho Chi Minh," p. 209) implies that the meeting never took place. Eventually, a telephone was seized during an attack on a local village, which allowed a linkup between Giap's headquarters and Ho Chi Minh's office outside the village—see Giap, "Ho Chi Minh," p. 209. The village of Tan Trao is about thirteen miles east southeast of the provincial capital of Tuyen Quang and slightly to the north of Highway 13 (Patti, *Why Viet Nam?*, p. 550, n1).

55. Allison Thomas, in U.S. Senate Committee on Foreign Relations, The United States and Vietnam, 1944–1947, 92d Congress, 2nd sess., Staff Study no. 2, April 3, 1972, pp. 285–87. In Thomas's report dated September 17, 1945, he described the camp where they arrived: "The camp was located on the side of a hill in a bamboo forest at the end of Kimlung gorge about one kilometer from the small village of Kimlung. Kimlung itself is located 27 kilometers almost due east of Tuyen Quang and about 47

kilometers northwest of Thai Nguyen" (ibid. p. 257). Also see comments by Henry Prunier, a member of the team, at OSS-Vietminh Conference, September 23, 1997. Ho's culinary arrangements were recounted by Kim Hien at ibid., September 22, 1997.

56. Patti, *Why Viet Nam?*, pp. 127–29. For a discussion of French awareness of the identity of Ho Chi Minh and the political orientation of the Vietminh Front, see Alain Ruscio, *Les Communistes français et la guerre d'Indochine, 1944–1954* (Paris: L'Harmattan, 1985), pp. 54–61. Some French officials suspected that Ho was Nguyen Ai Quoc, but others insisted that he had died in a Hong Kong jail in the 1930s. In fact, the Sûreté was now well aware that he had survived the period of imprisonment in Hong Kong and had chaired the meeting at Pac Bo in 1941. See Service de la Sûreté au Tonkin à Résident Supérieur Tonkin, no. 11914–S, June 6, 1941, in dossier labeled "1106 Nguyen Ai Quoc," in SPCE, Carton 369, CAOM. The ICP veteran Nguyen Khanh Toan informed Ruscio that no one in Chongqing at the end of the Pacific War knew who Ho was. For a different view, see Marr, *Vietnam 1945*, p. 337.

57. Cited in Shaplen, *Lost Revolution*, p. 29. Also see Fenn, *Ho Chi Minh*, p. 81. Thomas's report is in Senate Committee, *U.S. and Vietnam*, p. 245. Phelan was apparently less impressed with some of Ho Chi Minh's colleagues, who "go charging around with great fervor shouting 'independence,' but seventy-five percent of them don't know the meaning of the word" (ibid., p. 207).

58. Giap, "Ho Chi Minh," pp. 210–11.

59. Marr, *Vietnam 1945*, citing William Broyles, Jr., *Brothers in Arms: A Journey from War to Peace* (New York: n.p., 1986), p. 104. See also Richard Harris Smith, *OSS: The Secret History of America's First Central Intelligence Agency* (Berkeley, Calif.: University of California Press, 1972), p. 332. The medic who diagnosed Ho, Paul Hoagland, later suggested that he felt that his own treatment had been instrumental in saving Ho's life, and Vietnamese sources today appear to concede that fact—see *The Washington Post*, December 13, 1969, and comments by Trieu Duc Quang at OSS-Vietminh Conference, September 22, 1997.

60. Nguyen Luong Bang, "Gap Bac o Tan Trao" [Meeting Uncle at Tan Trao] in *Tan Trao, 1945–1985* (Ha Tuyen, 1985), p. 52, cited in *BNTS*, vol. 2, p. 258. Also see Tran Trong Trung, "92 ngay dem: Bac Ho o Tan Trao" [92 days and nights: Uncle Ho at Tan Trao], *Tap chi Lich su Quan su* [Journal of Military History], April 1995.

61. Hoang Van Hoan, *Drop in the Ocean*, p. 213.

62. *Histoire de la révolution*, pp. 119–20. A somewhat longer version appears in *Van kien Dang (1930–1945)*, vol. 3, pp. 410–11. One of Ho's stratagems for winning the support of other Party leaders was apparently to play up the issue of Allied support. According to Patti (*Why Viet Nam?*, p. 551), the National Uprising Committee consisted of Truong Chinh, Vo Nguyen Giap, Tran Dang Ninh, Le Thanh Nghi, and Chu Van Tan. For the debate over strategy at the meeting, see Nguyen Luong Bang, "Moi vstrechii c tovarishchim Ho Shi Minh," [My meeting with comrade Ho Chi Minh] in *Nash Prezident Ho Shi Minh* [Our president Ho chi Minh] (Hanoi: Foreign Languages Press, 1967), pp. 97–99. See also *Récits de la résistance Vietnamienne (1925–1945)* (Paris: François Maspero, 1966), pp. 19–22.

63. Tran Trong Trung, "92 ngay dem," pp. 15–17. Nguyen Luong Bang, "Mes rencontres avec l'Oncle Ho," in *Souvenirs*, p. 76. This is a slightly different version of the article in *Nash Prezident* cited in the previous note. For an account of the congress by a participant, see Tran Huy Lieu, "Di du Tan Trao" [Going to Tan Trao], in *NCLS*,

no. 17 (August 1960). Henry Prunier recalls that as the U.S. contingent filed by the congress hall en route to Thai Nguyen, they noticed portraits on the wall of the meeting hall. Among them was a portrait of General Claire Chennault, but Ho's was not among them (Prunier remarks at OSS Vietminh Conference, September 23, 1997). Also see Patti, *Why Viet Nam?*, p. 134.

64. The complete appeal is contained in *Van kien Dang (1930–1945)*, vol. 3, pp. 404–5. For the ceremony, see Nguyen Luong Bang, in "Mes rencontres," p. 77.

X | *The Days of August*

1. For an estimate of the number of deaths, see David G. Marr, *Vietnam 1945: The Quest for Power* (Berkeley, Calif.: University of California Press, 1995), p. 104. Shipments of grain to the north were hindered by a variety of factors, including U.S. air attacks, the mining of Haiphong harbor, and Japanese requisitions of all large vessels for their own use—see the memoirs of Lt. General Nguyen Quyet, "Hanoi in August," in *Hanoi Moi*, August 26–31 and September 4, 1980, translated in JPRS, no. 81,203, July 2, 1982.

2. *Histoire de la révolution d'août* (Hanoi: Foreign Languages Press, 1972), pp. 125–26; Vo Nguyen Giap, "Ho Chi Minh: Père de l'armée révolutionnaire du Vietnam," in *Souvenirs*, p. 212; remarks by Henry Prunier at OSS-Vietminh Conference, September 23, 1997.

3. See Nguyen Khang, "Hanoi khoi nghia" [The Hanoi uprising], in *Nhung ngay thang tam* [The Days of August] (Hanoi: Van hoc, 1961), pp. 125–27. According to Khang, by the end of 1944 the Party had already enrolled about three thousand members in its organizations, and was able to buy weapons or obtain them from secret supporters in the native army. The terrorist units were selected from the most enthusiastic members of the Youth National Salvation Association, who were released from other duties and placed under the direct control of the regional committee.

4. Ibid., p. 133; Nguyen Quyet, "Hanoi in August."

5. Tran Huy Lieu, *Lich su thu do Ha noi* [A history of the city of Hanoi] (Hanoi: n.p., 1960), pp. 213–15; Nguyen Khang, "Hanoi khoi nghia," pp. 133–34. Nguyen Quyet, "Hanoi in August."

6. See Tran Van Giau, *Giai cap cong nhan Viet Nam* [The Vietnamese working class], vol. 3, *1939–1945* (Hanoi: Su that, 1963), pp. 238–43; Nguyen Quyet, "Hanoi in August."

7. Tran Van Giau, "Mot so dac diem cua khoi nghia thang tam 1945 o Nam bo, Sai gon" [A few remarks about the August 1945 Revolution in Saigon], *Tap chi Lich su Dang* [Party History Review], no. 34 (June 1990), pp. 4–10. Giau admitted (p. 5) that in 1945 non-Communist political elements outnumbered the ICP by a ratio of 10 to 1.

8. Tran Van Giau, *Giai cap cong nhan Viet Nam* [The Vietnamese working class], vol. 1 (Hanoi: Su that, 1957), p. 256. On Tran Van Giau, see Stein Tonnesson, *The Vietnamese Revolution of 1945: Roosevelt, Ho Chi Minh, and de Gaulle in a World at War* (London: Sage, 1991), p. 142; Tonnesson quotes Tran Van Giau as remarking that three hundred comrades in prison with him in 1940 were protected from the full force of the official represssion and constituted a sort of "reserve force" for the Party in its future rise to power. Pham Ngoc Thach was at this time an affluent medical doctor and a

French citizen, and some Party members questioned his fitness for Party membership—see the interview with Tran Van Giau in Marr, *Vietnam 1945*, p. 217.

9. Tran Van Giau, "Mot so dac diem," pp. 8–10; Archimedes L. A. Patti, *Why Viet Nam? Prelude to America's Albatross* (Berkeley, Calif.: University of California Press, 1980), pp. 182–89; Truong Nhu Tang, *Vietcong Memoir: An Inside Account of the Vietnam War and Its Aftermath* (San Diego: Harcourt Brace Jovanovich, 1985), p. 7.

10. Vo Nguyen Giap, *Unforgettable Days* (Hanoi: Foreign Languages Press, 1975), pp. 9–16; BNTS, vol. 2, p. 269; *Nhung su kien lich su Dang* [Events in the history of the party], vol. 1 (Hanoi: Su that, 1976), p. 660. For Ho's remark on the flooding, see Tran Dan Tien, in *Avec l'Oncle Ho* (Hanoi: Foreign Languages Press, 1972), p. 103. Ho Chi Minh's route from Tan Trao to Hanoi is traced in BNTS, vol. 2, 267–70. Also see Nguyen Quyet, "Hanoi in August." There is some disagreement on the date of Ho's arrival in Hanoi. Some sources give August 25, others the twenty-sixth. I am inclined to accept the former, since Archimedes Patti received an invitation to meet him at noon on August 26 and Ho was already settled in. Daniel Hémery contends that he arrived in Hanoi on August 21—see Hémery, *Ho Chi Minh: De l'Indochine au Vietnam* (Paris: Gallimard, 1990), p. 89.

11. Vo Nguyen Giap, *Unforgettable Days*, p. 22.

12. Patti, *Why Viet Nam?*, pp. 199–211.

13. In his memoirs, Bao Dai declared that the audience, most of whom were probably officials or courtiers, took the news of the abdication in stunned silence—see S. M. Bao Dai, *Le Dragon d'Annam* (Paris: Plon, 1980), pp. 117–21. Tran Huy Lieu provided his own version of the occasion in "Tuoc an kiem cua Hoang de Bao Dai" [The abdication of Emperor Bao Dai], in NCLS, no. 18 (September 1960), pp. 46–51. In Lieu's account, the voyage south was marked by exuberance on the part of the local population en route. After the abdication, the palace and the property therein, along with the imperial tombs in the mountains west of the city, were turned over to the local people's committee for safekeeping. In the awkward moments after the abdication, Lieu asked Bao Dai whether the domination of his country by the French and the Japanese had been painful. Bao Dai simply replied, "Yes, it was often painful" (see p. 50). In his own memoirs, Bao Dai described Tran Huy Lieu as "a seedy-looking runt who hid behind his dark glasses such a squint that it was not possible to look at him without embarrassment."

14. Vo Nguyen Giap, *Unforgettable Days*, pp. 24–25.

15. Hoang Van Hoan, *A Drop in the Ocean: Hoang Van Hoan's Revolutionary Reminiscences* (Beijing: Foreign Languages Press, 1988), p. 217; BNTS, vol. 2, p. 272; Vo Nguyen Giap, *Unforgettable Days*, pp. 25–26.

16. Vo Nguyen Giap, *Unforgettable Days*, pp. 27–28. The *place* was named after a French bishop in Indochina in the nineteenth century. Ho Chi Minh suggested that the spot be renamed Ba Dinh Square in honor of three villages in Thanh Hoa province that had fought against the French conquest in the late nineteenth century—see Kobelev, p. 174. For information on Ho's change of residence, see Georges Boudarel and Nguyen Van Ky, *Hanoi, 1936–1996: Du drapeau rouge au billet vert* (Paris: Editions Autrement, 1997), p. 99.

17. NR 63 from XUF, dated September 2, 1945, Box 199, Folder 3373, RG 226, USNA. For the size of the crowd, see Marr, *Vietnam 1945*, p. 530, fn 239; Marr estimates that the crowd was unlikely to have exceeeded 400,000, given the fact that the population of the city at that time was only about 200,000. According to some observers,

when the Allied planes passed overhead, Vietminh officials announced proudly, "Those are ours." I have taken the translation of Ho Chi Minh's speech from *Ho Chi Minh: Selected Writings* (Hanoi: Foreign Languages Press, 1977), pp. 55–56. Patti gives his own version (p. 250), taken verbatim and translated later into English. One Vietminh veteran recently recounted that when Ho's speech was broadcast at Tan Trao, villagers tried to open the radio—which they had never seen before—to see if they could find the speaker inside—comments by Tran Minh Chau, OSS-Vietminh Conference, September 23, 1997.

18. See *Histoire de la révolution*, pp. 120–21. According to Georges Boudarel, Ho's khaki suit was specially made at his own request. When his private secretary Vu Dinh Huynh, pleaded with him to buy a better suit and leather shoes, Ho refused and demanded something simple, practical, and comfortable, rather than expensive or elegant—see his comments in Boudarel, *Hanoi*, pp. 99–100. Ho remarked to Huynh that he had never worn a necktie, but that was certainly not true, as numerous photographs attest.

19. Vo Nguyen Giap, *Unforgettable Days*, pp. 39–41, and Bui Diem, *In the Jaws of History* (Boston: Houghton Mifflin, 1987), p. 39. One Vietnamese source states that in the fifteen provinces of the Red River delta the total rice harvest for the autumn of 1945 was only 500,000 metric tons, as compared with 832,000 the previous year—see Nguyen Kien Giang, *Viet Nam nam dau tien sau cach mang thang tam* [Vietnam in the years immediately following the August Revolution] (Hanoi: Su that, 1961), pp. 140–41, citing the newspaper *Su That* [Truth], December 12, 1945.

20. Nguyen Kien Giang, *Nam dau tien*, pp. 153–54, citing *Su That*, September 13, 1946.

21. Philippe Devillers, *Histoire du Vietnam, 1940–1952* (Paris: Editions du Seuil, 1952), p. 189; Nguyen Cong Binh, "Ban ve tinh chat cuoc cach mang thang tam" [On the nature of the August Revolution], in *NCLS*, no. 17 (August 1960), p. 4.

22. Patti, *Why Viet Nam?*, p. 284. According to Patti (p. 291), the total number of Chinese troops never exceeded 50,000. "Yesterday's elite corps" is a reference to disciplined troops who had arrived the day before and were stationed in the citadel or on the grounds of the governor-general's palace.

23. "Nghi quyet cua Toan quoc Hoi nghi Dang Cong san Dong duong" [Resolution of the National Conference of the Indochinese Communist Party], in *Van kien Dang (1930–1945)* [Party Documents (1930–1945)], vol. 3 (Hanoi: Ban Nghien cuu lich su Dang Truong uong, 1977), pp. 412–23, especially pp. 415–17.

24. Charles Fenn, *Ho Chi Minh: A Biographical Introduction* (New York: Scribner, 1973), p. 8.

25. See William Duiker, *U.S. Containment Policy and the Conflict in Indochina* (Stanford, Calif.: Stanford University Press, 1994), p. 27. The issue of trusteeships had been discussed at length at San Francisco and there was disagreement among U.S. officials as to whether the United States should insist on future independence or just self-government. The latter view prevailed, despite the plea by FDR adviser Charles Taussig that Roosevelt had insisted on independence. Other officials felt that Great Britain would not accept "independence" and that would wreck the whole concept. See William Conrad Gibbons, *The U.S. Government and the Vietnam War: Executive and Legislative Roles and Relationships*, vol. 1 (Princeton, N.J.: Princeton University Press, 1986), pp. 14–15.

26. Patti, *Why Viet Nam?*, p. 289. Patti's superiors in China felt that should the United States become involved in Franco-Vietminh negotiations, it could lead to "serious

trouble. See cable Davis to Heppner, September 1, 1945, Box 199, and Heppner to Davis, cable dated September 1, 1945, Entry 154, Box 18, both in Folder 3373, RG 226, USNA.

27. For a description of conditions in Saigon by an American observer, see the report by Captain J. Herbert Bluechel, dated September 30, 1945, in U.S. Senate Committee on Foreign Relations, *Causes, Origins, and Lessons of the Vietnam War*, 92d Congress, 2d sess., 1972, pp. 283–84. For criticism of Tran Van Giau within the ICP, see Marr, *Vietnam 1945*, p. 462.

28. An OSS detachment had been dispatched to Saigon with responsibility for investigating war crimes and prisoners-of-war conditions, and protecting U.S. property. For a source reflecting Gracey's point of view, see Peter M. Dunn, *The First Vietnam War* (New York: St. Martin's, 1985), especially p. 155.

29. Contemporary official reports of the attack are contained in Senate Committee, *Causes*, pp. 283–98. I have also drawn on the remarks by George Wickes at the OSS-Vietminh Conference, September 22–23, 1997.

30. Ho Chi Minh's letter, dated September 29, 1945, is in the Patti Collection. Gracey considered Dewey to be "an unpleasant man," while U.S. officers criticized Gracey for his "bull-like attitude." See the comments by Wickes, OSS-Vietminh Conference, September 22–23, 1997. According to Wickes, most of the other British officials were more sympathetic to the Vietnamese than was General Gracey. Also see Dunn, *First Vietnam War*, p. 156. For a report on the incident by Captain Bluechel, see Senate Committee, *Causes*, pp. 283–84, letter by Bluechel dated September 30, 1945.

31. Reported in telegram Paris to Secretary of State, October 12, 1945, RG 59, UPA.

32. Nguyen Kien Giang, *Nam dau tien*, pp. 117–18; untitled Vo Nguyen Giap article in *Cuu Quoc*, no. 83, October 5, 1945. For additional information on the religious sects, see Hue-Tam Ho Tai, *Millenarianism and Peasant Politics in Vietnam* (Cambridge, Mass.: Harvard University Press, 1983), and Jayne Werner, "Cao Dai: The Politics of a Vietnamese Syncretic Religious Movement" (Ph.D. diss., Cornell University, 1976).

33. Bao Dai, *Dragon*, pp. 130–31. The reference to opium is from Vu Thu Hien, *Dem giua ban ngay* [Between Night and Day] (Westminster, Calif.: Van Nghe, 1997), p. 108. Despite his efforts, Ho Chi Minh was apparently detained by the Chinese authorities on at least one occasion (ibid, p. 28). Still, Lu Han ceased calling him "Mr. Ho" and addressed him as "Chairman Ho"—see Mai Van Bo, *Chung toi hoc lam ngoai giao voi Bac Ho*" [I studied diplomacy with Uncle Ho] (Ho Chi Minh City: NXB Tre, 1998), p. 46.

34. Patti, *Why Viet Nam?*, p. 300.

35. Vo Nguyen Giap, *Unforgettable Days*, p. 68; Devillers, *Histoire*, p. 177; Mai Van Bo, *Chung toi hoc lam*, p. 46.

36. Sainteny's departure deprived Ho Chi Minh of one of his most conciliatory French adversaries. Sainteny had no liking for some of the more militantly anti-French members of the nationalist movement and observed in a report to Paris that should the new Vietnamese leaders (such as Ho Chi Minh) be driven into exile, they might return with French support to become "our best allies": Note of October 3, 1945 (SA1–02/3), cited in Philippe Devillers, *Paris: Saigon: Hanoi* (Paris: Gallimard, 1988), p. 98. He also remarked that the Vietnamese had no idea of the true meaning of independence, but were simply entranced by the symbolism of the word. Also see Patti, *Why Viet Nam?*, p. 299.

37. Telegram, Kunming (Sprouse) to Secretary of State, September 27, 1945, in RG 59, UPA. The report sent in early September was contained in Donovan letter to Ballantine, Director of the Division of Far Eastern Affairs, September 5, 1945, in ibid.

38. Memo from FE (Vincent) to U (Acheson), "Indochina," September 28, 1945, in RG 59, UPA. Ho Chi Minh confirmed that he was Nguyen Ai Quoc in a lengthy conversation with Patti on September 30—see Patti, *Why Viet Nam?*, pp. 371–73.

39. The quote is from Memo from Bonbright to Matthews (EUR), October 2, 1945, in RG 59, UPA.

40. "Possible Viet-Minh Representative en Route to Washington" (memo of conversation dated October 31, 1945), in ibid.

41. Remarks by Carlton Swift at OSS-Vietminh Conference, September 22–23, 1997. Ho's letter to Truman, dated October 22, 1945 is contained in Consulate General (Kunming) to Sec, October 24, 1945, in RG 59, UPA. Also see Patti, *Why Viet Nam?*, pp. 373–74.

42. See Truong Chinh, "The August Revolution," in *Truong Chinh: Selected Writings* (Hanoi: Foreign Languages Press, 1977), pp. 45–47. According to Nguyen Van Tran, Tran Van Giau also had some reservations about Ho's moderate strategy—see his *Viet cho me va Quoc hoi* [Letter to my mother and the National Assembly] (Garden Grove, Calif.: Van Nghe, 1996), p.152.

43. See, for example, Harold R. Isaacs, *No Peace for Asia* (New York: Macmillan, 1947). Isaacs had known Ho Chi Minh when he was living a shabby existence in Shanghai during the 1930s. During an interview with Isaacs at the Northern Palace in the fall of 1945, Ho laughed and said, "And now, I'm president of the provisional government of the RVN [*sic*]. They call me 'Excellency.' Funny, eh?" (p. 163).

44. Ibid., pp. 165, 177.

XI | *Reconstruction and Resistance*

1. Greg Lockhart, *Nation in Arms: The Origins of the People's Army of Vietnam* (Sydney: Allen & Unwin, 1989), p. 175; Yves Gras, *Histoire de la guerre d'Indochine* (Paris: Destins Croisés, 1992), p. 88, gives a figure of 30,000 Vietminh in the north alone.

2. According to Bao Dai, most of the members of the cabinet did not understand the humor in the comment, since they were from central Vietnam, where sausage made from dog meat was not a delicacy as in the north. For gold week, see Archimedes Patti, *Why Viet Nam? Prelude to America's Albatross* (Berkeley, Calif.: University of California Press, 1980), pp. 337–39. For information on the armed buildup, see Vo Nguyen Giap's *Unforgettable Days* (Hanoi: Foreign Languages Press, 1975), pp. 82–88.

3. Georges Boudarel and Nguyen Van Ky, *Hanoi 1936–1996: Du drapeau rouge au billet vert* (Paris: Editions Autrement, 1997), p. 103; Vu Thu Hien, *Dem giua ban ngay* [Between Night and Day] (Westminster, Calif.: Van Nghe, 1997), p. 227. Ngo Dinh Diem, of course, later served as president of the Republic of Vietnam (South Vietnam), thus emerging as Ho Chi Minh's main rival for the role of savior of the country.

4. See K.N.T., "Jours passés auprès de l'Oncle Ho," in *Avec l'Oncle Ho* (Hanoi: Foreign Languages Press, 1972), p. 352. For the meetings and nationalist demands, see Nguyen Kien Giang, *Viet Nam nam dau tien sau cach mang thang tam* [Vietnam in the first years following the August Revolution] (Hanoi: Su that, 1961), pp. 130–33.

5. See, for example, Hoang Van Hoan, *A Drop in the Ocean: Hoang Van Hoan's Revolutionary Reminiscences* (Beijing: Foreign Languages Press, 1988), p. 224. According to the Vietnamese historian Nguyen Kien Giang, some viewed the public dissolution as "an error in principle"—see his *Nam dau tien*, p. 130. The decree is located in *Van kien Dang (1945–1954)* [Party Documents (1945–1954)] vol. 1 (Hanoi: Ban nghien cun lich su Dang, 1979), pp. 19–20. Also see Philippe Devillers, *Paris-Saigon-Hanoi* (Paris: Gallimard, 1988), p. 108. According to Devillers, the decision may have been influenced by Tran Van Giau, who urged the formation of the broadest possible united front to lure moderates in the south.

6. "Khang chien kien quoc" [Resistance and reconstruction], in *Van kien Dang (1945–1954)*, vol. 1, pp. 21–35; Nguyen Kien Giang, *Nam dau tien*, p. 133.

7. Vo Nguyen Giap, *Unforgettable Days*, pp. 103–4. On the negotiations, see King C. Chen, *Vietnam and China, 1938–1954* (Princeton, N.J.: Princeton University Press, 1969), p. 129.

8. Vo Nguyen Giap, *Unforgettable Days*, p. 106. Lam Quang Thu, "Bac Ho tai ky hop dau tien cua Quoc hoi khoa I" [Uncle Ho at the first session of the National Assembly], in *NCLS*, no. 184 (January–February 1975), p. 8; Chen, *Vietnam and China*, pp. 129–30.

9. Chen, *Vietnam and China*, p. 130; Vo Nguyen Giap, *Unforgettable Days*, pp. 106–7. According to Giap, Nguyen Hai Than spoke in Chinese. When Ho offered him a large house and his own automobile, he was delighted and offered to tell Ho's fortune.

10. For de Gaulle's letter to Leclerc and other quotes, see Jacques de Folin, *Indochine, 1940–1955: La fin d'un rêve* (Paris: Perrin, 1993), pp. 130–33, citing Dossier E 166, Ministère des Affaires Etrangères. Hereafter MAE. See also Devillers, *Paris-Saigon-Hanoi*, p. 95.

11. According to de Folin, de Gaulle had instructed d'Argenlieu not to make a deal with the Vietminh, or to accept foreign mediation—see *Indochine*, p. 112.

12. Jean Sainteny, *Ho Chi Minh and his Vietnam: A Personal Memoir*, trans. Herma Briffault (Chicago: Cowles, 1970), p. 54.

13. Dossier E, 166–1, MAE, cited in de Folin, *Indochine*, p. 98.

14. Sainteny, *Ho Chi Minh* , p. 58. Bao Dai says that he met Sainteny on only one occasion, despite efforts by Sainteny to meet with him privately. He confirms that Ho insisted that all his colleagues address the ex-emperor by the honorific "Ngai." See Bao Dai, *Le Dragon d'Annam* (Paris: Plon, 1980), p. 134.

15. Bao Dai, *Dragon*, pp. 135–50. On one occasion during a cabinet meeting, a colleague from the VNQDD passed Bao Dai a book about Nguyen Ai Quoc and pointed to Ho Chi Minh. When Ho noticed the book in Bao Dai's hands, he gave him a malicious smile.

16. Caffery to Secretary of State, February 6, 1946, in book 8, p. 59, *United States Vietnam Relations, 1945–1967* (Washington, D.C.: U.S. government printing office, 1971). Hereafter USVN. Ho Chi Minh's letter to Truman is located in U.S. Senate Committee on Foreign Relations, *The United States and Vietnam, 1944–1947, 92d Congress, 2d sess., Staff Study no. 2, April 3, 1972, pp. 10–11*. Landon's reports to Washington are in *Foreign Relations of the United States*, 1946, 8: pp. 26–27. Ho Chi Minh's letter appears in OSS cable to Kunming dated February 28, 1946, S1–INT 32, Entry 140, Box 53, Folder 427, RG 226, USNA. Also see Vietnamese-language excerpts in *BNTS*, vol. 3, p. 121.

17. De Folin, *Indochine*, pp. 137–38, citing Thierry d'Argenlieu, *Chronique de*

l'Indochine, 1945/1947 (Paris: Albin Michel, 1985), p. 148. According to this source, d'Argenlieu and Leclerc detested each other, and the high commissioner once demanded the general's recall. Leclerc once took issue with de Gaulle's advice to restore order in the north before opening negotiations by saying that France lacked the power to do so.

18. Gras, *Histoire de la guerre*, p. 91.

19. Devillers, *Paris-Saigon-Hanoi*, p. 143; *BNTS*, vol. 3, pp. 147–48. Bao Dai recalls that the meeting took place on February 27—see his *Dragon*, pp. 150–51. See also Vo Nguyen Giap, *Unforgettable Days*, p. 145. In his *Ho Chi Minh*, Sainteny recalled that Ho had sometimes hinted that if an accord was to be reached, someone else might sign it (p. 60).

20. De Folin, *Indochine*, pp. 139–44. Pignon later remarked that if the French had wanted precision in the Sino-French treaty, it probably wouldn't have been signed—see ibid., p. 144, citing Note of July 4, 1946, by Pignon, MAE.

21. Vo Nguyen Giap, *Unforgettable Days*, pp. 159–66; *BNTS*, vol. 3, pp. 152–53. According to Lam Quang Thu, early in the morning Ho and others went to VNQDD headquarters to inform them that the meeting would be held a day early—see his "Bac Ho tai," p. 9.

22. Paul Mus, *Viet-Nam: Sociologie d'une guerre* (Paris: Editions de Seuil, 1952, p. 85. See also Kobelev, p. 192.

23. "Tinh hinh va chu truong" [Situation and recommendations], in *Van kien Dang (1945–1954)*, vol. 1, pp. 36–42. The resolution is dated March 3. Other sources declare that the meeting had been held on February 24. See *Toan Tap I*, vol. 4, p. 598, and *BNTS*, vol. 3, p. 148.

24. Sainteny, *Ho Chi Minh*, p. 62. Vo Nguyen Giap, in *Unforgettable Days* (p. 171), refers to Leclerc's request as well.

25. Frank White, in Senate Committee on Foreign Relations, *Causes, Origins, and Lessons of the Vietnam War*, 92d Congress, 2d sess., 1972, has an account—see p. 148. White dates the incident in December 1945, but is apparently mistaken. See the paper presented by Joseph Kelly, a U.S. observer, at the OSS-Vietminh Conference at Hampton Bays, N.Y., September 21–23, 1997.

26. Vo Nguyen Giap, *Unforgettable Days*, pp. 176–77, and Sainteny, *Ho Chi Minh*, pp. 62–64. The two accounts are roughly similar. Both make reference to the fact that at the last minute the Chinese persuaded Ho to sign. A cable to Washington by the U.S. diplomatic representative who attended the ceremony estimated that the referendum in Cochin China would probably be close—see Hanoi no. 37, dated June 5, 1946, in RG 59, UPA.

27. "Hoa de tien" [Conciliate to advance], in *Van kien Dang (1945–1954)*, vol. 1, p. 53. Ho's speech is reported in Vo Nguyen Giap, *Unforgettable Days*, p. 189, and Kobelev, p. 195; for a slightly different version, see Sainteny, *Ho Chi Minh*, p. 64. One contemporary recalls that when Ho Chi Minh visited the University of Hanoi to seek the support of the agreement, one student walked out of the shower in the dormitory completely naked in a patent effort to embarrass him. Ho recovered quickly and remarked: "Oh, it's you, little brother. You're always looking for a good laugh, aren't you?"—see Bui Diem, *In the Jaws of History* (Boston: Houghton Mifflin, 1987), p. 40.

28. Gras, *Histoire de la guerre*, p. 98.

29. Senate Committee, *Causes*, pp. 148–52. White places this dinner much earlier in time, but his comments suggest that it took place around Leclerc's arrival in March. Washington was apparently using OSS officers to provide information on Indochina,

since diplomatic offices had not yet been reopened. For the description of the city at the time of the arrival of the French, I have relied on the remarks of George Wickes at the OSS-Vietminh Conference, September 22–23, 1997.

30. Byrnes to French Ambassador Henri Bonnet, April 12, 1946, in USVN, book 8, part B.2, pp. 64–65. The telegram to Truman, dated February 28, 1946, is from OSS Kunming, SI-INT 32, Entry 140, Box 53, Folder 427, RG 226, USNA. A letter from Ho Chi Minh containing the same message, dated February 16, 1946, is in the Patti collection. Carlton Swift, Patti's immediate successor in Hanoi, says that he had been reprimanded by his superiors for giving his tentative agreement to the creation of a U.S.-Vietnamese Friendship Society (remarks by Swift at the OSS-Vietminh Conference, September 23, 1997).

31. Comments by George Wickes at the OSS-Vietminh Conference, September 22–23, 1997. Also see Gras, *Histoire de la guerre*, p. 98; Hoang Van Hoan, *Drop in the Ocean*, p. 231; and Sainteny, *Ho Chi Minh*, p. 67.

32. Vo Nguyen Giap, *Unforgettable Days*, pp. 221–22. Ho's remark to Salan can be found in Kobelev, p. 198. According to Gras, *Histoire de la guerre*, p. 111, the final decisions on the Dalat conference were not made until after the Ha Long Bay meeting.

33. Vo Nguyen Giap, *Unforgettable Days*, pp. 270–74; Nguyen Thanh, *Chu tich Ho Chi Minh o Phap* [Ho Chi Minh in France] (Hanoi: Thong tin Ly luan, 1988), pp. 168–69. In addition to chairman Pham Van Dong, members of the delegation were Hoang Minh Giam, Phan Anh, Ta Quang Buu, Nguyen Van Huyen, and Trinh Van Binh. Foreign Minister Nguyen Tuong Tam was scheduled to join the group, but declined at the last moment on the pretext of illness. He later admitted that he hadn't wanted to take part in the talks—see Hanoi to Department of State, no. 29, May 30, 1946, RG 59, UPA.

34. The loss of the eastern territories of Alsace and Lorraine to Germany after the Franco-Prussian War of 1870 had aroused a fierce sentiment of revenge among the French people, serving as a major factor in the outbreak of World War I. For Ho's remark, see Gras, *Histoire de la guerre*, p. 118, who cites Salan's *memoirs*. Gras points out that the French government did not intend to grant formal recognition to the new government until after a referendum. The trip is also traced in *BNTS*, vol. 3, pp. 216–21.

35. Ho was originally scheduled to stay in Cannes, according to Mai Van Bo— see his *Chung toi hoc lam ngoai giao voi Bac Ho* [I studied diplomacy with Uncle Ho] (Ho Chi Minh City: Tre, 1998), p. 60. There is some confusion over the accommodations in Biarritz. Several sources indicate that Ho stayed at the Carlton, which has now been transformed into a condominium. Jean Sainteny has recorded that Charles Tillon, minister of aviation in the Gouin cabinet, visited Biarritz in secret in order to determine "with his own eyes" in what conditions Ho was being held there. See Sainteny, *Ho Chi Minh*, p. 80. But Vietnamese sources state that he stayed at the Hotel Le Palais—see *BNTS*, vol. 3, p. 226, and Nguyen Thanh, *Chu tich Ho Chi Minh*, p. 169. Philippe Devillers says that the delegation was housed with Ho at the Carlton, but a U.S. diplomatic source reported that it was put up in a second-class hotel—see Devillers, *Paris-Saigon-Hanoi*, p. 289, and U.S. Embassy Paris to Department of State, no. 5411, June 15, 1946, RG 59, UPA.

36. Most of this material comes from Sainteny, *Ho Chi Minh*, pp. 74–75, who noted that the crew of the fishing boat was amazed at Ho Chi Minh's "sea legs" on the choppy waters of the Bay of Biscay, not realizing that he had spent several years at sea earlier in life. He adds that a wit later added the phrase "gone with the wind" to Ho's dedication at the restaurant in Biristou. Also see *BNTS*, vol. 3, pp. 226–32.

37. Sainteny, *Ho Chi Minh*, p. 76. The remark about Ta Thu Thau is in Gras, *Histoire de la guerre*, p. 118. Some Vietnamese sources hostile to Ho Chi Minh claim that he was responsible, directly or indirectly, for Thau's execution—see the article in *Chroniques Vietnamiens* (Fall 1997), p. 19.

38. Sainteny, *Ho Chi Minh*, p. 76–78. En route to Normandy, a second car, which was carrying a number of his aides, suddenly left the road and overturned in a ditch. No one was seriously hurt, but both Ho Chi Minh and Sainteny briefly wondered whether it had been a botched attempt on his life.

39. Nguyen Thanh, *Chu tich Ho Chi Minh*, pp. 202–3 (the article in *Le Figaro* is cited on p. 165). Sainteny, *Ho Chi Minh*, p. 77.

40. Leclerc apparently had obtained a copy of a message from Ho advising his colleagues to "be ready for any eventuality" during his absence in Paris. See Sainteny, *Ho Chi Minh*, pp. 81–82.

41. Nguyen Thanh, *Chu tich Ho Chi Minh*, p. 179. Also see Vo Nguyen Giap, *Unforgettable Days*, p. 299. Ho Chi Minh informed colleagues in later years that he was well aware of French efforts to seduce him by according him royal treatment in Paris, including the hanging of the Vietnamese flag next to the French tricolor—see Mai Van Bo, *Chung toi hoc lam*, pp. 60–61.

42. Sainteny, *Ho Chi Minh*, p. 71. The FCP's suspicion of Ho was reported in a cable to the State Department—see Paris to Department, June 16, 1946, RG 59, UPA. Historian Alain Ruscio surmises that, in his comments about fighting for Indochina, Thorez was referring not to the government in Hanoi, but to the radical nationalists; in general, he portrays relations between the two parties as amicable—see his *Les Communistes français et la guerre d'Indochine, 1944–1954* (Paris: L'Harmattan, 1985), p. 109. But Thorez later explained to journalist Philippe Devillers that his party had no intention of serving as the liquidator of the French presence in Indochina and that it ardently supported the vision of the tricolor flying over the far-reaching territories of the French Union around the globe—see Devillers, *Paris-Saigon-Hanoi*, p. 269.

43. *BNTS*, vol. 3, pp. 237–240; Ruscio, *Les Communistes*, p. 103; Kobelev, *Ho Chi Minh*, p. 201.

44. The American reporter was David Schoenbrun. Ruscio, *Les Communistes*, pp. 129–31; Nguyen Thanh, *Chu tich Ho Chi Minh*, pp. 187–89. When someone wondered whether he would accept a separate South Vietnam, Ho replied by asking rhetorically why they would not wish to join the rest of the country, since they shared the same language and the same ancestors—see Ruscio, *Les Communistes*, p. 131.

45. For Moutet's views, see the cable quoted in Devillers, *Paris-Saigon-Hanoi*, pp. 208–12.

46. Caffery to Burns, September 11 and 12, 1946, in RG 59, UPA. Also see *BNTS*, vol. 3, pp. 298–99, and Devillers, *Paris-Saigon-Hanoi*, p. 218.

47. DOS 241 to Reed in Saigon, August 9, 1946, in RG 59, UPA; Office Memo: Moffat to JCV-FE, August 9, 1946, in ibid. Both messages were drafted by Charlton Ogburn, later an outspoken critic of French policy in Indochina.

48. Many years later, Ho Chi Minh confided to younger colleagues that by the late summer of 1946 he was convinced that war was inevitable. "The situation was quite tense," he explained. "They were seeking to gain time to prepare an attack on us. We understood their plot and sought in turn to gain time to prepare ourselves." See Mai Van Bo, *Chung toi hoc lam*, p. 61. The phrase "sorcerer's apprentice" is from Jean Sainteny, in his *Ho Chi Minh*, p. 88.

49. David Schoenbrun, *As France Goes* (New York: Harper & Bros., 1957), pp. 234–36.

50. Sainteny, *Ho Chi Minh*, p. 88–89, Hanoi 88 to Secretary of State, September 26, 1946, in RG 59, UPA. On the meeting with Moutet, see Vo Nguyen Giap, *Unforgettable Days*, pp. 333–35, citing an article in the French newspaper *Franc-Tireur*. According to Ruscio, Ho's secretary confided that the president really wanted peace—see *Les Communistes*, p. 114.

51. Sainteny, *Ho Chi Minh*, p. 90; Nguyen Thanh, *Chu tich Ho Chi Minh*, pp. 205–6; Vo Nguyen Giap, *Unforgettable Days*, p. 337; Stein Tonnesson, *1946: Déclenchement de la guerre d'Indochine: Les vêpres tonkinoises du 19 Décembre* (Paris: L'Harmattan, 1987), pp. 40–41. For the story of the incredible shrinking carpet, see David Halberstam, *Ho* (New York: Knopf, 1987), second edition, p. 89.

52. Tonnesson, *Déclenchement*, pp. 41–42. The French obtained copies of all of his messages from the *Dumont d'Urville* because he was compelled to use their military telegraph system. French agents also snuck into his room and photographed documents that he was carrying in a dispatch case (see ibid). There is some discrepancy on Ho's departure date. Most sources give the date as September 18, while Sainteny gives the nineteenth. According to Mai Van Bo, (*Chung toi hoc lam*, p. 64), Ho left Paris on the eighteenth for Marseilles and arrived in Toulon the next day.

53. Alain Ruscio, ed., *Ho Chi Minh Textes, 1914–1969* (Paris: L'Harmattan, n.d.), pp. 132–34.

54. *Avec l'Oncle Ho*, pp. 337–40.

55. Bernard B. Fall, *The Two Viet-Nams: A Political and Military Analysis* (New York: Praeger, 1964), p. 82.

56. Ho Chi Minh's arrival in Haiphong and Hanoi is reported in Giap's *Unforgettable Days*, pp. 342–47. The tumultuous return and the crowds surrounding the palace are confirmed by a U.S. diplomatic observer—see Hanoi 94, October 24, 1946, in RG 59, UPA.

57. For a variety of interpretations, see Sainteny, *Ho Chi Minh*, p. 90; Tonnesson, *Déclenchement*, p. 41; and Bui Diem, *In the Jaws*, p. 49. For Ho Chi Minh's own comments, see Mai Van Bo, *Chung toi hoc lam*, p. 65. Ho added that it was nice to sail on a ship as a passenger for a change.

58. Vo Nguyen Giap, *Unforgettable Days*, pp. 283–86. The VNQDD headquarters was at 132 Minh Khai Street. Responsibility for these clashes has always been a matter of controversy. It is worth noting, however, that both French and U.S. diplomatic sources put most of the blame for fomenting disorders on nationalist elements—for one account, see Hanoi to Secretary of State, June 18, 1946, in RG 59, UPA.

59. A bonze is a Buddhist monk. Nguyen Binh (real name Nguyen Phuong Thau) is truly one of the bêtes noires of the Vietnamese revolution, but surprisingly little is known about his life. For Ho Chi Minh's directive, "Reduce the Campaign of Terrorism," see Extrait de télegrammes décryptés, 2ème Bureau no. 2186/2, dated April 15, 1946, in dossier labeled "1946–1949," in SPCE, Carton 366, CAOM.

60. Truong Chinh, "The August Revolution," in *Truong Chinh: Selected Writings* (Hanoi: Foreign Languages Press, 1977), pp. 62, 73. U.S. intelligence sources reported a comment by Pham Van Dong that Ho had gone to Paris "suffering from the illusion that national liberation could be wrested from an imperial power by negotiations"—see To NA, Mr. Bond from SY Jack D. Neal, "The Position of Ho Chi Minh," June 15, 1950, RG 59, UPA. Contemporary French sources now began to speak increasingly of

the existence of rival factions within the Party and the Vietminh leadership. There is some evidence from Ho Chi Minh himself to the contrary. In a conversation with General Raoul Salan en route to France in late May, Ho remarked that "Giap is totally devoted to me. He only exists as a result of my support. He, like the others, can do nothing without me. I am the father of the revolution"—see de Folin, *Indochine*, p. 165, citing Salan's memoirs. Such blunt comments, however, do not sound much like Ho Chi Minh.

61. Information on his sister's visit was provided by officials at the Ho Chi Minh Museum in Kim Lien. Also see *BNTS*, vol. 3, pp. 366–67 and *BNTS*, vol. 10, pp. 490–92. According to one hostile source, Dat came under suspicion from Party members during the Franco-Vietminh conflict, but because of his relationship to Ho Chi Minh no one who was aware of the relationship dared interfere—see *China News Analysis*, December 12, 1969.

62. Gras, *Histoire de la guerre*, p. 135.

63. As it turned out, because of the onset of war this constitution was never formally promulgated. Truong Chinh's comments are in "The August Revolution," pp. 62–63.

64. Gras, *Histoire de la guerre*, pp. 147–48. According to Philippe Devillers, the fighting was difficult to defuse because Colonel Dèbes, confident that he was adequately covered by Valluy in Saigon, had adopted an arrogant attitude toward the Vietnamese—see *Paris-Saigon-Hanoi*, pp. 240–49. The number of dead resulting from the shelling of the city has long been a matter of dispute. Many sources listed the number of those killed in the thousands, but some French sources put the figure at 200 or 300. See, for example, de Folin, *Indochine*, p. 179. Abbot Low Moffat, the U.S. diplomat who arrived in Hanoi a few days after the incident, reported an estimate of 2000. In a letter to French Prime Minister Léon Blum, Ho Chi Minh gave a figure of 3000. For a discussion of the issue, see Tonnesson, *Déclenchement*, pp. 104–6. For an overview of the issues surrounding the incident by U.S. Consul O'Sullivan in Hanoi, see Hanoi Dispatch 12 to Secretary of State, December 1, 1946, RG 59, UPA. For other accounts, see Sainteny, *Ho Chi Minh*, p. 91, and Tonnesson, *Déclenchement*, pp.81–120.

65. Confidential Reed November 7, 1946, from Saigon, in RG 59, UPA, Hanoi to Secretary of State, November 23, 1946, in RG 59, UPA; Paris to Department, November 29, 1946.

66. A deserter from the Vietminh movement later declared to French interrogators that Ho was always "the uncontested chief of the Party" and used the extremists to play his own "double jeu" with the French and other foreigners. See "Déclaration sur la vie en zone viet minh du Haut Tonkin, Viet Bac: Ho Chi Minh," in Ministère des Relations avec les Etats Associés, DGD, Saigon, du 9 au 15 fevrier 1953. Moffat's report is contained in the Senate Committee, *U.S. and Vietnam,* appendix 2, pp. 41–42. In Senate hearings in 1972, Moffat expressed his sympathy for Ho and sensed he was in the presence of a great man—see Senate Committee, *Causes*, pp. 200–201. He had less liking for Giap, whom he described as "the typical Commie" (ibid., p. 202).

67. DOS Circular Airgram, December 17, 1946, in RG 59, UPA. In retrospect, Moffat may have regretted his comments, since he was very concerned at the rising anti-Communist hysteria in Washington in the fall of 1946. See his comments in Senate Committee, *Causes*, pp. 190–91.

68. Sainteny, *Ho Chi Minh*, pp. 92–93; Devillers, *Paris-Saigon-Hanoi*, p. 262. According to U.S. Consul O'Sullivan, there may have been a disagreement within the DRV leadership, with Ho Chi Minh wanting to make concessions to the French on the sit-

uation in Haiphong, and hard-liners like Vo Nguyen Giap opposed—see Hanoi 132 to Department of State, December 4, 1946, RG 59, UPA.

69. Hanoi 134 to Department of State, December 5, 1946, RG 59, UPA; Devillers, *Paris-Saigon-Hanoi*, pp. 266–68. The views of the French on separating Ho Chi Minh from radical forces in his government were reported by Ambassador Caffery in Paris 6019 to Department of State, December 7, 1946, RG 59, UPA. According to Caffery, the French were suspicious of Ho Chi Minh's motives, but felt that he sincerely hoped to carry out the modus vivendi when Caffery left Paris. Now he was under pressure from radicals. Bidault told Caffery that the French were prepared to return Cochin China to Vietnam, but only at an appropriate time and under the proper conditions.

70. Gras, *Histoire de la guerre*, p. 126. According to Vo Nguyen Giap, the first artillery companies were formed with heavy guns captured from the French and the Japanese; prior to the war, the munitions service had supplied the army with eighty anti-tank bombs—Vo Nguyen Giap, *Unforgettable Days*, pp. 398–99.

71. Devillers, *Paris-Saigon-Hanoi*, p. 270.

72. Ibid., pp. 275–76.

73. Ibid., pp. 291–95; Tonnesson, *Déclenchement*, pp. 184–85; Vo Nguyen Giap, *Unforgettable Days*, pp. 407–8. Ho's telegram was also given to O'Sullivan, who sent it to the U.S. Embassy in Paris.

74. The letter to Sainteny is quoted in Vo Nguyen Giap, *Unforgettable Days*, p. 413. Msg Ho Chi Minh à Léon Blum, December 18, 1946, transmis à Paris par tg de Saigon 2071, December 20, 1946, 03.40 Z (AN SOM, Tel 938, 3642 A); Ho's message to Blum is in Devillers, *Paris-Saigon-Hanoi*, pp. 295–96.

75. Sainteny's account is in *Ho Chi Minh and . . .* , pp. 96–97.

76. This meeting is reported in Ngoc An, "Them tu lieu ve hoi nghi Van Phuc va 'loi keu goi toan quoc khang chien" [Additional material on the Van Phuc meeting and the "appeal for a war of national resistance"], in *Tap chi Lich su Quan su* [Journal of Military History], no. 36 (December 1988). According to this source, Ho drafted the appeal himself on the evening of December 18; some Vietnamese sources wrongly date the meeting itself on that date. Also see Devillers, *Paris-Saigon-Hanoi*, pp. 297–99.

77. Sainteny, *Ho Chi Minh*, pp. 97–98. According to Devillers (*Paris-Saigon-Hanoi*, pp. 297–298), there was a brief glimmer of hope that hostilities could be avoided. During the afternoon of December 19, Morlière (allegedly to demonstrate his sincerity) suddenly agreed to Giap's request to order a demobilization of French troops in the capital region. Party leaders thereupon decided to cancel their plans for an attack that evening. But at about 5:00 P.M. a French double agent informed Morlière about the original Vietnamese plans for an attack, and the general ordered his troops to resume their combat positions. In response, the Vietnamese returned to their original plan.

78. For Ho's use of Sun-tzu, see Ho's comments on October 11, 1946, cited in *BNTS*, vol. 3, p. 315. For other examples of his use of Sun-tzu, see ibid., pp. 217, 222.

XII | *The Tiger and the Elephant*

1. For an English-language version of the December 22 statement, see JPRS, no. 50,557, Translations on North Vietnam, no. 725, "Historic Documents of the ICP." On June 4, 1954, French General Alessandri told U.S. diplomat Robert McClintock

that the French had obtained a copy of the Vietminh war plan sometime in 1947. The plan, Alessandri noted, was deceptively simple—to create a base area in the Red River delta, as a source of manpower and provisions, and to open lines of communication with China, as the primary source for equipment. It would be a war of maneuver, with the Viet Bac as the main battleground and safe haven. See Saigon dispatch 570 to Department of State, June 4, 1954, RG 59, UPA.

2. According to Georges Boudarel, columns of Vietminh troops passed under the span of the Paul Doumer Bridge and then crossed the Red River at a point midway between two French posts farther up the river; their exodus was facilitated by the heavy smoke which blanketed the city, from fires set by Vietminh sapper units earlier in the day—see Georges Boudarel and Nguyen Van Ky, *Hanoi, 1936–1996: Du drapeau rouge au billet vert* (Paris: Editions Autrement, 1997), p. 118.

3. The tract, titled "Appel au peuple de France," is contained in Alain Ruscio, ed., *Ho Chi Minh: Textes, 1914–1969* (Paris: L'Harmattan, n.d), pp. 135–36. It began appearing on the streets of the capital shortly after the outbreak of conflict. Also see Yves Gras, *Histoire de la guerre d'Indochine* (Paris: de Noel, 1992), p. 160. Ho's letters are contained in Hanoi 851 to Secretary of State, April 24, 1947, in RG 59, UPA.

4. Quoted in Gras, *Histoire de la guerre*, p. 160. In a telegram to Ho Chi Minh that was routed through General Valluy, Blum took a hard line, insisting on an immediate cessation of hostilities for negotiations to resume; no violation, he warned, could be accepted—see Philippe Devillers, *Histoire du Vietnam, 1940–1952* (Paris: Editions du Seuil, 1952), p. 299.

5. Stein Tonnesson, *1946: Déclenchement de la guerre d'Indochine: Les vêpres tonkinoises du 19 décembre* (Paris: L'Harmattan, 1987), pp. 245–46; for Ho's letter, see Philippe Devillers, *Paris-Saigon-Hanoi* (Paris: Gallimard, 1988), p. 321, citing Letter from Ho Chi Minh to Moutet, January 3, 1947, in *Recueil Varet*, p. 277.

6. Devillers, *Paris-Saigon-Hanoi*, p. 324; Gras, *Histoire de la guerre*, p. 161.

7. Paris 1007 to Department of State, March 6, 1947, in RG 59, UPA.

8. There are many sources for Mus's meeting with Ho. The original version is in "Entrevue du Président Ho avec le représentant du Haut Commissaire Bollaert," undated, in dossier labeled "Ho Chi Minh 1947–1948," in SPCE, Carton 370, CAOM. For a U.S. account of the discussions, see Hanoi A13 to Department of State, June 20, 1947, RG 59, UPA. O'Sullivan described the meeting as "cordial."

9. Marshall's cable to Paris is in Secretary of State to Caffery, February 3, 1947, RG 59, UPA. Earlier messages are found in Department of State to Paris no. 74, January 8, 1947, and no. 431, February 3, 1947, in ibid.

10. Ho's interview was with Harrie Jackson of the Associated Press. The Pham Ngoc Thach affair is discussed in some detail in Mark Bradley's "An Improbable Opportunity: America and the Democratic Republic of Vietnam's 1947 Initiative," in Jayne Werner and Luu Doan Huynh, eds., *The Vietnam War: Vietnamese and American Perspectives* (Armonk, N.Y.: M.E. Sharpe, 1993). In a cable to Washington on April 17, Ambassador Stanton reported that he had recently received two letters from Thach. The first, dated April 12, transmitted a memorandum on the conflict in Indochina and was also sent to O'Sullivan in Hanoi in January for transmission to the State Department. On the twenty-fourth, Stanton reported that Thach had informed Colonel Law that the Vietnamese were disillusioned with the FCP, which had betrayed them by approving French military measures in Indochina. Thach described the United States as a vigilant defender of the Atlantic Charter and the only country that could bring the hostilities to an end.

See Bangkok 289, dated April 17, 1947, and no. 851, dated April 24, 1947 to Secretary of State, along with accompanying documents, in RG 59, UPA.

11. For references, see William Duiker, *U.S. Containment Policy and the Conflict in Indochina* (Stanford, Calif.: Stanford University Press, 1994), pp. 58–60, and Bradley, "Improbable Opportunity," pp. 18–23.

12. Sources on military problems encountered by the Vietminh during the early years of the war are Truong Chinh's *The Resistance Will Win*, translated in *Truong Chinh: Selected Writings* (Hanoi: Foreign Language Press, 1977), pp. 175–76, and *Cuoc khang chien than thanh cua nhan dan Viet Nam* [The sacred war of the Vietnamese people], vol. 1 (Hanoi: Su that, 1958), pp. 238–39.

13. For changing Vietminh military tactics during the late 1940s, see Vo Nguyen Giap, *People's War, People's Army* (New York: Praeger, 1962), p. 92.

14. Cited in Gras, *Histoire de la guerre*, p. 196.

15. For a description of Ho's life in the jungle, see "Déclaration sur la vie en zone viet minh du Haut Tonkin, Viet Bac: Ho Chi Minh:" in Ministère des Relations avec les Etats associés, DGD, Saigon, du 9 au 15 fevrier 1953.

16. *Cuoc khang chien than thanh*, vol. 1, p. 239.

17. For an excellent overview of this process, see Motoo Furuta, "The Indochinese Communist Party's Division into Three Parties: Vietnamese Communist Policy Toward Laos and Cambodia," in Motoo Furuta and Takashi Shiraishi, eds., *Indochina in the 1940s and 1950s* (Ithaca, N.Y.: Cornell University Southeast Asia Program, 1992), pp. 143–63.

18. In June 1954, the American Embassy in Tokyo transmitted a document from Taipei sources providing the texts of five secret agreements allegedly reached between 1940 and 1952. One was signed in June 6, 1948, somewhere in Yunnan and provided for mutual recognition and a formal military alliance between the two parties. Recent information on the limited links between the two countries makes it likely that this was an agreement between local operatives in the area, but Vo Nguyen Giap confirms that cooperation began to take place at the leadership level beginning in early 1948—see his *Duong toi Dien Bien Phu* [The road to Dien Bien Phu] (Hanoi: Quan doi Nhan dan, 1999), p. 13. Also see AmEmbassy Tokyo to Department of State, dispatch 1671, June 10, 1954, RG 59, UPA. For information on the Independence Regiment, see Am-Consulate Hanoi, January 8, 1951, dispatch transmitting a report by French Captain Augier, in ibid. Augier was a specialist in Chinese affairs, and his report stressed that Chinese activities along the border near the Tonkin Gulf were making the Vietminh so nervous that they eventually disbanded the regiment. U.S. diplomats suspected, probably correctly, that both the French and the Nationalist Chinese were making a major attempt to influence U.S. policy by pointing to Chinese influence over the Vietminh and thus tended to discount such warnings. Information from Chinese sources, however, suggests that such low-level contacts did indeed exist at the time; nevertheless, in the light of recent information, the 1948 alliance seems unlikely. On these early contacts, see Luo Guibo, "Lishi de Hui-tan" [Historical recollections], in *Zhongguo waijiaoguan tsongshu* (Beijing: Zhong hua Publishers, 1995), pp. 163–64. The establishment of radio links is recounted in *HZYZ*, p. 123.

19. *Foreign Relations of the United States (1949)*, vol. 7, pt. 1, pp. 140–41. On the change in French military leadership in Indochina, see Gras, *Histoire de la guerre*, pp. 264–67. For Vo Nguyen Giap's reported visit of April 1949, see the note on Sino-Vietnamese military operations, in SPCE, Carton 366, CAOM. According to this source,

a joint conference held at Jingxi that month agreed to a fusion of the armies of the two countries and broad cooperation along the border. Another document in the French archives indicates that in early January 1950, Vietnamese Party leaders rejected a Chinese proposal to fuse the armies of the two countries. I have been unable to find any confirmation of this document, which appears to predate the formal signing of an aid agreement between Vietnamese and Chinese Party leaders—perhaps it refers to the decisions reached in Jingxi in April. See no. 995/TNH, Parti Communiste, Dong Duong Cong San Dang [*sic*], "Résolutions prises en séance plenière de l'Assemblée des Conseillers tenue le 3 janvier 1950."

20. This report is contained in a dossier labeled "1950," in SPCE, Carton 366, CAOM. Vietnamese sources confirm the existence of this meeting—see *BNTS*, vol. 4, p. 308. Also see Vo Nguyen Giap, *Duong toi*, p. 10.

21. Cited in Gras, *Histoire de la guerre*, p. 272.

22. "Déclaration sur la vie"; Gras, *Histoire de la guerre*, p. 272.

23. Ho Chi Minh's letter and the mission are reported in Luo Guibo, "Lishi," pp. 150–51. Also see *HZYZ*, p. 21, and *HZYZ*, p. 124. The two delegates were Le Ban (Li Bishan) and Nguyen Duc Rui. Le Ban, a southerner, settled in China before World War II but returned to Vietnam in 1947. Rui was reportedly a merchant in Hanoi. French intelligence wrote about the trip in a report dated October 3, 1949, in SPCE, Carton 366, CAOM. On the meeting of the DRV Council of Ministers held on August 18, see SF de Tonkin, September 3, 1949, in ibid.

24. Gras, *Histoire de la guerre*, p. 286. Truong Chinh's article is in *Cuoc khang chien than thanh*, vol. 2, pp. 293–98. On Liu Shaoqi's famous trade union speech, see Melvin Gurtov, *The First Vietnam Crisis: Chinese Communist Strategy and United States Involvement, 1953–1954* (New York: Columbia University Press, 1967), pp. 7–8. Also see King C. Chen, *Vietnam and China, 1938–1954* (Princeton, N.J.: Princeton University Press, 1969), pp. 14–20.

25. *Vietnam: Nhung su kien (1945–1986)* [Vietnam: Historical events (1945–1986)] (Hanoi: Nha xuat ban Khoa hoc Xa hoi, 1990), pp. 49–50. Gras, *Histoire de la guerre*, p. 287.

26. Luo Guibo, "Lishi," pp. 151–53. According to Luo, electronic communications had been restored between the two parties in the late 1940s, but were still not functioning smoothly, and most communications were apparently carried by messengers.

27. Ibid, pp. 157–60; Gras, *Histoire de la guerre*, p. 287. Chinese escorts had surmised that Mr. Ding was actually Ho Chi Minh and reported that fact to the authorities—see Vo Nguyen Giap, *Duong toi*, pp. 13–14. For the meeting in the Viet Bac in mid-December, see *BNTS*, vol. 4, p. 376.

28. Hoang Van Hoan *A Drop in the Ocean: Hoang Van Hoan's Revolutionary Reminiscences* (Beijing: Foreign Languages Press, 1988), pp. 275–78; *BNTS*, vol. 4, p. 399; Vo Nguyen Giap, *Duong toi*, p. 14. In his telegram to Mao reporting Ho Chi Minh's arrival in Beijing, Liu Shaoqi indicated that Chinese leaders had listened with sympathy to their visitor's request for assistance—See *Liu Shaoqi Nianpu (1898–1969)* [Liu Shaoqi's chronicle (1898–1969)] (n.p.: Central Documents Press, 1996), p. 241.

29. Ho's letter was reported on Radio Moscow on August 29, 1949—see SPCE, Carton 56, CAOM. Also see Georges Boudarel, *Autobiographie* (Paris: Jacques Bertoin, 1991), p. 90. A U.S. diplomat in Moscow reported attending a lecture by a Soviet official on February 23, 1950. The speaker remarked that Vietnam was a "party of a new type which is in the process of transforming itself into a party of the Marxist type."

There were, the speaker noted, compulsory lectures on Marxism for members of the Communist Party. The strategy was for Communists to "unite temporarily in a national party with any working class parties." The Vietnamese Party, he concluded, differed from those in Eastern Europe, which were "much further developed" than in Vietnam, which had not yet established a dictatorship of the proletariat or a people's democracy. I was told by a Vietnamese specialist in Moscow that there were no Soviet contacts with Ho Chi Minh until 1949, and that Stalin had been skeptical of a Vietminh victory before that.

30. Jerrold L. Schector with Vyacheslav V. Luchkov (tr. and ed.), *Krushchev Remembers: The Glasnost Tapes* (Boston: Little, Brown, 1990), pp. 154–55. For the story of the helicopter, see Wu Xiuquan, *New China Diplomacy*, cited in Harrison Salisbury, *The New Emperors* (Boston: Little, Brown, 1992), p. 93. Also see his *Eight Years in the Ministry of Foreign Affairs* (Beijing: n.p., 1985). Hoang Van Hoan's son told Vietnam specialist Christopher Goscha that in 1950 neither Stalin nor Mao Zedong was convinced that Ho Chi Minh was a genuine Marxist-Leninist.

31. Interview with Do Quang Hung in Hanoi, December 15, 1990.

32. Luo Guibo, "Lishi," p. 161. Stalin explained his decision on the grounds that Soviet attentions were focused on their new allies in Eastern Europe. According to one source, Ho Chi Minh asked Stalin for equipment sufficient to arm ten infantry divisions and one artillery regiment—see Vo Nguyen Giap, *Duong toi*, pp. 14–15.

33. For a convincing discussion of Mao Zedong's worldview at that time, see Chen Jian, "China and the First Indo-China War," *China Quarterly* (March 1993), pp. 88–91. Also see his *China's Road to the Korean War: The Making of the Sino-American Confrontation* (New York: Columbia University Press, 1994). Ho Chi Minh's new role as director of operations for Communist Parties in the region comes from "Déclaration sur la vie."

34. Robert M. Blum, *Drawing the Line: The Origins of the American Containment Policy in Asia* (New York: Norton, 1982), p. 122. The possibility of Ho-Bao Dai talks came from Indian sources and was reported in "The Position of Ho-Chi-Minh," in To NA Mr. Bond from SY Jack D. Neal, dated June 16, 1950, RG 59, UPA. Ho firmly denied to another journalist that he would deal with traitors like Bao Dai—see the article in *Khong Dich* (June 12, 1949), contained in high commissioner's report dated April 17, 1950, in SPCE, Carton 366, CAOM.

35. Secretary of State to Gibson, May 20, 1949, in FRUS, 1949, vol. 7 (East Asia), pt. 1, pp. 29–30.

36. Cited in Duiker, *U.S. Containment Policy*, p. 81.

37. Luo Guibo, "Lishi," pp. 163–68. As always, Ho Chi Minh was solicitous of the comfort of his guests, instructing his private secretary, Vu Dinh Huynh, to make sure that Luo and his colleagues were given appropriate accommodations: "With me it doesn't matter, but with others it has to be just right. They care about things like that." See Vu Thu Hien, *Dem giua ban ngay: Hoi ky chinh tri cua mot nguoi khong lam chinh tri* (Westminster, Calif.: Van Nghe, 1997), p. 108.

38. See Truong Chinh, "Hoan thanh nhiem vu chuan bi chuyen manh sang tong phan cong" [Complete the task of preparation, switch strongly to the general counteroffensive], in *Van kien Dang (1945–1954)*, vol. 2, part 2, pp. 265–338. The DRV decision to move to the general offensive sometime in 1950 was reported by the New China News Agency shortly after. See the report by U.S. Consul Edmund Clubb, in Peiping [Bejing] to Secretary of State, no. 395, February 25, 1950, RG 59, UPA.

39. Vo Nguyen Giap, *Nhiem vu quan su truoc mat chuyen sang tong phan cong* [The

military task in preparing for the general counteroffensive] (Hanoi: n.p., 1950). French intelligence sources obtained a July 15, 1950, report from the ICP Central Committee to the Vietminh leadership in the south that described the general offensive as taking place in several stages and involving arduous sacrifices—see Saigon to Secretary of State, August 21, 1950, RG 59, UPA. Documents from the Third National Conference can be found in *Van kien Dang (1945–1954)*, vol. 2, part 2, pp. 241–431.

40. Liu Shaoqi cabled Ho Chi Minh reporting the appointment of General Wei; see *Liu Shaoqi nianpu*, p. 247. Liu's comment on the global significance of the assignment is in ibid., p. 256. Also see Hoang Van Hoan's article in *Beijing Review*, November 23, 1949. For a lengthy analysis of Chinese assistance to the Vietminh during this period, see Qiang Zhai, "Transplanting the Chinese Model: Chinese Military Advisers and the First Vietnam War, 1950–1954," *The Journal of Military History* (October 1993). Also see Furuta, "Indochinese Communist Party's Divisions," p. 150. French intelligence reports on the new China connection were relayed to U.S. officials, who reacted initially in a low-key manner and expressed skepticism that China was about to become directly involved in the conflict. An undated message from the State Department to the U.S. Embassy in Paris in the summer of 1950 remarked that a Chinese invasion was unlikely in light of historic Vietnamese suspicions of the Chinese. At most, the writer noted, the two were cooperating to achieve common goals. See For Bruce from Secretary, undated, drafted by Gibson, August 15, 1950, in RG 59, UPA.

41. *Zhongguo junshi guwentuan fang Ywe kang fa douzheng shishi* [The Chinese Military Advisory Group in Vietnam during the Anti-French War] (Beijing: Liberation Army Publishers, 1990), pp. 44–46. See also *ZYG*, p. 28, and Gras, *Histoire de la guerre*, pp. 315–16. According to an informer, Party leaders gave some consideration to establishing an external headquarters at Guilin in order to strengthen contacts with Beijing and also to facilitate Ho Chi Minh's activities to promote revolution elsewhere in Southeast Asia. See BR no. 9426 du Service de Sécurité du Haut Commissariat au Nord Vietnam, July 13, 1950, in dossier labeled "Ho Chi Minh années 1949 à 1953," in SPCE, Carton 370, CAOM.

42. Truong Chinh, "Chuyen manh sang tong phan cong" [Vigorously switch to the general counteroffensive] in *Van kien Dang (1945–1954)*, vol. 2, part 2, pp. 264–338. Also see Motoo Furuta, "Indochinese Communist Party's Division," pp. 157–58. Furuta points out that the ICP had technically adopted the concept of a "growing over" of the Vietnamese revolution as early as 1948, but had refrained from taking key steps to bring theory closer to reality until the beginning of the new decade.

43. According to a defector who had once been well placed in the movement, after Ho's return from his 1950 trip to Moscow and Beijing, chief responsibility for formulating the Party's domestic agenda was turned over to General Secretary Truong Chinh—see "Déclarations sur la vie." For some of the press reports mentioned in this paragraph, see the extract from the Bangkok journal *The Democrat*, June 1950, and the *Journal d'Extrême Orient*, June 13, 1950, and Saigon cable no. 1644 dated March 13, 1951, all in SPCE, Carton 366, CAOM. For Figuères's visit to Vietnam, see Jean Lacouture, *Ho Chi Minh: A Political Biography*, trans. Peter Wiles (New York: Vintage, 1968), pp. 185–87. According to the French journal *Aux Ecoutes*, Moscow warned Ho that the final objective of the revolution was not national independence, but the advent of world communism, and advised him to accept Chinese advice and assistance. Whether this report has any basis in fact, there seems little doubt that both Moscow and Beijing

continued to harbor doubts about Ho Chi Minh's intentions. See the folder on the Figuères visit in SPCE, Carton 366, CAOM.

44. Translation of an extract from the journal *Gia Dinh* dated November 16, 1950, annex to "Note pour le Conseiller Politique" no. 1257/C/SG, I, February 23, 1951, in dossier labeled "1951," in SPCE, Carton 366, CAOM.

45. For an account, see Vo Nguyen Giap, *Duong toi*, pp. 17, 41–43. Also see *Chen Geng Riji* [Chen Geng's Diary], vol. 2 (Beijing: People's Liberation Army Press, 1984), p. 37.

46. Manila 788 to Secretary of State, October 2, 1950, RG 59, UPA.

47. See Heath to Secretary of State, November 4, 1950, in *United States–Vietnam Relations, 1945–1967* (Washington, D.C., U.S. Government Printing Office, 1971), book 8, pp. 405–8. Also see Heath to Secretary of State, October 15, 1950, RG 59, UPA.

48. Hoang Van Hoan, *Drop in the Ocean*, pp. 295–96; Vo Nguyen Giap, *Duong toi*, pp. 12, 36–44; Ngoc Chau, *Chiec ao Bac Ho* [Uncle Ho's Jacket] (Hanoi: Thanh nien, 1987), p. 60; Boudarel and Ky, *Hanoi*, p. 123; Chen Jian, "China," pp. 93–94. For Chen Geng's criticisms of Vietminh performance—and there were many—see Qiang Zhai, "Transplanting the Chinese Model," pp. 700–703, and *Chen Geng Riji*, pp. 38–39. According to the latter source, many of these ideas were apparently passed on to Ho and Giap prior to Chen's departure. They "happily" accepted his suggestions. According to Vo Nguyen Giap (*Duong toi*, p. 14), Ho Chi Minh had considerable respect for Chen Geng, and had initially requested that he head the original Chinese delegation to Indochina in early 1950.

49. According to Vo Nguyen Giap, at the end of the successful border offensive Chen Geng recommended a three-pronged attack similar to the recent campaign in the vicinity of the Red River delta sometime the following year—see *Duong toi*, p. 99. The role of Chinese advisers—and their superiors in Beijing—in planning the offensive is described briefly in *Zhongguo junshi*, p. 27. Senior Chinese military planners apparently gave their approval to the plan, although it should be noted that in a letter to Ho Chi Minh in December, Liu Shaoqi had expressed Beijing's agreement with Ho's declared intention to fight a protracted war based on a policy of self-reliance. Liu expressed confidence that, with the assistance of Chinese advisers, such a strategy would eventually succeed, but only if it were carried out on the basis of careful planning and painstaking efforts to improve the effectiveness of the movement. Liu also stressed that all Chinese suggestions should be adapted to conform with conditions inside Vietnam—see *Liu Shaoqi nianpu*, telegram of December 8, 1950, p. 265. Doubts within the Vietminh leadership about the likelihood of a successful offensive are discussed in Vu Thu Hien, *Dem giua ban ngay*, pp. 361–62.

XIII | *A Place Called Dien Bien Phu*

1. Ngo Van Chieu, *Journal d'un combattant Viet-minh* (Paris: Editions du Seuil, 1957), p. 154.

2. Hanoi 366 to Secretary of State, January 23, 1951, RG 59, UPA.

3. Chen Jian, "China and the First Indo-China War," *China Quarterly* (March 1993), p. 95; Yves Gras, *Histoire de la guerre d'Indochine* (Paris: de Noel, 1992), pp. 383–84; *Zhongguo junshi guwentuan fang Ywe kang Fa douzheng shishi* [The Chinese Military

Advisory Group in Vietnam during the Anti-French War] (Beijing: Liberation Army Publishers, 1990), pp. 30–31. For the meeting of Party leaders in April, see *BNTS*, vol. 5, pp. 43–46. According to Saigon 1580 to the Secretary of State, dated March 10, 1951, RG 59, UPA, local journals reported that Giap had committed suicide. For the reaction of Chinese advisers, see Qiang Zhai, "Transplanting the Chinese Model: Chinese Military Advisers and the First Vietnam War, 1950–1954," *The Journal of Military History* (October 1993), p. 704.

4. Georges Boudarel, *Autobiographie* (Paris: Jacques Bertoin, 1991), pp. 406–7. One of the key texts used in the program, *Reform Work Methods*, was a direct translation of Liu Shaoqi's *Lun Dang* [On the party], which was used for the same purpose in China— see *HZYZ*, p. 130.

5. For one report on his fate, see Saigon ARMA, MC 361–51, dated December 13, 1951, RG 59, UPA. According to sources in Hanoi, one of the members of the team that escorted Nguyen Binh to the north was Le Duan, later Ho Chi Minh's successor as Party general secretary. Other sources say Nguyen Binh had been under suspicion for months, because he was "too tough." For reports of Sino-Vietnamese friction, see Saigon 928 to Secretary of State, October 27, 1951, and Hanoi 536, April 4, 1951, both in RG 59, UPA.

6. For Truong Chinh's report to the Congress, see *Ban ve cach mang Viet Nam* [On the Vietnamese revolution] (Hanoi: 1956], p. 6. Also see Ken Post, *Revolution, Socialism, and Nationalism in Vietnam*, vol. 1 (Aldershot, U.K.: Dartmouth, 1989), pp. 172–73.

7. For the captured document, see U.S. Department of State, *Working Paper on North Viet-Nam's Role in the War in South Viet-Nam* (Washington, D.C., 1968), appendix item no. 1, p. 2–2.

8. This captured document was reported to Washington by U.S. Consulate in Hanoi no. 10, July 12, 1950, RG 59, UPA. The three countries, it stated, were contiguous and should mutually aid one another in every field to fight the imperialist invader and provide mutual assistance in building "new democracies." Party directives were to be valid for action throughout Indochina, but should be applied according to the situation in each country. According to the document, the Democratic Federation of Indochina would not be created until the independence of all three countries had been achieved. Then each would join the new federation on its own volition.

9. Extract from *Bulletin des Ecoutes Viet-minh* no. 1211 dated April 26, 1951, in dossier labeled "1951," in SPCE, Carton 366, CAOM. For some of the rumors regarding Ho Chi Minh, see Saigon 220, June 12, 1950, RG 59, UPA. French media and intelligence sources reported that Ho had been replaced by the militant Truong Chinh—see the *Journal d'Extrême Orient*, June 11, 1950. A newspaper in Thailand said that Stalin had ordered the eviction of Ho Chi Minh from the Party because he refused to follow the Soviet line.

10. For references to Sino-Vietnamese discussions of the campaign, and Ho's trip to Beijing, see *Zhongguo junshi*, pp. 52, 56–57; also see Qiang Zhai, "Transplanting the Chinese Model," pp. 706–7, and Chen Jian, "China," pp. 96–97. According to these sources, Beijing refused a Vietnamese request to dispatch Chinese troops from Yunnan province to take part in a future attack on Lai Chau.

11. For rumors of Ho's death, see the paper by Edmund Gullion attached to Memo, Far East (Allison) to Sec, January 28, 1953, and Memo to Undersecretary titled "Intelligence Note," April 9, 1954, both in RG 59, UPA. According to the latter, no reliable

source had seen him since May 1947, when he had tuberculosis. Also see Joseph Starobin, *Eyewitness in Indochina* (New York: Cameron & Kahn, 1954).

12. This information was printed in the Chinese newspaper *People's Daily*. See "Bulletin officiel du New China News Agency" (trad. française), January 12, 1951, in dossier labeled "1951," in SPCE, Carton 366, CAOM. Also see "Bulletin des renseignements," no. 88 (September 10, 1951), in ibid. For his frequent change of residence, see *BNTS*, vol. 5, p. 153.

13. For an interview with a Vietminh defector on conditions in liberated areas, see Hanoi 34, March 25, 1952, in RG 59, UPA. For a more favorable view, see Starobin, *Eyewitness*, especially pp. 82–89 (Starobin, a journalist with ties to the U.S. Communist Party, spent several weeks in the liberated area in the spring of 1953).

14. Duong Van Mai Elliott, *The Sacred Willow: Four Generations in the Life of a Vietnamese Family* (New York: Oxford University Press, 1999), pp. 234–35.

15. Cited in Bernard B. Fall, *The Vietminh Regime: Government and Administration in the Democratic Republic of Vietnam* (Ithaca, N.Y.: Cornell University Southeast Asia Program, 1954), p. 109. For a classic account of the land reform program from a critical point of view, see Hoang Van Chi's *From Colonialism to Communism: A Case History of North Vietnam* (New York: Praeger, 1964). On pp. 182–83, Chi quotes Ho Chi Minh as having observed that when you need to straighten a curved piece of bamboo, it is necessary to bend it in the opposite direction and hold it a while. Then it will slowly straighten up.

16. Edwin E. Moise, *Land Reform in China and Vietnam: Consolidating the Revolution at the Village Level* (Chapel Hill, N.C.: University of North Carolina Press, 1983), p. 168; Starobin, *Eyewitness*, pp. 88–91.

17. For the full text, see *Public Papers of the Presidents: Dwight Eisenhower, 1953*, pp. 12–34.

18. Ambassador in France (Dillon) to Secretary of State, July 22, 1953, in *Foreign Relations of the United States, 1952–1954*, vol. 13 (Indochina), pt. 1, p. 693. From Saigon, U.S. Ambassador Donald Heath angrily took the editors of *Life* to task for their pessimistic view of the situation, and the latter eventually agreed to publish his response, "France Is Fighting the Good Fight," in September; however, the author of the original article, Douglas Duncan, defended himself and claimed that it reflected the views of most U.S. military officers in Indochina. In exasperation, Henry Luce, the publisher, complained to State Department officials that he was being accused by his own subordinates of ignoring lower-level views. See Saigon 391, September 3, 1953, and 397, September 4, 1953, both in RG 59, UPA.

19. See Han Huaizhi, comp., *Dangdai Zhongguo jundui de junshi gongzuo* [The military activities of the contemporary Chinese army], vol. 1 (Beijing: Social Sciences Press, 1989), p. 529. Also see *Zhongguo junshi*, pp. 89–90.

20. *Zhongguo junshi*, p. 90. According to Han Huazhi, *Dangdai*, vol. 1, p. 530, the attack on Dien Bien Phu was suggested to Vo Nguyen Giap by his Chinese advisers. Beijing indicated that a victory at Dien Bien Phu could have strong political and international significance. Also see Hoang Van Thai's article in *Vietnam Courier* (March 1984), pp. 19–23, and Vo Nguyen Giap's *People's War, People's Army* (New York: Praeger, 1962), p. 148.

21. For the Chinese viewpoint, see François Joyaux, *La Chine et le règlement du premier conflit d'Indochine: Genève 1954* (Paris: Sorbonne, 1979), pp. 68–71. Also see Zhai Qiang, "China and the Geneva Conference of 1954," *The China Quarterly*, no. 129 (March 1992), p. 107.

22. For a similar conclusion, see Qiang Zhai, "Transplanting the Chinese Model," pp. 708–9.

23. In actuality, Ho had not rejected the idea of peace talks, but had simply stated that they should take place only under highly favorable conditions—see *Toan Tap I*, vol. 6, p. 459. For the TASS report, see Joyaux, *La Chine*, p. 68; also see U.S. Embassy Saigon, dispatch 208, October 11, 1951, and U.S. Ambassador in Moscow (Bohlen) to Department of State, September 3, 1953, both in RG 59, UPA. On French peace feelers, see Jacques de Folin, *Indochine 1940–1954: La fin d'un rêve* (Paris: Perrin, 1993), p. 261.

24. This report is contained in Saigon Joint Weeka 49, December 7, 1953, in RG 59, UPA. The interview was summarized in U.S. Embassy (Stockholm) to Department of State, November 29, 1953, in RG 59, UPA. In an editorial that accompanied the interview, *Expressen* expressed some skepticism about Ho Chi Minh's sincerity and indicated that the article seemed to be "inspired by Moscow." For a Vietnamese-language version, see *Toan Tap I*, vol. 6, pp. 494–96.

25. *Toan Tap I*, vol. 6, pp. 430–42.

26. *Chu tich Ho Chi Minh voi cong tac ngoai giao* [Chairman Ho Chi Minh and foreign relations] (Hanoi: Su that, 1990), p. 143.

27. Zhai Qiang, "China and Geneva Conference," p. 108; Nikita Khrushchev, *Khrushchev Remembers* (Boston: Bantam, 1971), pp. 532–34. Chen Jian, "China in the Vietnam Wars," in Peter Lowe (ed.), *The Vietnam War* (New York: St. Martin's, 1998), p. 159. According to this author's source, the Vietnamese apparently agreed.

28. Stanley Karnow, *Vietnam: A History* (New York: Viking, 1983), p. 191.

29. Ho's letter is quoted in *Chu tich Ho Chi Minh*, p. 142, citing *Lich su Dang Cong san Viet Nam* [A history of the Vietnamese Communist Party] (Hanoi: Su that, 1984), p. 691; For Zhou Enlai's message, see *Zhongguo junshi*, p. 99. The figures on Chinese aid are from ibid. According to one Chinese source, from 1950 to 1954 China provided the Vietminh with 116,000 rifles and 4,630 cannons, equipping five infantry divisions, one engineering and artillery division, one anti-aircraft regiment, and one guard regiment. See Han Huaizhi, *Dangdai*, vol. 1, pp. 520–22.

30. Sniping between Beijing and Hanoi over the relevance of Chinese advice to conditions on the battlefield has been common since the end of the Vietnam War. For Vietnamese complaints, see Georges Boudarel, "Comment Giap a failli perdre la bataille de Dien Bien Phu," *Le Nouvel Observateur*, April 8, 1983.

31. Jay Taylor, *China and Southeast Asia* (New York: Praeger, 1974), pp. 13–14; Bernard B. Fall, *Hell in a Very Small Place* (Philadelphia: Lippincott, 1966), p. vii; Henri Navarre, *Agonie de l'Indochine* (Paris: Plan, 1956), p. 181, and Vo Nguyen Giap, *People's War*, p. 179.

32. According to Chinese documents, on January 24 the Central Military Commission in Beijing instructed Chinese advisers to propose a cautious "bit by bit" strategy at Dien Bien Phu to their Vietminh colleagues. See *Zhongguo junshi*, p. 98, and Qiang Zhai, "Transplanting the Chinese Model," p. 709.

33. President Eisenhower's indecision over how to respond to the situation in Indochina has been the subject of considerable scholarly interest. I have dealt with the issue in my *U.S. Containment Policy and the Conflict in Indochina* (Stanford, Calif.: Stanford University Press, 1994), chapters 5 and 6. For Nixon's private comment, see de Folin, *Indochine*, p. 254, citing telegram 2414 from the French Embassy in Washington, April 8, 1954, MAE.

34. Philippe Devillers and Jean Lacouture, *La Fin d'une guerre: Indochine 1954* (Paris: Editions du Seuil, 1960), p. 149; Vo Nguyen Giap, *People's War*, p. 153; *Zhongguo junshi*, pp. 102–3. Surviving French prisoners of war were released after the signing of the Geneva Agreement in July.

35. For a brief excerpt to that effect by the Party secretariat and dated May 1, 1954, see *Chu tich Ho Chi Minh*, p. 144.

36. According to U.S. Embassy Saigon telegram 2312, dated May 10, 1954, in RG 59, UPA, French intelligence sources estimated that nine Vietminh infantry battalions—the equivalent of one division—could be transported from Dien Bien Phu to the delta in ten days. The entire Vietminh force of twenty-seven battalions could arrive in three weeks' time. There were already an estimated sixteen Vietminh battalions in the area. Some French officers were less pessimistic. General René Cogny, one of Navarre's senior military commanders, was convinced that the Vietminh needed time to regroup and would not attack the Red River delta until at least October, predicting that he could hold the area temporarily if provided with needed reinforcements—see Saigon 2363, May 12, 1954, in RG 59, UPA. Vietminh sources confirm his estimate, conceding that logistical problems alone would have prevented a successful assault on the Hanoi region until at least 1955.

37. Chen Jian, "China," p.108. Many years later, Mao Zedong conceded to Ho Chi Minh that the Chinese diplomatic strategy at Geneva had perhaps been faulty—see Odd Arne Westad et al., *77 Conversations between Chinese and Foreign Leaders on the Wars in Indochina, 1964–1977* (Washington, D.C.: Cold War International History Project/ The Woodrow Wilson Center, 1998), p. 134.

38. For a detailed analysis of the meeting, see Joyaux, *La Chine*, pp. 251–54. In a cable from London, the U.S. Embassy reported that Zhou told Nehru that China was agreeable to neutralist governments in Laos and Cambodia, on condition that neither should be turned into bases for hostile acts against China. He stated further that the Vietminh would agree to cease large-scale military operations if the French did so as well, and that the DRV would respect a division of Vietnam into separate regroupment zones. See U.S. Embassy, London to Department of State, no. 32, July 2, 1954, in RG 59, UPA.

39. After the meeting, the VWP Politburo instructed Pham Van Dong to adopt a more conciliatory position. See Qiang Zhai, *China and the Vietnam Wars, 1950–1975* (Chapel Hill: University of North Carolina Press, 2000), pp. 60–62. Also see Joyaux, *La Chine*, pp. 262–64; Chen Jian, "China," p. 109; *77 Conversations*, p. 134.

40. Pham Van Dong's reluctance to compromise, a consequence of the Vietminh victory at Dien Bien Phu, is explored in Qiang Zhai, *China and the Vietnam Wars*, pp. 61–62, and Chen Jian, "China and the Vietnam Wars, 1950–1975," pp. 159–161, and Chen Jian, "China . . . ," p. 109, citing Qu Xing, "On Zhou Enlai's Diplomacy," p. 258, and Shi Zhe, *Together with Historical Giants*, p. 557. Also see Zhai Qiang, "China and Geneva Conference," p. 111, citing Shi Zhe, "Rineiwa huiyi Sanj," [Random recollections of the Geneva Conference] in *Ran wu* (January 1989), p. 43.

41. Wang Bingnan, *Zhongmei huitan jiunian huigu* [Recollections of nine years of Sino-U.S. talks] (Beijing: Shijie Zhishi Publishing, 1985), p. 13.

42. Report to the Sixth Plenum in *Ho Chi Minh: Selected Writings* (Hanoi: Foreign Languages Press, 1977), pp. 181–83. See the comment by the Vietnamese diplomat Mai Van Bo that international factors intervened to prevent a total victory at Geneva, in his

Chung toi hoc lam ngoai giao voi Bac Ho [I studied diplomacy with Uncle Ho] (Ho Chi Minh City: Tre, 1998), p. 80.

XIV | *Between Two Wars*

1. Ho's speech before city officials is printed in *Toan Tap I*, vol. 7, pp. 49–51. For the arrival of Vietnamese troops and the reference to Ho's arrival in the city, see Hanoi 278 to Department of State, October 10, 1954, and Hanoi 314 to Department of State, October 20, 1954, both in RG 59, UPA. Also see Joint Weeka, October 24, 1954, in ibid. Ho Chi Minh's rules of behavior to civilian and military personnel are listed in *BNTS*, vol. 5, p. 540. For his decision to refuse the use of the palace for his private residence, see the *Vietnam Courier* (May 1985), p. 3.

2. Reported in Hanoi 318, dated October 21, 1954, in RG 59, UPA. For Nehru's visit, see Joint Weeka 43, October 24, 1954. Ho's speech welcoming Nehru is in *Toan Tap I*, vol. 7, pp. 52–53.

3. Jean Sainteny, *Ho Chi Minh and his Vietnam*, trans. Herma Briffault (Chicago: Cowles, 1972), p. 117. According to Sainteny, Vietnamese soldiers stationed outside the U.S. consulate carefully registered the license numbers of the automobiles transporting guests to this party.

4. For the eight-point decree, see Memo, Joseph Yager, to Ambassador Johnson, dated July 16, 1954, in RG 59, UPA.

5. *Toan Tap I*, vol. 7, pp. 20–27.

6. For a reference to the number of trained administrators, see Ken Post, *Revolution, Socialism, and Nationalism in Vietnam*, vol. 2 (Aldershot, U.K.: Dartmouth, 1989), p. 54. For remarks on why so many refugees left for the South, see Mieczyslaw Maneli, *War of the Vanquished* (New York: Harper & Row, 1971), pp. 38–39.

7. The law on People's Councils was passed by the National Assembly in July 1957, and the first elections were held in November—see Post, *Revolution*, vol. 2, p. 55.

8. *Toan Tap I*, vol. 7, pp. 20–27.

9. One of those weighing in on the issue is Carlyle Thayer, who estimates that in 1954 there were about 100,000 Vietminh supporters in the Southern provinces and 90,000 of these went to the North—see his *War by Other Means: National Liberation and Revolution in Viet-Nam 1954–1960* (Sydney: Allen & Unwin, 1989), p. 18. On Ho's confidence regarding the elections, see Vu Thu Hien, *Dem giua ban ngay* [Between Night and Day] (Westminster, Calif.: Van Nghe, 1998), p. 230.

10. Ironically, however, Vietminh sources had predicted as early as the fall of 1950 that the United States would eventually replace Bao Dai with Ngo Dinh Diem. See Saigon 245 to Secretary of State, October 10, 1950, in RG 59, UPA. For information in State Department archives on Diem's activities in the United States and his appointment as prime minister, see Memorandum of Conversation, Ngo Dinh Diem with Gibson and Hoey of PSA, January 15, 1951; Saigon 2363, June 30, 1951; Memo PSA (Bonsal) to FE (Allison), January 16, 1953; Paris 1076 to Secretary of State, September 14, 1953; Paris 4530 to Secretary of State, May 25, 1954; Paris 4538, May 26, 1954; Paris 4756 to Secretary of State, June 8, 1954, in ibid. For reaction in Saigon to his appointment, see Saigon 2819 to Secretary of State, also in ibid. For his view that the South Vietnamese were too easygoing either to become soldiers or to resist Communist subversion, see Saigon 105 to Secretary of State, July 8, 1954, RG 59, UPA. Only six

of seventeen portfolios in his first cabinet went to southerners. The comment about the "messiah without a message" was Robert McClintock's—see Saigon 48 to Secretary of State, July 4, 1954, RG 59, UPA.

11. *BNTS*, vol. 5, pp. 563–64, 568. Thayer, *War by Other Means*, p. 26. For a Ho Chi Minh interview with a French journalist, in which he offered such concessions, see *Toan Tap I*, vol. 7, pp. 68–70. For the reaction by Dulles and other U.S. officials, to Diem's decision, see William J. Duiker, *U.S. Containment Policy and the Conflict in Indochina* (Stanford, Calif.: Stanford University Press, 1994), p. 215.

12. The quote from Molotov is in Thayer, *War by Other Means*, pp. 35–37. For Ho's activities in China, see *HZYZ*, pp. 143–47. Ho's speech on his return to Hanoi is printed in *Toan Tap I*, vol. 7, pp. 286–89. Also see *ZYG*, p. 65. According to Mieczyslaw Maneli, then the Polish representative on the ICC in Hanoi, Moscow adopted a cautious attitude on Vietnam after the Geneva conference, supporting the Vietnamese position on issues relating to the settlement, but not at the expense of their new foreign policy promoting peaceful coexistence—see Maneli, *War of the Vanquished*, p. 24. For Soviet reservations about the ideological line in the DRV, see ibid., p. 36. For the international context, see R. B. Smith, *An International History of the Vietnam War*, vol. 1, 1955–1961 (New York: St. Martin's, 1983), pp. 30–33, 62.

13. Ta Xuan Linh, "How Armed Struggle Began in South Vietnam," *Vietnam Courier* (March 1974), p. 20, cited in *No Other Road to Take: Memoirs of Mrs. Nguyen Thi Dinh*, trans. Mai V. Elliott (Ithaca, N.Y.: Cornell Data Paper No. 102, 1976), p. 12.

14. Neil Sheehan, *After the War Was Over: Hanoi and Saigon* (New York: Vintage, 1992), p. 77.

15. An English-language version of the speech is in *Ho Chi Minh: Selected Writings* (Hanoi: Foreign Languages Press, 1977), pp. 188–91. Also see *Toan Tap I*, vol. 7, pp. 329–32.

16. Post, *Revolution*, vol. 1, pp. 267–68.

17. Bernard B. Fall, ed., *Ho Chi Minh on Revolution: Selected Writings, 1920–1966* (New York: Praeger, 1967), p. 12. For Ho's private comments, see Vu Thu Hien, *Dem giua ban ngay*, p. 221, and his article in *Chroniques Vietnamiennes* (Fall 1997), p. 12. Also see Edwin E. Moise, *Land Reform in China and North Vietnam: Consolidating the Revolution at the Local Level* (Chapel Hill, N.C.: University of North Carolina Press, 1983), pp. 191, 239–41.

18. Le Duc Tho, "Lam the nao de phat dong chien tranh du kich o Nam bo" [How to carry out guerrilla warfare in the South], in *Cuoc khang chien than thanh cua nhan dan Viet Nam* [The sacred war of the Vietnamese people], vol. 3 (Hanoi: Su that, 1958), pp. 289–92. Also see Georges Boudarel, *Cents fleurs écloses dans la nuit du Vietnam: Communisme et dissidence, 1954–1956* (Paris: Jacques Bertoin, 1991), p. 171.

19. Bui Tin, *Following Ho Chi Minh: Memoirs of a North Vietnamese Colonel* (Honolulu: University of Hawaii Press, 1995), p. 23; *BNTS*, vol. 5, p. 559; *Nhan Dan*, November 19, 1954.

20. Duong Van Mai Elliott: *The Sacred Willow: Four Generations in the Life of a Vietnamese Family* (New York: Oxford University Press, 1999), pp. 344–45. Also see Moise, *Land Reform*, chapter 11.

21. See Moise, *Land Reform*, pp. 218–22, and Boudarel, *Cent Fleurs*, p. 177. For an example of Le Van Luong's views, see his "Vi sao phai chinh Dang" [Why the Party must be purified], in *Cuoc khang chien than thanh*, vol. 3, p. 293–302. Le Van Luong

was the younger brother of Nguyen Cong Hoan, a popular writer of fiction who remained in the North after the Geneva conference.

22. "Speech at the recapitulative meeting of the second phase of land reform, Thai Nguyen, Bac Giang," in *Toan Tap I*, vol. 7, pp. 112–21. Also see Post, *Revolution*, vol. 1, pp. 273, 289; Boudarel, *Cents fleurs*, pp. 177–78, 188.

23. Bui Tin, *Following Ho*, pp. 28–29; Vu Thu Hien, *Dem giua ban ngay*, p. 224; Moise, *Land Reform*, pp. 218–22.

24. *Toan Tap I*, vol. 7, pp. 179–82. For a discussion of the seventh plenum and its decisions, see Post, *Revolution*, vol. 1, p. 271.

25. Cited in Post, *Revolution*, vol. 1, p. 272.

26. Ibid., p. 274. Ho's speech is contained in *Toan Tap I*, vol. 7, pp. 354–59. The comparison with a bowl of soup is cited in Georges Boudarel, "Ho Chi Minh," in George Fischer, ed., *Hommes d'état d'Asie et leur politique* (Paris: Université René Descartes, 1980), pp. 127–28.

27. Post, *Revolution*, vol. 1, p. 274; "Bai noi chuyen tai hoi nghi can bo cai cach mien bien" [Speech to a conference of reform cadres in maritime areas], in *Toan Tap I*, vol. 7, pp. 413–16. Vu Dinh Huynh's plea is cited in Vu Thu Hien, *Dem giua ban ngay*, p. 225.

28. Cited in W. R. Smyser, *The Independent Vietnamese: Vietnamese Communism Between Russia and China, 1956–1969* (Athens, Ohio: Ohio University Center for International Studies, 1980), pp. 5–6. According to Georges Boudarel, when a reporter from Radio Moscow asked Truong Chinh for his views on the decisions reached at the Twentieth Congress, Chinh had responded with an ambiguous remark about "the analysis of the new situation leading to very profound theoretical remarks and resolutions on audacious tasks"—see Boudarel, *Cent fleurs*, p. 193. Vu Thu Hien claims that only members of the Politburo and the Secretariat received copies of the de-Stalinization speech—see *Dem giua ban ngay*, p. 101.

29. Vu Thu Hien, *Dem Giua Ban Ngay*, p. 333; "Vu Thu Hien parle," in *Chroniques Vietnamiennes* (Fall 1997), p. 13.

30. "Loi be mac Hoi nghi lan thu 9 (mo rong) cua Ban chap hanh Trung uong Dang Lao dong Viet Nam" [Concluding speech at the Ninth (Enlarged) Plenum of the Party Central Committee], in *Toan Tap I*, vol. 7, pp. 426–30.

31. Boudarel, *Cents fleurs*, pp. 199–200. Ho Chi Minh's letter is "Thu gui hoi nghi tong ket cai cach ruong dat dot 5" [Letter to summary conference of land reform wave 5], in *Toan Tap I*, vol. 7, pp. 460–61.

32. The speech is in *Toan Tap I*, vol. 7, pp. 506–9. The concept of the "mass line," adopted from Chinese practice, called for a policy of responding to the immediate aspirations of the people (from the masses to the masses) at the early stage of the socialist revolution.

33. *Nhan Dan*, October 30, 1956, quoted in Thayer, *War by Other Means*, 89–90. I have used Thayer's translation.

34. Moise, *Land Reform*, pp. 244–46; Post, *Revolution*, vol. 1, p. 280; *BNTS*, vol. 7, p. 364.

35. *BNTS*, vol. 7, p. 334. Also see Vu Thu Hien, *Dem giua ban ngay*, pp. 457–58. For a brief discussion of how ordinary Vietnamese assessed Ho Chi Minh's responsibility for the campaign, see Elliott, *Sacred Willow*, pp. 343–44.

36. Post, *Revolution*, vol. 1, pp. 282–83. For Chinh's response to the dismissal, see

Bui Tin, *Following Ho*, p. 31, and Hoang Gian, "Une goutte bleu dans le grand ocean," in *Chroniques Vietnamiennes* (Winter–Spring 1988), p. 23.

37. For the speech, see *Toan Tap I*, vol. 7, pp. 585–86. Fall, *Ho Chi Minh on Revolution*, pp. 277– 81, has an English version. Moise, *Land Reform*, pp. 246–50, also has lengthy excerpts from this speech. For the notes on Quynh Luu, see ibid., pp. 258–60.

38. Boudarel, *Cents fleurs*, pp. 202–4. For various estimates of the numbers killed and punished, see ibid., p. 203–4. Boudarel cites a source to the effect that Ho Chi Minh himself admitted that 12,000 to 15,000 had been erroneously executed—see p. 203. For a lower estimate, see Moise, *Land Reform*, pp. 218–22.

39. Post, *Revolution*, vol. 1, p. 287.

40. Nguyen Manh Tuong, *Un excommunie. Hanoi: 1954–1991: Procès d'un intellectuel* (Paris: Que Me, 1992), p. 9.

41. Boudarel, *Cent Fleurs*, p. 143. Information in the above paragraphs comes from *Post*, vol. 1, pp. 280–90, and vol. 2, pp. 156–57, and Boudarel, *Cent Fleurs*, passim. Also see Hirohide Kurihara, "Changes in the Literary Policy of the Vietnamese Workers' Party, 1956–1958," in Takashi Shiraishi and Motoo Furuta, ed., *Indochina in the 1940s and 1950s* (Ithaca, N.Y.: Cornell University Southeast Asia Program, 1992), pp. 165–96. For Truong Chinh's comment about freedom of speech, see Nguyen Van Tran, *Viet cho me va Quoc hoi* [Letter to My mother and the National Assembly] (Westminster, Calif.: Van Nghe, 1996), p. 275.

42. See Bui Tin, *Following Ho*, pp. 36–37.

43. Ibid., pp. 32–33; Vu Thu Hien, *Dem giua ban ngay*, p. 322.

44. U.S. Department of State, *Working Paper on North Viet-Nam's Role in the War in South Viet-Nam* (Washington, D.C., 1968), appendix item 204. For a discussion, see William Duiker, *The Communist Road to Power in Vietnam*, 2d ed. (Boulder, Colo.: Westview Press, 1996), pp. 186–87.

45. Vietnam News Agency, April 3, 1956. For Hanoi's initial reaction to the new Soviet policy and Mikoyan's visit, see Smyser, *Independent Vietnamese*, pp. 6–7, and Ang Cheng Guan, *Vietnamese Communists' Relations with China and the Second Indochina Conflict, 1956–1962* (Jefferson, N.C.: McFarland, 1999), pp. 19–20. According to Russian Scholar Ilya Gaiduk, Truong Chinh may have been one of the doubters, expressing skepticism to a Soviet official in 1955 that a peaceful solution to the problem was possible. See his "Developing an Alliance: The Soviet Union and Vietnam, 1954–1975," in Peter Lowe (ed.) *The Vietnam War* (New York: St. Martin's, 1998), p. 141.

46. I have used the English version of the speech in Fall, *On Revolution*, pp. 269–71. For the Vietnamese version, see *Toan Tap I*, vol. 7, p. 427.

47. For the poem, see Hoang Van Chi, "Collectivization and Rice Production," *The China Quarterly* (January–March 1962), p. 96. For Ho's letter, see *Toan Tap I*, vol. 7, pp. 453–57. The letter is given in English in Fall, *On Revolution*, pp. 272–74. The quote about "simple thoughts" is from a *Nhan Dan* editorial on July 22, 1956.

48. *Toan Tap I*, vol. 7, pp. 462–64; William S. Turley, *The Second Indochina War: A Short Political and Military History, 1954–1975* (New York: New American Library/ Mentor, 1986), p. 22.

49. The pamphlet appears in its original Vietnamese form, as *Duon loi Cach mang mien Nam*, in the Race documents, a collection of materials deposited by Jeffrey Race with the Center for Research Libraries, Chicago, Illinois. Also see Turley, *Second Indochina War*, p. 22.

50. For an inside comment, see Vu Thu Hien, *Dem giua ban ngay*, p. 107. For a more detailed analysis of the Zhou visit, see Thayer, *War by Other Means*, pp. 98–100, and Ang Cheng Guan, *Vietnamese Communists' Relations*, pp. 43–45. Thayer has pointed out that the final communiqué contained a reference to the five principles of peaceful coexistence and the dangers of chauvinism (an obvious slap at the USSR), but the words "great nation" were not included.

51. It should be noted that not all members of the southern leadership wished to adopt a more aggressive approach in using violence to oppose the Diem regime. For a discussion of varying views, see Duiker, *Communist Road*, pp. 190–92. Ho's National Assembly speech can be found in English in Fall, *On Revolution*, pp. 277–81.

52. Vu Thu Hien, *Dem giua ban ngay*, pp. 352–53.

53. *BNTS*, vol. 6, p. 472.

54. Smyser, *Independent Vietnamese*, p. 18.

55. Gérard Tongas, *L'Enfer communiste au Nord Vietnam* (Paris: Nouvelles Editions Delmesse, 1960), pp. 85–86. Though the accuracy of Tongas's account has been questioned by some observers, in the light of recent evidence much of it appears worthy of credence. However, Tongas dates Voroshilov's visit in September, rather than in May. I have found no record of a second visit in 1957.

56. His speech, given on the anniversary of the declaration of Vietnamese independence, is in *Toan Tap I*, vol. 7, pp. 771–81. Included in the delegation for the round of state visits were Minister of Culture Hoang Minh Giam, ex-ambassador to China Hoang Van Hoan, and Vice Minister of Health Pham Ngoc Thach.

57. Smyser, *Independent Vietnamese*, p. 19. For the Chinese account, see Thayer, *War by Other Means*, p. 171.

58. See Truong Chinh, "Let Us Be Grateful to Karl Marx and Follow the Path Traced by Him," a speech broadcast on Radio Hanoi in September 1968 and translated in *Vietnam Documents and Research Notes* (U.S. Mission in Vietnam, Saigon), document 51, p. 16. For the German and Italian reports, see Smyser, *Independent Vietnamese*, p. 19.

59. See Smyser, *Independent Vietnamese*, p. 19, citing *Ho Chi Minh: Selected Works*, vol. 4 (Hanoi: Foreign Languages Publishing House, 1960), pp. 277, 278–83.

60. Post, *Revolution*, vol. 2, p. 151, citing *Fifty Years of Activity of the Communist Party of Vietnam* (Hanoi, n.p.: 1979), p. 135.

61. Cited in Post, *Revolution*, vol. 2, p. 151. Party control over the military forces, a tradition in Marxist-Leninist organizations, was especially sacrosanct in Vietnam, where senior military officers also served in leading positions in the Party.

62. Ibid., pp. 153–55. Ho's New Year's message is in *Toan Tap I*, vol. 8, pp. 20–27.

63. For this extraordinary tale, which has the ring of veracity, see Vu Thu Hien, *Dem giua ban ngay*, pp. 605–9. The fiancé's letter is contained in "Lettre de larmes et de sang," *Chroniques Vietnamiennes* (Fall 1997), pp. 8–11.

64. Post, *Revolution*, vol. 2, pp. 153–55.

65. "May kinh nghiem Trung quoc ma chung ta nen hoc" [Some Chinese experiences that we should study], cited in *BNTS*, vol. 7, pp. 111–12; Post, *Revolution*, vol. 2, p. 176. Also see articles dated December 7 and 26, 1957, January 7, February 1, and March 1, 1958, in ibid., and *Toan Tap I*, vol. 8, pp. 1–5.

66. Post, *Revolution*, vol. 2, p. 155. David W. P. Elliott, "Revolutionary Reintegration: A Comparison of the Foundation of Post-Liberation Political Systems in North Vietnam and China" (Ph.D. dissertation, Cornell University, 1976), p. 417.

67. Post, *Revolution*, vol. 2, p. 176; Tran Luc, "China's Experience with Agricultural Collectivization," *Nhan Dan*, December 25, 1958, cited in ibid., p. 199; Thayer, *War by Other Means*, p. 181.

68. *Cuoc khang chien chong my cuu nuoc 1954–1975* [The Anti-U.S. war of National Salvation, 1971–1975] (Hanoi: Quan doi Nhan den, 1980), p. 35.

69. Carlyle Thayer reports that Ho received a welcome in India similar to that accorded previously to South Vietnamese President Ngo Dinh Diem; for a brief discussion, see his *War by Other Means*, pp. 166–67. Also see Ang Cheng Guan, *Vietnamese Communists' Relations*, pp. 76–77. India's attitude toward the Vietnam issue was more complicated than it often appeared on the surface. While Nehru had had little respect for the Bao Dai government and gave firm diplomatic support to the Vietminh cause during the Franco-Vietminh conflict, in private talks with U.S. or other Western officials he expressed concern over the possible implications of a Vietnam united under an aggressive Communist government in Hanoi. India thus played somewhat of a deceptive game, supporting the DRV in public, but expressing more reservations privately.

70. "A Party Account of the Situation in the Nam Bo Region of South Vietnam, 1954–1960," p. 41. This undated document, a copy of which is in my possession, was discovered by South Vietnamese armed forces during an operation in the early 1960s.

71. Tran Van Giau, "Great Strategic Effect of the Guerrilla War in South Vietnam Through Ten Years of Armed Struggle," *NCLS* (July 1969), pp. 19–32, as translated in JPRS, no. 49,387, Translations on North Vietnam, no. 639. The captured document titled "Party Account" contains statistics on Party losses during this period; in some base areas in the northern suburbs of Saigon, such as Go Vap, Ba Diem, and Gia Dinh, the Party apparatus was virtually eliminated—see pp. 11, 26, and 36–37.

72. The captured document is the so-called CRIMP document, a Viet Cong report seized by South Vietnamese armed forces during Operation CRIMP in 1963 and contained in Department of State, *Working Paper on North Viet-Nam's Role*, appendix item no. 301, p. 5.

73. Ho Chi Minh's comments are cited in *Chu tich Ho Chi Minh voi cong tac ngoai giao* [Chairman Ho Chi Minh and foreign relations] (Hanoi: Su that, 1990), p. 174.

74. *Cuoc khang chien chong My*, pp. 49–50.

75. For the various positions in this controversy, see (among others) George McT. Kahin, *Intervention: How America Became Involved in Vietnam* (Garden City, N.Y.: Doubleday, 1987), and Thayer, *War by Other Means*.

76. Thayer, *War by Other Means*, p. 185; Smith, *International History*, vol. 1, p. 157; Ang Cheng Guan, *Vietnamese Communists' Relations*, pp. 103–5.

XV | *All for the Front Lines*

1. Cited in Le Duan, *Thu Vao Nam* [Letters to the South] (Hanoi: Su that, 1985), p. 31. This book is a collection of highly revealing letters that were written by General Secretary Le Duan to leading Party officials in South Vietnam over a period of nearly two decades. An abridged English-language version, *Letters to the South*, was also published (Hanoi: Foreign Languages Press, 1986).

2. Ang Cheng Guan, *Vietnamese Communists' Relations with China and the Second Indochina Conflict, 1956–1962* (Jefferson, N.C.: McFarland, 1997), pp. 86–87; *ZYG*, pp. 66–67. According to the latter source, the VWP submitted two memoranda to Beijing

during the summer of 1958 asking for Chinese advice on the dual issues of socialist transformation and national unity. In their reply, the Chinese emphasized that their advice was tentative, and not based on careful study.

3. Cited in James Walker Trullinger Jr., *Village at War: An Account of Revolution in Vietnam* (New York: Longman, 1980), p. 71. The reference to Ho Chi Minh is interesting, since official propaganda in the DRV stressed that President Ho's only family was the Vietnamese people as a whole.

4. Cited in David Chanoff and Doan Van Toai, *Vietnam: A Portrait of Its People at War* (London: I. B. Tauris, 1996), pp. 151, 153.

5. Nguyen Thi Dinh, *No Other Road to Take* (Ithaca, N.Y.: Cornell University Southeast Asia Program, 1976), pp. 65, 69–70. Madame Dinh later became minister of defense in the Provisional Revolutionary Government, formed by Party sympathizers in 1969.

6. Some observers have argued that Le Duan's comments indicated that Hanoi continued to advocate a policy of peaceful reunification, but this misreads the underlying message contained in this speech, which was probably directed above all to Moscow and Beijing. In a letter written in early 1962 to Nguyen Van Linh, then the senior Party official in the South, Duan explained that he had become convinced by the late 1950s that political struggle had to be supplemented by military operations to bring about the collapse of the Diem regime. See Le Duan, *Thu Vao Nam*, letter of February 1962, pp. 51–70.

7. *BNTS*, vol. 7, p. 307.

8. Ibid., pp. 320–47; Ang Cheng Guan, *Vietnamese Communists' Relations*, pp. 120–28; *HZYZ*, pp. 151–52.

9. *HZYZ*, p. 156; *BNTS*, vol. 7, pp. 367–70; Ang Cheng Guan, *Vietnamese Communists' Relations*, pp. 128–29. For Ho's view of Chinese arrogance, see Vu Thu Hien, *Dem giua ban ngay* [Between Night and Day] (Westminster, Calif.: Van Nghe, 1997), p. 108; this source also gives Party veteran Tran Huy Lieu's remarks on one occasion when he had been angered by his treatment at the hands of Chinese officials: "I'm like Uncle Ho, I shit on the celestial court, I'm a nationalist!" (p. 109).

10. For Ho's comments within the Politburo on domestic issues, see the meetings of April 7, 13, and 16, 1959, and May 14, 1959, in *BNTS*, vol. 7, pp. 270–94 and 310. He also addressed these issues in his speech at the Sixteenth Plenum in April and at a conference on rectification the following month. See "Dien van khai mac Hoi nghi lan thu 16 cua ban chap hanh trung uong Dang (khoa II)" [Opening speech at the Sixteenth Plenum of the Party Central Committee (second session)] in *Toan Tap I*, vol. 8, pp. 388–90, and "Bai noi tai lop chinh huan khoa II cua bo cong an" [Remarks at the second session of the Ministry of Public Security on Rectification] in ibid., pp. 429–32.

11. *Toan Tap I*, vol. 8, pp. 763–73. For an English translation of the speech, see Bernard B. Fall, ed., *Ho Chi Minh on Revolution: Selected Writings, 1920–1966* (New York: Praeger, 1967), pp. 313–319. For an English version of the proceedings of the conference, see *The Third National Congress of the Vietnam Workers' Party*, 3 vols. (Hanoi: Foreign Languages Press, 1960). The *Nhan Dan* editorial mentioned in the previous paragraph appears in W. R. Smyser, *The Independent Vietnamese: Vietnamese Communism Between Russia and China, 1956–1969* (Athens, Ohio: Ohio University Center for International Studies, 1980), pp. 40–41.

12. Pham Hung was born in Vinh Long province, in the Mekong delta. There has

been considerable speculation as to Nguyen Chi Thanh's origins: most reliable evidence suggests that he was born in poor peasant family near Hué, in central Vietnam, but other sources suggest that he came from more affluent means and had a rather mysterious past. See Vu Thu Hien, *Dem giua ban ngay*, p. 359. As we shall see, Nguyen Chi Thanh would soon emerge as the dominant figure involved in drafting military strategy in the South, replacing Vo Nguyen Giap. Ho Chi Minh's role in the selection of Le Duan as first secretary is a matter of debate. Some observers in Hanoi privately suggest that he approved the decision because of Duan's role in the South, while others hint that he might have preferred Giap, his old comrade-in-arms.

13. Chen Jian, "China's Involvement in the Vietnam War, 1964–1969," *The China Quarterly*, no. 142 (June 1995), p. 338. For a Vietnamese version of the nature of Chinese advice given to DRV leaders in May, see *The Truth About Vietnamo-Chinese Relations over the Past Thirty Years* (Hanoi: Ministry of Foreign Affairs, 1979), pp. 31–32. In their report to Moscow on the Third Congress, Soviet diplomats in Hanoi did note that new First Secretary Le Duan had placed significant emphasis on the issue of national reunification. See Ilya V. Gaiduk, "Developing an Alliance: The Soviet Union and Vietnam, 1954–1975," in Peter Lowe (ed.) *The Vietnam War* (New York: St. Martin's, 1998), p. 142.

14. There is some discrepancy between various sources on what actually transpired at that briefing. On the formation of the NLF, see Truong Nhu Tang, *Vietcong Memoir: An Inside Account of the Vietnam War and Its Aftermath* (San Diego: Harcourt Brace Jovanovich, 1985), pp. 76–80.

15. For references to the January Politburo meeting, see *Cuoc khang chien chong My cuu nuoc, 1954–1975* [The Anti-U.S. Resistance War for National Salvation, 1954–1975] (Hanoi: Quan doi Nhan dan, 1980), pp. 74–75. Ho Chi Minh's comments are in *BNTS*, vol. 8, pp. 21–22. Le Duan followed up the meeting with a lengthy letter on the subject to Nguyen Van Linh in the South–see his *Thu Vao Nam*, letter of February 7, 1961, pp. 35–36.

16. Chinese leaders were also unhappy with Ho's efforts to straddle the issue. See Qiang Zhai, *China and the Vietnam Wars, 1950–1975* (Chapel Hill: University of North Carolina Press, 2000) pp. 87–88. For Ho's suspicions of Mao Zedong, see Vu Thu Hien, *Dem giua han ngay*, p. 229. Still, while in Moscow, Ho appealed to Khrushchev to compromise with Beijing, since China was a large country with an important role in the world; when the Soviet leader countered that the USSR was an important country as well, Ho responded, "For us, it is doubly difficult. Don't forget, China is our neighbor"—see Ang Cheng Guan, *Vietnamese Communists' Relations*, p. 168.

17. For the October 1961 Politburo meeting and Ho's recommendations, see *BNTS*, vol. 8, p. 150. For its directives to the South, see "Situation of the Revolution in South Vietnam," an unpublished document sent to the southern leadership sometime in 1962. Also see the directive of the Politburo meeting held in February 1962, contained in *Mot so van kien cua Dang chong My cuu nuoc, 1954–1965* [Party documents on the anti-U.S. National Salvation Movement, 1954–1965], vol. 1 (Hanoi: Su that, 1985), pp. 137–57.

18. Hanoi's hope that Washington could be lured into accepting a compromise agreement in South Vietnam similar to that reached in Laos in July 1962 is discussed in Le Duan's letter of July 1962 to Nguyen Van Linh (alias Muoi Cuc), in his *Thu Vao Nam*, pp. 63–66. Hanoi had already begun to recruit an "under the blanket" group of sympathetic neutralists among exile groups in France in preparation for such an eventuality.

19. *BNTS*, vol. 8, pp. 367–68.

20. Ibid., pp. 322–23.

21. *Beijing Review*, November 23 and 30, December 7, 1979. Also see *ZYG*, p. 67, Smith, *International History*, vol. 2, pp. 87–88, and Chen Jian, "China's Involvement," p. 359. For a discussion of the "hangman's noose" strategy, see Mao Zedong's speech to the Supreme State Council in September 8, 1958, in *Jianquo yilai Mao Zedong wengao* [Mao Zedong's proclamations since the formation of the country], cited in ibid.

22. Smyser, *Independent Vietnamese*, pp. 63–64; Chen Jian, "China's Involvement," pp. 359–60, citing Qu Aiguo, "Chinese Supporters in the Operations to Assist Vietnam and Resist America," *Junshi Shilin* [The Circle of Military History], no. 6, p. 40. Smyser suggests that Ho Chi Minh was more cautious in his comments than were other Vietnamese leaders, but the evidence is inconclusive (see pp. 65–66). Many years later, official sources in Hanoi would charge that the Chinese were trying to seize the leadership of the world revolution and form a new Comintern dominated by Beijing—see *Truth About Vietnamo-Chinese*, p. 33.

23. Mieczyslaw Maneli, *War of the Vanquished* (New York: Harper & Row, 1971), pp. 127–28. Maneli stated that Ho Chi Minh appeared somewhat intimidated by the conversation. Also see Gareth Porter, "Coercive Diplomacy in Vietnam: The Tonkin Gulf Crisis Reconsidered," in Jayne Werner and David Hunt, eds., *The American War in Vietnam* (Ithaca, N.Y.: Cornell University Southeast Asia Program, 1993), pp. 11–12. Ho Chi Minh may have made a similar offer to negotiate through the left-wing Australian journalist Wilfred Burchett—see *Foreign Relations of the United States (1961–1963)*, vol. 4, *Vietnam, August–December 1963*, p. 85.

24. Vu Thu Hien, *Dem giua ban ngay*, p. 230. According to Hien, Ho Chi Minh disliked war and turned to it only as a last resort. Le Duan, on the other hand, relied on war to achieve his objectives. The secret directive sent to the South mentioned in this paragraph was the CRIMP document. Ho Chi Minh's interview with the Japanese journalist is reported in *BNTS*, vol. 8, pp. 484–85.

25. *BNTS*, vol. 8, 492–93. It was at this meeting that he predicted future coups in Saigon. Plenary sessions of the Central Committee are dated from the time of the last previous National Congress of the Party. In this case, the latest Party Congress had been held in September 1960.

26. Donald Zagoria, *Vietnam Triangle: Moscow/Peking/Hanoi* (New York: Pegasus, 1972), p. 109, citing Thanh's article, "Who will win in South Vietnam," in the July 1963 issue of *Hoc Tap*.

27. The rumor about replacing Ho Chi Minh is contained in Nguyen Van Tran, *Viet cho me va Quoc hoi* [Letter to my mother and the National Assembly] (Garden Grove, Calif.: Van Nghe, 1996), p. 328. Also see Georges Boudarel and Nguyen Van Ky, *Hanoi, 1936–1996: Du drapeau rouge au billet vert* (Paris: Editions Autrement, 1997), pp. 144–46. For a remark about his loss of sagacity, see "Vu Thu Hien parle," *Chroniques Vietnamiennes* (Fall 1997), p. 13. An evaluation of the roles played by Pham Van Dong, Truong Chinh, and Vo Nguyen Giap is contained in Vu Thu Hien, *Dem giua ban ngay*, pp. 25–26, 275, 296, and 337, and Nguyen Van Tran, *Viet cho me*, p. 328.

28. "Vu Thu Hien parle," p. 13; Vu Thu Hien, *Dem giua ban ngay*, p. 362; Nguyen Van Tran, *Viet cho me*, pp. 328–29; Boudarel and Ky, *Hanoi*, p. 146.

29. The debate over the circular was apparently also a bitter one. On one occasion, Ho Chi Minh lamented the vituperative comments issued in the meeting and reminded delegates that disagreement among Marxist-Leninists must be kept within the bounds

of fraternal love and comradeship. That, he said, was an "inalterable principle" (*thien kinh dia nghia*). With Marxism-Leninism to illuminate the road, Ho concluded, the Communist revolutionary movement would certainly prosper and develop. See his comments at the meeting of December 7, 1963, in *BNTS*, vol. 8, p. 490. Copies of the resolution and the circular letter were later captured by South Vietnamese forces, and are published in English translation in *Vietnam Documents and Research Notes* (U.S. Mission in Vietnam, Saigon), documents 96 and 99. The removal of the reference to Khrushchev was reported by Hoang Van Hoan in his article, "Une goutte d'eau dans le grand ocean," in *Chroniques Vietnamiennes* (Winter–Spring 1988), p. 24.

30. Vu Thu Hien, *Dem giua ban ngay*, p. 354. According to Georges Boudarel, Giap was so shaken by the results of the Ninth Plenum that he went into isolation and played the piano to calm his nerves—see Boudarel and Ky, *Hanoi*, p. 146. The most prominent victim of the purge was the academic Hoang Minh Chinh. A leading academic and a hero of the anti-French resistance movement, Chinh had spent considerable time in the Soviet Union and had close connections to Giap. In late 1963 he was asked by Truong Chinh to draft the resolution to be presented to the Ninth Plenum in December. At the plenum it was eventually rejected as "revisionist" in tone, and Hoang Minh Chinh was sentenced to a lengthy prison term. Some suspect that he was deliberately targeted for punishment because of his relationship to Giap and critical view of the current leadership—see, for instance, Bui Tin, *Following Ho Chi Minh: Memoirs of a North Vietnamese Colonel* (Honolulu: University of Hawaii Press, 1995), pp. 55–56, and Georges Boudarel, *Cent fleurs écloses dans la nuit du Vietnam: Communisme et dissidence, 1954– 1956* (Paris: Jacques Bertoin, 1991), pp. 257–58. Others purged during this period were Ung Van Khiem, a Foreign Ministry official, and Bui Cong Trung, a veteran Party member.

31. Bejiing had attempted to consolidate its reputation as a proponent of revolution in the Third World by convening a secret meeting of Asian Communist Parties in Guangdong province in September 1963. Ho Chi Minh was in attendence. At the conference, Zhou Enlai promoted revolutionary struggles in rural areas throughout the region. See Chen Jian, "China and the Vietnam Wars, 1950–1975" in Peter Lowe (ed.), *The Vietnam War*, p. 164. For editorials published in Hanoi during and after the December meetings in Moscow, see Smyser, *Independent Vietnamese*, pp. 71–72. Smyser surmises that this visit took place at Soviet invitation. In a new year's message to the Soviet people, Ho Chi Minh praised the successes of the USSR in building a modern, technologically advanced socialist society, but obliquely noted that the national liberation struggle was succeeding around the world and more countries were gaining freedom from imperialist oppression—see *Toan Tap I*, vol. 9, pp. 626–27.

32. Ho Chi Minh, "Bao cao tai hoi nghi chinh tri dac biet" [Speech at special political conference], in *Toan Tap I*, vol. 9, pp. 661–81. His closing remarks to the conference, contained in ibid., pp. 682–83, praised the delegates for their unity of spirit and determination.

33. For a good example of Ho's *Nhan Dan* articles, see the article dated May 29, 1964, in ibid., pp. 735–38. On Americans' fear of death, see the meeting of December 9, 1963, in *BNTS*, vol. 8, p. 492.

34. The first PAVN units apparently left in September or October and arrived at the end of the year. See Gareth Porter, "Coercive Diplomacy," p. 13. I have seen no evidence about Ho Chi Minh's role in reaching the decision. According to one source, however, in late September he advised his colleagues that they should prepare to deal

with the worst-case scenario, since the U.S. plot to destroy North Vietnam was a strategical and not a tactical decision—see the Politburo meeting of September 26, 1964, in *BNTS*, vol. 9, p. 130.

35. In his conversation with Mao Zedong, which took place in mid-August, Le Duan informed his host that the DRV intended to send one division of PAVN troops to the South. He also confirmed that the initial decision to attack the U.S. warships in the Tonkin Gulf had been made by the local commander on the spot. Mao responded that according to information available to Beijing, the U.S. charge that a second attack had taken place was based on misinformation in Washington. See "Mao Zedong and Pham Van Dong, Hoang Van Hoan," meeting of October 5, 1964, in Odd Arne Westad et al., *77 Conversations Between Chinese and Foreign Leaders on the Wars in Indochina, 1964–1977* (Washington, D.C.: Cold War International History Project/The Woodrow Wilson Center, 1998), p. 74; also see fn 117.

36. See *Vietnam Documents and Research Notes*, document 67 (September 1969), p. 7. According to another source, Moscow promised to support a general offensive in South Vietnam should it prove necessary—see Gareth Porter, *A Peace Denied: The United States, Vietnam, and the Paris Agreement* (Bloomington, Ind.: Indiana University Press, 1975), p. 23. The Russian scholar Ilya Gaiduk contends that three senior leaders of the DRV—Le Duan, Pham Van Dong, and Vo Nguyen Giap—had agreed to seek a restoration of the traditional evenhanded balance in relations with China and the Soviet Union: comment by Ilya Gaiduk at the LBJ Library Conference on the Vietnam War, October 17, 1993.

37. The directive is contained in *Nhung su kien lich su Dang* [Important events in the history of the Party] (Hanoi: Su that, 1976), vol. 3, p. 315. Polish diplomat Mieczyslaw Maneli has said that Hanoi previously avoided attacks on Americans in order to avoid provoking Washington; he claims Ho Chi Minh was opposed to the use of indiscriminate terrorism as a means of realizing national objectives: see Maneli, *War of the Vanquished*, p. 156. As a young foreign service officer at the U.S. Embassy in South Vietnam at the time, I had my own personal experience with the rapid turnover of governments in Saigon. On a Friday early in 1965 I left the country for a weekend in Bangkok. On Saturday a coup overthrew the government in Saigon. On Sunday, the new leaders were themselves evicted from power. I returned on Monday to discover that I had missed an entire government in the short life of South Vietnam.

38. Le Duan, *Thu Vao Nam*, letter to Xuan [Nguyen Chi Thanh], of February 1965, p. 96. Ho's comment on Binh Gia appeared in an article in *Nhan Dan*, January 7, 1965.

39. For an insightful analysis of Soviet policies during this period, see Ilya V. Gaiduk, "The Soviet Policy Dilemma in the Vietnamese Conflict," in Lloyd C. Gardner and Ted Gittings, eds., *Vietnam: The Early Decisions* (Austin: University of Texas Press, 1997), pp. 207–18. For Zhou Enlai's visit to Hanoi in March, see *77 Conversations*, pp. 77–78.

40. For Ho Chi Minh's reaction to the U.S. air strikes, see *BNTS*, vol. 9, p. 130. His February warning about the United States is in ibid., p. 197. For the resolution issued at the end of the Eleventh Plenum, see *Mot so van kien*, vol. 1, pp. 311–27. Ho Chi Minh spoke at the opening of the meeting, but his contribution to the debate is not clear. From the sources available he appears to have supported the prevailing approach—see *BNTS*, vol. 9, pp. 215–17. Ho was especially concerned to prepare the population of North Vietnam for the sacrifices ahead and suggested the convening

of a special political conference to mobilize support for the new line—see ibid., pp. 207–9.

41. Ho's interview with the Japanese journalist is contained in *Toan Tap I*, vol. 10, pp. 79–84 (see especially p. 82). Was the ambiguity in Hanoi's peace terms over the timing of the U.S. withdrawal deliberate, or a consequence of divergent views in Hanoi and the NLF leadership? I have long been inclined to believe the former, on the grounds that the timing and scope of peace talks were probably viewed as an affair for the Party leadership to determine. But it is worthy of note that in December 1965 Ho Chi Minh complained that it was important that announcements by the NLF must be coordinated with those of the DRV in order to present a unified position. Perhaps he was expressing irritation in Hanoi that the NLF sometimes adopted diplomatic positions without first consulting Party leaders in the North. See *BNTS*, vol. 9, pp. 338–39.

42. Le Duan, *Thu Vao Nam*, letter of May 1965; see also George Herring, ed., *The Secret Diplomacy of the Vietnam War: The "Negotiating Volumes" of the Pentagon Papers* (Austin: University of Texas Press, 1983), pp. 42–44.

43. Meeting of Liu Shaoqi with Le Duan, April 8, 1965; Mao Zedong with Ho Chi Minh, May 16, 1965; Zhou Enlai and Deng Xiaoping with Ho Chi Minh, May 17, 1965, all in *77 Conversations*, pp. 85–87. Ho's visit to China in May was treated as a brief vacation to celebrate his birthday—see *BNTS*, vol. 9, pp. 244–45; *HZYZ*, p. 250; and Vu Ky, *Bac Ho viet di chuc* [Uncle Ho writes his testament] (Hanoi: Su that, 1989), pp. 44–45. For an analysis of the relationship between China's policies in Vietnam and the Cultural Revolution, see the introductory comments by Odd Arne Westad in *77 Conversations*, pp. 8–20.

44. Meeting of Zhou Enlai with Ayub Khan, April 2, 1965, in *77 Conversations*, pp. 79–85. Also see Chen Jian, "China's Involvement," pp. 368–69. For Edgar Snow's interview with Mao Zedong, see *Truth About Vietnamo-Chinese*, pp. 35–36, and Edgar Snow, *The Long Revolution* (London: Hutchinson, 1973), p. 216.

45. Chen Jian, "China's Involvement," pp. 380–81. According to Odd Arne Westad, Lin Biao's famous article was actually a collective effort—see *77 Conversations*, p. 10.

46. *77 Conversations*, p. 90.

47. For his views on conditions for negotiations, see the Politburo meetings of December 1965, in *BNTS*, vol. 9, pp. 338–53. It is interesting to note that Ho considered the most important reason to bring an end to the U.S. bombing campaign was to facilitate the shipment of troops and matériel to the South—see the Politburo meeting of October 18, 1966, in ibid, pp. 485–86. On demonstrating Hanoi's firmness, see the Politburo meeting of July 31, 1965, in ibid, pp. 280–81. On promoting the peace movement in the United States, see the Politburo meeting of December 30, 1965, in ibid, pp. 350–51.

48. The date of Ho Chi Minh's conversation with Zhou and Deng is not clear from the context, but it probably took place in May 1965. For Le Duan's speech responding to the Lin Biao article, see William J. Duiker, *The Communist Road to Power in Vietnam*, 2d ed. (Boulder, Colo.: Westview Press, 1996), pp. 269–70. For other discussions between Chinese and North Vietnamese leaders on their tense relationship, see Zhou Enlai and Le Duan et al., April 13, 1966; Mao Zedong and Zhou Enlai with Pham Van Dong, April 10, 1967; and Deng Xiaoping with Le Duan, September 29, 1975; all in *77 Conversations*, pp. 90, 104, and 195. In a conversation with a visiting Vietnamese delegation in April 1967, Zhou Enlai conceded that in the past the CCP

had followed erroneous advice from Soviet leaders like Joseph Stalin, but he insisted that in the end they had learned to rely on their own instincts.

49. For a brief overview of the abortive peace feelers, known as Operation Marigold, see George C. Herring, *LBJ and Vietnam: A Different Kind of War* (Austin: University of Texas Press, 1994), pp. 104–7. Also see the Politburo meeting of December 11, 1965, cited in *BNTS*, vol. 9, p. 336. A Vietnamese version of Ho's letter is in *Toan Tap I*, vol. 10, pp. 461–62.

50. *BNTS*, vol. 9, pp. 437–38; Jean Sainteny, *Face à Ho Chi Minh* (Paris: Seghers, 1970), p. 190.

51. For information on the stilt house, see *Noi o va lam viec cua Chu tich Ho Chi Minh tai phu chu tich* (Hanoi: Ho Chi Minh Mausoleum, 1984), p. 9.

52. Vu Ky, *Bac Ho Viet Di chuc*, pp. 35–36.

53. The trip is recounted in ibid, pp. 38–48. Some of the Confucian (and Mencian) phrases quoted by Ho Chi Minh included "Fear not poverty, only fear injustice," "People are the root of the country," and "The interests of the people come first, those of the country come next, and those of the king come last." Ho demonstrated equal respect for the fifteenth-century Vietnamese scholar-patriot and war strategist Nguyen Trai. In February 1965 he visited the shrine to Nguyen Trai at Con Son and spent considerable time at Trai's tombstone. According to Vu Ky, Ho had deep respect for Nguyen Trai's dedication to duty and his commitment to the cause of Vietnamese independence.

54. The source for this curious story is Quan Yan's "Tao Zhu ji mi" [The riddle of Tao Zhu], *Xinan junshi wenxue* [Xinan Military Literature] (Chengdu) no. 72 (1995), pp. 53–55. Tao Zhu served as Party chief in Guangdong before being purged during the Cultural Revolution. It was there that he became closely acquainted with Ho Chi Minh. From the context, I have set the date for this incident to the spring and summer of 1966. According to this article, Ho probably wanted a companion from Guangdong because he still cherished the memory of his first wife, Tang Tuyet Minh. Other sources provide no explanation as to why the role could not have been played by a Vietnamese. The Chinese government had gone to the trouble of locating three possible candidates before dropping the idea. On hearing about the project, Zhou Enlai had expressed concern that it could arouse anti-Chinese feelings within the Vietnamese Party leadership in Hanoi.

55. Ho's message to the Vietnamese people, "Con co gi gui hon doc lap tu do" [Nothing is more important than independence and freedom], was printed in *Nhan Dan*—see *Toan Tap I*, vol. 10, pp. 374–77. Also see Quan Yan, "Tao Zhu," p. 55.

56. *Giu yen giac ngu cua Nguoi* [Preserving Ho's remains] (Hanoi: Quan doi Nhan dan, 1990).

57. *BNTS*, vol. 10, pp. 40–41, 93–95, 111. Ho Chi Minh's letter to Johnson in March is reproduced in *Toan Tap II*, vol. 12, pp. 230–32. For a discussion of the diplomatic exchange, see Herring, *LBJ and Vietnam*, pp. 108–11.

58. *BNTS*, vol. 10, pp. 156–57, 159; *Giu yen*, pp. 16–17. Fidel Castro has reportedly told acquaintances that on several occasions during his final years, Ho had to be physically restrained from joining groups about to depart for the South—see the article by Michael Salmon in *Vietnam Today* (April 1980), p. 2.

59. *BNTS*, vol. 10, p. 195.

60. Vu Ky, *Bac Ho viet di chuc*, p. 71; Hoang Van Hoan, *A Drop in the Ocean: Hoang Van Hoan's Revolutionary Reminiscences* (Beijing: Foreign Languages Press, 1988), p. 334.

61. The Chinese had been advising their North Vietnamese allies to adopt a tough position on negotiations since the expansion of the war in 1965. During discussions on the issue in April 1968, Zhou Enlai warned Pham Van Dong that the Tết offensive had not been a decisive victory and that, in appearing anxious to open peace talks, Hanoi had lost the initiative to Washington. In a talk with PRC Foreign Minister Chen Yi in October, Le Duc Tho pointed out that the DRV had erroneously followed Chinese advice to compromise at the Geneva conference in 1954. See meetings of Zhou Enlai with Pham Van Dong, April 13 and 17, June 29, and October 17, 1968, in 77 *Conversations*, pp. 123–29, 137–38, 140.

62. *Testament du President Ho Chi Minh* (Hanoi: Central Committee of the Vietnamese Communist Party, 1989).

63. *Giu yen,* pp. 17–18. To deal with the heat, Ho ordered a palm leaf cut for his use as a fan. To avoid confusing his leaf from those of his colleagues, he burned the letter "B" [Bac?] on the leaf.

64. Ibid., pp. 19–20.

EPILOGUE | *From Man to Myth*

1. The quotation from India is cited in *Ho Chi Minh* (Hanoi: Social Sciences Commission, 1989), p. 82. The Uruguayan editorial appeared in the journal *People* (Montevideo) on September 4, 1969. Both newspaper reports are quoted in *The World Praises and Mourns President Ho Chi Minh* (Hanoi: Su that, 1976). The Soviet reaction is cited in Kobelev, p. 236.

2. Duan's speech is contained in *Testament du President Ho Chi Minh* (Hanoi: Central Committee of the Vietnamese Communist Party, 1989), pp. 57–64.

3. See *Giu yen giac ngu cua Nguoi* [Preserving Ho's remains] (Hanoi: Quan doi Nhan dan, 1990), pp. 36–39, 92–93. According to an account by the Australian journalist Malcolm Salmon, as soon as news of Ho's death arrived in Moscow, Soviet leaders called Hanoi to emphasize the importance of taking immediate action to preserve his remains. Because the Politburo had not yet decided whether to build a mausoleum, Soviet specialists flew in to carry out the preservation procedure before a decision to erect a mausoleum had actually been reached. In the meantime, the body was kept on ice. See Malcolm Salmon, "Memories of Ho Chi Minh," *Vietnam Today*, April 1980, p. 3.

4. For the construction of the mausoleum, see *Giu yen*, pp. 95–122. For the comments of Hue-Tam Ho Tai, see her "Monumental Ambiguity: The State Commemoration of Ho Chi Minh," in K. W. Taylor and John K.Whitmore, eds., *Essays into Vietnamese Pasts* (Ithaca, N.Y.: Cornell University Southeast Asia Program, 1995), p. 281.

5. Facsimiles of the original Vietnamese-language versions and French-language translations of Ho Chi Minh's testament are contained in *Testament du President Ho Chi Minh*. Also see Bui Xuan Quang, "The Publication of Ho's Last Will: Background to Deception," *Vietnam Commentary* (March–April 1990), pp. 4–6. Professor Quang, citing an article by Hoang Van Hoan, charges that Le Duan did not even inform his colleagues in the Politburo of the existence of earlier, untouched versions of Ho's testament and showed them only a typed version that he had witnessed and signed.

6. See *Our President Ho Chi Minh* (Hanoi: Foreign Languages Press, 1970), pp. 188–95. For one example of the decision to perpetuate his ideas, see *Nghien cuu tu tuong Ho*

Chi Minh [Studying the thought of Ho Chi Minh], 2 vols. (Hanoi: Ho Chi Minh Institute, 1993).

7. For a brief description, see "The Ho Chi Minh Museum," *Vietnam Courier* (May 1986), p. 6. In a visit to Hanoi shortly before completion of the museum, I had the good fortune of making the acquaintance of several craftsmen from Czechoslovakia who were working on some of the displays inside the building. They told me that although the official intent was to portray the evils of twentieth-century capitalist society, in their own work they had sought surreptitiously to portray a more positive impression of the times. For a comment, see Hue-Tam Ho Tai, "Monumental Ambiguity," p. 283.

8. Vo Nguyen Giap was dropped from the Politburo at the Fifth Party Congress in 1982. He was later given a position as chair of a committee to promote technological development.

9. This "devil's bargain" was clearly asserted in the new constitution approved in 1991. See *Socialist Republic of Vietnam: Constitution* (Hanoi: Foreign Languages Publishing House, 1992).

10. *Testament*, pp. 5–10, Hoang Van Hoan's article in *Beijing Review*, September 14, 1981, and Vu Ky, *Bac Ho viet di chuc* [Uncle Ho writes his testament] (Hanoi: Su that, 1989).

11. Charles Fenn, "Trial Run to Doomsday," pp. 238–39 (manuscript provided by Charles Fenn).

12. Extrait du Journal *l'Union Française*, May 20, 1947, in dossier labeled "Ho Chi Minh 1947 à 1948," in SPCE, Carton 370, CAOM. Also see Vincent Hugeux, "Entretien avec Vu Thu Hien," *Politique Internationale*, no. 77 (Autumn 1997), p. 272, and Miec-zyslaw Maneli, *War of the Vanquished* (New York: Harper & Row, 1971), p. 153.

13. I was interested to discover on a recent trip to Hanoi that some Vietnamese scholars have fallen victim to the same myth of Ho's special attachment to the United States. When some of them asked me why Presidents Roosevelt and Truman had not replied to Ho Chi Minh's letters requesting recognition of the DRV, I reminded them that Joseph Stalin had not answered Ho's appeals either. It is significant that Ho Chi Minh's many articles criticizing various aspects of American society, written of course under a pseudonym, have never been translated into English.

14. See Murray Hiebert, "Farewell Saigon," *Far Eastern Economic Review* (Hong Kong), May 10, 1990, pp. 29–30. Also see "Price of Heresy," ibid., December 19, 1991, p. 9. For a reference to that early love interest, see Trinh Quang Phu, *Tu Lang Sen den ben Nha Rong* [From Lang Sen to the Nga Rong Pier] (Ho Chi Minh City: Van hoc, 1998), p. 93. For the remark about the need for myths, see Olivier Todd, "The Myth of Ho Chi Minh: Height of Misinformation," *Vietnam Commentary* (May-June 1990), pp. 13–14.

15. For Sidney Hook's ideas on the subject, see his *The Hero in History* (Boston: Beacon Press, 1943).

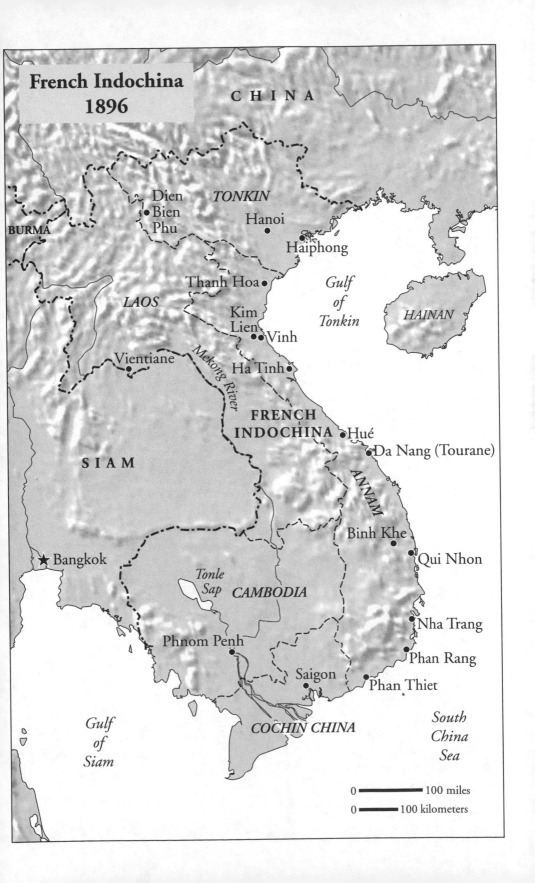

French Indochina
1896

CHINA

TONKIN

Dien
Bien
Phu

Hanoi

BURMA

Haiphong

Thanh Hoa

LAOS

Kim
Lien

Gulf
of
Tonkin

HAINAN

Vinh

Vientiane

Ha Tinh

FRENCH
INDOCHINA

Hué

SIAM

Da Nang (Tourane)

ANNAM

Binh Khe

Bangkok

Tonle
Sap

CAMBODIA

Qui Nhon

Phnom Penh

Nha Trang

Phan Rang

Saigon

Phan Thiet

COCHIN CHINA

Gulf
of
Siam

South
China
Sea

Mekong River

0 ▬▬▬ 100 miles

0 ▬▬▬ 100 kilometers

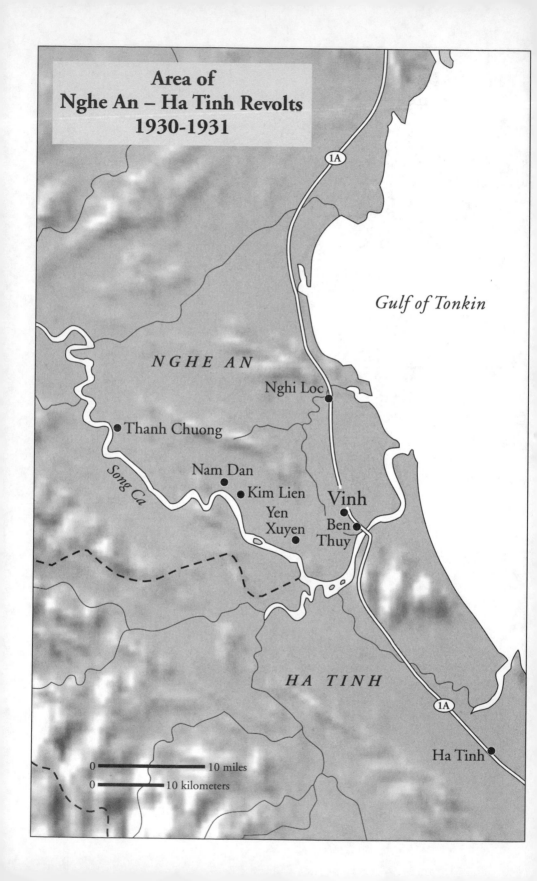

**Area of
Nghe An – Ha Tinh Revolts
1930-1931**

1A

Gulf of Tonkin

N G H E   A N

Nghi Loc

Thanh Chuong

Song Ca

Nam Dan

Kim Lien

Yen
Xuyen

Vinh

Ben
Thuy

H A   T I N H

1A

Ha Tinh

0 — 10 miles

0 — 10 kilometers

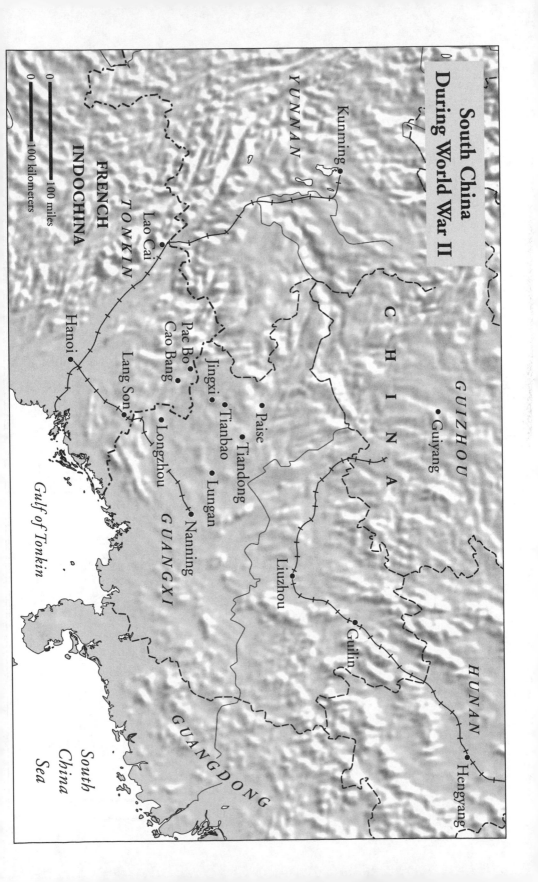

South China
During World War II

FRENCH
INDOCHINA

0
0
100 miles
100 kilometers

YUNNAN

Kunming

TONKIN

Lao Cai

Hanoi

Pac Bo
Cao Bang

Jingxi

Lang Son

Tianbao

Longzhou

Paise

Tiandong

Lungan

Nanning

GUANGXI

CHINA

GUIZHOU

Guiyang

Liuzhou

Guilin

HUNAN

Hengyang

GUANGDONG

Gulf of Tonkin

South
China
Sea

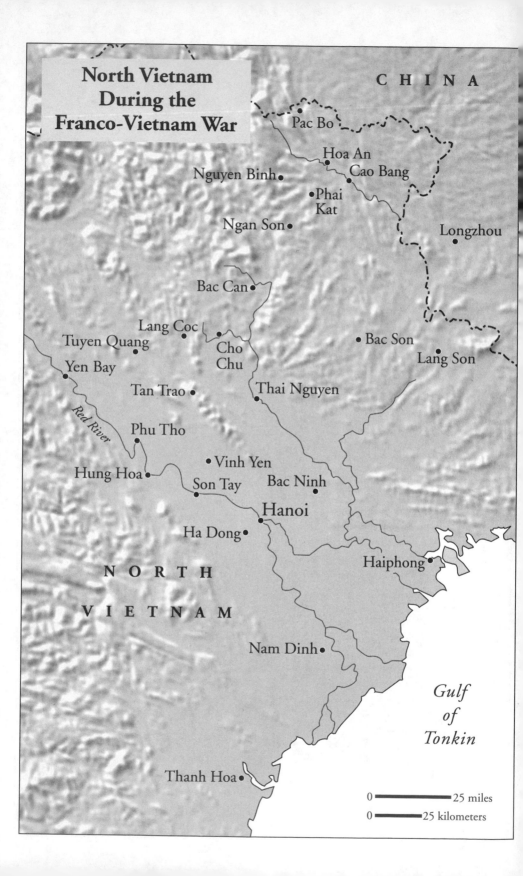

North Vietnam During the Franco-Vietnam War

C H I N A

Pac Bo

Hoa An

Cao Bang

Nguyen Binh

Phai
Kat

Longzhou

Ngan Son

Bac Can

Lang Coc

Cho
Chu

Bac Son

Tuyen Quang

Lang Son

Yen Bay

Thai Nguyen

Tan Trao

Red River

Phu Tho

Vinh Yen

Hung Hoa

Son Tay

Bac Ninh

Hanoi

Ha Dong

Haiphong

N O R T H

V I E T N A M

Nam Dinh

*Gulf
of
Tonkin*

Thanh Hoa

0 ━━━━━ 25 miles

0 ━━━━━ 25 kilometers

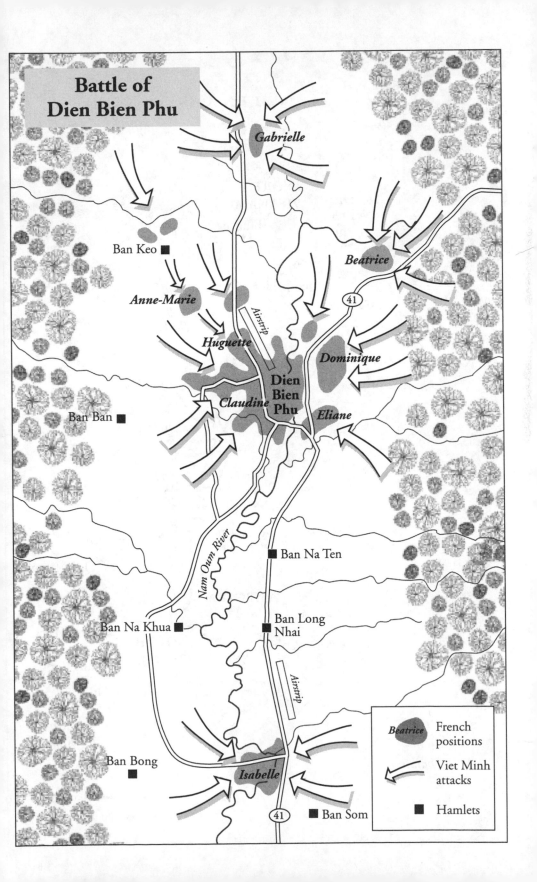

Battle of Dien Bien Phu

Gabrielle

Ban Keo ■

Beatrice

Anne-Marie

41

Airstrip

Huguette

Dominique

Dien Bien Phu

Ban Ban ■

Claudine

Eliane

Nam Oum River

Ban Na Ten ■

Ban Na Khua ■

Ban Long Nhai ■

Airstrip

Ban Bong ■

Isabelle

41

Ban Som ■

Beatrice — French positions

— Viet Minh attacks

■ Hamlets

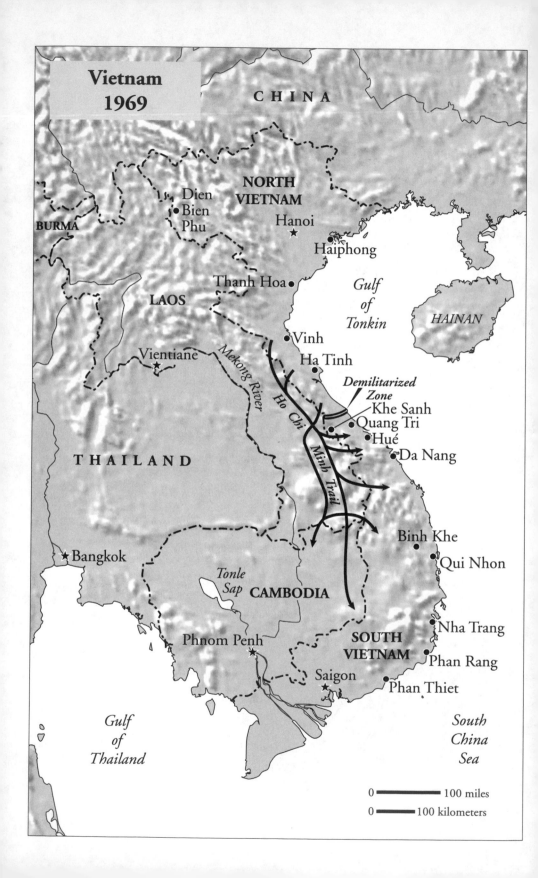

**Vietnam
1969**

CHINA

NORTH
VIETNAM

BURMA

Dien
Bien
Phu

Hanoi

Haiphong

Thanh Hoa

LAOS

*Gulf
of
Tonkin*

HAINAN

Vinh

Ha Tinh

Vientiane

Mekong River

*Demilitarized
Zone*

Khe Sanh

Quang Tri

Hué

THAILAND

*Ho Chi
Minh Trail*

Da Nang

Bangkok

*Tonle
Sap*

CAMBODIA

Binh Khe

Qui Nhon

Phnom Penh

SOUTH
VIETNAM

Nha Trang

Saigon

Phan Rang

*Gulf
of
Thailand*

Phan Thiet

*South
China
Sea*

0 ———— 100 miles

0 ———— 100 kilometers

INDEX

PHOTOGRAPHIC CREDITS

| Section I

"A view of downtown Hanoi . . .": From the collection of the author.

"Adjacent to the French sector . . .": From the collection of the author.

"A portrait taken of Ho Chi Minh's father . . .": By permission of Vietnam News Agency.

"After Nguyen Sinh Sac married Hoang Thi Loan . . .": By permission of the author.

"In this room in the house of his father-in-law . . .": By permission of the author.

"When Nguyen Sinh Sac took his family to live in Hue . . .": By permission of the author.

"A view of the small apartment . . .": By permission of Ho Chi Minh Museum, HCMC.

"The well-known scholar and revolutionary patriot . . .": By permission of Centre des Archives Outre-mer (Provence).

"After his triumphant return home from Hue . . .": By permission of the author.

"In the fall of 1907, Nguyen Sinh Sac enrolled . . .": By permission of the author.

"In June 1911, Ho Chi Minh sailed from Nha Rong . . .": By permission of the author.

"The French steamship *Amiral Latouche-Treville* . . .": By permission of Vietnam News Agency.

"Shown here is a copy of the demands . . .": By permission of Vietnam News Agency.

"A fellow classmate of Nguyen Sinh Sac . . .": By permission of Centre des Archives Outre-mer (Provence).

"At the Villa des Gobelins . . .": By permission of the author.

"A view of the main conference hall . . .": By permission of Vietnam News Agency.

"Under the suspicious eyes . . .": By permission of Vietnam News Agency.

"A view of Ho Chi Minh's apartment . . .": By permission of Vietnam News Agency.

"A cartoon by Ho Chi Minh . . .": By permission of Vietnam News Agency.

"During his years in Paris, Ho Chi Minh . . .": By permission of Centre des Archives Outre-mer (Provence).

"Ho Chi Minh shortly after his arrival . . .": By permission of Vietnam News Agency.

"On his arrival in Moscow in the summer . . .": By permission of Vietnam News Agency.

"In this building, the Comintern headquarters . . .": By permission of Ho Chi Minh Museum, HCMC branch.

"In the summer of 1924, Ho Chi Minh . . .": By permission of Vietnam News Agency.

"In December 1924, Ho Chi Minh left . . .": By permission of Vietnam News Agency.

"Ho Chi Minh with students and faculty members . . .": By permission of Centre des Archives Outre-mer (Provence).

"One of the brightest young stars . . .": By permission of Vietnam News Agency.

"One of the first female members . . .": By permission of Vietnam News Agency.

"In early June 1931, Hong Kong newspapers . . .": By permission of Patti Archive University of Central Florida.

"After his release from a Hong Kong prison . . .": From the collection of the author.

"In August 1945, Ho Chi Minh sent a letter . . .": By permission of Charles Fenn.

| Section II

"In this building, located in the heart of . . .": From the collection of the author.

"On August 19, 1945, crowds began to . . .": By permission of Vietnam News Agency.

"In late August, units of Vo Nguyen Giap's . . .": By permission of Patti Archive University of Central Florida.

"On August 26, 1945, a Vietnamese delegation . . .": By permission of Patti Archive University of Central Florida.

"On his secret return to Hanoi in mid-August 1945 . . .": By permission of the author.

"Built by the French at the beginning of the twentieth century . . .": By permission of Patti Archive University of Central Florida.

"On September 2, 1945, on a hastily-erected pavilion . . .": By permission of Vietnam News Agency.

"Shortly after declaring Vietnamese . . .": By permission of Vietnam News Agency.

"President Ho Chi Minh and his chief advisers . . .": By permission of Patti Archive University of Central Florida.

"A view of President Ho Chi Minh . . .": By permission of Vietnam News Agency.

"Ho Chi Minh prior to his departure . . .": By permission of Vietnam News Agency.

"En route to France to attend . . .": By permission of Corbis Sygma.

"In early June 1946, the French representative . . .": By permission of Corbis Sygma.

"During the days leading up to the opening . . .": By permission of Corbis Sygma.

"During the summer and fall of 1945 . . .": By permission of Patti Archive University of Central Florida.

"After the creation of the Provisional Republic . . .": By permission of Patti Archive University of Central Florida.

"Vietminh troops passed under the Long Bien . . .": From the collection of the author.

"In the fall of 1950, Vietminh forces . . .": By permission of Vietnam News Agency.

"After the outbreak of war in December . . .": By permission of Vietnam News Agency.

"In November 1953, Ho Chi Minh . . .": By permission of Vietnam News Agency.

"The French fort at Dien Bien Phu . . .": By permission of Vietnam News Agency.

"After planning their spring 1954 . . .": By permission of Vietnam News Agency.

"With victory over the French . . .": By permission of Vietnam News Agency.

"The elaborate Presidential Palace, in a garden . . .": By permission of the author.

"In this small stilt house built in the style . . .": By permission of the author.

"Ho Chi Minh inspecting one of the . . .": By permission of Vietnam News Agency.

"Ho Chi Minh presenting his political . . .": By permission of Vietnam News Agency.

"Although relations between Ho . . .": By permission of Vietnam News Agency.

"During the 1960s, Ho Chi Minh . . .": By permission of Vietnam News Agency.

"On the grounds of the Presidential . . .": By permission of Vietnam News Agency.

"During his last years in Hanoi, Ho Chi Minh . . .": By permission of the author.

"In the last years of his life, Ho Chi Minh . . .": By permission of Vietnam News Agency.

"The Ho Chi Minh Trail served as . . .": By permission of Vietnam News Agency.

"When U.S. bombing raids approached . . .": By permission of the author.

"In 1976, this mausoleum was erected in Ba Dinh . . .": By permission of the author.

"In the late 1980s the Ho Chi Minh Museum was built . . ." By permission of the author.

William J. Duiker is Liberal Arts Professor Emeritus of East Asian Studies at The Pennsylvania State University. He was a member of the History Department at Penn State until his retirement in the spring of 1997. A former foreign service officer with posts in Taiwan and South Vietnam, he currently specializes in the history of modern Vietnam and China, with a secondary interest in world history. In 1994, he was named Liberal Arts Professor of East Asian Studies at Penn State, and was awarded a Faculty Scholar Medal for Outstanding Achievement in the spring of 1996.

Professor Duiker has written several books and articles on subjects related to modern China and Vietnam. His *The Communist Road to Power in Vietnam* (Westview, 1981) received a Choice Outstanding Book Award for 1982–1983, and a second award when it was published in a second edition in 1996. Other recent books include *U.S. Containment Policy and the Conflict in Indochina* (Stanford, 1994) and *Sacred War: Nationalism and Revolution in a Divided Vietnam* (McGraw-Hill, 1995). In recent years he has developed a strong interest in world history and with colleague Jackson Spielvogel published a textbook entitled *World History* (West, 1994). A third edition will appear in the fall of 2000.

While at Penn State, he served as chairman of the East Asian Studies Program, as well as director of International Programs in the College of Liberal Arts. He is currently a regular lecturer for the Foreign Service Institute in Washington, D.C., and lives on the Outer Banks in North Carolina.